MACROMEDIA® FREEHAND® 9

Digital Illustration

PRENTICE HALL
Upper Saddle River, NJ 07458

Library of Congress Cataloging-in-Publication Data

Macromedia FreeHand 9: Digital Illustration/Against The Clock
p. cm.
ISBN 0-13-032524-4
1. Computer Graphics 2. FreeHand (Computer File)
I. Against The Clock (Firm)
T385.M322. 2001
006.6'869—dc21

00-061966

Executive Editor: Elizabeth Sugg
Developmental Editor: Judy Casillo
Supervising Manager: Mary Carnis
Production Editor: Denise Brown
Director of Manufacturing and Production: Bruce Johnson
Manufacturing Buyer: Ed O'Dougherty
Editorial Assistant: Lara Dugan
Formatting/Page Make-up: Against the Clock, Inc.
Prepress: Photoengraving, Inc.
Printer/Binder: Press of Ohio
Cover Design: Joe Sengotta
Icon Design: James Braun
Creative Director: Marianne Frasco

Prentice Hall International (UK) Limited, London
Prentice Hall of Australia Pty. Limited, Sydney
Prentice Hall Canada Inc., Toronto
Prentice Hall Hispanoamericana, S.A., Mexico
Prentice Hall of India Private Limited, New Delhi
Prentice Hall of Japan, Inc., Tokyo
Pearson Education Asia Pte. Ltd., Singapore
Editora Prentice Hall do Brasil, Ltda., Rio de Janeiro

10 9 8 7 6 5 4 3 2 1

ISBN 0-13-032524-4

Contents

Acknowledgements

I would like to give special thanks to the writers, illustrators, editors, and others who have worked long and hard to complete the Against The Clock series. Foremost among them are Doug Borton, Robin McAllister, Dean Bagley, Gary Goodenough, and Don Poyssick.

Thanks to the dedicated teaching professionals whose comments and expertise contributed to the success of these products, including Doris Anton and Kathy Besthorn of Wichita Technical College.

And a big thanks to Cynthia Toomey, copy editor and final link in the chain of production, for his help in making sure we said what we meant to say.

Thank you to Judy Casillo, developmental editor, and Denise Brown, production editor, for their guidance, patience, and attention to detail.

— Ellenn Behoriam, July 2000

PURPOSE

The Against The Clock series has been developed specifically for those involved in the field of graphic arts and now — video and multimedia production. Many of our readers are already involved in the industry in advertising and television production companies, in multimedia, and in the world of Internet web design. Others are just now preparing themselves for a career somewhere in these professions.

This series of courses will provide you with the skills necessary to work in this fast-paced, exciting, and rapidly expanding business. While many people feel that they can simply purchase a computer and the appropriate software and begin designing and producing high-quality presentations, the real world of multimedia production and professional communications requires a far more serious commitment.

THE SERIES

The applications presented in the Against The Clock series stand out as the programs of choice in professional graphic arts environments.

We've used a modular design for the Against The Clock series, allowing you to mix and match the drawing, imaging, and page-layout applications that exactly suit your specific needs.

Titles available in the Against The Clock series include:

Macintosh: Basic Operations
Windows: Basic Operations
Adobe Illustrator: Introduction and Advanced Digital Illustration
Macromedia FreeHand: Creating Digital Illustrations
Adobe InDesign: Introduction and Advanced Electronic Mechanicals
Adobe PageMaker: Introduction and Advanced Electronic Mechanicals
QuarkXPress: Introduction and Advanced Electronic Mechanicals
Microsoft Publisher: Creating Electronic Mechanicals
Microsoft PowerPoint: Presentation Graphics with Impact
Microsoft FrontPage: Designing for the Web
Macromedia Painter: A Digital Approach to Natural Art Media
Adobe Photoshop: Introduction and Advanced Digital Images
Adobe Premiere: Digital Video Editing
Macromedia Director: Creating Powerful Multimedia
File Preparation: The Responsible Electronic Page
Preflight: An Introduction to File Analysis and Repair
TrapWise and PressWise: Digital Trapping and Imposition

We've designed our courses to be cross-platform. While many sites use Macintosh computers, there is an increasing number of graphic arts service providers using Intel-based systems running Windows (or WindowsNT). The books in this series are applicable to either of these systems.

All of the applications that we cover in the Against The Clock series are similar in operation and appearance whether you're working on a Macintosh or a Windows system. When a particular function does differ from machine to machine, we present both.

ICONS AND VISUALS

Pencil icon indicates a comment from an experienced operator. Whenever you see the pencil icon, you'll find corresponding sidebar text that augments or builds upon the subject being discussed at the time.

Bomb icon indicates a potential problem or difficulty. For instance, a certain technique might lead to pages that prove difficult to output. In other cases, there might be something that a program cannot easily accomplish, so we might present a workaround.

Pointing Finger icon indicates a hands-on activity — whether a short exercise or a complete project. Note that sometimes this icon will direct you to the back of the book to complete a project.

Key icon is used to point out that there is a keyboard equivalent to a menu or dialog-box option. Key commands are often faster than using the mouse to select a menu option. Experienced operators often mix the use of keyboard equivalents and menu/dialog box selections to arrive at their optimum speed.

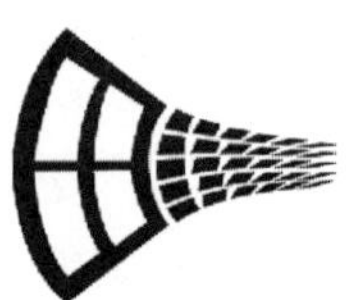

If you are a Windows user, be sure to refer to the corresponding text or images whenever you see this **Windows** icon. Although there isn't a great deal of difference between using these applications on a Macintosh and using them on a Windows-based workstation, there are certain instances where there's enough of a difference for us to comment.

Book Walk-Through

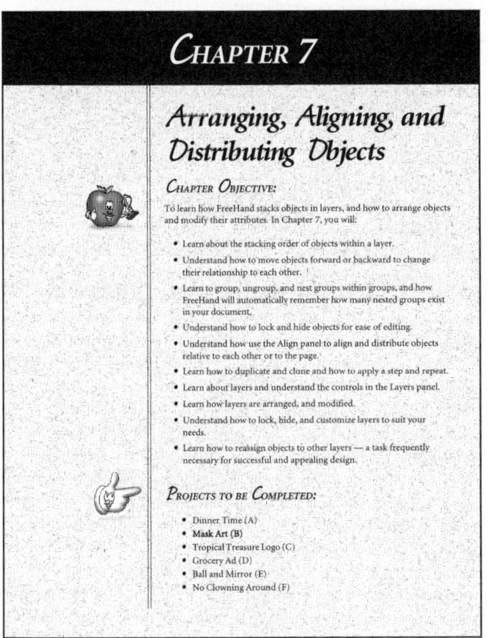

Chapter 7

Arranging, Aligning, and Distributing Objects

Chapter Objective:

To learn how FreeHand stacks objects in layers, and how to arrange objects and modify their attributes. In Chapter 7, you will:

- Learn about the stacking order of objects within a layer.
- Understand how to move objects forward or backward to change their relationship to each other.
- Learn to group, ungroup, and nest groups within groups, and how FreeHand will automatically remember how many nested groups exist in your document.
- Understand how to lock and hide objects for ease of editing.
- Understand how use the Align panel to align and distribute objects relative to each other or to the page.
- Learn how to duplicate and clone and how to apply a step and repeat.
- Learn about layers and understand the controls in the Layers panel.
- Learn how layers are arranged, and modified.
- Understand how to lock, hide, and customize layers to suit your needs.
- Learn how to reassign objects to other layers — a task frequently necessary for successful and appealing design.

Projects to be Completed:

- Dinner Time (A)
- Mask Art (B)
- Tropical Treasure Logo (C)
- Grocery Ad (D)
- Ball and Mirror (E)
- No Clowning Around (F)

Chapter openers *provide the reader with specific objectives.*

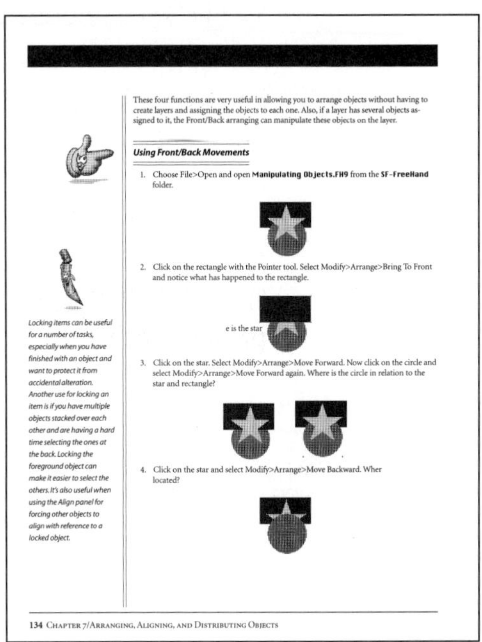

These four functions are very useful in allowing you to arrange objects without having to create layers and assigning the objects to each one. Also, if a layer has several objects assigned to it, the Front/Back arranging can manipulate these objects on the layer.

Locking items can be useful for a number of tasks, especially when you have finished with an object and want to protect it from accidental alteration. Another use for locking an item is if you have multiple objects stacked over each other and are having a hard time selecting the ones at the back. Locking the foreground object can make it easier to select the others. It's also useful when using the Align panel for forcing other objects to align with reference to a locked object.

Using Front/Back Movements

1. Choose File>Open and open **Manipulating Objects.FH9** from the **SF-FreeHand** folder.
2. Click on the rectangle with the Pointer tool. Select Modify>Arrange>Bring To Front and notice what has happened to the rectangle.

e is the star

3. Click on the star. Select Modify>Arrange>Move Forward. Now click on the circle and select Modify>Arrange>Move Forward again. Where is the circle in relation to the star and rectangle?
4. Click on the star and select Modify>Arrange>Move Backward. Wher located?

134 Chapter 7/Arranging, Aligning, and Distributing Objects

Sidebars and hands-on activities *supplement concepts presented in the material.*

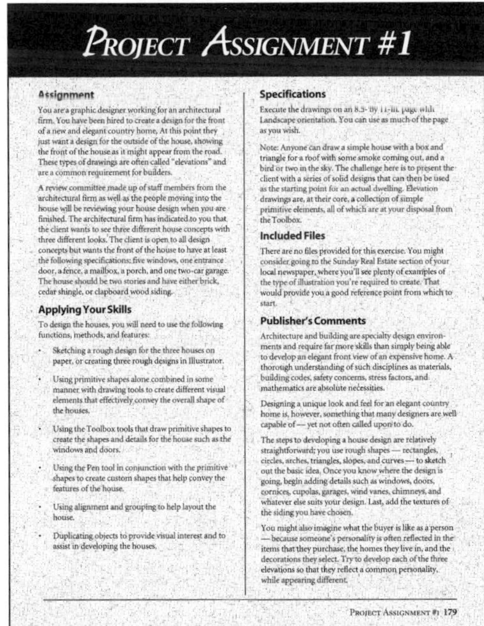

Project Assignment #1

Assignment

You are a graphic designer working for an architectural firm. You have been hired to create a design for the front of a new and elegant country home. At this point they just want a design for the outside of the house, showing the front of the house as it might appear from the road. These types of drawings are often called "elevations" and are a common requirement for builders.

A review committee made up of staff members from the architectural firm as well as the people moving into the house will be reviewing your house design when you are finished. The architectural firm has indicated to you that the client wants to see three different house concepts with three different looks. The client is open to all design concepts but wants the front of the house to have at least the following specifications: five windows, one entrance door, a fence, a mailbox, a porch, and one two-car garage. The house should be two stories and have either brick, cedar shingle, or clapboard wood siding.

Applying Your Skills

To design the houses, you will need to use the following functions, methods, and features:

- Sketching a rough design for the three houses on paper, or creating three rough designs in Illustrator.
- Using primitive shapes alone combined in some manner with drawing tools to create different visual elements that effectively convey the overall shape of the houses.
- Using the Toolbox tools that draw primitive shapes to create the shapes and details for the house such as the windows and doors.
- Using the Pen tool in conjunction with the primitive shapes to create custom shapes that help convey the features of the house.
- Using alignment and grouping to help layout the house.
- Duplicating objects to provide visual interest and to assist in developing the houses.

Specifications

Execute the drawings on an 8.5- by 11-in. page with Landscape orientation. You can use as much of the page as you wish.

Note: Anyone can draw a simple house with a box and triangle for a roof with some smoke coming out, and a bird or two in the sky. The challenge here is to present the client with a series of solid designs that can then be used as the starting point for an actual dwelling. Elevation drawings are, at their core, a collection of simple primitive elements, all of which are at your disposal from the Toolbox.

Included Files

There are no files provided for this exercise. You might consider going to the Sunday Real Estate section of your local newspaper, where you'll see plenty of examples of the type of illustration you're required to create. That would provide you a good reference point from which to start.

Publisher's Comments

Architecture and building are specialty design environments and require far more skills than simply being able to develop an elegant front view of an expensive home. A thorough understanding of such disciplines as materials, building codes, safety concerns, stress factors, and mathematics are absolute necessities.

Designing a unique look and feel for an elegant country home is, however, something that many designers are well capable of — yet not often called upon to do.

The steps to developing a house design are relatively straightforward; you use rough shapes — rectangles, circles, arches, triangles, slopes, and curves — to sketch out the basic idea. Once you know where the design is going, begin adding details such as windows, doors, cornices, cupolas, garages, wind vanes, chimneys, and whatever else suits your design. Last, add the textures of the siding you have chosen.

You might also imagine what the buyer is like as a person — because someone's personality is often reflected in the items that they purchase, the homes they live in, and the decorations they select. Try to develop each of the three elevations so that they reflect a common personality, while appearing different.

Project Assignment #1 179

Project assignments *allow you to use your imagination and your new skills to satisfy a client's publications needs.*

Step-by-step projects *result in finished artwork — with an emphasis on proper file construction methods.*

The Projects You Will Work On

In addition to explantory text and illustrations, ATC course materials have been constructed with two primary building blocks: exercises and projects. Projects always result in a finished piece of work — digital imagery typically built from the ground up, utilizing photographic-quality images; vector artwork from illustration programs; and type elements from the library supplied on your CD-ROM.

This course, *Macromedia FreeHand: Creating Digtial Illustrations*, uses several step-by-step projects on which you will work during your learning sessions. (There are also open-ended project assignments immediately preceding the two reviews.) You will find images of the step-by-step projects that you will complete by the end of the course displayed on the inside front and back covers of the book. Here's a brief overview of each:

Project A: Dinner Time

Using basic shapes, lines, and the drawing tools, a scene of pets at dinner is created. This project emphasizes the importance of using and combining primitive elements. All the drawing tools are used to create the scene, giving students an opportunity to experience the feel of the tools as they create.

Project B: Mask Art

In the Mask Art project, colorful shapes are created, duplicated, stacked, and positioned to create an effect similar to building designs from colored construction paper. This project makes extensive use of fill and stroke attributes, and also incorporates type converted to outlines. The drawing is developed in stages, with the mountains coming first and the other elements created individually, colored, and then positioned to complete the illustration. The positioning of the elements relative to each other — the so-called "stacking order" — is a critical technique.

Project C: Tropical Treasure Logo

Designing a logo that speaks elegantly of a company isn't easy. Here, you will create a retailer's logo block called *Tropical Treasure* using type, an illustration of the little treasure chest in the copy line, bordering rules, and a "deck" ("*Gifts from the Sea*"). This is a type-intensive project, with shadow techniques derived from using layers of overlapping type.

Project D: Grocery Ad

There are many reasons to use FreeHand as a page layout tool. The Grocery Ad is a prime example of how FreeHand can be used to stramline the production of a relatively complex one-page newspaper advertisement. The project requires extensive use of precise grids and guides to split the page into regions and layers, and the project relies on the use of rows and columns. Large font sizes that require exact specifications are used. Additionally, the use of type on a path is incoporated to help create an attractive headline.

Project E: Ball & Mirror

The Ball & Mirror image begins with using alignment techniques followed by the creative use of combining paths to create objects. There is also extensive use of the Freehand tool for a hand-drawn look of the mirror cracks. The mirror frame and reflection represents the creative use of a linear gradient, while the ball uses a radial gradient altered with the Gradient tool.

Project F: No Clowning Around

Both primitive shapes and the Pen tool are used to draw this clown. Elements are combined to create complex shapes. Understanding the stacking order of elements is very important to the successful completion of this project. The project also makes extensive use of FreeHand's ability to show and hide selected elements, aiding the artist in viewing the work without interference.

FOR THE STUDENT

On the CD-ROM you will find a complete set of the Against The Clock (ATC) fonts, as well as a collection of data files used to construct the various exercises and projects.

The ATC fonts are solely for use while you are working with the Against The Clock materials. These fonts will be used throughout both the exercises and projects.

A variety of student files have been included. These files are necessary to complete both the exercises and the step-by-step projects.

FOR THE INSTRUCTOR

The Instructor Kit consists of an Instructor's Manual and an Instructor's CD-ROM. It includes various testing and presentation materials in addition to the files that come standard with the student books.

- **Overhead Presentation Materials** are provided and follow along with the course. These presentations are prepared using Microsoft PowerPoint and are provided in both native PowerPoint format as well as Acrobat Portable Document Format (PDF).
- **Extra Projects Assignments** are provided along with the data files required for completion. These projects may be used to extend the course, or may be used to test the student.
- **Finished artwork (in PDF format)** for all projects that the students complete is supplied on the CD-ROM.
- **Test Questions and Answers** are included on the instructor CD-ROM. These questions may be modified, reorganized, and administered throughout the delivery of the course.

Our History

Against The Clock (ATC) was founded in 1990 as a part of Lanman Systems Group, one of the nation's leading systems integration and training firms. The company specialized in developing custom training materials for such clients as *L.L. Bean, The New England Journal of Medicine, Smithsonian,* the *National Education Association, Air & Space Magazine, Publishers Clearing House,* The *National Wildlife Society, Home Shopping Network,* and many others. The integration firm was among the most highly respected in the graphic arts industry.

To a great degree, the success of Lanman Systems Group can be attributed to the thousands of pages of course materials developed at the company's demanding client sites. Throughout the rapid growth of LSG, Founder and General Manager Ellenn Behoriam developed the expertise necessary to manage technical experts, writers, editors, illustrators, designers, layout artists, and the rest of the chain of professionals required to develop highly effective training materials.

Following the sale of the Lanman Companies to World Color, one of the nation's largest commercial printers, Ellenn embarked on a project to develop a new library of hands-on training materials engineered specifically for the professional graphic artist. A large part of this effort is finding and working with talented professional artists, writers, and educators from around the country. The result is the ATC training library.

Doug Borton

Doug Borton of Kellogg Community College in Battle Creek, Michigan, has been teaching college courses and workshops for five years. In the process of instructing others, he has created various how-to guides and training manuals. Doug has been using FreeHand since it was first introduced to the graphic arts community. Doug is an active traditional and digital artist in his local community. He has shown his artwork at various galleries and art shops.

Robin McAllister

Robin McAllister has been speaking and writing about creating effective pages since before desktop publishing was invented. In the process of teaching others, he has written various how-to guides and training manuals. Rob serves as a contributing editor for numerous publications and publishers, and has authored a variety of desktop publishing and prepress titles.

In addition to serving as senior project manager for Against The Clock, Rob is the team leader for America Online's Applied Computing Community, and a contributing editor for *Printing News* and *Electronic Publishing.*

Getting Started

Platform

The Against The Clock series is designed to apply to both Macintosh and Windows systems. Macromedia FreeHand runs under Macintosh, Windows 98, Windows 2000, and Windows NT. There are separate student files for Macintosh and Windows students.

Naming Conventions

In the old days of MS-DOS systems, file names on the PC were limited to something referred to as "8.3," which meant that you were limited in the number of characters you could use to an eight-character name (the "8") and a three-character suffix (the "3"). Text files, for example, might be called *myfile.txt*, while a document file from a word processor might be called *myfile.doc* (for document). On today's Windows systems, these limitations have been, for the most part, overcome. Although you can use longer file names, suffixes still exist. The Macintosh does not rely on the file extension at all. You see the characters as part of the file name.

When your Windows system is first configured, the Views are normally set to a default that hides these extensions. This means that you might have a dozen different files named *myfile*, all of which may have been generated by different applications and consist of completely different types of files.

You can change this view by double clicking on *My Computer* (the icon on your desktop). This will open the file. Select View>Folder Options. From Folder Options, select the View tab. Within the Files and Folders folder is a checkbox: Hide File Extensions for Known File Types. When this is unchecked, you can see the file extensions. It's easier to know what you're looking at if they're visible. While this is a personal choice, we strongly recommend viewing the file extensions. All the files used in this course have been named using the three- or four-character suffix.

Key Commands

There are two keys generally used as *modifier* keys — they do nothing when pressed, unless they are pressed in conjunction with another key. Their purpose is to alter the normal functions of the other key with which they are pressed.

The Command (Macintosh) or Control (Windows) key is generally used when taking control of the computer. When combined with the "S" key, it functions to save your work. When combined with "O," it opens a file; with a "P," it prints the file. In addition to these functions, which work with most Macintosh and Windows programs, the Control key may be combined with other keys to take control of specific functions in FreeHand.

Another special function key is the Option (Macintosh) and Alt (for alternate) (Windows) key. It, too, is a modifier key, and you must hold it down along with whatever other key (or keys) is required for a specific function. The Option and Alt keys are often used in conjunction with other keys to access typographic characters having an ASCII number higher than 128. Under Windows, they are used in conjunction with the numeric keypad. For example, Alt-0149 will produce a bullet character. Alt-F4 will close the program. The Option key is combined with alphanumeric keys, instead of the numeric keypad. Option-8, for example, will produce a bullet.

The keys on the top row of the keypad, F1–F12, also accomplish specific tasks in conjunction with the computer. F1 will bring up the Help menu. F6 and Shift-F6 will move elements to the front or the back of a "stack" of text and graphic objects.

The Macintosh and Windows access context-sensitive menus in similar but different ways. On the Macintosh, holding down the Control (not the Command) key while clicking the mouse button will bring up context-sensitive menus. Under Windows, this is accomplished by clicking the right mouse button (right-clicking). We generically call accessing the context menu "context-clicking."

The CD-ROM and Initial Setup Considerations

Before you begin using your Against The Clock course book, you must set up your system to have access to the various files and tools to complete your lessons.

Student Files

This course comes complete with a collection of student files. These files are an integral part of the learning experience — they're used throughout the course to help you construct increasingly complex elements. Having these building blocks available to you for practice and study sessions will ensure that you will be able to experience the exercises and complete the project assignments smoothly, spending a minimum of time looking for the various required components.

In the Student Files folders, we've created sets of data. Locate the **SF-FreeHand** folder and drag the icon onto your hard disk drive. If you have limited disk space, you may want to copy only the files for one or two lessons at a time.

We strongly recommend that you work from your hard disk. However, in some cases you might not have enough room on your system for all the files we've supplied. If this is the case, you can work directly from the CD-ROM.

Creating a Project Folder

Throughout the exercises and projects you'll be required to save your work. Since the CD-ROM is "read-only," you cannot write information to it. Create a "work in progress" folder on your hard disk and use it to store your work. Create it by context-clicking, while at your desktop, then selecting New Folder (Macintosh) or New> Folder (Windows). This will create the folder at the highest level of your system, where it will always be easy to find. Name this folder "Work in Progress".

Fonts

You must install the ATC font library to ensure that your lessons and exercises will work as described in the course book. These fonts are provided on the student CD-ROM.

Instructions for installing fonts are provided in the documentation that came with your computer. In general, drag them into your System>Fonts folder on the Macintosh, or, under Windows, from your Start>Settings>Control Panel>Fonts, select File>Install New Font. Navigate to the Fonts folder on the CD, select the fonts, and click OK.

System Requirements

On the Macintosh, you will need a Power PC 604 processor or above, running the 8.5 operating system or later; 64 MB of RAM; a monitor with a resolution of at least 800 × 600 or greater; Adobe PostScript Level 2 or higher printer; and a CD-ROM drive. You will need 105 MB of free hard drive space for installation.

On a Windows operating system, you'll need a Pentium II or faster processor; Windows 98/NT 4.0, or Windows 2000 or higher; 64 MB RAM; a monitor with a resolution of at least 800 × 600 pixels; Adobe PostScript Level 2 or higher printer; and a CD-ROM drive. You will need 105 MB of free hard drive space for installation.

Prerequisites

This book assumes that you have a basic understanding of how to use your system.

You should know how to use your mouse to point and click, and how to drag items around the screen. You should know how to resize a window, and how to arrange windows on your desktop to maximize your available space. You should know how to access pull-down menus, and how checkboxes and radio buttons work. Lastly, you should know how to create, open, and save files.

If you're familiar with these fundamental skills, then you know all that's necessary to utilize the Against The Clock courseware library.

Notes:

Introduction

An Introduction

FreeHand is a powerful application for creating commercial art and graphic illustrations. It also has comprehensive page layout tools that you can use to complete entire layouts. FreeHand 9's versatility is especially important for artists creating designs for printed publications, multimedia projects, and Internet content.

Graphic design, even with a computer, should begin traditionally with a few pencil sketches (called *thumbnails*). Thumbnails offer several ideas and concepts for presentation to your client. Once a design is chosen, it's easy for a skilled artist to bring the sketch to life in FreeHand. The finished project (called a *comp* or *mechanical*) can then be incorporated into other projects, or used as is.

Digital Graphic Images

Images that are created digitally are either object-oriented (vector) or bitmap (raster).

FreeHand is an *object-oriented* drawing program. Object-oriented drawing programs create artwork with graphic objects drawn as lines or curves. These lines and curves are known as *vectors*, and can be combined, colored, and modified in many ways to produce the desired effect that you require. Object-oriented images can also be scaled and printed in any size without a loss of quality.

Bitmap images can be created either by scanning a photograph, or by creating them in programs that use the raster format, such as Adobe Photoshop. As an artist and designer, you will be working frequently with raster images.

A bitmap image is a *map* composed of *pixels*, the simplest of which is one bit of information. Each pixel contains information in a *bit depth* that ranges from 1 to 32 bits. More information can be stored to represent the color of a specific pixel the higher the bit depth is. The most common bitmap image formats are TIFF, GIF, and JPEG. A common format on Windows computers is the BMP format; a common format on Macintosh computers is the PICT format, which can also store object-oriented images. Bitmaps cannot be scaled or printed in varying resolutions without a significant loss of quality, making them much less versatile than object-oriented images.

Step by Step

We feel very strongly that the best way to train you properly and efficiently in FreeHand 9 is to guide you through a structured and creative course with practical, hands-on exercises accompanied by annotated, lecture-style information. This introductory course moves step-by-step through the workings of FreeHand 9 with many exercises to help you understand, by practice, how to use the many features of the software. When you have completed this course, you will have a firm grasp on creating documents and be ready to begin developing your own designs.

Follow the exercises; study them closely. This is your career, and it is our desire to train you to be the best designer you can possibly be. If your computer already has FreeHand 9 installed, you're ready to begin. If not, install the program from the CD-ROM following the installation instructions included with your software package.

CHAPTER 1

FREEHAND WORKFLOW

CHAPTER OBJECTIVE:

To become familiar with FreeHand's operating environment, tools, and controls. In Chapter 1, you will:

- Begin to understand FreeHand's tools — panels, menus, Inspectors, toolbars, and document windows.
- Learn how the Toolbox can be modified and positioned.
- Understand why the most-used tool in FreeHand is the Pointer tool, and learn where and how it is used.
- Review the most basic commands an artist must remember when working in a graphic application: how to create, open, and save.
- Learn how to create and customize toolbars.
- Learn how to access the Document Inspector's numerous panels and sub-panels, and other panels that FreeHand offers.
- Explore FreeHand's menu structure — view what selections FreeHand provides, and explore its submenus.
- Learn about FreeHand's defaults, and how to customize them to your own specific tastes and standards.
- Learn a few basic drawing commands, and how to create custom views and windows of your document.
- Learn how to navigate your way through a FreeHand document.
- Learn to utilize Wizards (Windows version only).

PROJECTS TO BE COMPLETED:

- Dinner Time (A)
- Mask Art (B)
- Tropical Treasure Logo (C)
- Grocery Ad (D)
- Ball and Mirror (E)
- No Clowning Around (F)

FreeHand Workflow

This section guides you through some of the fundamental operations of FreeHand: creating and opening documents, saving them, and adjusting FreeHand's defaults to suit your preferences. You'll also learn how to navigate through a document and examine how FreeHand's tools are displayed and accessed.

The FreeHand Environment

In FreeHand you work with panels, menus, Inspectors, toolbars, and document windows, which include the pasteboard.

At the top of the screen is the Menu Bar, where most of FreeHand's major functions are accessed. The main document window (which only appears if you create a new document or open an existing one) contains all the document's pages and the Pasteboard.

Here's a representative look at FreeHand's environment for the Macintosh. Your screen might look a little different because many things such as panels and the Inspector can be placed anywhere on the screen, or may not appear in a new document unless you modify the FreeHand Preferences (explained later in this section).

Imagine the pasteboard as a storage area for anything you might want to use in your artwork. Things on the pasteboard won't print or otherwise appear in your document, but can be moved onto the page at any time.

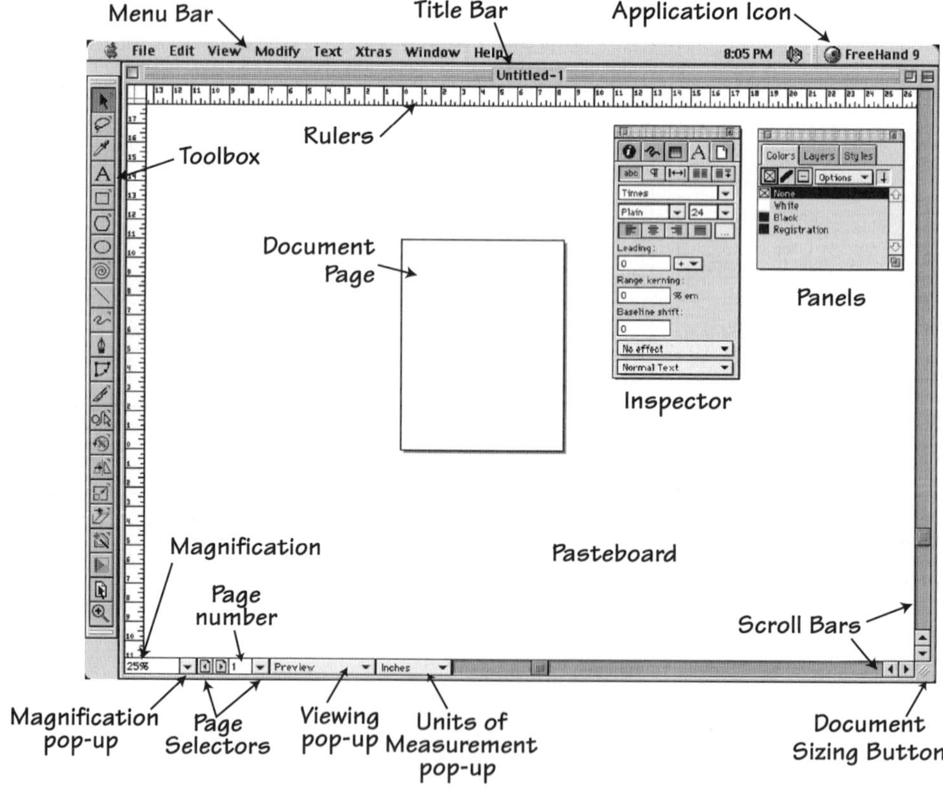

The image that follows is the Windows representation of the FreeHand environment. Most FreeHand operations are identical between the two versions, but there are subtle differences in their appearance.

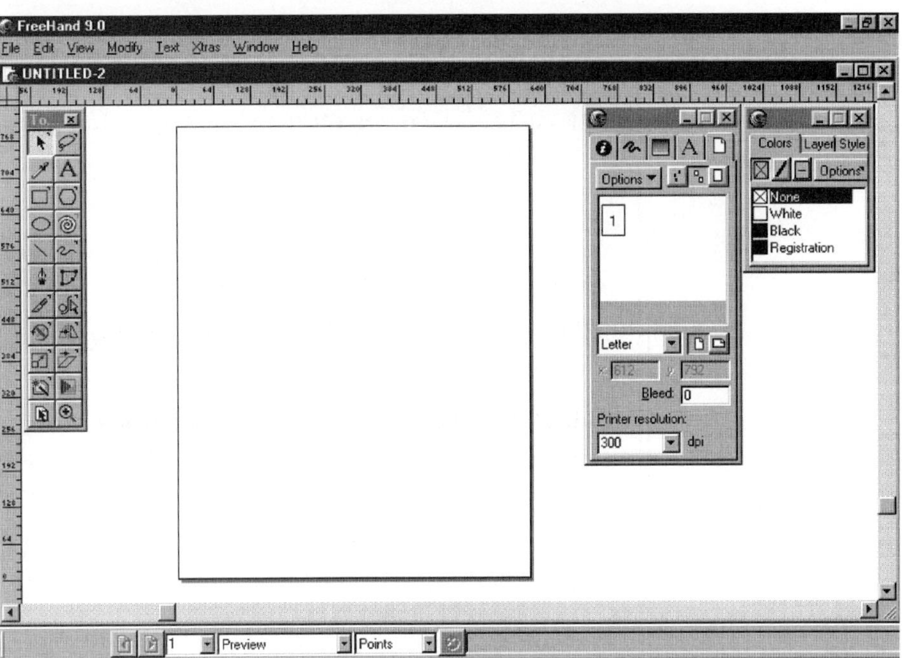

The Pointer Tool

The Pointer tool (the arrow that moves with your mouse) is the most fundamental tool in FreeHand, and the one you'll probably use the most. It is selected at the top of the toolbar and is used within a document to select and move objects; and in the rest of FreeHand it is used to make selections from menus, inspectors, and other controls.

Press Command-S (Macintosh) or Control-S (Windows) to save a document.

Creating, Opening, and Saving a Document

These most basic functions, plus a number of others, are all accomplished through the File menu. As you look at the upper portion of this menu, you will notice that these basic functions also have keyboard shortcuts because you use them so often.

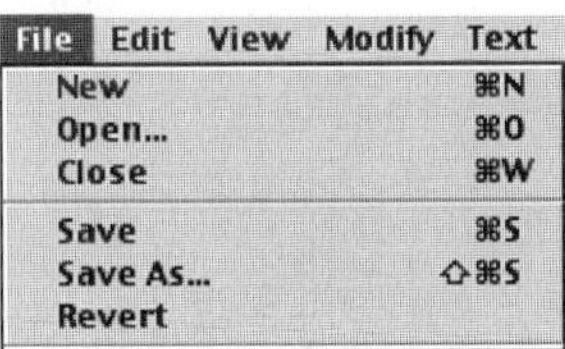

To create a new file, select File>New. You will be presented with a blank page, ready for you to create a new illustration. To open an existing document, select File>Open, then navigate to the folder in which the document has been placed. In this course, you will often be asked to open a file from your **SF-FreeHand** folder which is located on your student CD. To close a document without saving, select File>Close.

It is important to develop the habit of saving early and saving often. Hours of work can be lost in an instant if your computer locks up or the power fails and you forgot to save your work. This can easily happen when you get really wrapped up in what you are doing. By saving the document often, say, every five minutes, at worst you'll have to recreate five minutes worth of work if the power goes out. The easiest way to save is to take a moment and press Command-S (Macintosh) or Control-S (Windows).

However, when you have created a new document, this option is not available to you. You'll need to use the File>Save As command. Navigate to the folder in which you wish to store the document and give it a unique file name. During this course, you will often be asked to save a file to your **Work in Progress** folder, and will be using this command. Files may be saved as FreeHand Documents, FreeHand Templates (on which you may base other documents) or Editable EPS, which may be placed into page layout programs.

You may also find File>Revert useful. This is sometimes referred to as the "bail out" command, and it is used when work has been done to a document and you decide that you want to return the document to its most recent saved state.

Create and Save a FreeHand Document

1. Choose File>New to create a new document.
2. To save the document, choose File>Save As. Navigate to your **Work in Progress** folder that you created to save your work (you should have created this folder in the *Getting Started* section).

   The Save As dialog box appears. Click on the Format (Macintosh) or Save as type (Windows) pop-up menu to see the three formats for saving documents.

Both the Macintosh and Windows versions of FreeHand can open files created on either platform. Adding ".FH9" to the end of document file names ensures maximum compatibility across these two different computer platforms. The same applies for the ".FT9" file extension for FreeHand templates, which we will cover shortly. Refer to the Getting Started section for more information about file naming conventions. The file extensions are automatically created by the Windows version, but must be manually input on the Macintosh.

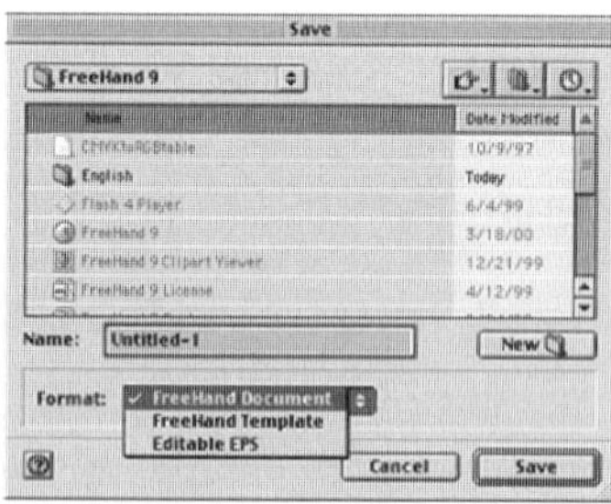

Macintosh

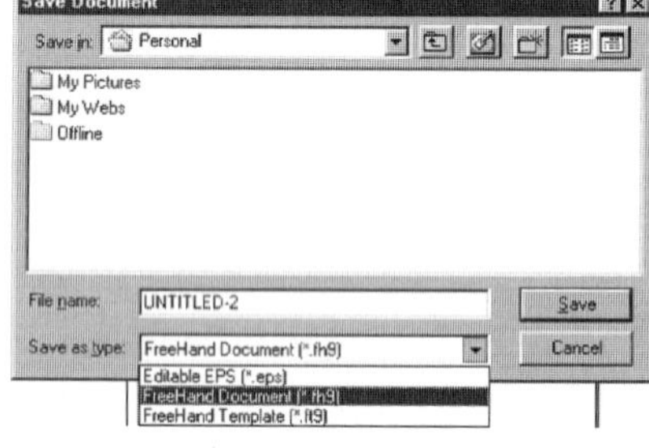

Windows

3. Select FreeHand Document. In the Save As section, name the file "FreeHand Document.FH9" and click Save.
4. This will save the original document. The new document name will appear in the Title Bar across the top of the document. Choose File>Save As again. This time, choose the FreeHand Template format. Name the file "FreeHand Template.FT9". Click Save. Notice that the name did not change in the Title Bar. The template was saved as an external copy of the document.
5. Choose File>Save As again. Click on the Format submenu to choose the Editable EPS option. Name the file "Editable.EPS". Click Save. The new document name will appear in the Title Bar. You have now saved the same document in three different formats. These file formats may not make much sense now, but we will cover them in later sections.
6. Close this document.

Opening a FreeHand Document

1. In the File menu, choose Open.
2. In the Open Document dialog box, navigate to the **SF-FreeHand** folder. When you click on a document name in this box, you have the option of showing a preview of the document. Not all files allow for a preview. If the file you have selected can not be previewed, text will appear indicating that no preview is available.

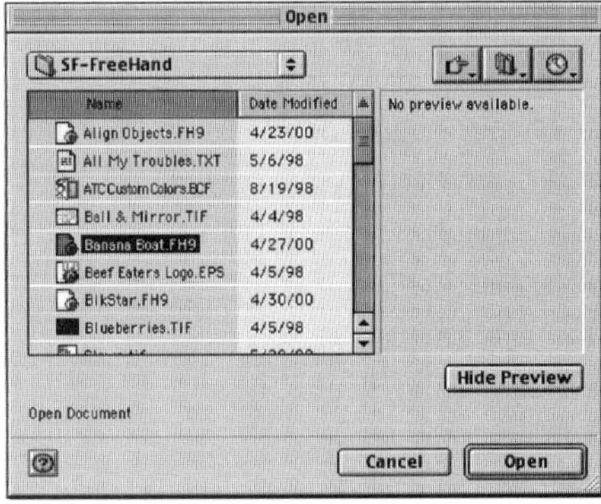

Macintosh

Hold the Spacebar to activate the scrolling Hand tool. It stays active as long as the Spacebar is held down.

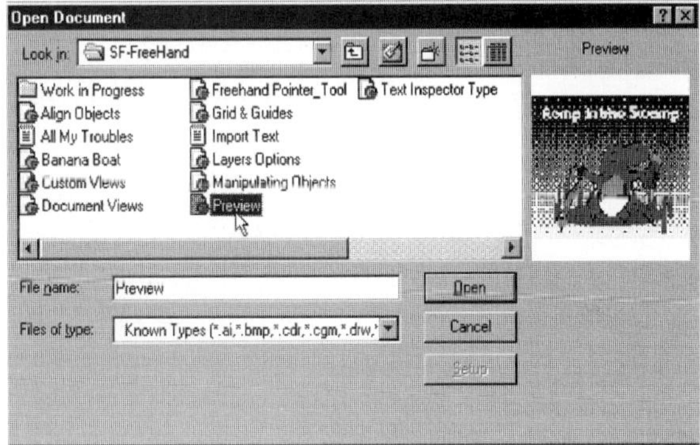

Windows

Randomly click on files that have an FH9 or FT9 extension — these are FreeHand documents and templates.

3. Select **Banana Boat.FH9** and click Open; the document opens and you can see the artwork inside. To see the entire page, select Fit Page in the Magnification pop-up.

Press Command-5 (Macintosh) or Control-5 (Windows) to switch to 50% magnification.

4. Choose File>Close to put the document away.

5. Choose File>Open again and open **Sky.EPS**. You will see a picture that you will use later within the Projects section of this course book. Because this file is in the EPS format, it can be placed into other applications such as PageMaker, InDesign, or QuarkXPress.

6. The upper-left (Macintosh) or right (Windows) square in the document's Title Bar is the Close box. Click on it to close the document.

7. Choose File>Open and select **FreeHand Template.FT9** — you created this file in the previous exercise.

   When the document opens, look at the Title Bar. What do you see? Why is the document named "Untitled"? Templates allow a document to be saved with graphics, type, and attributes set for use in the untitled copies of the original. You cannot automatically press Command/Control-S, but must choose "Save As" and enter a name to save the document. This eliminates the possibility of accidentally changing or ruining the original you worked so hard to produce.

8. Let's assume you want to make changes to an existing template. Choose View>Magnification and select 25%. While in the View menu, select Page Rulers>Show. Now choose Save As and save this file in FreeHand Template format, naming it "FreeHand Template.FT9". You will be asked if you want to replace the existing file of that name. Click Replace (Macintosh) or Yes (Windows).

9. Close the untitled document without saving. At the caution menu, click Don't Save (Macintosh) or No (Windows).

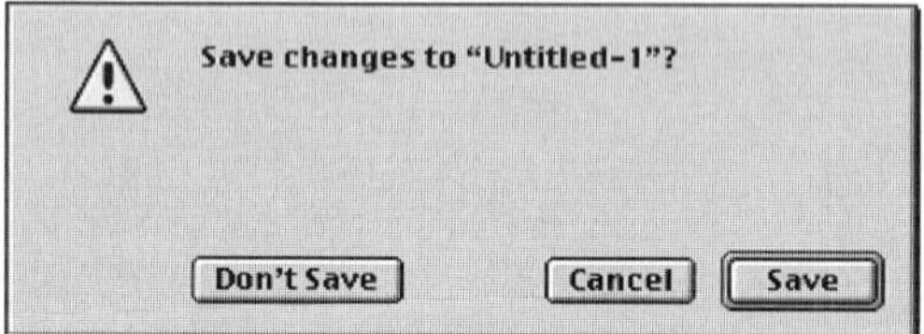

Explore the FreeHand Document

1. Choose File>Open to open **Document Views.FH9** from your **SF-FreeHand** folder.

2. In the menu bar, click on each menu and view what selections it contains. If any selections have a triangle, highlight them to see the submenus and what they offer.

Press Command-K (Macintosh) or Control-K (Windows) to toggle between Preview and Keyline mode.

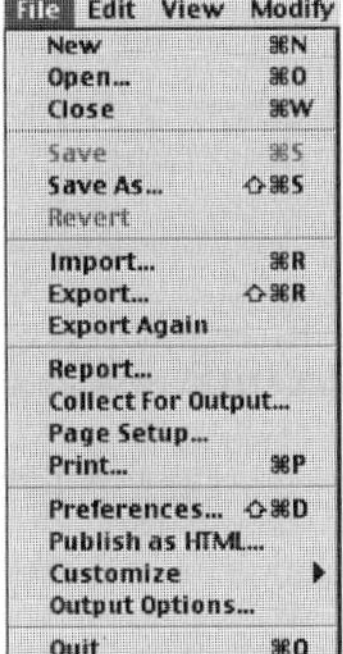

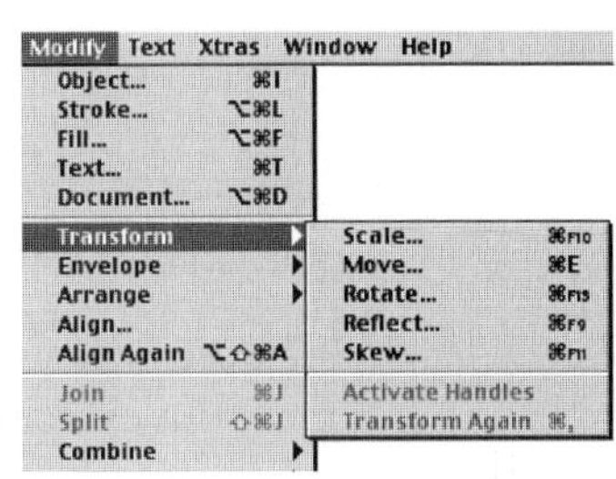

Macintosh

3. With the Pointer tool, click on the black square. Click on the Magnification pop-up menu at the bottom of the document window and select different percentages. Note how the document page enlarges or reduces.

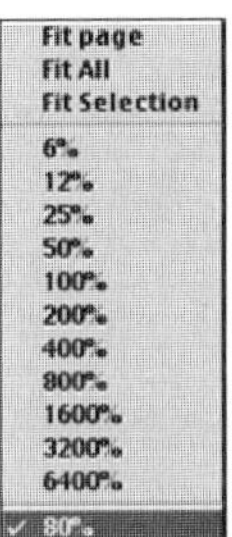

Macintosh

4. To the left of the Magnification pop-up menu is a field that shows the current percentage. Highlight this number with the mouse and type in 177. Press Return (Macintosh) or Enter (Windows) to apply; you will see the document change to this percentage. This is the way to achieve the exact magnification that you prefer.

5. Click on the View pop-up menu at the bottom of the screen to see your five options. Select Keyline and note how the square appears. For now, ignore the other options. Return to Preview mode.

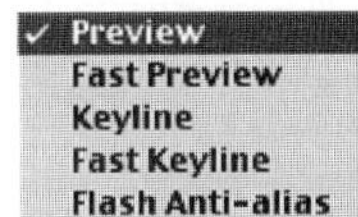

6. The View pop-up menu is not the only way to go from Preview to Keyline mode. You can select either in the View menu. Do this now by choosing View>Preview. When you select a mode, the menu item acquires a checkmark.

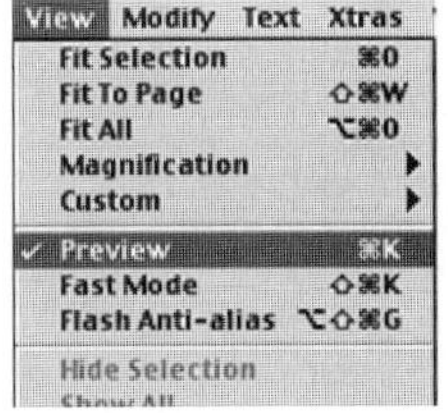

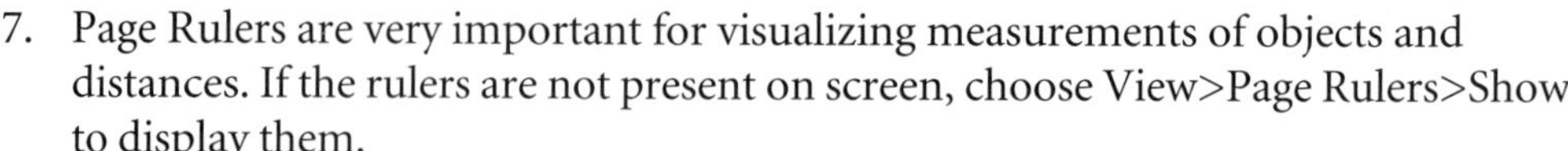

7. Page Rulers are very important for visualizing measurements of objects and distances. If the rulers are not present on screen, choose View>Page Rulers>Show to display them.

   Ruler increments have eight measurement units from which to choose. To change to a different measurement unit, access the Units pop-up menu at the bottom of the document window. Click on this pop-up menu to observe the units. Choose Inches and watch the rulers on screen change as well. Now select Points and observe the rulers. Reset the pop-up menu back to Inches.

A Kyu is a Japanese unit of measurement equal to 0.25mm.

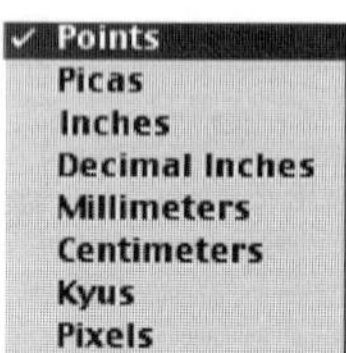

8. From the File menu choose Save As. When the dialog box appears, navigate to the your **Work in Progress** folder, type in the name "FreeHand Sample.FH9", and click Save.

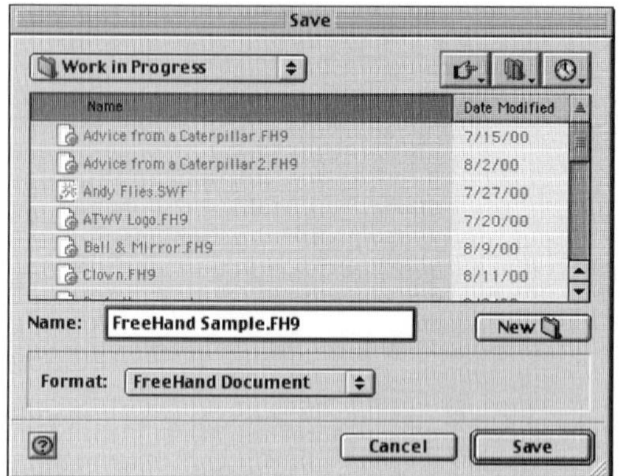

   Now look at the Title Bar of the document; the name has changed to the new name with which you saved the document.

9. Sometimes the page needs to be moved away from the panels and dialog boxes to better view the image. This is done either by the scroll bars or the Hand tool.

   The scroll bar consists of up/down arrows, the bar itself, and the scroll button on the bar.

Hold the Spacebar to activate the scrolling Hand tool. It stays active as long as the Spacebar is held down.

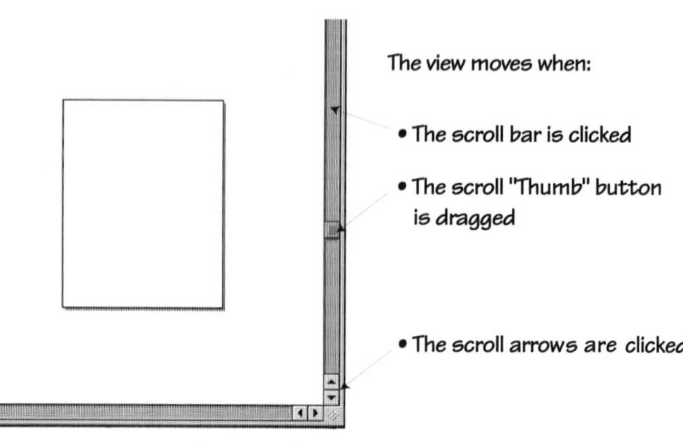

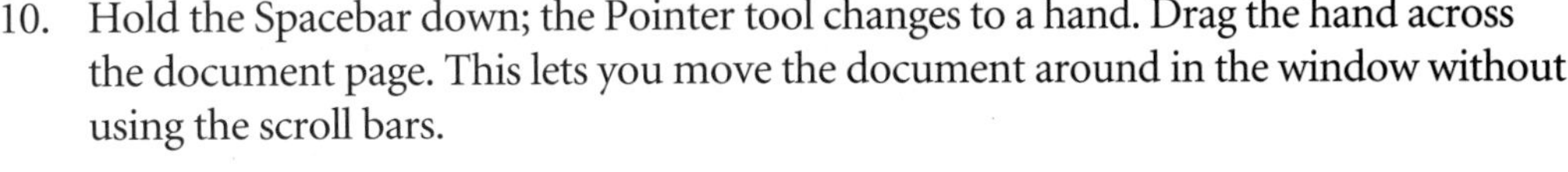

10. Hold the Spacebar down; the Pointer tool changes to a hand. Drag the hand across the document page. This lets you move the document around in the window without using the scroll bars.

11. Choose Window>Inspectors and select Document. Click on the Options feature and select Add pages.

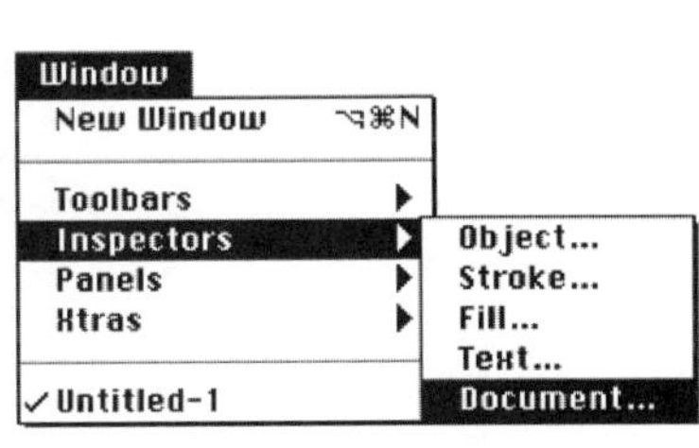

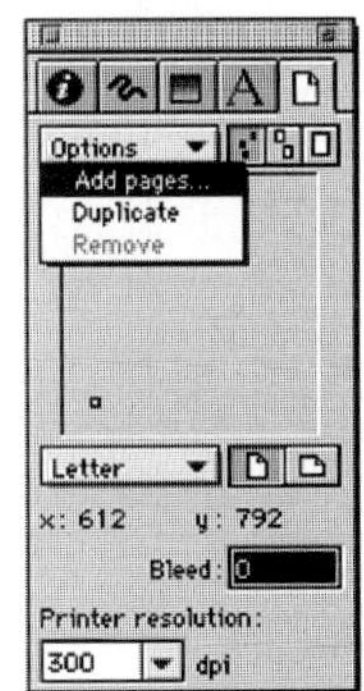

Press Command-5 (Macintosh) or Control-5 (Windows) to switch to 50% magnification.

12. In the dialog box, set the Number of pages to 4. Click OK.

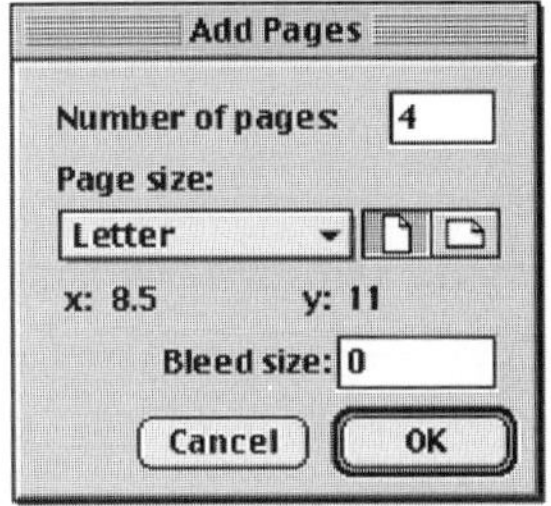

13. Use the Magnification pop-up menu at the bottom of the screen to view at 50%.

14. The page selection features at the bottom of the screen offer two ways to go to a page and tell you the page number you are currently on.

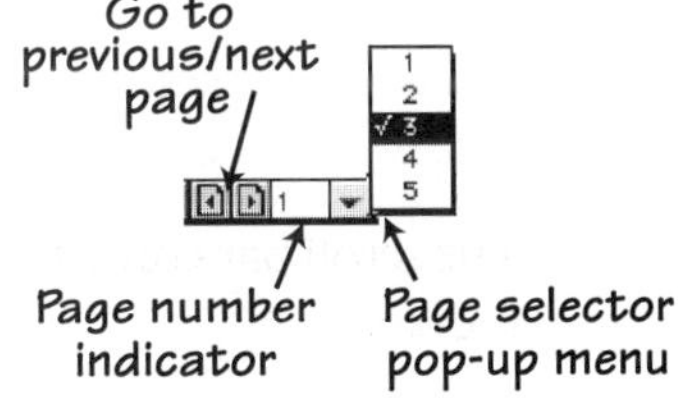

15. You have added four pages and are looking at a single page on the screen. What is the number of this page? Click on the Previous and Next page buttons to scroll through your pages.

    Observe how the page number changes as you move from page to page. Use the Selector pop-up menu to access different pages.

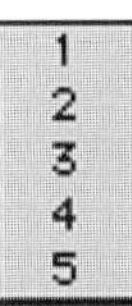

16. Close the document without saving.

Document Inspector

The Document Inspector is where you make most of the settings for the document's size, page orientation, *bleed,* and the number of pages in the document. You can also add, duplicate, and remove pages in the Inspector.

The Document Inspector presents a miniature view of the pasteboard with small icons (*thumbnails*) that represent each page of your document. Magnification settings for the pasteboard view are located at the top right of the Inspector. If your document contains lots of pages, they may not all fit within the pasteboard viewer at the larger viewing sizes.

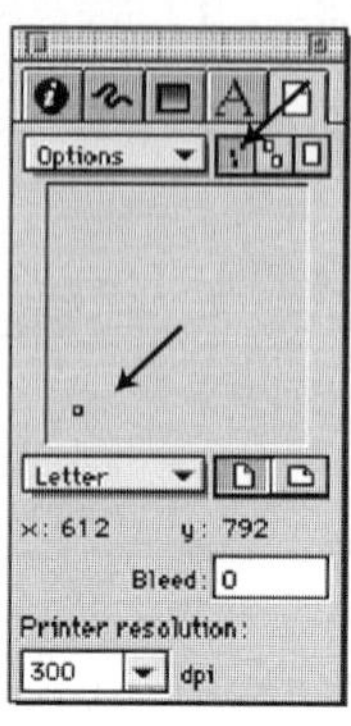

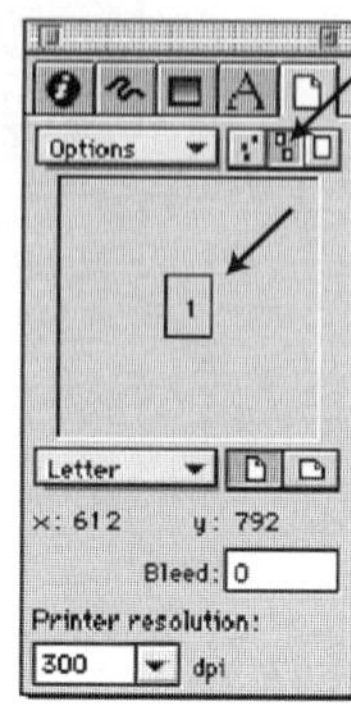

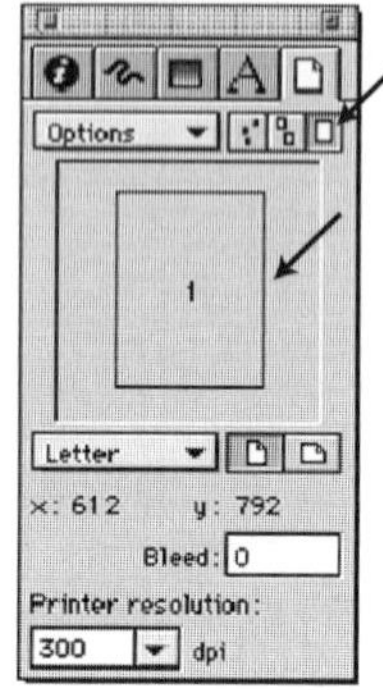

Use the Document Inspector

1. Create a new document by choosing File>New.
2. In the Magnification pop-up menu, set the page view for 25%. Choose Window> Inspectors>Document, if the Inspectors are not visible. The Inspector will appear on screen. Move the Inspector to the upper-right corner of the document. Set the measurement units to Inches from the Units pop-up menu.

Double-clicking on a page in the Document Inspector viewer brings the page in the document to the center of the drawing screen.

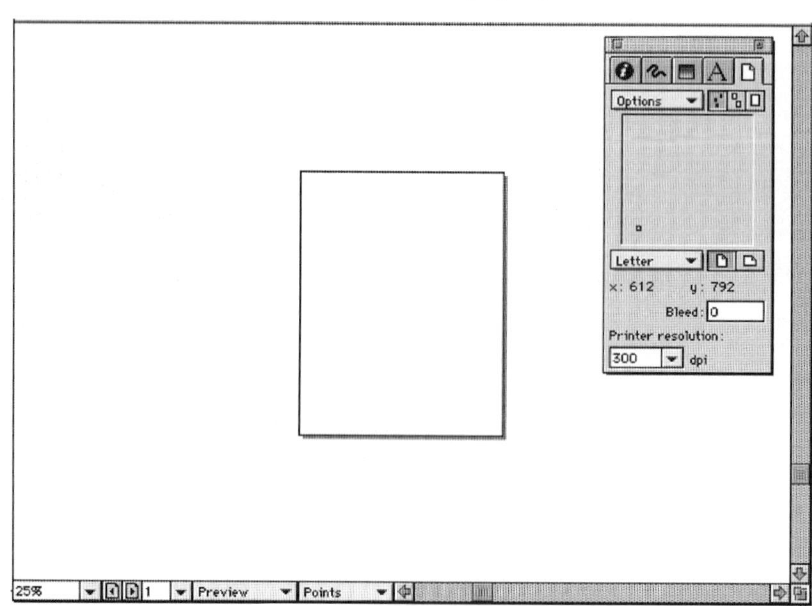

3. The three Thumbnail buttons allow you to move the page around on the pasteboard.

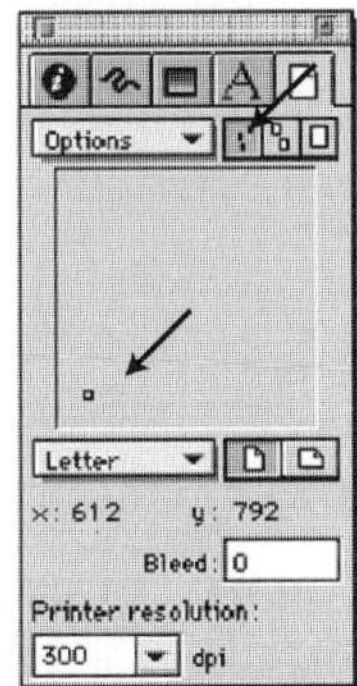

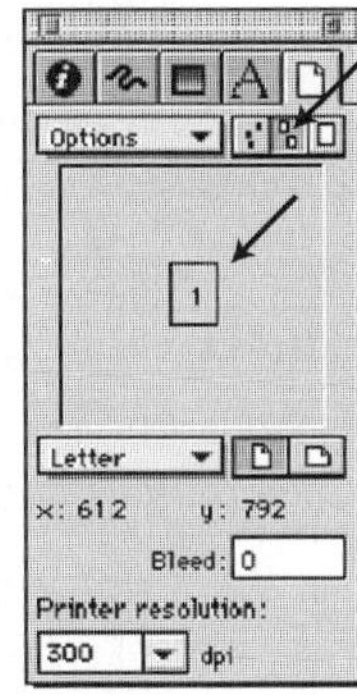

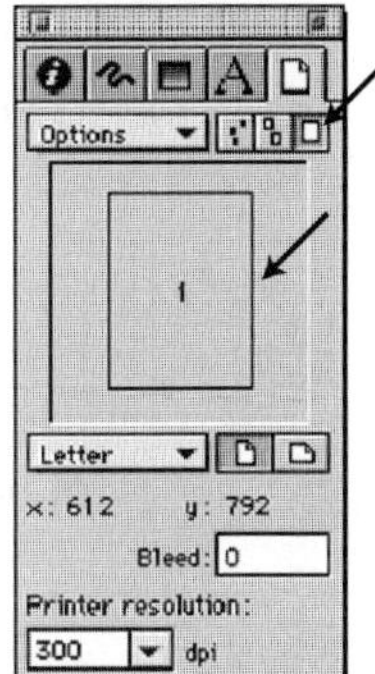

4. The default thumbnail view is the left one, next to the Options submenu. Click on the middle Thumbnail button. In the Viewer, move the page around watching how the actual page on the pasteboard moves. The actual page moves when you release the mouse button.

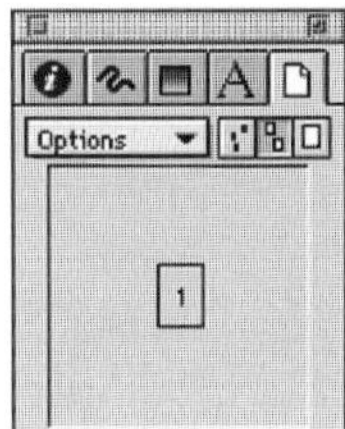

5. Click on the right Thumbnail button. In the viewer, move the page around to see how the document page moves.

6. Click on the Options submenu and select Add Pages. In the Add Pages dialog box, enter 5 and click OK.

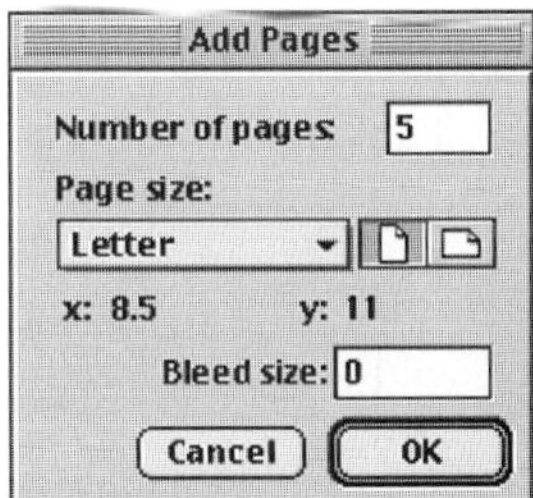

7. In the Document Inspector, click on the left view Thumbnail button. Five pages will appear on the pasteboard and in the Document Inspector, making six in all, counting the original. In the Document Inspector, the thumbnails will show one page that is darker than the others; this represents the current page.

Bleed *is the area around the page that will be trimmed off after the document is printed. This way, you can have artwork extending off the page and when the page is trimmed, the art will appear to extend exactly to the edge of the page.*

8. Click on this darker page in the viewer and move it up slightly. Notice how the corresponding page in the document moves up too.

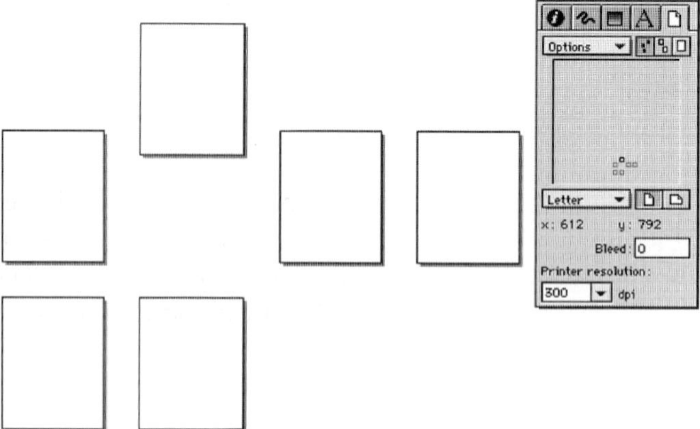

9. On the pasteboard, click on a different page. Notice how the corresponding page in the Inspector viewer becomes darker.
10. Select the Options pop-up menu in the Inspector and select Remove. The page on the pasteboard was removed and another page in the Inspector became the selected, darker page.
11. Navigate to the Page Size pop-up menu and select Legal. Note that only the one page size was changed. A FreeHand document can contain pages of several sizes.
12. Click on the other pages in the Inspector viewer. Each clicked page becomes darker, indicating it as the working page.
13. Click on the Landscape (horizontal) Orientation in the Inspector.

    The corresponding page on the pasteboard responds to the change in page orientation.
14. Click on the middle viewing icon in the Inspector; the selected page goes to the center of the viewer.
15. Remove all pages but one, using the Options submenu of the Inspector.
16. Choose View>Fit To Page. In the Status Bar, set the Units pop-up menu to Inches.
17. In the Inspector, enter 0.25 (inches) for Bleed. Press Return (Macintosh) or Enter (Windows) to apply. This will draw a gray outline around the page to show you how far the bleed extends.

    You have now experimented with the Document Inspector and observed how its various features work.
18. Close the document without saving.

FreeHand Defaults

FreeHand's default settings are stored in a file on your computer called FreeHand Defaults (Macintosh) or Defaults.FT9 (Windows). You might want to copy this file to a diskette should you ever want to revert back to the original settings. FreeHand uses this settings document each time you create a new file. But you can create your own settings file, set up the way you want to work, and FreeHand will use it for all new documents, instead of the original default settings file.

To select this default file use the File>Preferences>Document window, listed in template box under Document tab. FreeHand also uses this template file for all its settings when you create a new file. If you have other templates created with different settings they will be used if you type the document name in this box and then close Preferences.

Customizing Your Default Files

You can change nearly all FreeHand settings to be used as a default. For example, if you create a set of base colors that you will use often, you can create a new settings file that contains those colors. A settings file is simply a FreeHand template, and should be thought of in the same way as any other FreeHand template.

Change FreeHand Defaults

1. Choose File>Open. In the Open Document dialog box, navigate to the **English** folder in the **FreeHand 9.0** application folder and open the file **FreeHand Defaults**.

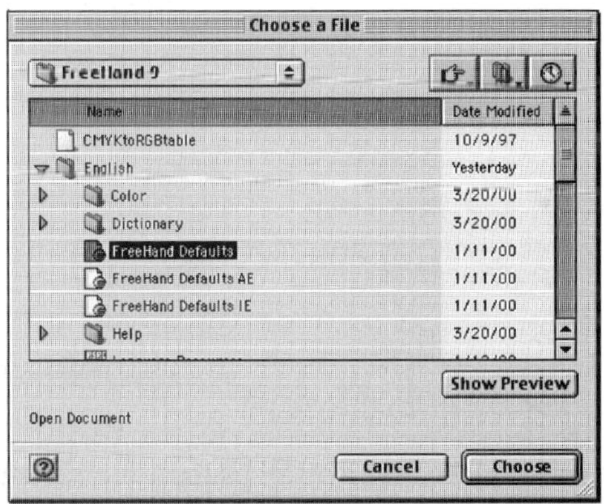

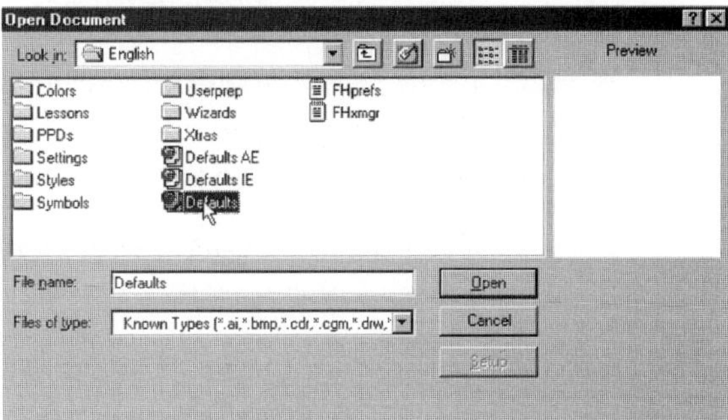

Macintosh (above) and Windows (below) FreeHand Default files.

2. When you open the **FreeHand Defaults** file, a new untitled document is created, because the default file is a template. All templates open as new, untitled documents. You could save this as a new template, then tell FreeHand to use it as the basis for all new documents by specifying the new template in the File>Preferences>Document settings.

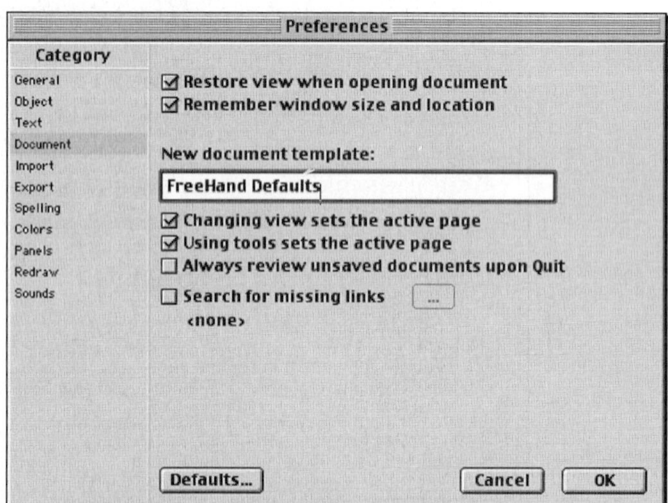

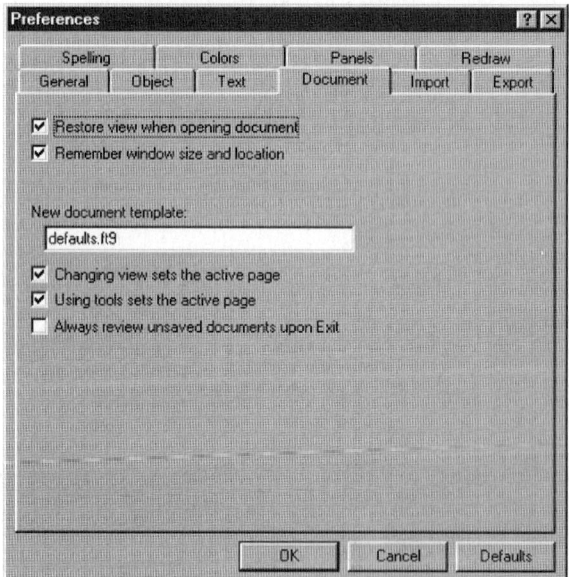

Macintosh (above) and Windows (below) Document Preferences

3. In this untitled document, make the following changes:

   - From the View menu, toggle on Page Rulers so the default document will automatically appear with rulers.

   - In the Units of Measurement pop-up menu at the bottom of the screen, set the units for Inches.

   - In the Magnification pop-up menu, set the percentage for 12%.

4. Your document should look something like the following image:

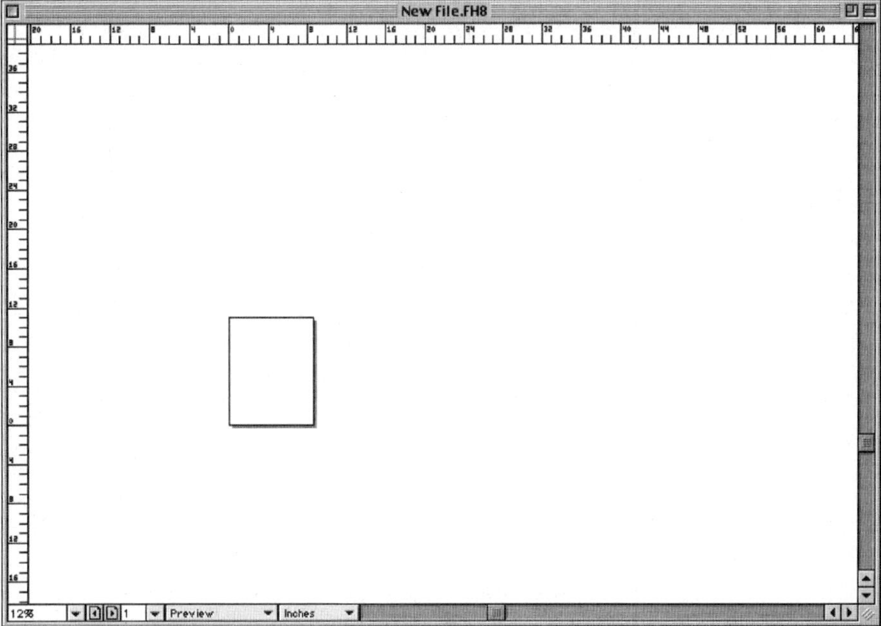

5. Choose File>Save As and select the FreeHand Template format. Save this default in the **English** folder inside the **FreeHand 9.0** folder. Name the file with your own name: "(Your Name) Defaults.FT9". Click Save. Close the Untitled file without saving. The Default file with your name is now available along with the FreeHand Defaults document in the **FreeHand 9.0** folder.

6. FreeHand will still use the FreeHand Defaults file as a guide to create new documents. How do you change to your own defaults?

7. Choose File>Preferences and click on the Document option. See New Document Template in the list? Underneath this heading is where you type the name of the file you want used as the default file for new documents. In this input area, replace FreeHand Defaults with "(Your Name) Defaults.FT9". Click OK to close the Preferences window.

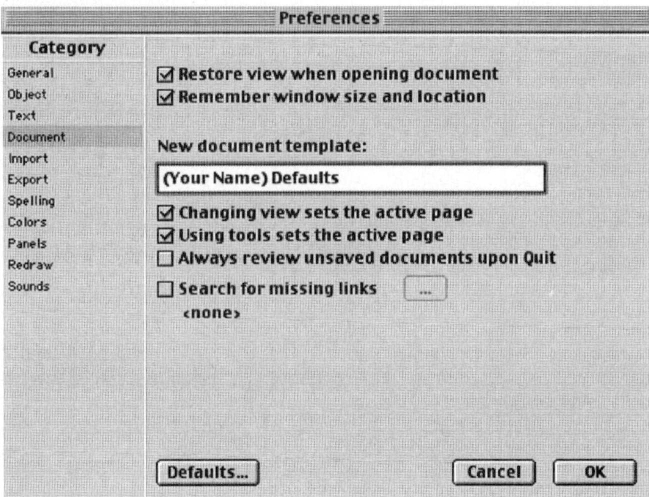

8. You do not have to restart the FreeHand application. Choose File>New to create a new document. When the document appears on your screen it uses the new defaults.

   Creating default documents is useful for customizing features you want in all new documents. You can create and store as many as you want, using Preferences to select which one to use.

Creating default documents is useful for customizing features you want in all new documents. You can create and store as many as you want, using Preferences to select which one to use.

9. Return to File>Preferences>Document and type "FreeHand Defaults". Click OK.
10. Close the untitled document without saving.

The Status Bar (Windows)

The Windows version of FreeHand adds a floating Status Bar that incorporates Magnification, Page Selector, View, and Units pop-up menus. It also displays the status of any actions in progress, menu selections, and which tool is currently active.

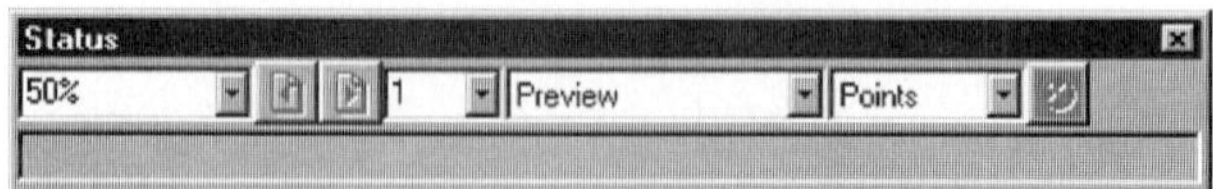

Wizards (Windows Only)

FreeHand's Wizard buttons access its help menus and allow you to quickly select and create basic page layout and panel content options for commonly used types of documents.

The first menu screen that appears when you open FreeHand is the Welcome Wizard. This uses menus for creating or finding documents, or for launching the FreeHand Help menu.

The templates on the FreeHand CD-ROM are pre-built documents that you can use for many types of layouts, such as business cards, forms, stationery, and other types of documents. These always open as new, untitled documents to preserve the original. Templates have the extension ".FT9".

The Welcome Wizard

The Welcome Wizard buttons launch the Help system, help you find previously created FreeHand documents, and assist with creating new documents.

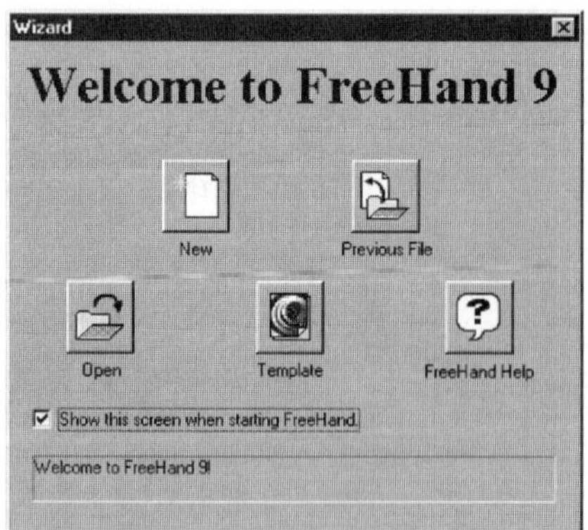

The Welcome Wizard buttons perform the following functions:

- New — creates a new document, using the FreeHand page default settings. This is the same as choosing File>New.
- Previous File — finds and opens the last FreeHand 9 document that was open. Previous files can also be found under the main File menu just above the Exit command.
- Open —displays the Open Document dialog menu.

- Template — prompts you to locate the FreeHand Templates folder. This folder is on the FreeHand CD-ROM, unless you copied it to your hard drive. It is not copied to the hard drive during a normal installation. When a folder is selected, the Open Document dialog menu is displayed.

- FreeHand Help — displays the FreeHand 9 interactive help menu. This is the same as choosing Help>FreeHand Help.

FreeHand Help

The FreeHand Help menu displays button links to FreeHand's interactive help menus. Clicking on Overview, Reference, How To, or Trouble opens a list of related help or information topics.

- Scripting — explains how to access Macromedia Script Editor to create Java Scripts, which can automate frequently-used operations.

- Web Links — displays Macromedia's home page web address.

- Show Me Movies — plays the movies *Using the Color Main Menu* and *Using the Layers Main Menu* provided on the FreeHand application CD-ROM.

- Text, Drawing, and Layout buttons in focus on — display sample screens with interactive components that link to content area information or procedures. Click on any of the page components with the Hand icon to display the list of related help topics.

- Index — opens the Help Index window. Help topics are listed by contents, general topic categories, a word based Index, and a word(s) Find listing that displays the desired word or phrase information and lists of related help topics.

Choosing A Wizard

If you decide not to use the Welcome Wizard to create a FreeHand document, there is a second Wizard menu available to help make your document setup quick and easy. The Choose a Wizard menu, found under Help>Wizards, offers four new buttons for the creation of special content-based documents.

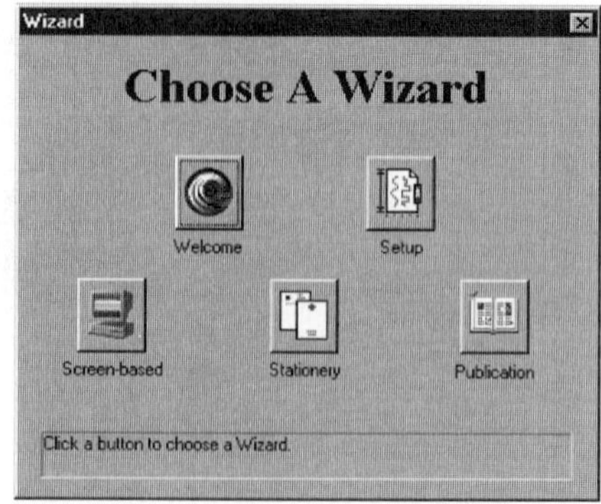

- Welcome — opens the Welcome wizards menu.
- Setup — creates an illustration-based document, either FreeHand or technical. Select colors for the Color List, color mode, default unit of measurement, page size, and orientation.
- Screen-based — creates a document optimized for either Internet or multimedia/image graphics. Choose colors for the Color List and set on screen page size and orientation.
- Stationery — creates common business page layouts including letterheads, envelopes, business cards, diskette labels, and mailing labels. Select colors for the Color List and browse through several layout samples.
- Publication — creates multiple-page documents. Select the page size, number of pages and orientation, colors to be included in the Color List, the default unit of measurement, and preformatted type and graphic styles available in the Colors/Layers/Styles panel.

Each Wizard document topic directs you through a series of interactive screens that allow you to select page options and panel contents specific to the document type of your choice.

Choose the Stationery Wizard

1. From the Help>Wizards>Choose a Wizard dialog box, click the Stationery Wizard button. Select Letter for your page size and click Next.

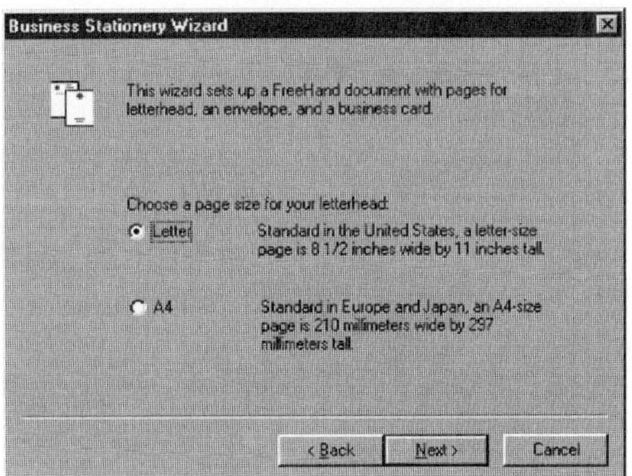

2. Click Yes for the selection of colors in your Color List, but don't select a Color List. Click Next.

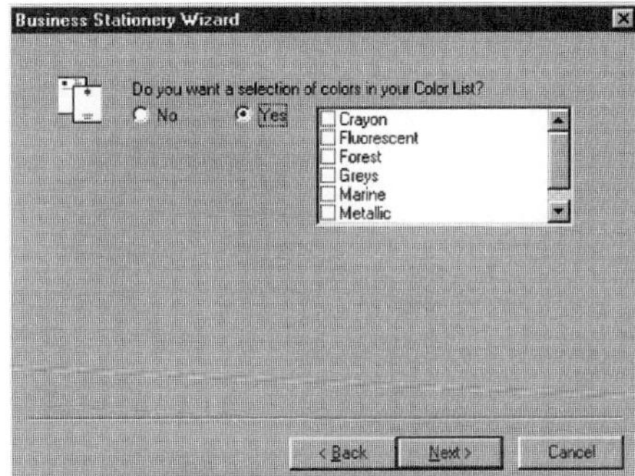

3. Select Layout Ideas and Corporate as your display sample, then click Next.

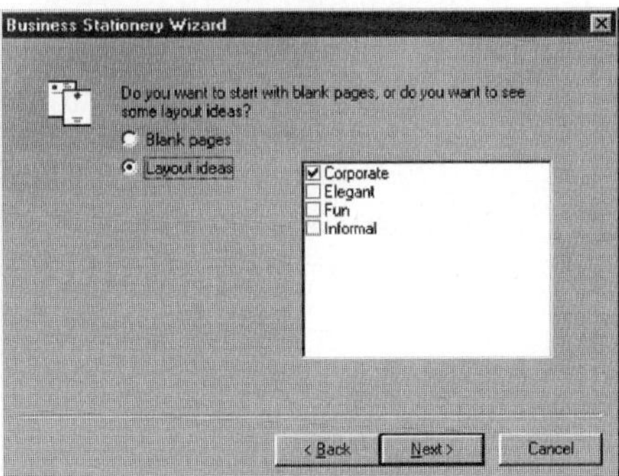

4. The Attributes menu should appear as follows:

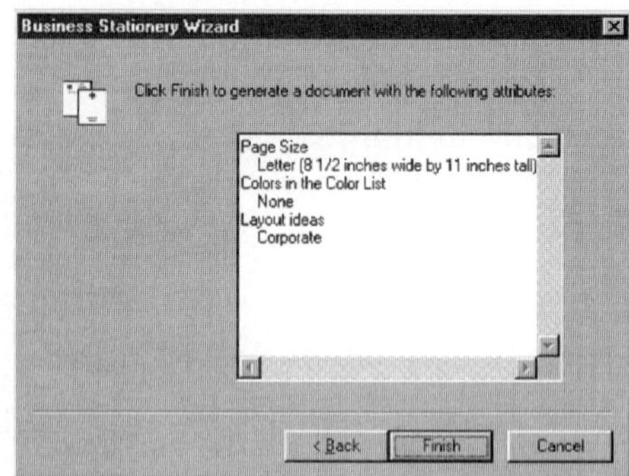

5. Click Finish. Your document screen should display the following:

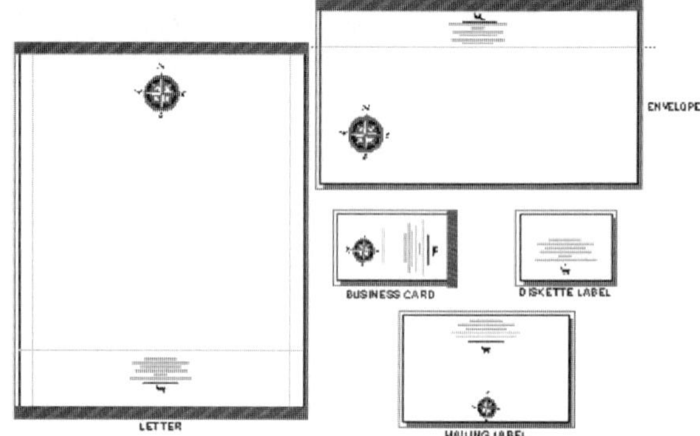

   You just created a FreeHand document called Corporate. Any of the objects on the pages (text or graphics) can be selected and altered.

   You should see five pages of varying sizes. Use the Text tool to highlight the dummy text. You could delete this text and replace it with your own information.

6. Open the Color List panel. Note there are three spot colors used in this document. If you edit and change one of these colors, all the objects on all pages with that color applied to them will automatically reflect the change.
7. Open the Document Inspector. Double-click on any of the Page icons displayed in the panel. The screen fills with that particular page.
8. Close the document without saving.

Use the Publication Wizard

1. In the Choose a Wizard selection screen, click Publication Wizard and create a four-page, letter-size, tall document. Click Next.
2. Click Yes for a selection of colors in your Color List and check Black plus 3 Spot Colors. Click Spot to answer "Do you plan to print with spot inks or process inks?" Click Next.

3. Choose Picas as your unit of measure. Answer Yes to "Do you want to start with some graphic and text styles in your Styles panel?" and check the Newsletter style. Click Next.

4. Your attributes should contain the following:

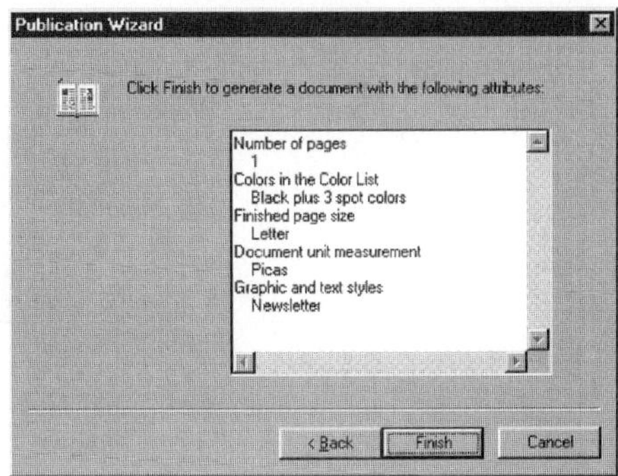

5. Click Finish.

6. Open the Styles panel and examine the list of predefined type styles listed. Select Normal text from the Styles list and open the Edit menu under the Options button. Most of the text styles are based on the Normal text style. Select a typeface from the Font menu and click OK.

7. Select Article from the Style list and open the Edit menu. Examine the Style/Parent/Next relationship; the same Normal text-based font is selected.

8. Close the document without saving.

Summary

You have learned to open, save, and close documents, and have discovered the difference between documents and templates. You have explored magnification and view options and have learned to use the Document Inspector. You have also customized some of FreeHand's defaults and have explored Wizards and the Help menus. You are now prepared to explore FreeHand's working environment.

Notes:

CHAPTER 2

The FreeHand Working Environment

CHAPTER OBJECTIVE:

To become familiar with FreeHand's operating environment, tools, and controls. In Chapter 2, you will:

- Begin to understand FreeHand's working environment and the tools that you work with in FreeHand (panels, menus, inspectors, toolbars, and document windows), and where to access them.
- Learn how the Toolbox can be modified and positioned, and how tool defaults can be changed.
- Learn how to create and customize toolbars.
- Learn how to access FreeHand's numerous panels and sub-panels.
- Be introduced to FreeHand's five Inspectors.
- View what menu selections FreeHand provides, and explore its submenus.
- Learn a few basic drawing commands, and how to create custom views and windows of your document.
- Learn about FreeHand's five viewing modes, and how to enlarge or reduce your document view.

PROJECTS TO BE COMPLETED:

- Dinner Time (A)
- Mask Art (B)
- Tropical Treasure Logo (C)
- Grocery Ad (D)
- Ball and Mirror (E)
- No Clowning Around (F)

The FreeHand Working Environment

FreeHand contains a powerful workshop of tools, panels, operations, and features. Once you become familiar with a particular operation, it usually becomes second nature. For example, if you have a car, you jump in, start it up, and take off. You don't think too much about shifting, braking or steering — you just do it. The same principle applies to learning an application such as FreeHand.

The most important features of FreeHand are the:

- Toolbars
- Inspectors
- Panels
- Menus

The Toolbars

Toolbars are useful for accessing features and functions found in the menus and panels. Toolbars are accessed through the Window menu.

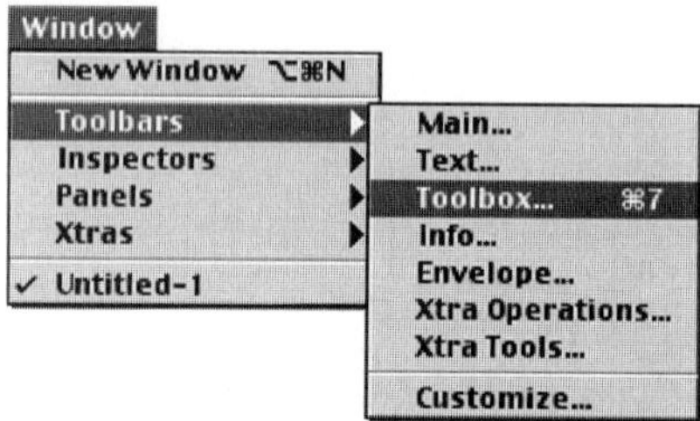

Imagine the pasteboard as a storage area for anything you might want to use in your artwork. Items on the pasteboard won't print or otherwise appear in your document, but can be moved onto the page at any time.

The Windows version of FreeHand also lists the Status Bar in the Toolbars menu.

These are the Toolbars that are available:

- Main Toolbar
- Toolbox Toolbar
- Envelope Toolbar
- Xtra Tools Toolbar
- Text Toolbar
- Info Toolbar
- Xtra Operations Toolbar
- Status Bar (Windows only)

Flexibility of Toolbars

Toolbars can be maneuvered around the FreeHand environment, positioned at the extreme top or left side of the screen, or as a floating unit in the document.

When positioned at the top of the screen, the Toolbars are accessible, but out of the way. They may appear to be different depending on their position.

Drag on these areas to maneuver toolbar on screen

When you drag on either end of the toolbar and move it into the document window, the appearance changes to look like the picture below. The top box closes the toolbar; the bottom box resizes it to several other configurations.

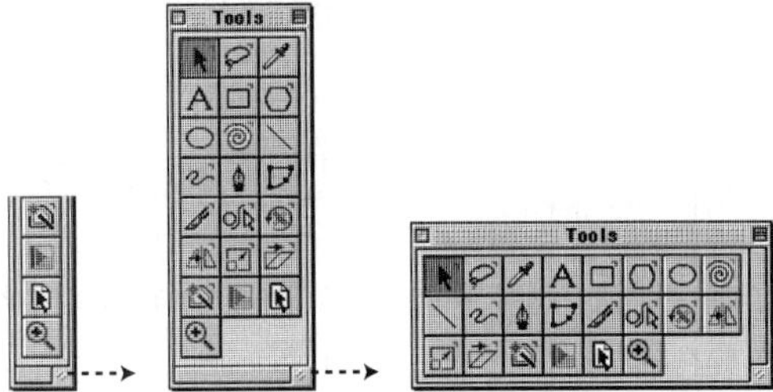

Main Toolbar

The Main Toolbar gives you immediate access to the menu functions by clicking on the icons located there. To avoid having to guess what a tool does, you can select File> Preferences>Panels>Show Tool Tips. With this option on, a tool identifier appears when the Pointer passes over the tool.

Press Command-S (Macintosh) or Control-S (Windows) to save a document.

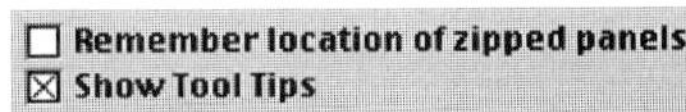

Shown below is the Main Toolbar with its default icons that are present when FreeHand is first installed and launched; they can be customized with Window>Toolbars>Customize.

This is how the Main Toolbar looks when located out of the way across the top of the document window. The Toolbox is located in one column down the left side of the document window.

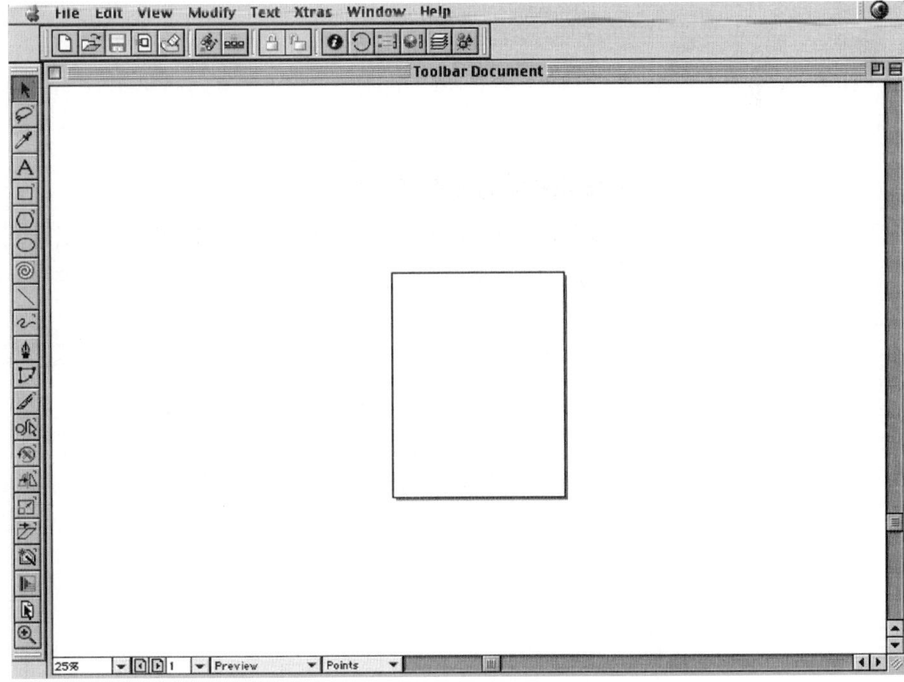

The Toolbox

The Toolbox is one of FreeHand's panels. It contains many tools used for drawing lines and shapes, placing text, reshaping and sizing objects, and otherwise modifying your artwork. The toolbox contains the following 22 tools:

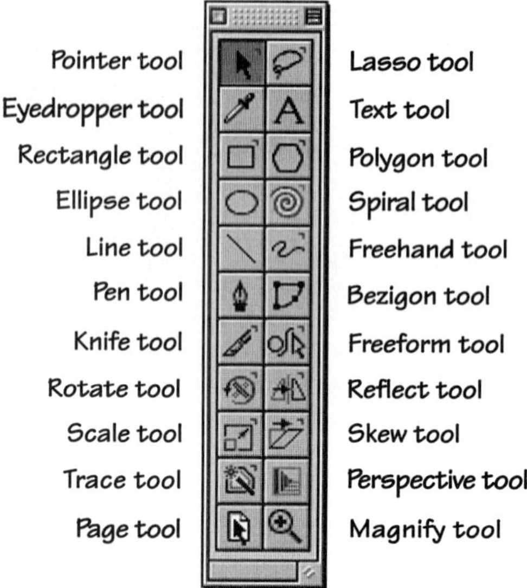

Toolbox Options

Most tools — the Pointer, Lasso, Rectangle, Polygon, Spiral, Freehand, Knife, and Freeform tools — have small triangles in the corners of their tool icons. Double-clicking this icon will display a dialog box.

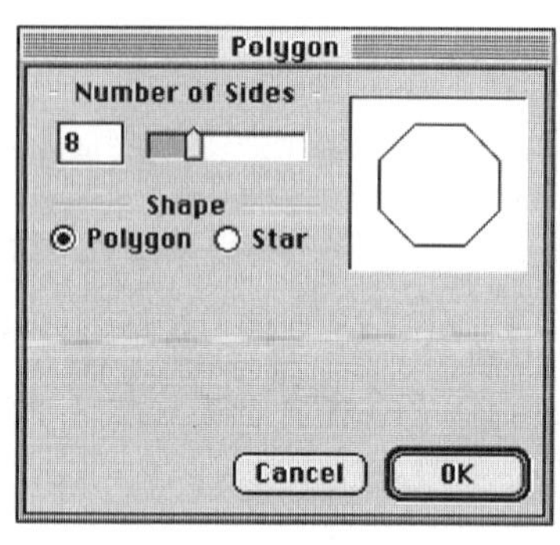

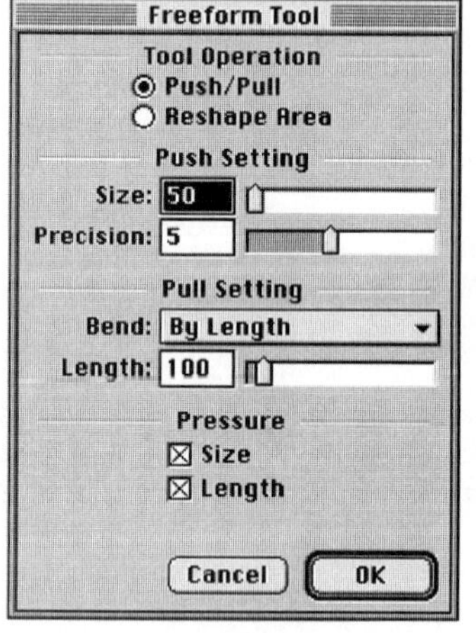

The transformation tools — Rotate, Reflect, Scale, and Skew — all have this triangle symbol, and this brings up the Transform panel, set for the tool you double-clicked on.

The Toolbox has traditionally been positioned on the left side of the FreeHand screen. You can move it to the top of the screen, or anywhere that suits your work pattern

Manage the Toolbox

1. From the File menu, select New to create a new document.
2. A single page untitled document will appear. The Toolbox should be on the left side. If the Toolbox is not present, navigate to Window>Toolbars>Toolbox.

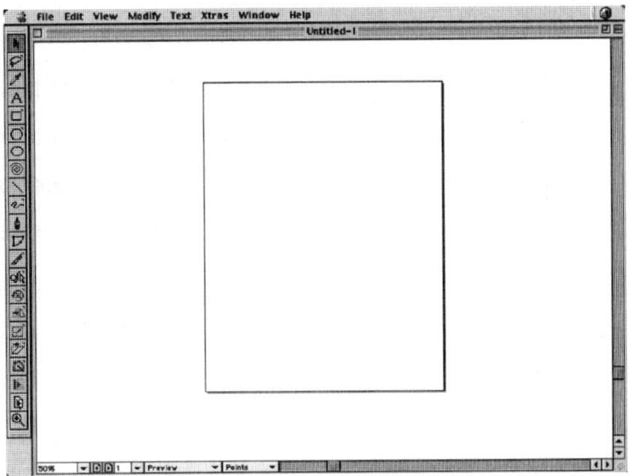

3. In the Toolbox, click on the border just above the Pointer tool and drag the cursor up to the top of the document window. Release the mouse button. You have now moved the Toolbox to another position across the top.

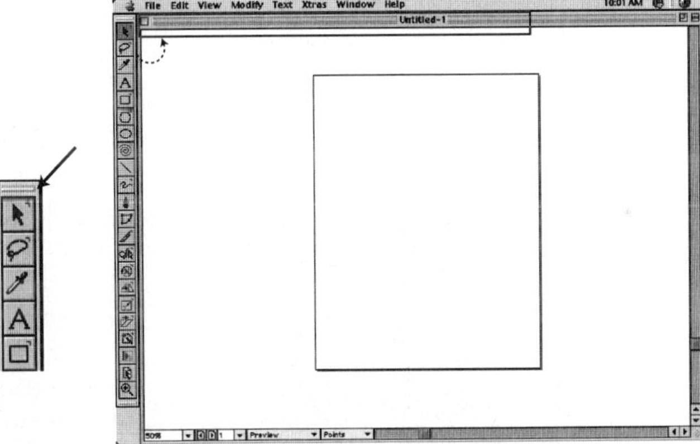

4. Click on the area to the left of the Pointer tool and move the cursor downward to the left to return in to its original position.

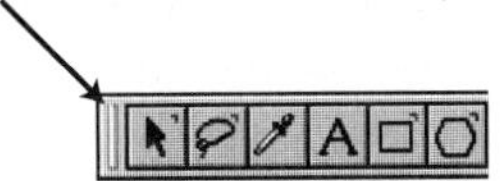

5. With the Toolbox located on the left side of the screen, it is difficult to see its bottom portion. The top border above the Pointer tool is the area you click to drag the Toolbox. Click here and drag to move the Toolbox into the document area. You want to see the bottom of the Toolbox, so that when you move the outline of the Toolbox, you are certain that the top of it touches the Title Bar of the document. This is tricky because if you go too high, the Toolbox will move to a Horizontal position.

If you can't see any portion of the Toolbox, click on the Sizing button at the bottom right corner of the document; this will bring the Toolbox into view.

6. When positioned, release the mouse button. If the Toolbox disappears, don't panic. For some reason, it has become hidden by the document window itself. Click on the bottom right sizing box of the document window, and it will come forward.

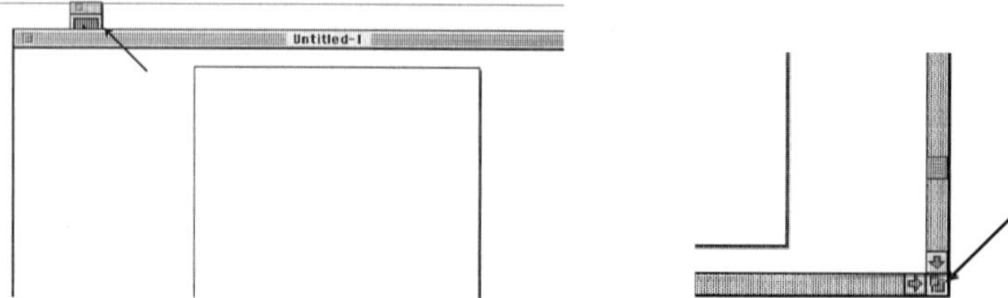

7. With the Toobox located away from the left side of the screen, it takes on a different look. Click on the bottom right box and drag to the right. You will see the moving outline change on screen. Release the mouse button to see the new configuration. Experiment with using this box to reshape the Toolbox. Leave the Toolbox reshaped for the next step.

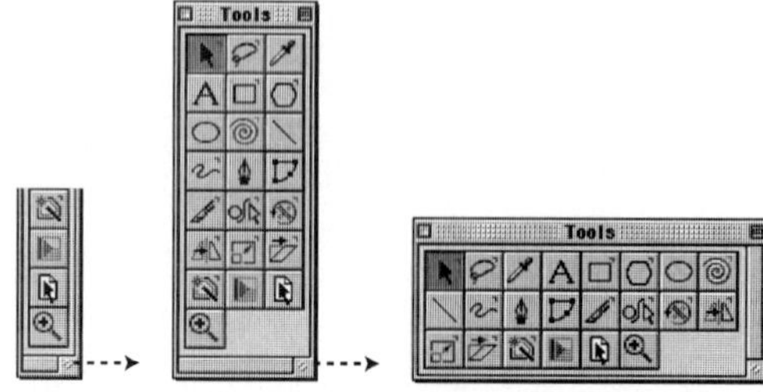

8. By clicking on the Title Bar of the Toolbox, you can drag it to any location of the document window. Don't click the Toolbox's close box; it puts the Toolbox away. Drag the Toolbox to other areas of the document, release the mouse button, then drag again.

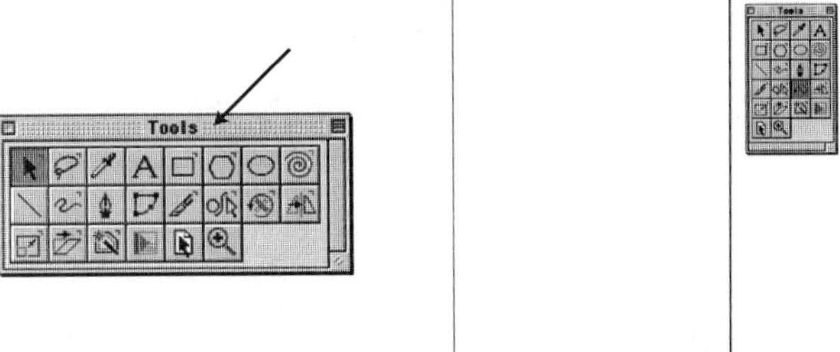

9. Drag the Toolbox back to the left side of the screen so that it snaps to the vertical position without any buttons.

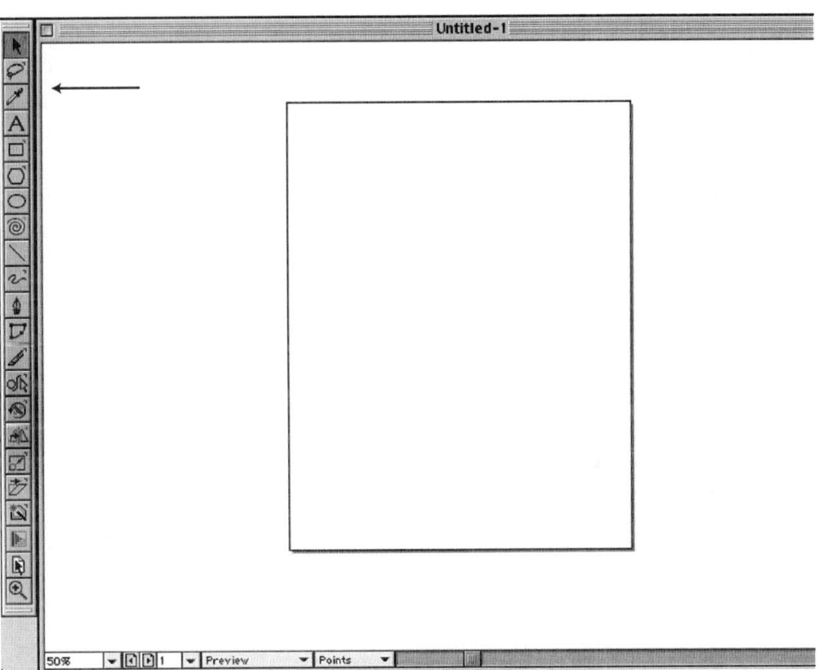

Press Command/Control-7 to toggle the Toolbox on and off.

10. Navigate to the Window>Toolbars menu and select Toolbox to toggle it off, removing it from the screen.

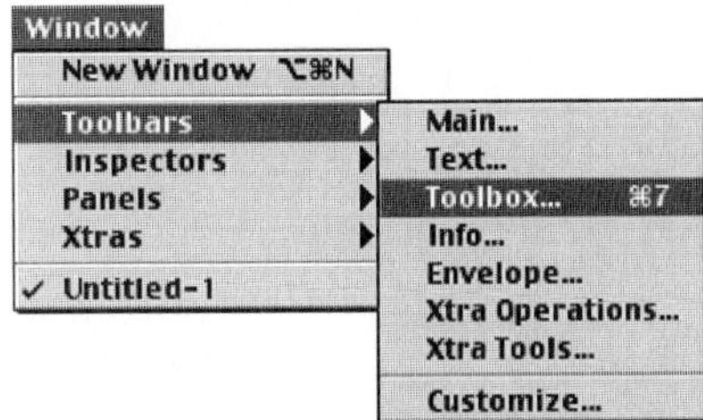

11. Return to the same menu and toggle the Toolbox on, bringing it back to the screen.

12. You have now seen the various ways to manage the Toolbox. Close the document without saving.

The Text Toolbar

The Text Toolbar offers the basic typographic settings you can apply to all selected text.

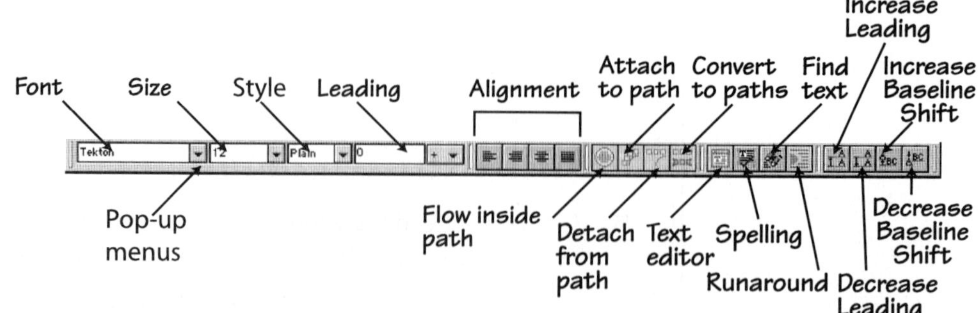

The Text Toolbar positions below the Main Toolbar in the extreme top of the screen. They both can fit in this location above the document window.

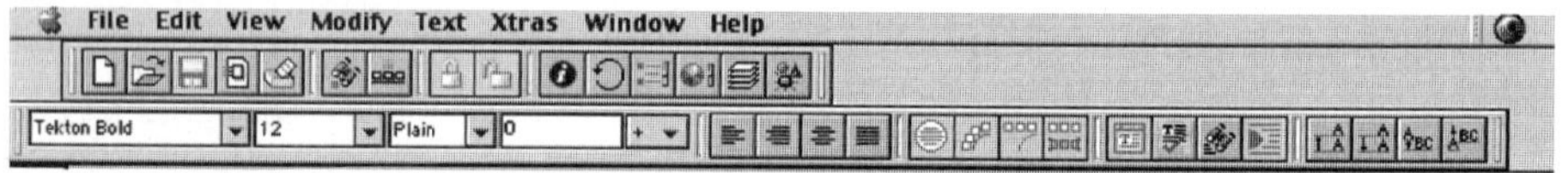

The Info Toolbar

The Info Toolbar shows what type of object is selected, its Lock status, the x,y page location of the cursor, change in an object's position, angle, and center of rotation. When an object is being created, it also reflects its height and width.

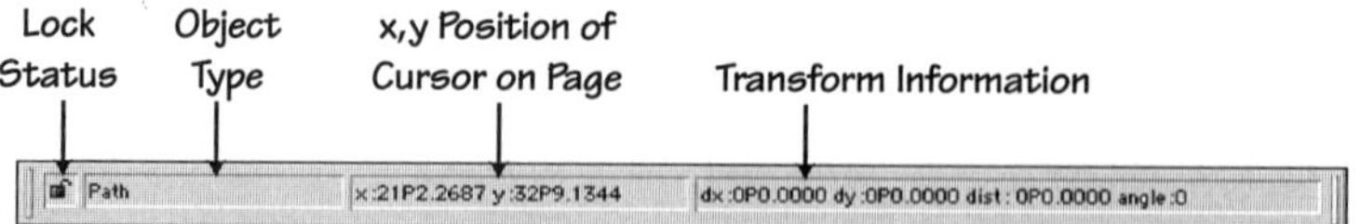

Customizing the Toolbars

From the Windows menu you can select Toolbars>Customize to modify the toolbars. You can customize them through the lists (A) on the left side of the window. Features of the chosen list appear as icons in the right side of the window (B). You can add features by dragging the desired icon up into the toolbar. You can remove features by dragging their icons out of the Toolbar.

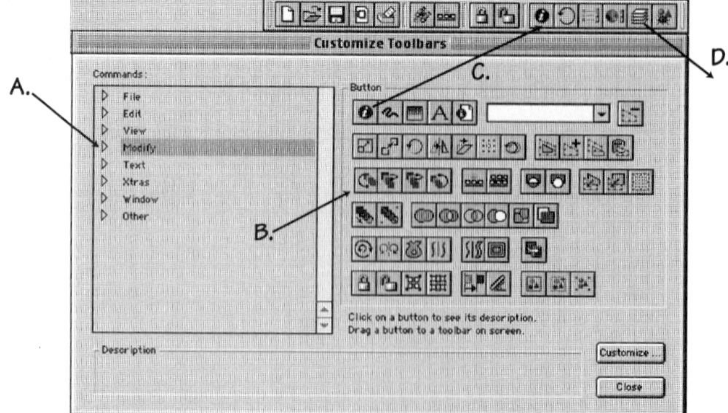

A. *Menus are selected from this list*
B. *Menu items are represented by icons*
C. *Icons are dragged to add them to the toolbar*
D. *Toolbar items are removed by dragging the icon from the toolbar*

Preferences>Panel>Show Tool Tips must be selected if you want to know the names or functions of icons in the Toolbars.

Customize the Main Toolbar

1. Choose File>New to create a new document.
2. Select File>Preferences>Panels and make certain that Show Tool Tips is clicked.
3. If the Main Toolbar is not on screen, choose Window>Toolbars>Main.
4. Display the customizing dialog box with Window>Toolbars>Customize.
5. In the left side of the window you will see the menu names. Click on any of these menu names to see the toolbar icons representing functions that may be performed.

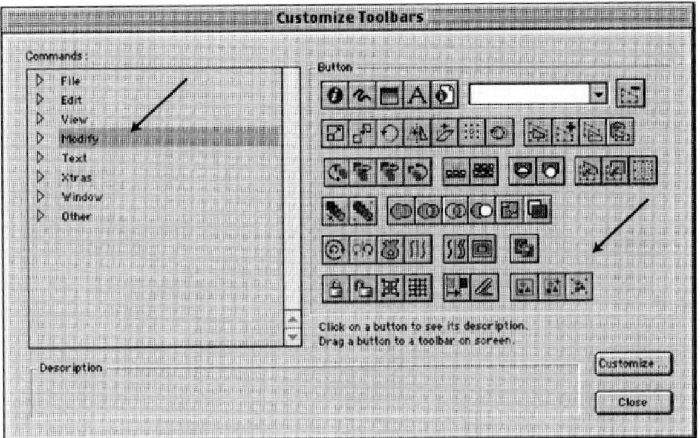

6. Click on the name Other in the list of menus; this is for functions other than those found in the menus. They range from page navigation to inspectors to tools found in the Toolbox. Touch the Pointer tool to the first icon at the top and leave it there a few seconds. A tool tip will pop out, identifying the icon.

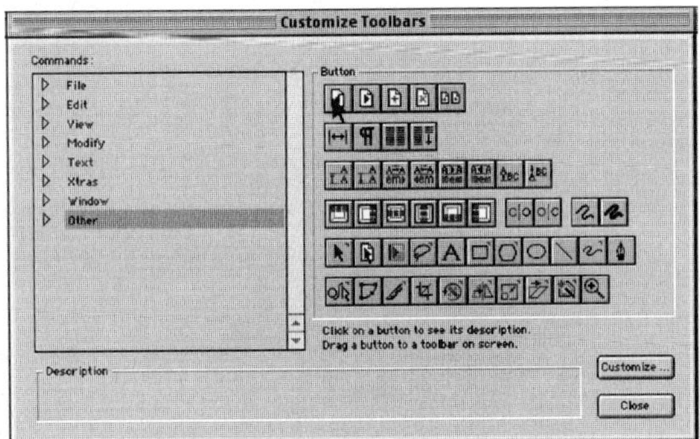

7. To remove any icon from a toolbar, simply drag it out with the Customize Toolbars dialog box open. Do this now. Click on the Find Graphics icon in the Main Toolbar and drag it out of the toolbar. Release the mouse button; it is no longer in the toolbar.

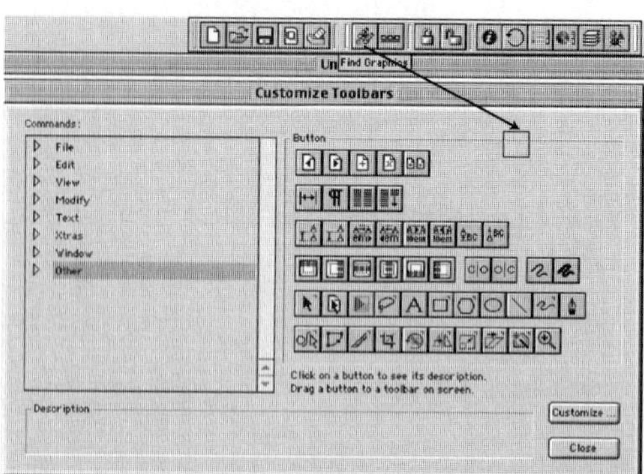

8. Click on the Edit menu name in the left side list. In the second row of icons, touch (don't click) the Pointer tool to the sixth icon to see its name, Paste In Front. Drag this icon up to the toolbar to the left of the icon with the padlock symbol (Lock).

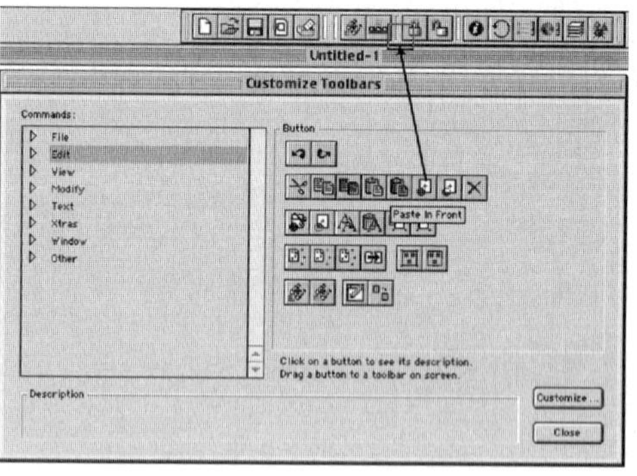

To re-establish default toolbars, click Reset in the Custom Toolbars menu.

9. Click on the View menu name in the list. Click and drag the 400% View icon up to be next to the Lock icon.

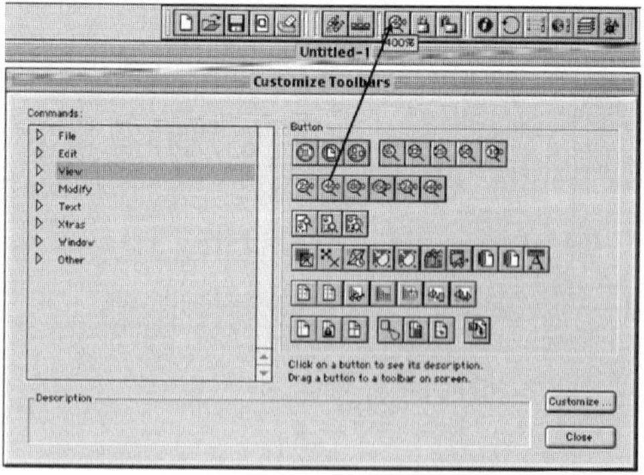

The keyboard shortcuts to access the panels are:

Layers:
Command-6 (Macintosh) or Control-6 (Windows).

Styles:
Command-3 (Macintosh) or Control-3 (Windows).

Color List:
Command-9 (Macintosh) or Control-9 (Windows).

Color Mixer:
Shift-Command-C (Macintosh) or Shift-Control-9 (Windows).

Tints:
Shift-Command-Z (Macintosh) or Shift-Control-3 (Windows).

Halftones:
Command-H (Macintosh) or Control-H (Windows).

Align:
Option-Command-A (Macintosh) or Alt-Control-A (Windows).

Transform:
Command-M (Macintosh) or Control-M (Windows).

Symbols:
No shortcut available.

10. You have now received an introduction to customizing the Toolbars. Drag the Paste In Front and 400% View icons out of the Toolbar to return the Main Toolbar to it original state. From the Edit list, drag Find Graphics back into the Toolbar. Close the document without saving.

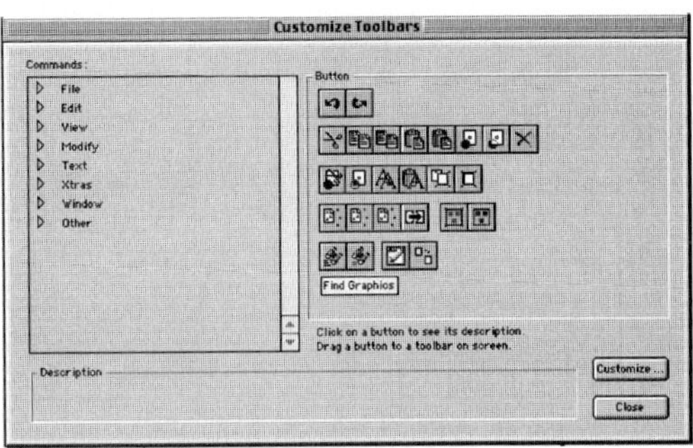

Panels

Panels float on top of the pasteboard and can be dragged and placed anywhere on your screen. Panels are customizable tabbed windows that can be moved, separated, or combined by dragging their tabs.

All panels can be moved and hidden. To hide all panels, choose View>Panels or press F12. Press F12 to show all the panels previously open.

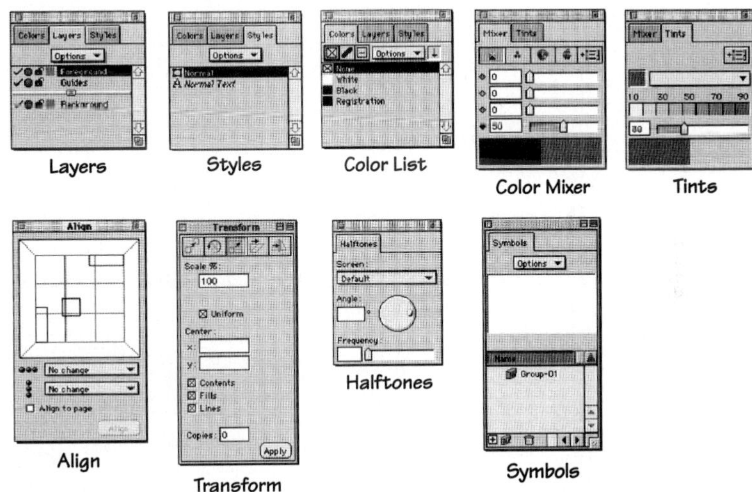

- Layers — is used to create, manage, and maneuver through layers to increase the productivity of the artist.
- Styles — holds text and graphics styles.
- Color List — shows all colors in use in the document, and is used to access colors. The Options pop-up menu manages colors and external libraries of color.
- Color Mixer — allows creation of colors using CMYK, RGB, HLS, the system (Macintosh or Windows) Color Picker. Colors created may be added to the Color List.

- Tints — allows creation of tint percentages of existing colors. Tints created may be stored in the Color List.
- Align — is where selected objects are aligned and distributed.
- Transform — is used to access the Transformation tool dialog boxes.
- Halftones — controls the shape, angle, and frequency of halftone screens.
- Symbols— stores reusable images, animations, or buttons. Symbols may be imported and exported for use in other documents.

Inspectors

Most tasks that you perform in FreeHand involve the use of the Inspector panels. The Inspector is a multi-panel, floating control center from which you select a particular Inspector panel by clicking on the panel's tab.

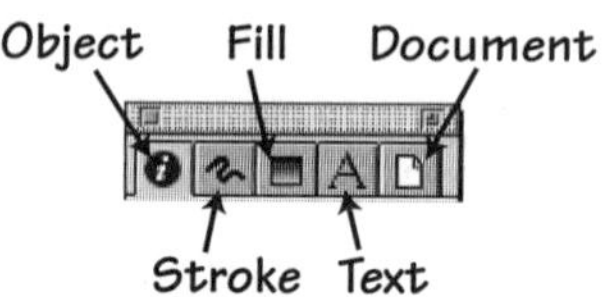

When an Inspector tab is clicked, one of the following Inspectors appears:

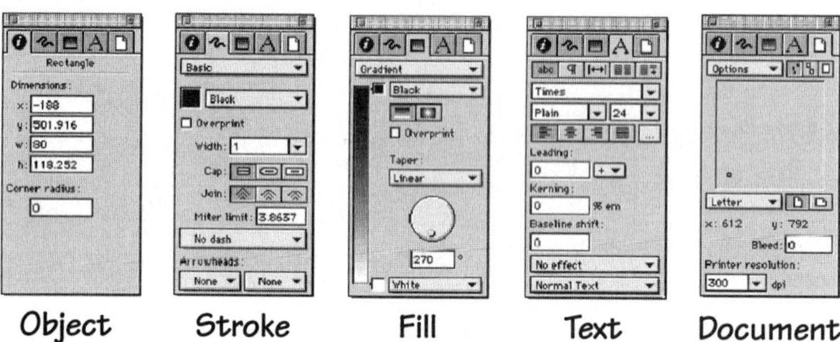

- Object Inspector — tells what type of object is selected; gives dimensions, x,y locations, and other information about the structure of the object; and closes paths.
- Stroke Inspector — applies colors and special visual effects, assigns width to the selected path, defines endcap and joint mitre, and creates arrowheads and dashed lines.
- Fill Inspector — applies colors and special fill effects and creates and alters gradients.
- Text Inspector — assigns typographic settings to selected text, text attributes, paragraph attributes, horizontal spacing, rows and columns, and copy fitting.
- Document Inspector — lets you control the pages of a document, including the number of pages, size, orientation, bleed, and printer resolution.

The keyboard shortcuts to access the Inspectors are:

Object Inspector:
Command-I (Macintosh) or Control-I (Windows).

Stroke Inspector:
Option-Command-L (Macintosh) or Alt-Control-L (Windows).

Fill Inspector:
Option-Command-F (Macintosh) or Alt-Control-F (Windows).

Text Inspector:
Command-T (Macintosh) or Control-T (Windows).

Document Inspector:
Option-Command-D (Macintosh) or Alt-Control-D (Windows).

FreeHand Menus

You have seen Toolbars, Panels, and Inspectors and noted their uses and customizing qualities. Some of these features are not available in a menu, such as setting the stroke width of a path, which can only be performed in the Stroke Inspector.

Other than these few exceptions, many of the panel and toolbar features are found in corresponding menus. For example, if you want to apply a font, point size, alignment, or other specifications, you could easily pull down the Text menu and use the appropriate text features.

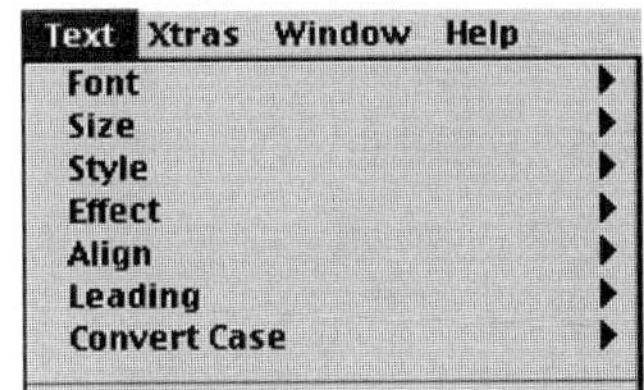

Submenus

Some menu selections have a triangle to the right of the name indicating that there are more available options. When one of these items is selected, its submenu appears. You can then drag the mouse into this menu to make a selection.

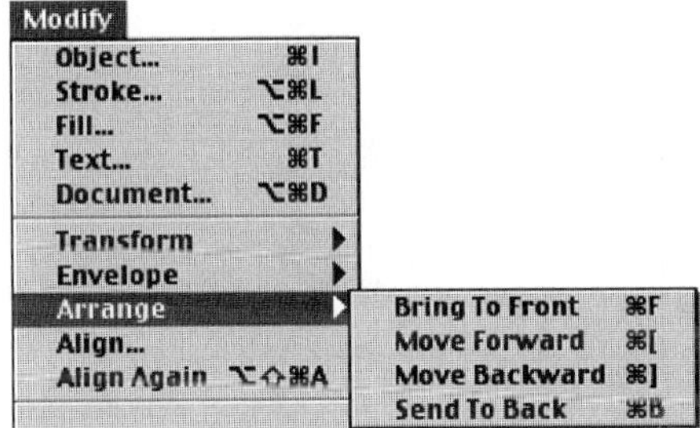

Viewing Modes

FreeHand allows you to see your documents and designs in a variety of different views. In addition to page magnification, there are the View menu selections, four viewing modes, Custom Views, and New Window.

The five viewing modes are the most important for seeing what you are designing, making certain that you are achieving the colors and effects you desire, and providing a reasonable idea of how the job will look when printed. They are Preview, Fast Preview, Keyline, Fast Keyline, and Flash Anti-alias.

View Pop-up Menus

The View pop-up menu in the lower part of the document window accesses the five viewing modes. The different viewing modes affect the on-screen representation of your artwork, not data or print quality.

If Fast Preview is still taking too long to paint the screen, going to Keyline mode will allow you to move objects around faster without the repainting that occurs in Preview mode.

Preview

When you work in Preview mode, the display shows you most fills as they will look when sent to the printer. The exceptions to this are the PostScript fills and strokes that must be printed for viewing.

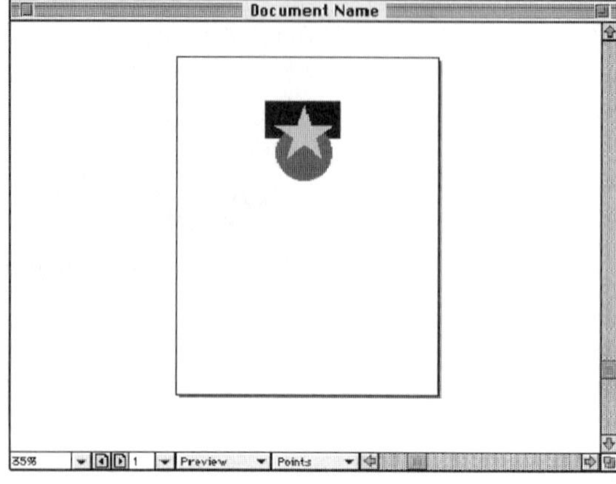

Image in Document

The Printed Page

Fast Preview

Certain features, such as gradients, can take a lot of time to paint on the screen, especially if there are many objects colored with these features. FreeHand has added the Fast Preview to expedite the screen's redraw function.

Fast Preview presents text below 50 pt. as a gray band, and reduces the number of steps in a blend or gradient to 10 to decrease the time it takes for the screen to redraw.

Preview mode

Fast Preview mode

Press Command-K (Macintosh) or Control-K (Windows) to switch between Preview and Keyline modes.

Keyline View

It is possible to see a path's anchor points and segments in Preview mode, but for fine-tuning of paths it is best to view them in Keyline mode. This viewing mode very clearly shows the points and segments without their fills or strokes.

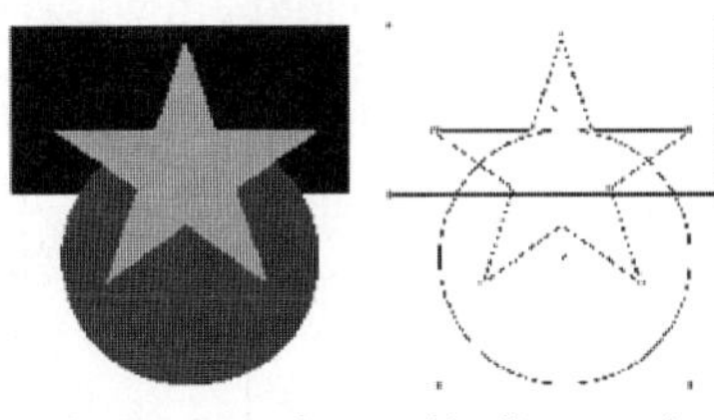

The ability to isolate individual elements in a complex drawing is very important. You can see the constructing anchor point and segments of the paths, and click on them easily in Keyline mode when they might be obscured in Preview mode.

Fast Keyline

Fast Keyline shows grayed (*greeked*) text below 50 pts., and reduces the number of steps in a blend to 10 to speed screen redraw.

Text is legible

Keyline mode

Text Greeks gray

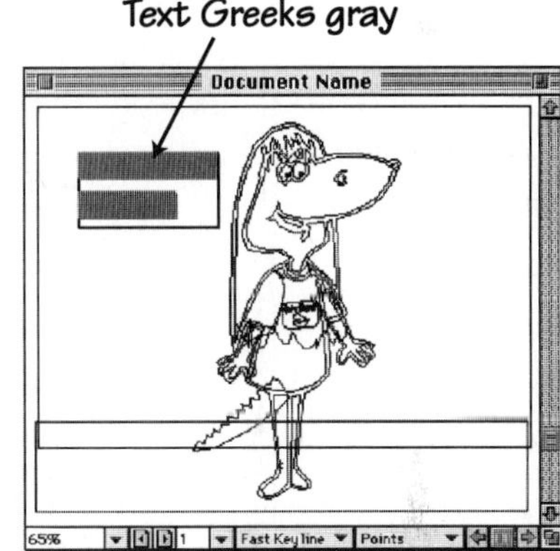

Fast Keyline mode

Flash Anti-alias

Flash Anti-alias shows how your illustration will look in Flash, a vector-based animation program, without leaving FreeHand.

Using the Five Viewing Modes

1. Open the file **Preview.FH9** from your **SF-FreeHand** folder.

2. When first opened, the document will be in Preview mode.
3. Use the View pop-up menu at the bottom of the screen to navigate to Fast Preview.
4. Note that the headline became grayed out and, instead of being a smooth blend of color, the gradient was reduced to 10 steps.
5. Go back to Preview mode. Note how much better the illustration looks.
6. Select Keyline mode in the pop-up menu.

7. In Keyline mode you will never see colors of any kind. This is a preview of the raw structure of anchor points and segments.
8. In the View pop-up menu, choose Fast Keyline. Even in Keyline mode, the headline is grayed out.
9. Return to Keyline mode, observe the images, then switch to Flash Anti-alias mode.
10. Use the View pop-up menu to select Preview mode. You have now worked with the five main viewing modes of FreeHand.
11. Close the document without saving.

Custom Views

You can create a Custom View in the View menu if there are certain locations or magnifications of a document that you access often. When accessed, custom views go instantly to this created view when needed.

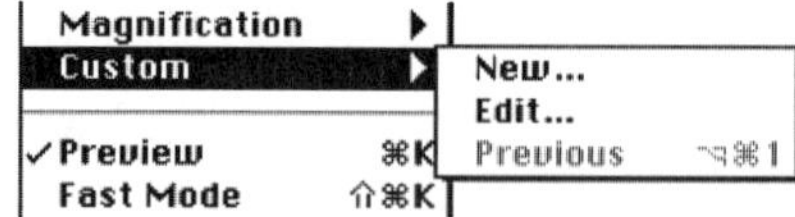

Creating Custom Views

The procedure to create a Custom View is simple enough. After you've arranged the document window to a view you like, you would choose View>Custom>New.

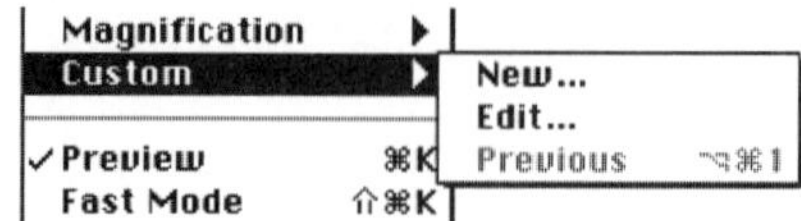

The New View window appears in which you can name the view appropriately for the view's function.

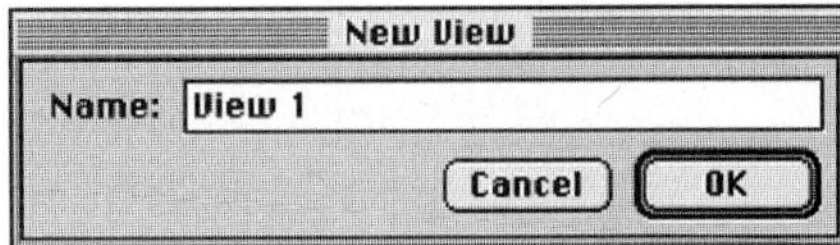

The advantage to this feature is that regardless of the magnification percentage or the location of the document on which you are working, you are instantly taken to that exact location and viewing percentage if you choose View>Custom and select the named view.

You can create multiple views and select them this way at any time.

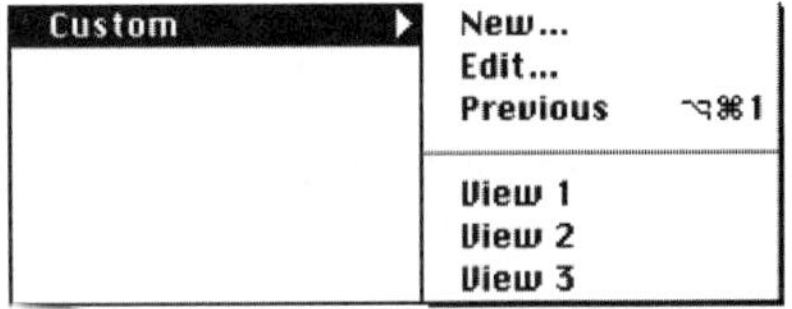

Editing Custom Views

There might be times that you want the custom view to be modified slightly so you can work or see the design better. This is done by going to the custom view in the View>Custom menu. For example, we might go to View 2.

You could then rearrange the screen to your new desired view. Then, View>Custom>Edit Views would be selected. The Edit Views dialog box would appear. The View 2 would be clicked on in the view list, and Redefine clicked. After this modification, View 2 would be set to incorporate your new changes.

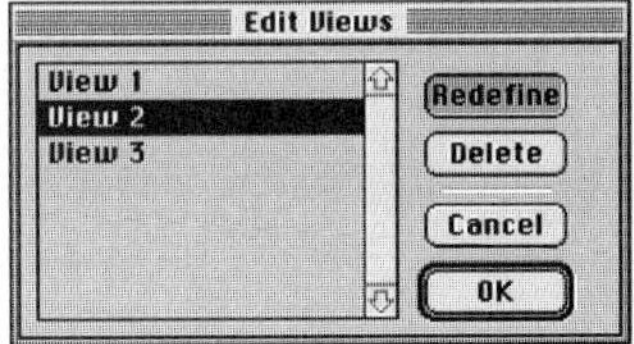

Create, Modify, and Delete Custom Views

1. Open the file **Custom Views.FH9** from your **SF-FreeHand** folder.

Press Command (Macintosh) or Control (Windows) plus one of the following numbers to zoom in or out:

5	*50%*
1	*100%*
2	*200%*
4	*400%*
8	*800%*
0	*fit in window*

2. Use the Magnify tool to draw a marquee around the large top star to zoom in on it.

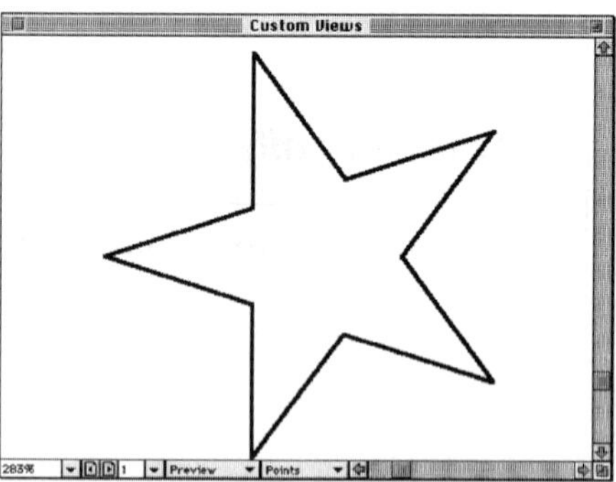

3. Select View>Custom>New, and in the New View window, name the view "Stars Closeup" and click OK.

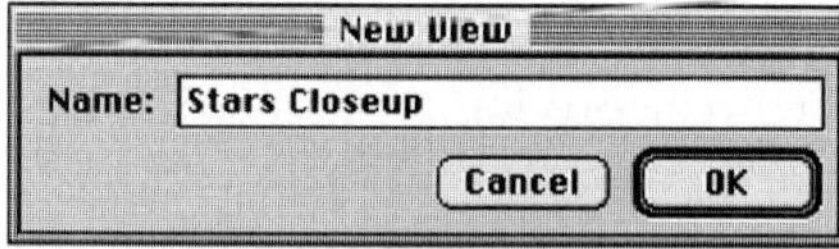

4. Select the Magnification field at the lower left of the screen and set the view for 13% by typing the number in the entry field.
5. Select View>Custom>New and name this view "Stars 13%". Click OK.
6. Use the Magnification pop-up menu to go to 50% view.
7. Go to View>Custom and select the Star Closeup view.

8. This is the zoomed-in view that you created in step 3.

Whether you apply a custom view to a new window, or just use magnification tools to zoom in to a location, you can have several of these windows on screen for design purposes.

9. Select View>Custom and select the Stars 13% view. The magnification will change to only 13%.
10. You can make as many custom views as you want, but your document will only show one view at a time. If you need to see multiple views at the same time, you must use New Window.
11. Leave the document open for the next exercise.

The Magnify Tool

The Magnification tool enlarges (plus sign) or reduces (negative sign) the view of your artwork on the page. Specific objects or locations can be isolated and magnified by dragging a *marquee* around the object.

Use the Magnify Tool

1. With **Custom Views.FH9** open, select the Magnify tool and click on the page. Observe how the view enlarged; look at the magnification percentage in the lower-left corner of the document to see how much it has enlarged.
2. Hold the Option (Macintosh) or Alt (Windows) key so that the Magnify tool has a negative (–) symbol in it and click again; the view will reduce in size. Observe its percentage in the lower-left corner.
3. Drag a marquee around the upper-left corner of the page. It will zoom up to an enlarged view. Note the size of the page.
4. Hold the Option/Alt key and drag another marquee around the page corner. The view will reduce in size. Observe its percentage in the lower-left corner.
5. You have now seen how the Magnify option works.
6. Close the document without saving.

The plus (+) and minus (-) symbols can be toggled by pressing the Option/Alt key when using the Magnification tool.

New Window

If you use custom views, you can only see one custom view at a time. The New Window command allows you to create other view windows of the same document and assign one of the custom views to each. You can then view the same document in many different perspectives on screen at the same time.

New Window, though, is not dependent upon Custom Views. Each of the New Window views appears in a different document window, but is a representation of the original document. Any changes made to these extra viewing window objects will affect the actual document.

In this example, three new windows were created and zoomed to different viewing levels. Notice that they are named appropriately. The original document will have a "1" after its name. The second window has a "2", and so on.

A marquee is the visual representation of a selection, represented by a dashed line.

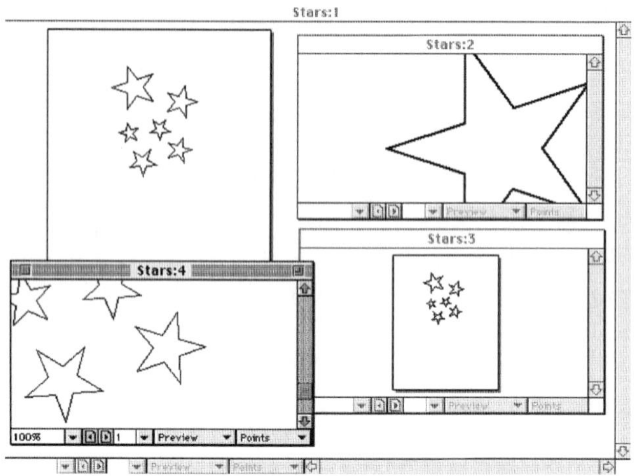

If you have several new windows active, and they get lost behind other document windows, it is simple to access them. Select the Window menu and the active new windows will be listed for selecting.

Manage New Windows

1. Open the document **Custom Views.FH9** from your **SF-FreeHand** folder.

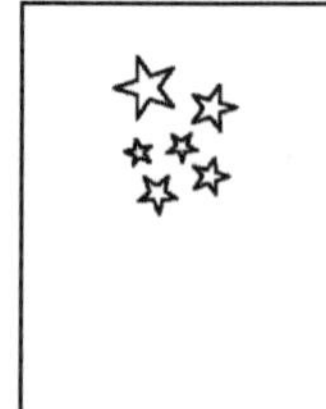

2. From the Window menu choose New Window. A new window representing this same document will appear. Notice that it completely covers the original window.

Creating new windows is convenient when you want to see the same document in both Preview and Keyline mode at the same time.

3. With the Magnification pop-up menu go to 25% view. Resize the window down to a smaller size and move it to the upper-right corner of the first window.

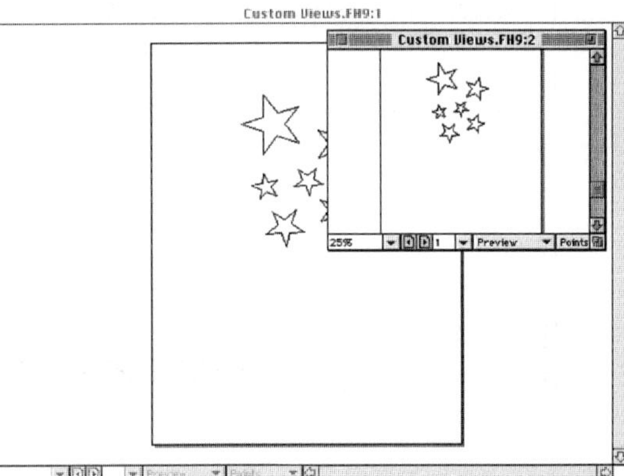

4. From the Window menu select New Window again. A new window will appear, but it covers the second window. Each new window always appears in front of the active window, and it will always be the same size as the source window.

5. This is New Window "3". Resize and drag it down under Window number 2 and use the Magnification pop-up menu to go to 200% screen view.

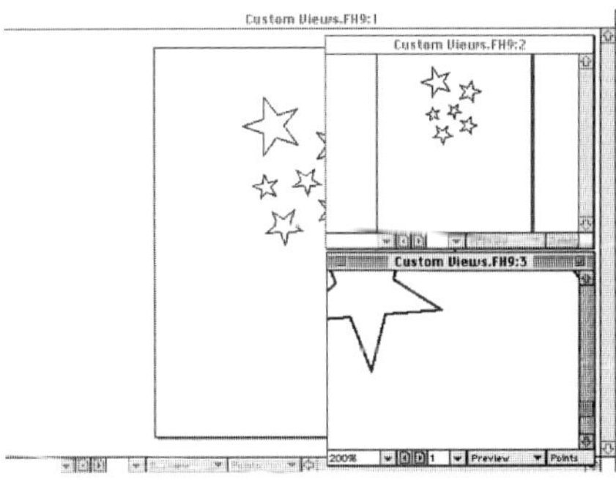

6. Select Window>New Window again. The new window will appear in front of Window 3. Resize and drag new window 4 over to the left. Use the Magnification pop-up menu to go to 50% screen view. Also, use the View pop-up menu to go to Keyline view.

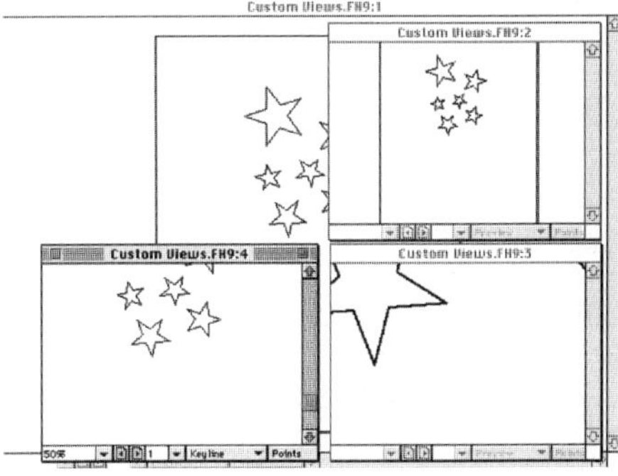

7. You have now created three different windows of the same document, all viewed at the same time. Each window shows a completely different display of the same document.
8. Close the document without saving.

Summary

In this chapter, you have learned to manage FreeHand's toolbars, in particular, the Main Toolbar, the Toolbox, and the Text Toolbar. You have learned how you may customize the toolbars for specific working environments. You have also become familiar with the nine panels and five viewing modes that you will work with in FreeHand. You have learned how to create and edit custom views, and to open a new window to provide a separate simultaneous view of your document. You are now ready to explore the grids, guides, and rulers that will enable you to effectively work with your documents.

Chapter 3

Rulers, Grids, and Guides

Chapter Objective:

To learn to use FreeHand's rulers, grids, and guides to position elements on the page, and to modify them so they comply with the needs of your workflow. In Chapter 3, you will:

- Learn how to use the page rulers to position elements on the page and to create custom page rulers.
- Become familiar with the use and positioning of the Zero Point for ease of positioning elements on the page.
- Learn about layers — one of FreeHand's most useful design aids and understand the various controls in the Layers panel.
- Learn the importance of how layers are arranged, and the different methods in which they can be arranged and modified.
- Understand how to lock, hide, and otherwise customize layers to suit your personal needs.
- Learn to create a custom scale, such as would be used for technical illustration.
- Learn how to reassign objects to other layers — a task frequently necessary for successful and appealing design.
- Learn the importance of guides; how to show and hide guides, create and modify guides, and understand how guides relate to layers.
- Learn to use the Guide Manager to precisely position guides.
- Learn to use and modify the document grid; learn to modify the grid from its plotted and set size.

Projects to be Completed:

- Dinner Time (A)
- Mask Art (B)
- Tropical Treasure Logo (C)
- Grocery Ad (D)
- Ball and Mirror (E)
- No Clowning Around (F)

Rulers, Grids, and Guides

Rulers, grids, and guides are useful tools for visually laying out your documents. As with so many of FreeHand's functions, they may be customized to match your working habits. While they provide a visual representation of the page, they are most effective when used in conjunction with the Info toolbar and the Object Inspector, when precise placement of objects is desired.

The Page Rulers

Grids and guides reference the Page Rulers, which you can turn on or off by selecting View>Page Rulers>Show.

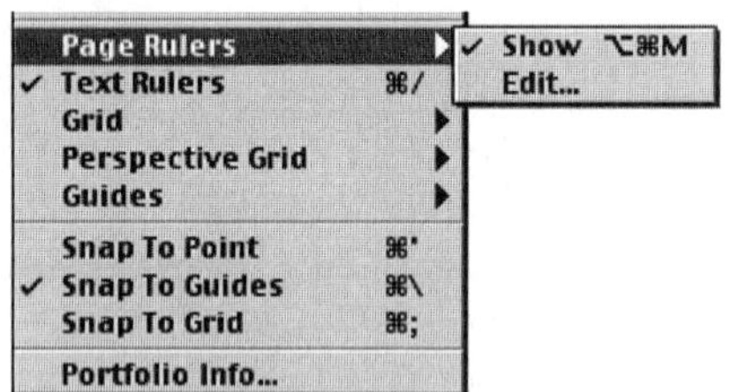

In most cases, the page rulers directly reflect the units of measurement set in the Status Bar pop-up menu. The standard units of measurement are Points, Picas, Inches, Decimal inches, Millimeters, Centimeters, Kyus, and Pixels. However, these are not the only available units of measurement. Technical illustrators, such as architects and engineers will appreciate FreeHand's ability to create relational units of measurement, such as 0.25″ = 1′. The rulers may be customized through View>Page Rulers>Edit.

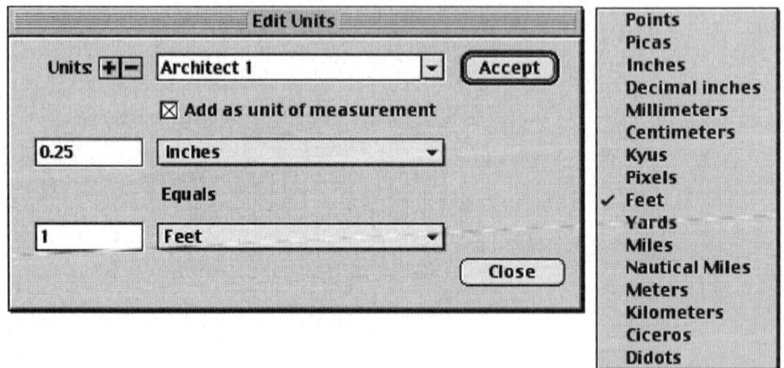

The intersection of the two rulers, the Zero Point, moves along with the rulers, which is useful for referencing measurements not based on the page boundaries.

The Ruler Zero Point

The Zero Point of the rulers can be moved to any part of the document, for ease in measuring. You can move it when the rulers are on by clicking in the upper-left corner of the document where the two rulers meet and then dragging to the desired location. Numbers above and to the right of the Zero Point are positive numbers; numbers below and to the left of the Zero Point are negative numbers.

The default location of the Zero Point is the lower-left corner of the document page. If you have changed the Zero Point and want it back to the default position, double-click on the Zero Point icon where the rulers meet in the upper-left corner of the screen.

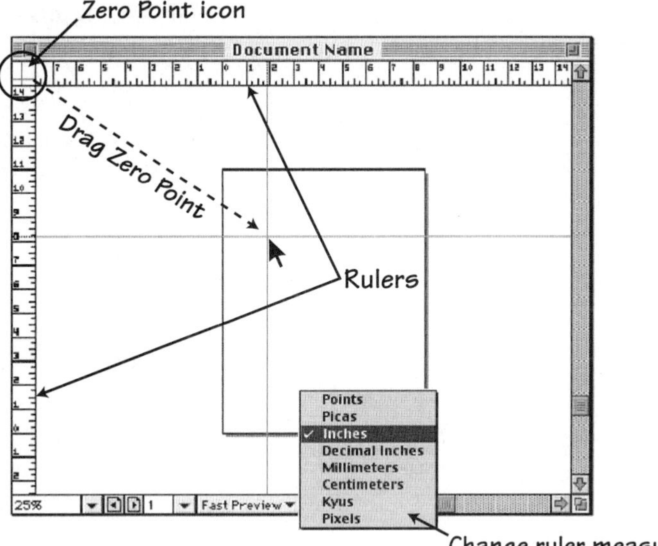

Set the Zero Point

1. Select File>New to create a new document.
2. Select View>Page Rulers and turn on the page rulers. The Zero Point is in the upper-left corner of the document where the rulers meet.
3. Click the mouse on the Zero Point and drag it onto the page. Observe the position of the intersecting guides as you move the mouse around.
4. Choose a location where you want the Zero Point to be relocated, then release the mouse; the zeroes of the rulers have now changed.
5. You do not have to drag the Zero Point back to its original position. Double-click on the Zero Point in the upper-left corner to reset the Zero Point back to the original position.
6. Notice how the zeroes of the rulers return to the default position.
7. You have now seen how you can drag the Zero Point to any other location in the document.
8. Close the file without saving.

Use the Rulers

1. Open the document **Office Design.FH9** from your **SF-FreeHand** folder. We have provided you with a number of icons that you can place in the office you're going to design.
2. From the Units pop-up menu at the bottom of the page, select Inches as your unit of measurement.

3. Select View>Page Rulers. If Show is not checked, click on it to select it now.
4. Click on the Zero Point's cross-hairs and drag them to the intersection of 3 inches on the horizontal ruler and 2 inches on the vertical ruler.

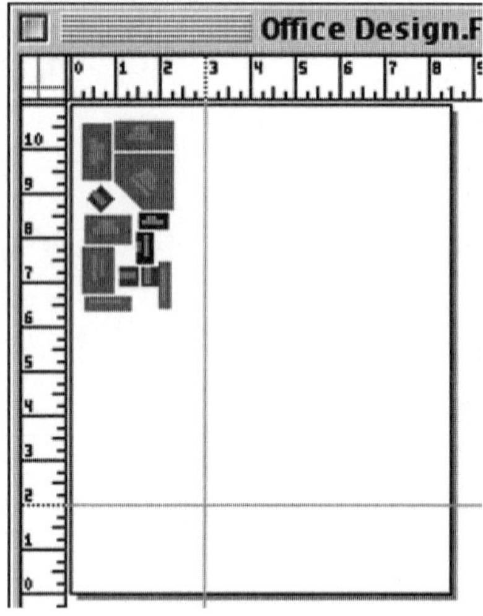

5. We're going to change to a custom scale. Select View>Page Rulers>Edit.
6. In the first window, type "Interior Design" in place of "Custom 1" and click the Add as unit of measurement box.
7. Type 0.25 in the next dialog box, and choose Inches from the drop-down menu.
8. Type 1 in the last dialog box and choose Feet from the drop-down menu.

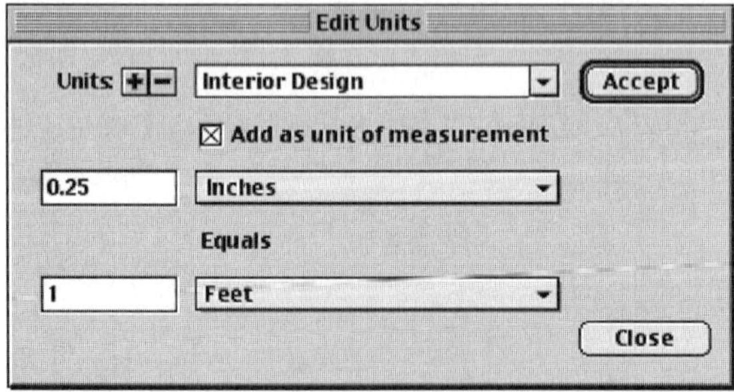

9. Click Accept, then Close.
10. From the Unit pop-up menu, select Interior Design as your new unit of measurement.
11. From the Toolbox, select the Rectangle tool.

12. Click and drag a rectangle of any size on the page.

13. If it is not already visible, select Window>Inspectors>Object.
14. In the Object Inspector, type the following in the respective dialog boxes:

    x: 0, y: 0, w:12, h: 12

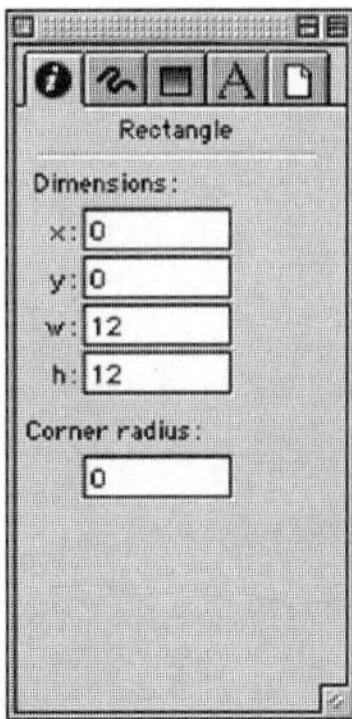

    This will create a 12′×12′ square at the scale of 0.25″=1′.

15. Arrange the furniture to your liking. Use as much or as little as you think is appropriate. Save the document to your **Work in Progress** folder.

Guides

Use guides to visually aid you in page layout. These non-printing blue lines can be located anywhere on the document page and may be straight or curved. The guides should be a color that will not appear to be part of the illustration. If you're using a blue similar in color to the guide's color, change the guide color at Preferences>Colors, then double-click on Guide Color to bring up a Color Picker.

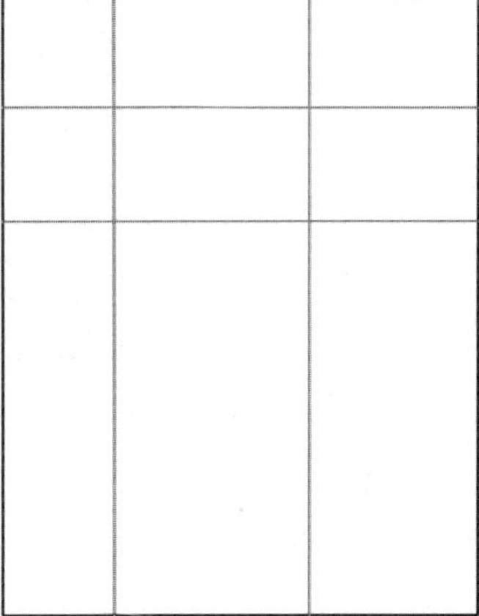

Show/Hide Guides

When you create a new document, the guides are visible by default. You can Show/Hide Guides by toggling View>Guides>Show. A checkmark next to Show signifies that guides are visible.

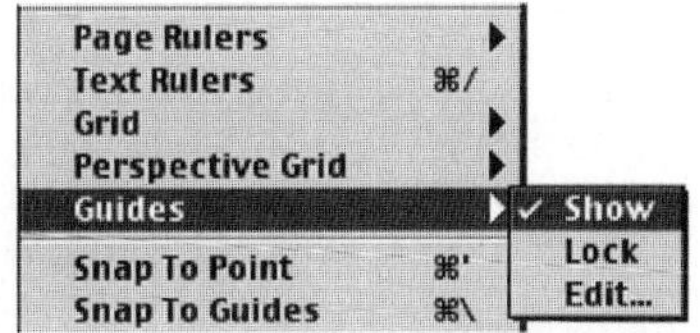

Guides and Layers

The guides can also be shown or hidden by clicking the checkmark symbol on the Guides layer in the Layers panel. This is the Show/Hide icon. When the checkmark is not visible, the guides are hidden. The Padlock icon locks the guides.

The Guides layer in the Layer panel cannot be deleted.

We will discuss layers in detail in Chapter 8, Advanced Drawing Features

Creating Guides

Guides can be created using three different methods:

- Page Rulers — When guides and rulers are visible new guides may be added. Simply drag guides from the horizontal or vertical Page Rulers to the desired position.
- Converting Paths — Paths created with the FreeHand drawing tools can be assigned to the Guides layer in the Layers panel.
- Guides dialog box — Accessed through View>Guides>Edit, this dialog box allows you to create or modify the characteristics of existing guides, or to add guides at specific locations and increments. When you click Add, the Add Guides dialog box will display to allow you to adjust your settings.

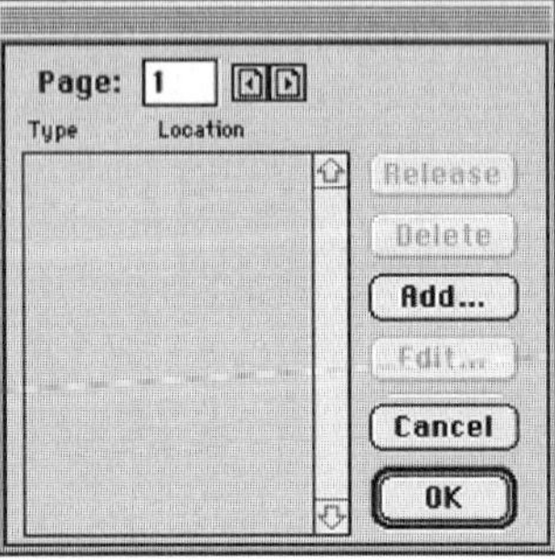

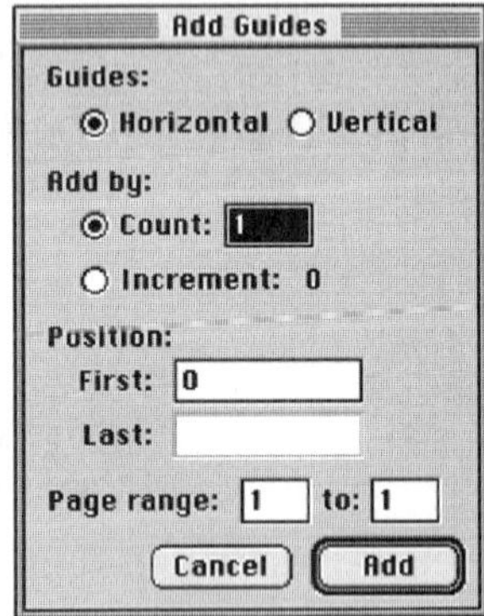

Guides Dialog Box

From the Guides dialog box you can add, delete, and modify guides. This box can be accessed by using View>Guides>Edit, or by double-clicking on any guide on the page.

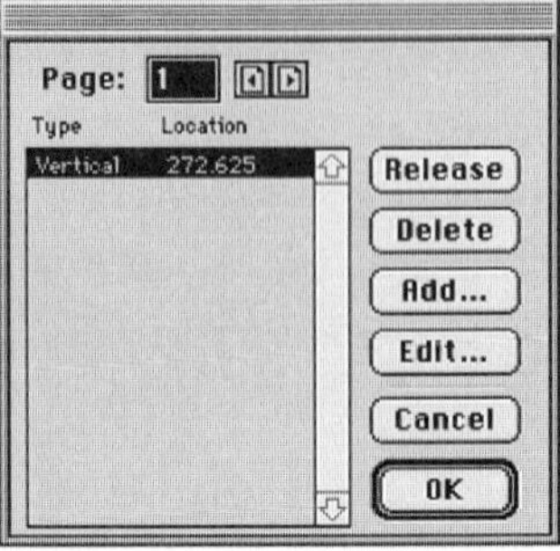

The Guides dialog box displays guide data for only one page of your document at a time. Enter the page you wish to modify or use the Next/Previous page buttons. The location that corresponds with the orientation (Horizontal, Vertical, or Path) of the guide will be shown in the unit mode you selected. The orientation is listed under Type.

When the guide you wish to change in this window is highlighted, all buttons will be available for use:

Use the Guides dialog box for exact positioning of new guides.

- Release — Use this button to turn the selected guide into a path.
- Delete (Macintosh) or Remove (Windows) — Use this button to delete all selected guides.
- Edit — Edit the location of a guide by clicking this button and typing the new location in the dialog box.
- Add — This button opens the Add Guide dialog box , where you may create your own guides numerically by specifying origin and quantity.

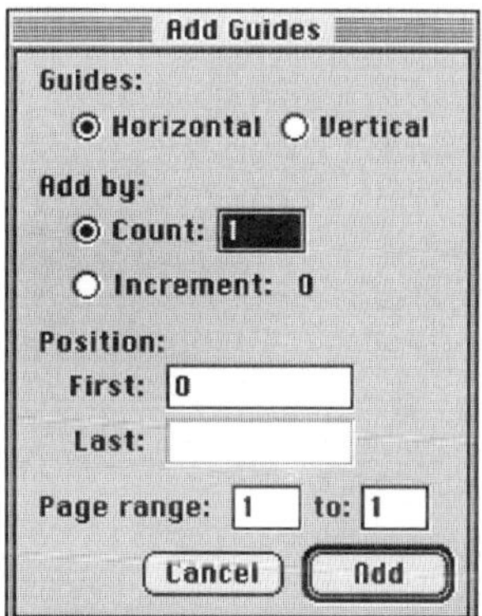

- Guides — Choose an orientation, either horizontal or vertical.
- Add by — Count allows you to choose how many guides will appear. Increment specifies the distance between multiple guides to create a grid or the basis for a form.
- Position — Set the first and last horizontal and vertical page position for the number of guides specified in this dialog box.
- Page range — Select the pages to which you wish to apply the guides.

Releasing a guide turns the guide into a FreeHand path. If you made an object into a guide, this will convert it back to an object that may be edited.

Removing Guides

Removing guides is as simple as creating them. To remove a guide manually, just click and drag it off the page. This is true for ruler guides as well as paths turned to guides.

To remove guides in the dialog box, click on the guide listed in the Type column. The dimmed buttons (Release or Delete) will activate and you can release the guide or delete it.

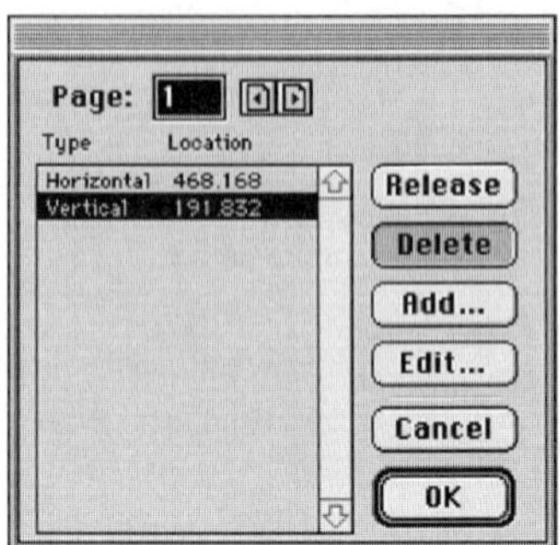

Controlling Guides

Guides come with a few more options that make them even more useful. You can have objects "snap" like a magnet when they are moved close to the guides, lock the guides to protect them from modification, and change the color from blue to any color you desire.

"Snapping" is like a magnetic force that attracts the object to the guide when it is a certain distance away. Choose View>Snap To Guides or press Command-\ (Macintosh) or Control-Alt-G (Windows).

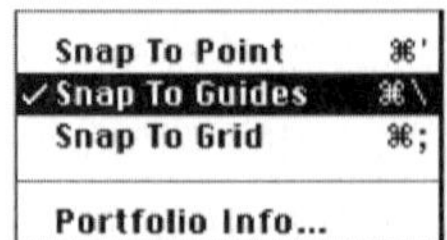

You can customize the sensitivity of guides by specifying a "Snap Distance" in screen pixels through File>Preferences>General. The default value is 3; smaller values make the guides less sensitive and larger values cause objects to snap to the guide from a greater distance. If you are trying to place objects near the guide, you may find it best to turn Snap To Guides off, or to decrease the sensitivity.

Locking Guides

If you find yourself accidently moving your guides after precisely locating them, Lock them from modification. Select View>Guides>Lock or lock the Padlock for the Guides layer in the Layers panel.

Create and Modify Guides

1. Select File>Open and navigate to **Grid & Guides.FH9** in your **SF-FreeHand** folder.

2. In the Magnification pop-up menu in the lower left of the screen, set the percentage for 50%.

3. Select View>Page Rulers>Show to toggle the rulers on-screen. Set the measurement units for Inches.

4. Click on the vertical ruler at the left side of the screen and drag a guide onto the page, matching it to the 4.25 inch mark on the horizontal ruler at the top of the document. Click on the horizontal ruler and drag a guide down onto the page, matching the 5.5 inch mark of the vertical ruler as you can see in the following image. The place where the two guides meet in the middle marks the center of the page. This is the ruler-dragging method.

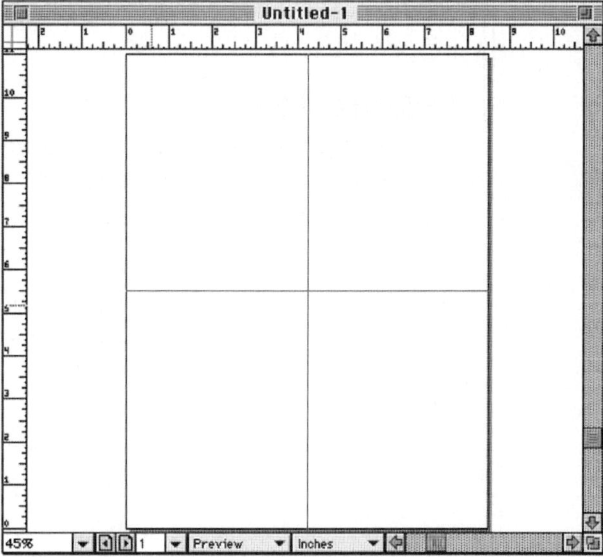

If the blue color of the guides is confusing because of the nature of your illustration, change it. From File>Preferences>Colors, change the "Guide color" by double-clicking on its swatch to access the system color palette.

5. Sometimes custom guides need to be created from paths. Select the square on the page.
6. Select Window>Panels>Layers to open the Layers panel. You will notice that it has three layers: Foreground, Guides, and Background.

7. With the square selected, click on the Guides layer to assign the square. Click the checkmark on the Guides layer. This is the Show/Hide button. What happened to all the guides on the page? Click this button again.
8. Click on the square guide and move it around the page. Click on the Padlock icon on the Guides layer. Try to move the square guide; try to move any of the guides. The clicked padlock locked them. Click this again to unlock the guides.

   You now have three guides on the page: the vertical, horizontal, and the square. Let's assume you want the square turned back to a path for use in a design. How do you convert back to paths? You do this in the Edit Guides dialog box, accessed through either View>Guides>Edit or by double-clicking on the guide in question.
9. Double-click on the square guide to display the dialog box listing the guides by their type or measurement location; the Path option will be highlighted. Click Release, then click OK.

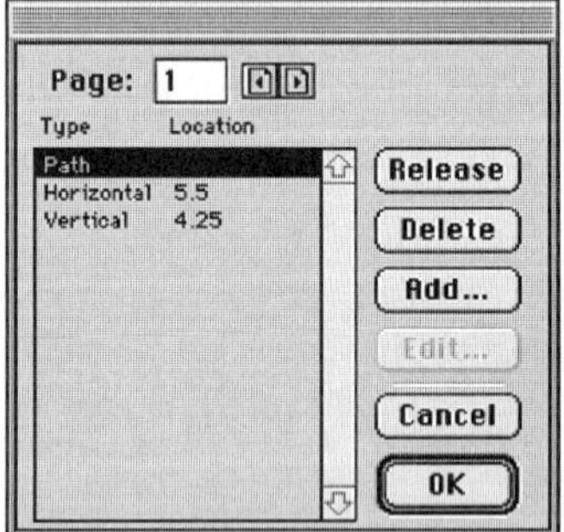

10. What happened to the guide? It reverts back to an object. Choose Edit>Undo to make the path a guide again.
11. Click on the vertical guide and drag it off the page. What happened to it? Drag the horizontal guide off the page. Guides are deleted by dragging them off the page.
12. Double-click on the square guide to display the Edit Guides dialog box.
13. Click on the Path item in the Type column. Click the Delete (Macintosh) or Remove (Windows) button, then click OK. The guide has been deleted from the page.
14. Keep the document open for the next exercise.

Create Guides with Add Guides

1. Continue working in the open document, Grids & Guides.FH9.
2. You should be looking at a blank page with no guides or paths.
3. Select View>Guides>Edit to show the Edit Guides dialog box. Click on the Add button to display the Add Guides dialog box.

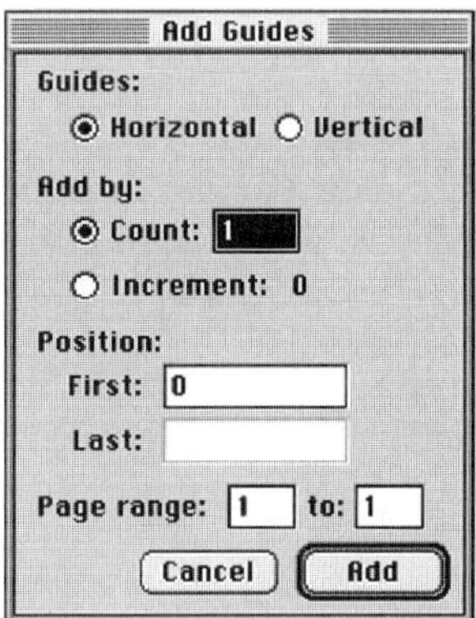

4. Apply the following settings:

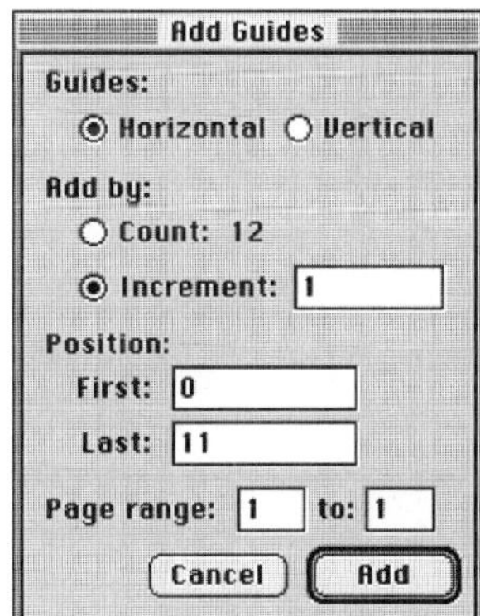

Guides: Horizontal

Add by Increment: 1. The guides will be placed at one-inch increments, since you have the units set for inches. This automatically calculates the number of guides to be placed and displays that number in the Count information.

Position: First: 0, Last: 11. We will place a guide at the very top and the very bottom of the page.

Page Range: 1 to 1, since this is a single-page document.

Click Add.

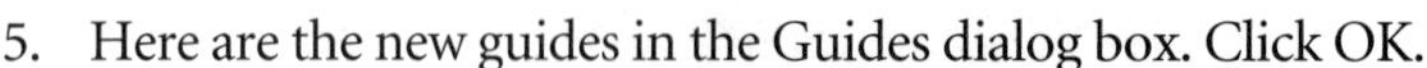

5. Here are the new guides in the Guides dialog box. Click OK.

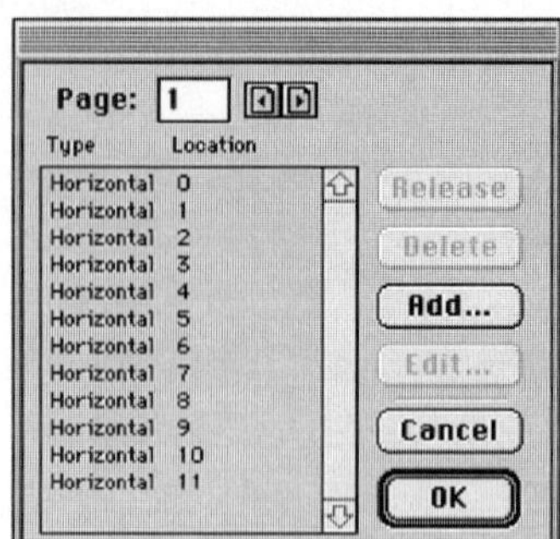

6. You will see the guides on the page.

Use the Guides dialog box for exact positioning of new guides.

7. Double-click on any of the guides with the Pointer tool to display the Edit Guides dialog box. Click the Add button.

8. Enter the following settings:

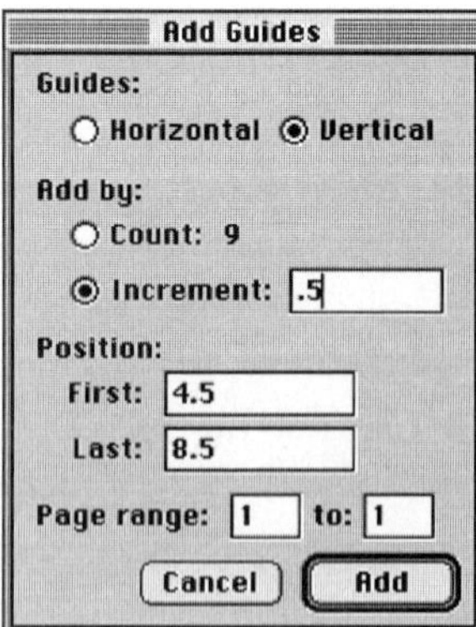

Guides: Vertical

Add by Increment: .5

Position First: 4.5, Last: 8.5

Click Add.

9. You will see the Guides dialog box. Click OK.

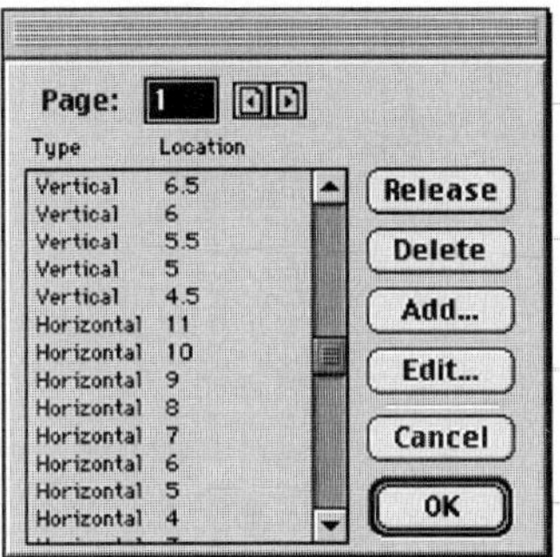

10. Here's the page with your custom-made guides:

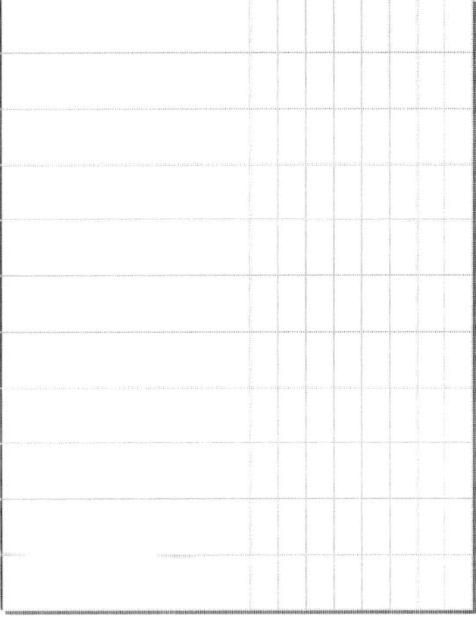

11. Close the document without saving.

Grids

The FreeHand Grid is a background of horizontal and vertical dotted lines set as a background (non-printing) alignment tool. The grid is plotted at a set size, but you can alter these settings.

Releasing a guide turns the guide into a FreeHand object. If you made an object into a guide, this will convert it back to an object for further editing.

Show/Hide Grids

Like guides, grids can be toggled on and off by choosing View>Grid>Show. When you launch a new document the grid is off. Choose View>Grid>Show to display the non-printing grid.

Editing the Grid

Think of a grid as dotted lines that turn your page into graph paper. The increments between the horizontal and vertical parallels are exactly the same. The value can be set by selecting View>Grid>Edit.

Remember that the value entered into this box depends on what unit of measurement you have set. The following shows the default setting for inches:

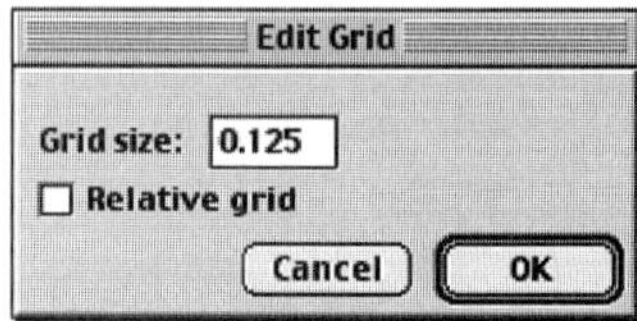

The color of the grid defaults to red, but this can be changed by making a new color setting in Preferences>Colors.

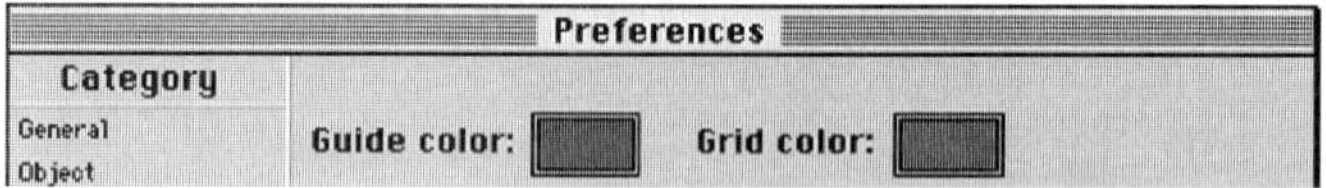

Snapping

Grids can snap objects, much like guides. You activate this feature by choosing View>Snap To Grid or press Command-; (Macintosh). Snapping attaches objects to the nearest intersection on the grid. Everything from charts to business cards and logos to multimedia projects such as web graphics and marketing materials can benefit from using a grid for your layout. The grid is the most basic and powerful tool available to a designer.

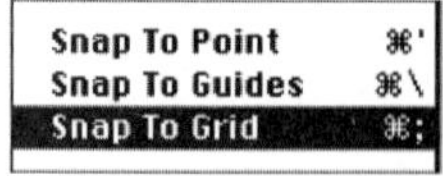

Perspective Grid

The FreeHand Perspective Grid allows you to create customized perspective grids as a background of lines that create one, two, or three perspective vanishing points. The grid is plotted at a set size, but you can alter these settings. We will discuss perspective in Chapter 8, Advanced Drawing Features.

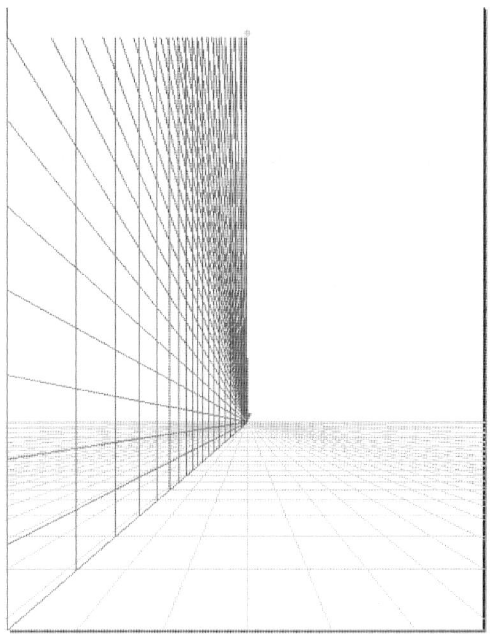

Show/Hide Perspective Grids

Like grids, perspective grids can be toggled on and off by choosing View>Perspective Grid>Show. When you launch a new document the perspective grid is off.

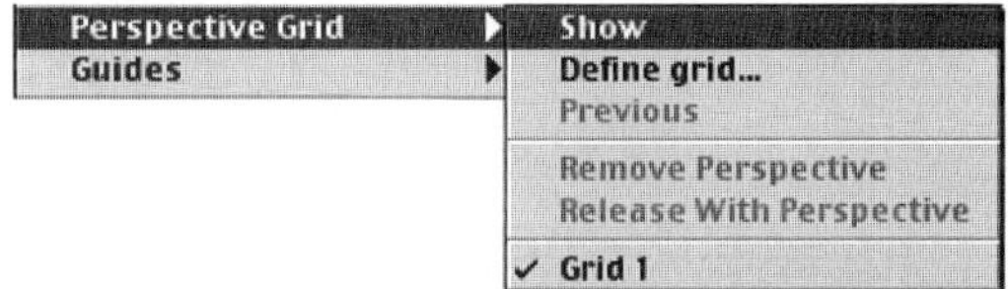

Defining Perspective Grids

Customize the perspective by choosing View>Perspective Grid>Define Grid. The Define Grid options let you set the number of vanishing points from 1 to 3. You can also type in the grid cell size and choose the grid colors.

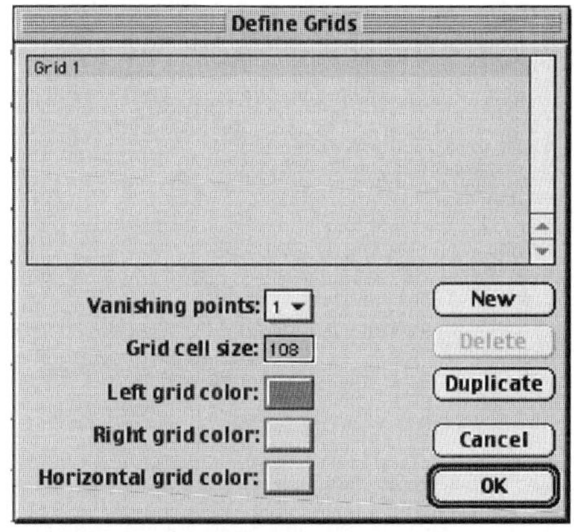

Use Grid and Guides

1. From the File menu, select New to create a new document.
2. Use the Magnification pop-up menu to set the view for 50%.
3. Select View>Grid>Show.

4. You will see the grid appear on the page in its assigned color and on the pasteboard in black.
5. Set the Units pop-up menu for Inches. Select View>Grid>Edit to display the dialog box for customizing the grid's increments. Specify the Grid increment based on the measurement units selected in the Units pop-up menu.
6. Set the Edit Grid defaults to 0.125 inches.

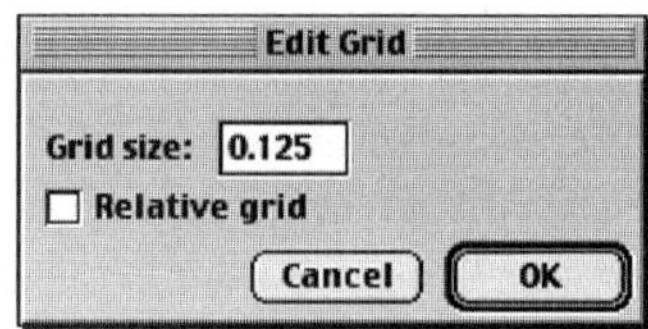

7. Experiment with this dialog box. Change this Grid size to any other number you wish and click OK. View the grid on screen.
8. After you have an idea of how the grid can be changed, change the Grid size back to 0.125 inches and click OK.
9. The grid is useful for giving you a guide-like system to use for placement and measurements without having to drag out Guides to create one. Unlike guides, you can't move the grid.
10. Select View>Grid>Show to turn the grid off. You can see how simple it is to control and edit the grid.
11. Close the document without saving.

Summary

You have learned to work with rulers, grids, and guides, customizing their use to your needs. You have learned to create custom rulers to allow you to do technical drawing, positioning the Zero Point on a page for ease of use. When working with guides, you have learned to create and modify guides singly and several at a time, through the Add Guides dialog box. You are now ready to learn to use FreeHand's drawing tools.

CHAPTER 4

Drawing Basics

CHAPTER OBJECTIVE:

Learning more about drawing basics briefly covered in Chapter 3, and expand the material to cover most aspects of FreeHand illustration techniques. In Chapter 4, you will:

- Learn the fundamentals to create, edit, and compose basic shapes — the first step in drawing with FreeHand.
- Learn about and use the basic line drawing tools.
- Learn about basic shapes, the most-used shapes for commercial art, design, printing, or advertising.
- Learn the features of the tools that draw basic shapes.
- Learn how to create a closed path with straight lines.
- Learn about the two methods of moving objects and practice using them.
- Learn how to use the three drawing tools, where to access them, and their many features.

PROJECTS TO BE COMPLETED:

- **Dinner Time (A)**
- Mask Art (B)
- Tropical Treasure Logo (C)
- Grocery Ad (D)
- Ball and Mirror (E)
- No Clowning Around (F)

Drawing Basics

Now that you know how to work with FreeHand, we can begin drawing. This chapter teaches you how to create basic shapes, how to edit them, and helps you understand the components of the drawn objects.

Primitive shapes — rectangles, ellipses, and polygons — are the most basic and most frequently used elements. Complex shapes are drawn in FreeHand using Bézier points and line segments. FreeHand gives us a number of tools that make creating even complex images relatively easy.

Basic Shapes Drawing Tools

Basic shapes are sometimes taken for granted. However, imagine having to draw a simple border with pen and ink. You would have to measure from the edge of the page to each starting point and mark the corner points (using non-reproducible blue pen or pencil). Then you would have to draw each line separately and accurately. If the pen blobbed, or if you overdrew the corner, you'd have to start all over again.

With FreeHand, you could define the page size as exactly the ad size, then select the Rectangle tool, begin dragging from the upper-left corner, and release the mouse when the cursor reached the lower-right corner of the page. As an alternative, you could use a larger page size and create the border to the appropriate dimensions, adjusting them in the Object Inspector if you discovered they were a bit off.

There are five tools in the Toolbox for drawing basic shapes. When using the Line tool, Spiral tool, Rectangle tool, Ellipse tool, and Polygon tool, you simply drag the tool cursor on the page and the specified shape is created.

 The Line Tool

The Line tool is used to draw straight lines at any angle, which may be constrained to 45° increments simply by holding down the Shift key. To draw from a center point, hold down the Option/Alt key. The Line tool works in conjunction with the Stroke Inspector, which is used to assign color, width, endcap characteristics, dashes, and arrowheads.

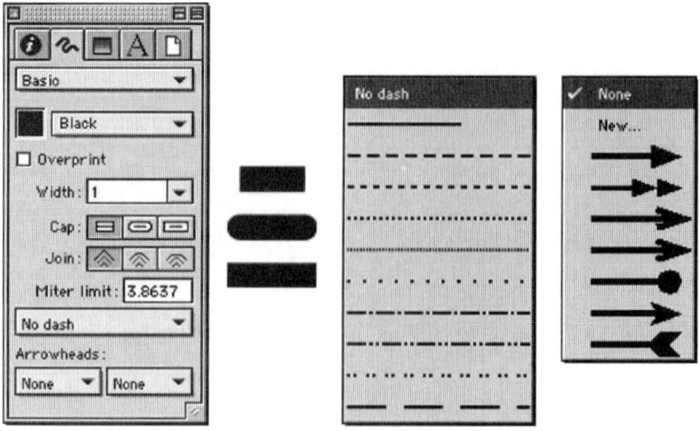

The Spiral Tool

The Spiral tool is used to draw spiral lines. The spiral is defined in the Spiral dialog box, which is accessed by double-clicking on the Spiral tool.

The Spiral type option allows you to draw a spiral with rotations that are equal in distance from one another or spirals with expanding space between them. The Draw by option allows you to draw spirals based on the number of rotations or by increments, based on the unit of measurement you have selected. The Draw from option provides three starting points for the spiral: the center, edge, or corner. The Direction option allows you to define your spiral as clockwise or counter-clockwise.

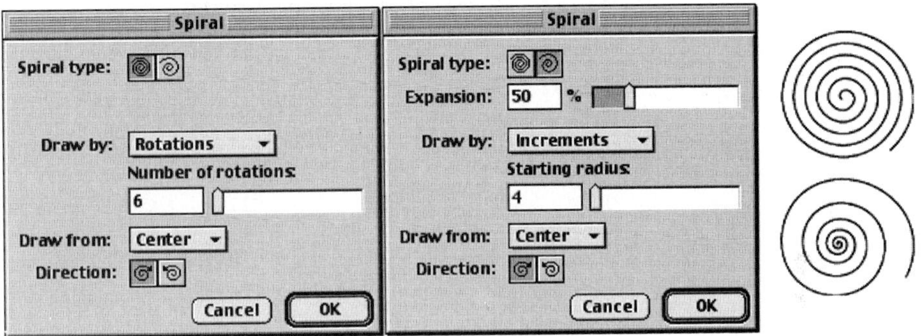

Consistent or expanding spirals are drawn based on the settings in the Spiral dialog box.

Use Basic Line Drawing Tools

1. Choose File>New to create a new document.
2. Set the units of measurement to Inches from the pop-up menu.
3. Click on the Line tool in the Toolbox to select it.

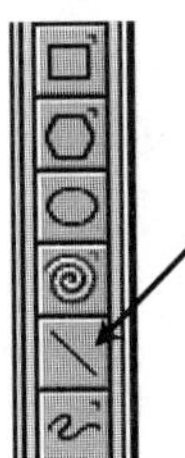

4. Click and drag a line to a length of 2 inches and release the mouse. Click again and drag at an angle. Press the Shift key to constrain the line to a 45° angle as you drag.

5. Double-click on the Spiral tool in the Toolbox to display its dialog box.

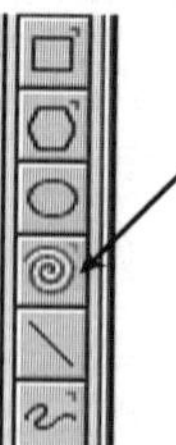

6. Select the left (even) Spiral type, Draw by Rotations, and assign 3 rotations. Leave the defaults of drawing from the center and a clockwise spiral.

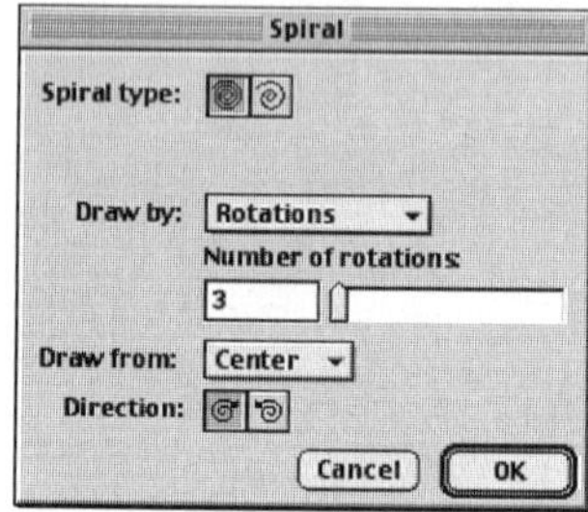

7. Click the cursor on the page and drag. Notice that no matter what size spiral you create, it will have only 3 rotations. Move the cursor around in a circle to position the end of the spiral in different locations. Hold down the Shift key and constrain the spiral to movement in 45° increments.
8. Return to the Spiral dialog box and experiment with other settings.
9. Close the document without saving.

Corner radius is the size of a circle with the described radius. A rectangle with a corner radius of 0.25" could hold a circle 0.5" in diameter in the corner.

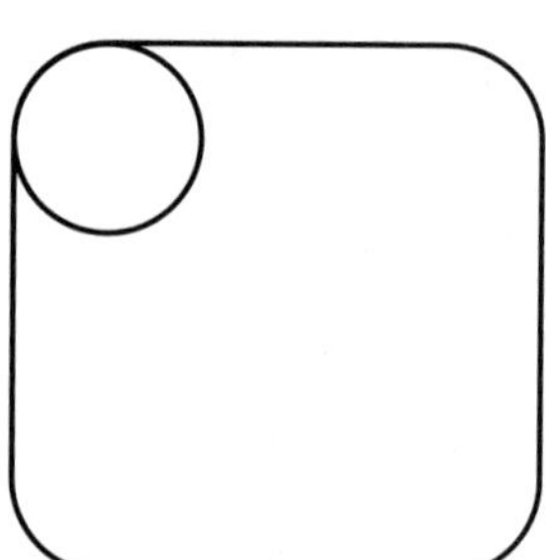

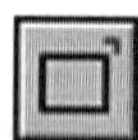

The Rectangle Tool

The Rectangle tool is used to draw rectangles that may be constrained to squares by holding the Shift key while drawing the objects. Holding the Option/Alt key causes the rectangle to be drawn from the center.

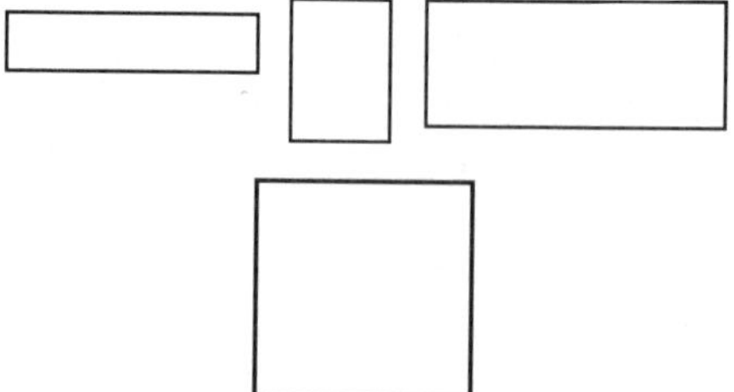

Rounded Corners

Double-clicking on the Rectangle tool in the Toolbox will access the Rectangle Tool dialog box, which allows you to assign a corner radius to the rectangle.

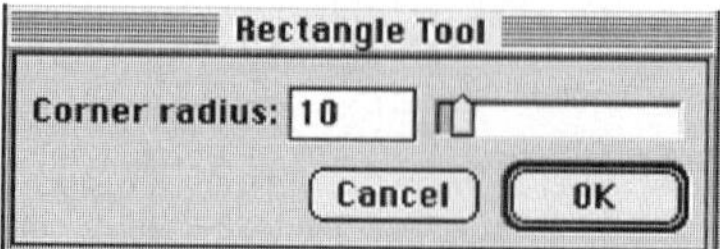

Once the corner radius is set, all rectangles will be drawn with this radius until you change the setting. The radius is based on the units of measurement you have selected.

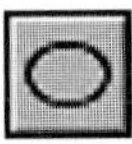 The Ellipse Tool

The Ellipse tool is used to draw elliptical shapes that may be constrained to circles by holding down the Shift key while drawing the objects.

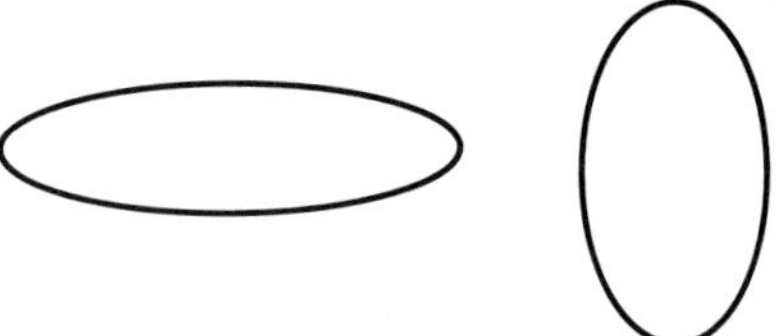

When the Option/Alt key is pressed, the ellipses are drawn from the center.

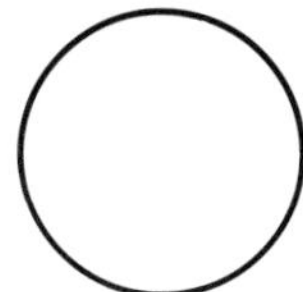

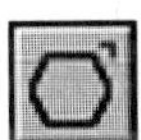 The Polygon Tool

The Polygon tool is used to draw a variety of geometric shapes.

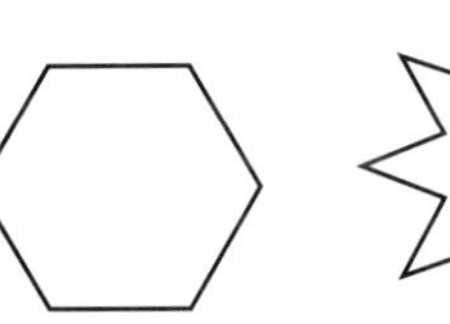

Double-clicking on the Polygon tool in the Toolbox will access the Polygon dialog box. When the Polygon shape is selected, equilateral polygons of 3 to 20 sides are drawn. When the Star shape is selected stars with 3 to 20 points are drawn. You may use FreeHand's default (Automatic) or create stars with more acute or obtuse angles by clicking Manual and using the slider. Polygons and stars are drawn from the center by default.

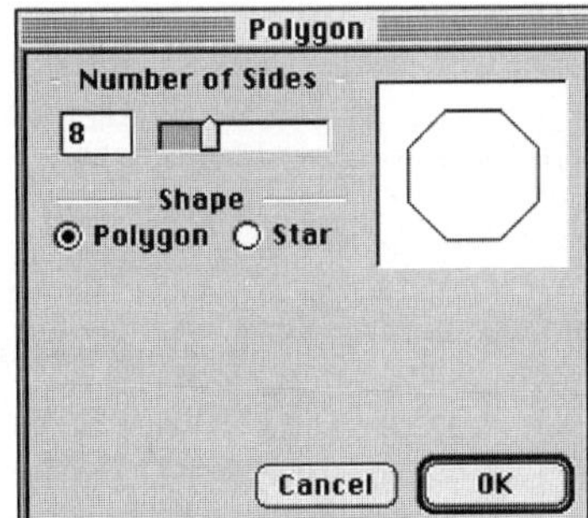

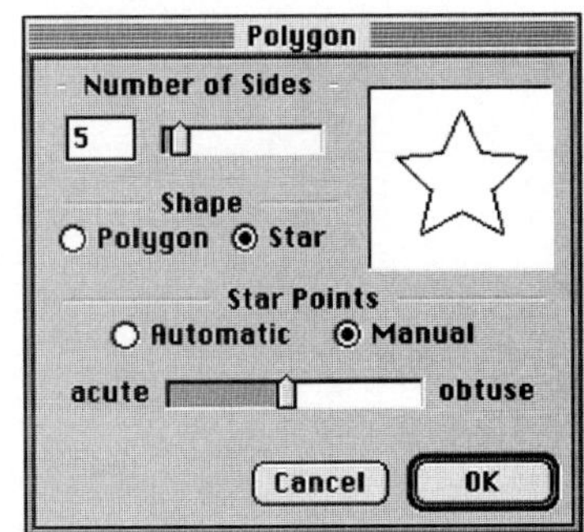

Use Basic Shape Tools

1. Choose File>New to create a new document.
2. At the top of the Toolbox, below the Text tool, are a variety of drawing tools that produce paths and objects using different techniques.

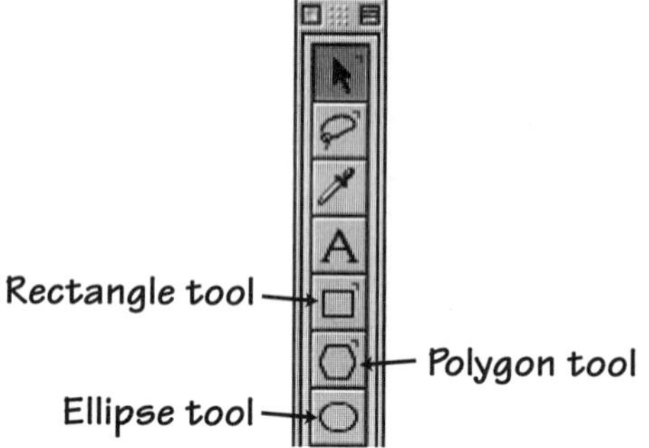

3. Click on the Rectangle tool. Click and drag on the document page to draw a rectangle. Draw another rectangle on the page, but this time hold the Shift key as you drag. This will make it a square. Hold the Option/Alt key to draw the rectangle/square from the center outward.

4. Click on the Polygon tool. Click and drag across the page to draw an unconstrained polygon. Draw another polygon, holding the Shift key to constrain the image.

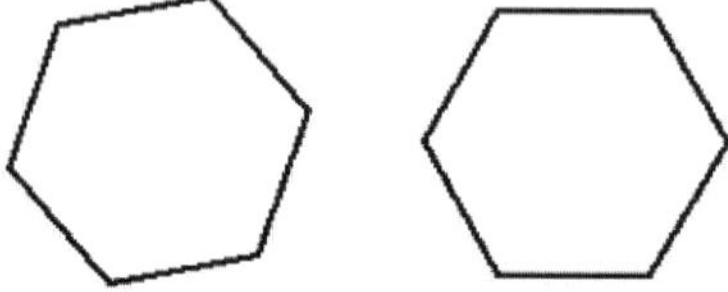

5. Double-click on the Polygon tool in the Toolbox.
6. The Polygon dialog box appears. Set the shape to Star with 5 points. Click OK.

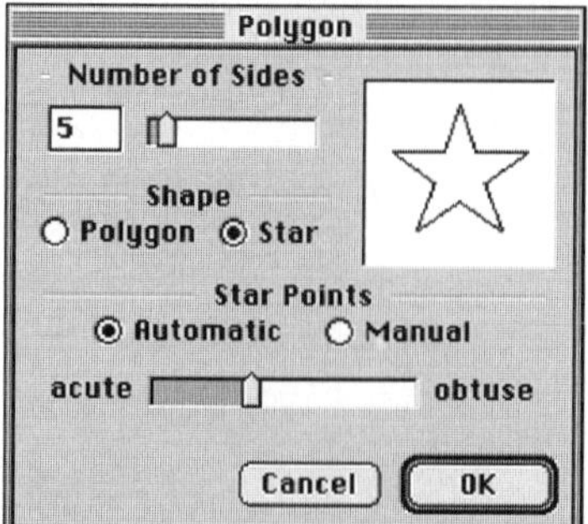

7. Now click the Polygon tool on the page and drag to see what sort of star you are creating. Experiment by holding the Shift key to constrain the star's rotation as you draw the star shape.

8. Click on the Ellipse tool.

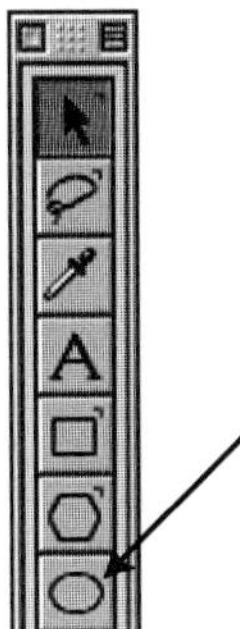

9. Click the Ellipse tool on the page and drag to create ellipses. Hold the Option/Alt key to draw the ellipse starting from the center.

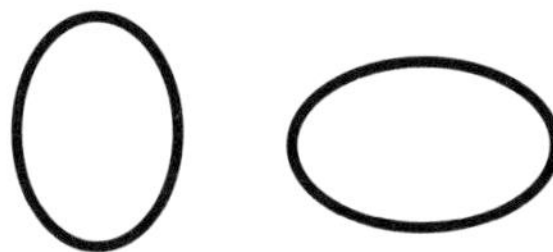

10. Draw an ellipse holding the Shift key to constrain it to a circle. Draw another circle from the center.

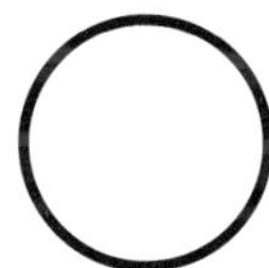

11. Close the document without saving.

Composition of Your Artwork

Your artwork can exist on many different planes called Layers. Within each layer you can have placed images, drawn vector paths, text, and other objects. Most objects in FreeHand are made of points, segments, and fills.

Segments connect points that define an outer border of an object (easily seen in Keyline mode) that can be filled (easily seen in Preview mode) with a multitude of different colors and patterns. All points that make up an object rest on a single layer within FreeHand.

FreeHand uses mathematical equations to place the object at the specified location. This location is determined by its Cartesian coordinate (x,y), which can be anywhere on the pasteboard. The measurement system is chosen from the Units pop-up menu.

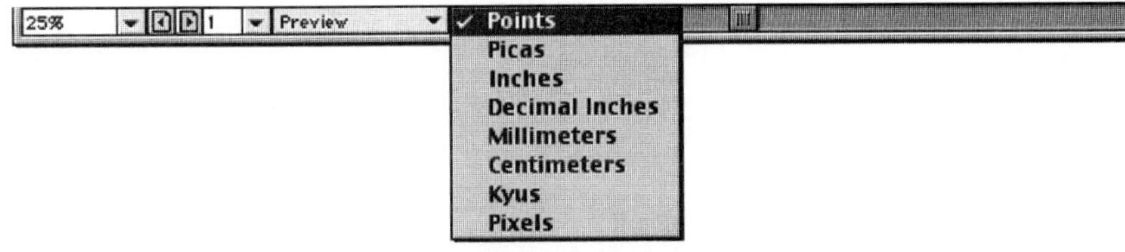

Points

All objects drawn in FreeHand contain points. The individual points determine the boundaries of an object.

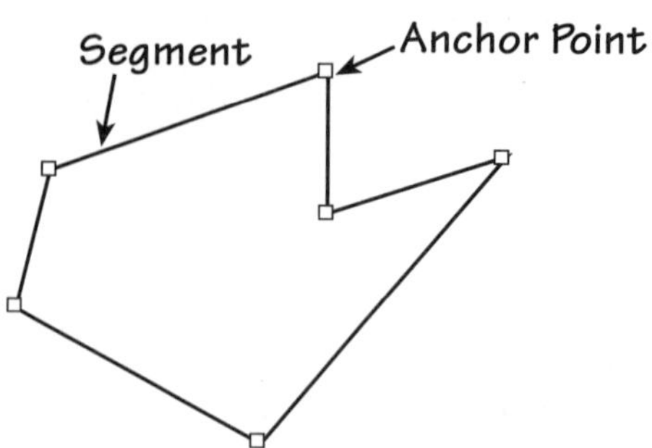

There are three types of points: corner points, curve points, and connector points. A corner point joins two straight segments, or may be used when there is an abrupt shift in direction between two curved segments. A curve point joins two curved line segments, where a flowing line is desired. A connector point joins a straight path to a curved path, creating a smooth connection between the segments. The type of point used may be changed in the Object Inspector.

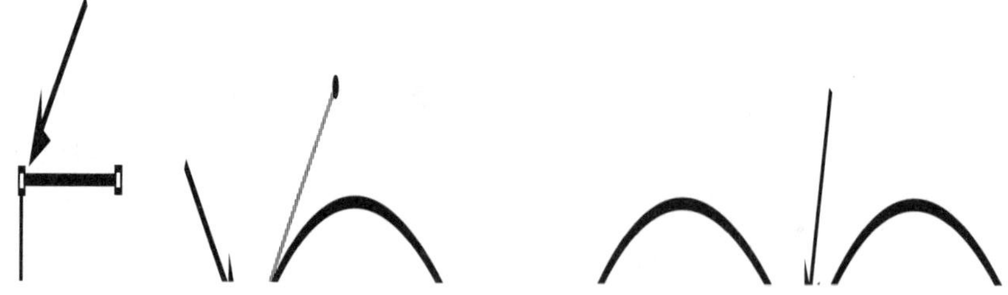

Points are placed by drawing with FreeHand's variety of drawing tools.

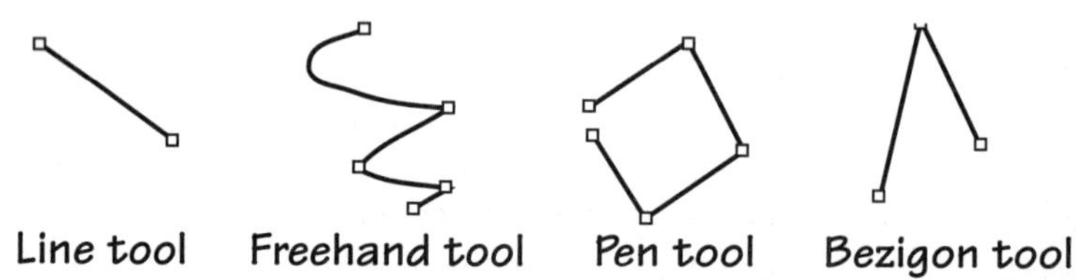

Segments

When you connect two points, a segment occurs. Segments are defined by the relationship between two points. There are only two types of segments: the straight segment and the curved segment. In FreeHand, segments are also called paths.

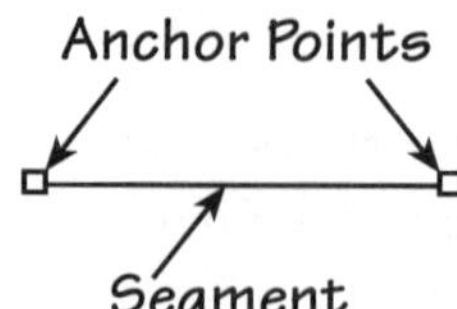

An object can be considered either open or closed. If an object is open, there is not a common beginning and end point. An example of an open path would be a straight line. When an object is closed there is a common beginning and end point. Fills can only be applied to a closed path.

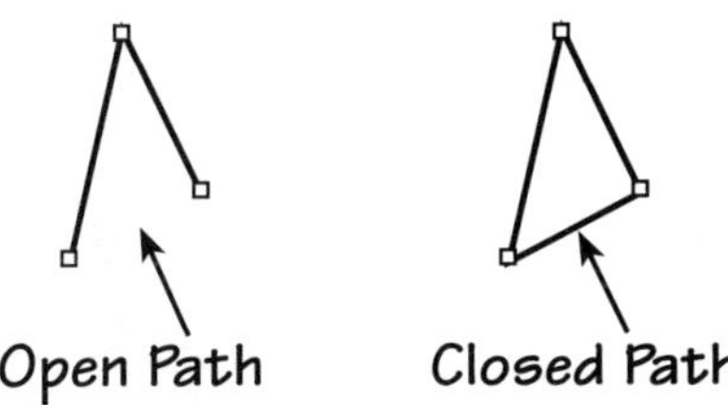

Fills

The third component of an object is its fill. Fills are set from the Fill Inspector. There are many types of fills that can be applied. Fills are best viewed when in Preview mode.

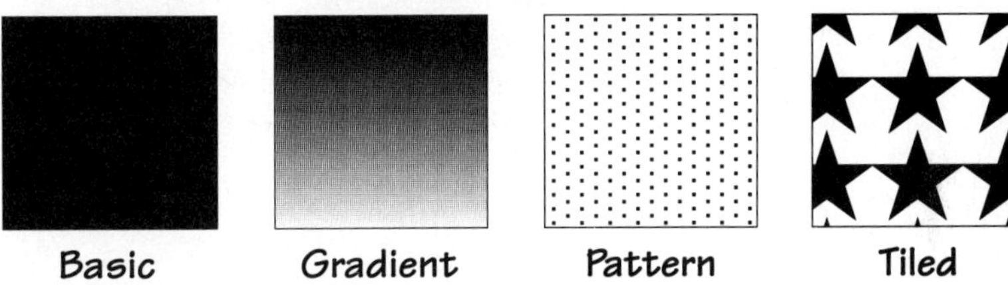

The Pointer Tool and Object Inspector

The Pointer tool and the Object Inspector work hand in hand. When an object is selected with the Pointer, its data is displayed in the Object Inspector.

 Pointer Tool

The Pointer tool is used to select, move, and alter objects. To select an object, click the Pointer tool on a path or on a filled object. Clicking in an unfilled object will not select it. You can select multiple objects by drawing a selection marquee around them. When objects are selected using the marquee method, all the objects to be selected must be surrounded by the marquee. However, the Pointer tool may be made contact sensitive, so that objects must simply be touched by the Pointer tool to be included in the selection. To do so, double-click the Pointer tool and check Contact Sensitive in the Pointer Tool dialog box.

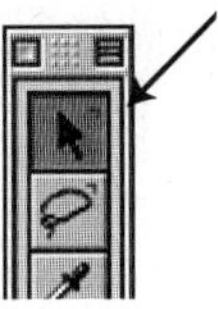

When the Even/Odd Fill box is selected, overlapping portions of closed paths become transparent at their intersections.

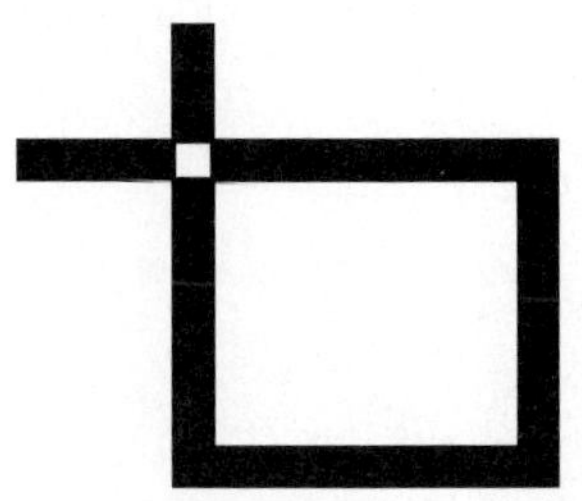

Object Inspector

Path and point information is shown in the Object Inspector.

If a path is the selected object, it will tell you the number of points in the path, the type of fill, whether or not the path is closed, and the flatness of the object.

If a point on the path is selected, it will also tell you the type of point, allow you to collapse the point's handles individually, allow you to automatically adjust the handles of a point in relation to preceding and following points, and provide the x,y coordinates of the point.

If the selected object is a rectangle or an ellipse, the Object inspector provides the x,y coordinates, the width, and the height of the object. The x,y coordinates are defined as the lower-left edge of the bounding box.

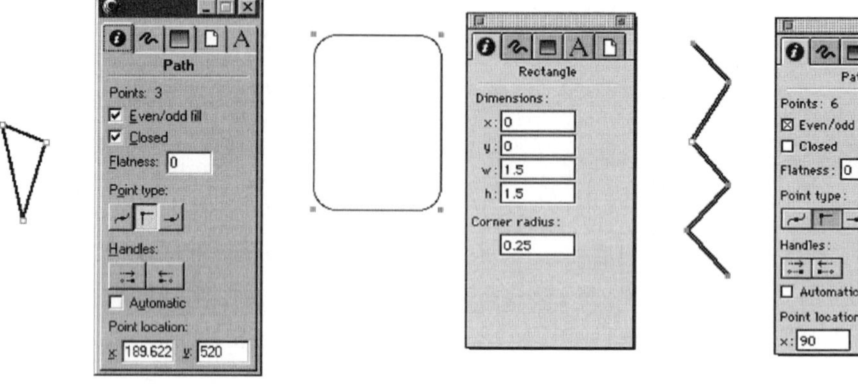

Windows Macintosh

Use the Pointer Tool

1. Open the file **FreeHand Pointer Tool.FH9** from the **SF-FreeHand** folder.

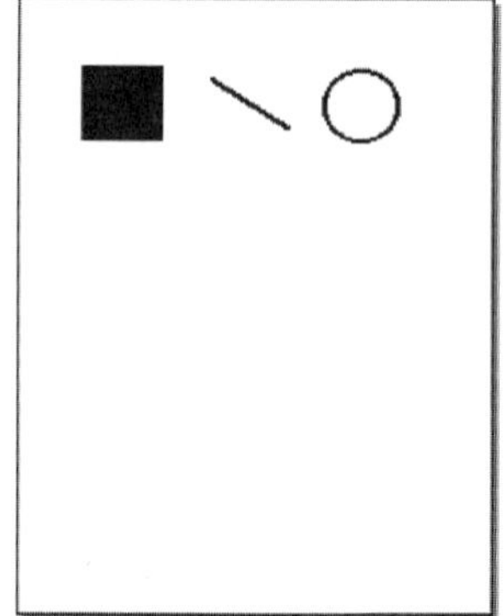

2. Select Window>Inspector>Object to access the Object Inspector.
3. With the Pointer tool, click on the black square. The Object Inspector displays the object's coordinates, width, and height.

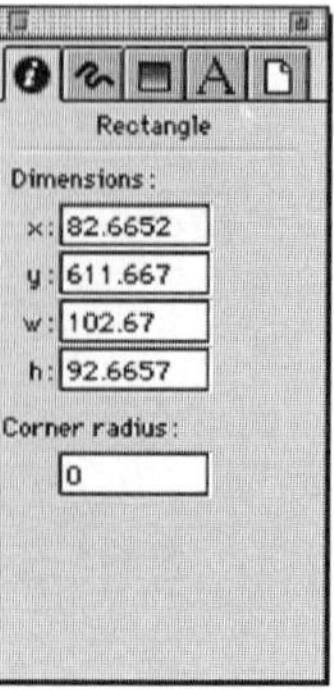

By default, the Zero Point of a page (x: 0/y: 0) is the lower-left corner. If the Zero Point is moved, positions above and to the right are positive (x: 20/y: 20) and positions below and to the left are negative (x: –20/y: –20).

4. Click on the black square and hold the mouse button down, without moving, until the cursor becomes a cross with arrowheads.
5. Move the square slightly to the left. Observe how the coordinates change in the Object Inspector.
6. Click on the middle object — the single line. See how different its information is in the Object Inspector. Remember, the path is not closed.

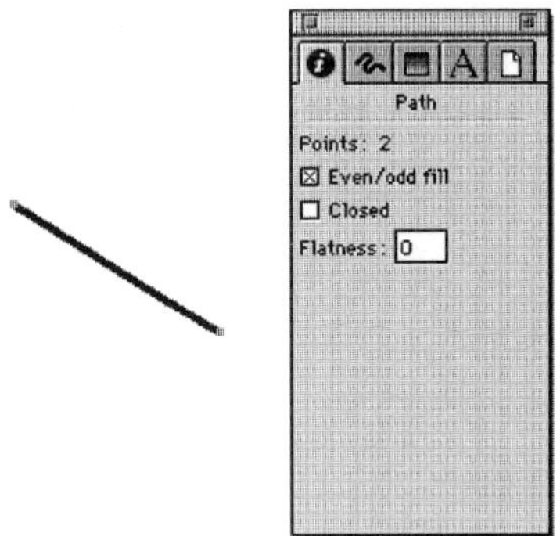

7. With the Pointer tool, draw a marquee around this middle object. The Object Inspector now gives information about the line's endpoints.

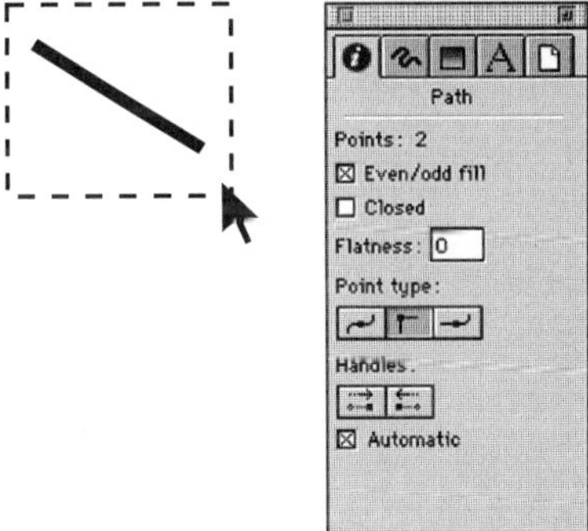

8. Click on the circle object. Observe how similar its information is to the square; however, circles do not have a corner radius.
9. You have now seen how the Pointer tool and the Object Inspector can show you information about objects that would not readily be visible. You will learn to apply changes in upcoming exercises.
10. Keep the document open for the next exercise.

Moving Objects with the Pointer Tool

There are two ways to select and move objects with the Pointer tool. They are very different in appearance and give you more control over positioning the object when you move it. The two methods are to click and hold the mouse on the object or to quickly move the bounding box.

The Click-hold Method

When you click on an object without moving it and hold the mouse button down for a few seconds, the cursor turns into a cross with arrowheads.

The object is ready to relocate, and the advantage to this method is that you can see the object as you move it. In this example, the circle was clicked and held until the cross appeared (A), then the circle was moved (B).

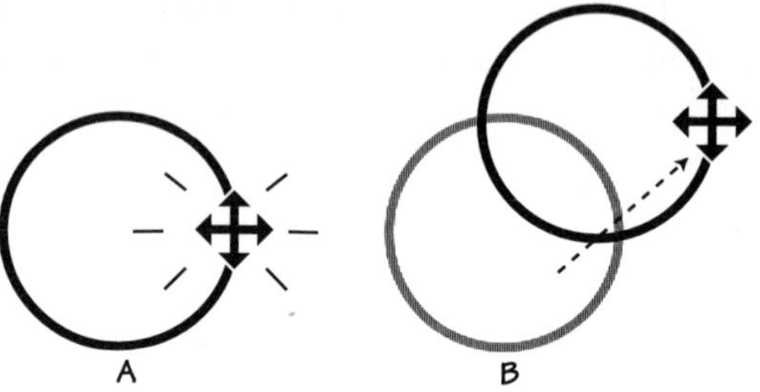

The Quick-move Method

Every object or group of objects has a *bounding box*. The bounding box shows the outer perimeter of the objects, but it doesn't appear until you move the object with the quick-move method.

Bounding boxes of various objects.

The secret to moving objects and seeing only their bounding box is tricky. You must be comfortable with using a mouse. The idea is to begin the move as soon as you click on the object in one sweeping movement.

When you succeed in selecting the object this way, you will only see its bounding box, not the paths of the object. This is used mostly for more precision alignment. When the edge of the bounding box touches a target path or guide, you know the object's extreme dimensions are in place.

In this example, the circle was quickly clicked on and moved in one sweep. The cursor remained a Pointer arrow, and the moving object became the bounding box. When the mouse is released, the object will be moved.

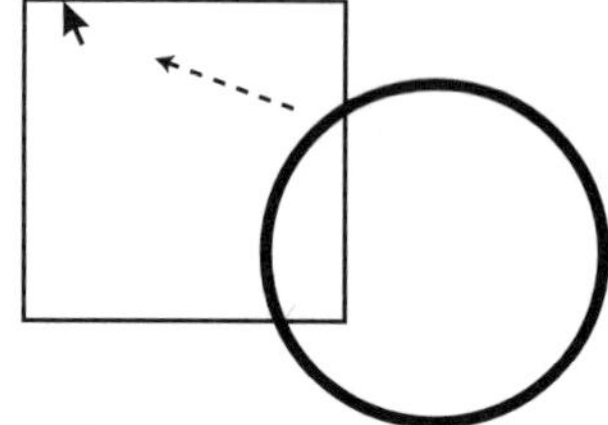

Use the Two Movement Methods

1. Continue working in the open document **FreeHand Pointer Tool.FH9**.
2. Click on the black square with the Pointer tool but do not move it. Hold the mouse button down for a few seconds and you will see the cursor turn into the cross with arrowheads.
3. Continue holding the mouse button and move the square around on the page. Drag the square over the other two objects on the page to see how the dragged image alters when it touches other objects. End this move with the square under the line and the circle. Release the mouse button.

4. Click on the square again and drag it toward the circle. Notice how the original image remains as you move the object. Also notice the visual effects seen on-screen as the various objects touch and overlap.

5. Release the mouse and select Edit>Undo.
6. With the Pointer tool, perform a quick select-move on the line object; the bounding box appears as the moved object. Release the mouse to see how the line was moved. Select Edit>Undo.

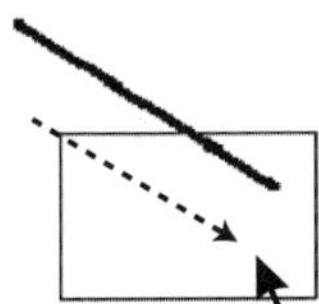

7. Quickly select-move the circle so that you see only its bounding box. Move this around on the page and over other objects to see how their appearance does not change.

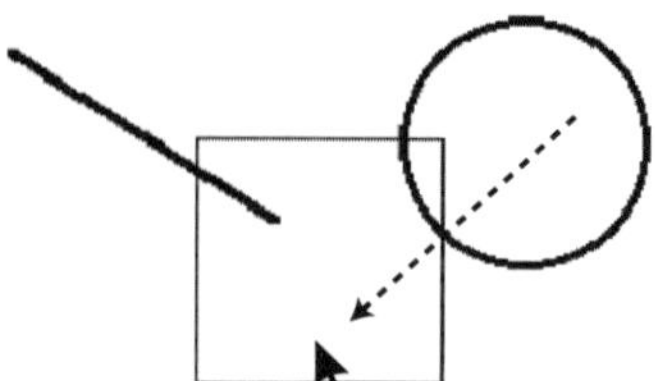

8. Release the mouse.
9. You have now experienced and observed the two methods of using the Pointer tool to move objects.
10. Close the document without saving.

The Drawing Tools

There are three drawing tools in the Toolbox — the Freehand tool, Pen tool, and Bezigon tool — that allow you to draw lines and shapes, each a little differently.

The Freehand Tool

Using the Freehand tool is very much like drawing with a pencil. It is totally unrestricted, but you may add some controls such as straight and constrained line segments. To draw a straight line segment, press and hold the Option/Alt key. To constrain the straight line to 45° angles, press Shift-Option/Alt.

As is the case with other drawing tools, the Freehand tool can be customized by double-clicking on the tool in the Toolbox. In the Tool Operation section, when the Freehand option is selected, the line drawn is of uniform weight. The Precision option defines how many control points will be placed on the path, based on settings from 1 to 10. A setting of 1 places fewer control points, while a setting of 10 places many points on the path. The Draw dotted line option shows the line you are drawing as a dotted line; when the mouse button is released, the line appears as a solid line. If a closed shape (one that may be filled) is drawn, a small solid box will appear when the cursor is in the correct position to close the shape.

When Variable stroke is selected in Tool Operation, a number of other controls are made available. The "line" created when Variable stroke is selected is actually a closed path consisting of an inner and outer line, plus a fill; that's how the variation in the width of the line is accomplished. As a result, it is possible to draw a line that is one color on the edges and a different color in between. When this is done, a crisscross pattern will occur where lines overlap. When Auto remove overlap (slow) is checked, this crossover path is deleted, creating a composite path. In the Width section, Minimum and Maximum slidebars control the width of the line when you are using a pressure-sensitive tablet. When more pressure is exerted on the pen, a wider path results. You can use the arrow keys on your keyboard to accomplish this also: the right key makes the line wider, the left key makes the line narrower.

The Tool Operation Calligraphic pen controls is similar to the Variable stroke, except that you may create a fixed width in addition to the minimum/maximum line width. An Angle selection controls the angle of the Freehand tool to create the effect of drawing with a calligraphic pen.

Use the Freehand Tool

1. Select File>New to create a new document.
2. Double-click on the Freehand tool to access the Freehand Tool dialog box. Set the Tool Operation to Freehand and the Precision to 5.

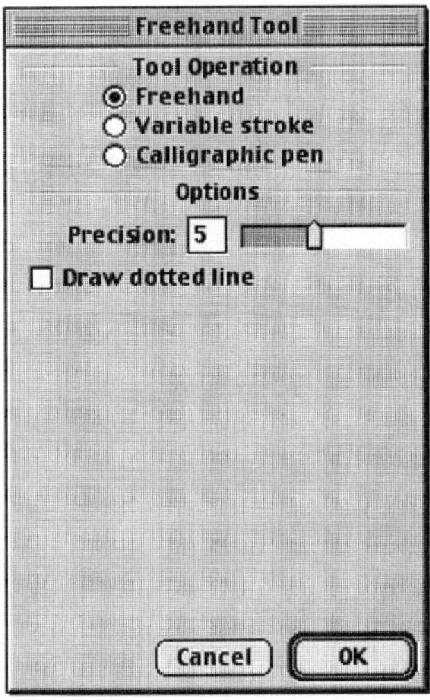

3. Click on the page and practice drawing several shapes.

4. Double-click on the Freehand tool to access the dialog box again. Set the Tool Operation to Variable stroke, leave the Precision at 5, and set the Width Minimum at 11 and the Maximum at 39.

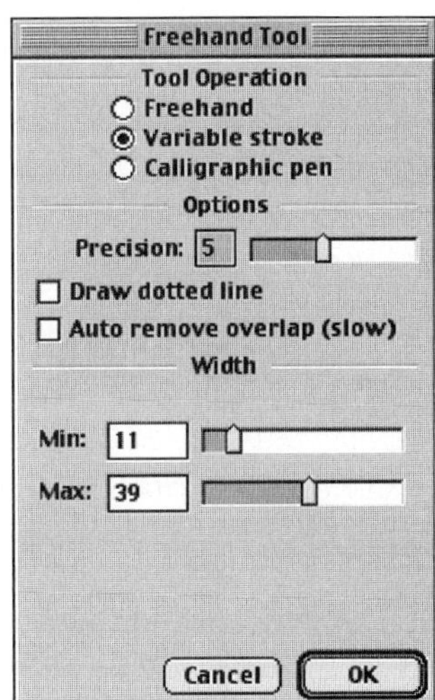

5. Experiment with drawing a number of lines, then try to imitate the one below. Be sure to press the Left Arrow key to reset to 11 each time you draw another variable line.

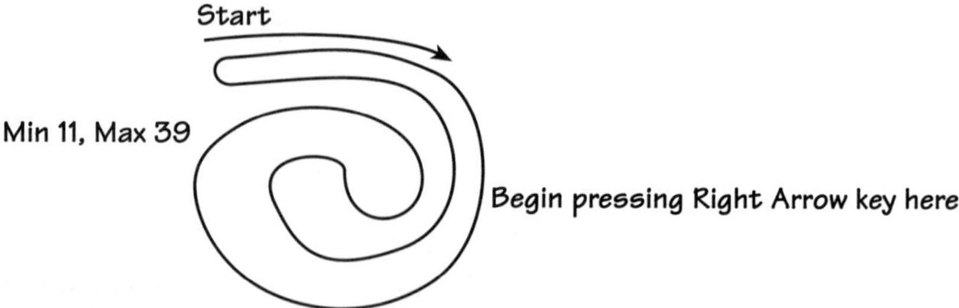

6. Double-click on the Freehand tool to access the dialog box again. Set the Tool Operation to Calligraphic pen, with the Precision set at 5. Set the Width to Fixed, with a value of 16. Leave the Angle at its default of 45°.

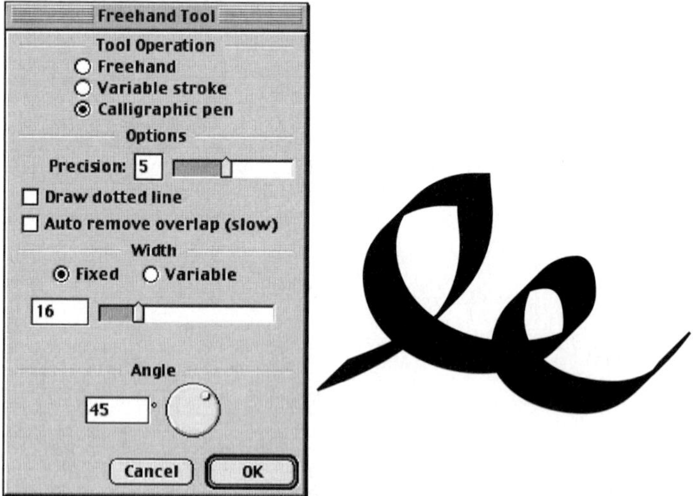

7. From the Colors panel (Windows>Panels>Color List), set both the Fill and Stroke to Black.

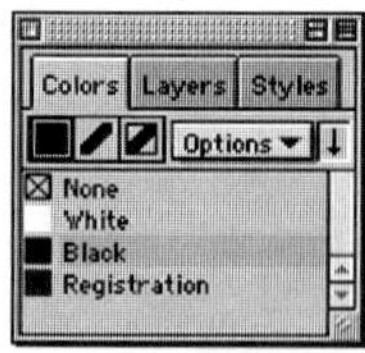

8. Play with the Calligraphic pen until you have the feel of it, then write your name. (Hint: some letters, like "o" are best created with two strokes.)

9. Close the document without saving.

The Pen Tool

The Pen tool is the most versatile of FreeHand's drawing tools, and it takes the most practice to learn to use well. A simple way to think of drawing with the Pen tool is as a game of connect-the-dots. First, you click to create your first anchor point (first dot). You then select where you want your next point to be and click again. When the second point is made, FreeHand connects the points with a line segment, or path. When a point is clicked and dragged with the Pen tool, it creates a curve. A path can be lines, curves, or a combination of both.

If the Shift key is held down when clicking to the next point, the movement is constrained to 45° increments. A series of points may create a zigzag effect. This is called an open path, and cannot be filled with a color. When a closed path is created, the small box appears next to the cursor, as with the Freehand tool. You will work with curves in a later section.

The Bezigon Tool

The next drawing tool in the Toolbox (after the Pen tool) is the Bezigon tool. The technique is to click with the Bezigon tool the same way you clicked the Pen tool. It can create both open and closed paths but will not draw curves like the Pen tool.

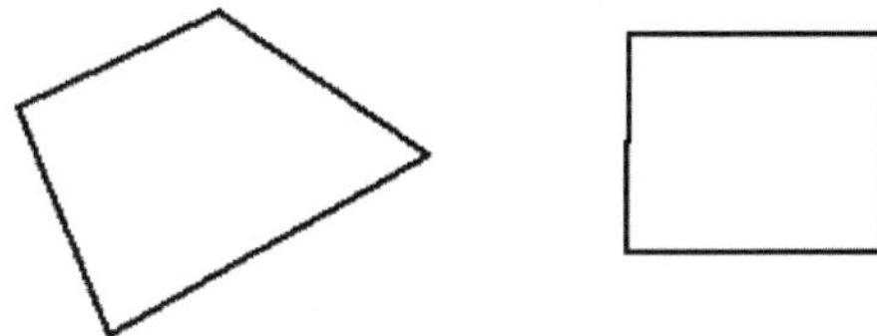

If you hold the Shift key while clicking, it will constrain the lines to 45° increments. Experiment with the Bezigon tool, creating a variety of shapes.

Use the Pen and Bezigon Tools

1. From File>New, create a new document.
2. Select the Pen tool from the Toolbox.
3. Create a zigzag shape, by simply clicking the mouse to create a series of straight paths.
4. Hold down the Shift key and note how the zigzag shape is constrained.
5. Rather than simply clicking, click and drag one of the anchor points. Note how it affects the shape of the curve.

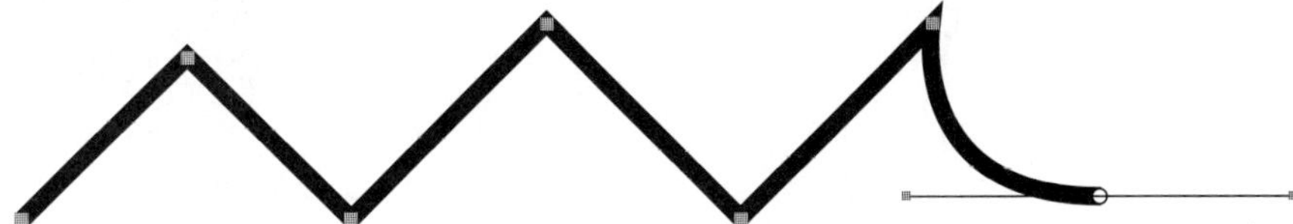

6. Deselect the path by clicking in an empty area of the page. Now click three points to create the first two sides of a triangle.
7. Position the cursor over the beginning point to finish the triangle. When the square appears next to the cursor, click to close the path.
8. Select the Bezigon tool.
9. Experiment with creating a zigzag shape, and add some constrained points.

10. Click the Bezigon tool and drag it. What happens? Instead of creating a curve as the Pen tool does, you are simply moving the point.
11. Deselect the path by pressing the Tab key. Click four points to form the first three sides of a 4-sided polygon. Note that when you close the shape, the same box appears next to the cursor.
12. Close the document without saving.

Summary

In this chapter you began to use FreeHand's drawing tools. You experimented with the basic shapes tools: the Line, Spiral, Rectangle, Ellipse, and Polygon tools, and used the breadth of their capabilities. You also explored the varieties of settings available with these tools. You then used the drawing tools: the Freehand, Pen, and Bezigon tools. You experimented with a variety of settings and used the tools to create a variety of effects. You are now prepared to create objects to which you can apply color.

Complete Project A: Dinner Time

CHAPTER 5

Painting FreeHand Objects

CHAPTER OBJECTIVE:

To learn many of the available techniques and methods for adding color and patterns to objects. In Chapter 5, you will:

- Learn how to paint the objects that you have created in FreeHand, applying colors to enhance your design.
- Learn how to create new colors, and select colors from predefined libraries.
- Learn how to use and understand the Color Mixer and Tint Mixer.
- Understand what gradients are, and how to create and apply them.
- Understand the many important functions of the Fill Inspector; become comfortable with Basic, Custom, Gradient, Pattern, PostScript, Textured, and Tiled effects on objects.
- Learn how to create patterned fills and how to modify them through the Fill Inspector.
- Become comfortable with the Color List; how to use it, and how to access the Color List if you don't want to use Inspectors.
- Become comfortable with the aspects of the Stroke Inspector.
- Learn about Endcaps and Joins and how they are used to structure the flow of an object

PROJECTS TO BE COMPLETED:

- Dinner Time (A)
- Mask Art (B)
- Tropical Treasure Logo (C)
- Grocery Ad (D)
- Ball and Mirror (E)
- No Clowning Around (F)

Painting FreeHand Objects

While drawing shapes using the variety of FreeHand tools is an interesting pastime, we could reasonably argue that a simple line drawing is, well, colorless. FreeHand allows us to add color to objects in a variety of ways.

In addition to simply coloring objects, FreeHand gives us the opportunity to add textures, gradients, pattern tiles, lens effects, and more. The creative application of strokes and fills can mean the difference between a good illustration and a dynamic one.

Color may be applied to either the object's fill or its stroke. The fill is the area inside a closed path; it may be colored with a color, tint, gradient, pattern, texture, or tile. Fills are controlled by the Fill Inspector. The stroke is the attribute applied to the line of a path. This can be a color, tint, or pattern. Strokes are controlled by the Stroke Inspector.

Objects can have a fill, stroke, or both applied. The star below was painted three different ways.

Stroke only
3 pt. Black

Fill only
40% Black

Stroke 3 pt. Black
Fill 40% Black

Understanding Color

Although we can communicate effectively in black and white, color adds dimension to our documents. However, color appears different on the printed page than it does on a monitor — in fact, it may look different from monitor-to-monitor. When colors are chosen for print, they should be selected from printed samples; when they are chosen for use on the web or in multimedia, they may be properly selected from screen representations of the colors.

Remember, only closed paths can be filled in FreeHand.

The Color Models

FreeHand mixes color using four color models: CMYK, RGB, HLS, and the system Color Picker for either Macintosh or Windows. CMYK, the subtractive primaries (additive secondaries), combines the pigments cyan, magenta, yellow, and black; when all pigments are removed, the result of which is white. RGB, the additive primaries, combines the colors of light: red, green, and blue; when all colors are added, the result is white. HLS defines color by it hue, luminance, and saturation. The Macintosh and Windows Color Pickers allow you to select colors based on those system standards.

CMYK 

The CMYK color model is based on the absorption and reflection of light, as opposed to the transmission of light used in the RGB model. A portion of the color spectrum is absorbed when white light strikes ink-coated paper. The color that is not absorbed is reflected.

Theoretically, a mixture of equal parts of cyan, magenta, and yellow would produce black. Pigments, however, as opposed to light, are not pure, so the result of mixing these colors is muddy brown. To obtain vibrant colors, we add black to the palette. CMYK is also called process color.

Process color is used to print documents that contain multiple distinct colors, or that contain color photos. A pattern of dots in varying sizes (called a rosette) fools the eye into thinking that, although it is actually seeing cyan, yellow, magenta, and black dots, it is seeing distinct colors. The resolution of these dots, when used in the printing process, is described in lines per inch (lpi).

RGB 

The RGB color model is capable of displaying many more colors than the CMYK model. Red, green, and blue light, when added in equal quantity, result in white. Where they overlap, they create a version of the additive secondary colors: cyan, magenta, and yellow. RGB colors are the colors of light used in monitors and scanners.

The RGB model should be used when documents will be distributed electronically and viewed on monitors, such as CD distribution, or publication on the internet.

Indexed color is a subset of RGB and is used to create GIF files. Indexed color is used in drawn images with areas of flat color. The greatest number of colors that may be contained in an indexed color image is 256. When creating indexed color images, you should always use the Web Safe Color Library, found in FreeHand's Color List panel.

HLS 

The HLS color model uses the properties of hue, saturation, and luminance to describe color. Hue is the property we refer to when we call a color by its name: red, purple, or teal, for example. Hue is defined as beginning from red (0°) and travelling counterclockwise around the color wheel. Luminance, or value, is the amount of white or black added to the pure color. A luminance of 50 means there is no addition of white or black. Luminance of 100 is pure white, and luminance of 0 is pure black. Saturation is the clarity of the color. Color is dulled by the introduction of elements of the color opposite it in the color wheel. When the center of the wheel is reached, the color becomes a neutral gray.

Like RGB, this is a good color model to use when documents will be distributed electronically and viewed on monitors.

System Colors 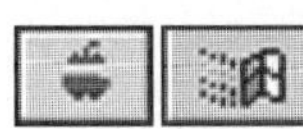

The Apple and Windows Color Pickers allow you to choose from a library or libraries that are specific to their operating system. Like RGB and HLS, these colors are based on light and may not print as you would expect.

Although you can apply colors directly to an object from the Color Mixer, it is better to apply colors from the Color List to maintain consistency throughout the document. In addition, colors from the Color List may be imported to other documents.

The Color Mixer

The Color Mixer is used to create or modify colors, using the color models we have discussed: CMYK, RGB, HLS, and the System Color Picker. The colors created can then be added to the Color List or can be applied directly to an object. Select Window>Panels to access the Color Mixer. Here are the features of the Color Mixer, with the CMYK Color Mixer's options visible :

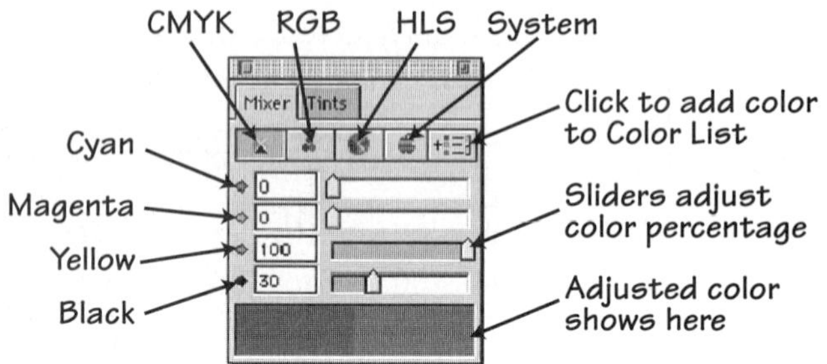

Building Colors

Different processes are employed when building colors in the four Color Mixers. Mixing higher percentages of color in the CMYK mode produces darker colors. Mixing higher amounts (in levels of 0–255, rather than percentages) of RGB color produces lighter tones. In the HLS mode, an angle is first chosen, then a luminance, or brightness percentage, then a saturation, with the brightest color having a saturation of 100% and a neutral gray resulting with a saturation of 0%. In any of the panels, the numbers may be typed in, if the value is known, or the interactive display may be used.

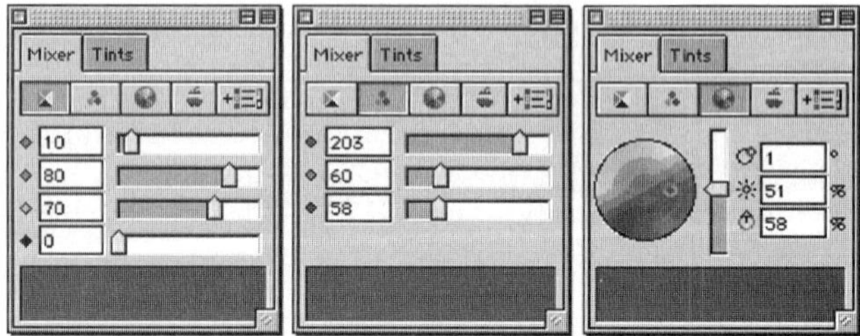

In the example above, an identical color, brick red, is displayed on (left to right) CMYK, RGB, and HLS Color Mixers. Note the difference in how the color was achieved.

Create Colors by Mixing

1. From File>New, create a new document.
2. Select Windows>Panels>Color Mixer and Windows>Panels>Color List.
3. We're going to create two new colors in our document: a medium teal and a soft peach. Be sure that the CMYK mode is selected in the Color Mixer and, either using the sliders or simply typing percentages into the dialog boxes, enter:

   C: 60, M: 20, Y: 20, K: 0

   Depending on how your monitor is set, the color you created may or may not look like teal to you. We defined it from a printed color swatch.

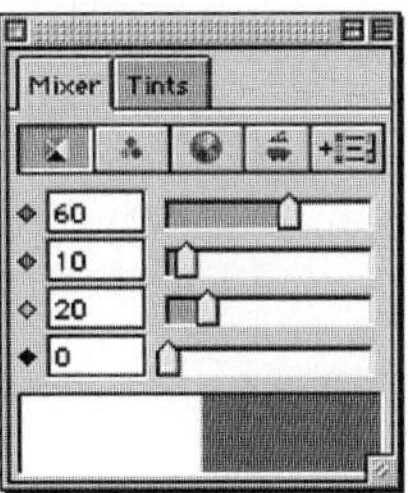

The notation "60c 20m 20y 0k" refers to the percentage of each process color used in the new color. 0c 0m 0y 100k is 100% black; 0c 100m 100y 0k is a bright red; 25c 0m 95y 5k is a yellowish-green color. Experiment with the Color Mixer to see what new colors you can create with different percentages of process colors.

4. Click the Add to Color List button. A dialog box will appear giving you the option of Process or Spot color. Leave the color definition as Process and click Add.

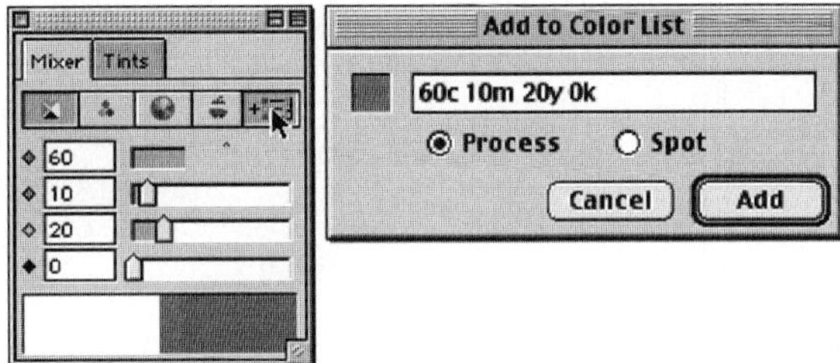

5. With the new color in the list, click on the name of the color to select it, then triple-click and type " - Teal" following the CMYK description, to give it an easier-to-remember reference.

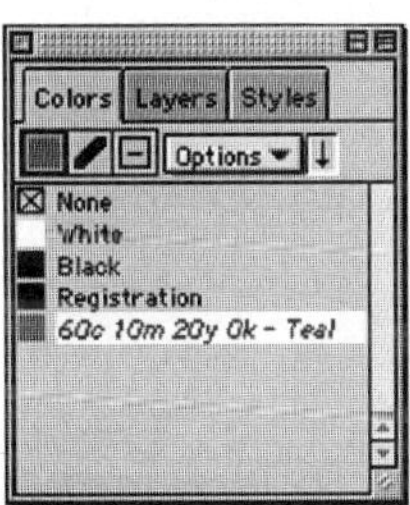

6. Now we'll create the peach. Set the colors as:

   C: 0, M: 10, Y: 10, K: 0

   Click on the Add to Color List button, and choose a Process color. Add the easy-to-remember description " - Peach" after the CMYK description.

7. Save the file to your **Work in Progress** folder as "Working Color.FH9".

Tints

Tints are described in percentages of an original color: either one that has been created in the Color Mixer or one that has been selected from one of the color libraries. They are defined through the Tint panel and applied directly to the object or added to the Color List.

There are three ways to create tints:

- Click on the percentage boxes listed in the panel.
- Enter numeric percentages in the field to the left of the slider.
- Drag the slider to achieve the desired tint.

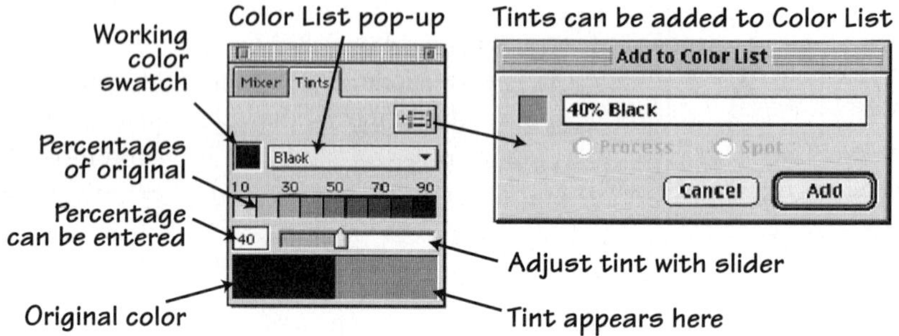

When working with colors that will be used for printed documents, it is best to work with an actual swatch book that shows the tint, rather than using the monitor as a guide. Tints are best applied to spot colors, not process colors. In order to achieve an accurate representation of light process colors, it is best to use a good reference and build the color by its CMYK values, rather than attempting to render it as a tint.

We will work with tints after we have selected some spot colors.

The Color List

The Color List is the panel in which you keep all the colors used in your FreeHand document. It is accessed through Windows>Panels>Color List. Use the Color List to drag a color onto an object's stroke or into its fill. Alternately, the object may be selected, the Stroke, Fill, or Both icon selected, and the color clicked on to apply it.

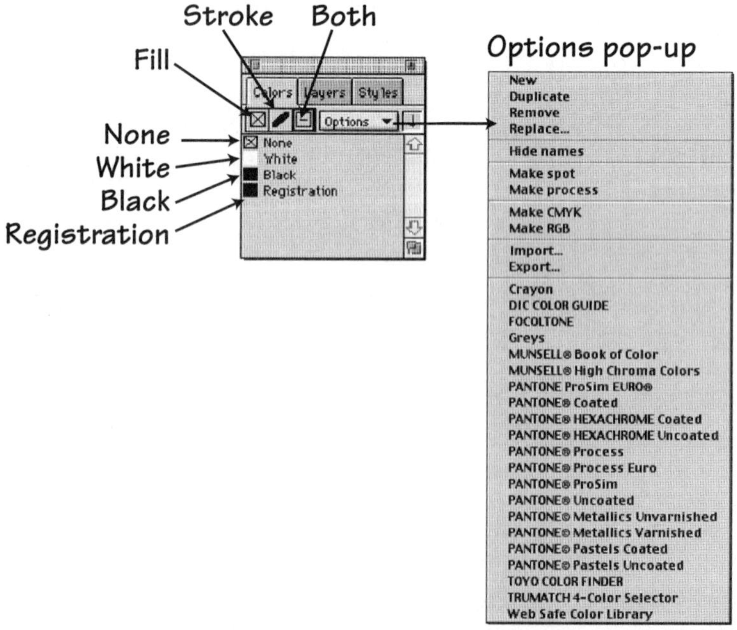

For predictable results in documents which will be printed, use spot colors only if you have a printed sample of the color, and if your printer uses that ink system. If your document will be used in multimedia or on the Web, other colors may be used, but you're best off using the Web Safe library.

By default, libraries are stored in your FreeHand 9>English>Colors folder.

The Color List contains all the colors you created in the Color Mixer and stored there. You may also select colors from standard libraries, accessed through the Options pop-up menu. When selecting a library for a print-related project, you should have a copy of the printed reference to the colors being used. You should also check with your printer to be sure they use the same inks that you specify. In the United States, Pantone inks have become the de facto standard.

Focoltone, Munsell, Toyo, Trumatch, Pantone Process, and the Greys libraries are all process colors. Pantone Hexachrome is a six-color system of printing to achieve a wider gamut of colors. The on-screen representation of some of these libraries may be defined as RGB. If the RGB symbol appears, the color must be converted to CMYK prior to printing. DIC (Dainippon Ink and Chemicals, Inc.) and most Pantone libraries are spot colors. The Crayon library is RGB, but may be converted to process. The Web Safe Color Library comprises the 216 colors that will display properly on both Macintosh and Windows computers.

How To Use The Color List

When applying colors using the Color List, you only have to be concerned with the Fill, Stroke, and Both buttons. Any object you select, including text highlighted with the Text cursor, will take on any color attributes when you drag the desired color swatch up to touch the appropriate button.

However, as you have noted, the Options menu gives you a number of other options. You can create a new color, based on the active color in the Color Mixer. You may duplicate, remove, or replace colors. You can hide the color names, working with swatches only. You also have the ability to make a process color spot, a spot color process and switch colors between RGB and CMYK.

Additionally, you can import and export libraries. To import a library, you would click Import, then locate the library file. To export a library, select Export, choose the colors you wish to include, then fill in the information requested in the dialog box. Click OK to export the library.

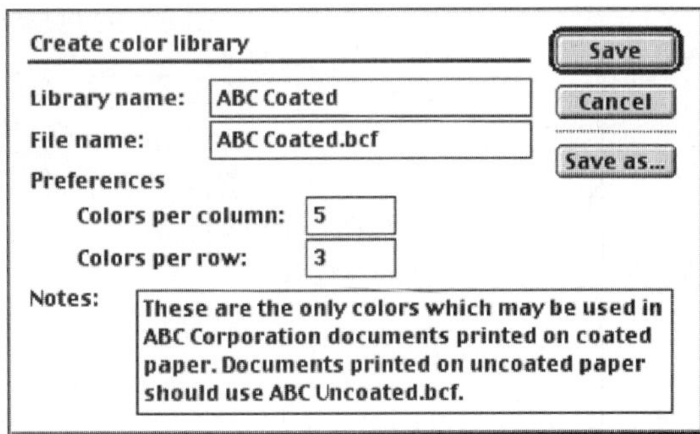

Some corporations have very specific rules as to how their corporate colors are to be used, even designating separate colors for coated and uncoated papers.

Select Colors from the Color List

1. With the document **Working Color.FH9** open, click on the Options pop-up menu in the Color List and select the Pantone Coated library.

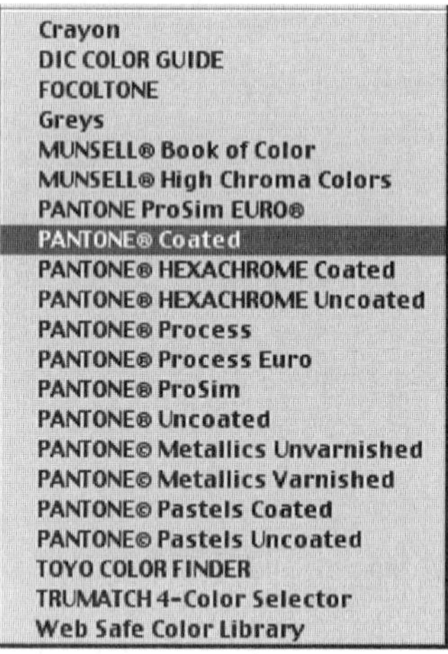

Process colors appear in the Color List in italics, while spot colors appear as Roman letters.

2. Using the scroll bar, scroll to Pantone 286 CVC. Click on it with the cursor, then double-click on it to add it to the library.

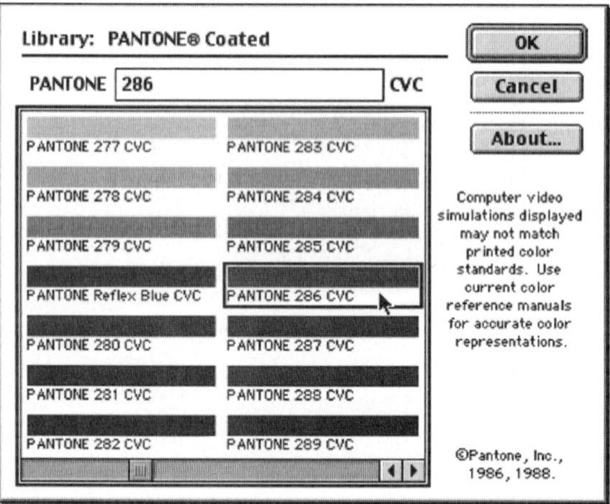

Pantone colors are usually referred to by the acronym PMS (Pantone Matching System), followed by their number or name. This is how we will usually refer to them in the future.

3. Go back to the Options menu and select the Pantone Coated library again. This time, we're going to select Purple. This color is located between Pantone 252 and 253, but rather than scroll to it, we're just going to type its name in the dialog box at the top of the screen. By the time you type "Pu" the library will have located the color for you.

4. Click OK to add the color to the list.

5. You have now added two spot colors to the Color List. Save the file and leave it open for the next exercise.

Create Tints

1. With the document **Working Color.FH9** still open, click on the Tints panel.
2. Drag the Pantone 286 CVC chip into the Tint panel's base color well.

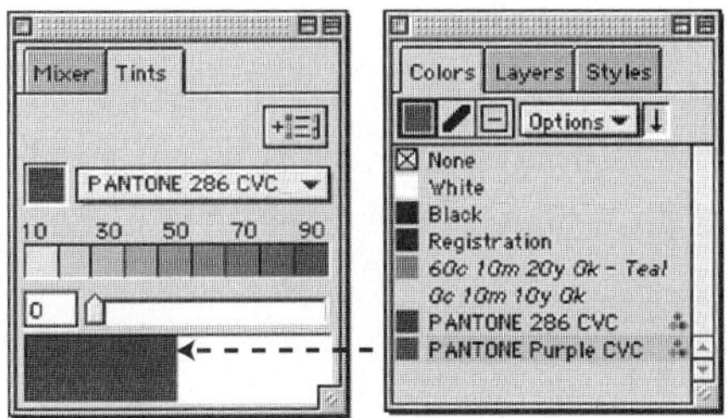

3. We'll make a 40% tint. Click the Tint Block between 30 and 50.

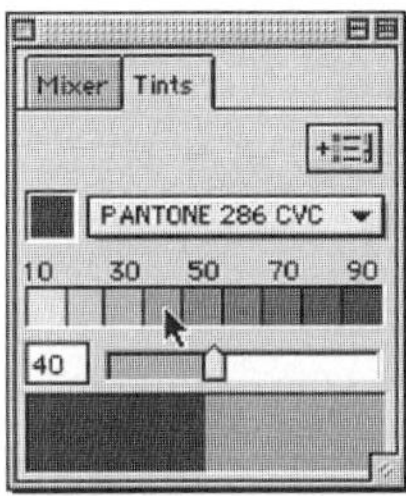

There are several ways to create tints in the Tints panel: The percentage buttons or, below them, the slider adjusts to a desired tint.

4. Add this tint by clicking the Add to Color List button and click Apply in the dialog box.
5. Let's add a tint of Purple. From the Tint panel's Color List pop-up menu, select Pantone Purple CVC.

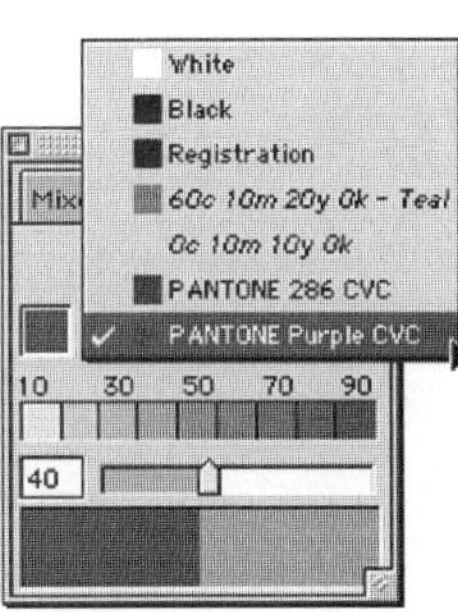

6. Type 35 in the entry field to assign a tint of 35%.

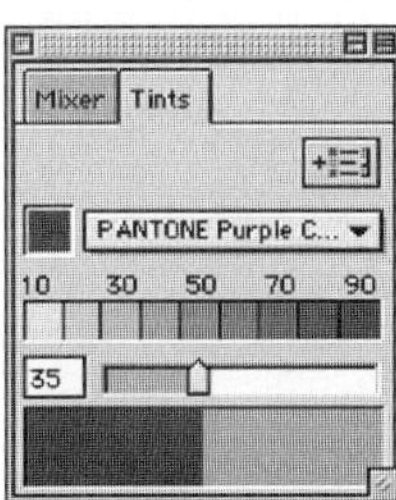

The numbered percentage boxes can be dragged to the lower-right sample box.

7. Click the Add to Color List button, then click Add to add this tint to the list.
8. Save the file and leave it open for the next exercise.

Export Colors from the Color List

1. With the document **Working Color.FH9** still open, select Export Colors from the Color List pop-up menu. The Export Colors dialog box will appear.
2. Click on all the colors in the list to select them and click OK.

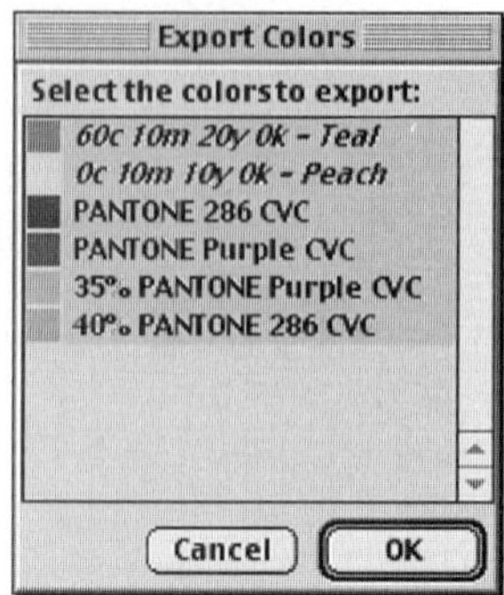

3. The Create Color Library dialog box will appear. Fill in the Library Name as [Your Name] Library, and the File Name as [Yourname.bcf]. Leave the Preferences as they are. Enter any notes you wish. Click Save As (Macintosh) or Browse (Windows) to save this library to your **Work in Progress** folder.

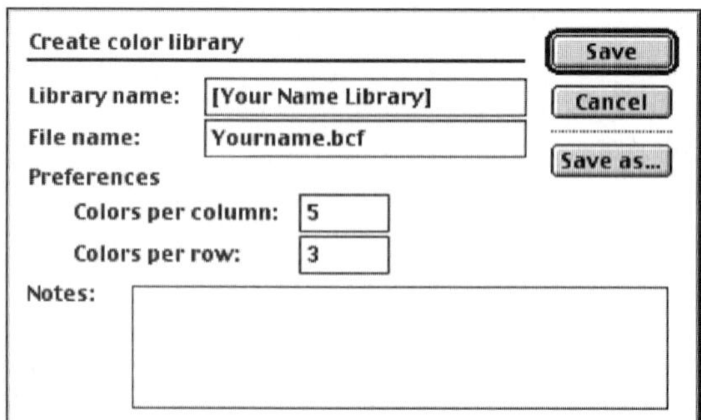

4. Let's see what the exported library looks like. From the Color List pop-up menu, select Import.
5. Navigate to your **Work in Progress** folder and select **[Yourname].bcf**. Click Open.

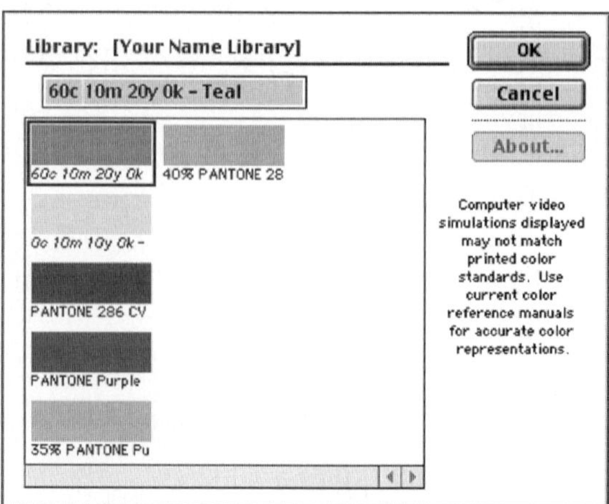

6. Note how the library looks, then click Cancel to close it.
7. Leave your document open for the next exercise.

Apply Colors from the Color List

1. With the document **Working Color.FH9** still open, select the Rectangle tool and create a rectangle approximately 3″× 2″ near the top of the page.
2. In the Color List, click on the Peach color and drag it inside the rectangle. Release the mouse button. The color fills the rectangle.
3. Now, let's apply Teal to the border. This is a little trickier. Drag the teal swatch on top of the border, and release. It may take you a couple of tries. By now you're probably thinking "there must be an easier way!"

Color Libraries contain predefined, industry-standard color swatches in the form of a Color System. In North America, the Pantone Matching System (PMS) is the most widely used color system; most of the others available in FreeHand are used in other parts of the world.

4. Draw an ellipse below the rectangle. Drag the 40% Pantone 286 CVC swatch to the Fill icon and release. The ellipse fills with the color.

5. Now drag the Pantone 286 CVC color swatch to the Stroke icon. This is much easier than attempting to drag the swatch over that narrow stroke, isn't it?
6. Let's assign both a stroke and fill simultaneously. Drag the Pantone Purple CVC swatch to the Both icon (the third box). Both stroke and fill become purple.

7. Deselect the ellipse. Save your document and leave it open for the next exercise.

Fills and Strokes

All closed objects created in FreeHand comprise fills and strokes. The stroke is the actual path you create with the drawing tool, and the fill is the area inside it. Sometimes the fill or the stroke are assigned "None" as a type, but they exist nonetheless.

If filling or stroking an object with only a basic color were the only decision that you would have to make when painting an object, life would be simple — and a bit dull. However, FreeHand's Fill and Stroke Inspectors provide a variety of effects in addition to standard fills of flat colors.

Fill Inspector

The Fill Inspector is accessed from Window>Inspectors. When the Inspector appears, it will default to None, meaning no fill (the object is transparent), unless a color is selected in the Color List. The pop-up menu at the top of the panel is used to apply the desired fill.

Fill Inspector

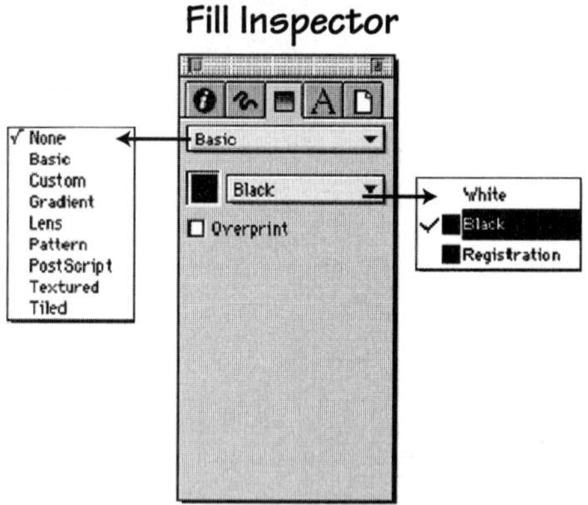

- Basic — A single color, either Process or Spot, is applied to the fill of the object. All colors accessible through the Fill Inspector must reside in the Color List.

- Custom — This PostScript fill can only be seen when the page is printed. It is a good idea to keep a reference to Custom fills, so they may be applied when appropriate.

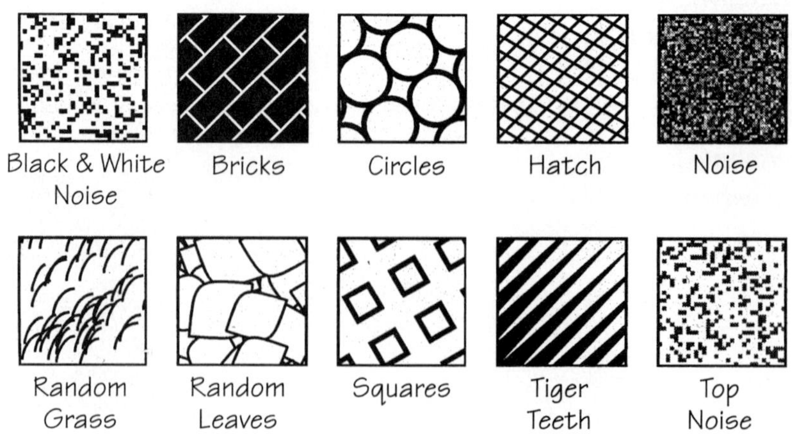

These are the ten Custom fills available through the Fill Inspector.

A linear taper creates the gradient in equal steps. A logarithmic taper creates small steps near the beginning of the gradient, becoming larger as they approach the other color.

There are three fills that you cannot see on-screen. Objects painted with these fills must be printed out before you can see what they look like. The three fills are: Custom, PostScript, and Textured.

- Gradient —This effect blends two or more colors to create a range of tones. Gradients can be linear or radial, determining the shape of the gradient, and they may have a linear or logarithmic taper. Either spot or process colors may be used to form the gradient.

- Lens — This assortment of six special effects perform visual enhancements such as transparency, magnification, inverting, and others. Lenses will be discussed in more detail in Chapter 8, Advanced Drawing Techniques.

Transparency

Magnify

Invert

Lighten

Darken

Monochrome

- Pattern — These bitmap patterns can be customized pixel by pixel. Patterns should not be used if the image is going to be printed at high resolution.

- PostScript — This effect requires knowledge of the PostScript language to apply the effect to the object. PostScript effects cannot be seen on-screen but appear when printed. These effects are actually written in PostScript code.

- Textured — A variety of textures can be applied to an object. It cannot be seen on screen, but the Inspector shows a sample of what the texture looks like. The textures are: Burlap, Coarse Gravel, Coquille, Denim, Fine Gravel, Heavy Mezzo, Light Mezzo, Medium Mezzo, and Sand.

- Tiled — Fill an object with multiple copies of another object, graphics, or text, that you create and paste into the Fill Inspector. Bitmap images, EPS, and other tiled fills may not be used to create a tiled fill.

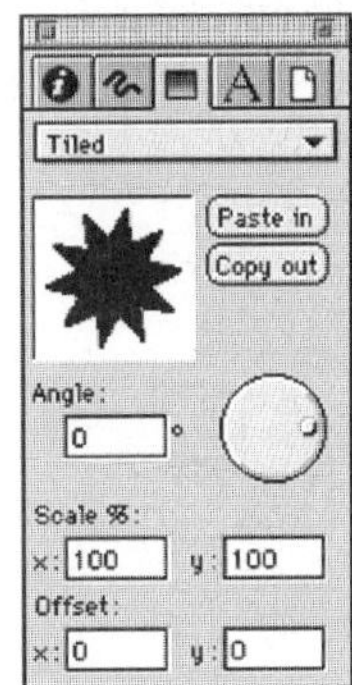

The following shows four of the Fill Inspectors in the pop-up menu:

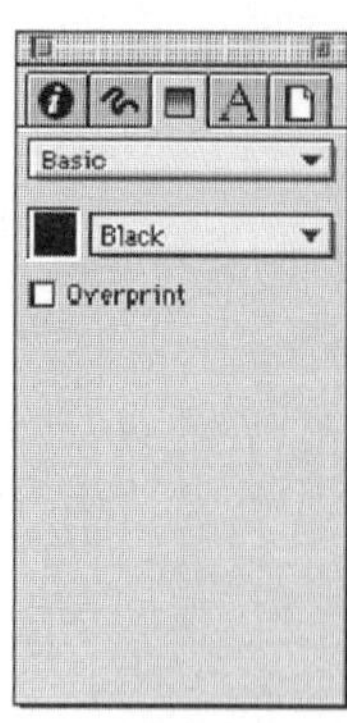

Basic

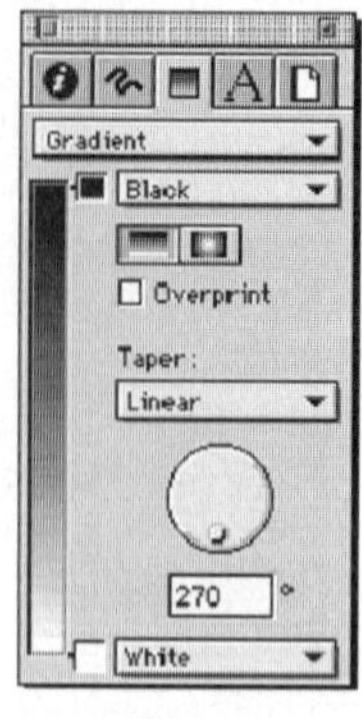

Gradient

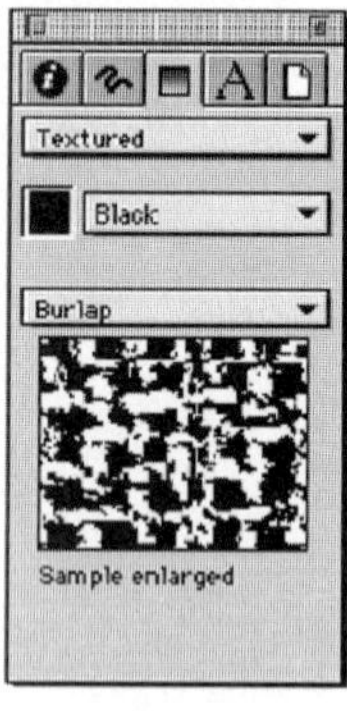

Texture

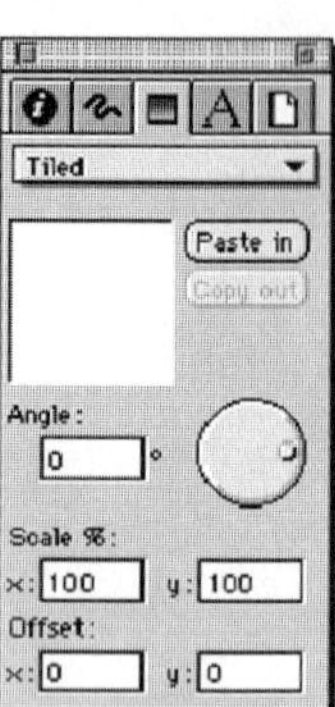

Tiled

Apply Color with the Fill Inspector

1. With the document **Working Color.FH9** open, create a new color. In the Color Mixer, with CMYK mode active, create a color of 100% Yellow and add it to the Color List as a Process color.
2. To get a feel for how the Fill Inspector applies color, create a new 2″× 2″ rectangle.
3. Access the Fill Inspector and select Basic from the pop-up menu. The square filled with yellow, because that color was still active in the Color List. This is not the color we want the rectangle to be.

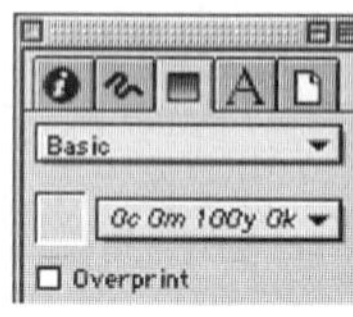

Clicking the Fill, Stroke, or Both buttons designates what part of the selected object will be painted.

4. From the Fill Inspector's Color List pop-up menu, select PMS Purple. The rectangle will take on the correct color.

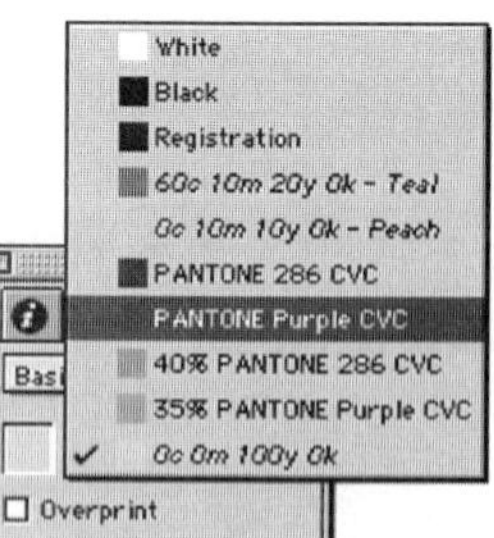

5. Back in the Color List, apply a color of None to the stroke.

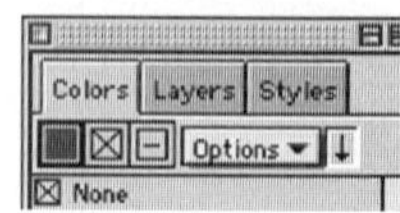

Selected objects can also be painted by clicking on the color name in the Color List.

6. Save the document and leave it open for the next exercise.

Creating Gradients

1. With the document **Working Color.FH9** open, draw a Rectangle, using the rectangle tool. Click the rectangle with the Pointer tool to select it.

2. Open the Fill Inspector.

3. Open the Color List. Use the Options menu to access the Crayon selection. Choose any two colors (holding the Command/Control key) from this assortment. Click OK.

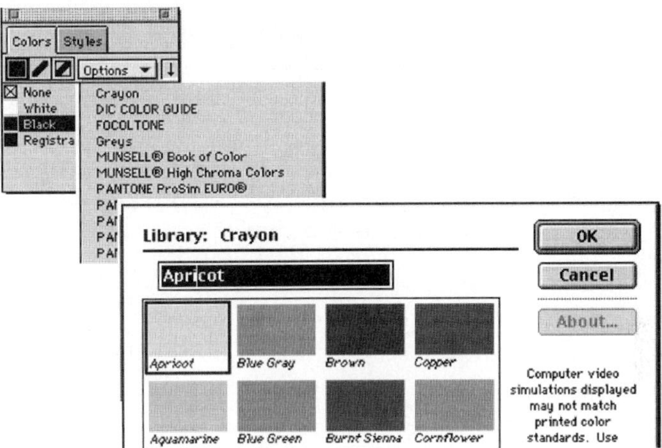

4. Click on the Gradient option in the pop-up menu. Be certain that the gradient is set to Linear.

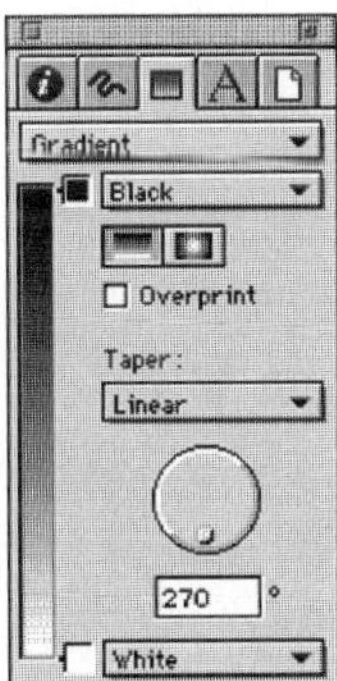

5. Drag one of the new colors from the Color List to the gradient's top drop box. Now drag the other color to the bottom drop box of the gradient. The rectangle now has a gradient comprising these two applied colors.

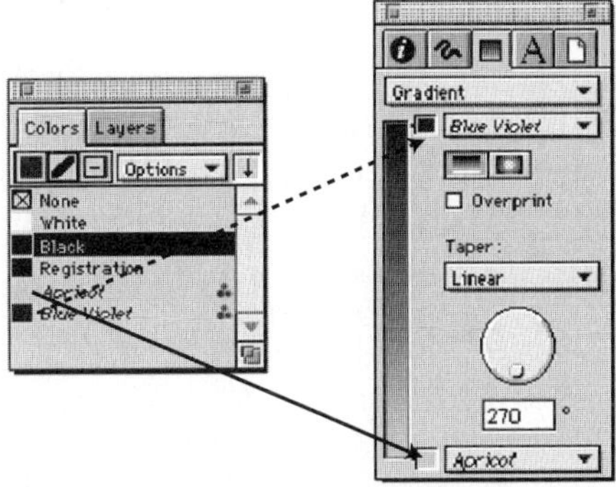

6. Select Edit>Undo. Repeat this operation with other colors and note the interaction between the colors.
7. Duplicate the rectangle and its gradient.
8. Set the gradient in the new rectangle with a Logarithmic taper and note the difference in effect.
9. Leave the document open for the next exercise.

Creating Radial Gradients

1. With the document **Working Color.FH9** still open, select the Ellipse tool, hold the Shift key, and draw a circle.
2. Fill the circle with a radial gradient fill, using two of the Crayon colors for the top and bottom drop boxes, and stroke of None.

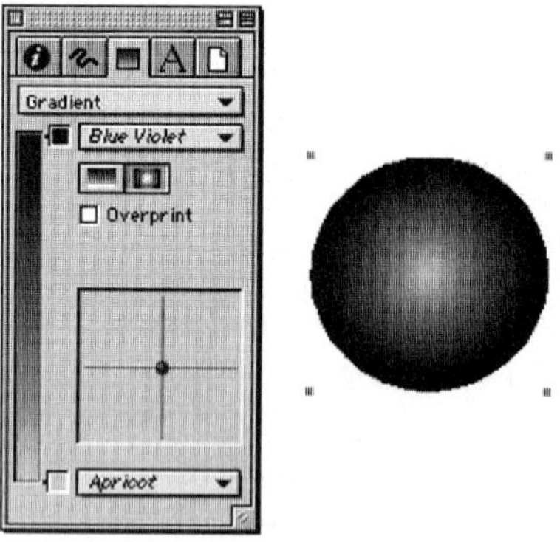

3. Click on the Point of Origin (the dot in the center of the crosshairs) in the Gradient Inspector, moving it down and to the left.

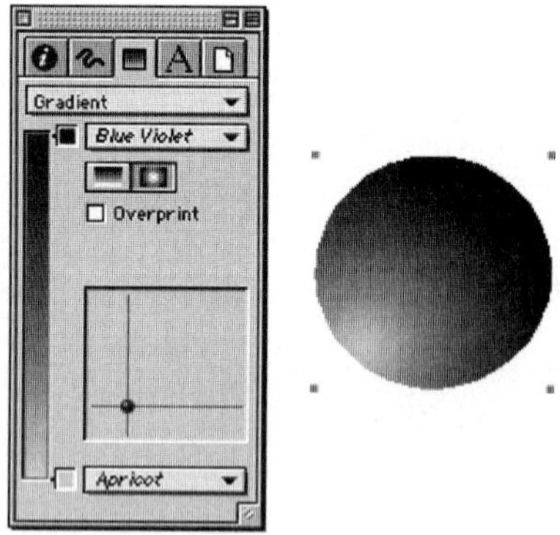

4. The center part of the radial gradient in the circle is moved to the same position. Practice moving the Origin Point in the Inspector and observe how this affects the radial gradient in the circle.
5. You can also add multiple colors to the gradient drop box by dragging colors into the drop box. To remove a color, just select it from the drop box and drag it off. Practice adding and deleting colors to the drop box.
6. Leave the file open for the next exercise.

Create a Multi-colored Gradient

1. With the document **Working Color.FH9** still open, create a new square.
2. Fill the square with a linear gradient fill, using Pantone 286 and Pantone Purple as the two fill colors.
3. From the Color List, click on the White swatch, drag it to the center of the gradient ramp, and drop it. What happens? You have created a 3-color gradient. Up to 99 colors may be added to a gradient.

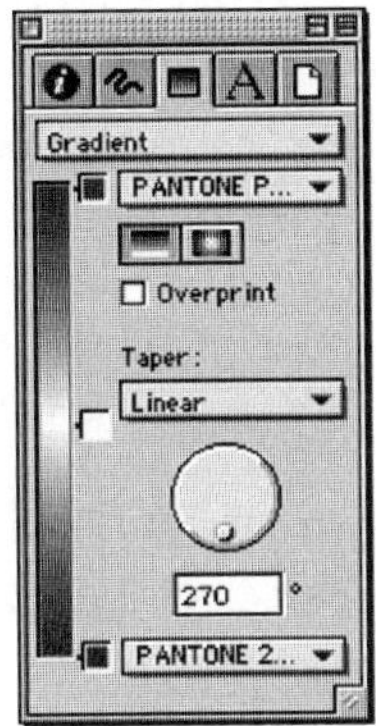

You should not mix spot and process colors in gradients. This would result in additional inks being added to the printing process.

4. Move the white swatch up and down the gradient ramp. Note how this affects the look of the gradient.
5. Drag the Purple swatch halfway down the gradient ramp toward the white swatch. What happens? The gradient between White and Purple is shortened, and the distance between the two Purple swatches is 100% Purple.

Never use colors from the crayon box in documents intended for print. Use only colors for which you have a printed sample for consistent, reliable results.

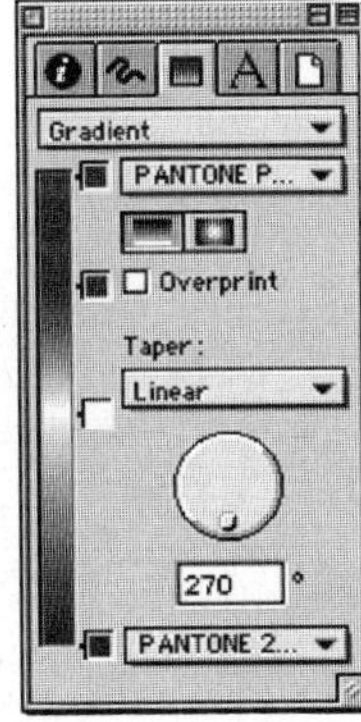

6. Save the file and leave it open for the next exercise.

Create Patterns in the Fill Inspector

1. Open the document **Working Color.FH9** from the **SF-FreeHand** folder, double-click on the Polygon tool and adjust the settings to produce a 5-pointed star.

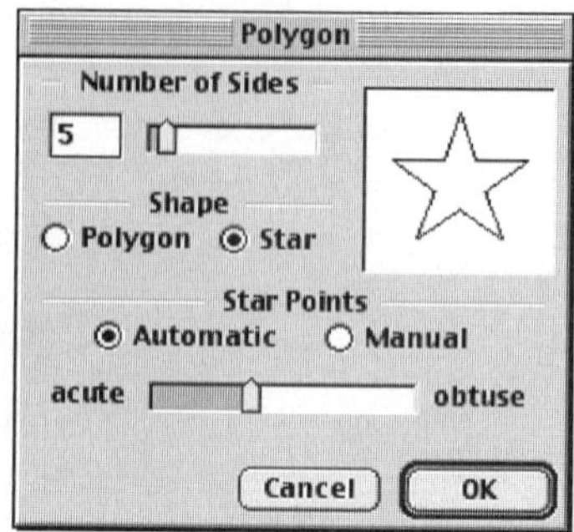

2. Holding down the Shift key to constrain it, drag a star approximately 1-in. wide. Assign it a fill of yellow and a stroke of None.
3. Select it with the Pointer tool and press Command/Control-C to copy it to the clipboard. Deselect the star.
4. Select the ellipse as the object to be filled with the Pointer tool. In the Fill Inspector, select Tiled as the fill type. Click Paste in. The ellipse is filled with the star as a repeating pattern.

With fills that include backgrounds, setting the x and y offsets to different numbers causes a clear band to appear between the tiles.

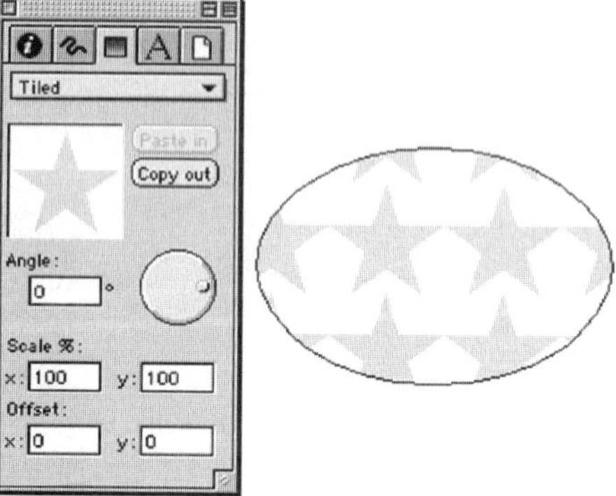

5. There's not a whole lot of excitement there. Let's set the angle to 30° and change the size of the stars to 50%, horizontally and vertically.

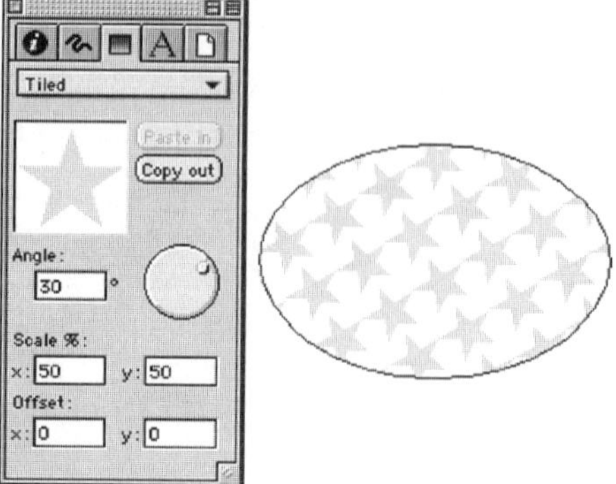

6. Let's see if we can make this fill even more interesting. Create three more stars at varying angles. Assign them a fill of yellow and a stroke of None.

7. Arrange all four stars in the purple square you created in the last exercise.

8. Using the Pointer tool, marquee the square with the stars and copy it to the clipboard.

9. Select the ellipse, then click Paste in the Fill Inspector. The ellipse is now filled with the purple background and the star pattern at the angle and percentage the fill was previously assigned.

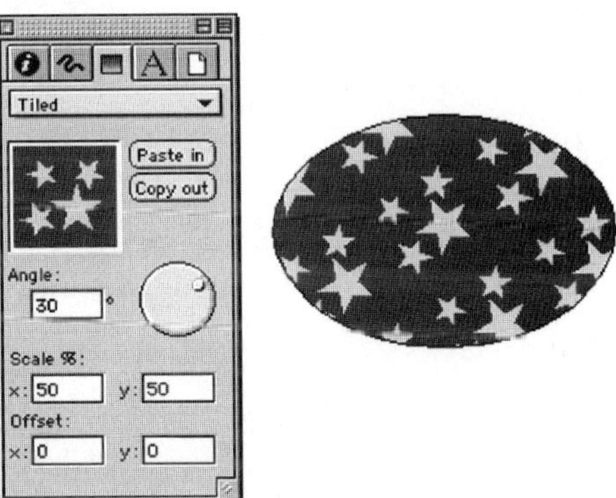

10. Change the offsets to x: 10 and y: 10 for a different look. What happens when you change the offsets to x: 10, y: 20?

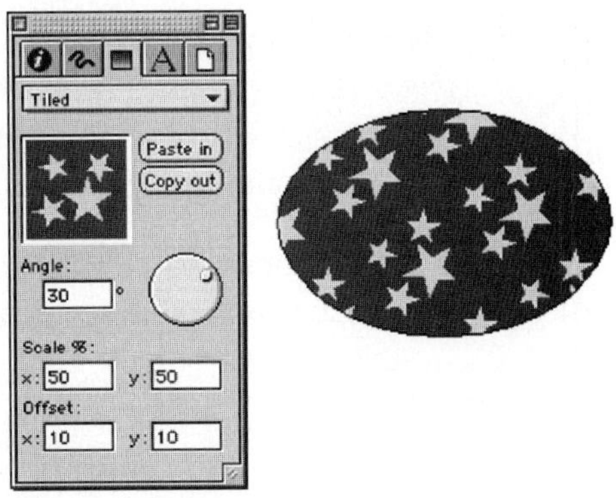

11. Save the document and leave it open for the next exercise.

Stroke Inspector

When you apply a color, pattern, custom, or PostScript visual effect to an object, it is applied to the defining path or segments that make the object. What determines the stroke, when painted, is the visual effect applied and the thickness or width of the stroke.

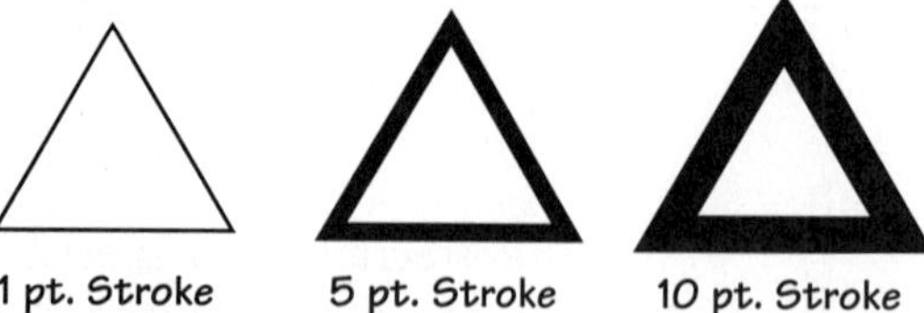

The Stroke Inspector offers a pop-up menu to select the type of stroke. Width affects the thickness of the line; End caps are the ends of an open path; and joins are the corners where paths meet at an anchor point. Dashed lines and arrowheads are other features that can be applied.

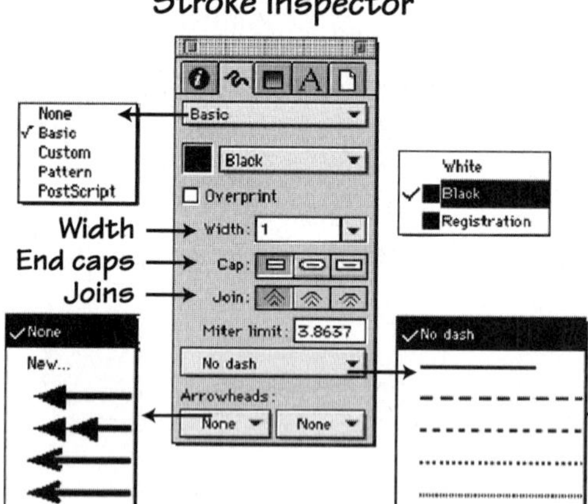

The Stroke Types

The Stroke pop-up menu offers five visual choices to apply to the path stroke as follows:

- Basic — applies simple color, either Process or Spot. Libraries of colors, such as Pantone, can be accessed through the Color List panel.
- Custom — is a PostScript fill that can only be seen when printed. These custom patterns are different from those available through the Fill Inspector; there is a preview for them.

- Pattern — accesses a variety of patterns that can be applied to the stroke. As with fill patterns, these should not be used when the document will be imaged to high resolution.

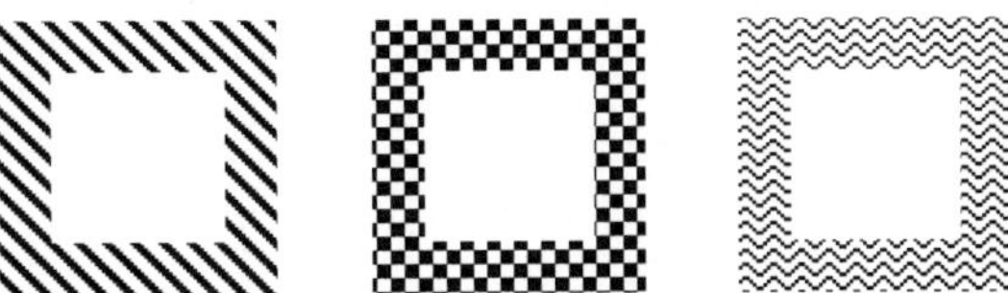

- PostScript — is a special effect that requires knowledge of the PostScript language to apply the effect to the object. It cannot be seen on-screen.

Stroke End Caps and Joins

End caps are defined by how they cap off the endpoint of open paths.

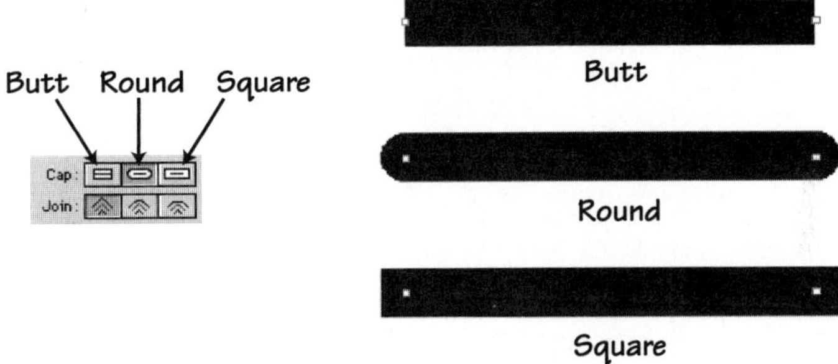

Joins affect the corner where two segments meet at an anchor point.

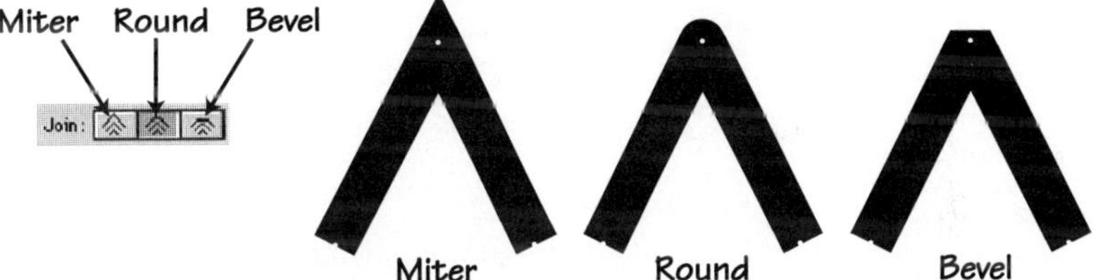

The miter limit determines when a mitered join will be altered to become a beveled join. As an angle becomes more acute, the miter becomes thicker, distorting the object. Miter limit calculates the allowable thickness of the miter, using the ratio of the thickness of the miter join to the thickness of the line. If the line is 4 pt. wide and the miter limit is 2, the join will become acute when the thickness of the apex of the line reaches 6 pt.

Stroke Extras: Dashes and Arrowheads

FreeHand offers a collection of 10 dashes and 7 arrowheads which may be added to a stroke's definition. You may also create custom arrowheads. For example, if you are working with floor plans, you may want an arrowhead that indicates a dimension, such as the following:

Work with Strokes

1. With the document **Working Color.FH9** open, draw a zigzag path with the Bezigon tool. By default, the path has butt end caps and mitered joins.
2. With the line selected, open the Stroke Inspector give the line a width of 12 pt., and apply rounded end caps. This often gives a thicker line a more finished look. Assign a Miter limit of 3.

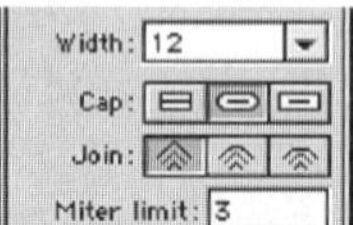

3. Zoom in to the highest percentage you can fit on your screen and still see an entire segment of the first zigzag.
4. Little by little, move the first endpoint nearer the second one, making the mitered join more acute. When the thickness at the apex of the miter join exceeds 15 pt. the join will change to acute.

5. Draw a smooth line with the Pen or Freehand tool and assign it a width of 2 pt. Apply each of the dash options to the line.

6. Choose an arrowhead and add it to the front of the line.

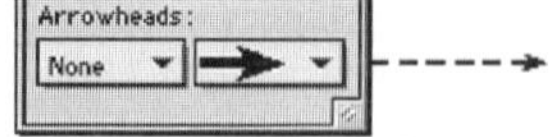

7. We'll make a new arrowhead for the back end of the line. From the Arrowheads pop-up menu, select New. The Arrowhead Editor appears.
8. From the Arrowhead Editor's toolbox, select the Pen tool. You'll want your line to abut the end on the line.

9. Place the first click near the top of the workscreen, hold down the Shift key to constrain to a straight line, and click near the bottom of the workscreen. You line should form a "T" with the existing line on the screen.

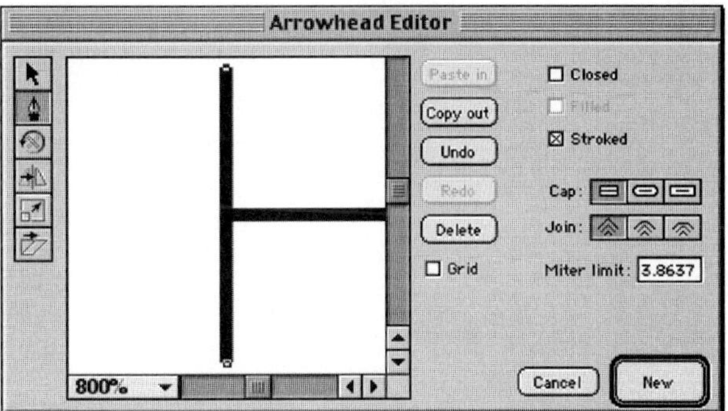

10. Click New and your arrowhead will be added to the list of arrowheads and to your line.

11. Save and close the document.

Summary

In this chapter you have learned to apply color and other elements to objects in a variety of ways. You have become familiar with the Color Mixer and the Color List, and you can create and apply color to objects using these panels. You have also learned to use the Fill Inspector and Stroke Inspector to add color, gradients, and patterns to fills and to modify the appearance of strokes. You are now prepared to create documents of greater complexity.

Notes

CHAPTER 6

Anchor Points, Paths, and Segments

CHAPTER OBJECTIVE:

To learn and master FreeHand's types of curves, anchor points, and paths, and the means by which they are modified. In Chapter 6, you will:

- Learn that a segment is the relationship between two points, and what the difference in these relationships means to you.
- Learn about the different kinds of anchor points.
- Understand how the curve, corner, and connector points are used to draw and alter curving segments.
- Learn how to select one or more anchor points in an object.
- Know how to join unconnected anchor points.
- Learn how to select, edit, and modify anchor points and their curves.
- Learn the easiest way to duplicate a path.
- Learn how to modify direction handles through the Object Inspector and become comfortable with path modification.
- Learn how to use the Freeform tool to alter anchors or entire paths — even possessing the ability to push and shove against a path to change it.
- Understand how to modify paths and segments by using the Knife tool; learn the difference between the Knife and Freeform tool.
- Learn how to draw curves.

PROJECTS TO BE COMPLETED:

- Dinner Time (A)
- Mask Art (B)
- Tropical Treasure Logo (C)
- Grocery Ad (D)
- Ball and Mirror (E)
- No Clowning Around (F)

Anchor Points, Paths, and Segments

It's necessary to know how to draw basic shapes and curves, but the real power of FreeHand's drawing tools is the ability to select and modify paths, segments of paths, and points. For example, to get an object "just right" it might be necessary to move one anchor point or adjust its curves. How do you select just one point?

The ability to single out and modify anchor points is the foundation to becoming a proficient designer in digital illustration.

Selecting a Single Anchor Point

Objects made with the Rectangle or Ellipse tools must first be ungrouped before individual anchor points can be selected. Objects made with the Polygon tool do not need ungrouping.

All objects contain points. Selecting a single anchor point is necessary when modifying an object by moving or deleting its points.

- You cannot click directly on the anchor point of an unselected path to select it. The path must first be selected by clicking on it with the Pointer tool, then any of its anchor points can be singled out by clicking on them. If you hold the Shift key, multiple anchor points can be selected.
- You do not have to select a path first if you draw a marquee around the anchor points you wish to select. However, you can't see the anchor point to select them unless the path is selected.
- Selected anchor points appear hollow.

The path must be selected before clicking individual anchor points

A marquee can select an anchor point without the path being selected

When anchor points have been selected, they appear hollow.

Adding Points to a Path

Adding anchor points is sometimes necessary depending upon the nature of your design. You can add more points to any path with the Pen tool.

- The path to receive the added points must first be selected with the Pointer tool; then the Pen tool or the Bezigon tool is clicked on the segment where you want to add the point. This will add an anchor point that can now be moved around or modified.

The path to receive the added points must first be selected.

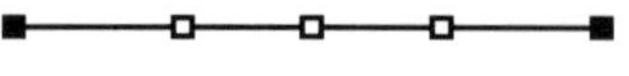

The Pen or Bezigon tool adds anchor points where clicked on the selected path.

Care should be taken when allowing FreeHand to arbitrarily add or delete points. Always review the results of automatic functions to ensure that alterations to your artwork are not unacceptable.

You can also add points to a path in the Xtras menu. You would select Xtras>Distort>Add Points to add an anchor point between each pair of existing points on your selected path.

Deleting Anchor Points

To delete a single anchor point of an object, select a single anchor point and press the Delete key to remove the point.

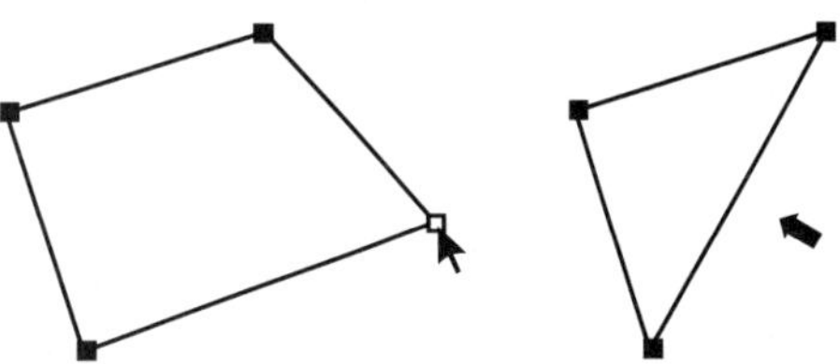

There is also a place to delete extraneous points on a path in the Xtras menu. Select the path that you want to delete points from and choose Xtras>Cleanup>Simplfy. A dialog box will pop up asking you for the amount of simplification you would like from 1 to 10, 10 simplifying the line the most. Choose an amount, click OK and the path is simplified.

Moving Segments of a Path

You cannot click directly on a segment to move it. Segments are controlled by their anchor points. To move a single segment, the anchor points on either end of the segment must be selected.

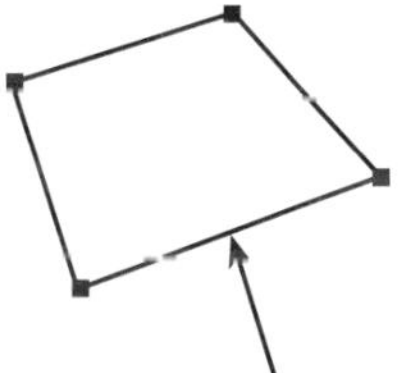

If this single segment were to require moving

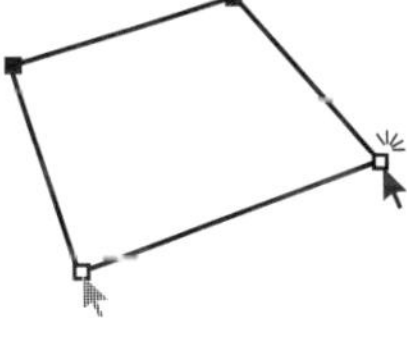

The two anchor points on either side of it must be individually selected

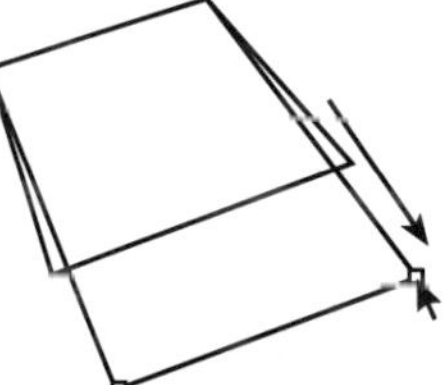

Then, by dragging on either anchor point, the segment will be isolated for moving

Because the Rectangle tool creates grouped objects by default, you only have to grab one of the corner points to adjust a segment's placement.

Connecting Anchor Points

Often, separate anchor points need to be connected to other points to complete a design or to close a path. This is not always as simple as it sounds because there are several ways to select and connect two points. It's important to get to know these techniques and when to use them.

- Use the Pointer tool to select the two anchor points of two separate paths, then choose Modify>Join to connect them. This can only be used for separate paths. It cannot be used to close a single path.
- Another way to close an open path is to click the check box next to the Closed option in the Object Inspector. This cannot be done with separate segments. It must be a single, open path.

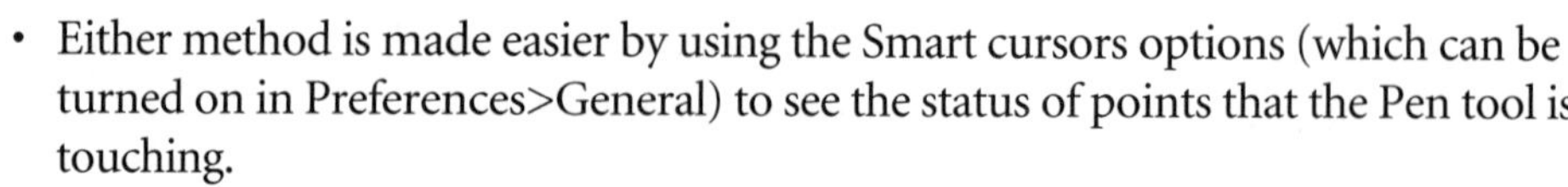

- Either method is made easier by using the Smart cursors options (which can be turned on in Preferences>General) to see the status of points that the Pen tool is touching.

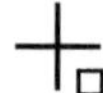

The hollow square means the Pen tool is going to create a new path

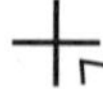

The angular "V" shape means that the Pen tool will continue the existing path

The black square means that the point the Pen tool is touching will close the path

Select, Edit, and Modify Anchor Points

1. Create a new document. With the Line tool draw an angled line approximately 2" long from top to bottom.

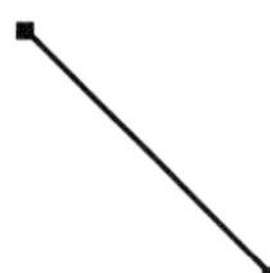

2. Select File>Preferences>General and verify that Smart cursors is clicked. Click on Object and select Option-drag copies paths (Macintosh) or Alt-drag copies paths (Windows). Press OK.

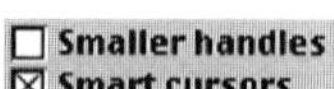

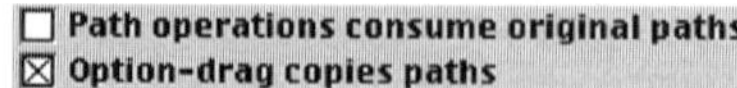

The easiest way to duplicate a path is to hold the Option/Alt key as you drag the object. Make certain that "Option/Alt-drag copies paths" is clicked in File>Preferences>Object.

☐ Path operations consume original paths
☒ Option-drag copies paths

3. With the Pointer tool, click on the segment of this single path. Hold the mouse button down until the cursor turns into a cross with arrowheads. Hold the Option/Alt key and the Shift key as you move the path. Drag the selected path 1 inch to the right. This will duplicate the path.

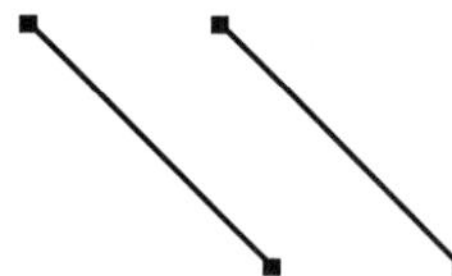

4. With the Pointer tool, marquee the two top anchor points of the paths to select them.

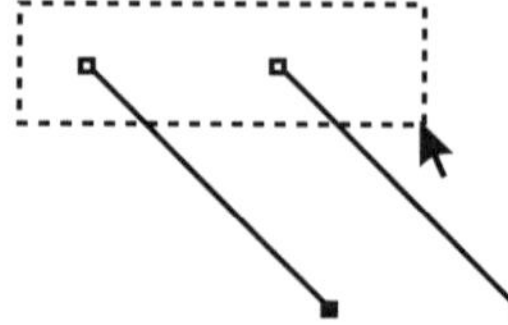

5. Select Modify>Join. The two selected points should be connected, yet the wrong points connected. The reason for this is path direction. When first drawn, the bottom points were the endpoints of the paths. You must reverse direction to put emphasis on the top points.

The keyboard shortcut for Undo is Command-Z (Macintosh) or Control-Z (Windows).

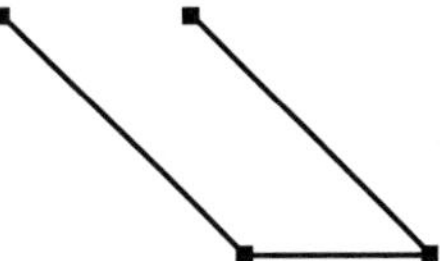

6. Select Edit>Undo.
7. Select both paths, then go to Modify>Alter Path>Reverse Direction. Again, marquee the top anchor points and go to Modify>Join.

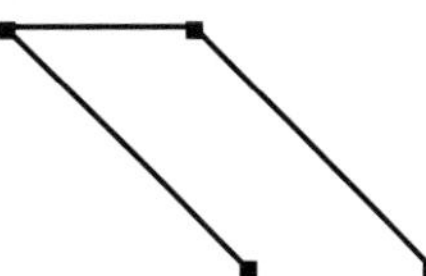

8. Don't bother selecting the bottom points and using Join. It only works on two separate paths. Your path is almost a closed path now. Closing this path actually can be done with three different methods.
9. To use the simplest method, select the path. Select the Object Inspector and click on the Closed box, you will see a closing segment appear. The object is now a closed path that can be filled. Select Edit>Undo.
10. Select the Pen tool and click its crosshair on one of the bottom anchor points. Now touch (don't click) the crosshair to the other bottom point; a black dot appears on the crosshair.

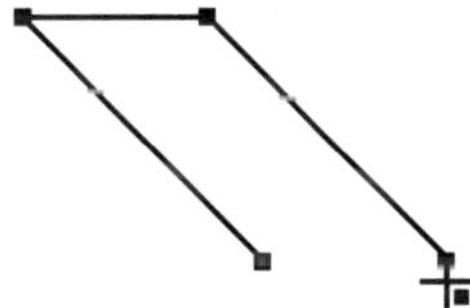

This tells you that this point will close the path when clicked. Click the Pen tool on this point. Notice how this new segment has closed the path. Select Edit>Undo.

11. The third method is only used in certain cases. With the Pointer tool, select and drag one of the bottom points so that it is directly over the other bottom point. Release the mouse; the path is now closed. Leave the path in this closed state and keep it selected.

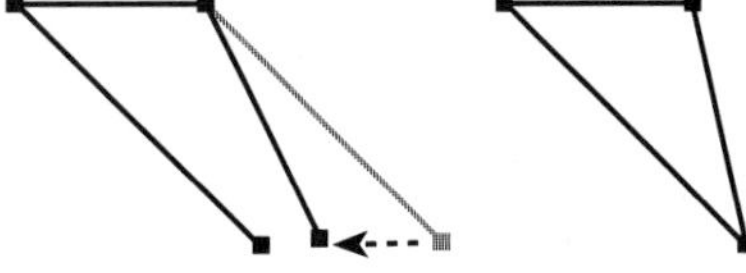

12. Access the Pen tool and click the crosshair on the middle of the left side segment. Click on this new point with the Pointer tool to select it, then drag the point to the lower left.

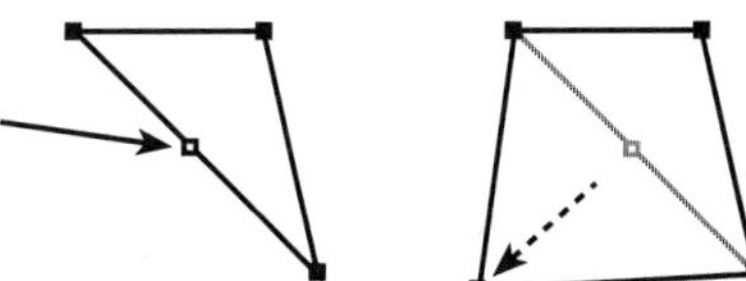

The keyboard shortcut for the Join command is Command-J (Macintosh) or Control-J (Windows).

You can easily select one or more objects and/or paths with the marquee, which appears when you click and drag over objects with the Pointer. To completely select an object (such as a group, primitive shape, or path) you must completely surround it with the marquee. You can select specific points on a path by drawing a marquee over the area containing the points you want. Note that the entire path will also be selected, but that the points you drew the marquee over will become hollow, which means you can now edit them as you wish.

13. Use the Pointer tool to select the path, then select the two bottom points. Drag one of the selected points to move the segment.

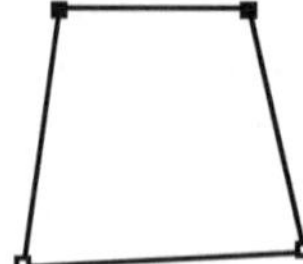

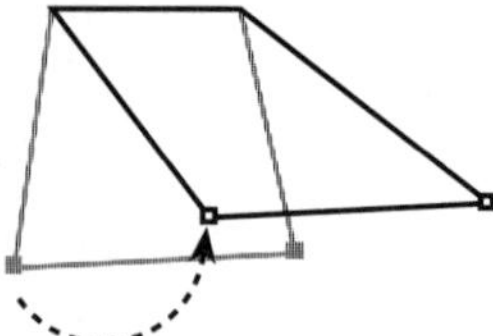

14. Let's imagine that the design now requires the bottom segment to be deleted. How do you delete a segment? Yes, you can delete anchor points, but if you delete the bottom anchor points you will not have much left to work with.
15. What if you toggled off the Closed box in the Object Inspector? Yes, this does delete one single segment. Will it be the right segment? Try it. Select the Object Inspector and uncheck the Closed box.

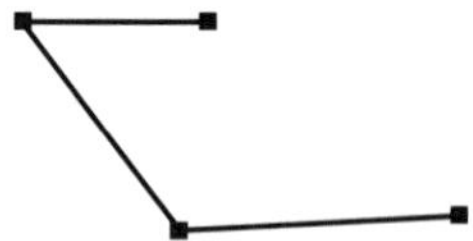

That was not the correct segment. Select Edit>Undo.

16. Select the path, then use the Pen tool to create a new anchor point on the bottom segment.

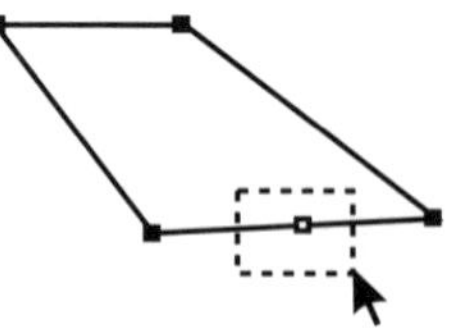

17. Select Modify>Split. The path will change slightly. Now marquee the same point again with the Pointer tool. Press the Delete key.

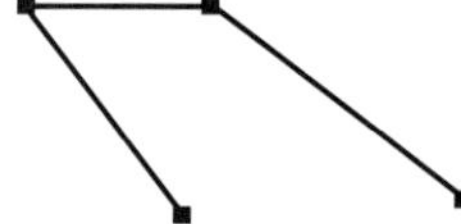

18. Now marquee the two left side anchor points, then press the Delete key.

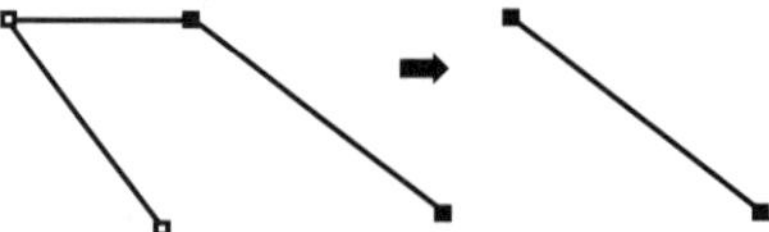

19. You have now created, added, deleted, moved, and modified anchor points.
20. Close the document without saving.

The keyboard shortcut for the Split command is Command-Shift-J (Macintosh) or Control-Shift-J (Windows).

Curve Basics

You use the Pen tool to draw curves as well as straight lines, but the big difference, as the saying goes, is all in the wrist. Curves are created when you click to create a new anchor point and drag the mouse to "pull" curve handles out of the point. The acuity and direction of the curve depends upon how you move the curve handles. Curves drawn with the Pen tool are mathematically represented as *Bézier* ("bez-yay") curves, named after the French mathematician Pierre Bézier, who developed them for automobile design.

Curve, Corner, and Connector Points

FreeHand can create three different types of points: curve points, corner points, and connector points.

- Curve points are drawn by clicking and dragging the Pen tool in the direction of the curve, and are identified by hollow circles when selected.

It's a good idea to have Smart cursors selected in Preferences>General.

With this option on, you can observe the crosshair when it touches the point where the path began. When the path touches, the small square dot will appear on the crosshair.

- Corner points are created by clicking (do not drag) the Pen tool on the page and are identified by hollow squares when selected.

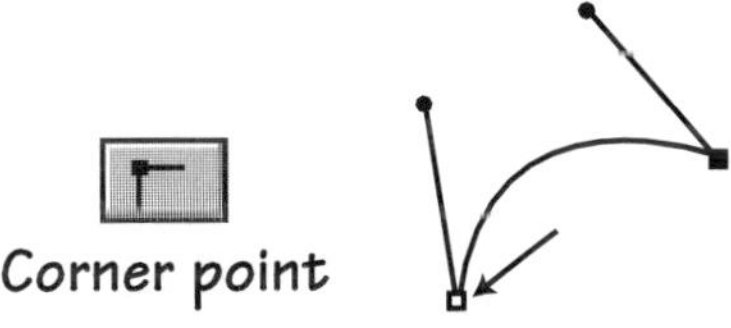

- Connector points create transitions between curved and straight path segments, identified by hollow triangles when selected.

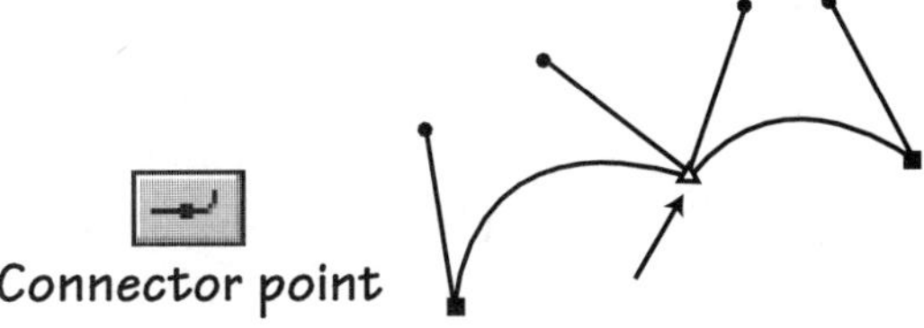

Draw Curves

1. Create a document. Select the Pen tool and drag it to create an anchor point.

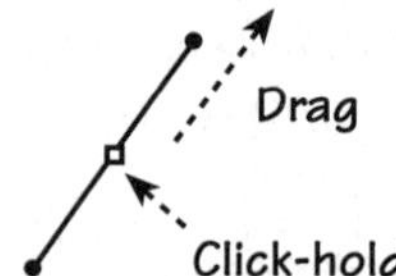

2. Move the mouse to the right. Hold the Shift key (to constrain) and single-click (don't drag). Click-hold on this second point and drag a control handle downward to the right. Release the mouse button. Move the Pen tool crosshair to the right, then single-click a third point. Press the Tab key to deselect. You should have an object looking something like the following:

If you have created a point without control handles and decide you need some afterwards you can "pull" a handle out of that point with the Pointer tool. Place the tool on top of the point. Hold the Option/Alt key and click and drag. Handles should appear on both sides of the point.

3. Click on the path with the Pointer tool, then click directly on the second point; its control handle will appear. Drag the handle so that the curve bends downward. Experiment with moving the handle to see how it affects the curve of the segment.

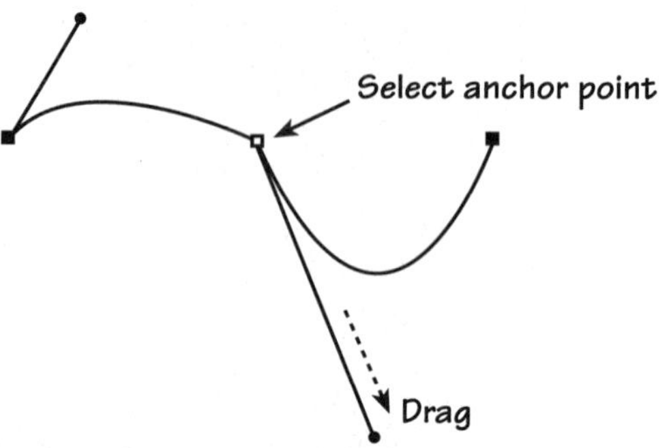

4. With the Pointer tool, click on the first point drawn; its control handle will appear. Drag the handle so that the curve bends upward, making the curve uplift to make a continuation of the curve from the other segment. Experiment with moving the handle to see how it affects the curve of the segment. You should have a curving object that appears as follows:

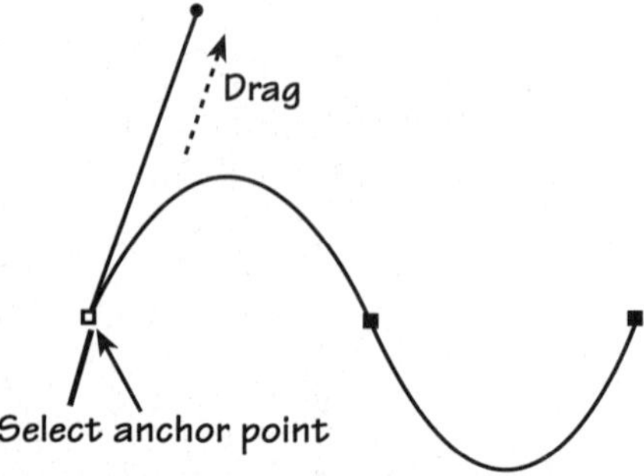

5. You have now had an opportunity to draw and alter curving segments.
6. Close the document without saving.

Create Consecutive Curved Lines

1. In the File menu, select New to create a new document.
2. Select the Pen tool and drag the crosshair on the page, pulling out direction handles. Release the mouse button.

Move the crosshair to the right and drag direction handles on this point. Release the mouse button.

Move the mouse to the right and drag direction handles on this point. Release the mouse button.

Move the mouse to the right and drag direction handles on this point. Release the mouse button. Move the crosshair to the right and make one final click. Select the Pointer tool for modifying the curves.

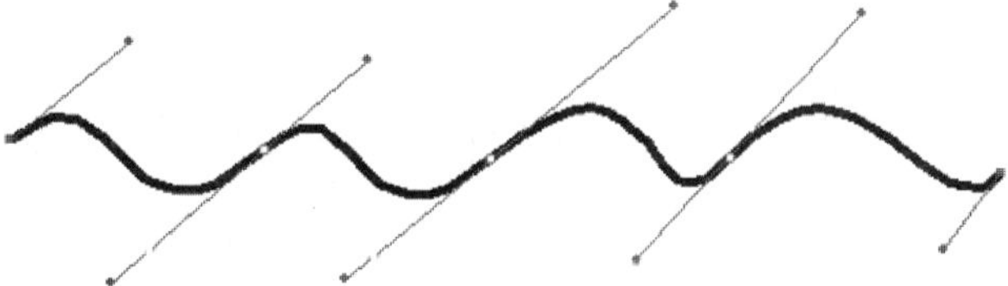

3. Each anchor point has direction handles that allow you to change the curves by moving them around. Select the different points and their handles. Pull and rotate the handles to see how the curves respond. When finished, delete the path.

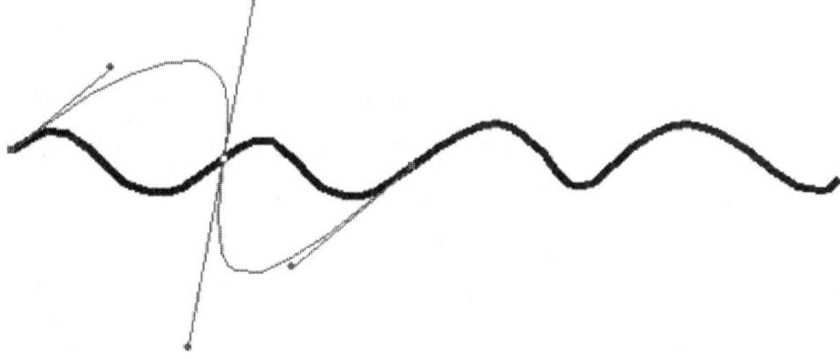

4. Select the Pen tool to create a new path. Drag the crosshair on the page to make the beginning point. Release the mouse. Move the crosshair to the right and, holding the Shift key to constrain, single-click the second anchor point.

5. Click and drag the crosshair on the endpoint you just made. This will continue the selected path. You will see a direction hand that will extend out of the clicked anchor point. Release the mouse button.

The next click will make a curving segment. Move the mouse slightly to the right, hold the Shift key and single-click an endpoint.

6. With the Pointer tool, click the middle anchor point and drag its direction handle upward.

7. With the Pointer tool, click the first anchor point and drag its direction handle upward.

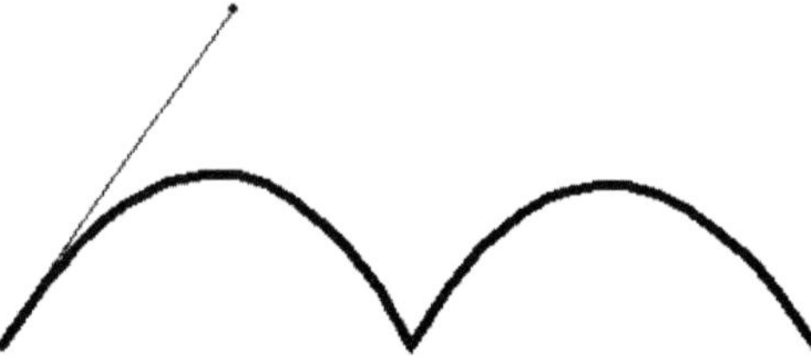

8. You have now created one path with two independent curves. When their direction handles are moved, they do not affect the adjoining curve.

9. Close the document without saving.

Combining Straight Lines with Curves

You will often want to create artwork that contains both straight lines and curves. This is easy to do by using FreeHand's ability to constrain an anchor point's curve handles to 45° increments.

Create a Closed Path with Straight Lines and Curves

1. Create a new FreeHand document.
2. With the Pen tool, single-click on the page to establish a beginning point. Move the mouse up ", then, holding the Shift key to constrain to a straight line, click again.

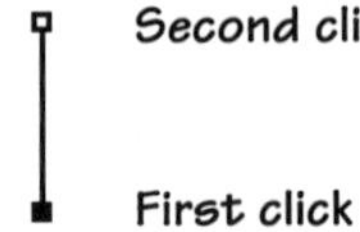

3. Move your mouse up and to the left of the second point. Click and drag upward to create a curve point.

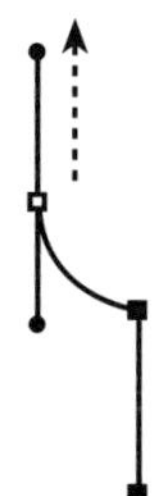

4. Move the mouse to the right, past the straight segment. Click and drag again to create the fourth point.

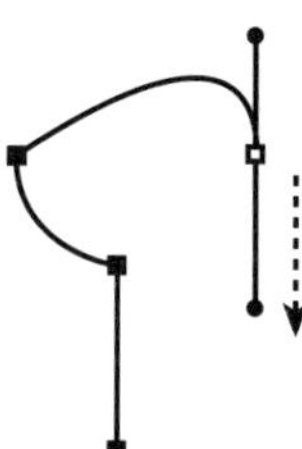

To change the direction of your control handles to create an independent curve "on-the-go" hold down the Option/Alt key after you've clicked your point. This will freeze the original handle of the curve and allow the new handle to swing around to where you want it for your next curve.

5. Move down and left, next to the second point you drew, and single-click.

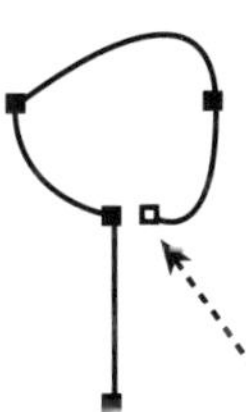

6. You need one last point. To draw this, move down, level with the first point, and click again while holding the Shift key.

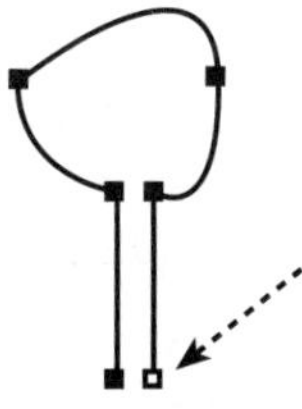

7. To finish your object, click the cursor on the first point you clicked with the Pen tool. You have now created a closed object that can be filled. Click on the curve points to access their control handles and fine-tune the object to look more rounded, as if it were an abstract tree to be used in an illustration or architectural design.

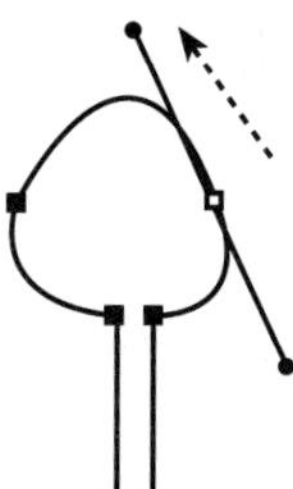

8. Close the document without saving.

Modifying Direction Handles

Once points have been drawn, the type of points can be changed with the Object Inspector. To do so, click on the Point type. A curve point will be rounder and smoother. A corner point should be used when two straight lines intersect. A connector point should be used when a curved line joins a straight line, or when an abrupt change of direction occurs.

Clicking on the Handles buttons collapses the right and left handles, depending on the path direction.

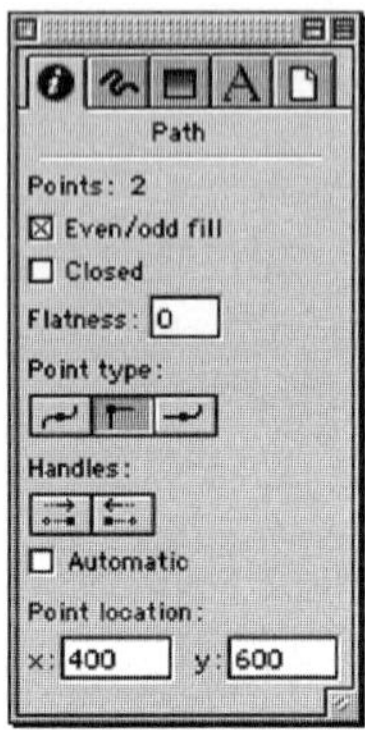

Modifying Curve Anchor Points

1. Create a new document. Select Window>Inspectors>Object to access the Object Inspector.
2. With the Pen tool, make an initial curve anchor point by clicking and dragging up and to the right. Move the mouse to the right, then, holding the Shift key to constrain, drag again to pull out the control handles. Move the mouse to the right and single-click a final endpoint.

3. Select the first anchor point, which, by default, is a curve point. Move its control handle to see how the curve is affected. You will notice that the line adjusts to the angle of the control handles. In the Object Inspector, click on the middle point type, which is the corner point. Move the same control handle to see if any changes were made to the curve. Don't be surprised if very little transpires. More will happen as you progress with the points and the Object Inspector.
4. Click on the third point type in the Object Inspector; this is the connector point. Notice how the segment changed on the path. Now try to move the handle; you will not have much success in maneuvering it. This is because connector points do exactly what the name implies: they connect two segments. This connector point is at the end of one segment.

5. With this point still selected, access the Pen tool and click down to the left of the connector point; a new point will appear with a segment between the two points. With the Pointer tool, click on the connector point and drag the control handle. Be aware that connector points are not very versatile, but they will alter the curve slightly. Work with its handle to see how far it will go.

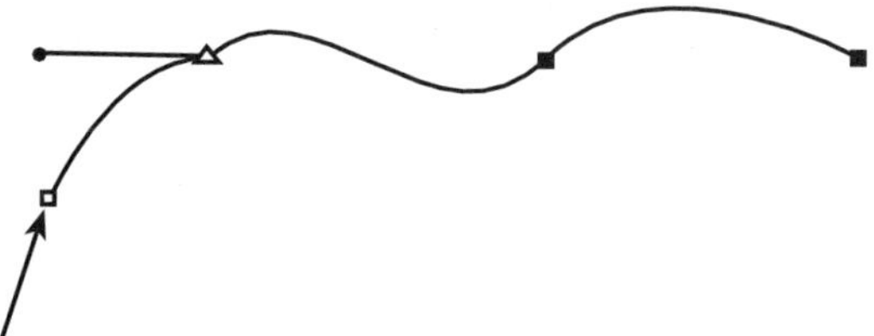

6. With the Pointer tool, select the anchor point to the right of the connector point. To see its control handles, look at the Object Inspector and notice how the point type changed to curve point.

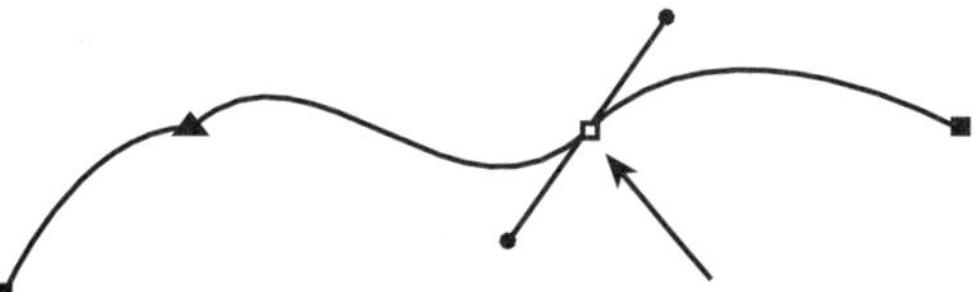

7. Click on the top handle and drag it downward. Notice how the segments on either side of the point were altered. This is one of the easiest ways to recognize a curve point, which behaves in the following manner:

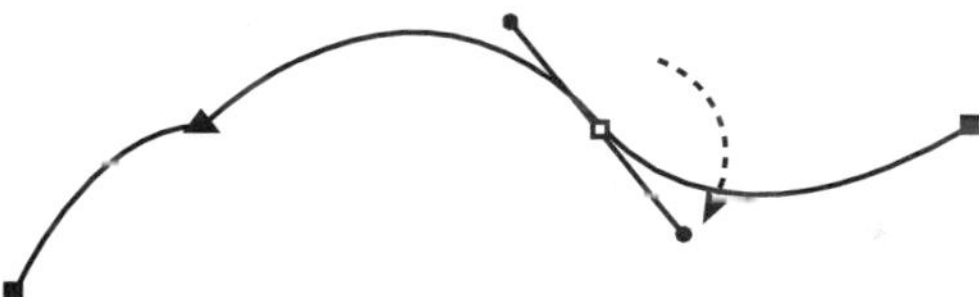

8. In the Object Inspector, click on the middle point type: the corner point. You will not see anything obvious happen to the path, but drag the topmost anchor point and observe how much of the path moves. The corner point does not control two segments at once. This is one of the ways to fine-tune only portions of a curved path.

9. Now, in the Object Inspector, click on the Connector point icon to change the selected point to flatten out the curve segment. Drag on the connector point's control handle to see just how much you can alter this type of anchor point.

10. Click on the Curve point icon in the Object Inspector to change the selected point back to its original state. Drag on the control handle to see how the point is back to its malleable state.

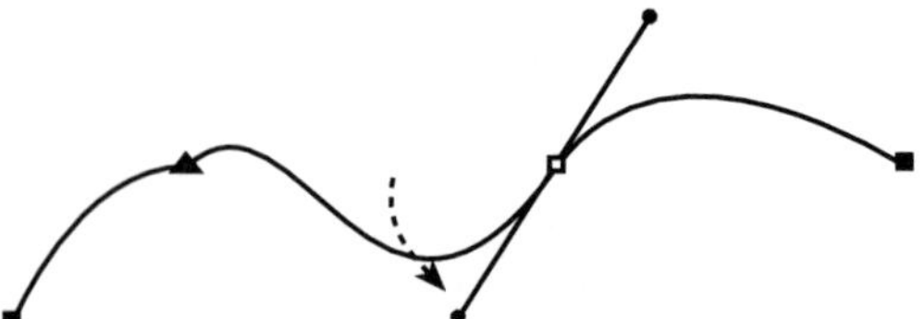

11. You have now worked with and observed how anchor points can be changed in the Object Inspector.

12. Close the document without saving.

Creating and Managing Anchor Points and Segments

1. From the File menu, select New to create a new document.

2. Select the Pen tool and click the crosshair once on the page; this will create the beginning point of the path. Move the mouse to the right and slightly upward. Click the second anchor point. Move the mouse to the right and downward, then click the third anchor point.

3. With the Pointer tool, click on the last point (endpoint) made to select it. Selected anchor points are hollow. If the clicked anchor point does not look hollow, click again. When selected, anchor points can be moved or deleted. Move the selected point to the upper right.

4. Select the middle anchor point and move it up slightly to the left.

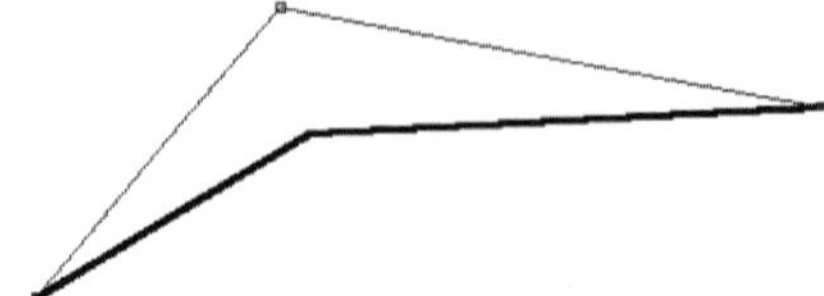

5. With the Pointer tool, select the path. With the Pen tool, click the crosshair on the middle of the second segment. This will add an anchor point.

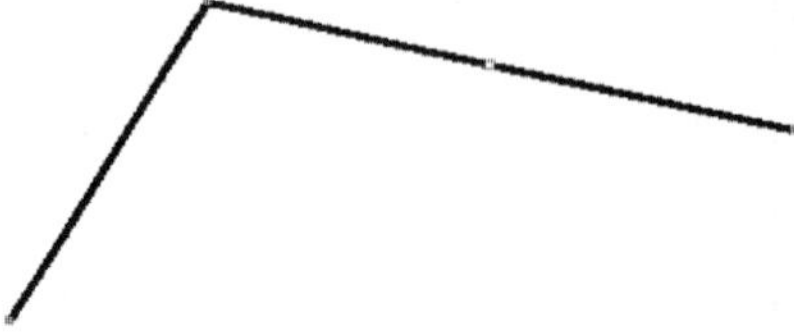

6. With the Pointer tool, drag this point downward.

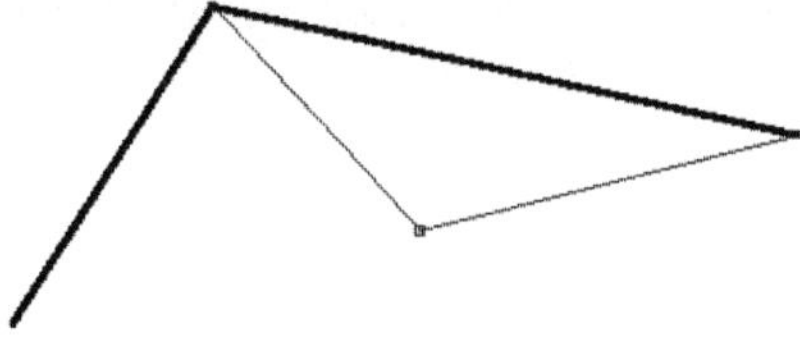

7. Keep the path selected and use the Pen tool to drag a direction handle from the right endpoint.

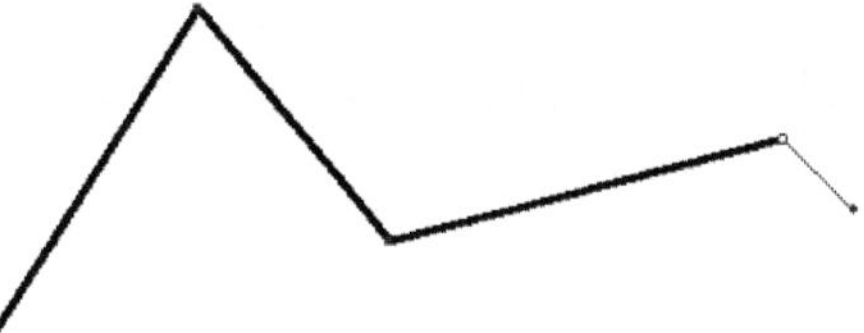

8. Move the Pen tool down and single-click an endpoint.

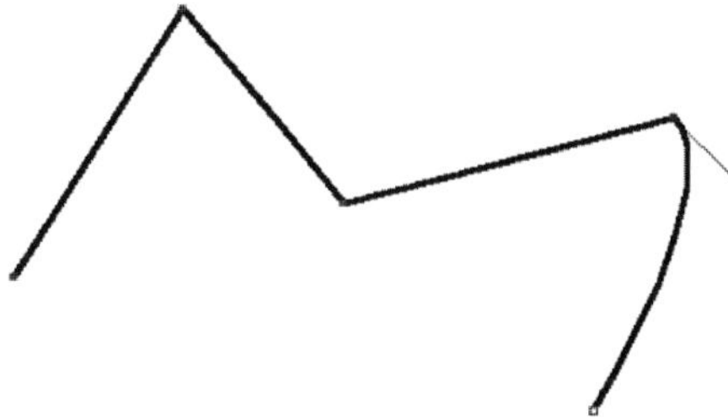

9. Click on the direction handle with the Pointer tool and pull it to the right to alter the curve of the segment.

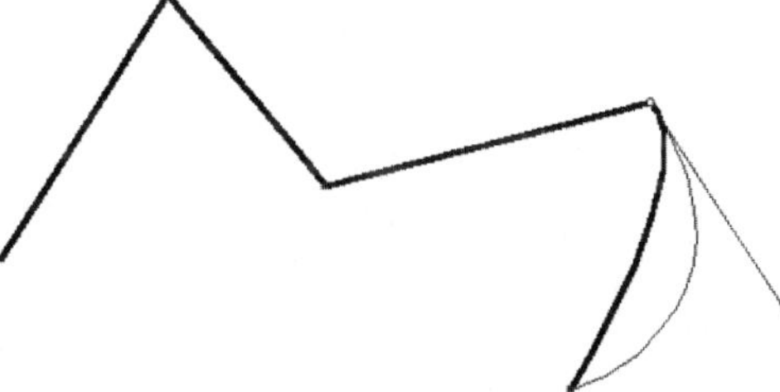

10. Marquee-select the new anchor point created in step 5. Delete this point.

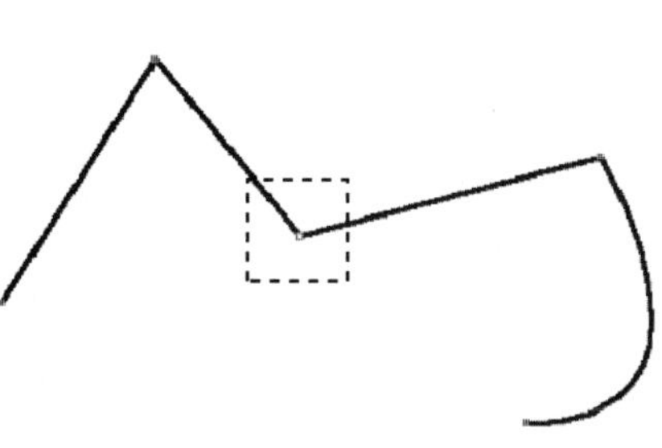

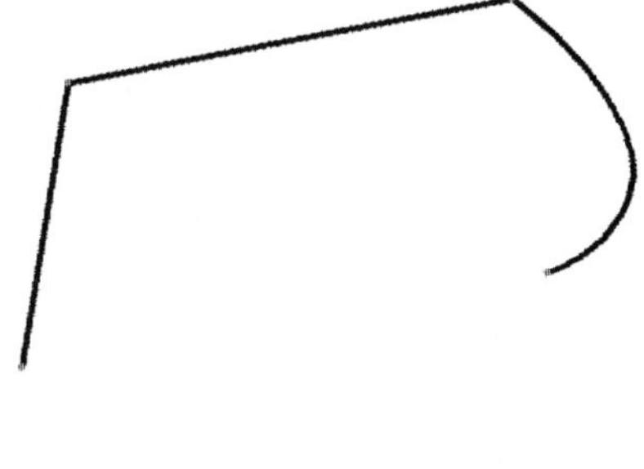

11. Click on the endpoint of the path to see the direction handle of the curving segment. Drag the handle to the right to round the curve more.

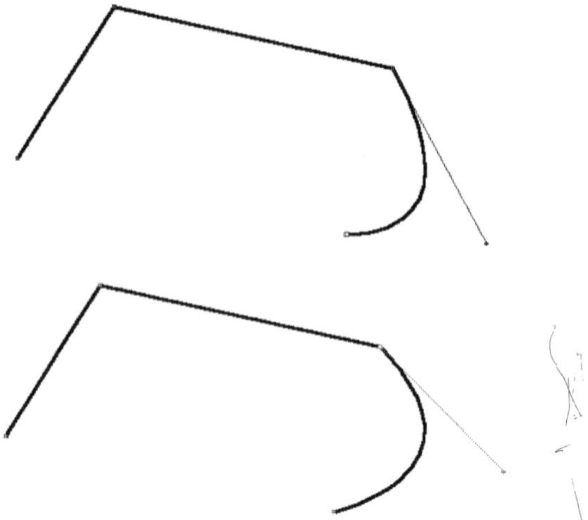

12. With the endpoint of the path still selected, select the Pen tool and click on the first-point you made. This final click has completed the closed path.

13. Close the document without saving.

The Knife Tool

Occasionally, you'll need to make more drastic changes to a path than simply moving a point around. The Knife tool can perform these alterations to a path without disturbing other points or control handles.

You can easily cut through an object with the Knife tool. Select the tool and drag the crosshair through the selected object. The path is split wherever the Knife tool crosses it, creating two or more separate, open or closed paths.

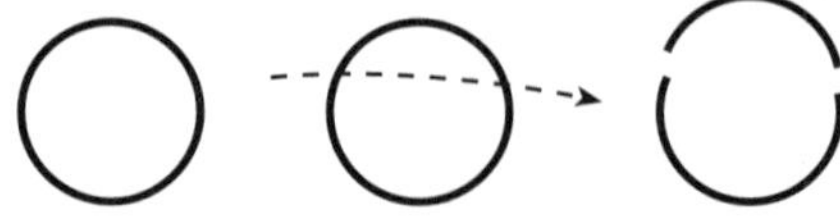

If you double click on the Knife tool icon in the toolbox, you will see a dialog box where you can customize how the knife will cut its objects.

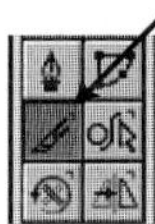

- Tool Operation — This option allows you to choose how your Knife tool will draw as it cuts, with freehand that can curve, or with straight cuts.
- Width — This option determines how wide the path that the Knife tool cuts with will be .
- Options — If the Close cut paths option is chosen you will create two separate closed paths in one cut with the Knife tool. If Tight fit option is chosen your cut will be very close to the line that you draw. Both can be on or off at any time and neither has any affect on the other.

The Freeform Tool

The Freeform tool can easily alter anchors or entire paths. Its most unusual ability lets you push and pull against a path to change it.

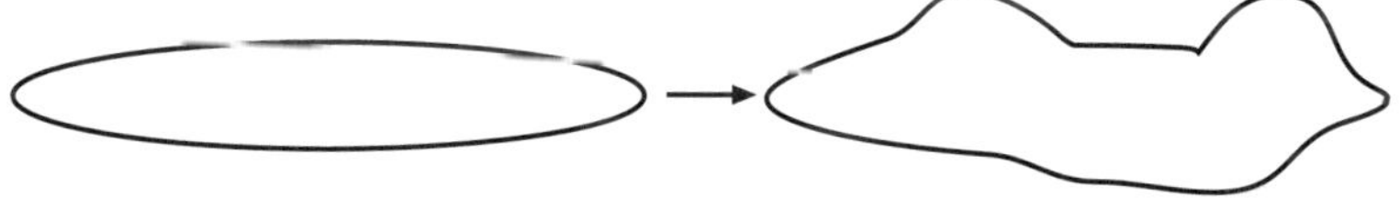

If you double-click on the Freeform tool icon in the Toolbox, you will see a dialog box where you can customize how you use this tool when distorting paths.

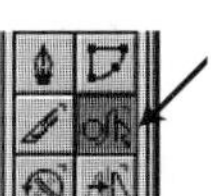

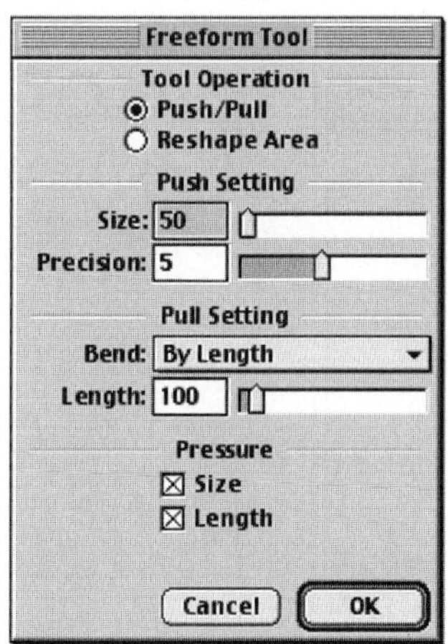

- Tool Operation — This option allows you to choose whether you will change a single path with the Freeform tool if Push/Pull is set or if you will change a whole area of a design if Reshape Area is set.

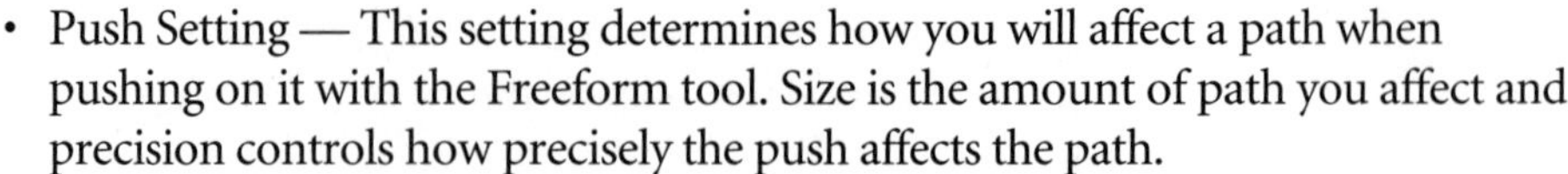

- Push Setting — This setting determines how you will affect a path when pushing on it with the Freeform tool. Size is the amount of path you affect and precision controls how precisely the push affects the path.
- Pull Setting — This setting determines how you will affect a path when pulling on it with the Freeform tool. Bend helps you to choose specifically how the path that you are pulling will bend. Your choices are By Length and Between Points. Length is the amount of path you will pull with the tool.
- Pressure — If you are using a stylus tablet to draw with, this setting determines how pressure will affect the path you are drawing.

Path Modifying Tools

1. From the File menu, select New to create a new document. The two path modifying tools are the Knife and Freeform tools.
2. With the Rectangle tool, draw a 1-in. square on the page.

3. The square is now selected. With the Knife tool, drag the crosshair in a sweep across the square. Make sure that Freehand is the only option on and that the width is set at 0 in the Knife tool dialog box before you make your cut.

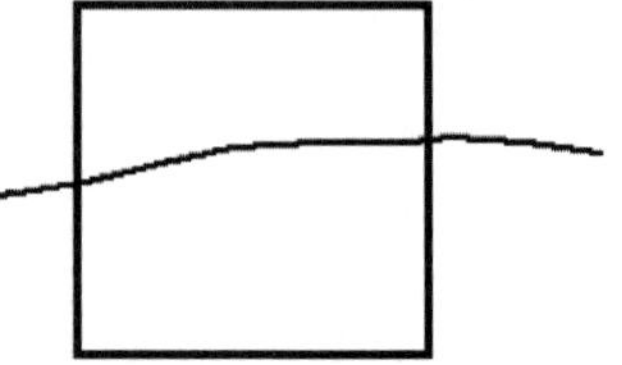

4. You have cut the selected path where the Knife tool touched it. Deselect the square and then click on the top part of the square with the Pointer tool. Press the Up Arrow key several times to see the separation. Delete this square and draw another one for the next step.

5. In the Knife tool dialog box change the setting to Straight. Select the square again. Drag the Knife tool across at an angle. Notice how the Knife cut remains straight, allowing you further control over where it cuts.

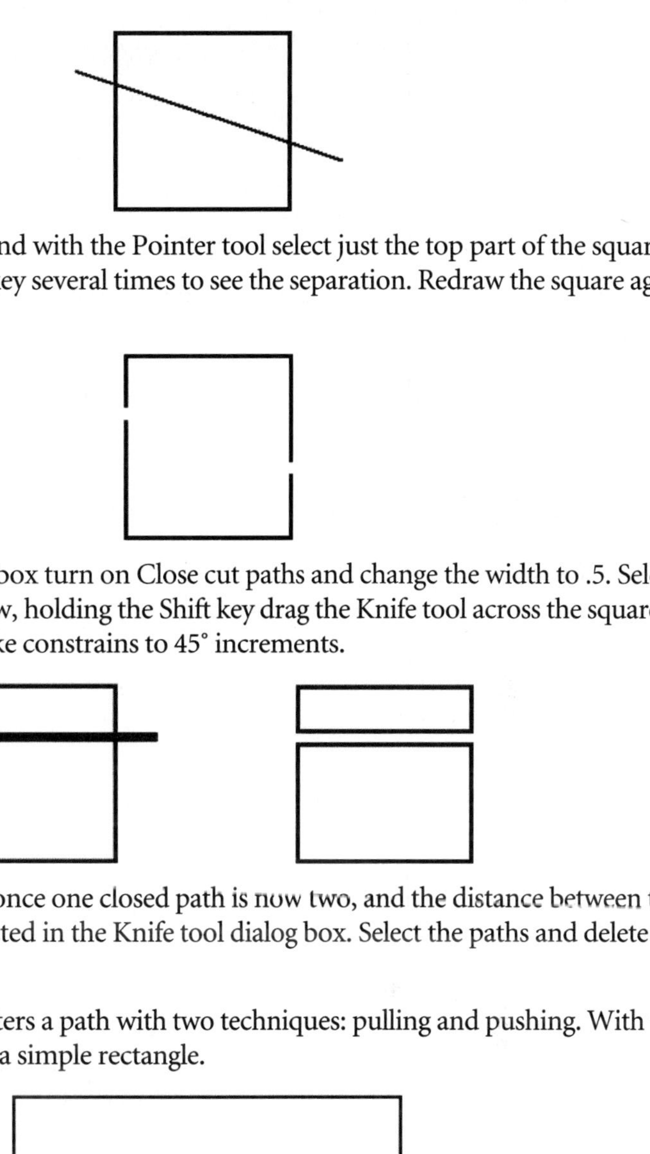

6. Deselect the square and with the Pointer tool select just the top part of the square and press the Up Arrow key several times to see the separation. Redraw the square again for the next section.

7. In your Knife dialog box turn on Close cut paths and change the width to .5. Select the square again. Now, holding the Shift key drag the Knife tool across the square. Notice the knife stroke constrains to 45° increments.

An object can be cut only if it is first selected.

8. The square that was once one closed path is now two, and the distance between them is the width you selected in the Knife tool dialog box. Select the paths and delete them.

9. The Freeform tool alters a path with two techniques: pulling and pushing. With the Rectangle tool, draw a simple rectangle.

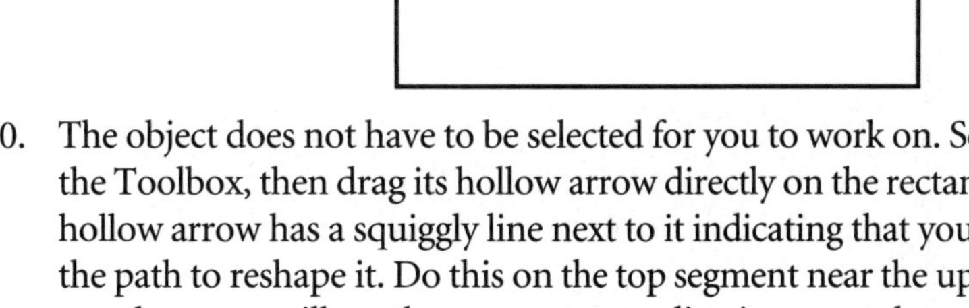

10. The object does not have to be selected for you to work on. Select the Freeform tool in the Toolbox, then drag its hollow arrow directly on the rectangle path. Note that the hollow arrow has a squiggly line next to it indicating that you can pull anywhere on the path to reshape it. Do this on the top segment near the upper-left corner. When you drag, you will see the segment extending in a curved manner.

To cut an object in half you must drag the Knife tool completely over the object, crossing the path on both edges.

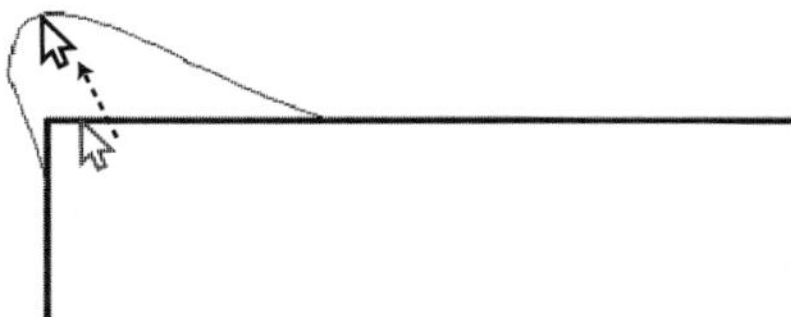

11. Release the mouse button. You will see the modified path and its new anchor points.

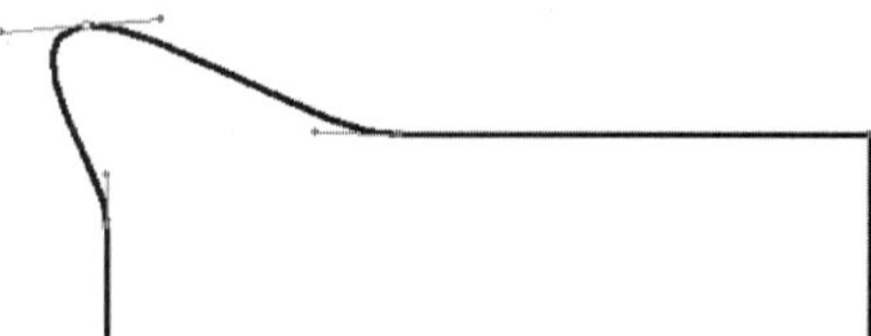

You can also cut straight with the Knife tool without changing the option in the dialog box. Hold down the Option/Alt key as you drag the Knife tool.

12. Drag the Freeform cursor on the bottom segment near the lower-left corner. This time hold down the Left Arrow key while dragging to make the pull area smaller and smaller.

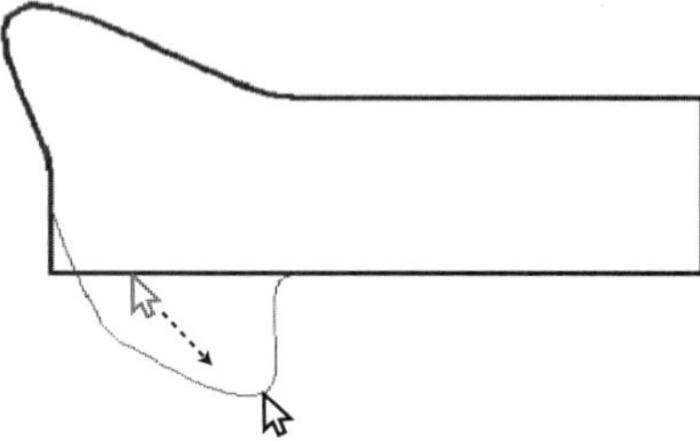

13. Release the mouse button. You will see the modified path and its new anchor points.

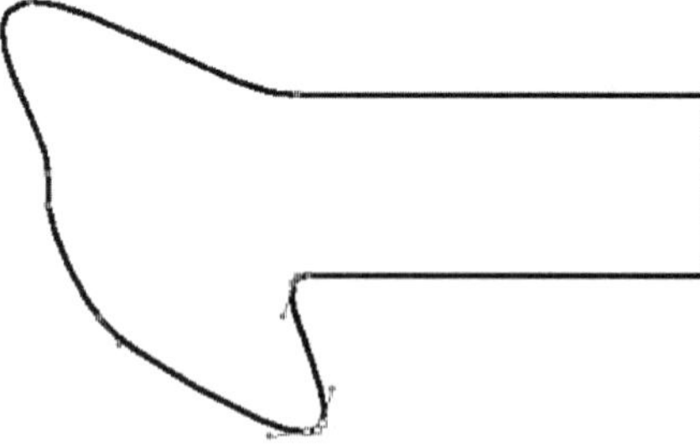

When cutting an object with the Knife tool, if you want the finished paths to hold color you must select Close cut paths in the dialog box. This will create closed paths that will hold a fill when the cutting is completed.

14. If you do not touch the path segments with the Freeform tool when you drag, its cursor turns into a hollow arrow with a circle next to it. This indicates you will push a path to alter it. Select the Freeform tool again and position its cursor inside the rectangle, but do not touch any segment.

    Drag upward and you will see the path extending along with the cursor.

15. Release the mouse button. Move the Freeform cursor under the rectangle and drag upward. Experiment changing the size of your Push tool by holding down the Right or Left Arrow key while you are pushing.

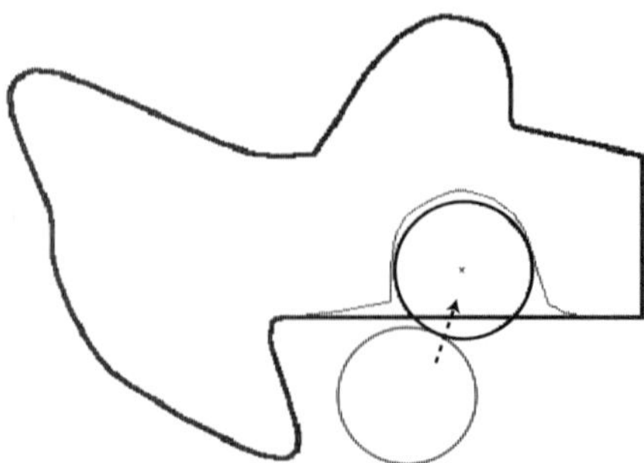

16. Release the mouse button. You will now see an entirely different shape than the rectangle you started with.

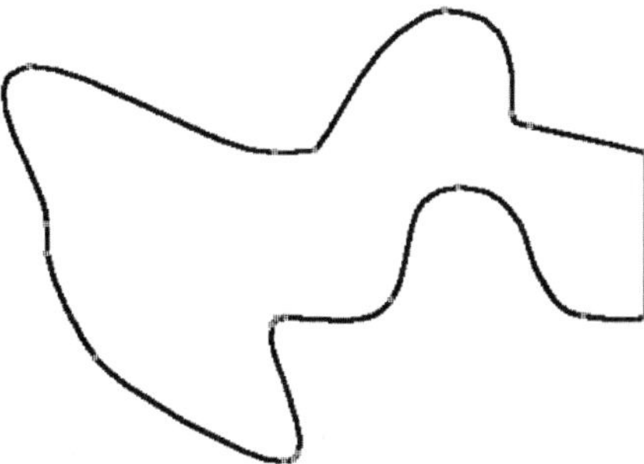

Besides setting the area you want to pull or push with the Freeform tool in the dialog box you can also adjust the size by using the right or left arrow key. Right would make the area bigger, left smaller.

17. You have now seen how the Knife and Freeform tools modify paths.
18. Close the document without saving.

Summary

In this chapter, you have learned to use FreeHand's collection of drawing and path-altering tools. You have learned to isolate anchor points and segments of a path and how to connect anchor points. You have learned how to work with Bézier curves, combining multiple curved paths in a smooth flow, or combining straight lines with curves. You have also learned how to create, modify, and manage anchor points and segments. You have explored and used the Knife and Freeform tools to modify paths. You are now ready to learn to manage the structure of your documents.

Notes:

CHAPTER 7

Arranging, Aligning, and Distributing Objects

CHAPTER OBJECTIVE:

To learn how FreeHand stacks objects in layers, and how to arrange objects and modify their attributes. In Chapter 7, you will:

- Learn about the stacking order of objects within a layer.
- Understand how to move objects forward or backward to change their relationship to each other.
- Learn to group, ungroup, and nest groups within groups, and how FreeHand will automatically remember how many nested groups exist in your document.
- Understand how to lock and hide objects for ease of editing.
- Understand how use the Align panel to align and distribute objects relative to each other or to the page.
- Learn how to duplicate and clone and how to apply a step and repeat.
- Learn about layers and understand the controls in the Layers panel.
- Learn how layers are arranged, and modified.
- Understand how to lock, hide, and customize layers to suit your needs.
- Learn how to reassign objects to other layers — a task frequently necessary for successful and appealing design.

PROJECTS TO BE COMPLETED:

- Dinner Time (A)
- **Mask Art (B)**
- Tropical Treasure Logo (C)
- Grocery Ad (D)
- Ball and Mirror (E)
- No Clowning Around (F)

Arranging, Aligning, and Distributing Objects

Without layers, manipulation of objects could be an incredibly tedious task. Since you now know how to create various objects, you need to know how to keep them organized. Objects in a layer are arranged in a stack. A layer can have many objects stacked on top of each other.

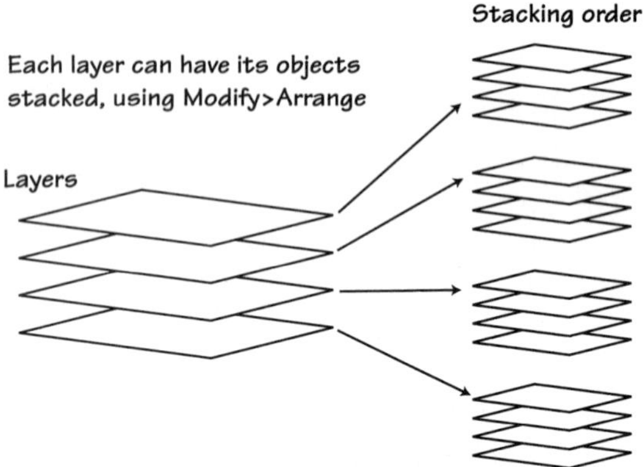

Every object in FreeHand has its own properties: its x,y coordinates on the page and its stroke and fill. It also has a relationship with other objects in the document: its stacking order from front to back, the alignment and distribution of space between objects, and its relationship to the page itself.

Objects can be arranged by moving them forward or backward within a layer. The stacking order tools are found in the Modify>Arrange menu.

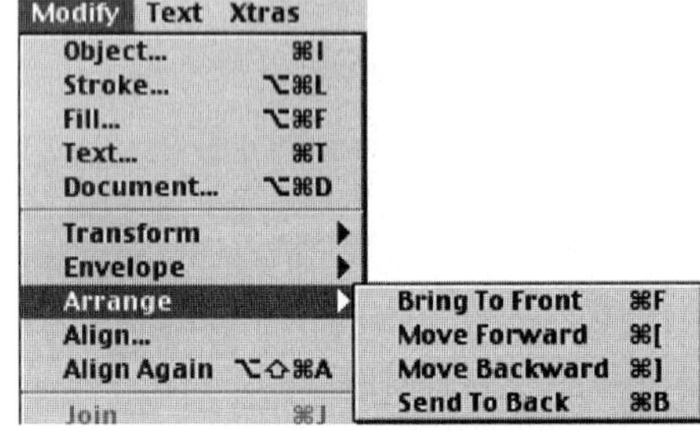

You can align and distribute objects in reference to each other and to the page. The Align panel allows you to align or distribute objects across a single axis or both axes as follows:

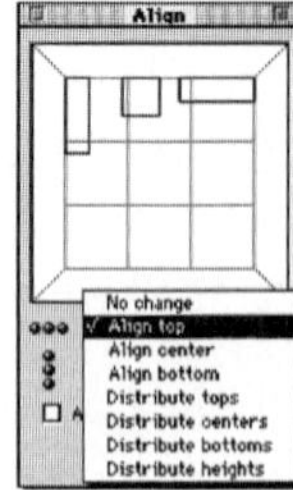

You can group multiple selected objects into a single combined object, and ungroup them as needed as follows:

Lock ⌘L
Unlock ⇧⌘L
Group ⌘G
Ungroup ⌘U

Arranging Objects

Each object sits either above or below other objects, even if the objects don't overlap. This order is determined by which object was drawn first. The sequence in which you draw objects will place them in a stacking order from bottom to top. Each new object drawn is automatically in front of all previous objects, unless the objects are created on other layers.

If you created a rectangle first, then a circle followed by a star, the star would be in front of the others. The rectangle, created first, would be in back.

There are four functions available in the Modify>Arrange menu. These four functions, called the Arrange commands, change the stacking order of objects. If you change the stacking order of objects that don't overlap, the change may not be apparent.

Move Forward, Move Backward

You can move an object forward or backward within a layer by choosing Move Forward or Move Backward. In this example, the rectangle (A) needs to be between the circle and the square in back. Without Move Forward/Backward, a lot of Send To Back and Bring To Front would have to be applied.

If the rectangle is selected, and Modify>Arrange>Move Backward is chosen, the rectangle moves backward by one object (B).

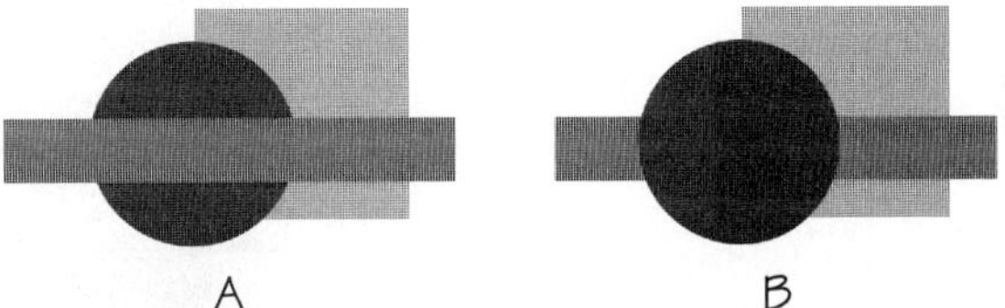

A B

Bring To Front, Send To Back

You can also move an object to the front or Back of a layer by choosing Bring To Front or Send To Back in the Modify>Arrange menu.

In this example the circle is behind all other objects (A) and needs to be in front. It would be time consuming to perform Move Forward as many times as needed. Instead, the circle was selected, then Modify>Arrange>Bring To Front chosen. This brought the circle all the way to the front (B).

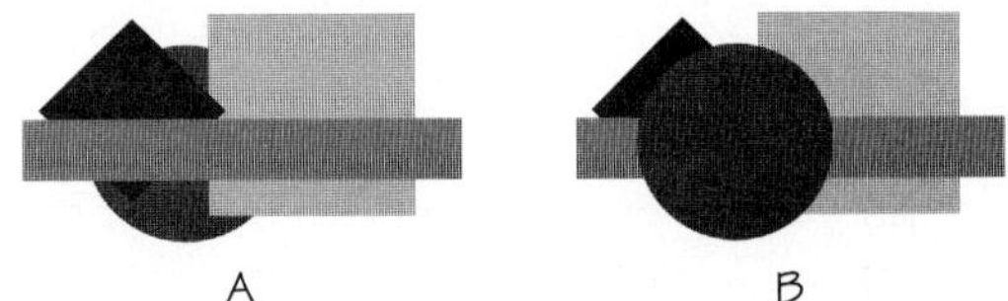

A B

These four functions are very useful in allowing you to arrange objects without having to create layers and assigning the objects to each one. Also, if a layer has several objects assigned to it, the Front/Back arranging can manipulate these objects on the layer.

Using Front/Back Movements

1. Choose File>Open and open **Manipulating Objects.FH9** from the **SF-FreeHand** folder.

2. Click on the rectangle with the Pointer tool. Select Modify>Arrange>Bring To Front and notice what has happened to the rectangle.

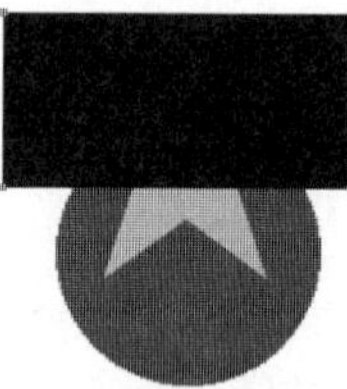

3. Click on the star. Select Modify>Arrange>Move Forward. Now click on the circle and select Modify>Arrange>Move Forward again. Where is the circle in relation to the star and rectangle?

Use these keyboard shortcuts to quickly arrange objects:

Cmd/Ctrl-F = move to front

Cmd/Ctrl-B = move to back

Cmd/Ctrl-[= move forward

Cmd/Ctrl-] = move backward

4. Click on the star and select Modify>Arrange>Move Backward. Where is the star located?

Locking items can be useful for a number of tasks, especially when you have finished with an object and want to protect it from accidental alteration. Another use for locking an item is if you have multiple objects stacked over each other and are having a hard time selecting the ones at the back. Locking the foreground object can make it easier to select the others. It's also useful when using the Align panel for forcing other objects to align with reference to a locked object.

5. With the star still selected, select Modify>Arrange>Move Backward again. Where is the star now?

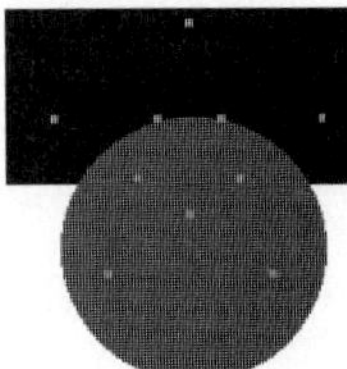

6. Click on the circle and the rectangle. Select Modify>Arrange>Send To Back.

7. You have now used the four arranging features available in the Modify>Arrange menu.
8. Keep the document open for the following exercise.

Locking and Unlocking Objects

FreeHand allows you to lock and unlock the position of individual objects with the Modify>Lock/Unlock options.

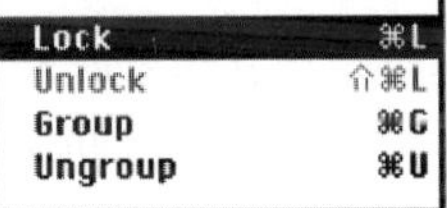

Locking an object doesn't mean you can't select it; you can click on the object and see its anchor points, but you cannot move or transform it. You can, however, still apply different fills or strokes to the locked object.

Locking and Unlocking Objects

1. Continue working in the open document, **Manipulating Objects.FH9**.

2. With the Pointer tool click on the star. Select Modify>Lock.
3. Drag a marquee around all three objects with the Pointer tool to select them.

4. Move the objects several inches to the right. What was the result? Did the star move with the other objects?
5. Choose Edit>Undo to undo the move. Deselect all the objects.
6. Choose Modify>Unlock. Why is it grayed out? If an object is locked, shouldn't this feature be accessible?
7. Click on the star, then select Modify>Unlock. Unlock is now accessible.
8. You have now observed and experienced how Lock/Unlock can make objects immune to movement or modifications.
9. Keep the file open for the following exercise.

The keyboard shortcuts for locking are Command-L (Macintosh) or Control-L (Windows).

To unlock a selected object, press Shift-Command-L (Macintosh) or Shift-Control-L (Windows).

Grouping and Ungrouping Objects

The Modify>Group feature combines several objects together into a single object; this makes performing the same tasks on multiple objects easy and faster.

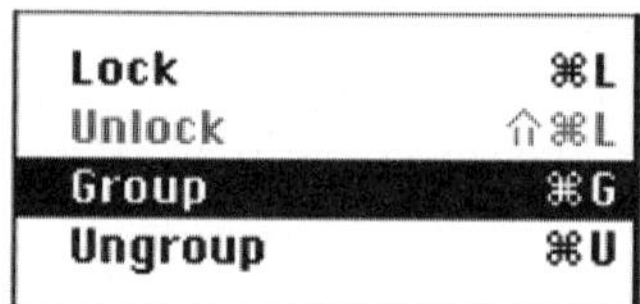

Objects must be selected to be locked or unlocked.

Nesting Groups

You can nest groups within groups. FreeHand remembers how many nested groups exist. If you need to ungroup them, you can do so at any time.

In the following example there are three ovals and three squares (A) that were grouped creating a group of ovals and a group of squares (B). The two groups were then selected (C) and grouped into a single object (D). Single and grouped objects have four corner handles to select them.

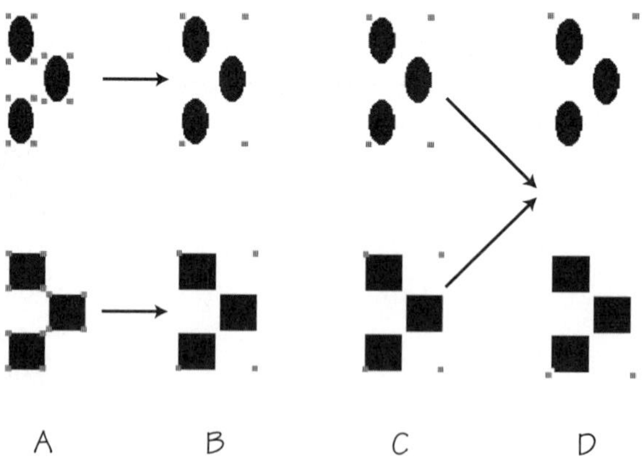

The keyboard shortcuts for grouping is Command-G (Macintosh) or Control-G (Windows).

Ungrouping

Grouped objects can be ungrouped by selecting the grouped object, then choosing Modify>Ungroup. Ungrouping will only undo the last grouping performed. All other groups will stay together until Ungroup is selected again.

In the following example, the nested grouped object was selected and ungrouped (A). The two previous groups become evident (B). Both groups are selected, then ungrouped, resulting in the original separate objects (C).

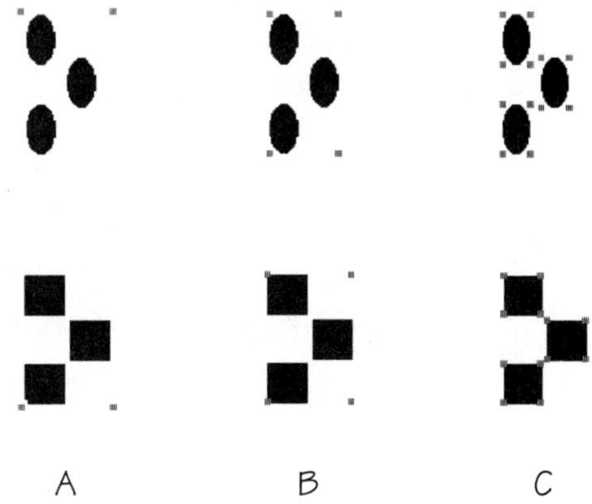

Group and Ungroup Objects

1. Continue working in the open document "Manipulating Objects.FH9".
2. Select the three objects; you will see all their anchor points.

3. Select Modify>Group. You will now see only the four corners of the bounding box of the grouped objects.

4. With the Pointer tool, select the group and move it around the page to see how the three objects move as one.
5. If you want to select a single object or line segment to modify, hold down the Option/ Alt key as you click on the circle; only the circle is selected.
6. Now add the Shift key as you click on the rectangle to select multiple objects. You can isolate objects in a group with these keys.

7. Release the keys and click away from the objects to deselect them.
8. With nothing selected, select Modify>Ungroup. Why isn't it accessible in the menu? Click on the grouped objects, then go back to Modify>Ungroup. You can now select Ungroup.
9. You have now seen how grouping combines objects, and how certain keys allow you to select individual objects in a group. You have also learned to ungroup combined objects.
10. Close the document without saving.

Aligning and Distributing Objects

The Align panel is accessed by selecting either Window>Panels>Align or Modify>Align.

The keyboard shortcut for accessing the Align panel is Option-Command-A (Macintosh) or Alt-Control-A (Windows).

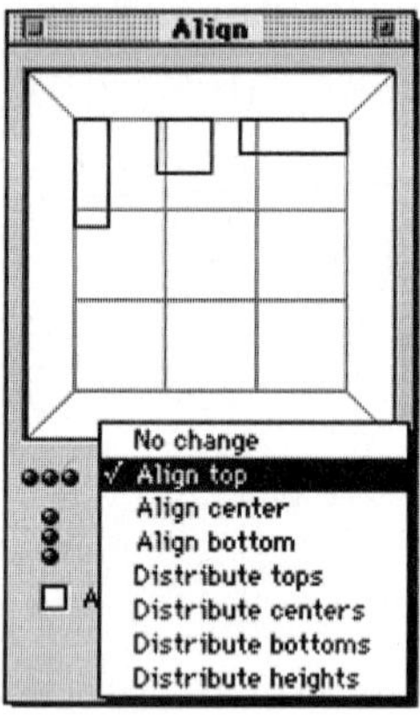

There are two ways to use the Align panel:

- Preview — by double-clicking the squares in the preview window.
- Pop-up menus — by using the pop-up menus in the panel.

Preview Method

If you prefer to work visually, you can single-click the regions to see alignments for selected objects, and double-click the region to apply the alignment. When each region is selected, you will see its specifications listed on the pop-up menus.

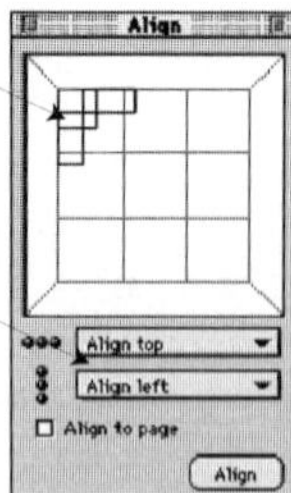

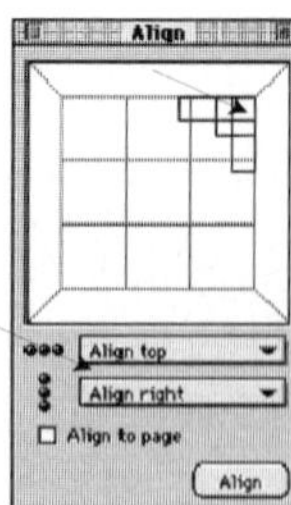

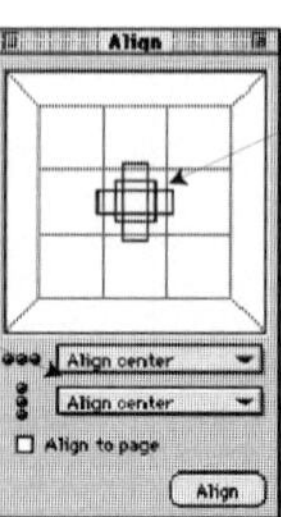

In this example, the three objects were selected (A). The preview window was clicked on to see a preferred alignment (B). The desired region was double-clicked, applying this alignment to the selected objects (C).

The preview method does not work well when the intent is only to align or distribute one element of the selected objects.

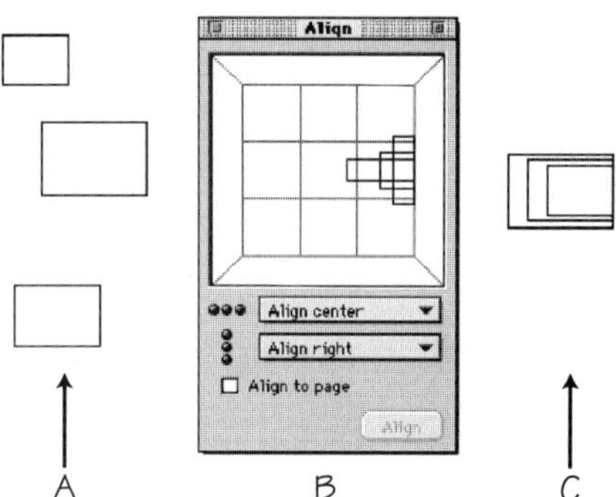

Pop-up Menu Method

If you prefer to make settings without visually manipulating the preview, make changes in the appropriate pop-up menu.

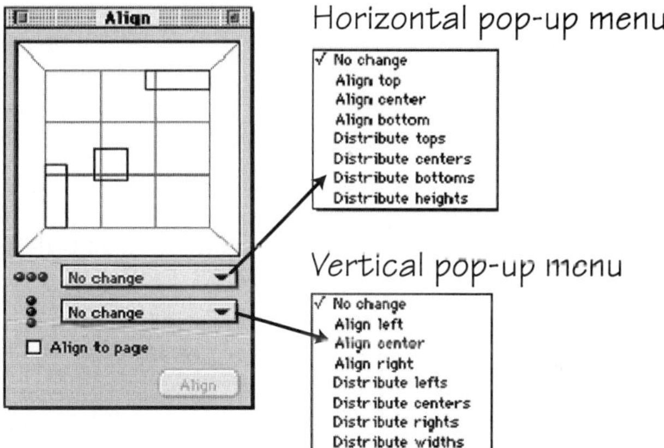

The Horizontal Align pop-up menu:

- No change — No changes are made to the vertical position of objects.
- Align top — All objects will align to the top of the highest object.
- Align center — The vertical center of all objects will become the alignment point.
- Align bottom — All objects align to the lowest point of the bottom object.
- Distribute tops — This determines the top of the highest and the lowest selected objects then distributes the tops of all other selected objects evenly between them.
- Distribute centers — This determines the centers of the highest and lowest selected objects then distributes the centers of all other objects between them.
- Distribute bottoms — This determines the bottoms of the highest and lowest selected objects then distributes the bottoms of all other objects between them.

- Distribute heights — This determines the bottom of the highest and the top of the lowest selected objects, then distributes the facing sides of the other objects between them.

The Vertical align pop-up menu:

- No change — No changes are made to the horizontal position of objects.
- Align left — All objects will align to the left of the leftmost object.
- Align center — Selected objects are aligned to the horizontal center of all objects.
- Align right — All objects align to the rightmost point of the furthest right object.
- Distribute left — This determines the leftmost and rightmost objects then distributes the lefts of objects between them.
- Distribute centers — This determines the leftmost and rightmost objects then distributes the centers of all objects between them.
- Distribute rights — This determines the leftmost and rightmost objects then creates an equal amount of space between the right edges of the objects.
- Distribute widths — This determines the right edge of the leftmost object and the left edge of the rightmost object then creates an equal amount of space between the facing edges of objects.

Align

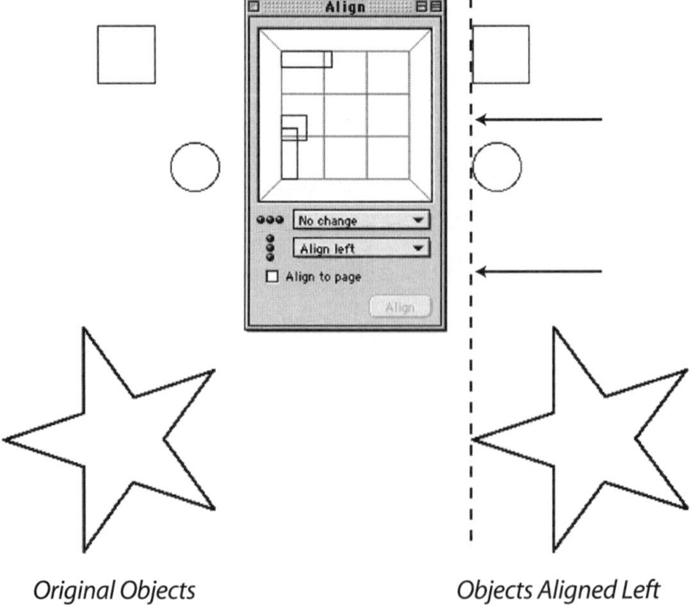

Original Objects *Objects Aligned Left*

Distribute

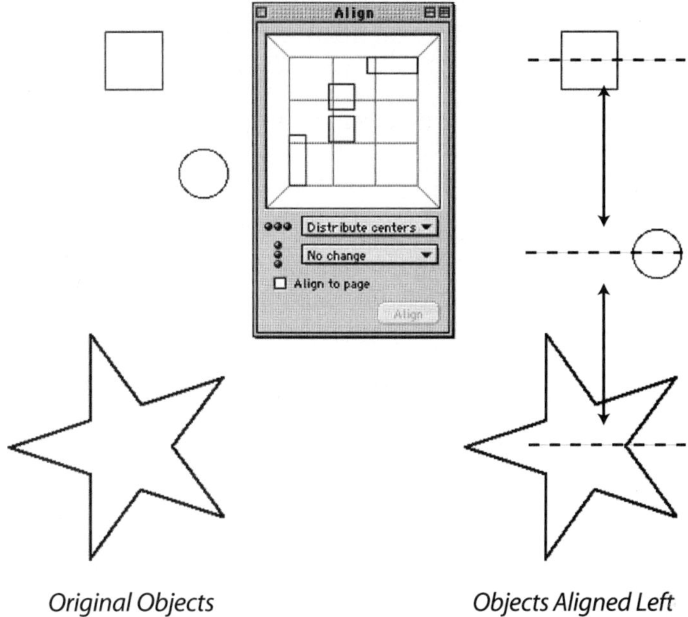

Original Objects *Objects Aligned Left*

Align to Page

When the Align to page option is checked, all selected objects are aligned or distributed in relation to the current page dimensions. If only one object is selected, Align to page must be checked to apply an alignment.

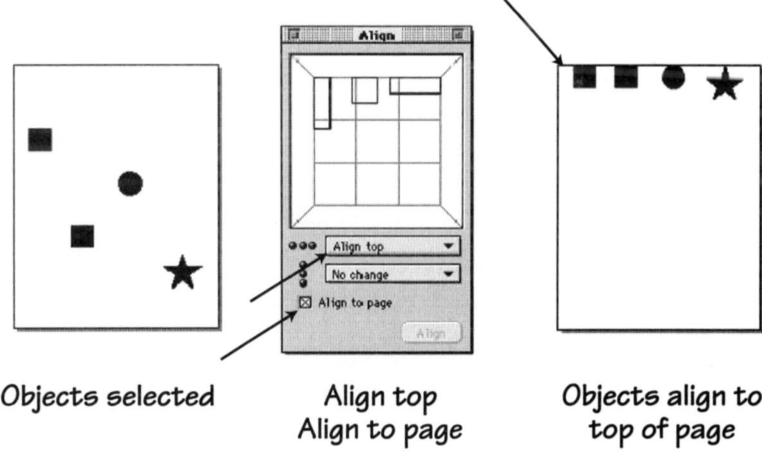

Objects selected

Align top
Align to page

Objects align to top of page

Align and Distribute with Preview Method

1. From your **SF-FreeHand** folder, open the file **Align Objects.FH9**.

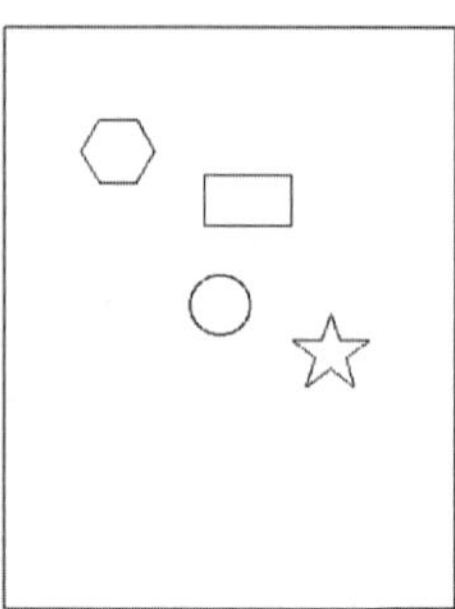

This is a great way to center an item or group of items on the page!

2. Click on each object, holding the Shift key to select them all, or choose Edit>Select All. Choose Modify>Align to display the Align panel.
3. Click on the various areas of the preview in the Align panel to see the alignments available. Align (Macintosh) or Apply (Windows) will apply these settings to the selected object, if clicked. Do not click now.

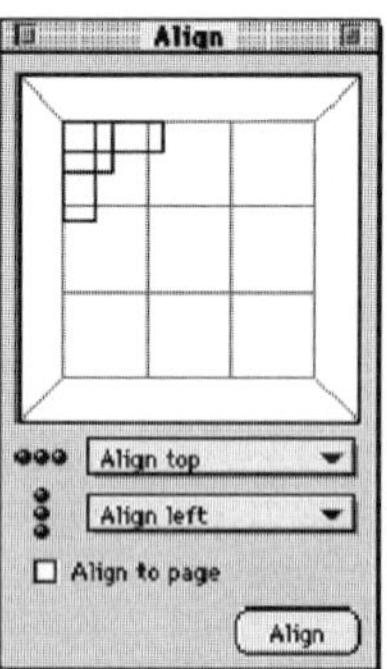

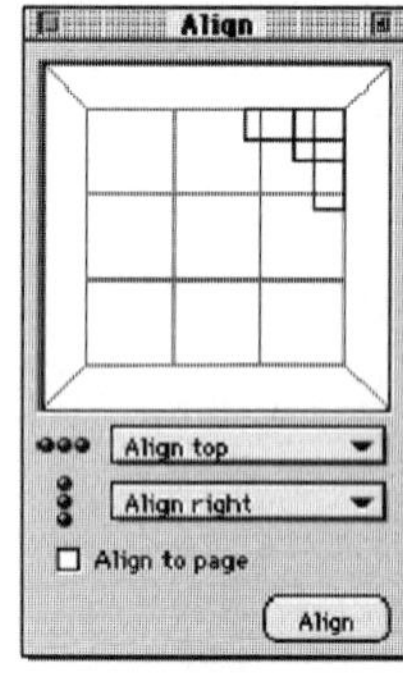

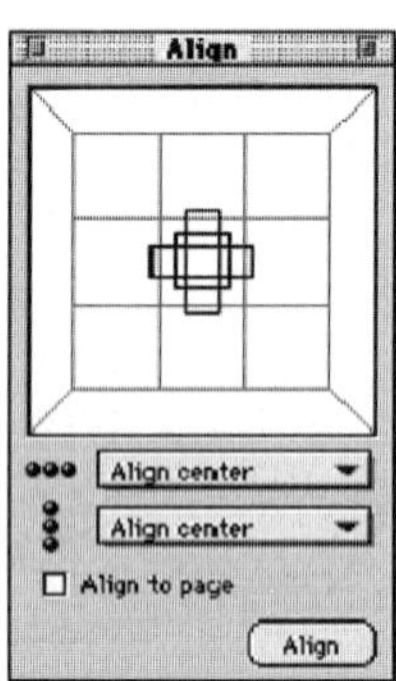

4. Double-click on any preview area you desire. Observe how the objects were affected by this method. Select Edit>Undo.
5. Double-click on a different area in the preview window. Note how the objects change with this alignment. Select Edit>Undo.
6. Click the Align to page option in the panel. Now double-click on a different area of the preview window. Notice how the alignment used the document page as a reference for its alignment. Select Edit>Undo.
7. Keep the document open for the next exercise.

Align and Distribute by the Pop-up Menu Method

1. Continue working in the open document "Align Objects.FH9", with the Align panel on screen.
2. Select all the objects in the document.

3. In the Horizontal pop-up menu, select Align top. Leave the vertical setting at No change.

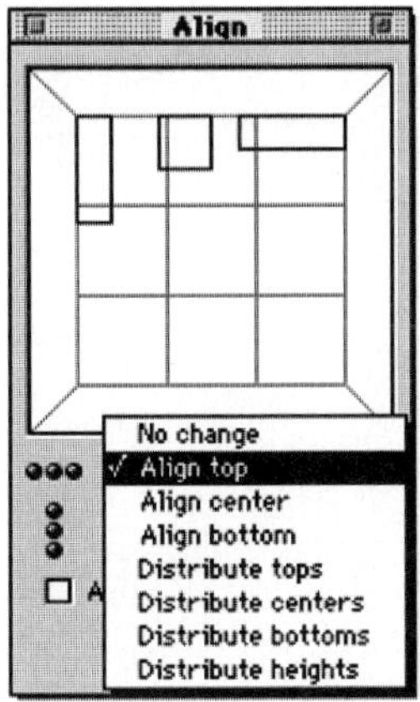

4. You might be puzzled as to why you see nothing happening on screen. You must click the Align or Apply button in the lower-right corner of the Align panel; you will then see the objects align across the top. Click the button now.

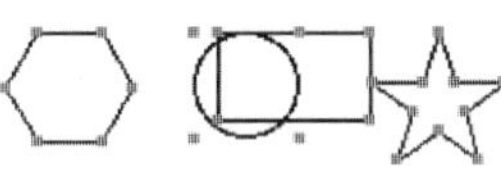

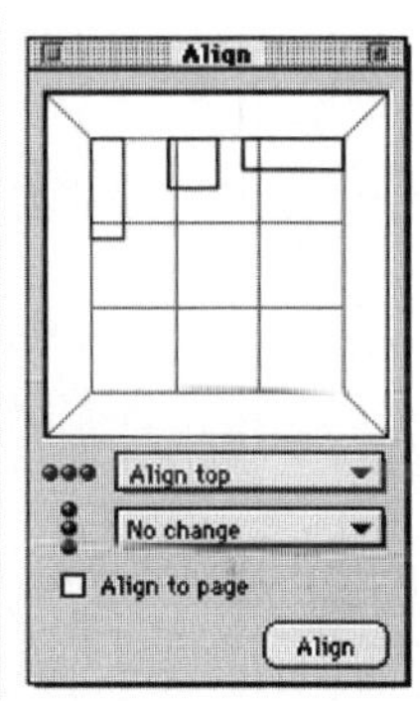

5. Select Edit>Undo, or Command/Control - Z.

6. With the objects still selected, navigate to the Vertical pop-up menu and select Align left. Set the Horizontal alignment for No change. Click Align, then Apply.

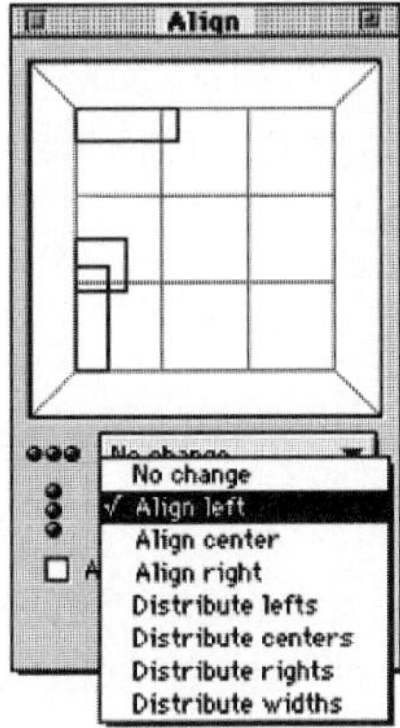

7. The objects will vertically align their left sides.

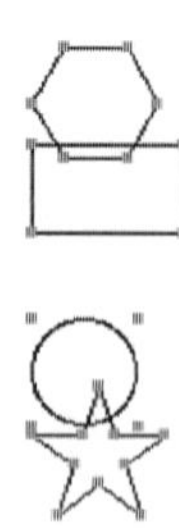

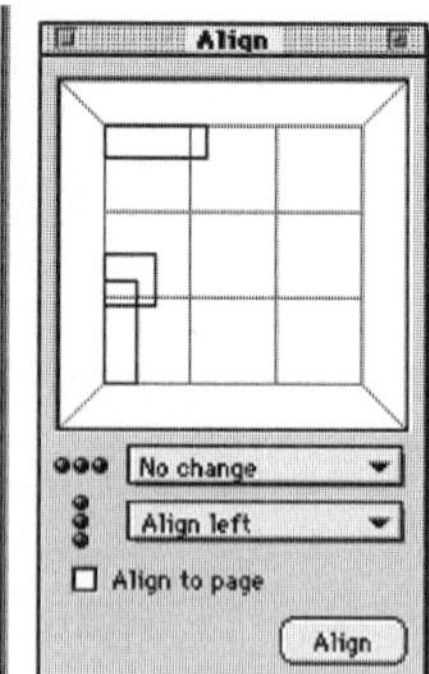

8. Click on the star and drag it down to the bottom of the page.

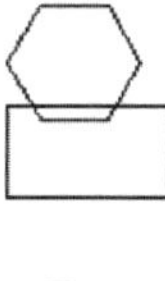

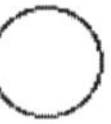

9. Select all the objects on the page. Set the Horizontal alignment for Distribute heights. This will distribute the objects up and down a vertical axis, evenly spaced based upon their heights.

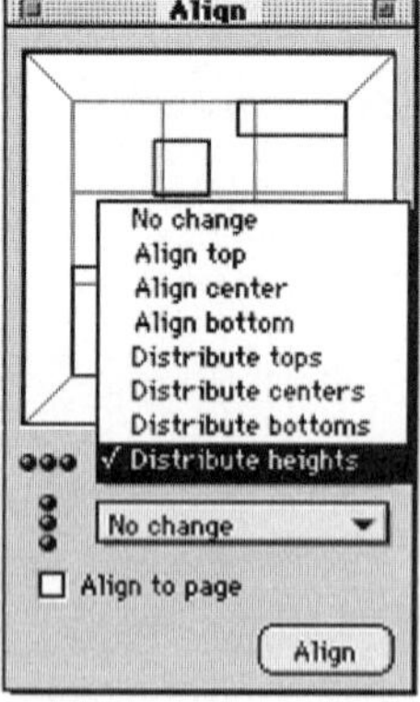

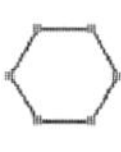

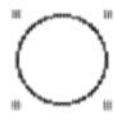

10. In the Align panel, there is an option called Align to page. If this is clicked, the objects will use the page as a guide for vertical or horizontal aligning. Select File>Revert to return the document back to its original state.

11. Select all the objects. In the Align panel, click on Align to page. In the Vertical pop-up menu, select Align left. In the Horizontal submenu, set No change. Click Align, then Apply. The objects will align left, but against the extreme left side of the page.

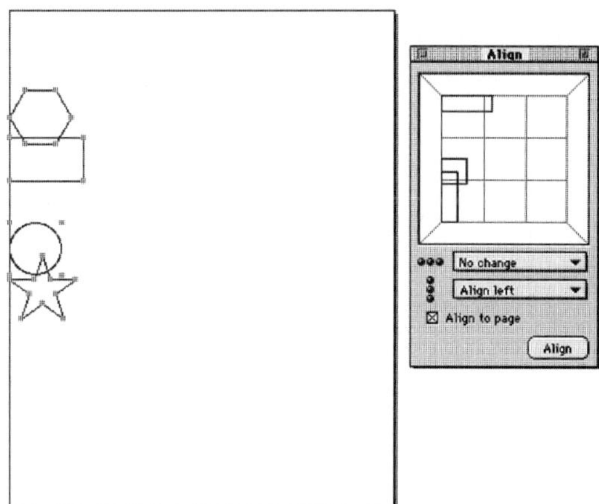

12. You have now experimented with the various alignment and distribution functions available in the Align panel. Close the document without saving.

Layers

Layers are one of FreeHand's most useful illustration aids — like a stacking order on steroids, and much more. Imagine a three-story building, layered vertically. Each floor has its own objects: people, offices, furniture and such, and these are independent of the same things on the other floors.

Layers are conceptually similar. If three layers are used in a document, each layer can have its own objects that can be created, modified, and manipulated independently of objects on other layers. Objects can be moved between layers, when necessary.

Layers are created and controlled in the Layers panel, by choosing Window>Panels>Layers.

The following graphic shows the controls in the Layers panel:

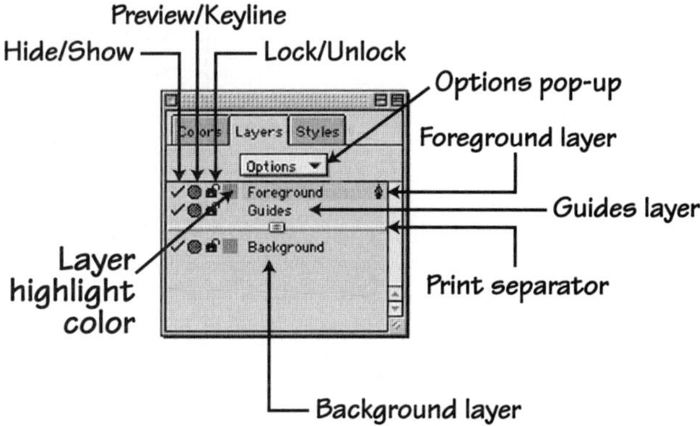

- Hide/Show — When a checkmark appears in the far left column, the objects on that layer are visible. You would uncheck the column to hide the layer, check it to show the layer.

- Preview/Keyline — When the Circle icon is solid, the layer is in Preview mode; when it is a hollow circle, the layer is in Keyline mode. Click the Circle icon to toggle between modes.

- Layer highlight color — This allows you to change the default selection color for each layer to help differentiate them. Each layer is assigned a different color.

- Lock/Unlock — When the Padlock icon is open, the layer is unlocked. When it is clicked closed, the layer may not be edited. Click the Padlock icon to toggle between locked and unlocked.

- Options pop-up — This menu offers several selections to create, duplicate, or remove layers; merge selected or foreground layers; turn all layers on or off; and move selected objects to the current layer.

- Foreground layer — This is the default layer created in all new documents.

- Guides layer — This default layer is used to create and manipulate page guides. Any vector path assigned to this layer turns into a guide. Ruler guides are shown, hidden, and locked on this layer. The guides layer is a non-printing layer.

- Separator — The Separator bar divides the layers into two groups: foreground layers, which display in full-intensity (above the bar) and background layers, which are dimmed non-printing layers (below). Except for the guides layer, all layers above the bar will print if they are visible.

- Background layer — This layer is used to hold objects that you want to appear grayed out for use as templates. Any object, whether vector or raster, will appear dimmed. Objects on the background layer do not print.

The Layers Options

Use the Options pop-up menu for adding, removing, duplicating, and viewing layers.

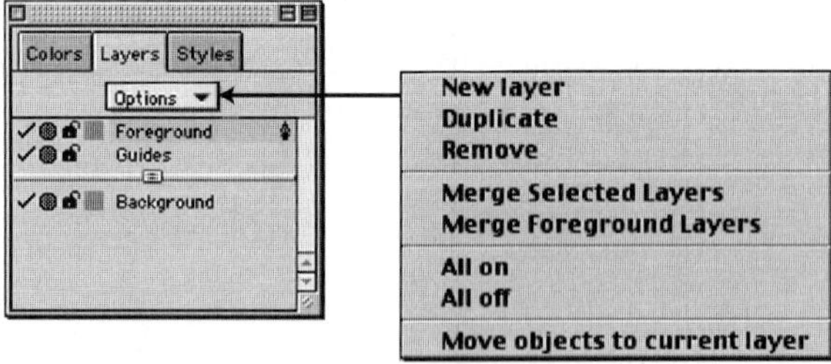

The Options pop-up menu offers the following selections:

- New layer — This option adds a new layer to your document.

- Duplicate — This option duplicates the currently selected layer.

- Remove — This option deletes the selected layers and all objects on those layers.

- Merge Selected Layers — All layers that are selected in the menu are merged into a single layer.

- Merge Foreground Layers — All layers that are above the separator bar are merged into one.
- All on — This option makes all layers visible.
- All off — This option hides all layers.
- Move objects to current layers — This option moves selected objects to the selected layer.

Managing Layers

When you begin working in a new document, all objects drawn will be placed on the foreground layer. The foreground layer is one of the three default layers. When you begin a new document, a foreground, background, and guides layer are created. All guides are assigned to the guide layer by default.

As a FreeHand operator you have the ability to change and manipulate these defaults, as well as defining your own working system. You can name and rename a layer at any time, place a layer in any order you want, or view layers as needed. The versatility of the environment allows you to express your creativity, with the fewest possible restraints.

Adding, Removing, and Duplicating Layers

1. Open **Layers Options.FH9** from your **SF-FreeHand** folder.

2. Press Command/Control-6 to access the Layers panel.
3. The objects, by default, are on the foreground layer; they need to be organized to be on separate layers.

4. In the Layers Options pop-up menu, select New layer to create a new layer.

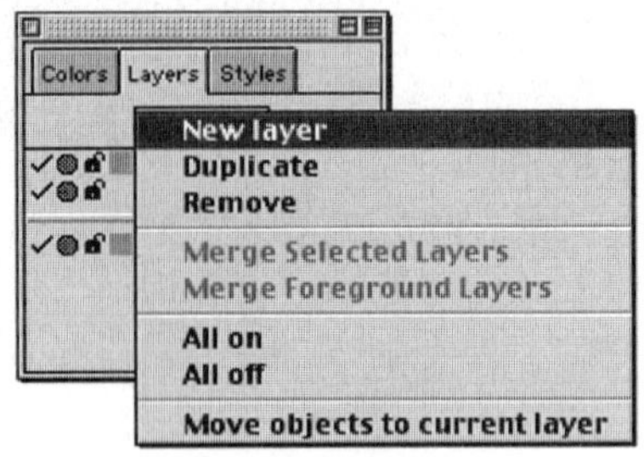

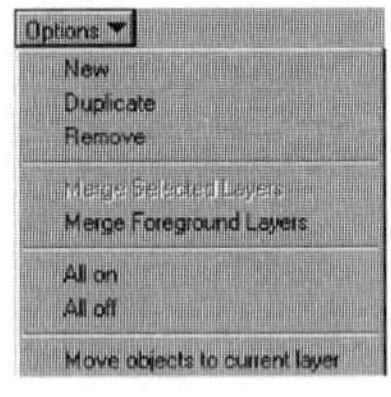

Macintosh *Windows*

5. Do this two more times to create new layers.

6. Double-click on Layer-3, rename it "Rectangle", then press Return/Enter to apply the change. Double-click on Layer-2 and rename it "Circle", pressing Return/Enter to apply. Double-click on Layer-1 and rename it "Star". Press Return/Enter to apply the change.

7. With the Pointer tool, click on the star that is peeking out from behind the top of the circle on the page. Click on the Star layer in the Layers panel.

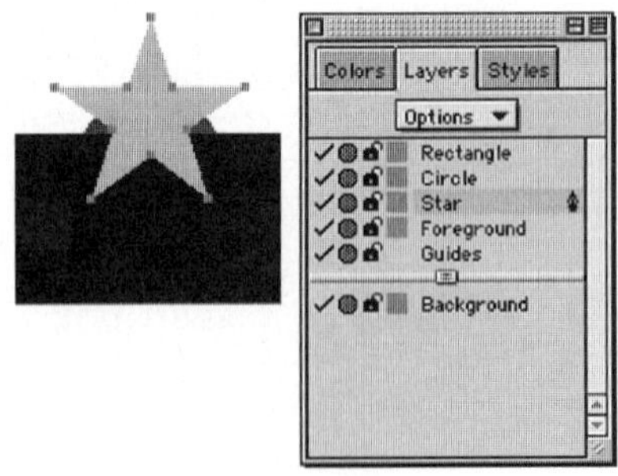

Click on the circle on the page, then click the Circle layer in the Layers panel. Now click on the rectangle on the page, and click on the Rectangle layer in the Layers panel. Press the Tab key to deselect everything. Notice that each element comes to the foreground when it is selected because it is being placed on a higher layer than the other objects on the page.

8. Click on the Foreground layer, then go to the Layers Options pop-up menu and select Remove to delete the layer.

9. Click on the Rectangle layer, then go to the Layers Options pop-up menu and select Remove to delete the layer. What warning did you get? Click Cancel so you don't delete the layer and its object. This is FreeHand's way of watching out for accidental deletion of useful objects.

10. Click on the rectangle on the page and the Rectangle layer in the Layers panel will become highlighted to show that this is the layer it is assigned to. Click on the star and observe the Layers panel change.

11. With the Star layer still highlighted, go to the Layer Options pop-up menu and select Duplicate. A new layer appears with the word "copy" in its name. Click on the star on the page and move it off to the right. What do you see? The Duplicate option not only duplicated the layer, but it made a copy of the object assigned to it.

12. Select Edit>Undo twice to undo the move and layer duplication.

13. You have now succeeded in using selections in the Layer Options pop-up menu and have observed how they affect the layers and objects in the document.

14. Keep the document open for the next exercise.

Layer Priority

The order in which the names appear in the Layers panel determines which layers are in front of or in back of others. The priority of layers is from the top of the layers list to the bottom. The layer at the top of the list contains the foremost objects. As the layers go down the list, the objects assigned to them are behind the objects belonging to the layers above them. The layer at the bottom of the list contains objects that are behind all others.

In this example the four objects are each assigned to their own layer. At the top of the layer list is the Circle layer. It is in front of the other objects.

If the Circle layer was dragged down to the bottom of the list, its object, the circle, would be behind the other objects.

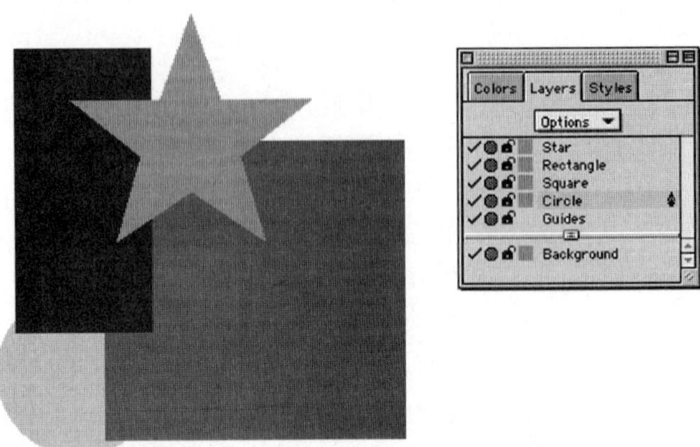

If the Square layer was dragged up to the top of the list, its contents would be in front of all the other objects. Notice where the square is now.

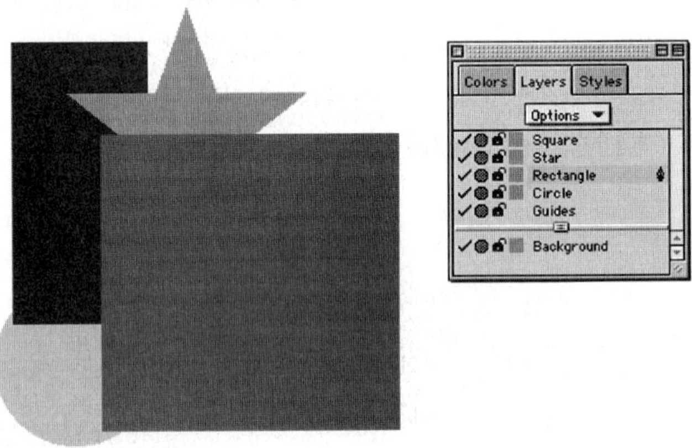

Rearranging Layer Priority

It is quite easy to change the order of the layers. Often one layer will need to be moved in front of another. Simply drag a layer to the location within the Layers panel that works best for your design.

It the following, it was desired to place the square object behind the star but in front of the rectangle. This was done in the Layers panel by dragging the Square layer below the Star layer but above the Rectangle layer.

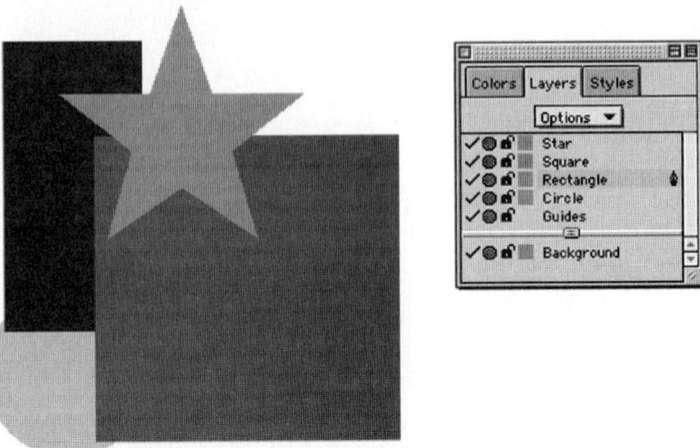

Using Layers to Organize Objects

1. Continue working in the open document, **Layers Options.FH9.**
2. In the previous exercise, you assigned each object to its own layer, but they still are not organized in layer priorities.
3. Drag the Star layer up to the top of the Layer panel.

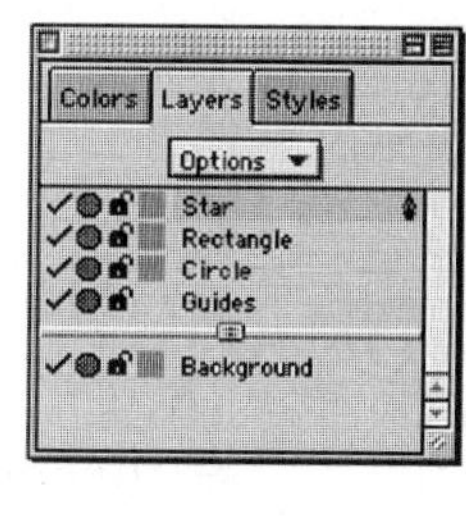

4. Drag the Rectangle layer down, just under the Circle layer.

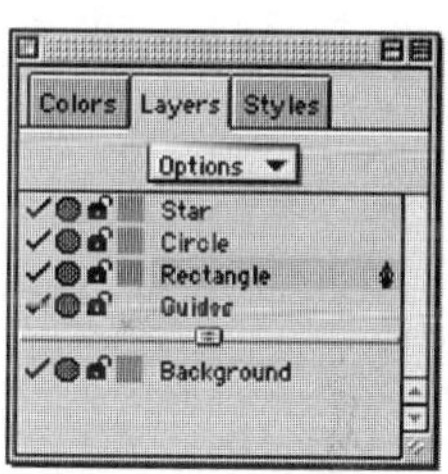

5. You have now succeeded in rearranging the objects in relation to their front/back positions by dragging the layers into a different order of priority.
6. Keep the document open for the next exercise.

Reassigning Objects to other Layers

As easily as layer order can be rearranged, so can the layer to which an object is assigned. Frequently an object will need to be moved to another layer. When an object is selected, the layer to which it is assigned becomes highlighted in the Layers panel. With the object still selected, click the other layer to which you want to move the object; the new layer will become highlighted to indicate the change.

In the following example the star was selected, showing the highlighted Star layer. The Rectangle layer was clicked to reassign the star to this layer, changing the star's position.

Be careful when you are clicking between layers in the Layers panel. If any objects are selected, you will unknowingly reassign them to other layers.

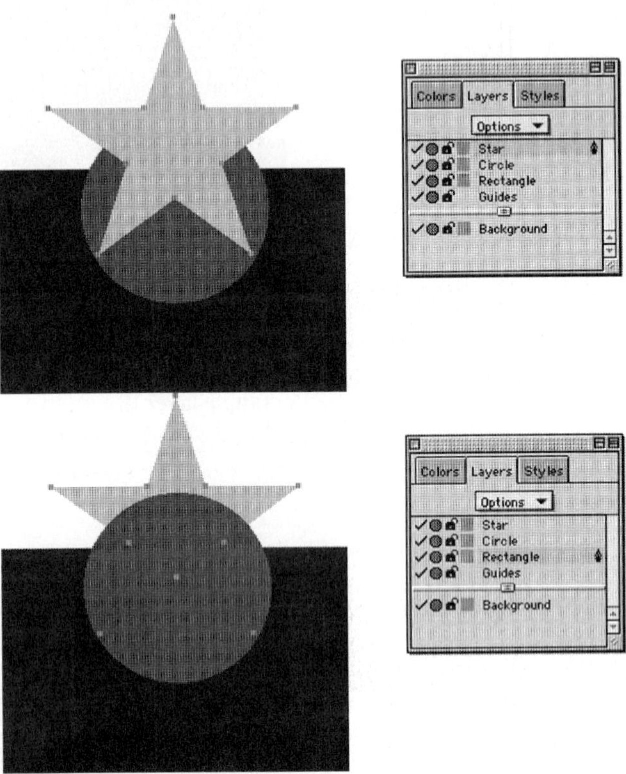

Settings for Work Efficiency

FreeHand allows individual layers to be hidden, viewed, locked, or modified. Learning when to change views and lock status is critical. Changing views too often leads to lost time; changing views too infrequently also equals poor productivity. The same goes for locking layers. Knowing when to change settings will eventually become instinctive.

Hide/Show

Change the visibility of a layer to see what it obscures. Toggle the checkmark on to show the layer; off to hide the layer.

Preview/Keyline

Use the Keyline/Preview toggle to easily select objects in complex drawings. The solid gray dot indicates that a layer is currently being viewed in Preview mode; an empty circle with a tiny "x" indicates Keyline mode.

In this example, the Star layer Preview/Keyline circle icon was clicked, which puts the star's layer into Keyline viewing mode.

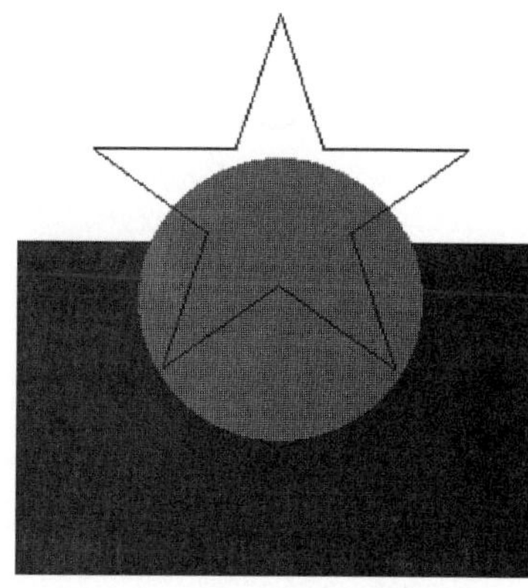

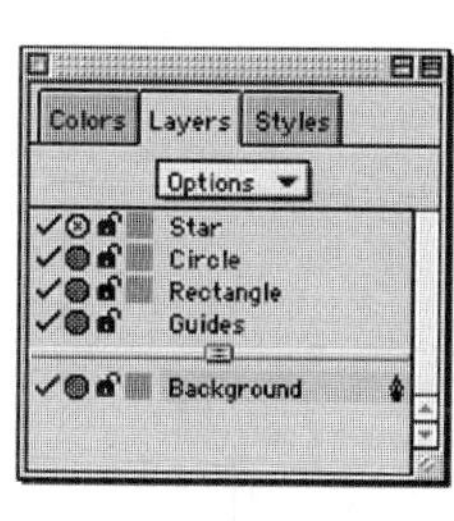

The Modify>Lock feature allows objects to be clicked on; while the Layers locking feature totally isolates the layer objects and will not allow them to be clicked on and selected.

Lock/Unlock

If you find yourself constantly selecting the wrong object, altering it by accident, then undoing, it's time to lock your layers. Plan ahead and use the Layers panel and its functions to your benefit. Allow yourself room to make changes. Sometimes locking entire layers is the only way to edit that one path that you can't ever seem to select. Click the Padlock icon to the left of a layer to lock it; click again to unlock it.

In the following example, the Star layer Padlock icon was clicked to lock the layer. All objects were selected and moved, but the locked star was not affected.

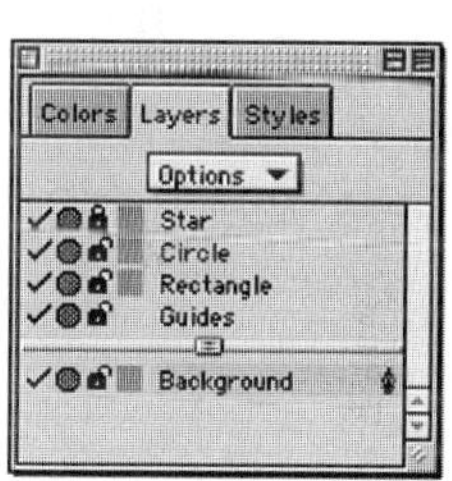

Locking, Viewing, and Previewing Layers

1. Continue working in the open document, **Layers Options.FH9**.
2. In the Layers panel, click the Padlock icon for the Circle layer.
3. Click the Hide/Show checkmark on the Rectangle layer to hide the object.
4. Click the Preview/Keyline circle icon for the Star layer to toggle the star to Keyline mode.

5. The design should look appear as follows:

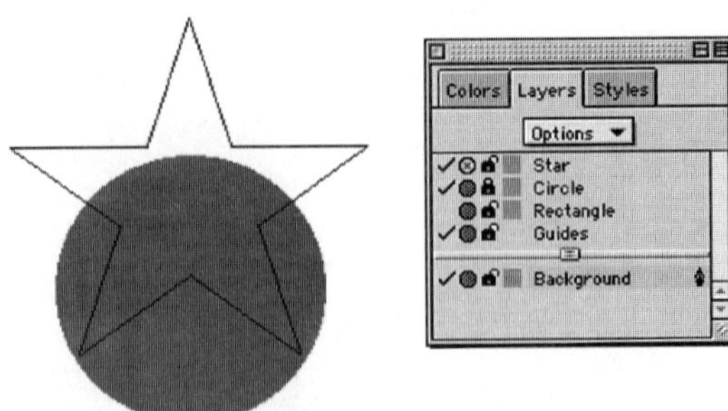

6. Try to click on the locked circle object and move it. What happened? Click on the Padlock icon on the Circle layer to unlock the circle. Now try to click on the circle and move it.
7. Click on the Preview/Keyline icon of the Star layer; the star's layer returns to Preview mode.
8. Click on the Hide/Show checkmark of the Rectangle layer; the rectangle's layer returns to view.
9. You have now used the Layers panel to control the objects and their attributes on the page.
10. Close the document without saving.

Summary

In this chapter you have learned about and performed a number of interactions between objects. You have explored the stacking order of objects with a single layer, and have learned how to move objects forward, backward, to the front and to the back. You have also learned how to lock, group, and ungroup objects. In addition, you have learned several methods of aligning objects with each other and with the page, and have practiced those methods.

You have progressed beyond working on a single layer, and have explored working with multiple layers, which includes viewing, locking and unlocking, and managing the layers of a document. You have learned about layer priority and have moved objects between layers.

Complete Project B: Mask Art

CHAPTER 8

Advanced Drawing

CHAPTER OBJECTIVE:

To work with the advanced drawing features of FreeHand that enable you to create special effects. In Chapter 8, you will:

- Learn to use the various Lens fills to enhance illustrations.
- Explore and use the Envelope features to distort objects.
- Work with the Perspective tool and the Perspective Grid.
- Learn to use one, two, or three vanishing points to achieve a variety of perspectives.
- Learn the variety of features of the Trace tool, and explore how to properly use it to convert objects.
- Use the Trace tool to trace line art and photographs, using appropriate tool settings.
- Understand and use Symbols and instances.

PROJECTS TO BE COMPLETED:

- Dinner Time (A)
- Mask Art (B)
- Tropical Treasure Logo (C)
- Grocery Ad (D)
- Ball and Mirror (E)
- No Clowning Around (F)

Advanced Drawing

So far, you've learned to work with the basic FreeHand shapes and to create straight and curved lines and closed shapes. You know how to fill shapes and modify strokes. You have also learned to manage documents using a variety of techniques. In this chapter, you will work with some of FreeHand's advanced tools to create special effects, perspective drawings, conversions of scanned images into vector drawings, and symbols and instances.

Using Lens Fills

In addition to the basic fills, gradients, patterns, and tiles, FreeHand has another means of applying effects to images: the lens. A lens is an effect that is overlaid on an image, causing an interaction between the object on top and the object below it, including imported bitmap and EPS images. Lens effects also interact between layers, even if the layer is locked. The lens effects are Transparency, Magnify, Invert, Lighten, Darken, and Monochrome.

The Lens Fill Inspector varies somewhat from lens to lens. You may choose a color when using the Transparency or Monochrome lenses. You may adjust the opacity of the color in the Transparency lens; the Monochrome lens uses the color values of the original to create a one-color rendition of an object for the area that falls under the lens area. The Magnify lens enables you to magnify the element under the lens from 2 to twenty times the size of the original. The Invert lens creates a negative of the portion of the image that is under the lens. Lighten and Darken lenses allow you to adjust the percentage from 0 (no change) to 100 (all white or all black).

With all lenses, the "center" of the lens may be positioned, by dragging or entering x, y coordinates, at any position on the page. The lens effect may be applied to objects only; for example, the monochrome lens would not apply color to a white background. Finally a lens effect may be converted into a snapshot of the image and placed anywhere on the page.

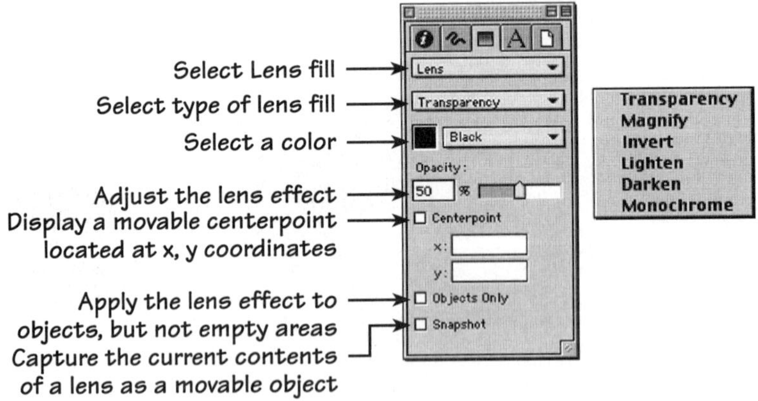

The Transparency Lens

A color is selected, then an opacity is chosen when using the Transparency lens. To create the illusion of transparency without changing an objects color, choose white. To convey the effect of two overlapping colors or beams of light, choose a color. The result will be similar to colored light striking on an image.

In this image, we placed a Transparency lens using White with an opacity of 50% around the smoke signals to create more a more “smokelike” appearance.

The Magnify Lens

This lens allows you to magnify a portion of the image from two to twenty times. When used with the Centerpoint or Snapshot option, it allows you to create a closeup of a portion of the image, while keeping the entire image in relative perspective.

Here, we placed a Magnify lens off to the side of the hummingbird. Using the Centerpoint option, we focused on the bird's head and beak.

The Invert Lens

Use the Invert lens to create a negative of your image. FreeHand uses the complimentary colors (those opposite a color on the color wheel) to determine the color's inverse.

We got fancy with this lens. First we drew a rectangle that completely encompassed the image. Then we drew a smaller rectangle in the center and, using the Punch option, created a compound object. We selected Objects Only with the Invert lens, so the white background would not be affected.

The Lighten and Darken Lenses

Each of these lenses goes from 0% to 100% addition of white or black, depending on whether you choose to lighten or darken the image.

In this image we used both the Lighten and Darken lenses. We lightened a beam of light at 25% from the moon, ending at the gondola. This was created by drawing an irregular polygon with the Pen tool. We then drew an irregular shape beneath the gondola and used the Darken lens at 50% to create a shadow.

Monochrome

The Monochrome lens creates a monochrome image from a multi-colored image. You may use any color in the document for the chroma of the final image. The effects are sometimes surprising. We are not showing an example of this lens because this book is in one color.

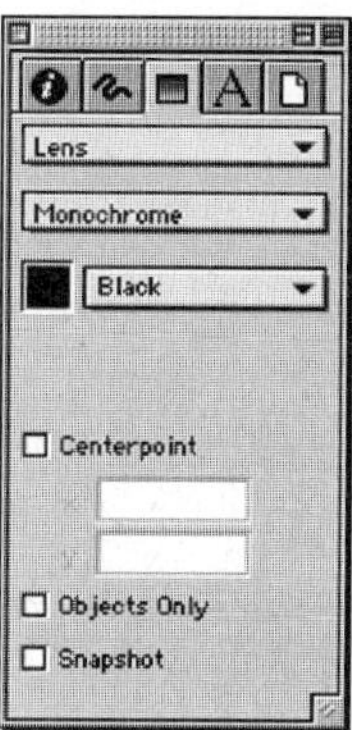

Use the Transparency Lenses

1. Open the document **Using Lenses.FH9** from your **SF-FreeHand** folder. The document should open to page 1. If it does not, select page 1 from the Document Inspector.
2. We have converted the type "Lincoln Walks at Midnight" to paths.
3. Click on the type and drag it on top of the Lincoln Memorial graphic.
4. From the Fill Inspector, set the fill type to Lens and the Lens type to Transparency. Keep the default transparency of 50%.

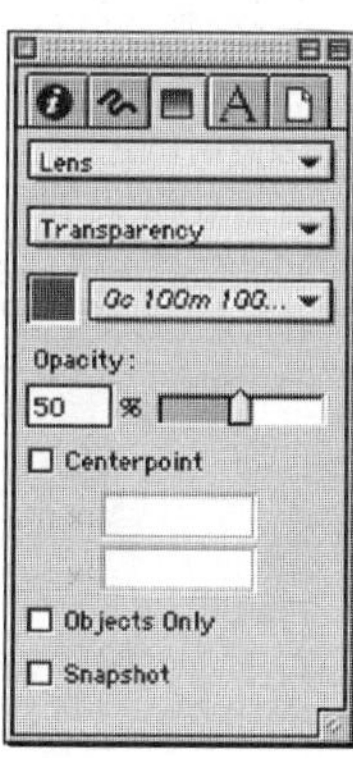

5. Notice how the letters are affected by the color of the image. They change color when crossing the white lines. Alter the opacity to achieve different effects.
6. Scroll down to the photo at the bottom of the page. We're going to zoom in on the key-grinding operation being performed in this photo.
7. Draw a circle to the right of the picture.

8. Assign it a lens fill of Magnify, and click the Centerpoint box.

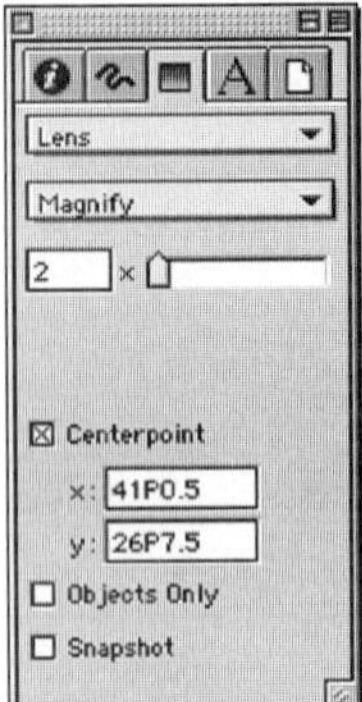

9. Drag the centerpoint from the circle to the keymaking operation

10. Experiment with other magnifications, if you wish.

11. From the Document Inspector, turn to page 2. The rest of the lenses affect color, so we'll work with them sequentially.

12. Draw a circle in the middle of the image. Assign it a stroke of None and a lens fill of Invert.

13. Sequentially assign the circle the Lighten, Darken, and Monochrome fills. Assign different percentages in the Lighten and Darken fills.

14. Close the document without saving.

Envelopes

In FreeHand, an envelope is an enclosure that contains one or more objects. The envelope allows you to distort and reshape the contents by changing the shape of the envelope. Changes are made to envelopes using any of FreeHand's path-related tools, such as the Pointer tool or the Pen tool. The Envelope toolbar is accessed through Windows>Toolbars> Envelope.

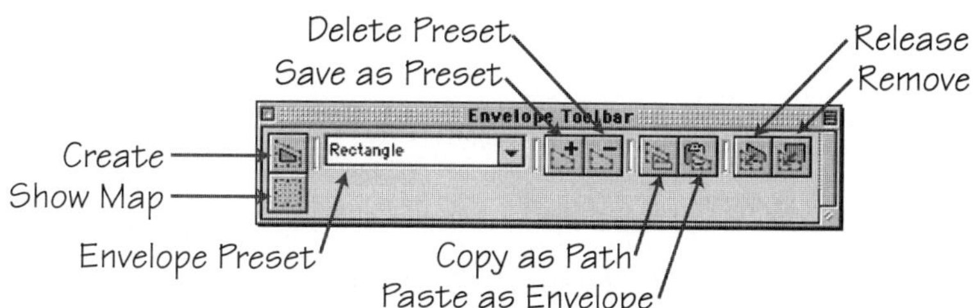

Envelopes are created with effects called presets. These are the standard presets:

Rectangle	Peak Left	Triangle
Fade Right	Peak Right	Hexagon
Fade Up	Arc	Octagon
Fade Left	Double Arc	4 Point Star
Fade Down	Reverse Arc	5 Point Star
Skew Right	Diamond	Heart
Skew Left	Circle	Starburst

Using the Envelope Tools

The Envelope tools allow you to create envelopes, copy envelopes as paths, and paste paths as envelopes. You may save any shape you have created as a preset, allowing you to use it again and again, and you may delete preset shapes. You may also release an object from an envelope, while retaining its effect, or you may remove the envelope effect from an object altogether. In addition, you may create a map of the envelope, which shows you the envelope's dynamics.

Create

After the object has been selected, and the envelope preset chosen, click the create button to apply the envelope. The distortions assigned by the preset will be applied. Further distortion may be applied to the object after the envelope has been selected.

Envelope Preset
This drop-down menu of the names or all presets (the 21 standard presets and any you create) shows a thumbnail of the preset effect when the mouse is run placed on the preset name.

Save as Preset
After a preset has been made and altered, this button may be pressed to add the new preset to the Envelope Preset list. Saved presets become a permanent part of the Envelope Preset list.

Delete Preset
Press this button to delete a preset from the Envelope Preset list. Presets deletions are permanent, but the effect of the preset on all objects to which it has been applied remains.

Copy as Path
When this button is pressed, the envelope becomes an editable path.

Paste as Envelope
This button allows you to apply any path to an object as an envelope.

Release
When this button is pressed, the preset envelope is removed from the object, and it can no longer be manipulated as a single object. The preset will remain in the Envelope Preset list.

Remove
Press this button to remove the actions of the preset envelope from an object. The preset will remain in the Envelope Preset list.

Show Map
When this button is pressed, you are presented with an overlay that shows graphically the distortions applied to the image.

You should always group objects (if multiple objects are selected) before applying a preset. If an image is constructed of multiple paths, they should be grouped, also. If they are not grouped, the Create command makes one envelope for each element, creating some interesting, but usually undesirable, effects.

A preset is selected from the Envelope Preset list.

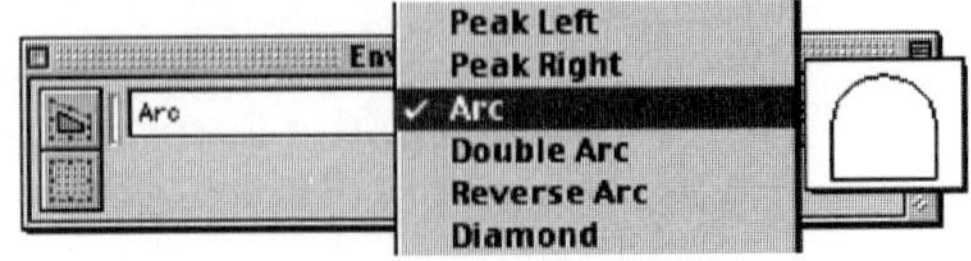

The Create button is pressed to apply the preset.

Alter the envelope further to achieve the effect you desire.

If you want to save the effect so that you can regularly apply it, click the Save as Preset button, name it, and add it to the Envelope list.

Place a Graphic in an Envelope

1. From your **SF-FreeHand** folder, open the graphic **Cruise Ship.FH9**. Select Window>Toolbars>Envelope to activate the Envelope toolbar.

2. Press Command/Control-A to select all elements of the graphic.

3. From the Envelope Preset menu, select Arc.

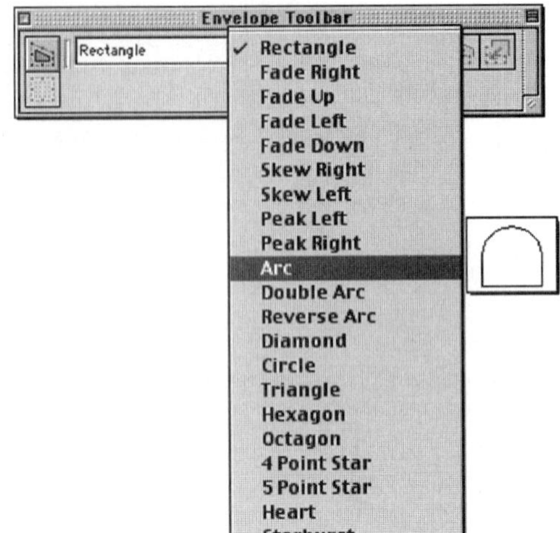

4. Press Create to apply the Arc preset to the image.
5. Oops! That wasn't what we wanted to happen. Press Command/Control-Z to undo the action.
6. With all elements still selected, press Command/Control-G to group the object. Now press Create.

7. Select the two middle anchor points on the right side of the image and pull to the right approximately 3/4″. Accuracy is not important here; we're looking for effect.

8. Work with the graphic until you're happy with it. If you create something really outlandish that you wish to get rid of, simply press Command/Control-Z.

9. To add this preset to the menu, press the Save as Preset button, and type your name into the New Envelope dialog box. Click OK.

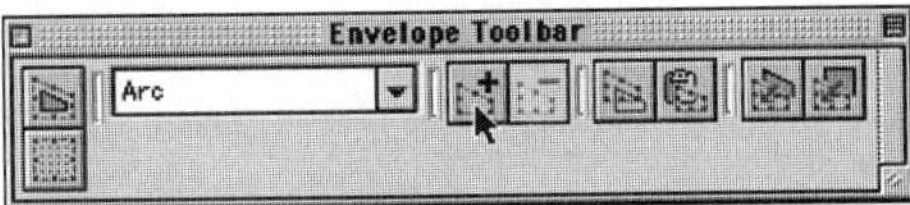

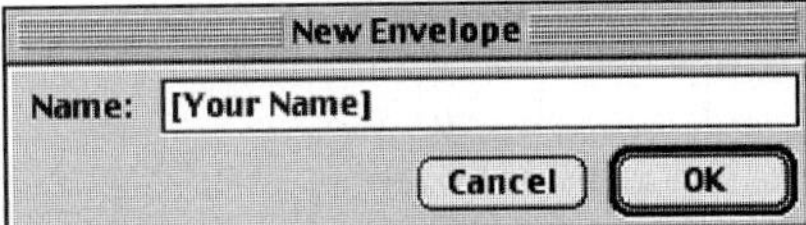

10. Save the document to your **Work in Progress** folder as "Envelope Cruise.FH9" and close the file.

More Work with Envelopes

1. From your **SF-FreeHand** folder, open **Red Car.FH9**.

2. Select All and group the objects.
3. Look at the Envelope toolbar. The envelope that you created is already at the top of the list, ready to be applied. Click Create to apply it.

4. What happens when you release the car from its envelope? Press the Release button and find out.

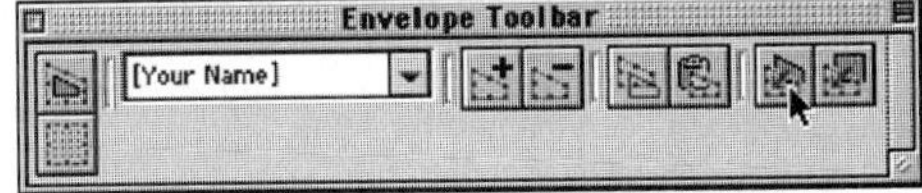

5. The envelope disappears and you are left with a grouped object that has the distortions of the envelope applied.
6. Press Command/Control-Z as many times as is necessary to reestablish the envelope. What do the envelope's distortions actually look like?

7. Click the Show Map button to see what your distortions look like in graphic form.

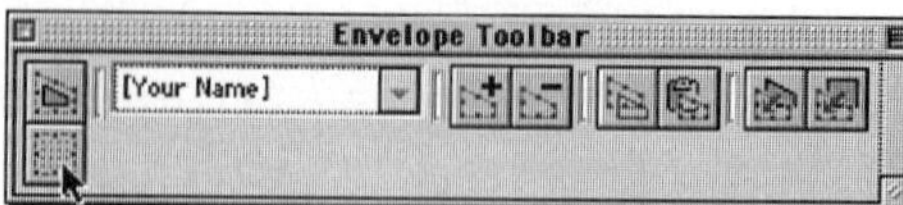

8. Press the Remove button to return the car to its original shape.

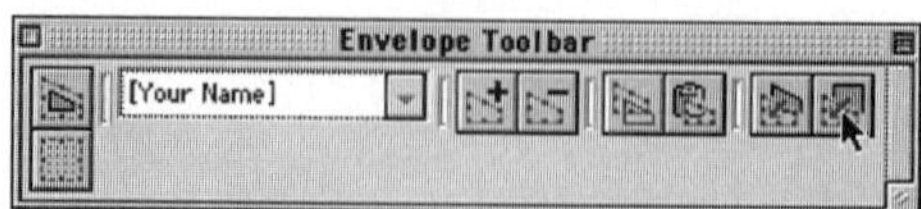

9. With the Pen tool or the Freehand tool, draw an irregular shape. Press Command/Control-C and copy it to the clipboard.

10. Click the Paste as Envelope button to create an envelope from the shape you drew.

11. Press the Save as Preset button to make this envelope usable. Assign it the name "Irregular".

12. Click on the car and assign it the Irregular envelope.

13. With the Irregular envelope still selected, press the Delete Preset button.

14. Notice that the shape did not change, even though the envelope was deleted from the envelope presets. Remove the [Your Name] envelope from the list as well.

15. Close the file without saving.

Envelopes work equally well with type, as you will see in the next section, Working with Perspective. Perspective grids use envelopes to achieve their effects.

Working with Perspective

The use of perspective in illustrations creates the illusion of three dimensions in two-dimensional space. Not only are objects in the foreground larger than those that appear to be farther away, but a single object that has dimension of its own becomes smaller as it approaches the vanishing point. So, even a single object, such as a building, a park bench, or a car may be placed in perspective.

When working with perspective in FreeHand, the perspective grid is used to define our field of perspective, and the Perspective tool is used to attach objects to the grid.

The Perspective Grid

The FreeHand Perspective Grid allows you to create customized perspective grids as a background of lines that form perspectives with one, two, and three vanishing points. A grid with one vanishing point has the perspective of either a left or right wall and the floor. A grid with two vanishing points has both left and right walls plus the floor. When a third vanishing point is added, the dimension of height is also brought into play.

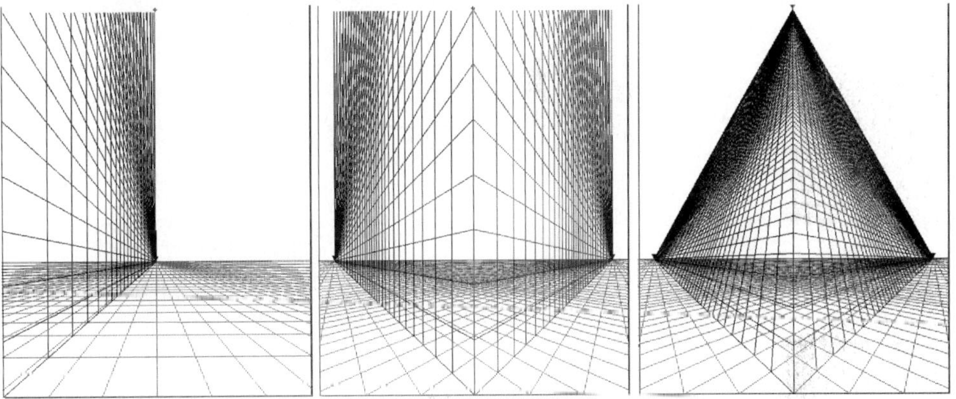

Perspective Grids showing (left to right) 1, 2, and 3 vanishing points.

A vanishing point is the point at which all grid lines touching that plane converge and the image disappears. Of course, unless we're illustrating scenes that involve "wide open spaces" such as roads, oceans, and prairies, we won't have a true "vanishing point." However, near objects will still be larger and far objects will be farther away.

You may have a number of perspective grids defined for any FreeHand document. This could be especially useful when documents have more than one page.

Show/Hide Perspective Grids

Like grids, perspective grids can be toggled on and off by choosing View>Perspective Grid>Show. When you launch a new document Perspective Grid is off.

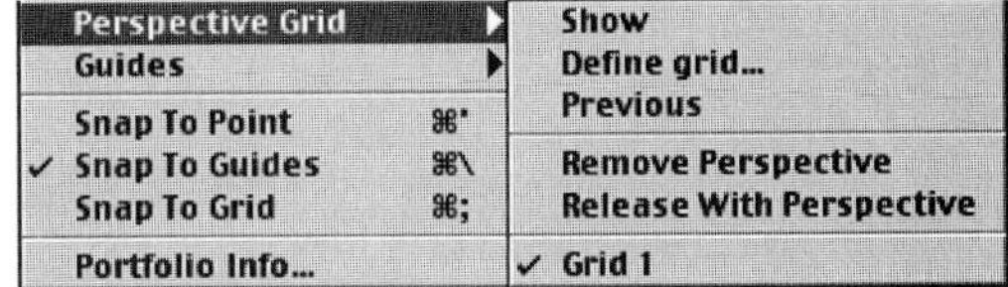

Defining Perspective Grids

Customize the perspective by choosing View>Perspective Grid>Define Grid. The Define Grids dialog box let you set the number of vanishing points from 1 to 3. You can also type in the Grid cell size and choose the grid colors.

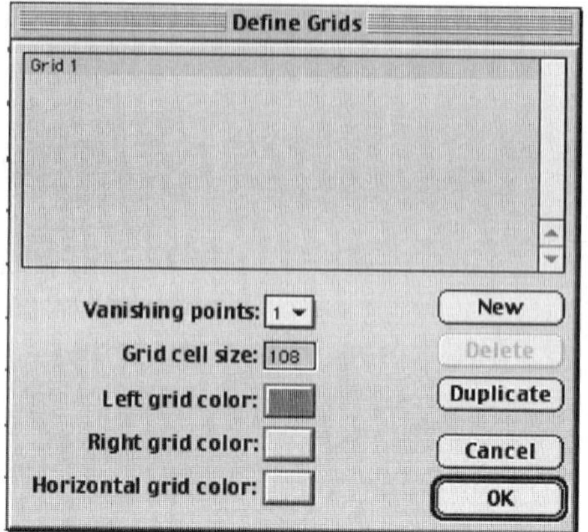

Use the Perspective Grid with the Perspective Tool

1. From the File menu, open **New Perspective.FH9** from your **SF-FreeHand** folder.

NEW

perspective

2. Select View>Perspective Grid>Show.

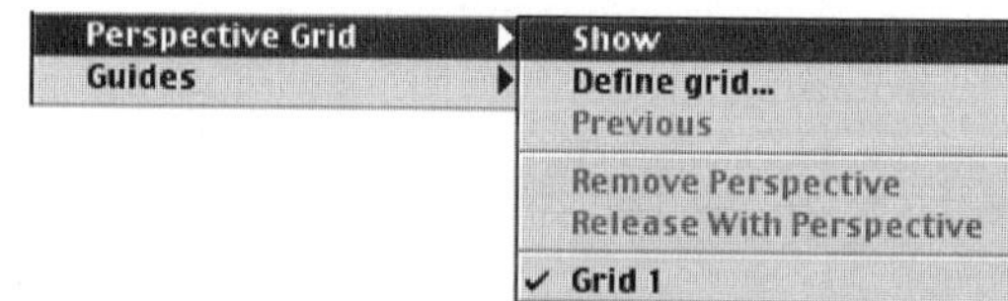

3. Select the Perspective tool from the Toolbox.

4. Select the text “New Perspective” with the Perspective tool.

5. While holding the mouse down, tap the Left Arrow key to attach the type to the perspective grid.

6. To modify the current perspective grid, use the Perspective tool and, while holding the Shift key, click and drag any part of the perspective grid. To maintain the object's relationship to the perspective grid, you must select both the attached object and the grid before dragging.
7. Select View>Perspective Grid>Define Grids.

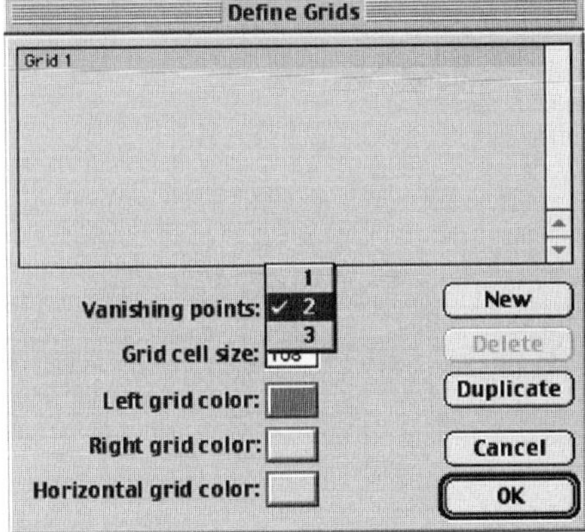

8. From the Define Grids dialog box, choose Vanishing points: 2 and click OK.

To remove an object from the perspective grid, select the object with either the Pointer tool or the Perspective tool, and choose View>Perspective Grid>Remove Perspective.

9. Select the text "New Perspective" with the Perspective tool and tap the Right Arrow key while holding the mouse down to move in line with the perspective grid.

10. Save the document to your **Work in Progress** folder and leave it open for the next exercise.

Put the Yard in Perspective

1. In the open document, **New Perspective.FH9**, go to page 2. You'll notice that it has a landscape orientation. From View>Perspective Grid>Define Grids, click New. This will create a new grid (Grid 2) with a single vanishing point. Triple-click on the name and rename it "One Vanishing Point". Name the other grid "Two Vanishing Points" just to keep them straight. Click OK.

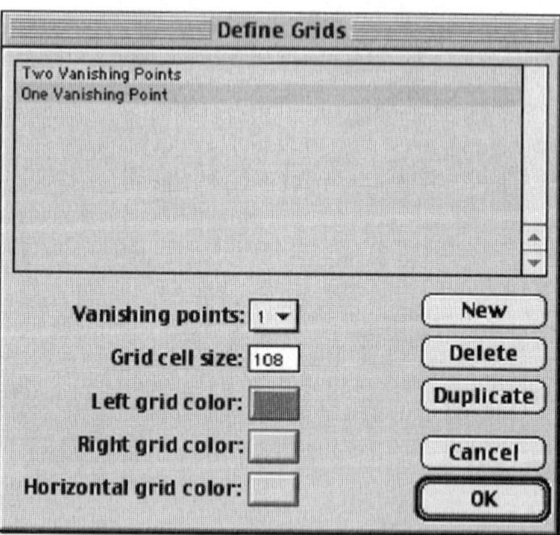

2. Select View>Perspective Grid>One Vanishing Point to view this grid. If the page rulers are not visible, from View>Page Rulers, select Show, and set the units of measurement to Inches.

3. With the Perspective tool, click on the diamond at the top of the perspective grid, above the vanishing point, and drag it to the top of the page. Then click on the outside left edge of the grid and drag it outside the page area to x= approximately -2. This alters our perspective just a bit.

4. First, let's put up the fence along the property line. You have one board for the fence on the left side of the page. Option/Alt-drag it onto the page. Click on the object with the Perspective tool, and press the Left Arrow key to attach it to the grid. Position it where the floor grid and the left wall grid meet at the edge of the page.

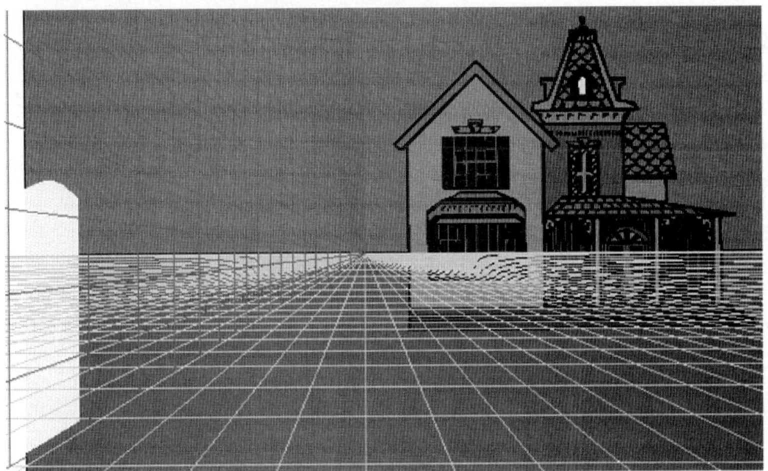

5. Option/Alt-drag a number of additional boards. Add them to the left wall to approximately the 3.5 mark on the horizontal scale. It's OK if there is a bit of space between the boards.

6. When the last perspective board is in place, switch to the Pointer tool and resize the board you have been copying from to the same height as the last board in the fence row. Set it next to the last board and Option/Alt-drag a copy of it to a position where the next fence piece would go. Command/Control-D to duplicate this action and extend the fence across the width of the "yard."

7. Marquee-select the row of fence and choose Modify>Arrange>Send To Back. Be sure to deselect the house, or you'll wonder why nothing is happening!

Use the keyboard commands for arranging the stacking order when possible:

Command/Control-F
Bring To Front
Command/Control-[
Move Forward
Command/Control-]
Move Backward
Command/Control-B
Send To Back

8. Size the tree to taste and place it behind the house. Duplicate it several times, disproportionately, then place a row of trees behind the fence, and another tree behind the fence and behind the house. You'll want to uncheck View>Perspective Grid>Show.

9. Add the bicycle, car, and dog to the scene. Size them appropriately to where they are placed in the scene. These elements are not appropriate for sizing using the perspective grid.

10. Save the file to your **Work in Progress** folder and close it.

In the preceding exercises, you have seen that the perspective grid and Perspective tool are powerful tools for adding perspective to an illustration. However, they may not be used for everything. Automation does not displace skills and experience.

Converting Images by Tracing

From time to time, you will most likely be given a scanned image or a drawing that you must scan, and you will be told that the image is to be converted to vector format. This happens often with company logos that were created prior to the mid-1980s.

You can import these images into a FreeHand document, then use the Trace tool as a first step toward converting them into vector graphics. The Trace tool will replicate the imported image as nearly as possible creating editable paths that can be filled or stroked.

The following are some factors to remember when tracing imported images:

- Tracing is not perfect. There's no magic method of converting scanned artwork into vector art. The Trace tool does a good job, but you *will* need to spend some time working on the results to ensure that it is workmanlike.
- Line art TIFF images give the best traced results.
- TIFF images in color, grayscale (8-bit), or line art (1-bit) may all be traced.
- Locked images and images on the background layer can be traced.
- The image does not have to be selected when traced.
- If you properly set up the trace parameters for the image you are tracing, you will achieve the best results.
- What you trace can only be as good as your scan. A scan of 300–600 dpi is appropriate. More resolution in the scan will result in FreeHand creating too many anchor points.

Autotracing looks at the artwork starting at the outer pixels and working inward to the center. Looking at the following sample, starting from the outer black pixels, the entire image would be traced in the following order:

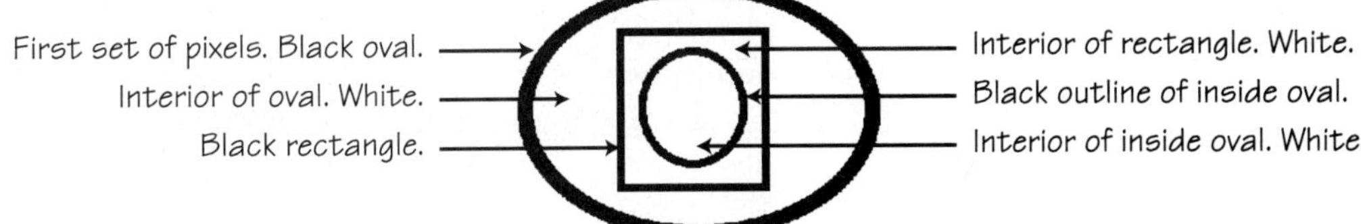

When a black-and-white image, such as this one, is traced, the Trace tool produces a variety of results, ranging from a nearly exact replica to a white circle with black stroke and a black rectangle inside, to a white circle with black stroke and, to all appearances, nothing inside. The results are dependent upon how the Trace tool is set for each type of image.

If you notice parts of the bitmap object that will not trace well, or might not provide you with the paths you need, you can make these alterations in a raster-oriented program such as Photoshop.

The Trace Tool 

When the Trace tool is double-clicked, it reveals a complexity that few would imagine, especially if they remember trace tools of the past that gave you few, if any, options.

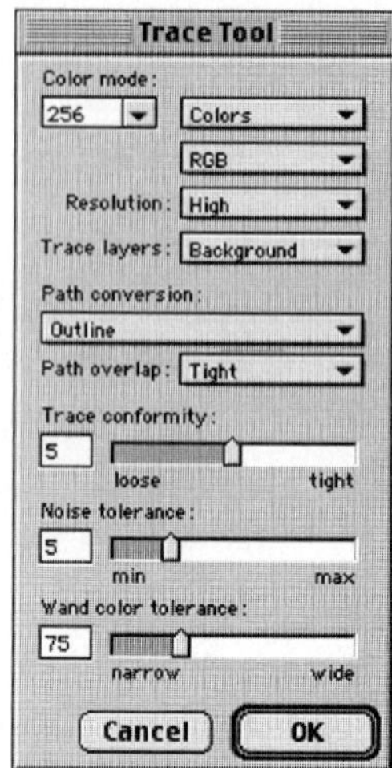

To achieve a good trace, that is both accurate and has as few points as possible, it is necessary to understand the controls available when using the Trace tool. The default settings provide good results when tracing bitmap and vector graphics, provided your computer has a reasonable amount of RAM.

Color Mode

Select the number of color levels you want to include. Levels higher than 16 (4-bit) require more RAM. The choices are 2, 4, 8, 16, 32, 64, 128, and 256. When tracing a black-and-white image, choose 2 for the most accurate tracing. If there are more colors in the original than 256, FreeHand will convert the excess color values to the nearest color value available.

Select the color representation of the resulting trace. The options are Colors and Grays. The Trace tool will convert a graphic from color to color, grayscale to grayscale, or color to grayscale.

You may also choose your color mode. If the resulting graphic will appear in print, choose CMYK. If it will appear in a multimedia presentation or on the Internet, choose RGB.

Resolution

The choices available are Low, Normal, and High. As you would expect, Normal will capture more detail than Low, and High will capture more detail than Normal. Using lower settings allows you to work with less RAM available. When working on the Macintosh, you may need to allocate more RAM to FreeHand if you use the High setting. If there is insufficient RAM available to use the setting you have chosen, FreeHand will use the highest setting for which sufficient RAM is available.

Trace Layers

In this section, you determine which layers you will trace. You may choose Foreground, Background, or All. It is a good idea to select Background. That way you can place the image to be traced on the background layer, lock it, and leave it there while you make any necessary adjustments to the tracing. If the background layer is locked, your tracing will be placed on a foreground layer.

Path Conversion

This important setting directs FreeHand how to generate the path, which may be an open or a closed path. The choices are Outline, Centerline, Centerline/Outline, and Outer Edge.

- Outline — When this method is chosen, FreeHand traces the outside borders of all the graphic elements. The traced objects are closed, filled paths. The Path overlap pop-up menu is displayed. Choose None when tracing logos, line art and text. Choose Loose when tracing continuous-tone images, to prevent spaces from developing between tones. Choose Tight for precise color tracing.

- Centerline — When this method is chosen, FreeHand traces at the center of the graphic strokes. It is best for tracing schematics and technical drawings that have almost no filled areas. Only outlines result from this tracing method. The Uniform lines checkbox is displayed. When the checkbox is displayed, the trace object will consist of uniform lines of one point, even if the original had lines of varying widths. When the checkbox is not displayed, open paths with varying stroke widths are generated.

- Centerline/Outline — When this method is chosen, FreeHand determines, on the basis of the information entered in the Open Paths Below dialog box, what attributes should be given each trace path. In the Open Paths Below dialog box, a value of 2 to 10 pixels may be entered. This value determines the value below which FreeHand will draw an open, stroked path, as opposed to a closed path.

- Outer Edge — When this method is chosen, FreeHand traces only the outer edge of the graphic, providing an accurate clipping path so that the original graphic may be pasted inside.

Trace Conformity

Using either the slider or entering a value from 0 to 10 in the dialog box, you define how closely the traced path will conform to the lines of the original graphic. A setting of 10 produces a tracing that closely conforms to the original, but may have too many anchor points.

Noise Tolerance

Using the slider or entry field, a value from 0 to 20 may be entered. This determines how much data FreeHand will keep with the file in the form of stray pixels (noise). The higher the setting, the more FreeHand ignores noise. Noise often occurs in bad scans or in scans from originals that are not crisp.

Wand Color Tolerance

This selection determines the Trace tool's sensitivity in selecting areas of contiguous color, through a color range of 0 to 255, with 0 being the most sensitive to color change and 255 being the least sensitive. This setting allows you to select specific areas of an illustration based on color. When the selection has been made, the selected area is clicked again, revealing the Wand Options dialog box, where you may choose to Trace selection or to trace only the edges of the selected areas by choosing Convert selection edge.

Trace Line Art

1. Choose File>New to create a new document.
2. Import and place the image **Little Nipper.TIF** from the **SF-FreeHand** folder. Click the Background layer in the Layers palette, and click the Lock button to lock the layer. This will force FreeHand to place the tracing on the foreground layer.

3. Double-click the Trace tool in the Toolbox. Set the Color mode to 16, Colors, RGB, the Resolution to Normal, Trace layers to Background, and Path conversion to Outline, with a Path overlap of None. Leave the Trace conformity and Noise tolerance settings at their defaults. Click OK.

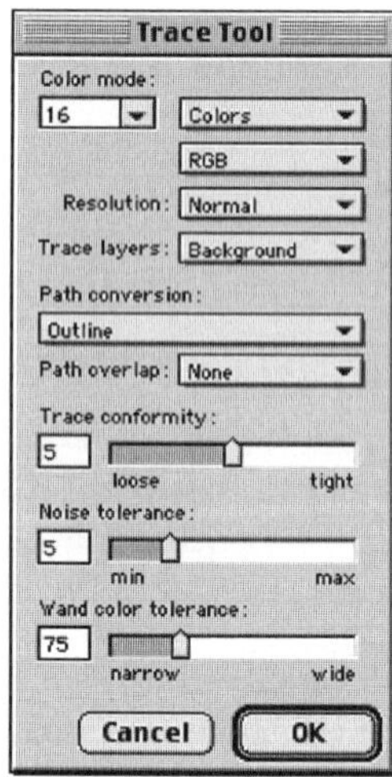

4. With the Trace tool active, drag a marquee around the image with the cursor. This will trace the bitmap pixels.

5. The image is traced and automatically selected. Move the paths off slightly to the right and compare this image with the one on the background layer. If you wish, unlock the image on the background layer and bring it to the foreground for comparison.

6. Click on Nipper's shirt and drag it to the right. What do you see? That black "undershirt" is the way FreeHand creates its paths in this drawing mode.

Press Command/Control-Z to put Nipper's shirt back on.

7. Select Keyline mode to see the paths more clearly. When selecting the paths to paint, it is sometimes easier to click on them in Keyline mode.

8. Revert to Preview mode.

9. From the Color List Options pop-up menu, select the Crayon library of colors. Holding the Shift or Control key, select the colors to paint the little critter. He is a little alligator, so select a dark green for the color of his skin. Use your imagination for the rest. When you're finished selecting, click OK.

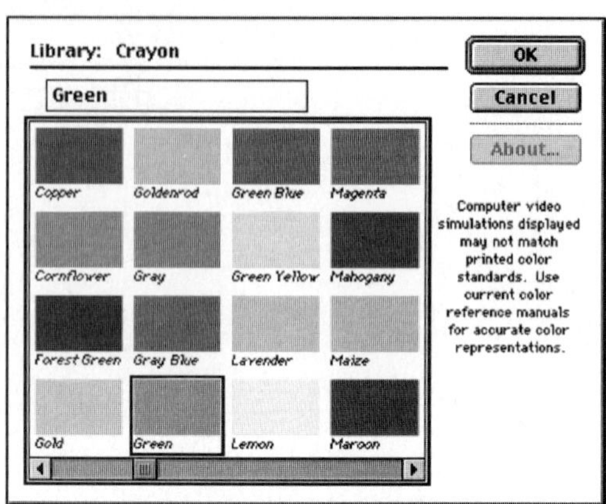

10. Use the new colors in the Color List, to paint the autotraced paths of the Little Nipper alligator.

11. When you finish, Save As the file in FreeHand Document format, naming it "Little Nipper.FH9", into your **Work in Progress** folder, and close the document.

Autotrace a Photograph

1. Create a new document. Click on the Background layer to make it the active layer.

2. Choose File>Import. Navigate to your **SF-FreeHand** folder and import **Girl in Hat.TIF**. She has been imported directly to the background layer. Lock the layer.

3. Double-click the Trace tool in the toolbox. Set the Color mode at 256, Grays, and RGB. Set the Resolution as Normal, the Trace layers as Background. Choose Outline as the Path conversion method, with a Loose path overlap. Leave the trace conformity and noise tolerances at their defaults. Click OK

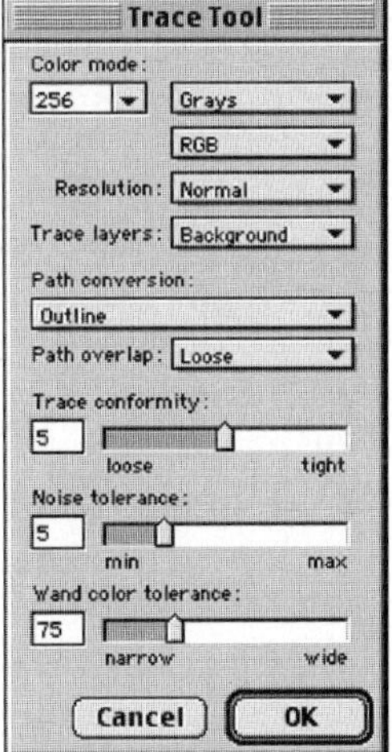

4. With the Trace tool, drag a marquee around the photo.

5. With the entire image still selected, drag the paths off to the right, so you can see the tracing result more clearly. (Click on an area that is gray, rather than in the cluster of anchor points.)

6. Press Tab to deselect the image.

7. With the Pointer tool, click on the brim of the hat and drag the selected path off to the right; click again on the hat brim and drag this path off to the left. This shows you how FreeHand separates the colors or shades of gray into separate paths.

8. Unlock the imported image and delete it from the background layer.
9. Save the file as "Girl in Hat.FH9" into your **Work in Progress** folder, then close the document.

Symbols and Instances

Symbols and instances help you reduce file size when using a graphic several times within a document. Instances are references to the original FreeHand object, which is stored in the Symbols panel. The Symbols panel is accessed by clicking the Symbols icon in the Main toolbar, or through Window>Panels>Symbol.

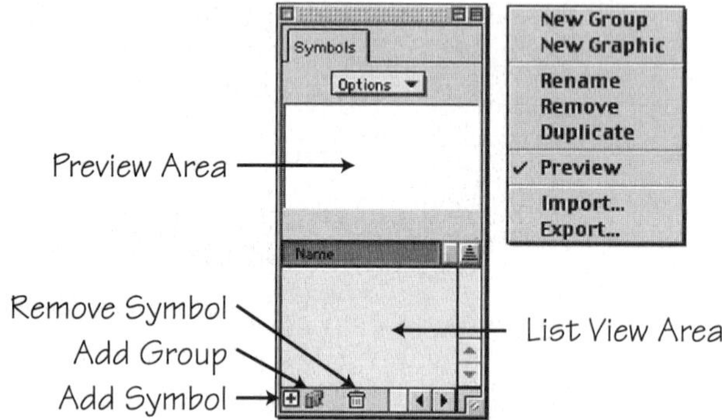

Symbols may be created from any object, text, or group by either dragging the item into the List View Area or by choosing Modify>Symbol>Convert to Symbol. Once an object has been converted to a symbol, all instances of the object may be converted back to objects or may be removed from the FreeHand document entirely.

You may have groups of objects within the Symbols panel; however, this is not particularly practical since symbol panels are created on a document-by-document basis and can be imported and exported between documents. Objects may be duplicated within the panel by selecting Options>Duplicate. To preview symbols, select Preview from the Options menu.

Create Symbols & Instances

1. From your **SF-FreeHand** folder, open the document **Symbols.FH9.**
2. If it is not already open, access the Symbols panel either by clicking on the Symbols icon in the Main toolbar or by selecting Window>Panels>Symbols.

3. From the Symbols>Options menu, select New Group.

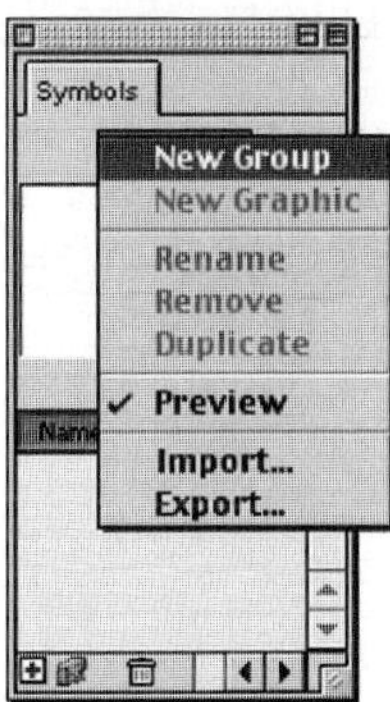

4. Click on the group in the Symbol palette to select it; from the Options menu select Rename, and type "Justice", replacing the name Group 1. Press Return/Enter.

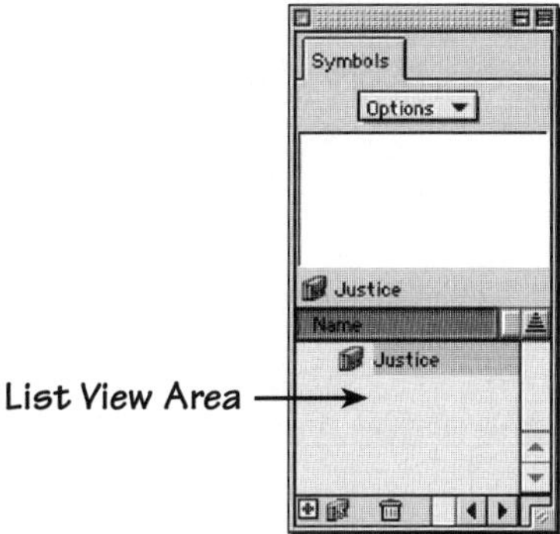

5. Click anywhere in the List View Area to deselect the Justice group, then click once on the New Group icon at the bottom of the panel to create a second group. Double-click on this group and name it "Politics".

6. With the Politics group selected in the List View Area, click on the elephant and, from the Options menu, select New Graphic. It will be added to the Politics group.

7. Double-click on the Graphic-0 icon to rename it "Elephant".

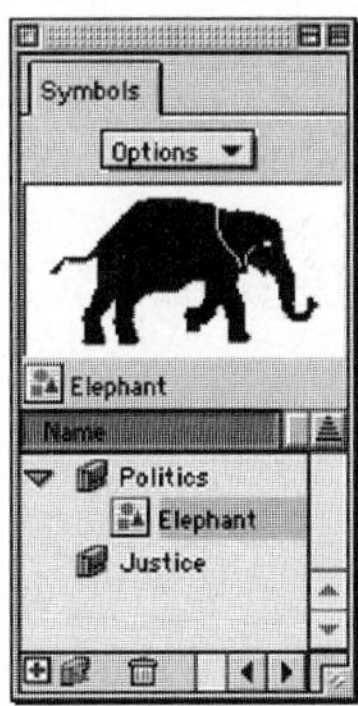

8. Click on the donkey and drag and drop it into the Politics group. Name it "Donkey". Drag the Vote 2000 graphic into the Politics group and name it "Vote 2000".

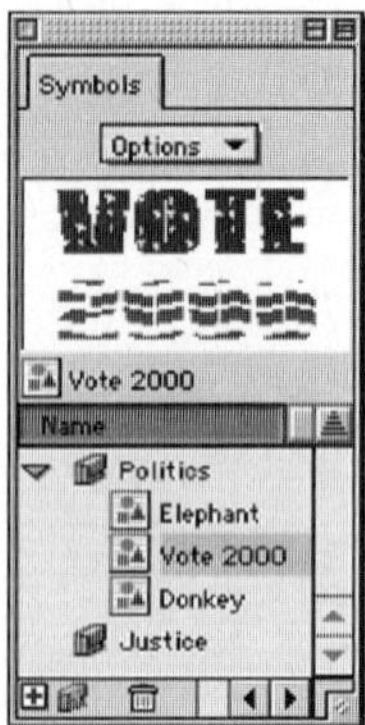

9. Drag the scales of justice, lawbooks and gavel, and "Equal Justice Under Law" slogan individually into the Justice folder, and name them "Scales", "Books & Gavel", and "Slogan".

10. From the Page Inspector Options menu, add a second page to the document and go to page 2.

11. Click on each item and drag it from its folder in the Symbols panel onto the page.

12. Let's remove an item. In the Symbols panel, click on "Vote 2000," then click the Delete icon. You have a choice as follows:

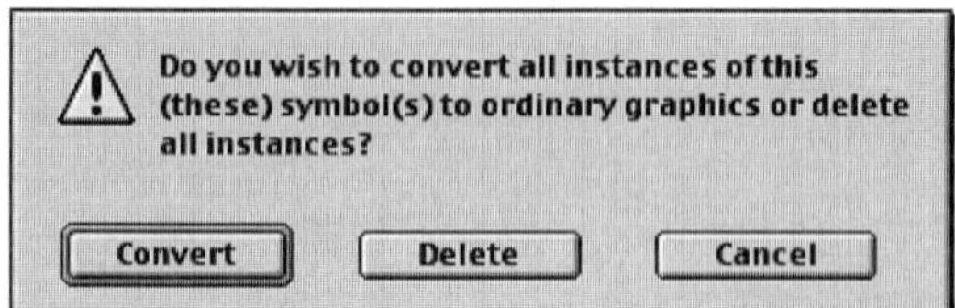

13. Select Convert/Release. The symbol is removed from the panel but is still in both places in the document.

14. Now select the "Books & Gavel" symbol. Click the Delete icon, but this time, choose Delete. It is completely removed from the document.

15. Close the file without saving.

Summary

In this chapter you have learned a number of more advanced skills. You have worked with lens fills. You have learned how to use the Envelope feature to apply distortions to an object. You have also applied the envelope in your use of the perspective grid and Perspective tool. You have learned to trace objects and to use the Trace tool to optimize the result of the operation. Finally, you have learned to use the Symbols panel to work more productively. You are now ready to learn to use FreeHand's text tools.

Project Assignment #1

Assignment

You are a graphic designer working for an architectural firm that has asked you to create a design for the front of a new house. At this point, they just want to have a design for the outside of the house, showing the front house as how it might appear from the road. This is a big account, and one that promises future work for the firm — and one which will really challenge your creative ability as a graphic designer.

A review committee made up of staff members from the architectural firm as well as the people moving into the house will be reviewing your house design when you are finished. The architectural firm has indicated to you that they want to see three different house concepts that give different looks to the client. The client is open to all design concepts, but wants the front of the house to have at least the following specifications: 5 windows, 1 entrance door, 1 picket fence, 1 mailbox, 1 porch, 1 two car garage, 2 stories and either brick or vinyl siding. The house should be drawn to the scale of 1/4″=1′

Applying Your Skills

To design the houses, you will need to use the following functions, methods, and features:

- Sketching a rough design for the three houses on paper, or creating three rough designs in FreeHand.
- Using primitive elements alone, or combined in some manner with drawing tools, to create different visual elements that effectively convey the overall shape of the houses.
- Use the basic shapes tools found in the Freehand Toolbox to create the shapes and details for the house such as the windows and doors.
- Utilize the Pen tool in conjunction with the primitive elements to create custom shapes that help convey the features of the house.
- Using alignment tools, grouping, and transformations to help layout the house.
- Applying color to the visual elements so that the house(s) each have a constant color theme.
- Cloning, reflecting, or skewing objects to provide visual interest and to assist in developing the houses.

Specifications

The houses you present should each be no larger than 6″ high at 100% and no more than 8″ wide at 100%. You should try to create each house on a new page in FreeHand.

It's challenging to create a simple yet elegant house that incorporates the specifications that the client demands. Here we're dealing with drawing basic shapes, and the ability to combine them together to create an image. Remember that you can send to back and bring to front images as you create them. You can also hide selected items. You also may need to use layers to place different shapes on dedicated layers.

Included Files

There are no files provided for this exercise. It is designed to provide you with an assignment wherein you create all the elements and graphics from scratch, using the tools and methods you've learned up to this point.

Publisher's Comments

For many professional designers, the opportunity to design something requiring creative ability — such as the front of a house for a client— represents a unique opportunity to apply their creating talents.

Creating a house design is a tremendous challenge; it must be simple, yet convey at a glance a personality. Simply seeing the house should invoke a warm feeling that a family could feel proud about when they pull into the driveway.

You aren't limited to just windows and doors either. Try to think of how you can use basic shapes to create a good house design — there are dozens of images that come to mind.

Remember too, that when you're presenting to a committee, it's likely that there will be different personalities coming into play — your challenge is to present three houses that are different from each other.

REVIEW #1

CHAPTERS 1 THROUGH 8:

In Chapters 1–8 we learned the basic operations necessary to create and work with a FreeHand document., including an understanding for the FreeHand working environment, and its menus, panels, and tools. We learned to use rulers, grids and guides as aids to working efficiently. We also learned how to use the basic tools and shapes to create images, to create images using anchor points and segments, and to paint those images. We learned how to manage single and multiple images on the page to speed workflow, and to use FreeHand's advanced drawing features to achieve special effects. Through this series of discussions and hands-on projects, you should:

- Be familiar with FreeHand's panels, menus, Inspectors, toolbars and document windows, and understand its underlying structure. You should be able to navigate through a FreeHand document. You should also understand and know how to customize FreeHand's Preferences.
- Know how to modify and position the Toolbox and to change the defaults of various tools. You have learned how to access the panels and sub panels and know how to use the five Inspectors. You have learned to create custom views, and have experienced working with the five viewing modes.
- Have learned how to use the rulers, in conjunction with guides, to accurately position elements on the page. You know how to create a custom scale, such as would be used for technical illustration. In addition you have learned to accurately position guides using the Guide Manager.
- Used the basic shape and drawing tools to create a variety of elements, including open and closed paths. In addition, you have learned two ways to move objects in your illustration.
- Know how to use the Color Mixer to create custom colors, and how to access the various color libraries and to add colors to the Color List. You have learned how to create a variety of fills and how many of them may be modified using the Fill Inspector. You have also learned to use the Stroke Inspector to work with the weight, color, endcaps, and joins of lines.
- Understand that segments are altered by working with the handles at the anchor points of the segment, and have learned to select, edit and modify these points. You have learned how to draw curved lines efficiently.
- Explored the stacking order of objects within a layer, and have learned how to use layers to manage illustrations. You know how to align and distribute elements within the layer.
- Used the various lenses to enhance illustration and explored the use of the Envelope and the Perspective Grid. Learned to convert images using the Trace tool, and experienced the variety of results achievable by altering its settings.

CHAPTER 9

Creating and Editing Text

CHAPTER OBJECTIVE:

To gain an understanding of how to work with text in FreeHand. In Chapter 9, you will:

- Begin to understand typography, and how to assign text attributes.
- Begin creating and formatting text as both an indepent design, or for incorporation into a design complete with graphics and other elements.
- Learn about the Text tool and the two types of text containers.
- Learn the importance of the Text Inspector's five sub-panels.
- Learn how to work with text outlines to create distinctive special effects.
- Import text from FreeHand, complete with the typography and effects you have created.
- Learn about several typographic special effects.
- Understand how to convert selected text into editable paths.
- Learn how to import text from word processing files.
- Learn how to link one text block to another.
- Learn how to meld text and graphics, so the elements interact with one another.
- Work with text on a path, and flow text into open and closed paths.

PROJECTS TO BE COMPLETED:

- Dinner Time (A)
- Mask Art (B)
- **Tropical Treasure Logo (C)**
- Grocery Ad (D)
- Ball and Mirror (E)
- No Clowning Around (F)

Creating and Editing Text

FreeHand offers sophisticated typographic features. Because of the variety of controls, words and text can be adjusted to fit practically any layout. Text can be created within a standard or an auto-expanding text block.

A standard text block is created by dragging the Text tool onto the page, or by entering dimensions in the Object Inspector, creating a text block of a finite size. The text block can be resized to smaller or larger dimensions by moving the corner handles of the block with the Pointer tool. This type of text container is well-suited to text that will continue for many lines.

An auto-expanding text block is created by clicking the Text tool on the page, when File> Preferences>New Text Containers Auto-expand is selected. This type of container has no defined right margin. As long as you continue to type, the container will get wider and wider, and you will need to press Return/Enter or Shift-Return/Enter to create more than one line of type. Even if the Pointer tool is used to adjust the size and shape of the container, the text will not wrap.

Assigning Text Attributes

Text is selected with the Text tool or with the Pointer tool. When selecting individual characters, words, or paragraphs, the Text tool is used. When selecting an entire text block, or several text blocks, the Pointer tool is used. Text attributes may be assigned from the Text menu, the Text toolbar, or the Text Inspector. All options are not available from any one of these selection areas.

Using the Text Tool

The Text tool allows you to highlight text to isolate letters, words, or paragraphs. You can apply any text attributes to highlighted text, except runaround and path functions. When you want to see the Text Ruler, you must select it in the View menu and click in the text block with the Text cursor.

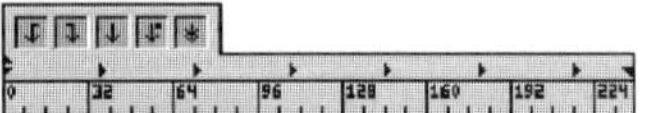

The Text Ruler is visible when the Text tool cursor is clicked inside the Text Block.

The Text tool cursor can highlight isolated letters and words in the text.

Selecting with the Pointer Tool

The Pointer tool can select the entire text block, or multiple text blocks. When the Pointer tool is used to select a text block, all text is affected by any changes made. Text blocks may be resized by clicking on the corner handles of the text block and dragging the text block inward or outward. If the side handles are selected, then the block is dragged, the letter space and word space are compressed with the line breaks remaining as they originally were.

When text blocks are resized using the corner handle, text is reflowed.

When text blocks are resized using the side handle, word and letter space is affected.

To flow text from one block to another, simply click the Linking box icon below the text block that has overflowed text and drag to the block to which you wish to link the text.

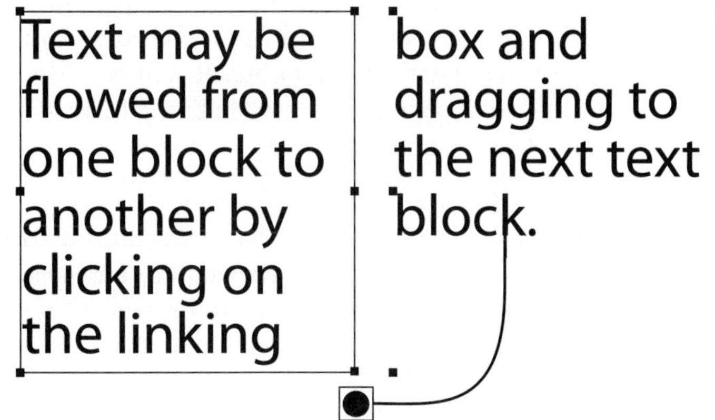

The Text Inspector

Once text has been selected, its attributes can be modified in the Text Inspector. You make choices for applying character attributes, paragraph attributes, spacing, columns and rows, and to copyfit text precisely. Across the top of the Text Inspector are five icons that, when clicked, give you more panels in which to make typographic changes.

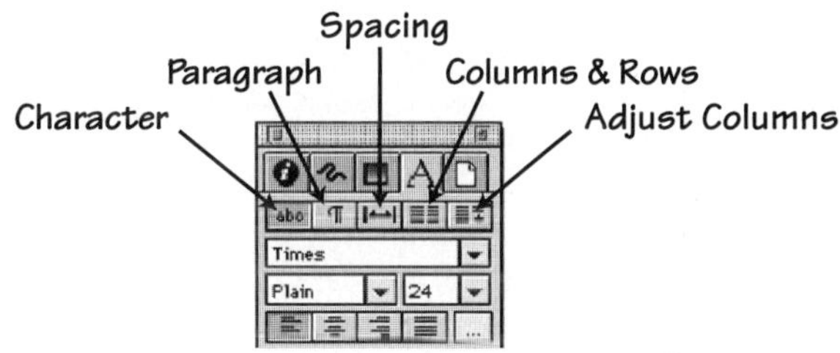

- Character — chooses the font, style (regular, italic, bold, bold italic), size, alignment, leading, kerning, tracking (range kerning), text effects, and paragraph styles.
- Paragraph — sets inter-paragraph spacing, indents, hyphenation, and hanging punctuation, and applies paragraph rules.
- Spacing — scales the width of letters horizontally, sets word and letter spacing, and keeps words and lines of text together (widow and orphan control).
- Columns & Rows — configures the text block into columns and rows and adjusts text flow.
- Adjust Columns —fits the copy to the layout by automatically adjusting the leading and/or by changing text size.

The Text Character Inspector

Use the Text Character Inspector to select the font, style, size, and alignment of the type. Define the leading as + (the point size plus a given number of points), = (a specific number in points), or % (a percent of the point size). When the Edit Alignment button is clicked the Ragged width and Flush zone may be edited. The Ragged width determines how much of a line, in percent of the full line length, must be filled, and does not affect the last line of text. The Flush zone determines at what point each line of text will become justified, and affects only the last line of text.

Kerning and tracking (Range kerning) is defined in percents of an *em* (the actual number of points in the point size) and the baseline shift is defined in the unit of measurement you have selected. Text effects and paragraph styles may be applied. Paragraph styles affect the entire paragraph, not just hightlighted characters.

Character

Font
Weight
Alignment
Leading
Kerning & Tracking
Baseline
Text Effects
Paragraph Style
Point Size

Times
Plain
24
Leading:
0
Range kerning:
0
% em
Baseline shift:
0
No effect
Normal Text

+
=
%

No effect
Highlight effect
Inline effect
Shadow effect
Strikethrough effect
Underline effect
Zoom effect
Graphic element
Edit...

Edit Alignment
Ragged width: 0
Minimum amount lines fill text container. 100% is full justification.
Flush zone: 75
Point at which last line in paragraph snaps to match the ragged width.
Cancel
OK

The Text Paragraph Inspector

Use the Text Paragraph Inspector to specify space above and below paragraphs and to specify the indent from the right and left and the indent for the first line. Indents are cumulative. If you specify a left indent of 2 picas and a first line indent of 3 picas, the first line will indent 5 picas from the left margin. You can also specify hanging punctuation. Hanging punctuation places certain punctuation marks outside the text block to give the aligned text a more even look. If rules are applied to the paragraphs, the text block must be selected with the Pointer tool, and a stroke weight must be applied.

These punctuation marks will "hang" outside the text block when hanging punctuation is specified:

Quotes " " ' '

Periods & Commas . ,

Colons & Semicolons : ;

Paragraph

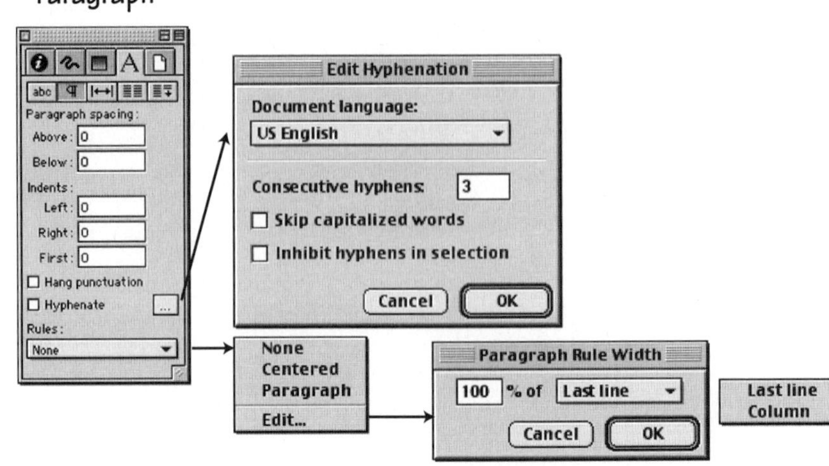

The Text Spacing Inspector

Use the Text Spacing Inspector to specify the horizontal scale of the letters and the word and letter spacing in percentages of the spacing defined by the type designer. You may also keep highlighted words together and specify the number of lines that will stay together.

Spacing

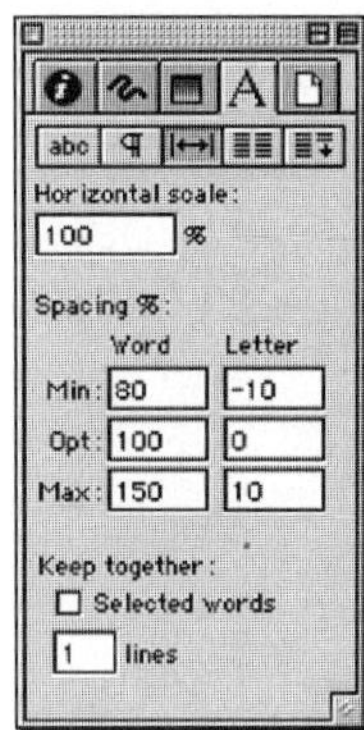

The Text Columns and Rows Inspector

Use the Text Columns and Rows Inspector to precisely define the number of columns (vertical) and rows (horizontal) you will have in a chart. The height, width, and spacing between columns can be precisely defined. This inspector is also used to define rules between columns and rows and to define the text flow — either horizontal or vertical.

Columns & Rows

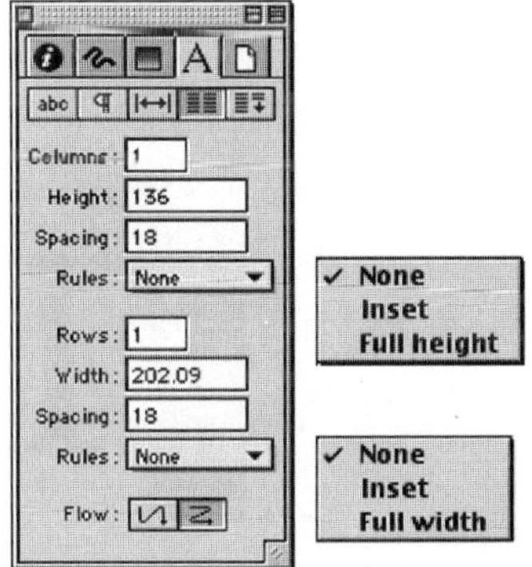

The Text Adjust Columns Inspector

In the Adjust Columns section, there are two check boxes, which may work independent of, or in collaboration with, one another. When Balance is checked, the same number of lines will be placed in both columns, justifying to the top of the column.

When the Modify leading box is checked, leading will be increased to justify the type vertically to the column, based on the Threshold percentage you select. 100% restricts the vertical justification to accepting only the leading value. When the Threshold percentage is set to 75%, a column that is 75% full of type will justify to the full column depth.

The Copyfit % will reduce or enlarge your type (and corresponding leading) by the minimum and maximum percentages you allow. All type in the text block will be enlarged or reduced by the same percentage.

The First line leading can be set to an absolute number; it maybe left at its default value, based on a percentage of the leading — generally the height of the capital letters of the typeface; or it may be set to a "+" value: the type size plus or minus a given number of points.

Adjust Columns

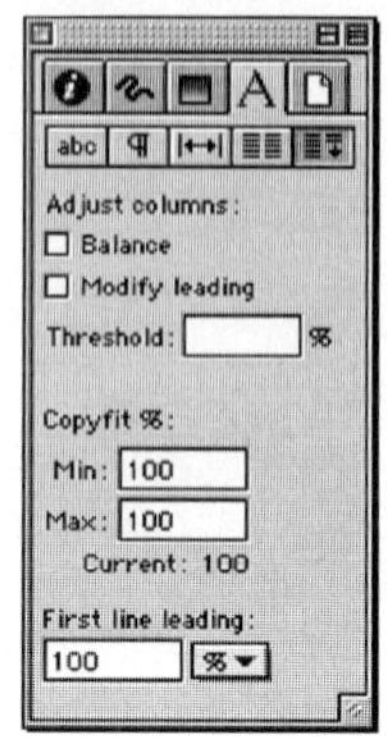

Text Character Settings

Typography is an extensive subject, the basics of which must be understood if you are to use FreeHand or any other illustration or page layout program effectively. Here, we will give you an overview of the various terms that you will encounter when working with type.

Type is designed for a variety of reasons, and with many different "looks." Ascenders, descenders, x-heights, and body clearance lines are variable design features. You cannot measure type with a ruler and achieve accurate results.

Point Size

The height of a letter is called the point size because the height of the letters, from the bottom of the descenders to the top of the body clearance line, is equal to the number of points of the type size. Hence, a 72 point letter is 72 points tall from the bottom of the descender to the top of the body clearance line.

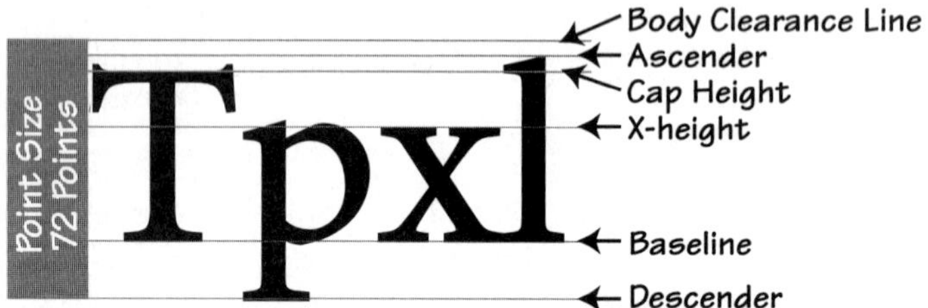

Leading

The spacing between lines of type is called leading. The leading will vary depending on the font used and its characteristics, as well as the look you are attempting to achieve.

A standard leading for long passages of text is 120% of the point size. In other words, if the body text is 10 pt., the leading would be 12 pt. It is not unusual for type to be set with looser leading. For example, 12 pt. type is often set with 15 pt. leading. When space is a concern, tighter leading is often used. Typographers use a form of shorthand when specifying type, using the slash (/) to divide the point size and leading. For example, "10/12" means to set 10 pt. type with 12 pt. leading.

Notice how the differences in leading change the readability of the following passage:

10 pt Minion Regular with 10 pt leading is what many people call "tight" line spacing. Too little linespacing creates dark, uninviting "color" that causes the eye to take in other lines.

10 pt Minion Regular with 12 pt leading is what many people call "normal" line spacing. A proper amount of linespacing allows the eye to travel easily from one line to the next.

10 pt Minion Regular with 15 pt leading is what many people call "open" line spacing. Too much linespacing creates disruptive jumps from line to line.

Kerning and Tracking

Kerning and tracking are adjustments of space between letters. Kerning is the adjustment of space between just two letters, while tracking is the adjustment of space across a range of characters. Positive values increase space between letters; negative values decrease space. All characters can be kerned or tracked, including punctuation and spaces.

Sometimes letters do not always fit with one another aesthetically. At other times, the letters in a paragraph need to be tightened or loosened to appropriately fit a text block.

This type has no kerning. The outside point of each letter abut.

WAT

This type is kerned with the parameters the designer built in.

WAT

This type is kerned tight, but not excessively.

W A T

This type is kerned loose. It loses readability.

While kerning and tracking are largely a matter of taste, the end result must be readable type. Most often, the kerning built into the typeface will be appropriate for passages of text.

Kerning can be performed in the following two ways:

Manual — Place the Text tool between the two letters or select a range of text and hold the Option (Macintosh) or Control-Alt (Windows) key(s) while pressing the Left or Right Arrow key. The Left Arrow key brings letters closer together while the Right Arrow key pushes them further apart.

Text Character Inspector — Enter the numeric amount of kerning the letter pair of selected text should receive. Negative numbers bring letters closer together; positive numbers push letters further apart.

Baseline Shift

At times you may need or wish to adjust the vertical position of a letter or letters. This is called a baseline shift, because it adjusts the character with relation to its baseline. The shift adjusts the character's relationship to the baseline in the unit of measure you have specified.

Alignment

Most reading material on the newsstands is aligned left, termed *flush left* by typographers. *Ragged right* is another term meaning the right margin is uneven, or ragged, as opposed to being flush with the margin. When type is *justified*, the margin is evenly aligned. Usually, when we speak of "justified" type, we mean that both the left and right margins are aligned.

The Text Character Inspector uses the following icons for setting text alignment.

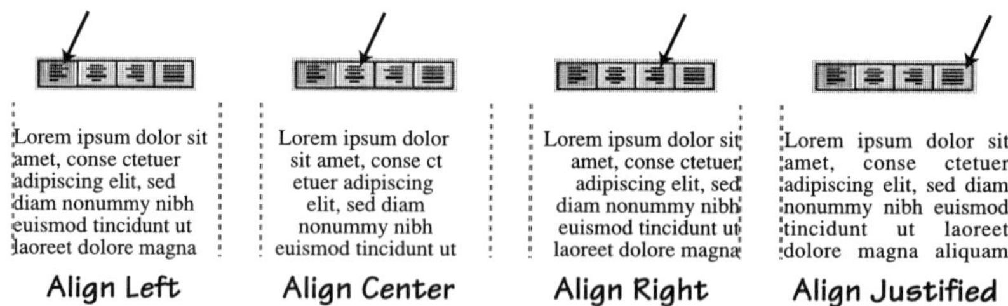

Text Effects

At the bottom of the Text Character Inspector window is a pop-up menu that allows you to apply special effects to the selected text. The Graphic Element option is for in-line graphics. Selecting Edit brings up the Run Around Selection dialog box when a graphic element is selected.

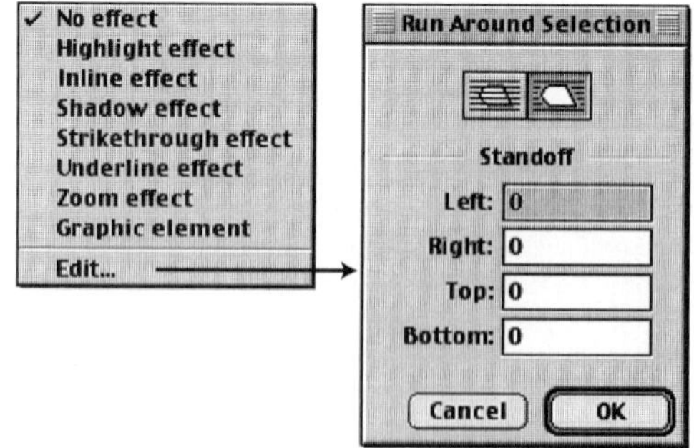

The following are some samples of what the effects look like. You may experiment with this feature to see how the effects appear. Text effects work only on type that has not been converted to outlines. Text effects will not carry through if the text is subsequently converted to outlines.

Create and Format Text

1. Select File>New or press Command/Control-N to create a new document.
2. Select the Text tool from the Toolbox.
3. In the upper-left corner of the page, click the Text tool to create an auto-expanding text block. The Text Ruler will appear above the text container.

4. Type the following text:

   "To sit in solemn silence, on a dull, dark dock. Awaiting the sensation of a short, sharp shock."
5. The text continued in one line. If you had kept typing, it would wrap to a second line when you reached the end of the pasteboard — about 56 inches later.

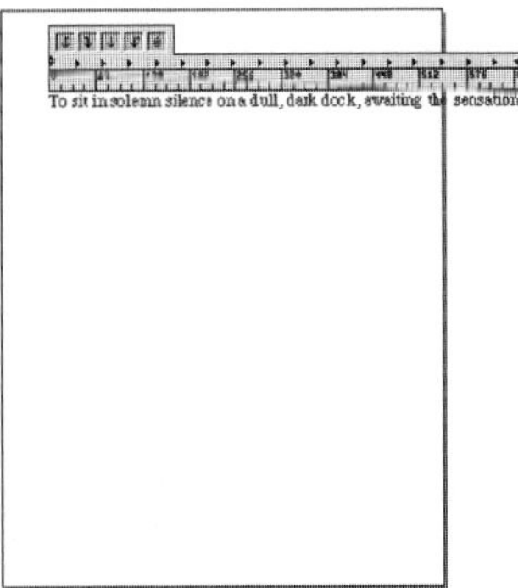

6. Click on the text block with the Pointer tool. Where did the Text Ruler go? Use the Pointer tool to move the corner handles of the text block to try to resize it. Did you succeed?
7. Select the Text tool and click after the word "dock." Press Return/Enter to create a line return.
8. Click on the text block with the Pointer tool. Select Edit>Cut.

To cut and paste using the keyboard instead of the menus, press:

Command/Control-X to cut and Command/Control-V to paste.

press Command/Control-Z to undo an action.

With the Text tool active, Press Command/Control-A to select all text.

Actions are said to be interactive when you actively cause them to happen, as opposed to automatic actions.

9. Select the Text tool. Click and drag a standard text block that is approximately 3-in. square. Click the Text tool in the block, then select Edit>Paste.

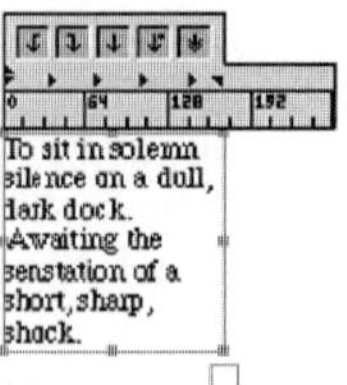

10. Click on the text block with the Pointer tool. In the Text Character Inspector, apply the settings Font: ATC Sands, Size: 9 pt., Leading: 11 pt. (Fixed "="). Notice how all the text is affected when selected in this manner.
11. Click on the Text tool, then highlight only the words "short, sharp, shock." In the Text Character Inspector, apply these settings: Font: ATC Coconuts Extra Bold, Size: 12 pt., Leading: 14 pt. (Fixed "="). Note that the change in leading affected the entire line.
12. Click on the text block with the Pointer tool. Click on and drag any of the corner handles to resize the block wider, then taller.
13. Click on the text block with the Pointer tool and drag it around the page.
14. Click on a side handle of the text block and drag it wider. What happened to the spacing of the text? This is one way to apply interactive range kerning (tracking). Select Edit>Undo, or press Command/Control-Z.
15. Click on a side handle of the text block and drag it wider, holding down the Option/Alt key. What was the spacing result? This is a method of interactively adjusting spacing between words.
16. Select the Text tool and click into the text block. Select Edit>Select>All. This is another way to select all the text in a block.
17. Close the document without saving.

Apply Character Settings to Type

1. From the File menu open the document **Text Inspector Type.FH9** from your **SF-FreeHand** folder. Set the units of measurement to Points.
2. With the Pointer tool, click on the text block. Select Window>Inspectors>Text to access the Text Inspector.

3. Apply these settings from the Text Character Inspector: Font: ATC Colada, Size: 10 pt., Leading: 14.5 pt. (Fixed), Alignment: Align Left.

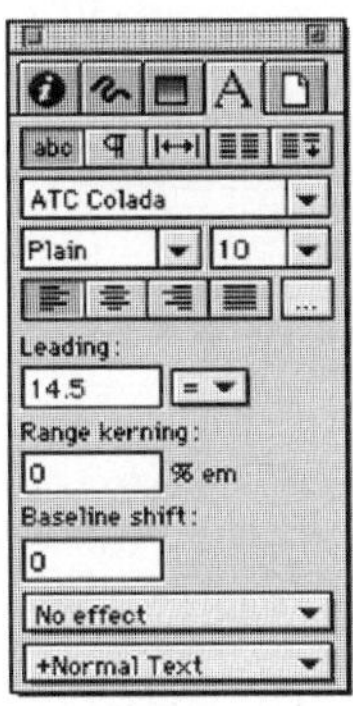

"All My Troubles
Seemed So Far Away"
by Dean Bagley

Sirens screamed and emergency lights flashed as firemen arrived on the scene and began unwinding yards of fire hose, donning their gas masks and chopping down a tall fence to get to the blaze. The neighbors who had called them peered over their wooden fences, gaping and pointing at what was surely the most horrifying spectacle ever to appear in their neighborhood.
Their adjoining neighbor, Walter Melon, had created a blazing bonfire in his backyard that was a veritable funeral pyre of books from his library. Self-help books he prized more than anything and read ravenously. And to make this entire scene seem even more like some fire-dance in a voodoo ritual, Walter was dancing around the inferno with a can of barbecue lighter fluid, sprinkling here and there and laughing a maniacal laugh that sent chills through the hearts of onlookers.
His light blue shirt was ripped and totally unbuttoned, stained with dark, hideous blotches. His stained white pants were becoming grayer by the minute from the smoke and ashes, all of which combined to make him look like the lone survivor of an airliner crash.

4. Use the Text tool to highlight the title and the author's name.

5. In the Text Character Inspector, apply these settings: Font: ATC Coconuts Extra Bold, Size: 14 pt., Leading: 18 pt. (Fixed), Alignment: Align Center.

6. With this text still selected, click on the Text Spacing Inspector and type 120 in the Horizontal scale field. Press Return/Enter to apply.

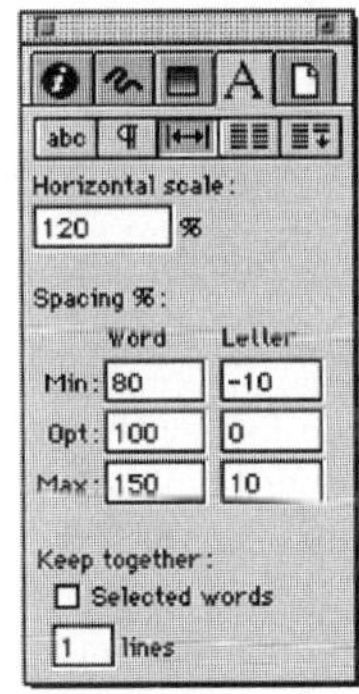

7. Highlight the title and apply these settings: Size: 18 pt., Leading: 27 pt.

8. Highlight the author's name, then apply a baseline shift of –10. This will move the line away from the title without changing the leading.

"All My Troubles

Seemed So Far Away"

by Dean Bagley

9. Now highlight the body text. Click on the Text Paragraph Inspector icon. In Paragraph spacing, type 10 in the Above field to assign a 10pt. space. In the Indents fields, type 10 for First to apply a first line indent of 10 pt. Press Return/Enter to apply it to the text.

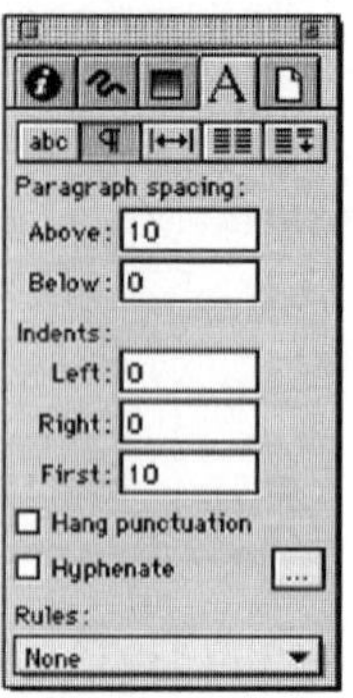

10. The text block should appear as follows:

"All My Troubles
Seemed So Far Away"

by Dean Bagley

Sirens screamed and emergency lights flashed as firemen arrived on the scene and began unwinding yards of fire hose, donning their gas masks and chopping down a tall fence to get to the blaze. The neighbors who had called them peered over their wooden fences, gaping and pointing at what was surely the most horrifying spectacle ever to appear in their neighborhood.

Their adjoining neighbor, Walter Melon, had created a blazing bonfire in his backyard that was a veritable funeral pyre of books from his library. Self-help books he prized more than anything and read ravenously. And to make this entire scene seem even more like some fire-dance in a voodoo ritual, Walter was dancing around the inferno with a can of barbecue lighter fluid, sprinkling here and there and laughing a maniacal laugh that sent chills through the hearts of onlookers.

His light blue shirt was ripped and totally unbuttoned, stained with dark, hideous blotches. His stained white pants were becoming grayer by the minute from the smoke and ashes, all of which combined to make him look like the lone survivor of an airliner crash.

11. Close the document without saving.

Text Paragraph Settings

The Type Paragraph Inspector allows you to apply settings that affect the entire paragraph, simply by placing the Text tool anywhere in the paragraph and entering the desired setting in the appropriate field. While you have used some of them incidentally in the previous exercise, we will review them here.

Paragraph Spacing

The Paragraph spacing fields allow you to add specific space above and below the paragraph, in addition to the leading values. So, if a paragraph that has 12 pt. leading and 6 pt. spacing is added above the paragraph, the baseline of the first line of the paragraph is 18 pt. below the baseline of the last line of type in the preceding paragraph. Space added below a paragraph has a similar effect. The two Paragraph spacing fields, Above and Below, have a cumulative effect, so you need to be careful when you use these features. Many typographers recommend using one or the other, but not both, to eliminate the possibility of error.

I. Down The Rabbit-hole
ALICE was beginning to get very tired of
had peeped into the book her sister was
book," thought Alice, "without pictures
So she was considering in her own mind
the pleasure of making a daisy-chain wo
White Rabbit with pink eyes ran close by
There was nothing so very remarkable in
itself, "Oh dear! Oh dear! I shall be too l
have wondered at this, but at the time it
waist-coat pocket, and looked at it, and

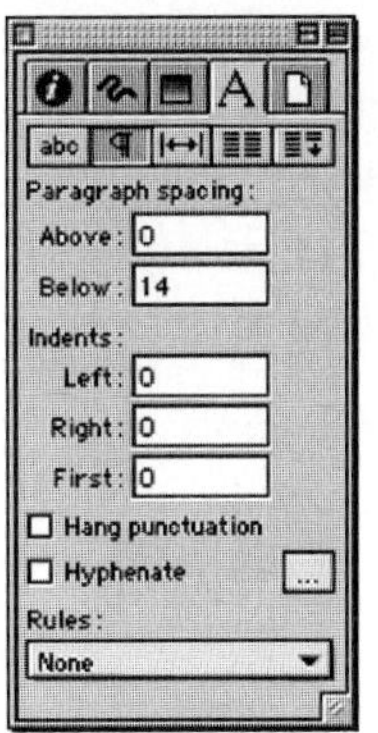

I. Down The Rabbit-hole

ALICE was beginning to get very tired of
had peeped into the book her sister was
book," thought Alice, "without pictures
So she was considering in her own mind
the pleasure of making a daisy-chain wo
White Rabbit with pink eyes ran close by
There was nothing so very remarkable in
itself, "Oh dear! Oh dear! I shall be too l
have wondered at this, but at the time it
waist-coat pocket, and looked at it, and

Here, paragraph spacing of 14 pt. Below was added to the headline.

Indents

Use these fields to enter indents that will affect the entire paragraph or the first line. Indents entered in the Left and Right fields shorten the line length from the left or right by the amount entered. The amount entered in the First field affects only the first line of a paragraph. Entering a first line indent in this field is preferred over pressing the Tab key to effect an indent.

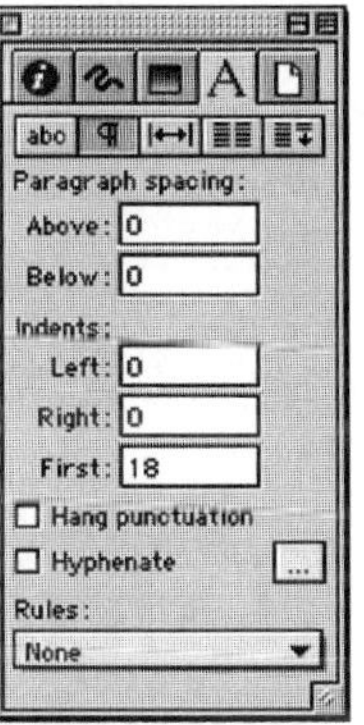

I. Down The Rabbit-hole

ALICE was beginning to get very tired of
had peeped into the book her sister was
book," thought Alice, "without pictures
So she was considering in her own
whether the pleasure of making a daisy-
suddenly a White Rabbit with pink eyes
There was nothing so very remarkab
say to itself, "Oh dear! Oh dear! I shall b
to have wondered at this, but at the tim
waist-coat pocket, and looked at it, and

In this example, the first paragraph was set to the full measure, and succeeding paragraphs were set with a first line indent of 18 pt.

Hanging Punctuation

Punctuation that hangs into the margin increases readability of display text, such as callouts. It allows the text to create an easy-to-read block, while the punctuation falls outside that area.

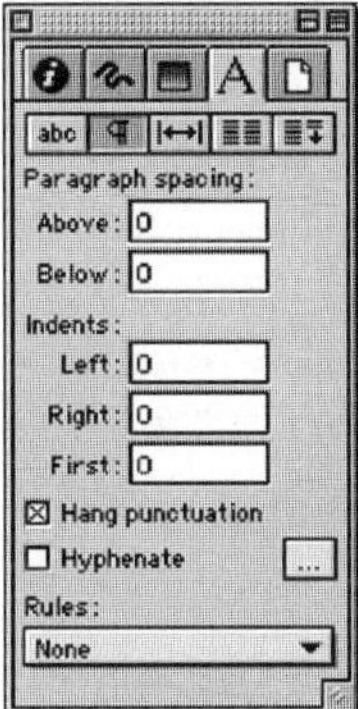

"After such a fall as this,
I shall think nothing of
tumbling downstairs!"

Hyphenate

When the Hyphenate box is checked in the Text Paragraph Inspector, hyphenation is turned on for the paragraph affected. You are able to select the language (if you have more than one language available), set the number of consecutive hyphens, prevent or allow the hyphenation of capitalized words, and disallow hyphenation of any selected text.

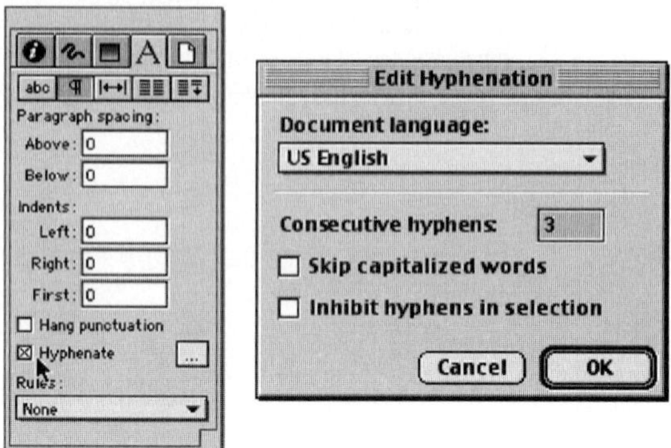

Rules

Sometimes it is desirable to attach a rule (line) to a paragraph, so that, if the paragraph is moved, the rule moves with the text. The rule may be centered, or may use the alignment of the paragraph. When a rule is selected, the edit item becomes selectable. Here, the rule may be designated as a percentage (up to 100%) of either the column width or the width of the last line in the paragraph. To make the rule visible, and to set its width, it is necessary to access the Stroke Inspector. Then you must access the Object Inspector and uncheck the Display border option.

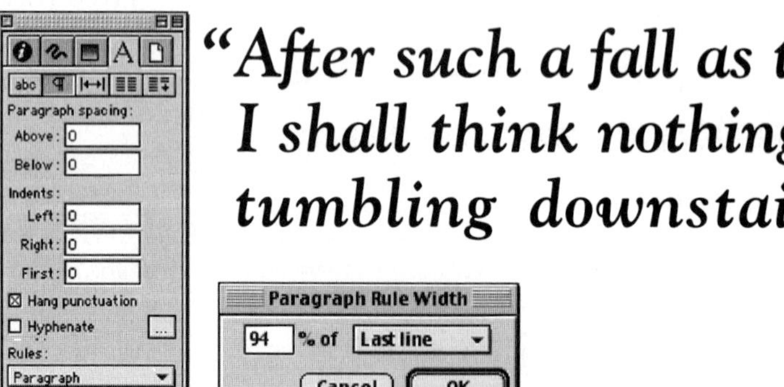

This rule below the callout created an interesting problem because of the hanging indent. A rule width of 94% of the last line gave us the results we needed.

Apply Text Paragraph Attributes

1. Open the file **Advice from a Caterpillar.FH9** from your **SF-FreeHand** folder. Set the units of measurement to Picas.
2. With the Text Paragraph Inspector open, place the Text tool in the title line ("5 Advice from a Caterpillar") and set Paragraph spacing Below at 1P3.

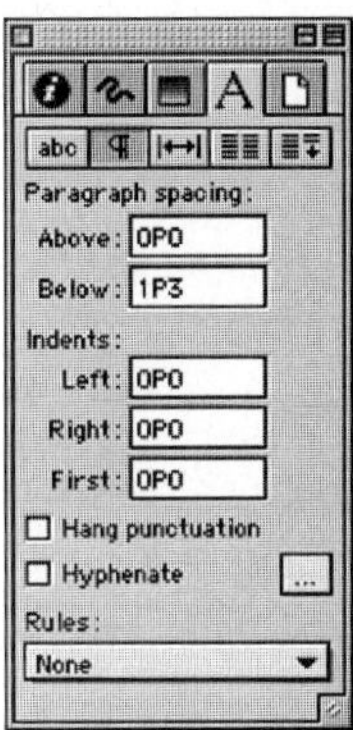

3. Highlight the text, beginning with the second paragraph ("Who are you?"...) through the last paragraph before the poem ("Alice folded her hands and began:"), and assign a first line indent of 1P6.

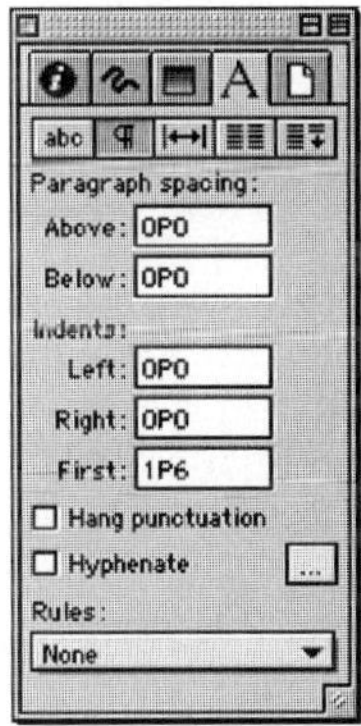

At this point your document should appear as follows:

5 Advice from a Caterpillar

The Caterpillar and Alice looked at each other for some time in silence: at last the Caterpillar took the hookah out of its mouth, and addressed her in a languid, sleepy voice.

'Who are you?' said the Caterpillar.

This was not an encouraging opening for a conversation. Alice replied, rather shyly, 'I-I hardly know, sir, just at present- at least I know who I was when I got up this morning, but I think I must have been changed several times since then.'

'What do you mean by that?' said the Caterpillar sternly. 'Explain yourself!'

'I can't explain myself, I'm afraid, sir' said Alice, 'because I'm not myself, you see.'

'I don't see,' said the Caterpillar.

'I'm afraid I can't put it more clearly,' Alice replied very politely, 'for I can't understand it myself to begin with; and being so many different sizes in a day is very confusing.'

'It isn't,' said the Caterpillar.

4. Now select all the paragraphs in the poem and set Paragraph spacing Above at 0P6 and Indent Left at 1P6.

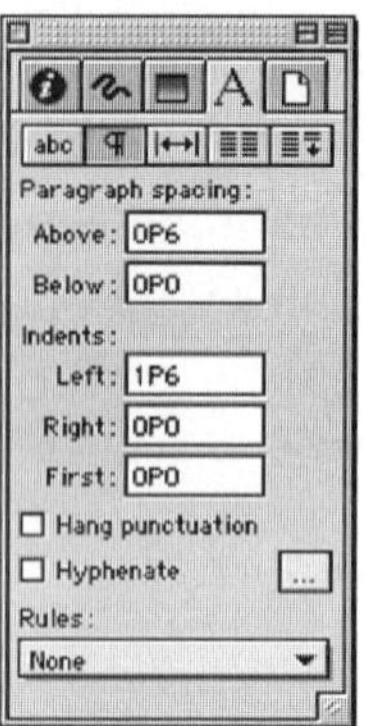

The poem should look like the following:

'Repeat, "You are Old, Father William,"' said the Caterpillar.
Alice folded her hands, and began:

'You are old, Father William,' the young man said,
'And your hair has become very white;
And yet you incessantly stand on your head —
Do you think, at your age, it is right?'

'In my youth,' Father William replied to his son,
'I feared it might injure the brain;
But, now that I'm perfectly sure I have none,
Why, I do it again and again.'

5. We want to apply a rule below the title. Place the Text tool in the title text. Select Rules> Paragraph from the Text Paragraph Inspector. Now select Rules>Edit. Click OK to accept the default to 100% of Last line. You'll notice that nothing happened.

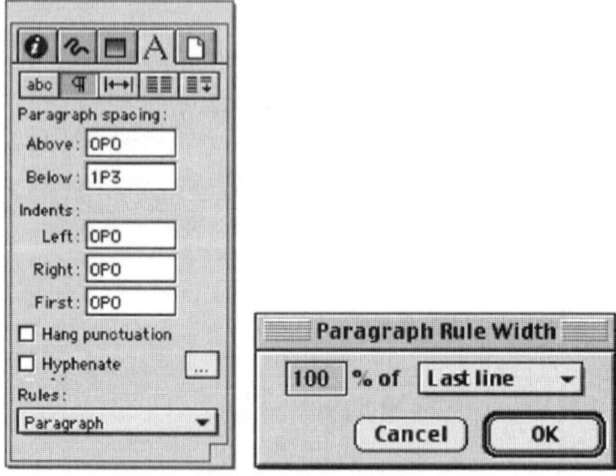

6. Switch to the Pointer tool and click on the text block to select it. Select the Stroke Inspector>Basic and assign a width of 0P2. Now there's a border around the entire text block.

7. Select the Object Inspector and deselect the Display border box.

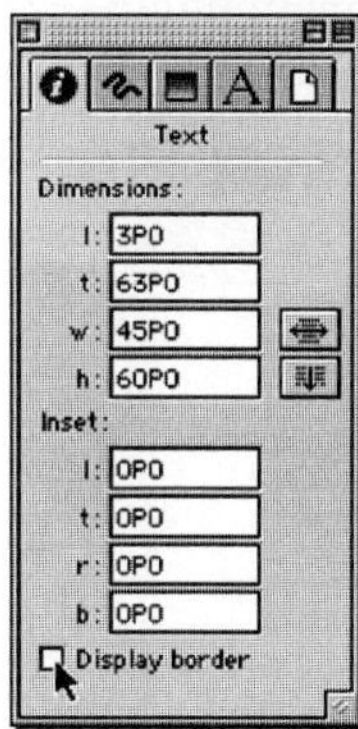

8. The title should look similar to the following:

5 *Advice from a Caterpillar*

The Caterpillar and Alice looked at each other for some time in silence: at last the Caterpillar took the hookah out of its mouth, and addressed her in a languid, sleepy voice.
'Who are you?' said the Caterpillar.
This was not an encouraging opening for a conversation. Alice replied, rather shyly, 'I-I hardly know, sir, just at present- at least I know who I was when I got up this morning, but I think I must have been changed several times since then.'

9. We'll revisit this document later. Save it to your **Work in Progress** folder and close it.

Text Spacing Settings

The settings in the Text Spacing Inspector are very helpful when producing longer documents and when you want repeatable results for scaling and word and letter spacing.

Horizontal Scale

Although you can scale text interactively, the result of doing so is arbitrary. If you wished to set a number of headlines with the same expansion or condensing of type, you'd have a difficult time if the interactive method was the only one available to you. Using the Horizontal scale %, simply type in the percentage to expand or condense the letters and you have a definable width to the type.

Spacing %

In this section, you tell FreeHand what the allowable parameters are to flow text. These percentages will be used first, before attempting to hyphenate a word (if hyphenation is turned on), or, if you are working with justified text, these parameters will be used to justify the left and right margins. Word spacing (space between words) is used before Letter spacing (space between letters).

In this section you tell FreeHand the minimum, maximum, and optimum word spacing and letter spacing, based on the spacing designed into the typeface by the designer. You will want to experiment on a typeface-by-typeface basis in order to arrive at acceptable limits.

Keep Together

You may highlight specific letters or words in the paragraph that must be kept together. Often this will be a person's or corporation's initials. You may also designate the number of lines in the paragraph that must remain together. This is called widow and orphan control.

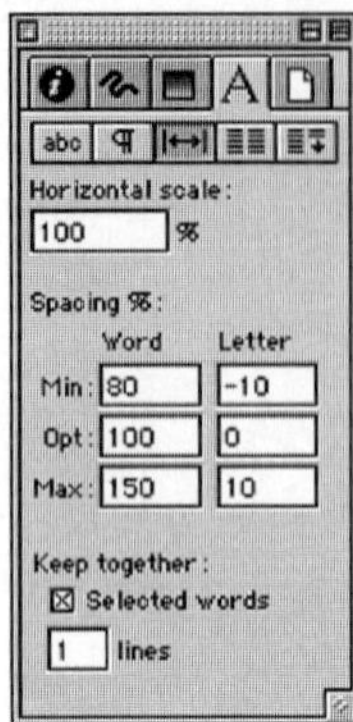

The poet was e
e cummings

The poet was
e e cummings

In this example, the initials of the poet e e cummings broke to different lines. We selected his name, then checked the Selected words box under Keep together for a much more acceptable presentation.

Text Columns & Rows Settings

Whenever you wish to set up linked equal partitions to a page of text block you can use the Text Columns & Rows Inspector. In it, you specify the number of columns and the number of rows. You can manually specify the height of the columns and the width of the rows. The Spacing fields define the space between columns and rows. Rules may be set between columns and rows. An Inset rule goes the height or width of each column or row; a rule that is set for full width goes the entire height of stacked columns or width of multiple rows.

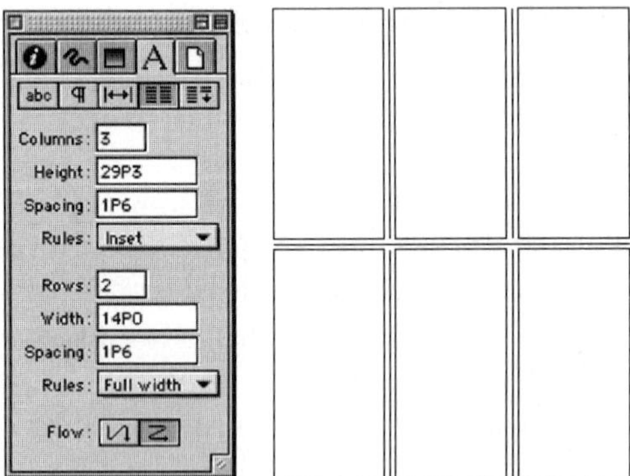

Note here that the rules between the columns go only the depth of each column, while the rule between the rows spans the full width of the text block.

Adjust Columns Settings

The settings in the Text Adjust Columns Inspector give a great deal of control over column balance and text fit. This is accomplished through balance, addition or subtraction of leading, and altering the text size.

Adjust Columns

When the Balance box is checked, FreeHand will put an equal number of lines of text in each column; if there are not enough lines to balance perfectly, one line will be removed from the last column or columns.

When the Modify leading box is checked, the Threshold % box also becomes available. If a column reaches that threshold — if at least that much of the column is filled with text — the text in the block will be justified vertically by adding equal amounts of leading between each line in the column.

When both the Balance and Modify leading boxes are checked, FreeHand will first put an equal number of lines in each column, then will justify the columns vertically.

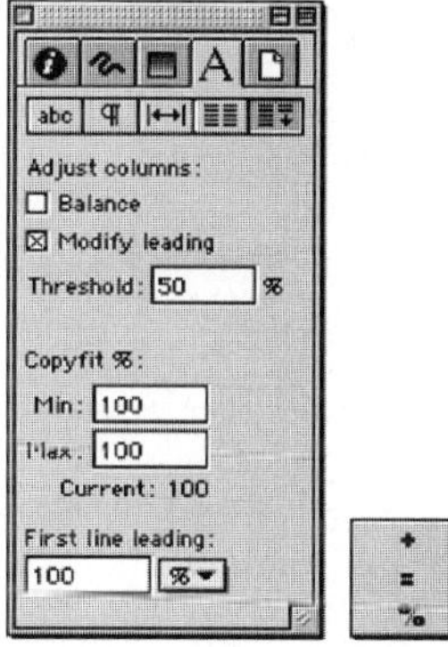

Copyfit %

With the Copyfit% selected, FreeHand will increase or decrease the point size of the text in order to fit it snugly within the text block. This option may be used in conjunction with the Adjust columns features.

First Line Leading

The position of the first line in relation to the top of the text block is determined by this setting. The default is 100% of the height of the capital letter, which is substantially less than the normal leading. The options available are % of size, = exact leading, and + or – a number of points based on leading.

Use Columnar Features

1. Open the document **Gaellic Tour.FH9** from your **SF-FreeHand** folder. Set the units of measurement to Picas. At the top of the page is a headline which has been converted to outlines. We will concern ourselves exclusively with the text.

2. With the Text Columns and Rows Inspector open, click on the text block and assign it 2 Columns with a Spacing of 1P0, and an Inset Rule. There are no rows to concern ourselves with. Notice that the rule goes all the way to the bottom of the text block.

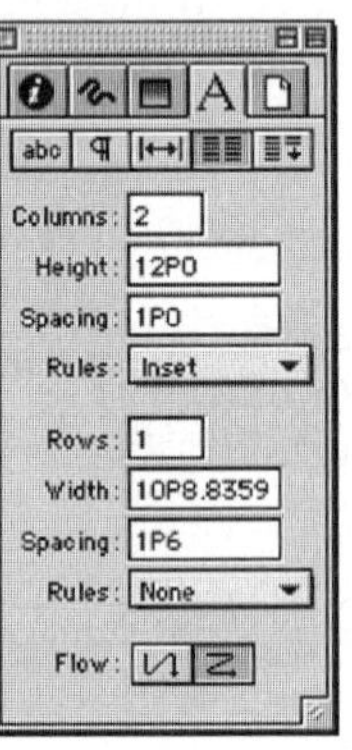

tour to the
land of the gaels

Our once-a-year two-week guided tour begins in Shannon. We motorbus through Ireland, including stops at Galway and Cork, a tour of the Waterford Crystal facility, and two glorious days in Dublin. I'll introduce you to some of my favorite pubs along the way.

Then it's off to Scotland for the rest of our time together. We'll take a ghost walk through Edinbugh and spend some time at the famous Edinburgh Military Tatoo (or you can take the time to do some shopping!). There will be a tour of the Glenkinchie Distillery. We'll also get a taste of the Western Highlands when we visit my ancestral home, Armadale Castle, on the Isle of Skye.

This tour is first-class accommodations all the way, with delightful meals, and shopping to die for.

August 8 – 22.

3. Switch to the Text Adjust Columns Inspector. Click on the Balance box to check it and note what happens. Now click Modify leading. Notice that the spacing is not what we would want. Since the ad is designed to be a specific size, we can vary the size of the text in order to fill the block.

4. Uncheck the Balance box, leaving Modify leading checked. In the Max Copyfit % field, type 120. Set the First line leading to 11= (Fixed).

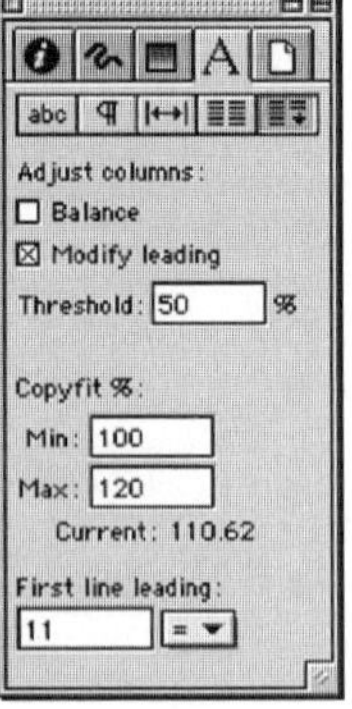

tour to the
land of the gaels

Our once-a-year two-week guided tour begins in Shannon. We motorbus through Ireland, including stops at Galway and Cork, a tour of the Waterford Crystal facility, and two glorious days in Dublin. I'll introduce you to some of my favorite pubs along the way.

Then it's off to Scotland for the rest of our time together. We'll take a ghost walk through Edinbugh and spend some time at the famous Edinburgh Military Tatoo (or you can take the time to do some shopping!). There will be a tour of the Glenkinchie Distillery. We'll also get a taste of the Western Highlands when we visit my ancestral home, Armadale Castle, on the Isle of Skye.

This tour is first-class accommodations all the way, with delightful meals, and shopping to die for.

5. The frame is filled satisfactorily. Normally, we'd concern ourselves with hyphenation problems, but for this exercise, save it to your **Work in Progress** folder and close.

Using Text Styles

While it is not difficult to assign text attributes, it is time consuming. Assigning a font, size, leading, indent, scale and color requires accessing three different Inspectors and the Color palette. FreeHand provides a means to assign multiple attributes at once through the Styles panel, which is accessed through Window>Panels>Styles.

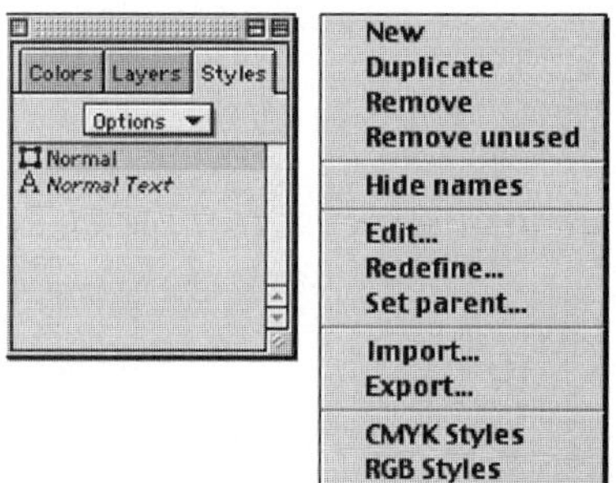

When Options>New is selected in the Styles palette, the style is named Style-1 by default. The name may be changed by triple-clicking on it and typing a new name. Attributes may be assigned from the appropriate Inspectors after selecting Edit from the menu, or they may be picked up from selected text. If a parameter is changed in the parent to a style, that change will be reflected in the style. CMYK styles and RGB styles are fills that may be applied to graphic styles.

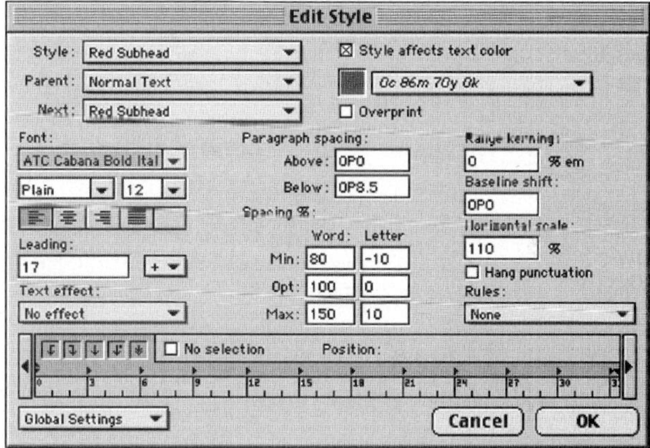

Styles are applied by selecting the style from the Styles palette with the Text tool in the paragraph to which the style will be applied, or they may be applied from the Text Character Inspector. Styles apply to entire paragraphs, not to individual words of selected text.

The Styles panel may also be used to apply graphic styles, such as fill and stroke parameters.

The Menu's Unique Features

Although most attributes can be applied to text using the various Inspectors, some features are available only from the Text menu or the Text Toolbar. These features include Convert Case, Special Characters, Text Editor, Spelling, Run Around Selection, Find and Replace (Edit Menu), in addition to the Path features, which we will discuss later in this chapter.

Convert Case

Sometimes it is necessary to change the case of the characters. Most often, this will be a change to small caps, but occasionally a typist will simply type in the wrong case, and the change must be made to fit the design parameters. Text may be changed as follows:

UPPER CASE — All letters are capitals.
lower case — All letters are minuscules, with no capitals.
Small caps — A smaller version of capital letters replaces minuscules.
Title Case — The first letter of each word is capitalized.
Sentence case — The first word of each sentence is capitalized

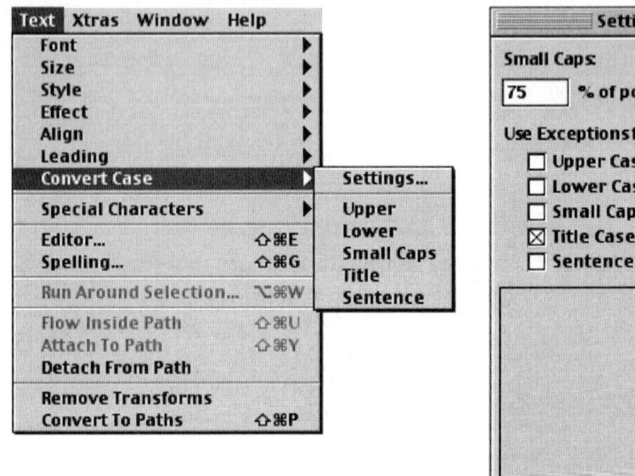

When the Settings menu is accessed, the size of small caps can be entered as a % of point size and exceptions may be added to a list, so the conversion will not affect those words. For example, prepositions and conjunctions are seldom capitalized in titles. When converting to lower case or sentence case, care should be taken that proper names are not inadvertently "uncapitalized."

To apply the case conversion, highlight the text to be converted and apply the appropriate Convert Case. Text added after a conversion will not be affected.

Special Characters

Some characters that are not a part of the standard keyboard may be added through Text>Special Characters. Many of them have keyboard commands, and, if you use these characters often, it is best to learn the keyboard shortcuts.

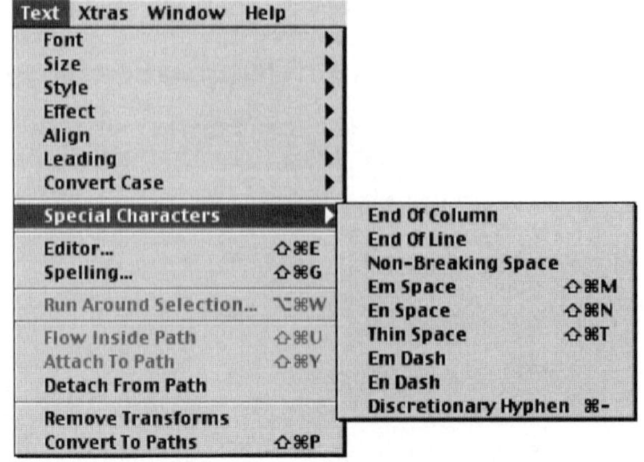

Use these shortcuts for special characters:

Macintosh

End of Line: Shift-Return
Em Space: Command-Shift-M
En Space: Command-Shift-N
Thin Space: Command-Shift-T
Em Dash: Option-Shift-Hyphen
En Dash: Option-Hyphen
Discretionary Hyphen: Command-Hyphen

Windows

End of Line: Shift-Enter
Non-Breaking Space: Control-Shift-H
Em Space: Control-Shift-M
En Space: Control-Shift-N
Thin Space: Control-Shift-T
Discretionary Hyphen: Control-Shift-Hyphen

Text Editor  and Spelling Feature 

Both the Text Editor and the Spelling feature are accessed through the Text menu. Because of the complexity of much of the work we do in FreeHand, and because we often apply special effects to text, it is often easiest to use the Text Editor to edit text. A text block must first be selected. All text in that block will appear in the Text Editor. When the text has been edited, clicking the Apply button allows you to see how the text will appear. To add the text and exit the Text Editor, click OK.

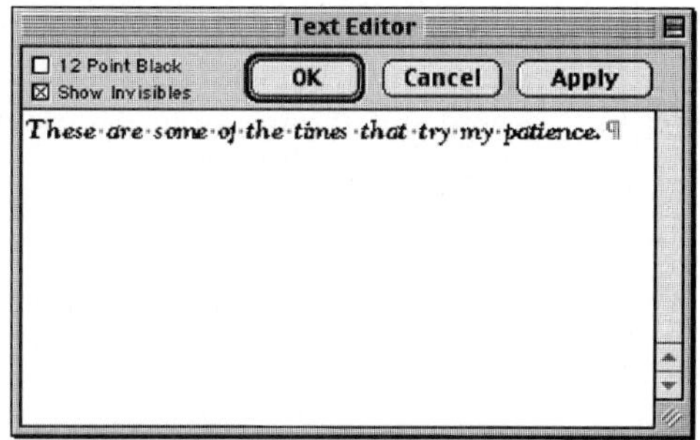

Spelling is particularly valuable when we have been performing last-minute edits to text. The text block may be selected with the Pointer tool, or the Text tool — the entire text block will be checked for correct spelling. To begin checking, click start. When a word is found, you have the option to select Ignore, Ignore all, Change, Change all, or to Add the word to the dictionary. You may also click on another word in the list and click the Suggest button to use the new word as the replacement word. Even though FreeHand is not a page layout program, using the spelling feature is a good habit to get into.

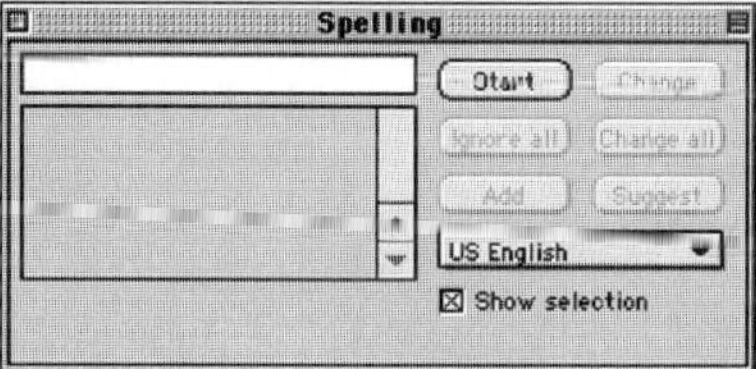

Run Around Selection 

When you integrate text and graphics, it is often desirable to run text around one or more sides of an object, whether it is an illustration created in FreeHand or a raster graphic you have imported. To do so, select Text>Run Around Selection. The left button (the default) causes text to flow over an object. When the right button is clicked, the runaround is activated. The text standoff (how near the text will come to touching the object) is entered in the Left, Right, Top, and Bottom fields. Click OK to apply the runaround.

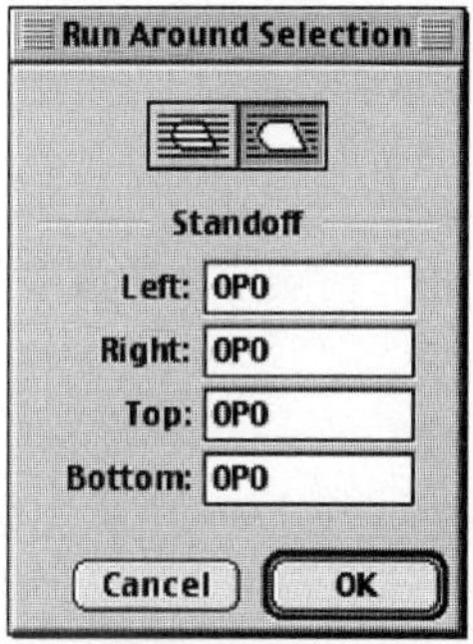

Find and Replace 

It is sometimes necessary to find and replace text, because of editorial changes, or because of errors. Edit>Find and Replace makes this easy to do. You enter the word you wish to replace in the Find field, and the word with which you wish to replace it in the Change to field. If there are several instances of the word, you may click either Find Next or Change all.

To further fine-tune a search, you may check the Whole word box. This will cause Find and Replace to find only instances where the characters are the entire word. For example, if Whole word is not checked and the word searched for is "port," the words "portable," "portage," and "report" would also be included in the search. You may also check Match case, which will cause only words with matching upper and lower case to be found. If the word Madras (the city in India) were searched for, madras (the material) would not be found in the search.

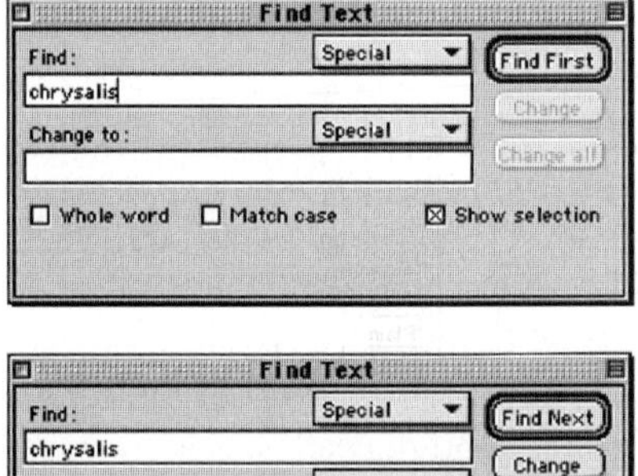

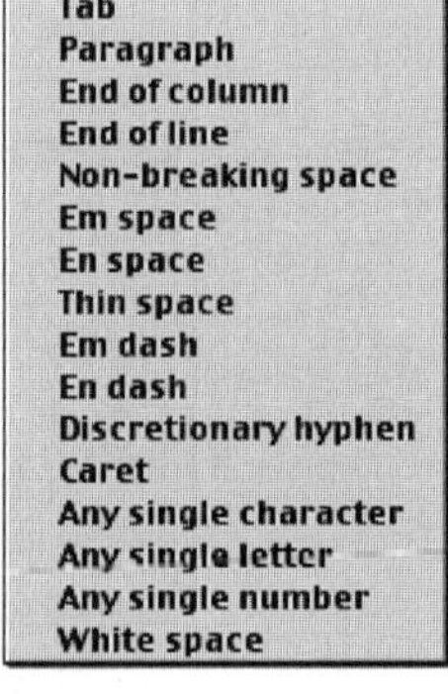

Work with Text Styles

1. Open the document **Advice from a Caterpillar.FH9** from your **Work in Progress** folder. The units of measurement should be set to Picas.
2. If it is not already open, select Window>Panels>Styles.

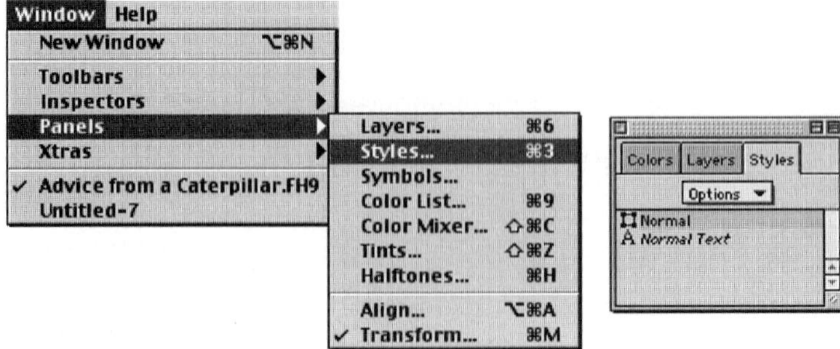

3. Place the Text tool in one of the paragraphs of the poem near the end of the document. From the Styles Options menu, select New.

4. Triple-click on Style-1 and rename this style "Poem".

5. Now select Edit from the Styles Options menu. Change the font to ATC Cabana Italic and click OK to accept the changes.

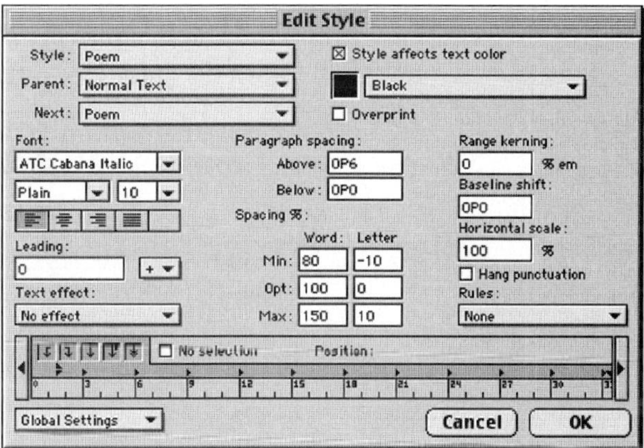

6. Select all paragraphs in the poem and click on the Poem style to apply the new parameters.

7. Select all the text of the poem and cut it from the document.

8. Shorten the main text block and create a new text block at the bottom of the page that is the same width as the main text block. Paste the poem text into this text block.

9. Select the Text Columns and Rows Inspector and set Columns: 2, Height 16P6, Spacing: 1P6.

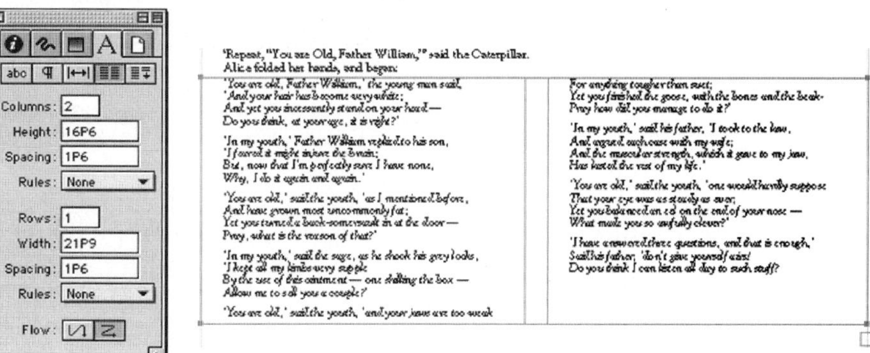

10. At the bottom of the first column is the first line of the fifth stanza. We want to move this together with the rest of the stanza. Place the Text tool in front of the line and select Text>Special Characters>End Of Column.

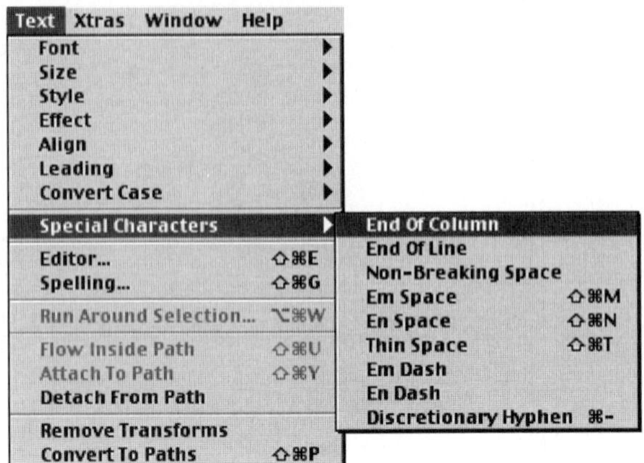

11. Now, move the graphic from the Pasteboard to the lower-right corner of the upper text block. With the graphic selected, Choose Text>Run Around Selection.

12. Set the object to runaround (the right button) and assign a Standoff of Left 1p6, Top 1p0. Click OK.

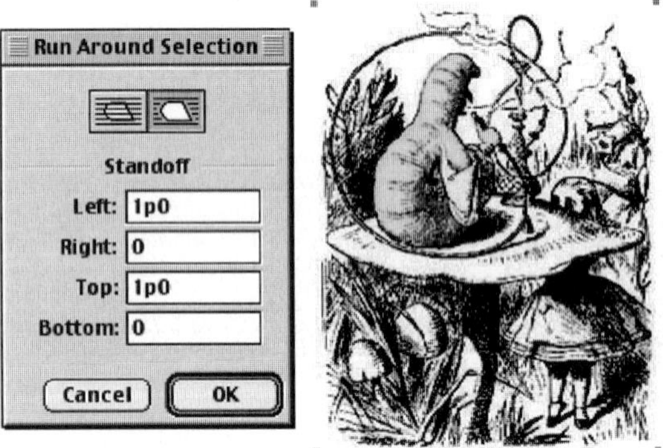

13. Save the document to your **Work in Progress** folder and close.

Working with Tabs

Tab rulers automatically appear above text blocks when View>Text Rulers is turned on and the Text tool is placed in the text block. Default tabs are placed at 1/2″ intervals. Five types of tabs may be created: Left Align, Right Align, Center Align, Decimal Align, and Wrapping tabs.

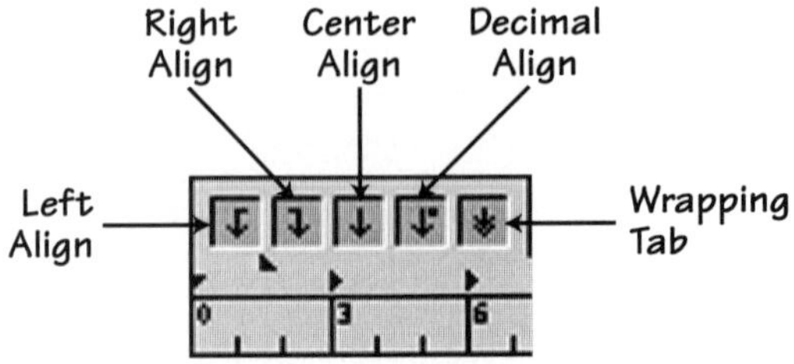

Tabs can be set for a single paragraph or for a range of paragraphs. When multiple paragraphs are selected and tabs are set, the tab settings apply to all selected paragraphs.

To set the Left, Right, Center, and Decimal align tabs, click on the Tab icon and drag it to the appropriate point in the Text Ruler. To set a Wrapping tab, you must set both the start and end positions of the text area. When the Tab key is pressed, the text will go to the first line of the next tab. When Return/Enter is pressed, the following line will take into account all lines of wrapping tabs.

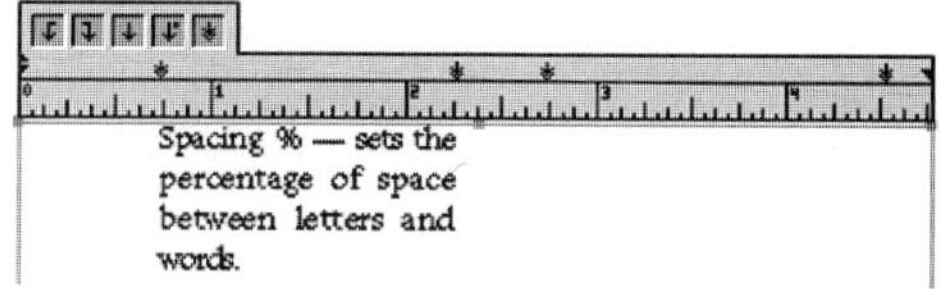

Use the Tab Functions

1. Open the document **Invoice.FH9** from your **SF-FreeHand** folder. Set the units of measurement to Picas and take a moment to look over the document.
2. Using the Text tool, select the column head text in the green box. From the Text Character Inspector, assign it a Baseline shift of –0P4.

3. Turn your attention to the text in the main text block. With the Text tool in the text block, press Command/Control-A to select all the text.
4. Set a Right align tab at 3P0, Wrapping tabs at 4P6 and 18P6, and Decimal align tabs at 21P6 and 25P6.

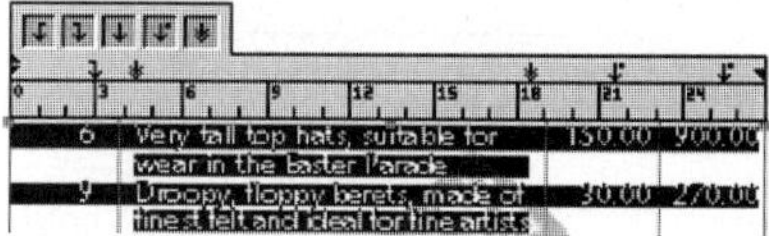

5. With the text still selected, access the Text Paragraph Inspector. Assign Paragraph spacing Below of 1P0.

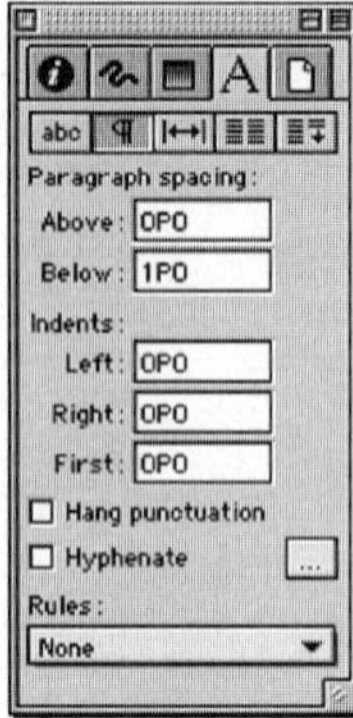

6. You've completed the invoice. Save the document to your **Work in Progress** folder and close the file.

The Hattery

1224 MadHatter Lane • Tieville, NY 13276
813/555-HATS

QTY	DESCRIPTION	PRICE	EXT
6	Very tall top hats, suitable for wear in the Easter Parade	150.00	900.00
9	Droopy, floppy berets, made of finest felt and ideal for fine artists	30.00	270.00
18	Baseball caps, all embroidered with the team's name — Mad Hatter's Toppers	9.95	179.10
	Total		1349.10
	Tax (very taxing)		114.67
	Grand Total		1463.77

Importing Text

Often, particularly with jobs containing longer passages of text, you will be supplied with text created in a word processing application. FreeHand supports both ASCII and Rich Text (RTF) formats for importing text, and preserves attributes applied to Rich Text. Once the text is imported, you can apply FreeHand's text attributes to any text.

Import a Text File

1. Create a new document.

2. From the File menu, select Import.

File	Edit View Modify Text
New	⌘N
Open...	⌘O
Close	⌘W
Save	⌘S
Save As...	⇧⌘S
Revert	
Import...	⌘R

3. Navigate to the **SF-FreeHand** folder and select the file **Import Text.TXT**. Click Open.

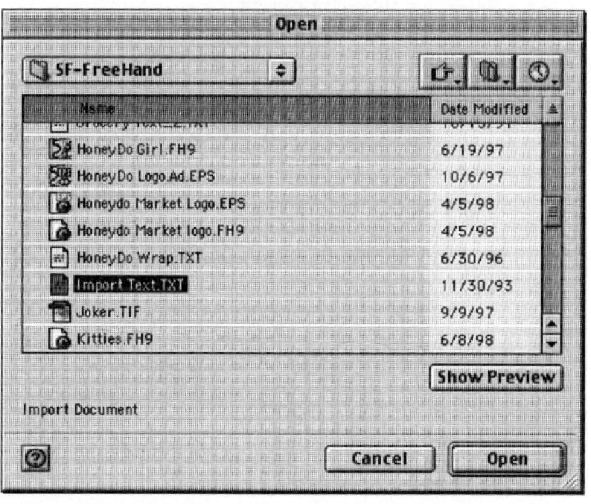

Press Command/Control-R to import text or graphics without using the menu.

4. This has returned you to the document page. With the Import cursor, draw a standard text block that is approximately 5″ wide and 7″ high. When you release the mouse, the text will appear in the block.

5. With the Text tool in the text, press Command/Control-A to select all the text.

6. Save the document to your **Work in Progress** folder as "Imported Text.FH9" and leave it open for the next exercise.

Linking Text Blocks

When a text block is not large enough to hold all the type imported into it, a dot will appear in the small box, called the linking box, at the lower-right corner of the text block. This is the text overflow indicator, telling you that there is more text, but there is no room in the text block to display it. When you see the text overflow indicator, you have the option of enlarging the text block or linking to another block of text.

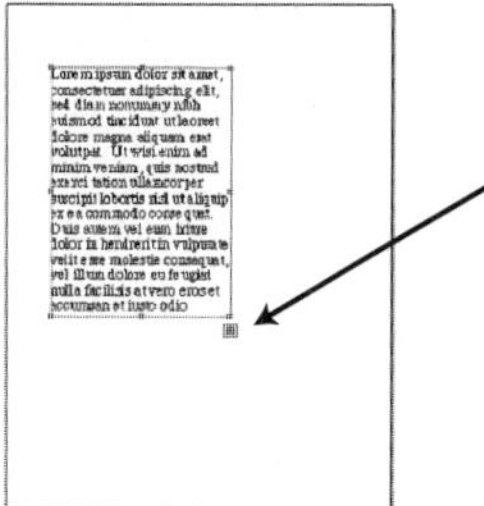

To link to another text block, you click on the overflow indicator and drag to a new text block. To unlink a text block, click on the Linking Box icon and drag to an empty area on the page.

Link Text Blocks

1. With the document **Imported Text.FH9** open, select the Rectangle tool and draw a rectangle about the same size as the text block.
2. With the Pointer tool, select the text block. Click on the text overflow indicator and drag the cursor into the empty rectangle.

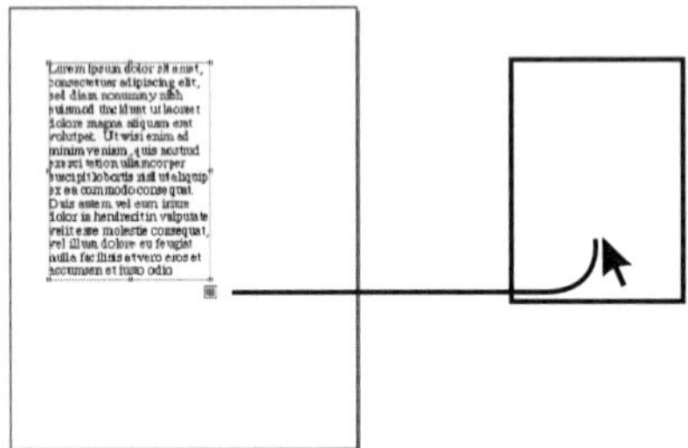

3. The rectangle will be converted to a text block, and the overflowing text will fill it, continuing the flow.

When a rectangle is used for linking text, simply set the fill and stroke to None after the text has been flowed.

4. Draw more rectangles and continue to flow the text this way until there are no more overflow boxes.
5. Save and close the file.

Special Effects with Text and Paths

FreeHand has two features that combine text with paths: Flow Inside Path and Attach To Path. Flow Inside Path will treat any open or closed path as a text block and flow the text inside that area. Attach To Path will allow the text to flow along a path.

Flow Inside Path 

To cause text to flow inside a path you need two elements: text and a path. The path may be created with any of FreeHand's drawing tools. To combine the two, select both the text and the path using the Pointer tool, then choose Text>Flow Inside Path.

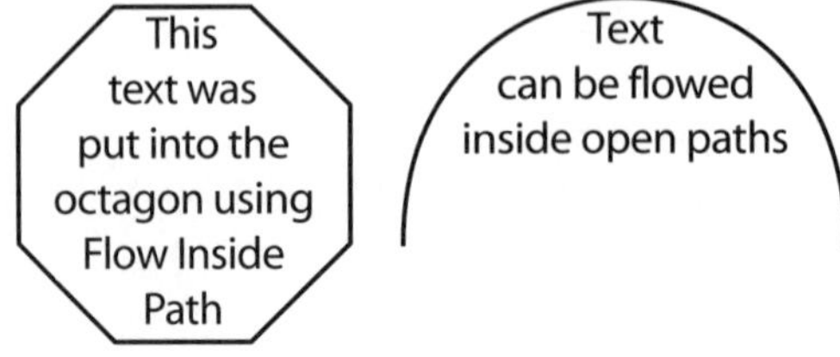

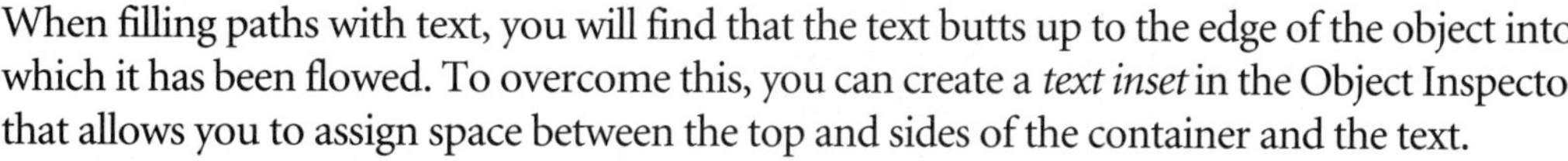

You may also use the tools in the Type toolbar to accomplish many of the functions noted here.

When filling paths with text, you will find that the text butts up to the edge of the object into which it has been flowed. To overcome this, you can create a *text inset* in the Object Inspector that allows you to assign space between the top and sides of the container and the text.

The Inset options are left (l), top (t), right (r), and bottom (b). The following example was given an inset of 0.05-in. to provide a little breathing room for the text inside the path. Text inset is specified in the current unit of measurement.

This text was placed with Fill Inside Path, then painted white to reverse out of the colored background.

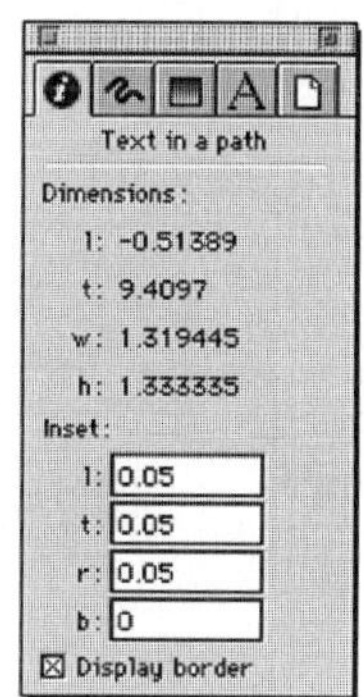

Place Text Inside a Path

1. Create a new document.
2. Select the Text tool from the Toolbox. Click and type the words:

   "To sit in solemn silence, on a dull, dark dock"
3. Using the Text Character Inspector, apply these settings: Font: ATC Cabana, Size: 14 pt., Alignment: Center.
4. Double-click on the Polygon tool. Set the Number of sides to 5 and the Shape to Polygon. On the page, draw a polygon 2″ wide.

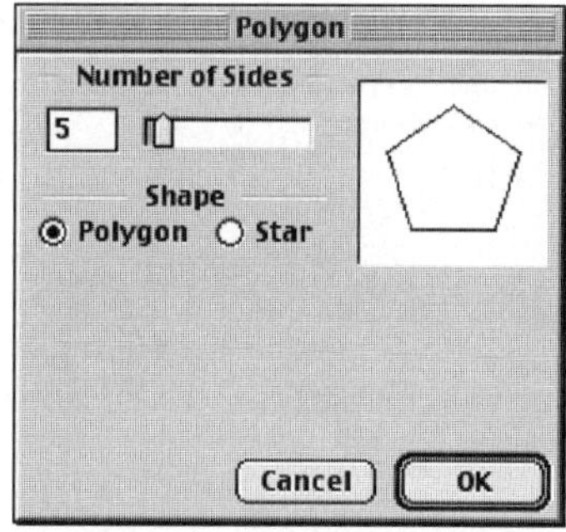

5. In the Color List, open the Crayon library and select Blue. Click OK.
6. Paint the polygon with a Blue fill and assign a stroke of Black, 1 pt. from the Stroke Inspector. Choose Edit>Copy to put a copy of the polygon on the clipboard.
7. Select both the text container and the polygon. Choose Text>Flow Inside Path. The text will fill the inside of the polygon.

8. Highlight the text with the Text tool and paint it with a White fill.
9. Click on the polygon with the Pointer tool and select the Object Inspector. The object appears as Text in a path. Set the units of measurement to Points.
10. Set the Inset as 5 pt. in all the inset fields.

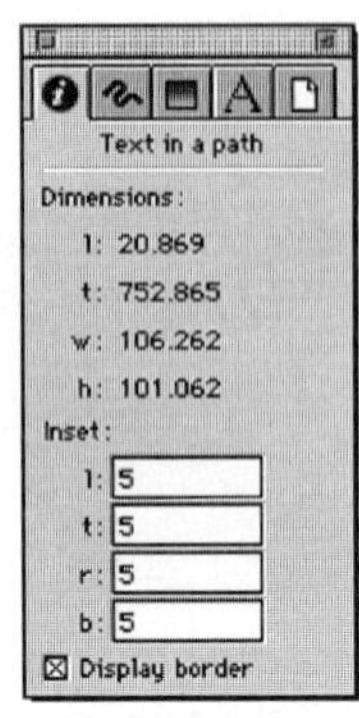

11. Close the file without saving.

Press Command/Control-C to copy any item to the clipboard.

Attach To Path 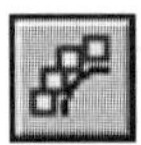 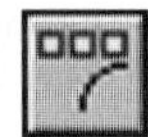

You can cause text to follow any closed or open path drawn in FreeHand by using the Attach To Path command. The process is similar to flowing text inside a path.

To flow text inside a path, press Command/Control-Shift-U.

First, you would type or import a line of text into a text block and draw a path with any of FreeHand's drawing tools. Select the text block and the object or path, then choose Text> Attach To Path. The text will flow along the path. If a closed path is drawn, text will flow along the top of the path. You can press Return/Enter and type a second line of text for closed paths, which will flow along the bottom of the path.

The alignment of the type to the path and its orientation are determined in the Object Inspector. Type may be aligned to the path by its baseline, ascender, or descender, either on top of the path or on the bottom of the path. It may be oriented as follows:

Rotate around path — The baseline of the characters are aligned to the path.
Vertical — The letters are absolutely vertical.
Skew horizontal — The letters slant outward.
Slew vertical — The letters slant inward.

When the Show path box is checked, the path will show behind the text.

Enter distances in the Left and Right fields to offset the left and right edges of the text from the left and right edges of the path.

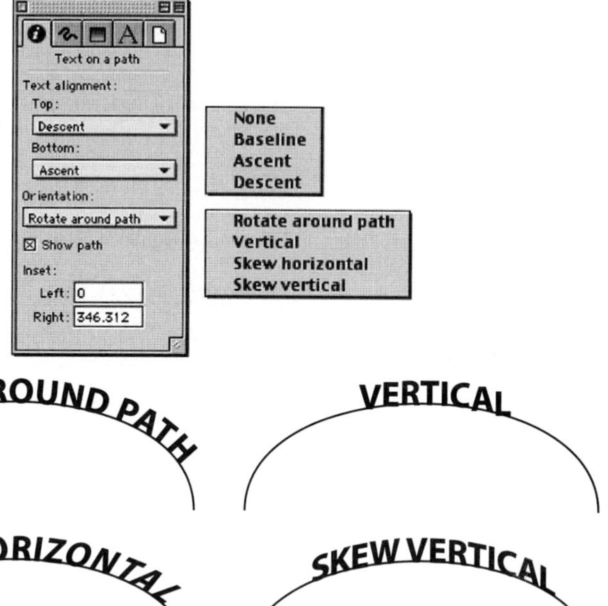

Attach Text to a Path

1. Create a new document, and set the units of measurement set to Inches.
2. Select the Text tool from the Toolbox. Click to create a text block. Type the words: "Robinson Crusoe Cruises take you over the waves!"
3. From the Text Character Inspector, apply these settings: Font: ATC Sea Breeze, Size: 12 pt.
4. With the Freehand tool, crate a wavy path that is 5″ wide.

5. With the Pointer tool, select the text box and the path.
6. Choose Text>Attach To Path.

7. From the Object Inspector, apply the three different alignments and four different orientations. Return to the default Rotate Around Path orientation.

To attach text to a path, press Command/Control-Shift-Y.

8. Hold down the Option/Alt key and click on the path. Choose Modify>Alter Path> Reverse Direction. What happens? The type flips upside down. Press Command/ Control-Z to undo the action.
9. Click on the triangle in the center of the path and move the text back and forth.
10. With the path selected, choose Text>Detach From Path to separate the text from the path. The text will return to its original text block and the path will reappear.
11. Draw a circle approximately 2″ in diameter.
12. With the Pointer tool, select the circle and the text. Attach the text to the path.
13. Place the Text tool between "Cruises" and "take" and remove the word space. Press Return/Enter. What happens? The type to the right of the Text tool is placed on the bottom of the path.

14. Check the Show Path box in the Object Inspector to display the path.
15. Close the file without saving.

Creating Paths from Text

If you want to create text with a distinctive look — perhaps for a logo — you may first want to convert the text to a path. Paths created from text function just as paths created using FreeHand's drawing tools. You can use the anchor points of the path to distort the letter form, and can apply gradients, tiled fills, and other effects.

Create Paths

1. Create a new document. Select Points as the unit of measurement.
2. Click the Text tool on the page to create a text block. On two lines type:

   TROPICAL
   TREASURE

3. Highlight the type with the Text tool and apply these settings from the Text Inspector: Font: ATC Jamaica, Size: 72 pt., Leave the Leading at 0+.

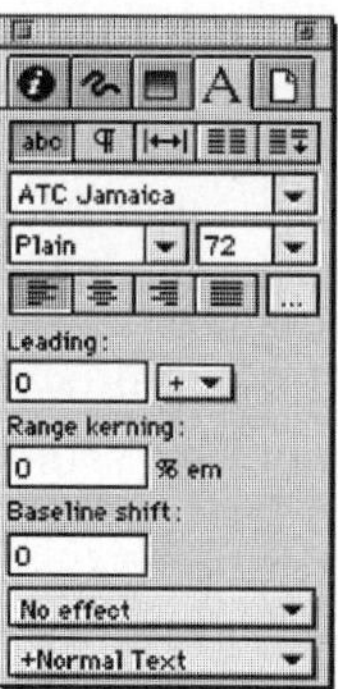

4. Click on the text block with the Pointer tool. Select Text>Convert To Paths. The letters will become filled paths. Select Keyline mode to view the path outlines.

TROPICAL
TREASURE

5. Click on the object with the Pointer tool. The letters (now paths) have been grouped into one object, as indicated by the four corner handles of the group. Select Edit>Copy to duplicate it for later use.

6. Select Modify>Ungroup. What happened?

7. Even though you ungrouped the object, each word is individually grouped. Select Modify>Ungroup again.

8. The letters are now separate objects. Click on any of the letters to see how their anchor points are visible to work with.

9. With the Pointer tool, click on the letter "T" in TROPICAL; you will see its anchor points. Select any one of the points and drag it to distort the path. Distort the other points of the "T" as well.

10. Click on the "O" in TROPICAL with the Pointer tool. Why don't you see anchor points? The "O" is grouped; it has corner handles. Certain letters in the alphabet are actually made up of two paths. The internal path is see-through, not white. This is an effect called a *composite* path. Letters such as "A," "B," "D," "O," "P," "Q," and "R" possess this internal path.

11. How do you split up the "O" to change it? With the "O" highlighted, select Modify>Split. This removes the compounding effect. You can now see both paths.

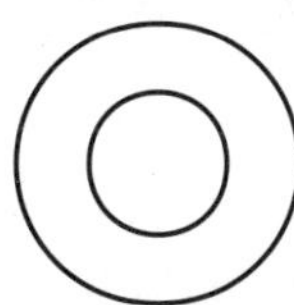

12. Click on the anchor points of the "O" paths with the Pointer tool to select and distort them.

13. Press Command/Control-A to select all text on the page and press the Delete/ Backspace key.

14. Press Command/Control-V to paste the outlines you copied previously. From the Color List, apply a fill of White and a stroke of 1 pt. Black. Change the viewing mode to Preview.

15. Keep the document open for the next exercise.

Create a Drop Shadow

1. In the open file, select the letter outline group and copy it, then select Edit>Paste Behind to paste the duplicate behind the group.

2. Once pasted, the duplicate will be the selected object. Press the Right Arrow button three times, then the Down Arrow button three times to move it three points to the right and three points down.

3. From the Color List Options menu, access the Crayon library. Select Gray and click OK. Paint the object with a fill of Gray and a stroke of None.

4. Let's give the text some more pizzazz. Go back to Color List>Options>Crayon library. Click on Blue, then hold down the Command/Control key and scroll through the list to Seafoam. Click on this color, then click OK to add both colors to the list.

5. Select the letters on the top. From the Colors List, change the stroke to None.

6. From the Fill Inspector, change the fill type to Gradient. Assign Blue to the top gradient swatch and Seafoam to the bottom swatch. Assign an angle of 0°.

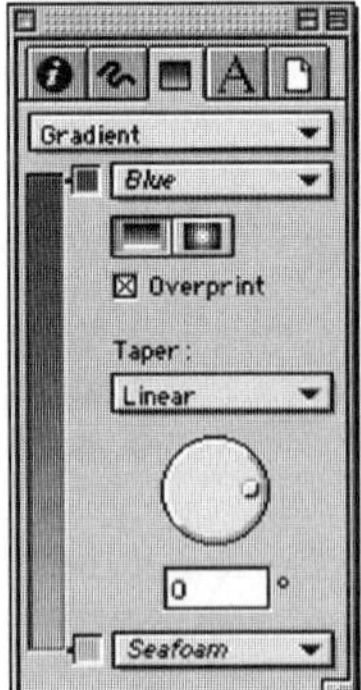

7. That would be fine, if that's what we wanted — but we really were looking for a smooth graduation across the entire word. Even though the letters are grouped, we can't apply the gradient to them as a unit. To achieve that, with the paths still selected, choose Modify>Join.

TROPICAL
TREASURE

8. Close the file without saving.

Summary

In this chapter you have used FreeHand's Text Inspectors: Character, Paragraph, Spacing, Columns and Rows, and Adjust Columns. You have created and edited text, used columnar features, and worked with the text adjustment tools. You have learned how to work with text styles and tabs, and how to import text saved in ASCII or RTF format. You have also learned to use text and graphics together, using the Run Around Selection feature. In addition, you have learned to flow text inside path and to attach and detach text from a path. You also can convert text to a path and work with the paths created.

Complete Project C: Tropical Treasure Logo

Notes:

CHAPTER 10

FreeHand as a Layout Tool

CHAPTER OBJECTIVE:

Learn to use FreeHand as a layout tool, creating single-page designs and multiple-page documents; learn the appropriate time to use FreeHand as a layout application to your advantage due to the unique features supplied by the application. In Chapter 10, you will:

- Learn that documents may be created with different page sizes within the same file.
- Learn about the Document Inspector — the primary tool for managing documents in FreeHand.
- Learn about bleed — a critical process in achieving your final printed output.
- Understand the importance of resolution when creating documents.
- Learn to create documents having a variety of text and graphic elements.

PROJECTS TO BE COMPLETED:

- Dinner Time (A)
- Mask Art (B)
- Tropical Treasure Logo (C)
- **Grocery Ad (D)**
- Ball and Mirror (E)
- No Clowning Around (F)

FreeHand as a Layout Tool

Imposition is the process of arranging a multiple-page document into the correct positions for printing on a press.

You can create many different page sizes from within a single FreeHand document. For example, you could have a single document that contains the entire corporate identity suite of documents — from business cards to envelopes, stationery, and oversized folders.

Press the Spacebar with any tool selected to activate the grabber hand and move the page around the screen.

FreeHand not only offers the tools needed to create single-page designs, but it can also be used to create multiple-page documents, such as booklets, brochures, and catalogs. Before deciding to use FreeHand as a page layout tool, determine whether or not you would be better off using a traditional page layout application, such as QuarkXPress, InDesign, or PageMaker. Use these guidelines to help you decide:

- If your project consists of many pages that are all the same size, such as a novel, catalog, or textbook, you should use a page layout application since they are better suited to long documents. Page layout programs feature Masters on which you can place guides, text, and objects that will be common to all pages in the document. Many page layout programs also allow you to create a table of contents, index, and other lists. They also allow for automatic page numbering.
- Printers often expect incoming documents to be in a QuarkXPress or PageMaker file, because, depending on the program used, many prepress operations such as trapping and imposition only work with page layout programs. In addition, FreeHand documents more than ten pages long can become very cumbersome to navigate.
- If your project consists of dissimilarly-sized pages (see sidebar) and there aren't that many pages, FreeHand might be a better choice.
- If the project is a single-page ad, many designers prefer to use FreeHand instead of a page layout application because they can draw and set type within the same program, and can export the file for inclusion in another document.

Document Preparation

When preparing pages for print in FreeHand or any other program you need to lay the proper groundwork. You should determine the size, orientation, and number of pages to be included in the finished document. In addition, you should create a system of layout guides and/or grids to use as aids in laying out the document.

Document Inspector

When working in FreeHand, the primary tool used for managing documents is the Document Inspector. Through this tool, you add and remove pages, change orientation from tall to wide, choose which page to work on, set bleed and choose different page sizes. An often-overlooked function of the Document Inspector is the Print Resolution setting. This does not, as you might suppose, set the printer's resolution. Instead, it uses the resolution to determine the number of steps to use for blends and gradient fills, and when sizing raster graphics.

Managing Pages with the Page Tool

You can use FreeHand's Page tool to click on FreeHand pages and move them around the screen with the mouse. You can also quickly delete FreeHand pages by selecting a page with the Page tool and pressing the delete key. You must always have at least one page; you cannot delete all pages in a document.

Using the ruler guides, you can set margins, the page center, folds, and other points of reference that require a vertical or horizontal orientation.

Managing Guides

Guides are directly associated with page rulers. The purpose of guides is to provide non-printing reference points to specific measurements on the page rulers. The Units pop-up menu at the bottom of the screen allows you to choose the measurement system that you prefer: Points, Picas, Inches, Decimal Inches, Millimeters, or a custom setting, such as 0.25″=1′.

The Guides dialog box displays data for each page of your document. Simply enter the page you wish to modify or use the Next/Previous page buttons. The location of the guide (horizontal, vertical, or path) will be expressed in the current unit of measurement.

Let's work with FreeHand's page layout features to create some documents similar to those that you will most likely create in the "real world." As you create these documents, remember that a consistent, planned approach is the most direct path to completing the job in a timely manner.

Create a Basic Ad Layout

The magazine's specifications for the ad you will prepare are: Size: 6½″×10″, Bleed: ⅛″, Resolution: 2540 dpi.

Page dimensions are always expressed by their x,y relationship; the width dimension precedes the height.

1. Create a new document. Turn on the page rulers and set the units of measurement for Inches.
2. Open the Document Inspector and set the page size for Custom, with a Portrait (tall) orientation. Set the page dimensions for x: 6.5, y: 10. Set the Bleed for 0.125 (the decimal equivalent of ⅛″. Set the Printer Resolution to 2540 dpi. Press Return/Enter to apply the settings.

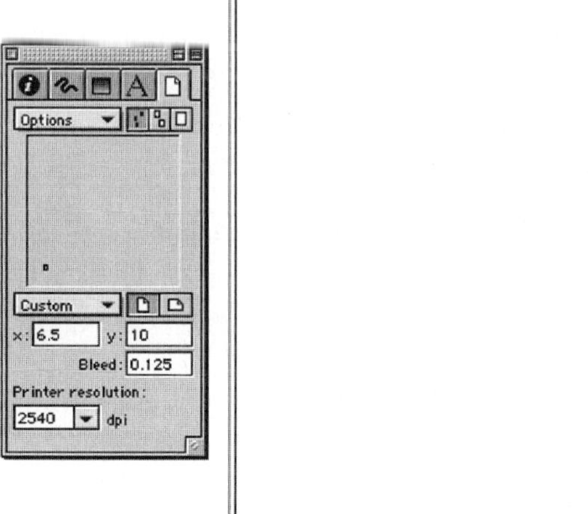

3. Set the guides to help you work quickly on the page. Drag a vertical guide to the 3.25″ position of the horizontal ruler and a horizontal guide to the 5″ position of the vertical ruler to establish the horizontal and vertical centers of the page.

4. Drag margin guides to 0.25 and 6.25 horizontal and 0.25 and 9.75 vertical to establish the text margins of the page.

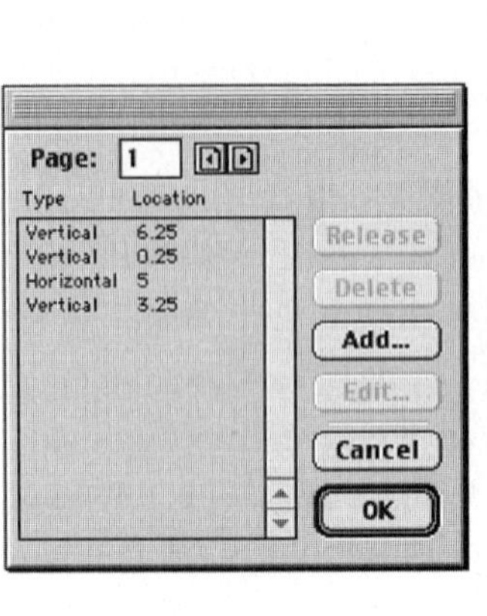

5. Save the document as "Travel Ad.FH9" to your **Work in Progress** folder.

You have set up the shell of your ad, with appropriate guides so you will be able to work on it quickly and efficiently. The next step in the process of completing the ad layout is to import graphics and text.

Import Graphics and Text

1. With the document **Travel Ad.FH9** open, navigate to your **SF-FreeHand** folder and import the first graphic, **Paradise.TIF**.
2. Position the cursor at the upper-left corner of the bleed area and click the mouse button. You'll notice that the photo fills the bleed area and comes to the middle of the page.

3. Let's set the main headline. With the Text tool, draw a text frame with the following parameters:

   l: 1P6 w: 36P0
   t: 29P6 h: 3P0

   You can double-check the positioning in the Object Inspector.

4. Click the Text tool in the text block and type: "The stuff that dreams are made of..." (Do not use the keyboard ellipse — that character is not included in the alphabet of the font we will use).

5. Select the text, and, in the Text Character Inspector, format the text as ATC Daquiri, 30 pt. Set Range Kerning to –4% em.

6. Press Command/Control-R to import **Travel Ad Text.RTF** from your **SF-FreeHand** folder.

7. Click the Import icon and draw a text block the following specifications:

   l: 1P6 w: 36P0
   t: 26P6 h: 24P6

   Double-check your positioning in the Object Inspector and make any corrections necessary.

8. From the Text Columns and Rows Inspector, assign this text block 3 columns with a spacing of 1P0 between them.

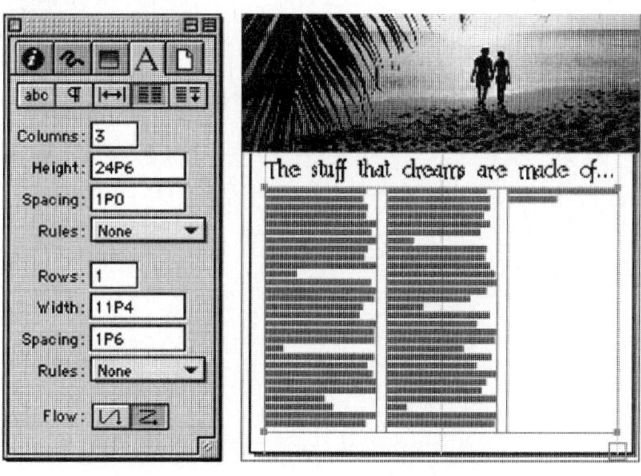

9. Save the document and leave it open for the next exercise.

With these elements in position, you're almost ready to begin composing the ad. First, however, you need to create the all-important client's logo.

Create the Logo

1. Open the file **Globe.FH9** from your **SF-FreeHand** folder. Set the units of measurement to Picas.
2. Using the Ellipse tool, create a circle 8P0 in diameter and position it on top of the globe image (x: 0P0, y: 76P0).
3. Switch to the Text tool and type the words "AROUND THE WORLD VACATIONS". Format them as ATC Jamaica, 16 pt., with Range kerning (tracking) or –5.

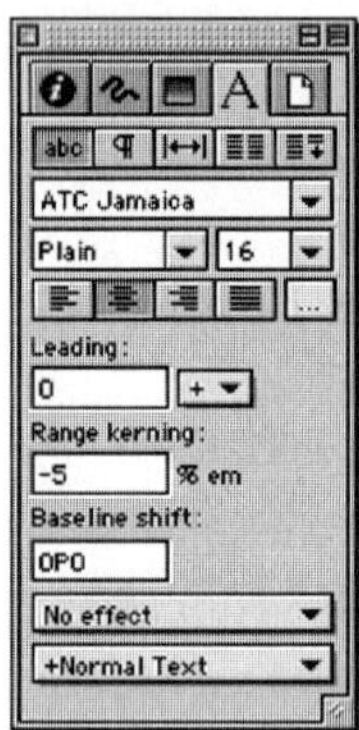

4. With the Pointer tool, select both the words and the circle. Choose Text>Attach To Path.

5. Switch back to the Text tool. Place it immediately in front of the "V" in "VACATIONS" and Delete/Backspace to remove the space in front of the word. Press Return/Enter to place the word at the bottom of the globe graphic.

6. Highlight the word "VACATIONS" with the Text tool, and, in the Text Character Inspector, assign a Baseline shift of -0P3 to move it as far from the globe as the rest of the text.

7. Switch to the Pointer tool. Press Command/Control-A to select all, and press Command/Control-G to group the logo.
8. Save the file to your **Work in Progress** folder as "ATWV Logo.FH9". Leave the file open.
9. With both **Travel Ad.FH9** and **ATWV Logo.FH9** open, drag the logo onto the pasteboard of the ad. You will position it later.
10. Close the **ATWV Logo.FH9** file and leave **Travel Ad.FH9** open for the next exercise.

Format the Ad

1. With **Travel Ad.FH9** open, select Window>Panels>Styles to make the Styles panel available for use.
2. Select all the text in the 3-column block and format it as ATC Cabana Normal/Plain, 9.5/11, with a First line indent of 1P0.

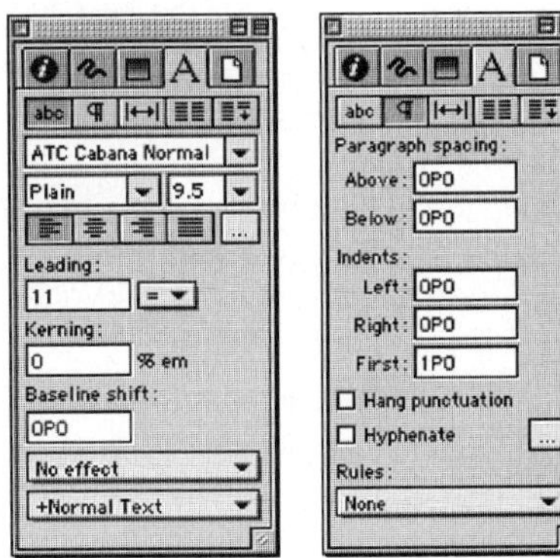

3. Place the Text tool in the first paragraph, and change the First line indent to 0P0.
4. With the Text tool still in that paragraph, select Styles>Options>New. Triple-click on the style name and change it to "T1". This will be the first line of text following a subhead.

5. Place the Text tool in the line "Sample the Culture," select the T1 style. This will remove the indent. From the Styles panel, select Options>New. Name the new style "Subhead".

6. Now select Styles>Options>Edit. Format the Font as ATC Mai Tai Bold and assign Paragraph spacing Above of 0.11. Click OK.

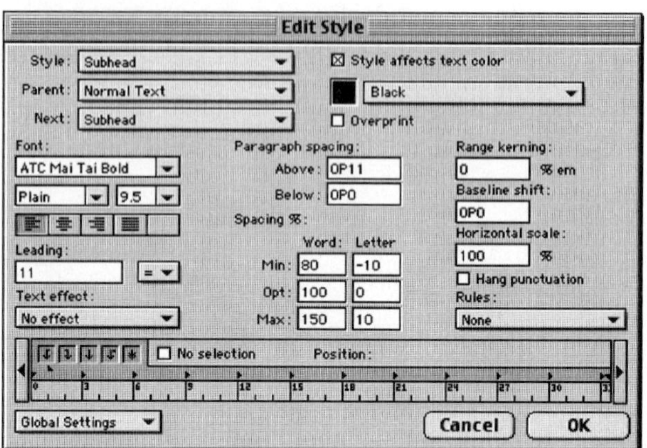

7. Apply the Subhead style to the paragraph that reads "Don't Miss These Other Attractions", and apply the T1 style to each paragraph immediately following the subheads.

8. With the Pointer tool, select the text block and shorten it so there are only two lines following the first subhead.

9. Place the Text tool in front of the fourth line in the second column and select Text>Special Characters>End Of Column.

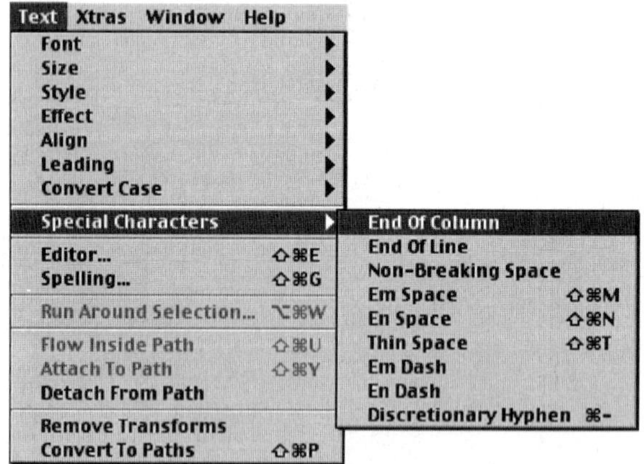

10. Create a separate text block on the pasteboard and type the following, line for line, with a hard paragraph return (Return/Enter) after the first line, and soft returns (Shift-Return/Enter) between the other lines:

Let us take you where you want to go!
Dockside Quay/Suite 100
Sarasota, FL 34231
941/555-2898

11. Select all the lines of type and format them as ATC Mai Tai Normal/Plain, 10/12, Centered.
12. Go back and select the first line of text and change its size to 8.5 pt. From the Text Paragraph Inspector, assign Paragraph spacing Below of 0P6.

Let us take you where you want to go!

Dockside Quay/Suite 100
Sarasota, FL 34231
941-555-2898

13. Position this text at the bottom of the second column, with the baseline of the telephone numbers aligning with the baseline of the text in the first and third columns.
14. Position the logo above the address text, with a "y" position of approximately 10P6.
15. With the Pointer tool, select the address text, logo, and the main text frame. Choose Modify>Align. On the vertical axis, choose Align Center to position them in the center of the page.

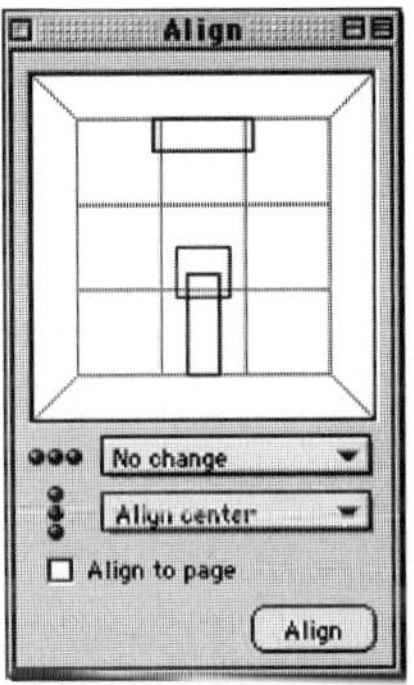

16. Save the document to your **Work in Progress** folder and close.

The stuff that dreams are made of...

The ocean holds an endless fascination — and Florida's Suncoast has more beaches than you can imagine! From Clearwater (voted #1 city beach in the country) and Dunedin's Honeymoon Island in the north to the pristine white sands of Siesta Key and beyond, the beautiful Gulf of Mexico beckons invitingly.

If you tire of baking in the sun and frolicking in the waves, you can stop in at one of the many beachside restaurants for a refreshing Key Lime Pie, a snack, or for liquid refreshment. Many establishments regularly feature up-tempo music on the patio.

For those "SPF 100" days that you really want to stay out of the sun, or in the rare event of a sunless day, you may want to experience the rest of what the area has to offer.

Sample the Culture
Experience the art exhibits and museums that abound in St. Petersburg and Sarasota, or drink in the variety of culture, from the honky tonks of Ybor City to the sponge docks of Tarpon Springs, to the music and theatre that abound in Tampa. Nightlife abounds — all year long, and most nights of the week. From jazz, to swing, to country, to an Irish pub or two. Pick the music you like, and the ambiance you're looking for.

Let us take you where you want to go!

Dockside Quay/Suite 100
Sarasota, FL 34231
941-555-2898

Don't Miss These Other Attractions
If you can't turn your back on an outlet mall, you'll be in seventh heaven! You'll find them all up and down the coast, just reeking with bargains.

And if you need to "get away" there's Busch Gardens in Tampa (with wild roller coasters, water rides, and an open-air zoo), and the attractions of Orlando are just a short car ride away.

What are you waiting for? We'll take you where you want to go — and Florida's Suncoast is just the beginning!

As you have seen, laying out an ad in FreeHand is simply a series of clearly-defined actions. You set your underlying layout, add graphics and text, then format the ad. However, some layouts are a little more complicated than the ad was. The mainstay promotional piece for many businesses is the 6-panel brochure. As you do this series of exercises, you will use most of the layout skills you have learned. Still, you will find each segment of the larger exercise a straightforward use of a skill group you have learned.

Establish the Brochure Format

1. Create a new document. Set the units of measurement to Picas.
2. Open the Document Inspector and choose the middle view. Set the document size as Letter, with a Landscape (Horizontal) orientation. Set the bleed as 0.125i and the Printer resolution to 2540 dpi.

Regardless of what unit of measurement you're working in, you can access other units. Typing 0.125i makes the bleed 0.125 inches. The Document Inspector will convert this to 0P9 — the equivalent in picas.

3. Set the margins for this page. Place horizontal guides at 1P6 and 49P6 and vertical guides at 1P6 and 64P6
4. From the Document Inspector, select Options>Duplicate. This will duplicate our page, complete with guides.

   Unfortunately, you can't fold a brochure in three even panels. That is because folders are mechanical devices, and the fold will vary a little bit. To allow for this, we make the panel that folds inside just a little bit narrower than the rest. Page 2 will be a mirror-image of page 1. We'll set our guides for the panels now.

It might seem easier to simply create three equal columns, but this doesn't work with the equipment use to mechanically fold brochures. The "tuck in" panel must be about 1/16" narrower than the other panels.

5. Select View>Guides>Edit. Select page 1. We'll add the guides that mark the folds and the live text area. Set vertical guides at 20P7, 22P1, 23P7, 42P8, 44P2, and 45P8.

6. Select page 2. Set the vertical guides at 20P4, 21P10, 23P4, 42P5, 43P11, and 45P5.

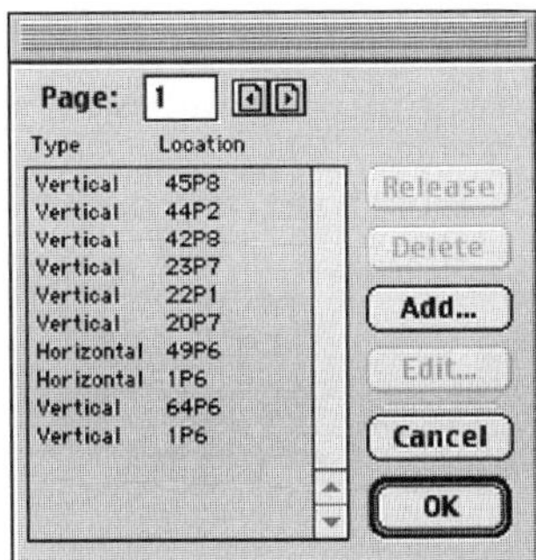

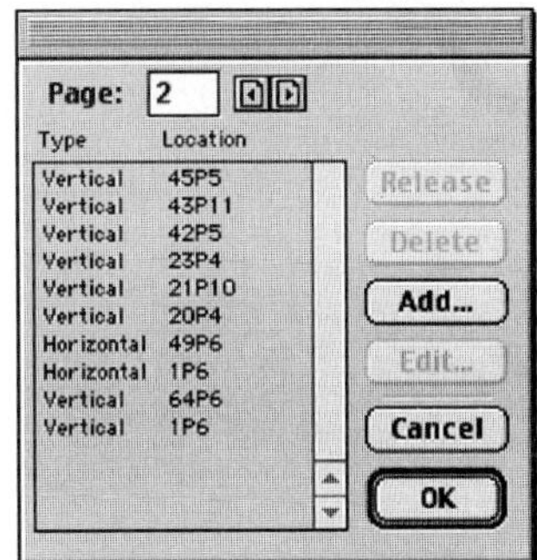

7. Choose View>Guides>Lock, so you won't accidentally move them.

8. Save your file as "Travel Brochure.FH9" to your **Work in Progress** folder and leave it open for the next exercise.

Establish the Color Scheme

Our brochure will use process color. There are three specific colors we will create in the Color Mixer and add to the Color List. If they are not open, activate them now from Window>Panels.

1. With **Travel Brochure.FH9** open, set the color specifications in the color mixer to C: 100, M: 0, Y: 75, K: 50. Click the Add to Color List icon. Name the color "Dark Green" and click Add.

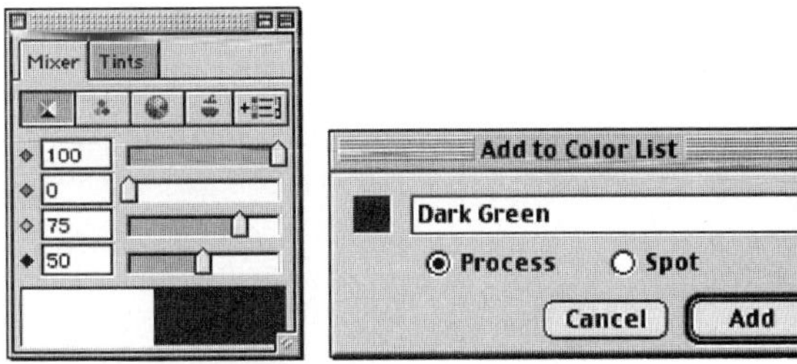

2. Create the two additional colors in the same manner:

   Dark Blue: C: 100, M: 75, Y: 0, K: 25
   Light Blue: C: 85, M: 35, Y: 0, K: 0

   Your Color List should look like the following when you are finished.

3. Close the Color Mixer. Save the document to preserve your changes.

Set Up Text Frames

1. In the Document Inspector, click on page 1 to make it the active page.
2. With the Text tool, drag a text frame the width and height of the live area in panels 2 and 3. Click on the Linking Box icon below panel 2 and drag the link to panel 3.

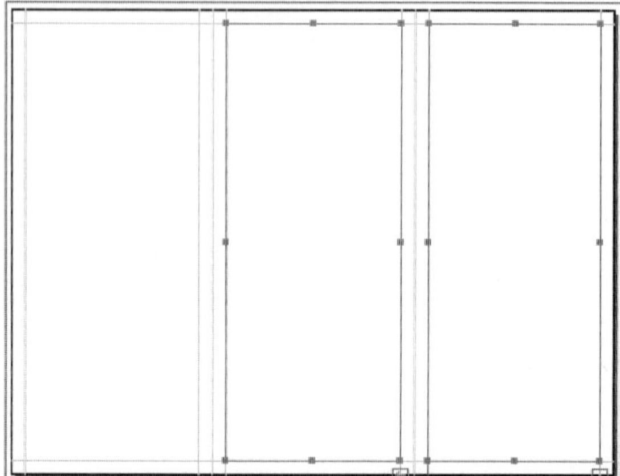

3. Deselect the frames. Select File>Import and import the file **Travel Brochure Text.RTF** from your **SF-FreeHand** folder into panel 1. Click on the overset text box and link to panel 2.

4. Select all the text and style it ATC Cabana Normal/Plain, 12/15.
5. Save the document to preserve your changes and leave it open for the next exercise.

Establish the Paragraph Styles

Your Styles panel is in the same group as the Color List, which should be open. If it is not, open the Styles panel from Window>Styles.

1. Place the Text cursor in the second paragraph and, from the Text Paragraph Inspector, assign a First line indent of 1P0.

2. With the cursor still in the second paragraph, select New from the Styles panel Options menu. Triple-click on the name to rename it "BT", for Body Text.

3. Place the cursor in the first paragraph, create a new style, and name it "BT1". This will be the first line of body text in the brochure and following a subhead.

4. Place the cursor in the "Meet Our Travel Specialists" line and create a new style. Name it "SH" for Subhead. Click Edit, and make the following adjustments to the style:

   Font: ATC Mai Tai Bold
   Color: Dark Green
   Above: 0P10, Below: 0P5

   Click OK when the adjustments have been made.

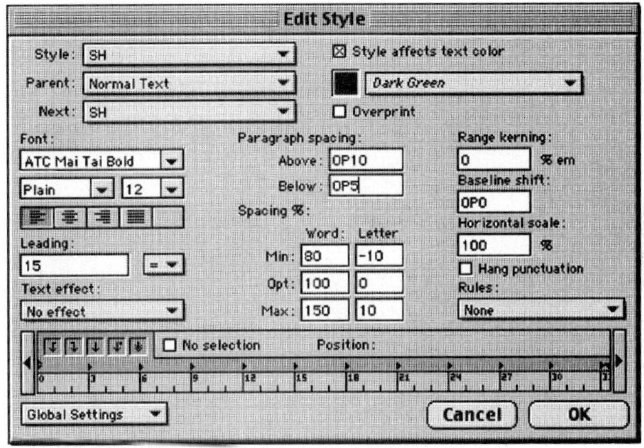

5. Click on the line of text "The British Isles" and, from the Text Paragraph Inspector, assign it a Left Indent of 3P0 and a First line indent of –0P9.

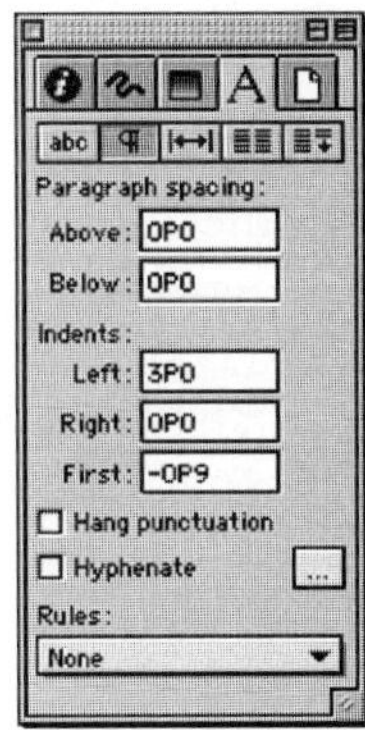

6. With the Text tool in this line, create a new style; name it "LB". This is the main bulleted list (list, bulleted) style.

7. Switch to the Pointer tool, and click in the margins to deselect all text. Click on the LB style and create a new style. Name this style "LB1". Edit it to have a Paragraph spacing Above of 0P7.5. This will be the first item of the bulleted list.

8. Create another style in the same way. Name it "LB2". Edit it to have Paragraph spacing Below of 0P7.5. This will be the last item of the bulleted list.

9. Click on the BT1 style to base the next style on it. Name the new style Bio and edit it to have a Paragraph spacing Below of 0P7.5.

When you are finished, your Styles panel should appears as follows.

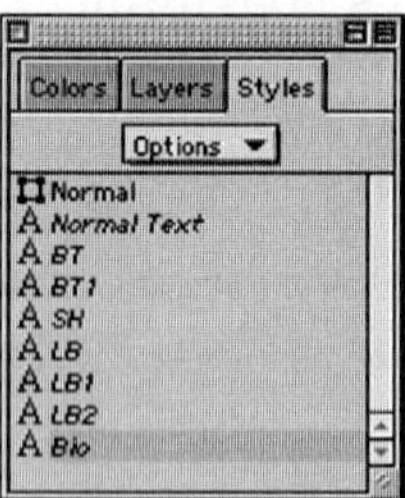

10. Save the document to preserve your changes and leave it open for the next exercise.

Style the Text

1. With the document **Travel Brochure.FH9** open, note that you have already applied styles (BT1, BT, and SH, respectively) to the first three paragraphs when you created the paragraph styles.
2. Place the Text tool in the "How Can We Serve You" line and apply the SH style.
3. Style the paragraphs in between the subheads with the Bio style. Style the following paragraph as BT1. This brings us down to our bulleted list — which has no bullets.
4. Place the Text tool at the beginning of the "Guided Tours" line and add the bullet character. Press Option-8 on the Macintosh, or if using Windows, hold down the Alt key and press 0149 on the numeric keypad, then release the Alt key.

   travel (but, of course, we'll be happy to book
   your travel for whatever reason).
   • Guided Tours
   The British Isles

5. Add bullets to the remaining lines in the list.
6. Style the "Guided Tours" line as LB1, the next 5 lines as LB, and the "Theater and On the Town" line as LB2.
7. Style the last paragraph BT1.
8. Save the document to preserve your changes. Leave it open for the next exercise.

Insert Graphics and Embellishments

1. With the document **Travel Brochure.FH9** still open, go to the first paragraph, with the Text tool, cut the letter "W" and paste it into its own text block.
2. Style the letter ATC Daquiri, 84 pt. From the Color List, assign it a fill and stroke of Dark Blue. From the Stroke Inspector, assign the stroke a width of 2 pt.
3. Select Text>Convert To Paths. Using the Pointer tool, place it with its baseline on the baseline of the fourth line of text.

3. Select Text>Run Around Selection. Set the object to runaround and the Right Standoff to 0P2. Click OK.

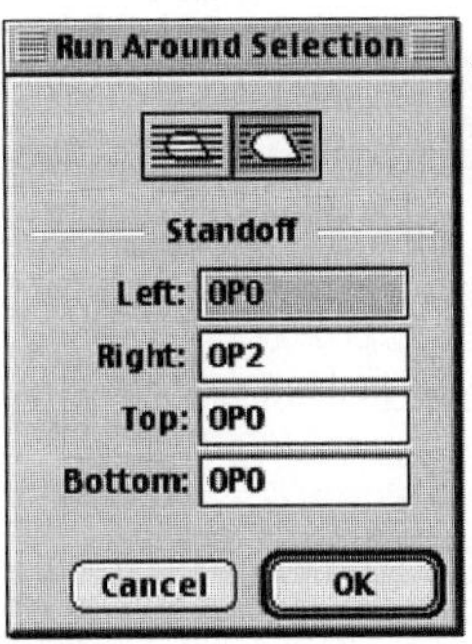

Whether your next vacation is designed to take you around the world in eighty days (more or less), or you're constrained to a long weekend closer to home, we're the people who can make your vacation fun, exciting, romantic, or relaxing — in other words, the kind of vacation you're looking to have. Located in "vacation central" — Florida's sunny Gulf coast, we're familiar with what people want from their vacations, and, with two decades behind us, we have the experience to help you maximize your vacation.

4. With the Text tool in the first paragraph, access the Text Adjust Columns Inspector and assign a First line leading of 24.6.

   Now it's time to add some photos.

5. From your **SF-FreeHand** folder, import **Judy.TIF**. Position it with the top of the photo approximately at the top of the capital letters in the first line of text of her bio (x: 1P6, y: 17p2). From Text>Run Around Selection, set the standoffs for Right and Bottom to 0P9, and click OK.

Run Around Selection
Standoff
Left: 0P0
Right: 0P9
Top: 0P0
Bottom: 0P9
Cancel
OK

Meet Our Travel Specialists

Judy, believe it or not, is our resident ski bum. Last winter she was the guide for six (count 'em) trips to the American Rockies and Sierras. This summer where else would she be but taking ski tours "down

6. From your **SF-FreeHand** folder, import **Max.TIF**, **Laurie.TIF**, and **John.TIF**. Place them in relative positions within their bios, and assign the same runaround standoffs.

7. It is obvious that there is not enough room for Glen's picture. Place the Text tool in front of the paragraph containing his bio and select Text>Special Characters>End of Column to force his bio to the next panel.

8. From your **SF-FreeHand** folder, import **Glen.TIF** in relative positions within his bio, and assign the same runaround standoffs.

9. From your **SF-FreeHand** folder, import **Your Vacation.TIF** at x: 45P8, y: 5P0. Assign a runaround standoff of 1P0 on the bottom.

   We're going to insert a teaser here.

10. With the Text tool, create a new text block with a width of 19P1 and a height of 4P0. Switch to the Pointer tool and, from the Fill Inspector, assign a fill of Dark Blue.

It's always a good idea to work with the Object Inspector open as much as possible. Sometimes it's a good idea to pull it out of its grouping so you'll always have it to refer to.

11. Switch to the Text tool and type the following, line for line:

    For your next vacation, call
    414/555-ATWV

12. Set the first line of text to ATC Mai Tai Bold, 10/18, and the second line to ATC Mai Tai Bold, 18/18. Color the text Light Blue. From the Text Adjust Columns Inspector, assign the First line leading to 18 pt. Center the text in the box.

13. Position this text block at the bottom of the second column.

Whether your next vacation is designed to take you around the world in eighty days (more or less), or you're constrained to a long weekend closer to home, we're the people who can make your vacation fun, exciting, romantic, or relaxing — in other words, the kind of vacation you're looking to have. Located in "vacation central" — Florida's sunny Gulf coast, we're familiar with what people want from their vacations, and, with two decades behind us, we have the experience to help you maximize your vacation.

We'll work with your desires (and your budget) to help you get the most from a guided vacation, a cruise, an "on your own" experience, or a combination of any of these.

Meet Our Travel Specialists

Judy, believe it or not, is our resident ski bum. Last winter she was the guide for six (count 'em) trips to the American Rockies and Sierras. This summer where else would she be but taking ski tours "down under" to the Chilean Andes and to New Zealand. Seems like all she knows how to do is take fun to the max!

And speaking of Max — she's a typical Floridian. Hates winter. (That's because she moved here from North Dakota about eight years ago.) Since she's been here she's been comfortable showing up at work in shorts and a polo shirt — except when she's having fun with our customers diving off the Keys, or sailing the Caribbean. Max is a registered dive instructor and holds her pilot's license for sailing craft. She also knows when the big fish are running for those of you who really enjoy big game fishing.

What can we tell you about Laurie, except that she's a Celtophile. Her specialty is trips to Ireland, Scotland, England, Wales, Australia and New Zealand. Whether it's helping folks get the most from their trip to "the Homeland" or accompanying them on cycling and hiking trips through the beautiful mountains, trying to spy Nessie, exploring the towns, or watching the changing of the guard at Buckingham Palace, she's right at home in the British Isles and Down Under.

John is our computer geek. He keeps track of all the best airfares and cruiseline fares, so we can pass them along to you. Like everybody else, he has a "life." In addition to living online, he's our resident expert on Florida theme parks — and has extended that expertise to cover other parks, like Colonial Williamsburg. Since we're so close, he's been known to take a mid-week theme park break, just to see what's new and exciting that he can share with you.

Glen is the person we all rely on to keep us together. He's the manager of the mailing list, keeper of the schedule — and all 'round expert on night life, concerts, and theatre. If you're planning an evening On the Town (New York, Chicago, San Francisco, Rome, or wherever) Glen will help you find the kind of fun you seek.

How Can We Serve You?

By now, you have a pretty good idea of what we can do for you. We specialize in vacation travel (but, of course, we'll be happy to book your travel for whatever reason).

- Guided Tours
- The British Isles
- Trips "Down Under"
- Dive Trips and Tours
- Sailing Trips
- Cruises
- Theatre and On the Town

Call us and see for yourself just how much fun you can have!

14. Save the file to your **Work in Progress** folder to preserve your changes. You're more than half finished.

Prepare a Special Offer

We want to give our customers something special to look for over the next few months. The Special Events panel requires some new styles, and we'll make it stand out with color as well.

1. With **Travel Brochure.FH9** open, go to page 2 by selecting it from the Document Inspector.

2. We want this panel to stand out, so we're going to make it a tint of Light Blue. With the Rectangle tool, draw a rectangle from the top left edge of the bleed area to bottom bleed at the fold mark of the first panel. The Object Inspector should read:

    x: –0P9 w: 22P7
    y: –0P9 h: 52P6

    Assign a stroke of None.

3. Activate the Color Mixer. Select the Tint panel and set the base color for Light Blue. Click the 30% swatch and drag it onto the rectangle you just created. Close the Color Mixer.

4. From your **SF-FreeHand** folder, import the document **ATWV Special Events.RTF.** With the Text tool, remove any extra spaces from the bottom of the set so as to avoid false "text overset" warnings.

5. From the Object Inspector, assign the text block the following parameters:

   x: 1P6 w: 18P10
   t: 49P6 h: 48P0

   Assign text insets of 0P6 to all four sides.

6. With the Pointer tool selected, click on the Stroke Inspector and select a Basic Stroke of 1 pt. Black.

7. From the Styles panel Option menu, create a new paragraph style named "BTS" (Body Text Special). Edit its format to ATC Mai Tai Normal/Plain, 9/11 with Paragraph spacing as 0P3.

8. Create a new style, based on BTS, named "BTS2". Edit its specifications to ATC Mai Tai Italic, 8/9, with Spacing Below as 0P5.

9. Create a new style, based on BTS, named "BTSH". Edit its specifications to ATC Mai Tai Normal/Plain, 10/11, with Above and Below of 0P5. Set the color to Dark Blue.

10. Create a new style, based on SH, name it "SH2". Set its specifications as ATC Mai Tai Bold, 14/14, with 0P0 Above and 1P2 Below. Set the alignment to Center and the Color to Dark Green.

11. Select the first paragraph, "Special Events Around the World" and assign it the SH2 style. Highlight all the text in this paragraph, and from Text>Convert Case, change the case to Upper.

It's better to drag the graphic into the file than to import it, creating a nested file. Often, nested files that have been rotated, or that contain type, print improperly.

12. Select the second paragraph and assign the BTSH style. Highlight the words "Caribbean Sail and Dive" and change them from Normal to Bold.

13. Assign the BTS style to the next paragraph.

14. The following paragraph should be formatted with the BTS2 style.

15. Format the next two events the same way: the event name as the BTSH style, the description as the BTS style, and the prerequisite as the BTS2 style.

SPECIAL EVENTS AROUND THE WORLD

Caribbean Sail and Dive. April 23 – 29.

ATWV's Max Taylor leads you in this 7-day, 6-night sail and dive in the pristine waters of the West Indies. You'll sail the 51-foot sloop Ligature, with a home port of Nassau, Bahamas. This combination sail and dive will provide a variety of experiences for all participants. We dive in the clear waters of the West Indies and come face-to-face with a variety of flora and fauna. A Gala in Nassau ends your week of frolic on and in the water. This tour fills up fast!

Beginning and intermediate sailors. Dive certification required. Call for rates and details.

16. Deselect the text block. Save the document and leave it open for the next exercise.

Add the Mailing Panel

This brochure is designed to be a self-mailer. The back panel is designated as the mailing panel. It needs to include the return address and the First Class Permit stamp.

1. With "Travel Brochure.FH9" open, open the document **ATWU Logo.FH9** from your **Work in Progress** folder. If you did not do the exercise to create this logo, you may use the document **Travel Logo.FH9** in your **SF-FreeHand** folder. Be sure the graphic is grouped. Drag the logo onto the page. Close the Travel Logo file.
2. Using the Object Inspector, scale the graphic so the width and height are each 9P0.
3. Double-click on the Rotate tool, and assign a Rotation angle of 90°.

4. Using the Object Inspector, position the logo at x: 23P5, y: 1P6.
5. Using the Text tool, create a text block approximately 9P0 wide and 4P0 in height. Type the following, line for line, with soft returns as line endings:

   Suite 100
   Dockside Quay
   Sarasota, FL 34231
6. Ensure that no style was applied. From the Text Character Inspector, format the text as ATC Mai Tai Normal, 12/15, and set the Alignment to Center.
7. Switch to the Pointer tool and rotate the text frame 90°. Position it below the logo at x: 33P0, y: 1P6
8. Create another text frame 6P0 × 6P0, with a top text inset of 0P5 and type the following line-for-line:

   Bulk Rate
   U.S. Postage
   PAID
   Permit #112
   Sarasota, FL
9. Format the text as ATC Mai Tai Normal, 10/12. Set the Alignment to Center.
10. Click on the Text Frame with the Pointer tool and, from the Stroke menu, assign a Black stroke of 0P1.
11. Rotate the block 90° and position it in the upper-left area of the mailing panel (x: 23P5, y: 43P6).

12. Save the document. There's just one panel to go — the easy one. Leave it open for the next exercise

Finish Up

1. Import the document **ATWV BroCover.TIF** from your **SF-FreeHand** folder. Position it so that it fills the right-hand panel from the fold mark to the bleed. Position it vertically as you see fit.

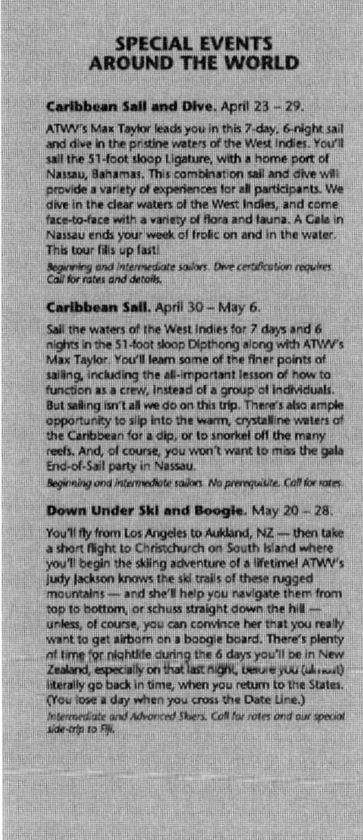

SPECIAL EVENTS AROUND THE WORLD

Caribbean Sail and Dive. April 23 – 29.

ATWV's Max Taylor leads you in this 7-day, 6-night sail and dive in the pristine waters of the West Indies. You'll sail the 51-foot sloop Ligature, with a home port of Nassau, Bahamas. This combination sail and dive will provide a variety of experiences for all participants. We dive in the clear waters of the West Indies, and come face-to-face with a variety of flora and fauna. A Gala in Nassau ends your week of frolic on and in the water. This tour fills up fast!

Beginning and Intermediate sailors. Dive certification requires. Call for rates and details.

Caribbean Sail. April 30 – May 6.

Sail the waters of the West Indies for 7 days and 6 nights in the 51-foot sloop Dipthong along with ATWV's Max Taylor. You'll learn some of the finer points of sailing, including the all-important lesson of how to function as a crew, instead of a group of individuals. But sailing isn't all we do on this trip. There's also ample opportunity to slip into the warm, crystalline waters of the Caribbean for a dip, or to snorkel off the many reefs. And, of course, you won't want to miss the gala End-of-Sail party in Nassau.

Beginning and Intermediate sailors. No prerequisite. Call for rates.

Down Under Ski and Boogie. May 20 – 28.

You'll fly from Los Angeles to Aukland, NZ — then take a short flight to Christchurch on South Island where you'll begin the skiing adventure of a lifetime! ATWV's Judy Jackson knows the ski trails of these rugged mountains — and she'll help you navigate them from top to bottom, or schuss straight down the hill — unless, of course, you can convince her that you really want to get airborn on a boogie board. There's plenty of time for nightlife during the 6 days you'll be in New Zealand, especially on that last night, [illegible] literally go back in time, when you return to the States. (You lose a day when you cross the Date Line.)

Intermediate and Advanced Skiers. Call for rates and our special side-trip to Fiji.

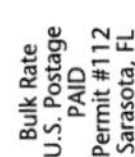

2. From Text>Spelling, check the spelling of both stories in the document.

3. Check the document for bad hyphenation or for kerning in headlines that you think should be repaired.

4. Save the document to your **Work in Progress** folder and close.

Creating a brochure in FreeHand is, as you see, demanding. However, when you use the tools at your disposal, the task is made much simpler. Using the techniques you have learned in these exercises will help you produce better-than-average publications.

Creating Longer Documents

FreeHand, while it can do larger documents, is not the program of choice. When possible, you should use a page layout program.

As we alluded to in the beginning of this chapter, it is possible to produce larger publications in FreeHand. The larger the publication is, the more planning is required. Doing the physical layout is not much more difficult than flowing text in a smaller document.

Although a larger document will usually contain many more styles than the documents we have been working with, the principles for working with them is the same. For practical purposes, a document larger than eight pages should be managed with a page layout program.

Create a Multiple-Page Layout

1. Create a new, letter-size document. Set the units of measurement for Inches and turn on the page rulers. Open the Document Inspector.

2. Using your method of choice, create ruler guides to show margins of 0.5″ around the page and horizontal and vertical guides to show the center of the page. You might want to try the method we used (shown below).

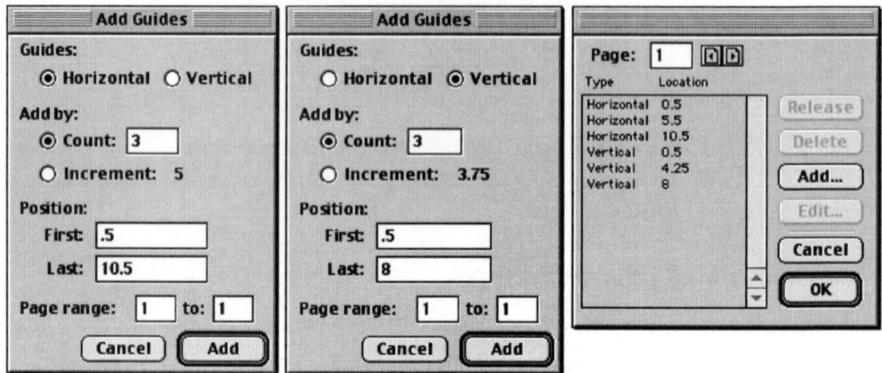

Here, we allowed FreeHand to do the calculations. We set three horizontal guides with the first at 0.5″ and the last at 10.5″. Then we set three vertical guides with the first at 0.5″ and the last at 8″. FreeHand did the calculations for us.

3. Save the document to your **Work in Progress** folder as "Multi-page Layout.FH9".

   Because you can't import text into a frame directly, we're going to duplicate this page first, then create a linking frame on page 2 to duplicate to the rest of the pages.

4. From the Document Inspector, select Options>Duplicate twice.

5. On page 3, draw a rectangle the width of the first column, inside the margins, from top to bottom. Its dimensions, viewed in the Object Inspector, should be as follows:

   x: 0.5 w: 3.75
   y: 0.5 h: 10

6. Set the fill and stroke of the rectangle to None.

7. From the Document Inspector, duplicate page 3 five times, to yield a total of 8 pages. You may want to click on the middle viewing button to increase the size of the pages in the Viewing Window. Pages may be positioned in the Viewing Window by dragging them.

8. From the View menu, choose Fit All to see all the pages in the document window.

9. Save the document and leave it open for the next exercise.

Add Text to the Document

1 In the Document Inspector, double-click on Page 1 of the open document to make it the active page, and to center it in the viewing area. Choose the Text tool and drag a standard text block the width of the margins. Type the following, line-for-line:

   All My Troubles
   Seemed So
   Far Away

A standard text block has a fixed size, and is created by dragging the Text tool on the page.

2. Highlight the text, and in the Text Character Inspector, format it as follows: ATC Plantation, 60/72, Aligned Center.

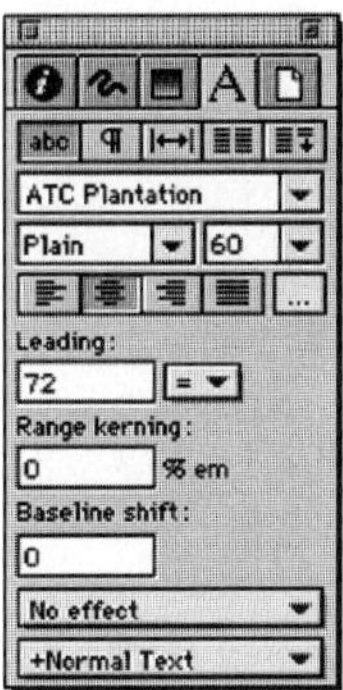

3. Press Command/Control, then click on the text block. The Text cursor will temporarily change to the Pointer tool, and you can move the text block to the upper center of the page.

4. Switch to Page 2, using either the Document Inspector or the Page Selector pop-up menu at the bottom of the page.

5. Import the text of the story, **All My Troubles.TXT**, from your **SF-FreeHand** folder.

6. On Page 2, drag the text cursor so it fills the left column, inside the margins, from top to bottom.

7. With the Text tool in the text, select Command/Control-A to select all the text. Format it from the Text Character Inspector ATC Sands 12/16, Align Left. From the Text Paragraph Inspector, apply Paragraph spacing Below: 0.1, First line indent: 0.15

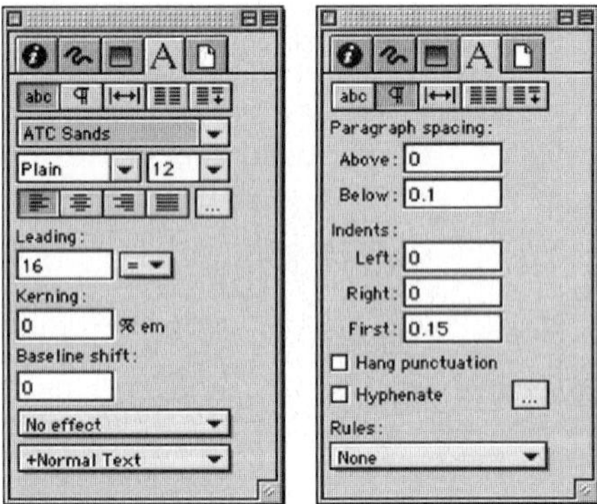

8. With the Pointer tool, click on the text block on page 2. You will see the *text overflow indicator* at the bottom right. Click and drag it into the rectangle on page 3. Continue flowing the text into the rectangles on the rest of the pages.

9. Click the Text tool in any text block. You can see the flow of text through the linked boxes. This is useful for keeping track of text in longer documents.
10. Select View>Guides and uncheck Show to view the pages you've created as they should appear when printed. Save and close the document.

The right hand column of these pages could be used to hold artwork that accompanies the text, or they could be used for notes.

Summary

In this chapter you have learned how to prepare straightforward ad layouts and more complex brochure layouts. You have also learned how to flow text within a larger document. You have experienced the details that you need to observe when working with documents larger than one page and documents that have many elements.

Complete Project D: Grocery Ad

Notes

CHAPTER 11

Transformation Tools

CHAPTER OBJECTIVE:

To learn the four transformational techniques with which you can drastically change an object. In Chapter 11, you will:

- Learn about the transformation tools with which you scale, rotate, skew, and reflect objects.
- Understand the three transformation modes; learn to use the tools in the Transform panel for precise operations.
- Learn how to manually rotate an object with the Rotate tool; how to create a design with the Rotate tool, and to understand the different features of the Rotate panel.
- Learn how to use the Refect tool to mirror a selected object across a specified axis; learn how to set the Reflect axis; understand how to reflect an object from the Transform panel; learn to to use Reflect to create symmetrical designs.
- Learn how to scale objects in the Scale panel.
- Understand how the Skew tool slants or obliques a selected object to create special effects; learn how to skew objects in the Transform panel.
- Learn how to use the Transform panel with repeating.

PROJECTS TO BE COMPLETED:

- Dinner Time (A)
- Mask Art (B)
- Tropical Treasure Logo (C)
- Grocery Ad (D)
- Ball and Mirror (E)
- No Clowning Around (F)

Transformation Tools

The FreeHand Toolbox includes a set of transformation tools that allow you to move, rotate, reflect, scale and skew objects. Transformations can be done interactively with the Toolbox tools, numerically using the Transform panel, or by performing multiple transformations interactively with the Interactive Transformer.

Transformation Modes

When a transformation tool is selected in the toolbox, the cursor changes to a crosshair that can be used to mark the origin of transformation. This is the center of the transformation, often called the origin point. The cursor is dragged on or around the selected object to perform the transformation.

If you double-click on a transformation tool in the Toolbox, the Transform panel with the available options appears. This is a more accurate means of making transformations. Move is arguably not really a transformation, but it's included in the Transform panel so you can precisely move objects.

Press Command/Control-M to open the Transform panel.

The Interactive Transformer appears if you double-click on an object with the pointer tool.

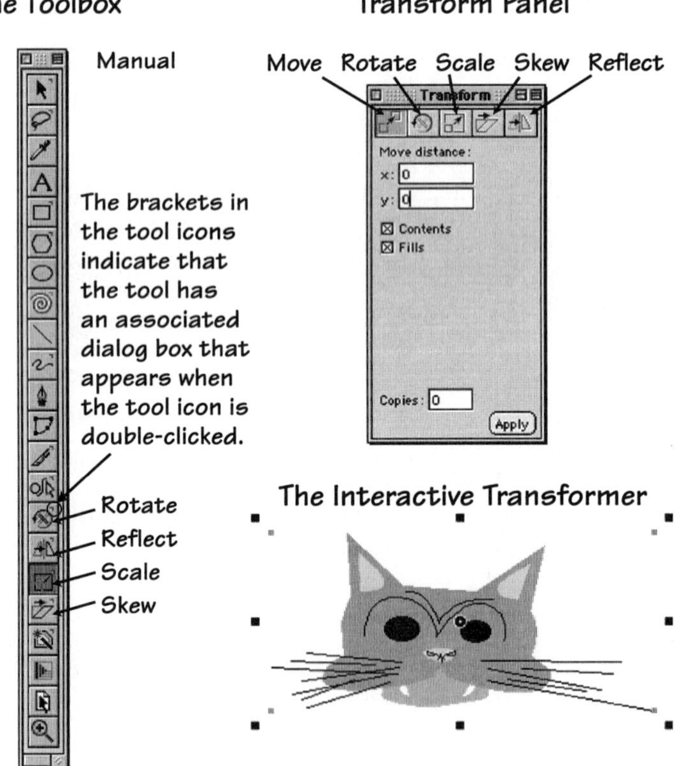

Positive degrees will rotate an object to the left; negative degrees will rotate it to the right.

Rotate

An object can be manually rotated by selecting the artwork, choosing the Rotate tool, and simply rotating the object. Rotation occurs around the point of origin, which is wherever you click the mouse in a simple rotation. Rotation can be accomplished through Window>Panels>Transform, or by using the Interactive Transformer, shown later in this section.

The following are the Rotate panel's options:

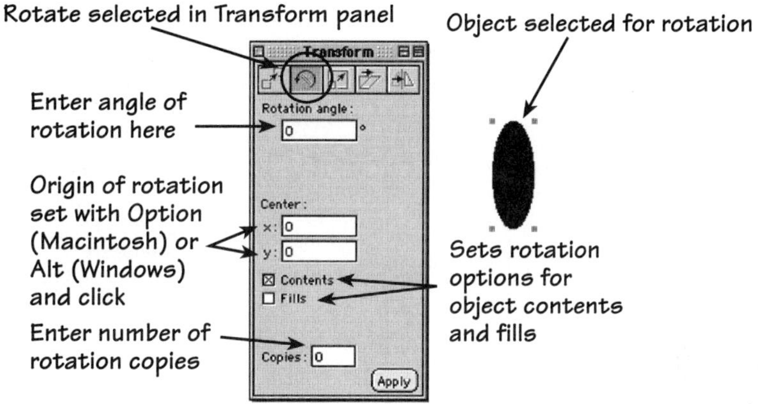

Create a Design with Rotate

1. Create a new document.
2. Use the Ellipse tool to draw an oval and fill it like the one shown below. Edit>Clone the oval to create a duplicate that will appear in the same spot as the original.

3. With one of the ovals selected, double-click on the Rotate tool to show the Transform panel. Click the crosshair underneath the oval while holding the Option/Alt key to set the origin of transformation.

Press Command/Control-= to clone an object. Cloning makes a duplicate of the object and places the duplicate exactly on top of the original.

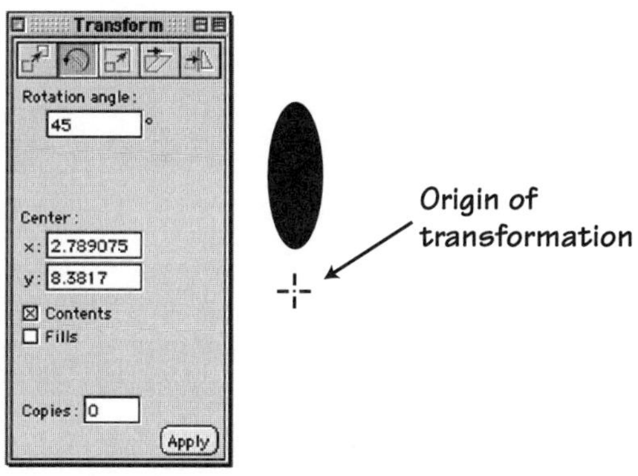

Double-clicking a transformation tool in the Toolbox sets the origin point to the exact center of the selected object(s).

In the Transform panel, type 45° for the Rotation angle. Click Apply (Macintosh) or Rotate (Windows). The clone rotates 45° to the left. If you had typed –45°, it would have rotated to the right.

4. Press Command/Control-D six times to complete the flower image.

5. Use the Ellipse tool to draw a circle for the center of this flower.

6. Edit>Select>All the objects and delete them.
7. Save the file in your **Work in Progress** folder as "Transforms.FH9". Keep the document open for the next exercise.

Reflect

The Reflect tool is used to mirror a selected object across a specified axis. You can set the Reflect axis in the dialog box, or set it manually by clicking the tool crosshair on the page while holding the Option/Alt key. Reflect is not available in the Interactive Transformer.

You can also reflect an object just by clicking the tool's crosshair near the selected object. The default reflection is 90°.

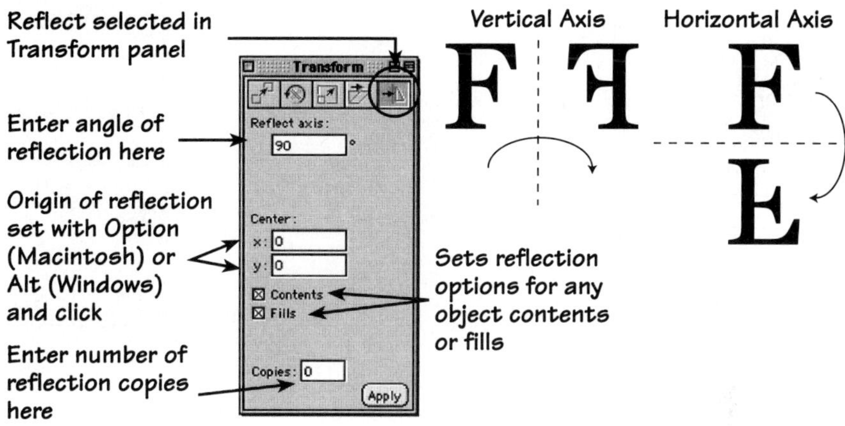

To make a reflection of an object, select the object, then open the Transform panel by double-clicking on the Reflect tool in the Toolbox. In the Transform panel, type the Reflect axis into the field. 90° produces a vertical reflection; 180° makes a horizontal reflection, and any other value will reflect the object around an imaginary axis of the specified angle.

The Reflect tool is very useful in generating symmetrical components, to make one side of an illustration look like a mirror-image of the other side.

Use Reflect to Create Symmetrical Designs

1. Continue working in the Transforms.FH9 file.
2. Use the Pen tool to create half a champagne glass.

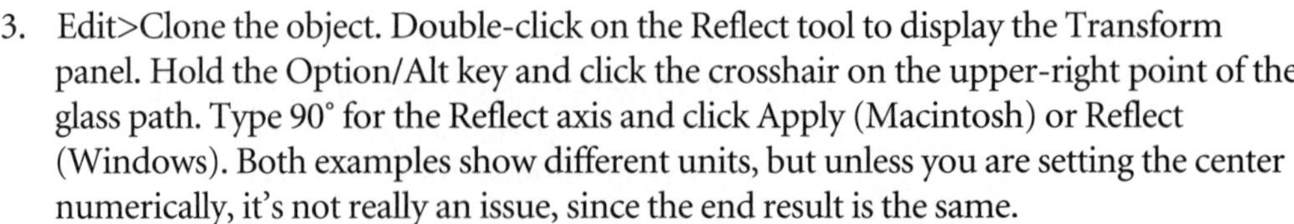

Joining objects is not like grouping them; if two objects are joined, they become one object; if they were grouped, they'd still be two objects after ungrouping.

3. Edit>Clone the object. Double-click on the Reflect tool to display the Transform panel. Hold the Option/Alt key and click the crosshair on the upper-right point of the glass path. Type 90° for the Reflect axis and click Apply (Macintosh) or Reflect (Windows). Both examples show different units, but unless you are setting the center numerically, it's not really an issue, since the end result is the same.

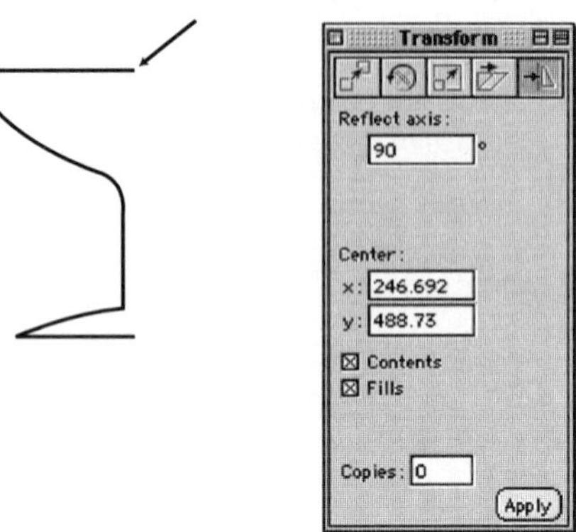

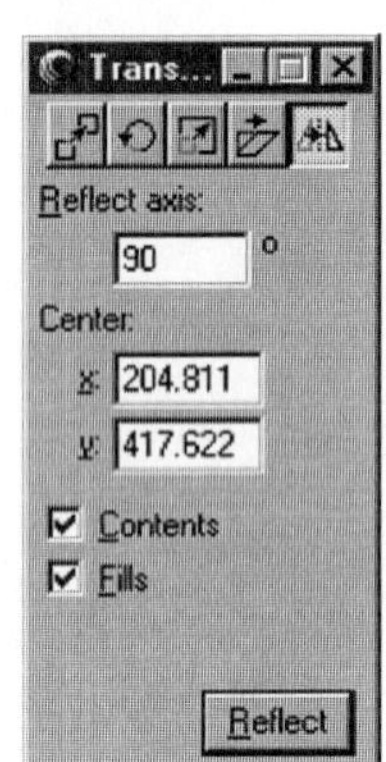

Macintosh Windows

4. The clone reflects across the vertical axis, originating the transformation from where you clicked the crosshair.

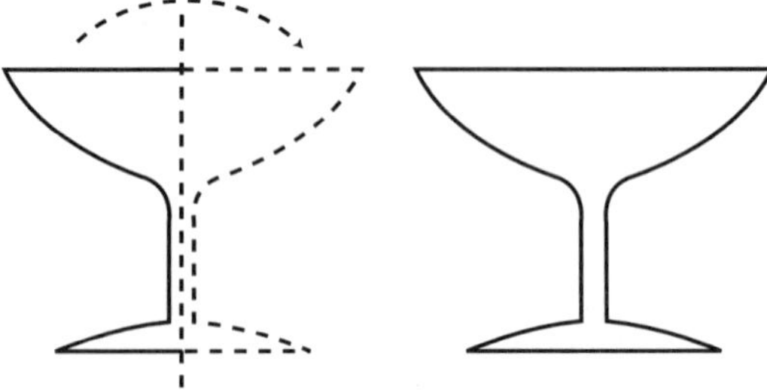

Remember that selected anchor points turn hollow, which shows that they can be edited, joined, moved, and so forth.

5. Select both halves of the glass. Select Modify>Join to join them. Then select the Object Inspector and click Closed, to make it a closed path.

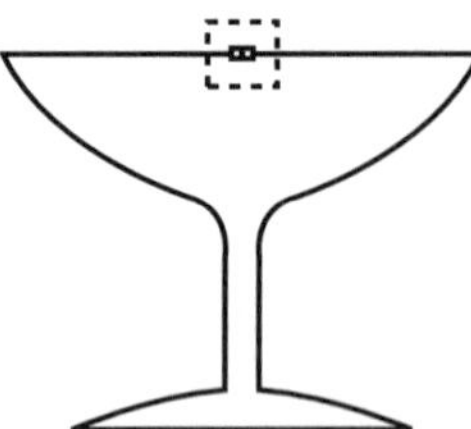

6. Keep the document open for the next exercise.

Scale

The Scale tool allows resizing of selected objects; the scaling can be uniform or not. Uniform scaling means that the object is scaled proportionally and will maintain the same aspects.

The following are the Scale panel options:

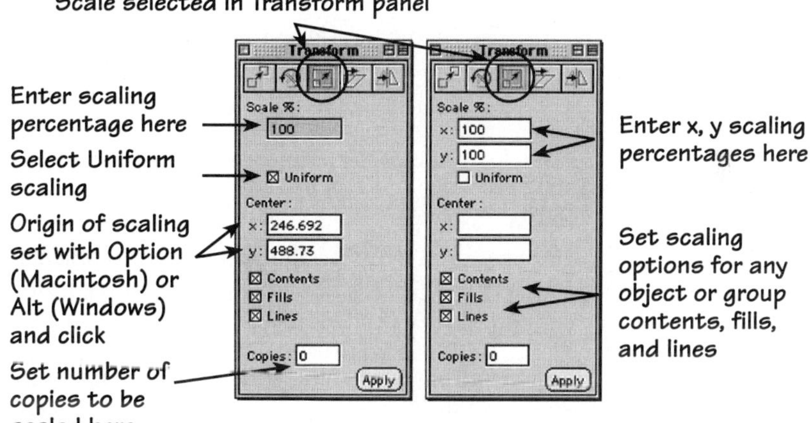

Scaling type and objects increases or decreases the thickness of any strokes in the object and increases or decreases the weight of type. When scaling type, try to avoid horizontal or vertical scaling, which can result in distorted letterforms.

To scale one or more objects, select them, then choose the Scale tool. Hold the Shift key while dragging to scale the object(s) proportionally; otherwise they will be scaled non-proportionally. Double-click on the Scale tool to show the Transform panel for scaling.

You can choose Uniform and type in the percentage of the desired scale. If you deselect Uniform, the x and y fields appear so you can use different horizontal and vertical scaling percentages. The default Center settings are the actual center of the object, so it will scale in position if you leave these settings alone. Enter the number of Copies you want scaled.

Scale Objects

1. Continue working in the Transforms.FH9 file.
2. With the Pointer tool, select the champagne glass.

3. Double-click on the Scale tool in the Toolbox to show the Scale panel. Select Uniform, then type 50 in the Scale % box. Click Apply (Macintosh) or Scale (Windows).

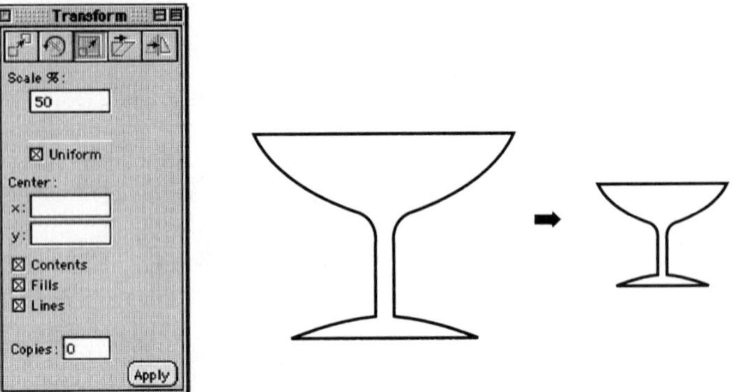

4. The champagne glass reduces 50% in size and doesn't change its relative position since no change in center was applied. Changing the center will scale the object and move the object to the specified coordinates relative to the object's center.

5. Keep the document open for the next exercise.

Skew

The Skew tool slants or obliques a selected object to create, for example, a reflected shadow of an object. Like the other transformational tools, you can use the Skew tool manually or with the Skew panel. Skew is not available in the Interactive Transformer.

You can easily skew an object by selecting the Skew tool and manually experimenting with different mouse moves to skew the object interactively.

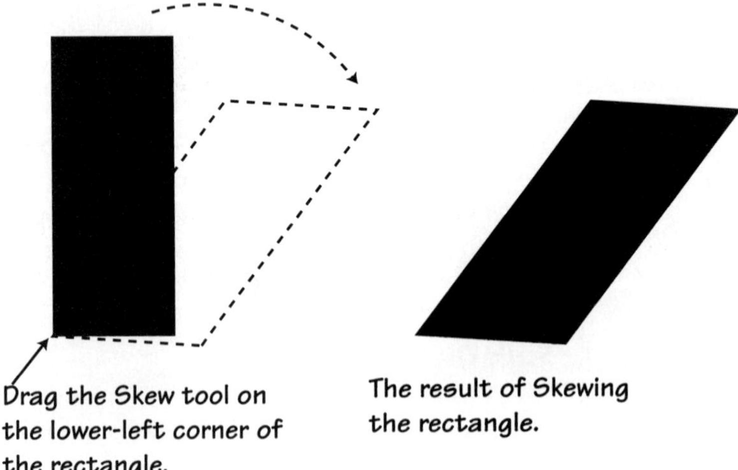

You can also use the Skew panel to set numeric skew angles and centers.

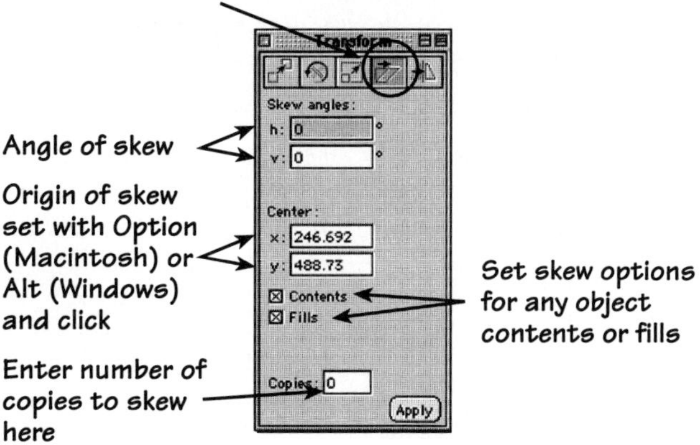

Skew Objects

1. Continue working in the Transforms.FH9 file.
2. Use the Pointer tool to select the scaled champagne glass.
3. Select the Skew tool. Click the crosshair on the bottom left point of the base of the glass. Drag the tool so that the glass begins to skew.

4. Move the mouse around while dragging to see how it affects the skewing procedure.
5. Click the crosshair on other points of origin and drag to see how the origin of transformation affects the skewing procedure.
6. Save and close the file.

Using the Interactive Transformer

The Interactive Transformer is activated when you double-click on an object with the Pointer tool. This allows you to make any number of successive transformations of an object before accepting any of the alterations made to the object. You can move, rotate, or reflect the object, and view the results. Only one Transform operation may be done at any one time.

You click and drag on the handles to scale the object. Click outside the bounds of the transformer to rotate the item with reference to the center point (the dot in the middle). You can move the center point anywhere within the bounds as a reference point for rotation. Click inside the bounds and you can move the object anywhere on the page. Simply moving the mouse over the various parts of the transformer will change it to the appropriate tool for moving, rotation, or scaling. Here's what the handles do:

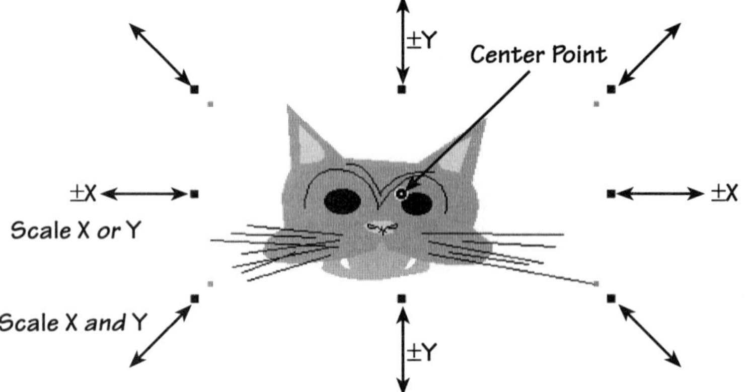

Confusing? Not really. Corner handles scale the image along the x and y axes (hold the Shift key down to scale proportionally). Handles on the top, bottom, and sides scale along either the x or y axis. Moving the pointer outside, near any handle, changes the cursor to a Rotation tool, and you can use any handle to rotate the object. Hold the Shift key to constrain rotation to 45° increments. It doesn't matter which handle you use for rotation; the object rotates only around the center point.

Moving the center point changes the reference for rotation. Here, the center point has been moved to the right, and rotation started from the lower-right corner. The cat rotates relative to the center point.

Use the Interactive Transformer

1. Create a new document.
2. Draw a star or any other shape you like.
3. Use the Pointer tool to double-click the shape with the Pointer tool to activate the interactive transformer.

4. Hold down the Shift key, then click and drag on the lower-right corner handle to scale the object proportionally.

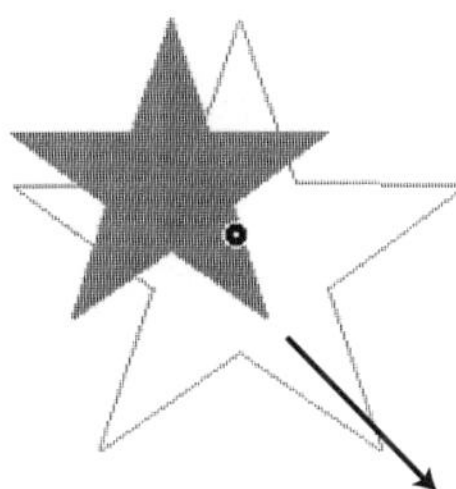

5. Move the center point anywhere within the bounds of the transformer, then rotate the object any way you like. Double-click to close the interactive Transformer.

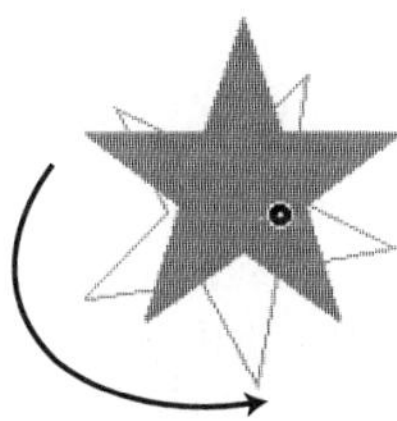

6. You've just seen a much faster, though less precise, way of scaling and rotating an object, instead of using the panels and tools. Close the file without saving.

Use the Transform Panel with Repeating

1. Create a new document.
2. With the Rectangle tool draw a 1″ square.
3. With the Pointer tool, Option/Alt-drag to duplicate the square to the right. Open the Transform panel.

4. Scale the clone (Uniform off): x/h = 55, y/v = 100.

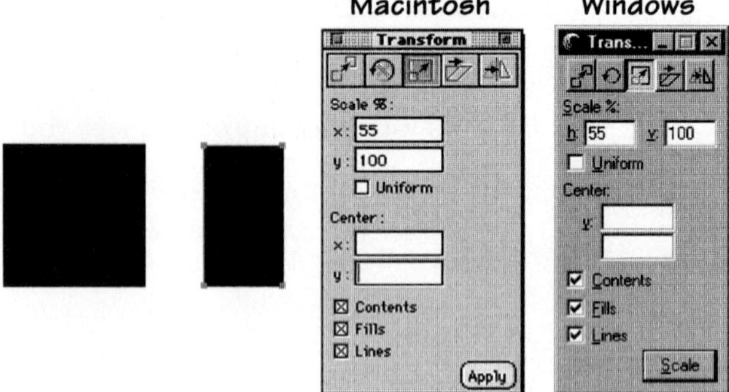

5. Rotate it 15°.

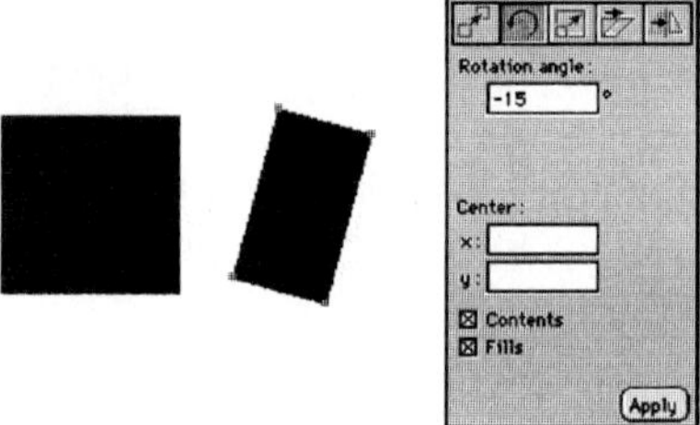

6. In Skew angles, apply: h = 9.926, w = -2.863.

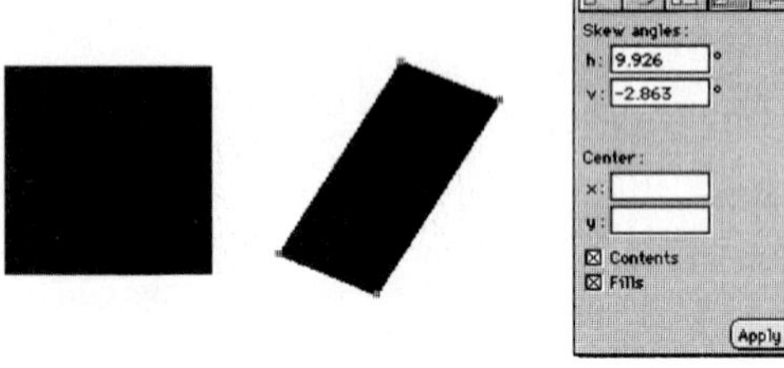

Press Command/Control-D to duplicate actions without using the menu.

7. Duplicate the transformations until the duplicates begin to disappear. The combined transformations cause distortion and give the perception of movement.

8. Close the file without saving.

Duplicating, Cloning, and Step and Repeat

Sometimes designs require objects to be duplicated either horizontally, vertically, or at an angle. It would be tedious to repeat the process of choosing menus and dialog boxes to repeatedly perform the same function, so FreeHand has automated this type of duplication as a step and repeat function.

There are two duplication commands: Duplicate and Clone.

Duplicate

The duplicate function works on different actions in different ways. If an object is selected, such as this square, the Duplicate command will make a copy offset from the original. If Duplicate is chosen a few more times, the duplication and offsetting will repeat.

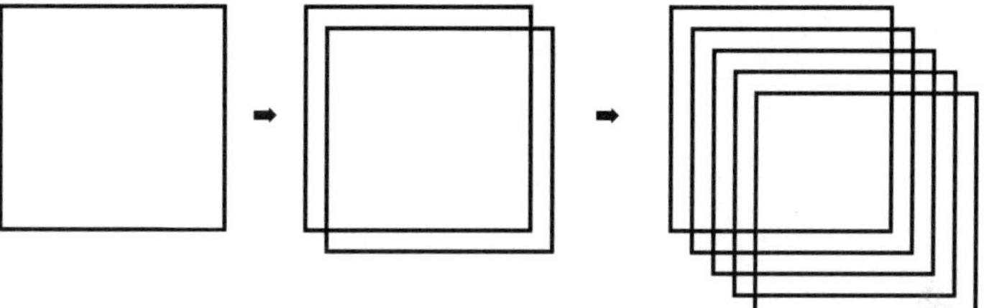

Holding the Option/Alt key while transforming an object makes a clone of the object, then performs the transformation on the clone. After you transform the clone, duplication will repeat the same transformation on all subsequent copies.

Duplication and transformation does not have to be performed in one action. In this example, the large square was rotated manually, then Scaled 70%. Duplication applied both the rotation and the scaling to all copies.

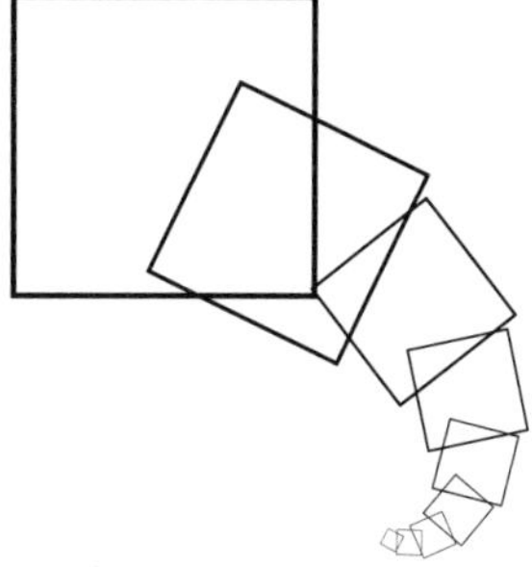

Clone

Cloning an object makes an exact copy and positions it on top of the original. This is particularly useful for duplicating objects in order to manually move copies to another position on the page, or to move a specific measurement, such as a drop shadow.

Dragging

There's another way of duplicating objects: drag them while holding the Option/Alt key. From File>Preferences>Object, check Option-Drag Copies Path (Macintosh) or Alt-Drag Copies Path (Windows) if you want to use this function.

You can add the Shift key to constrain the movement of the copy horizontally or vertically.

Use the Duplicate Command to Step and Repeat

1. Create a new document.
2. Draw a 2″ square with the Rectangle tool.
3. Press Command/Control-D to duplicate the object. Notice how the copy is offset from the original.
4. Duplicate again, four more times.
5. Watch how the offset of each duplicate changes.
6. Select the five duplicates and delete them. Select the original square.
7. While holding the Option/Alt key and holding the Shift key to constrain, drag the square to the side to make a duplicate.
8. Duplicate five more times to see the duplication and movement repeated each time.

9. Select all the squares but one and delete them.
10. Press Command/Control-= to clone the square directly on top of itself.
11. From the Transform panel, select the Move icon, and set the move for the x axis to 2.25″. Set the number of copies to 4. Click Apply/Move. This is a typical step-and-repeat to a defined distance.

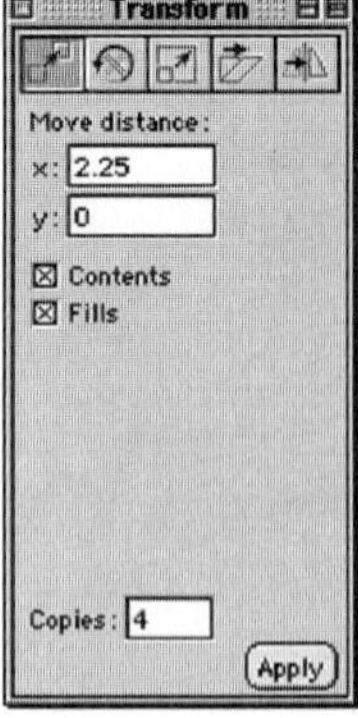

12. Double-click on the Polygon tool and set it for a five-pointed star. Draw a 1″ star on the page. With the star selected, choose the Rotation tool and rotate the star while holding the Option/Alt key for duplication. Open the Scale Transform panel and set the scale for 80%, then click Apply/Scale. Duplicate the copy five times to apply the selected rotate, duplicate, and scale settings successively to each copy.

13. Close the file without saving.

Summary

In this chapter, you have used FreeHand's tools to perform a variety of transformations. You have moved, scaled, rotated, reflected, and skewed objects. You have also used interactive rotation to alter an object. You have also become familiar with duplicating, cloning, and dragging objects to copy them, and you have used the duplicate command to step-and-repeat an object.

Notes

CHAPTER 12

Path Operations

CHAPTER OBJECTIVE:

To learn the assorted tools and techniques for altering paths and creating new objects from operations on paths. In Chapter 12, you will:

- Learn how path operations are preprogrammed operations, styles, and features that automatically perform very complicated tasks.
- Review the Xtra Operations toolbar and its tools, and learn how quickly its tools automatically perform operations on paths.
- Learn how to use the Xtras and Modify menus, as well as understand the Xtras window.
- Understand path-altering operations to simplify, reverse, and eliminate overlap in paths.
- Learn how to create blends.
- Learn how to use Expand Stroke to create composite paths.
- Understand what a composite object is, and how you can use it to enhance your design.
- Learn how to use Inset Path to create scaled replicas of paths; understand the use of Inset Path from both the Operations toolar and Inset Path dialog box.
- Learn how to attach blends to paths.

PROJECTS TO BE COMPLETED:

- Dinner Time (A)
- Mask Art (B)
- Tropical Treasure Logo (C)
- Grocery Ad (D)
- **Ball and Mirror (E)**
- No Clowning Around (F)

Path Operations

Path Operations are preprogrammed operations, styles, and features that perform work that would be very complicated if attempted by hand. They may be accessed in several locations. Many of them are actually FreeHand Xtras, but perform operations strictly on paths, so we're presenting them separately.

You will find most path operations tools under the Modify menu:

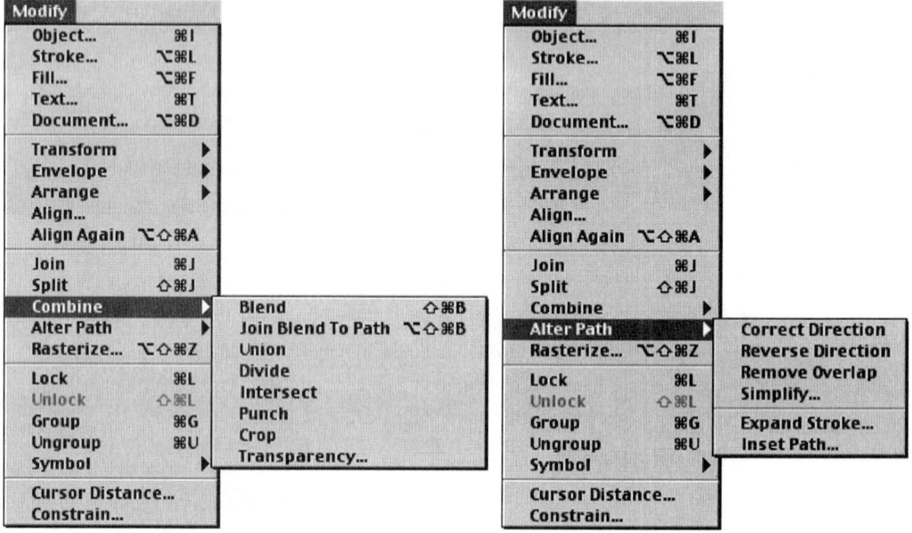

You will also find these tools under the Xtras menu:

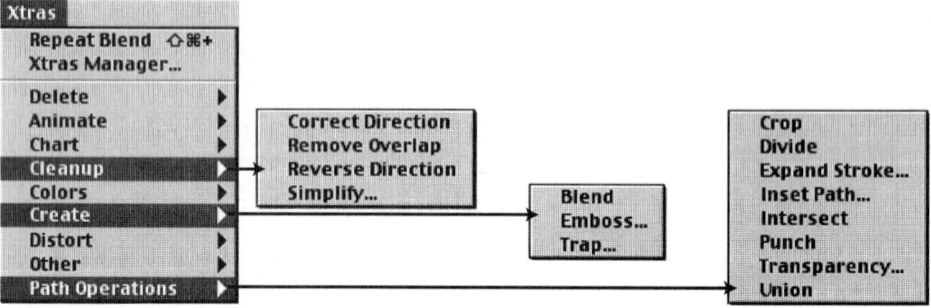

The floating Xtra Operations toolbar also gives you access to the majority of path operations. It is accessed through Window>Toolbars>Xtra Operations.

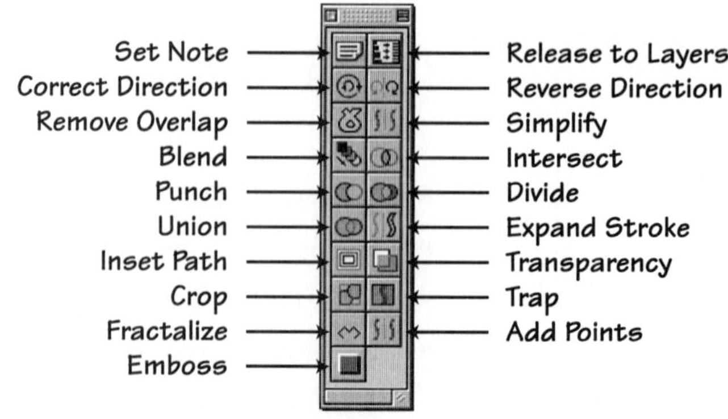

Xtra Operations Toolbar

These tools perform operations on paths in seconds that would take considerable time if done manually.

Some path operations combine objects, create new objects, or modify objects. Using the tools to effect these operations may require some experimentation in order to obtain the desired effect.

Depending upon how your preferences are set, you will achieve two separate results when using some of the path operations. When File>Preferences>Objects>Path Operations Consume Original Paths is checked, you will be left with only the results of the operation performed. When it is unchecked, you will have your original object(s) and the results of the operation.

Operations that Combine Objects

Some of the most-used path operations are those that combine two or more objects to produce a singe object with complex paths. The combining operations are accessed through Modify>Combine. You could also use the Xtras menu or the Xtra Operations Toolbar, the symbols for which we will reference as we introduce each tool.

Join and Split

Two operations that work effectively together are Join and Split. They are often used when text is converted to paths. As you discovered in Chapter 9, when text is converted to a path, it looks just like text.

TEXT TO PATH

However, after it is ungrouped, the paths can be split. This may be desirable to give special treatment to the characters.

TEXT T● PATH

In this example, the "O" was split, so it could receive different treatment.

When two elements are joined, the even/odd fill is restored.

TEXT T◆ PATH

In this example, the "O" received a diamond to replace the oval hole in the middle.

Blend 

A blend is a set of intermediate paths between two objects. Click on both objects before selecting Modify>Combine>Blend or clicking on the Blend icon in the Xtras toolbox. You control the number of intermediate steps in the Object Inspector, which will automatically display the blend characteristics. The beginning object will "morph" into the final object. If specific points on the object to be blended are selected, they will affect the outcome of the blend.

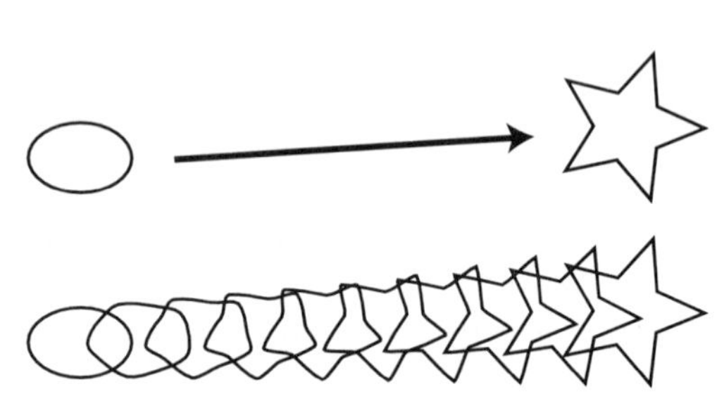

Press Command/Control-Shift-B to create a blend of two objects.

Join Blend To Path

This function, which does not have a complement in the Xtras toolbox, adheres a blend to a path, literally wrapping the blend along the contours of the path.

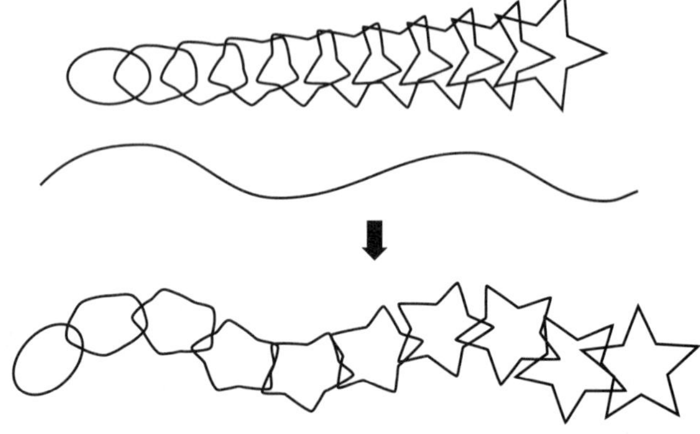

Union 

This operation creates a new path that is the combination of two or more closed paths. The stroke and fill of the new object is based on the attributes of the object that is lowest in the stacking order.

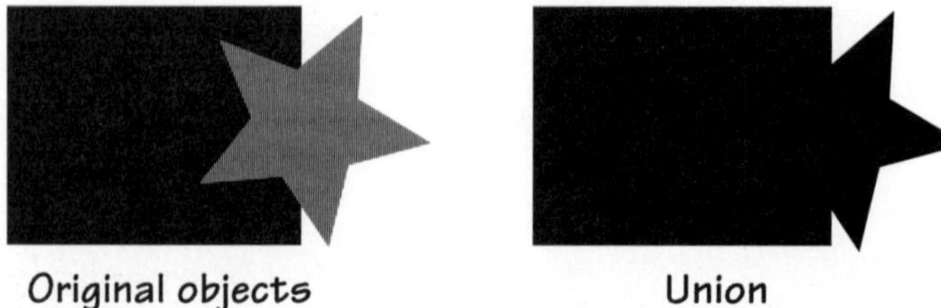

Divide  

This operation cuts overlapping sections of selected paths into new paths defined by the area of overlap. The original paths can be open, closed, or both. Stroke and fill of any new paths is based on the attributes of the object highest in the stacking order.

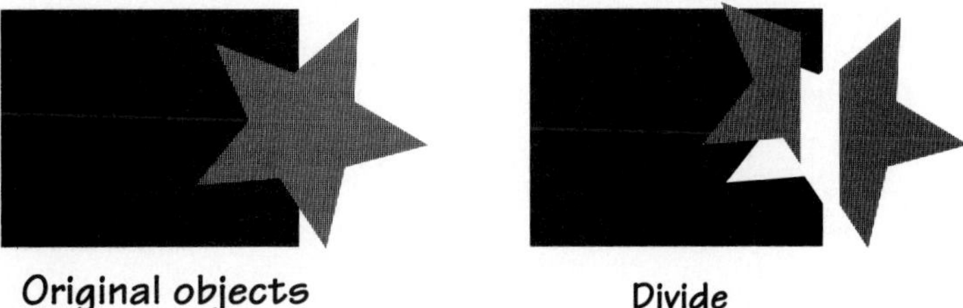

Intersect 

This operation creates a path based on the area in which two or more closed paths overlap each other. The stroke and fill of the new object is based on the attributes of the object that is lowest in the stacking order.

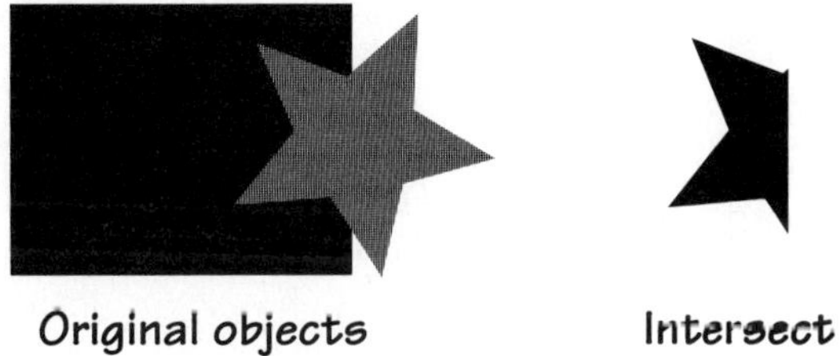

Punch 

This operation cuts the top path out of the selected closed path(s) underneath it, much like a cookie cutter. Stroke and fill attributes remain unchanged.

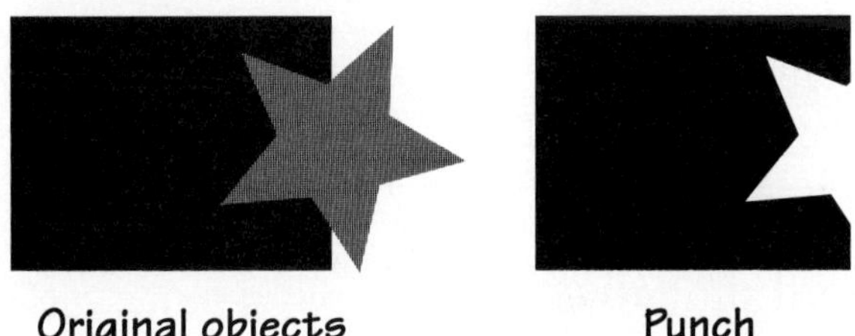

Crop 

This operation removes the portion of the selected, closed paths that are outside the area of the closed path highest in the stacking order. Stroke and fill attributes remain unchanged.

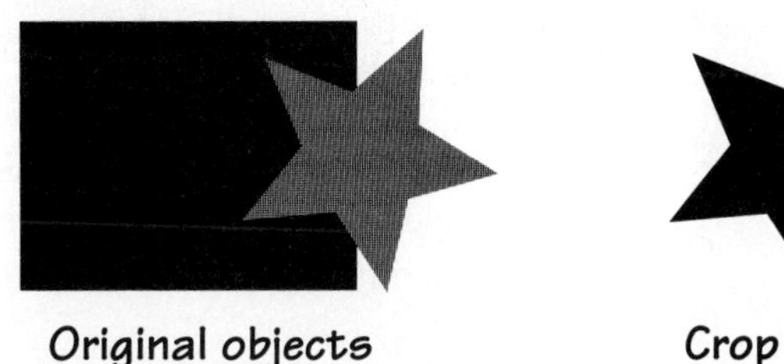

Transparency 

This operation uses basic fills in two or more closed paths, creating a third path that is a combination of the two colors filling the original paths. This new object really isn't transparent; it just looks that way because the color is an average of the objects' colors.

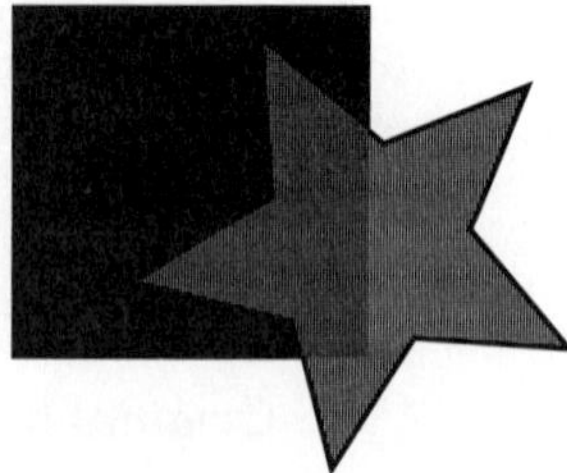

The percentage of transparency is controlled with the Transparency dialog box. Select the Transparency Xtra in the Operations Toolbar to show the Transparency dialog box. Higher values increase the level of transparency.

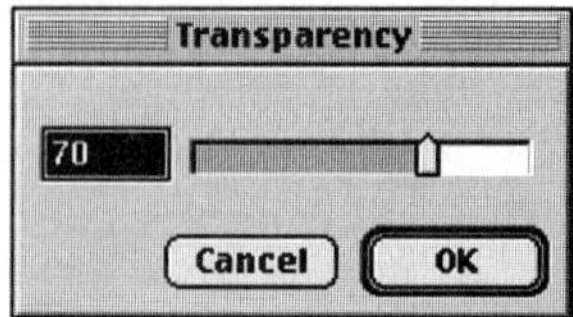

Note that this Transparency operation differs quite a bit from a lens applied in the Fill Inspector, which creates actual transparency in selected objects.

Work with Blends

1. Open the document **Blendit.FH9** from your **SF-FreeHand** folder.
2. With the Pointer tool, click on the first two ellipses and select Modify>Combine>Blend, or click the Blend tool in the Xtra Operations toolbar.

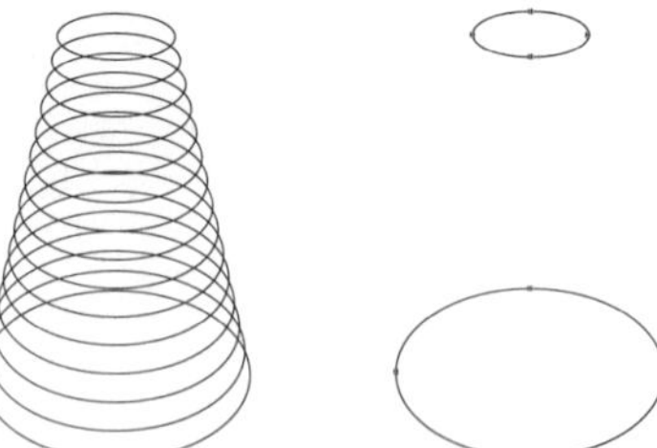

Your blend should appear similar to this. We have reduced the number of steps in the blend so you can see it more easily at this size.

3. Marquee the second and third sets of ellipses to select them. Choose Modify>Ungroup. Deselect.
4. In the middle set of ellipses, click on the back anchor point in the upper ellipse and shift-click the front anchor point in the lower ellipse. Apply the blend. Note the extreme difference in the shape of the blend.

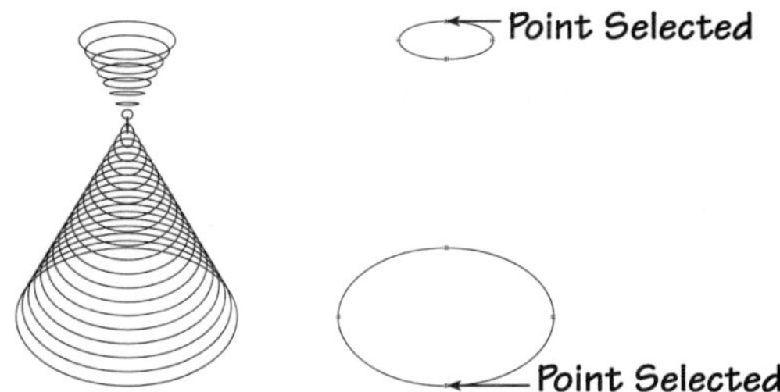

5. In the third set of ellipses, click on the front anchor point of the upper ellipse and shift-click the right anchor point in the lower ellipse. Apply the blend. Note again the change in shape.

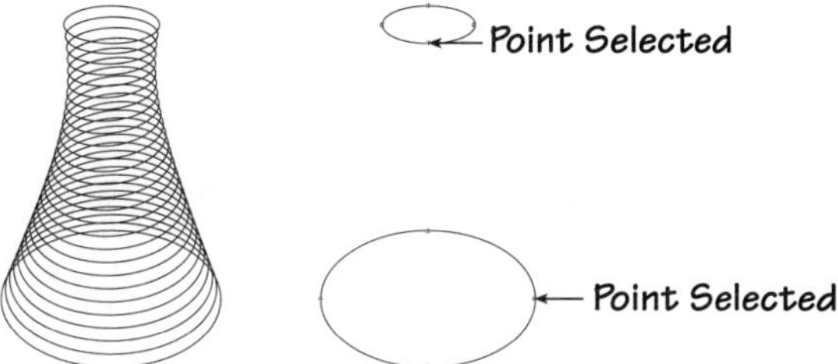

6. Near the bottom of the page are a square and a circle. Select the square and apply Magenta to its stroke. Apply Cyan to the stroke of the circle. Blend the two objects.

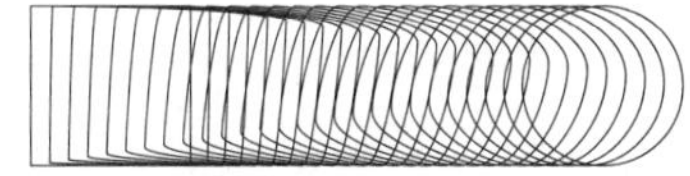

When objects of different shapes or different colors are blended, the shapes and colors change over the course of the blend.

7. Select the blended element and the path below it. Choose Modify>Combine>Join Blend To Path. In the Object Inspector, check Show path and click Rotate on path on and off to observe the changes that this choice makes in the blended object.

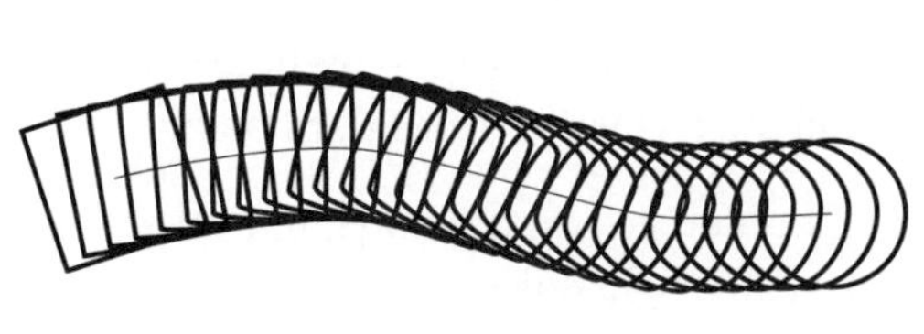

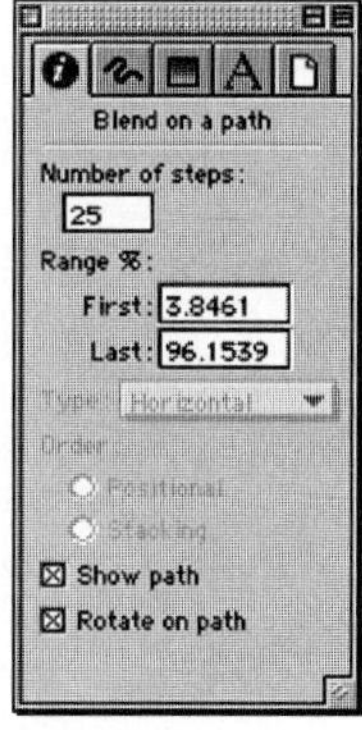

8. Hold down the Option/Alt key and click on the path to subselect the path. Press Modify>Alter Path>Reverse Direction. (We'll talk more about reversing direction in the next section.) The blend direction reverses.

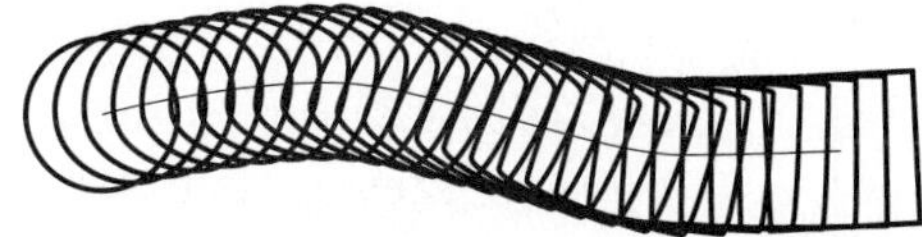

PostScript can only achieve a blend in color of 256 steps. If a step exceeds 2 pt. in width, the eye perceives it, and banding occurs.

One of the best uses of blends is to make a seamless gradation of color. While a gradient fill can do this, it will only work on a gradient up to 7″ on many of the imaging devices in use. However, we can "step" a blend in FreeHand. At the bottom of the page are four strokes, each 1.95 pt. wide. We will use these to create a seamless blend. Move the magenta and cyan blend so it is out of your way.

9. Select the two middle strokes and, from the Tint Mixer, assign them a color of 50% Black. Select the rightmost stroke and assign it a color of White.
10. Select the left stroke and the first middle stroke. Apply a blend, and adjust the steps to 256 in the Object Inspector.
11. Deselect the blend and select the remaining strokes, apply a blend, and adjust the steps to 256.
12. Position the ends of the blends atop one another and apply Modify>Group.
13. Close the file without saving.

Practice Combining Elements

1. Create a new document.
2. Select File>Preferences>Object. Select Path operations consume original paths if it is not selected.

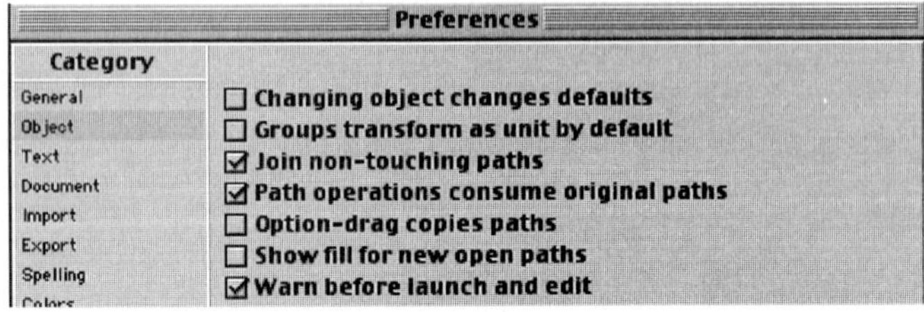

3. Select the Rectangle tool and draw a rectangle. Use the Color List>Options pop-up menu to access the Crayon library and select several light and dark colors. Click OK. Fill the rectangle with a dark color.
4. Double-click on the Polygon tool and set it to draw a star; then draw the star. Paint it with a light color from the Color List, then move it in front of the rectangle, overlapping it slightly.

Press Command/Control-Z to undo without using the menu.

5. With the two objects selected, click Union in the Operations Toolbar. Set your view for Keyline to see the result more clearly.

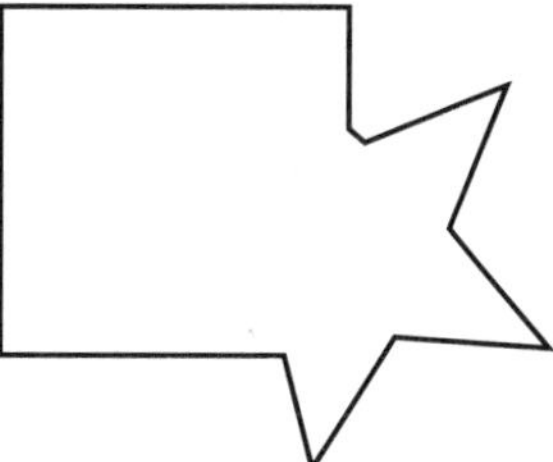

6. Select Edit>Undo to undo the operation. Return to Preview mode. Click on Divide in the Operations Toolbar. To see the resulting paths more clearly, move them apart.

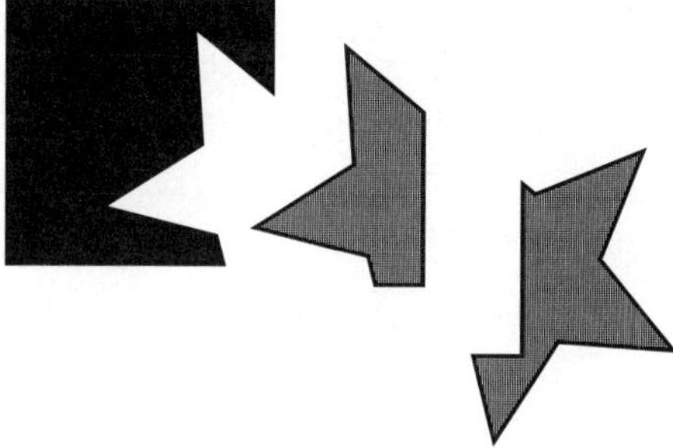

7. Select Edit>Undo to undo the moves and the Divide operation until you are back to your original two objects. Click Intersect in the Operations Toolbar.

8. Select Edit>Undo to undo the Intersect operation. Click Punch in the Operations Toolbar.

9. Undo the Punch operation and click Crop. This should be your result.

10. Undo the crop. Click on Transparency in the Operations Toolbar. Enter 15 in the dialog box and click OK. The two objects will turn into three. Move them apart with the Pointer tool to see how the transparency was accomplished.

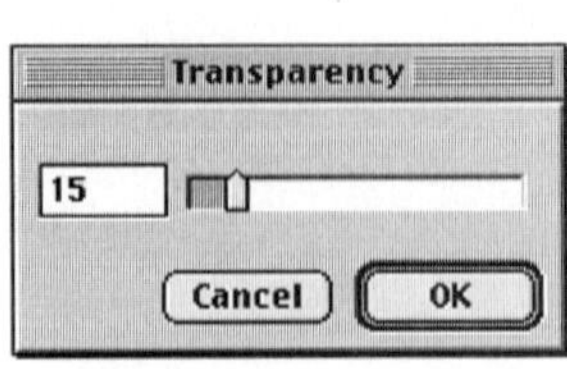

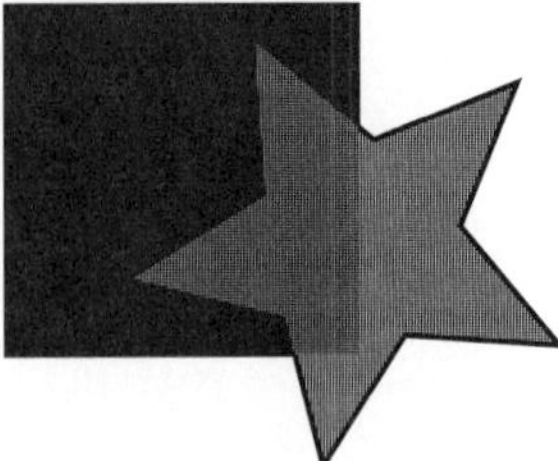

11. Close the document without saving.

Now that you've had a chance to experiment with the combining features, lets use them to create a cartoonish cat.

Build a Cat

1. Open the document **Build a Cat.FH9** from your **SF-FreeHand** folder.

   You have been supplied with most of the components needed to build your cat, using the skills you have just learned. The parts you have are the almost round face, the black ears, white eyes, and the green and yellow pupil components.

2. Position the ears as you feel is appropriate, and, with head and ears selected, choose Modify>Combine>Union.

3. Position the left eye. Press Command/Control-F to bring it to the front, then select Modify>Combine>Punch. Position the right eye and repeat the operation.

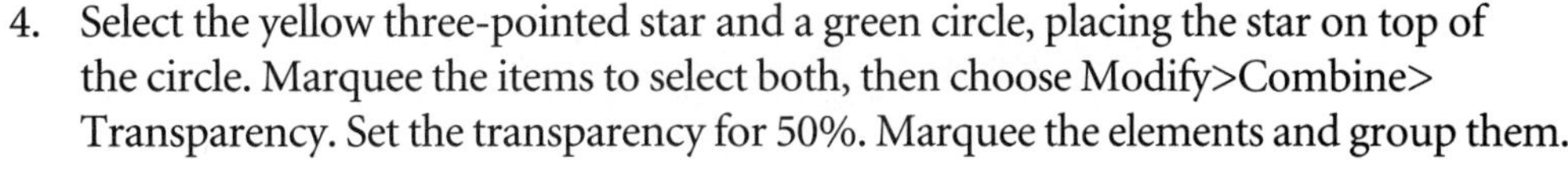

4. Select the yellow three-pointed star and a green circle, placing the star on top of the circle. Marquee the items to select both, then choose Modify>Combine> Transparency. Set the transparency for 50%. Marquee the elements and group them.
5. Press Option/Alt and drag a copy of this "eyeball."
6. Position the eyeballs above the eyes, and select Modify>Arrange>Send To Back. Select the eyeballs and the cat's face and select Modify>Group.
7. If you wish, give your cat some whiskers.

Press Command/Control-B to send an item to the back.

Press Command/Control-F to bring an item to the front.

Press Command/Control-G to group items.

8. Save to your **Work in Progress** folder.

Path-altering Operations

The Path-altering operations are accessed through Modify>Alter Path. You could also use the Xtras menu or the Xtra Operations Toolbar, the symbols for which we will reference as we introduce each tool.

Correct Direction 

The Correct Direction tool may be needed if a composite path's fill does not display as you expect. Some programs base their fills on winding — all paths go the same direction — as opposed to the even/odd fill that FreeHand uses. Even/odd fills produce alternate filled and transparent results when objects are combined.

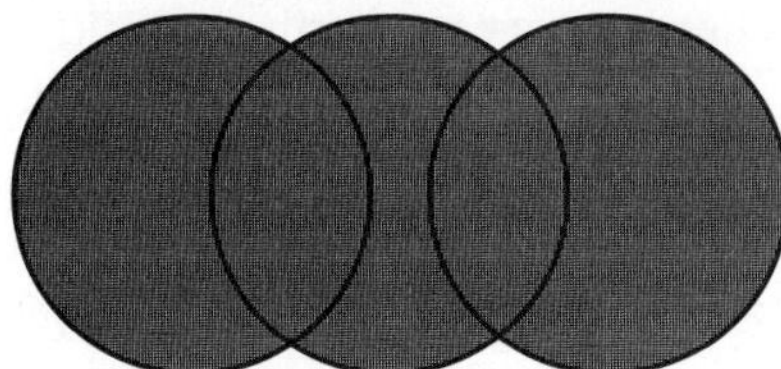

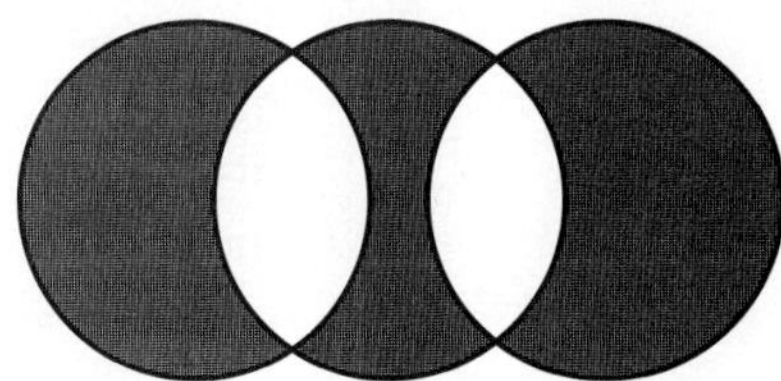

Reverse Direction 

Use this command to reverse the direction of any path.

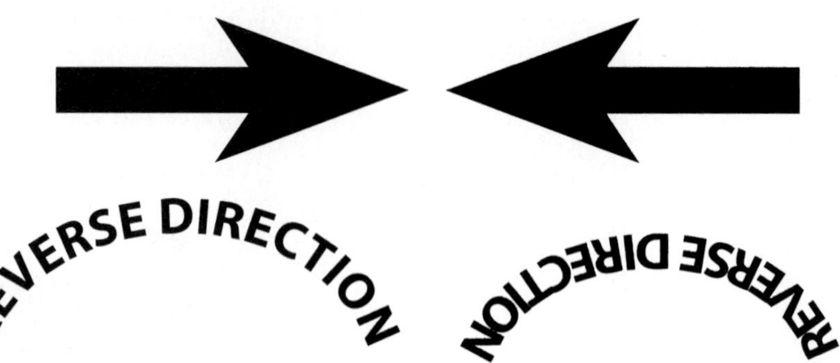

To reverse the direction of text on a path, hold down the Option/Alt key to subselect the path before choosing Modify>Alter Path>Reverse Direction.

Remove Overlap 

With a closed path that overlaps itself, Remove Overlap eliminates the crossover and unites everything into one or more paths. This is particularly useful in a situation such as this one, where there is an outline that interferes with the design.

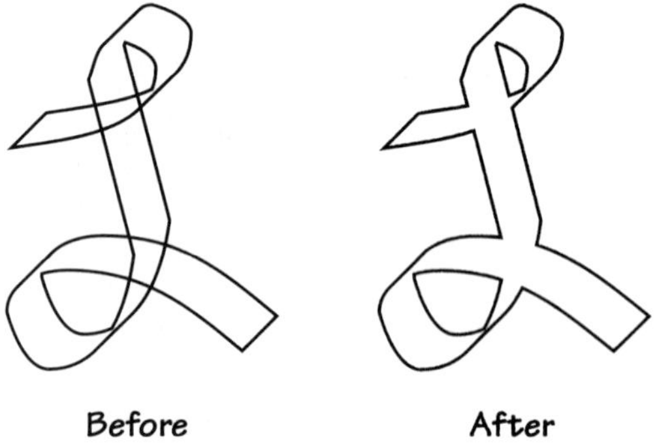

Before After

Simplify 

Simplify removes unnecessary points that should not affect the look of the line; the amount of change can be controlled through its dialog box. Double-click the Simplify Xtra icon to display the dialog box. Higher simplification values will result in more obvious changes in the object. You really only need to simplify a path if it contains an unmanageable number of points, or if your printer fails to print a complex path.

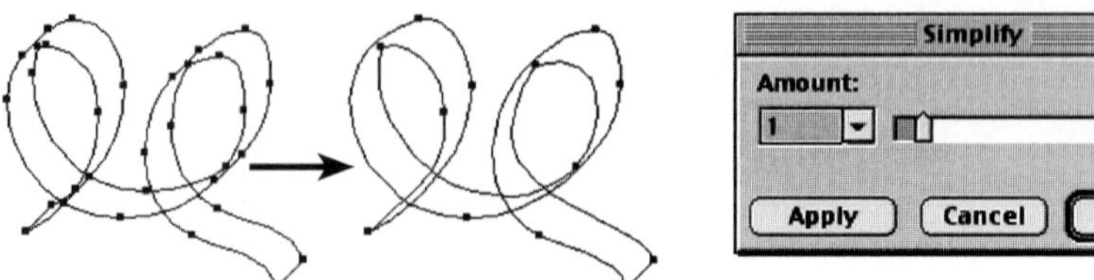

Expand Stroke 

Expand Stroke converts selected lines (strokes) to closed, sometimes composite paths. It's useful if you have sketched in some lines to make a rough object and later decide to convert them from lines to closed paths. You can also use this function if you want to use a fill type that is not available for a stroke, such as Gradient, Radial, Custom, and Texture. This function lets you create a closed path that looks like a stroke, and then fill it.

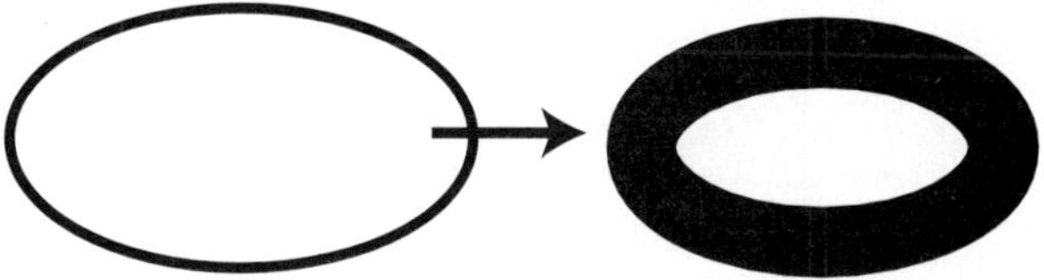

To expand a stroke to a closed path, select the object, choose Expand Stroke from the Operations Toolbar, and set the width of the new path in the dialog box.

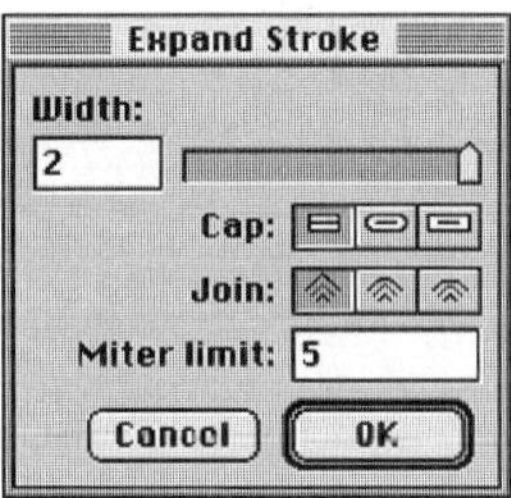

Macintosh

Windows

The result of using Expand Stroke on an already closed path is a composite object — an object that is made up of two paths.

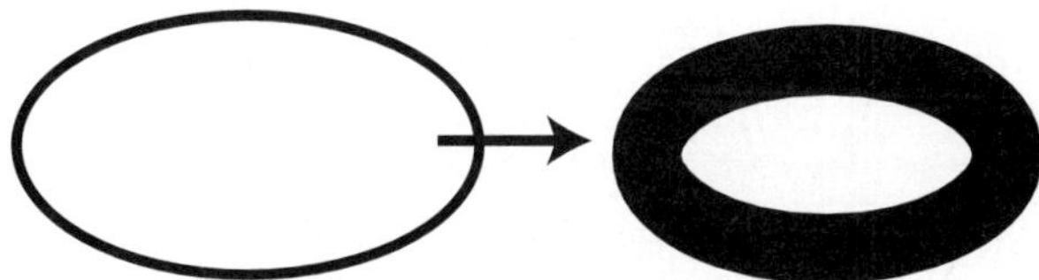

In Keyline mode, there is an inside and outside to the object. This is the same result you'd get if you used Modify>Join to combine the objects.

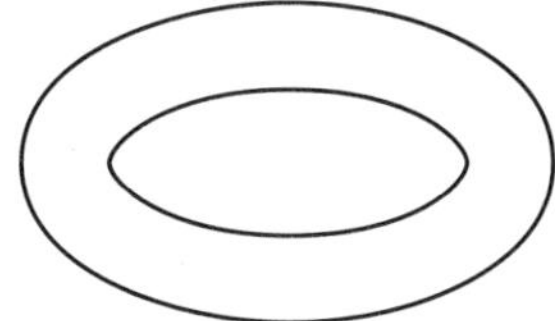

Composite objects have an inner path that is transparent. Background objects can then show through the opening.

You could use Modify>Split to separate the paths of the object , after which the inner path would no longer be transparent.

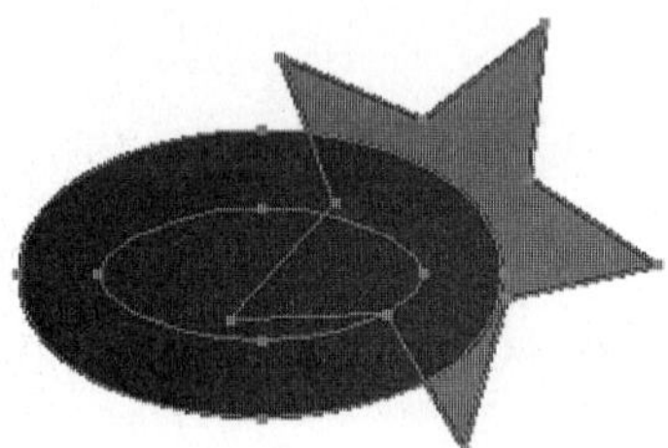

Expand Stroke Dialog Box

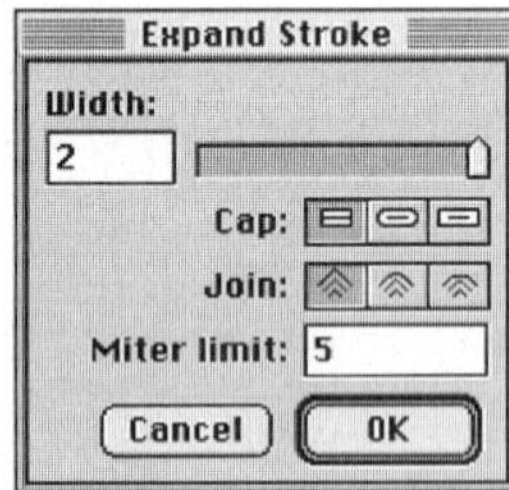

- Width — Enter a value here to set the thickness of the object that will be created. You can enter a value in any of FreeHand's units of measurement.
- Cap — This selection controls how the endpoint of an *open* path to be expanded is shaped. There are three options — butt, round, and square.
- Join — This selection controls the shape of a corner where two path segments meet. There are three options: miter, round, and bevel, which work just like those in the Stroke Inspector.
- Miter limit — The number entered here controls how far the stroke will extend before it converts to a bevel join. It is the ratio between the length of the miter join and the stroke width.

Here's a reminder of the Cap and Join options found in the Stroke Inspector:

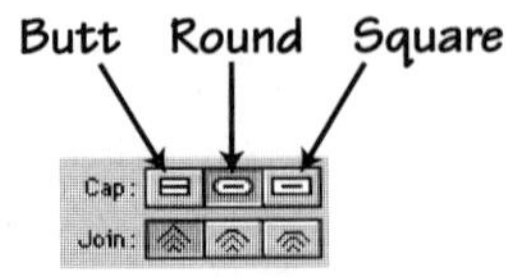

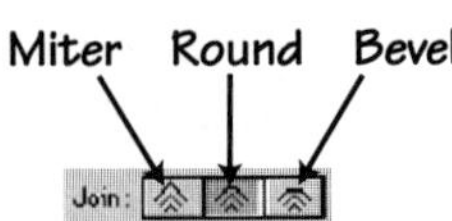

Using Expand Stroke and Blends

1. Create a new document. Set the measurement unit for Points.
2. Choose File>Preferences>Object. Select Path operations consume original paths if it is not already on.

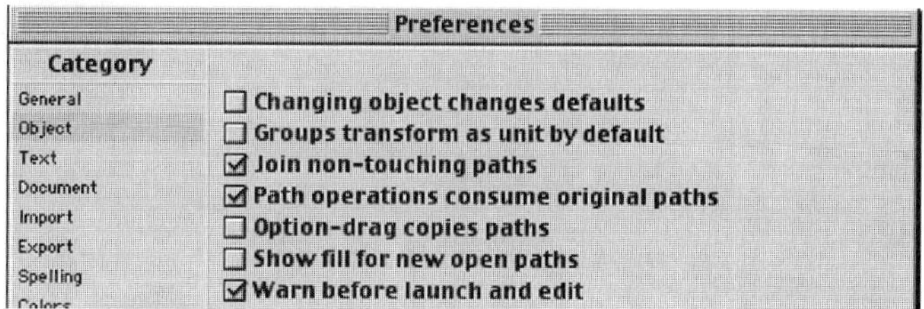

3. Draw an ellipse with the Ellipse tool. With the Color List set the fill as None and stroke as Black. Select Preview mode.

4. With the ellipse selected, select Modify>Alter Path>Expand Stroke.

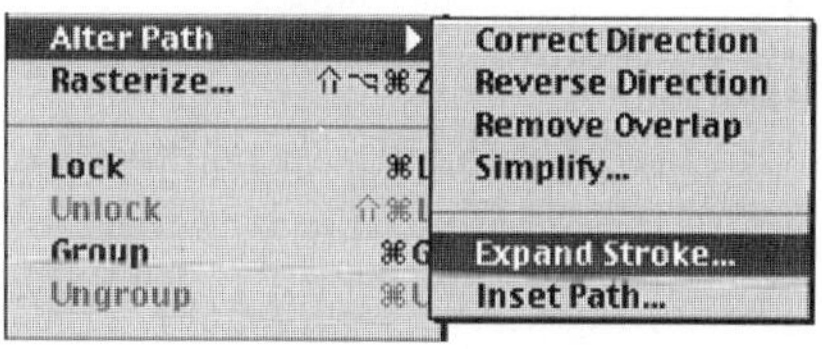

5. Enter 20 pt. for the Width.

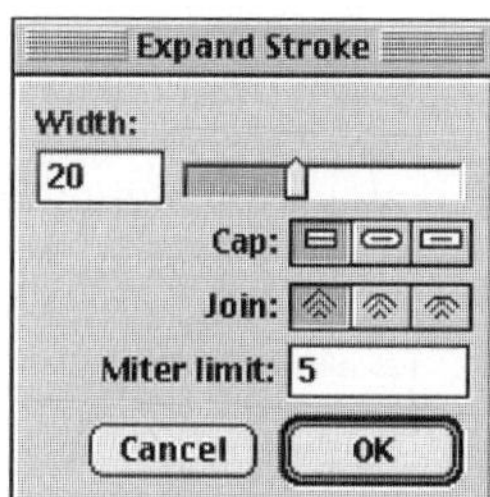

6. To see the object paths you have created, switch the viewing mode to Keyline.

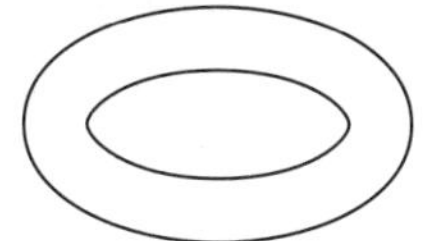

7. Go back to Preview mode. Open the Fill Inspector and try different fills on this object. Try some that you couldn't use with a stroke, such as a gradient.

8. Use the Polygon tool to draw a star and give it a solid fill. Move the star over to overlap the expanded ellipse and choose Modify>Arrange>Send To Back. The star will show through the opening in the expanded object because of the composite paths.

Press Command/Control-K to switch between Keyline and Preview modes.

9. Select the expanded ellipse and choose Modify>Split. This separates the two paths as in the following manner:

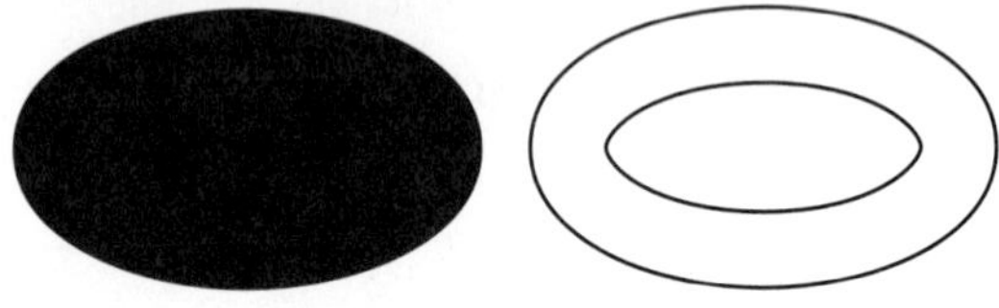

Split - Preview mode   Split -Keyline mode

10. Click on the outer path and choose Modify>Arrange>Send To Back. When split, it ends up in front of the smaller path because the inner path of a composite object always goes to the back, and filling it would obscure the inner path.
11. You have now taken a single path and created two custom paths with Expand Stroke. Imagine how you could create your own images using this useful operation.
12. Close the file without saving.

Inset Path

The Inset Path Xtra is also in the Xtra Operations Toolbar. It allows you to create enlarged or reduced duplicates of a closed path. You can specify the number of duplicates in the Inset Path dialog box. Here the star was inset with 3 Steps (meaning 3 duplicates), and was set for uniform size and 4 pt. Inset.

Original

3 steps, Inset 4 pt. Uniform

For some reason unknown to anyone except the original programmer, Inset Path uses positive values to make the insets inside the original object, and negative values to make an *outset* of duplicates. In this example, the same star was inset with a -4 pt. "inset." The same Join and Miter limit options found in the Stroke Inspector are available here.

Inset Path Dialog Box

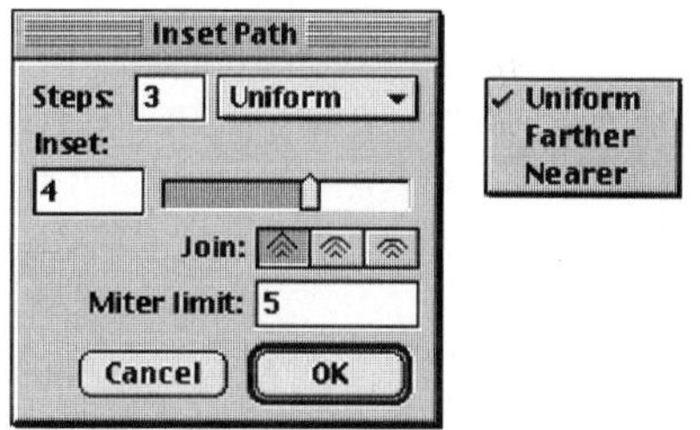

- Steps — This is the number of repeating paths that will be created.
- Inset — This distance, in the currently selected measurement units, separates the steps as they repeat.
- Join — This selection controls the shape where two path segments meet at a corner point. There are three options: miter, round, and bevel.
- Miter limit — This selection controls how far the stroke will extend before it converts to a bevel join. It is the ratio between the length of the miter join and the stroke width.
- Uniform, Farther, Nearer — This selection defines how the steps will be executed. Uniform means that the repeating steps will all be an equal distance apart, set in Inset. Farther makes each step close up the distance, becoming smaller as the steps repeat. Nearer makes each step increase the distance, becoming wider as the steps repeat.

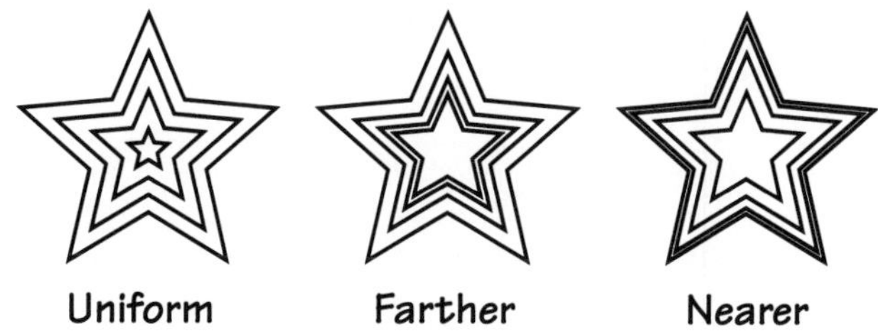

Using Inset Path

1. Create a new document. Set the measurement units to Points.
2. Select File>Preferences>Object. For this exercise, the Path operations consume original paths option should be turned off.

☐ Changing object changes defaults
☐ Groups transform as unit by default
☒ Join non-touching paths
☐ Path operations consume original paths

3. Double-click on the Polygon tool, and in the dialog box make its settings an 8-sided polygon. Click OK. Draw a polygon on the page that is approximately 2″ wide.

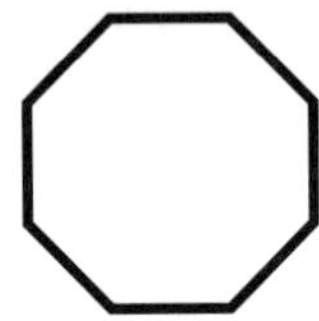

4. Open the Xtra Operations Toolbar by choosing Windows>Toolbars>Xtra Operations. With the polygon selected, choose the Inset Path Xtra from the Operations panel. Set the Steps for 9, Uniform, the Inset for 8, and click OK.

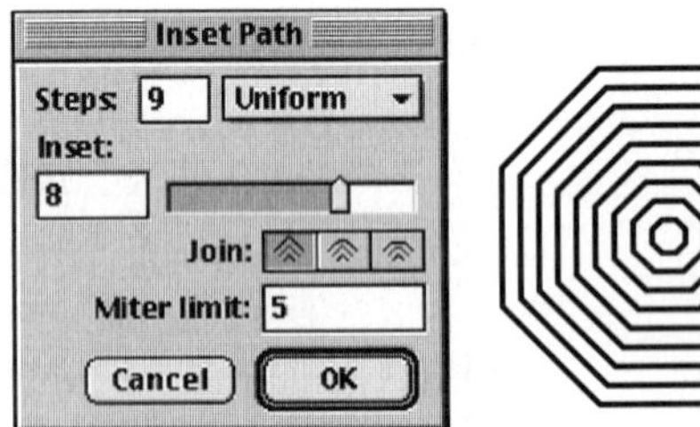

5. With the Pointer tool, click on the middle of this object and move it to the right. The Inset Path operation creates the duplicates as a group, leaving the original polygon alone.

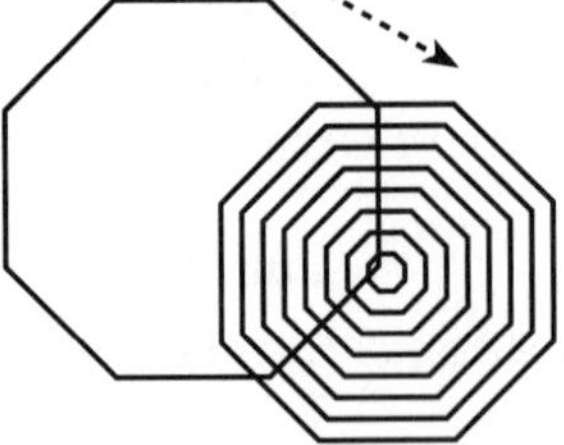

6. Select the grouped duplicates and delete them. Select the polygon. Select Modify>Alter Path>Inset Path again. Now set the Steps for 3, Uniform, and –4 for the Inset. Click OK. The negative number forced the inset outside of the original path.

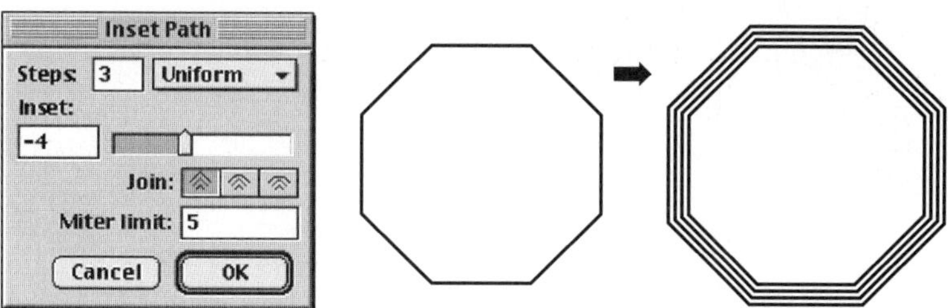

7. Select Edit>Undo and return to Modify>Alter Path>Inset Path. Make the settings of 8 Steps, Farther, and 8 Inset. Click OK.

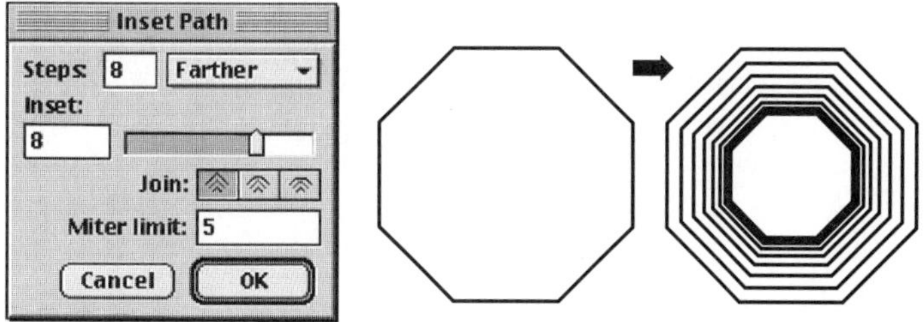

8. Select Edit>Undo and return to Modify>Alter Path>Inset Path. Make the settings of 8 Steps, Nearer, and –6 Inset. Click OK. Notice how the paths are closer together as they are duplicated toward the center of the object.

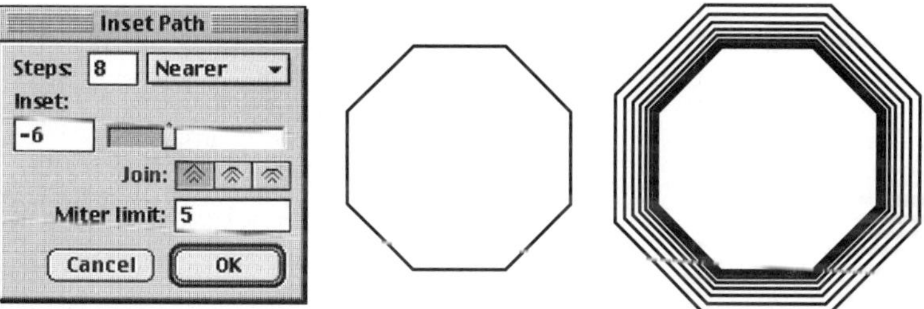

If you prefer to keep the original path along with the inset duplicates, make certain that Preferences> Object>Path operations consume original paths is turned off to avoid deleting the original.

9. Close the document without saving.

Summary

In this chapter, you have learned a variety of ways to combine and alter paths. These tools are accessed through the Modify menu, the Xtras menu, and the Xtra Operations toolbar. You have created a variety of blends and learned the importance of selecting the appropriate point of an object to ensure that the blend is the shape you expect. You have learned to blend from one color to another and to create a smooth gradient blend. You have also learned how to attach a blend to a path.

You have combined objects and created an element by combining objects. In addition, you have learned to use the Expand Stroke tool to achieve unique effects for "lines." You learned to use the Inset Path tool and discovered how it can be used most effectively.

Complete Project E: Ball and Mirror

Notes

CHAPTER 13

Xtras

CHAPTER OBJECTIVE:

To learn about the Xtras included with FreeHand, which accomplish a wide range of functions. In Chapter 13, you will:

- Learn about FreeHand's plug-in functions called Xtras; learn how to use Xtras to enhance standard features with special features.
- Find out what defines Xtras, and where to acquire new ones.
- Learn how to locate Xtras in the Xtras menu and the Xtra Tools Toolbar.
- Understand how to use the 3D rotation, smudge, fisheye lens, and bend Xtras to alter an object.
- Understand how to use the arc, spiral, shadow, chart, and mirror extras to create new objects based on either an existing object or from values that you supply.
- Understand how to use the graphic hose Xtra to "spray" objects across the page.
- Learn how to use the chart Xtra to create graphic bar charts.

PROJECTS TO BE COMPLETED:

- Dinner Time (A)
- Mask Art (B)
- Tropical Treasure Logo (C)
- Grocery Ad (D)
- Ball and Mirror (E)
- **No Clowning Around (F)**

Xtras

FreeHand has a number of plug-in functions called Xtras, which enhance the standard features with special features that have been requested by FreeHand users. You can further customize a design to meet your requirements by applying the appropriate Xtras.

A number of Xtras are standard features in FreeHand. You can purchase specialized plug-ins from Macromedia and third-party software developers. Adobe Illustrator filters can also be used in FreeHand. Xtras are stored in the FreeHand 9>English>Xtras folder.

The Xtras

There are too many Xtras to show how each one affects selected objects, but we will do an overview of some of the more frequently-used Xtras.

Xtras have their own menu in the Menubar. In Chapter 12, Path Operations, you looked at some of the Xtras in the Cleanup, Create, and Path Operations menus.

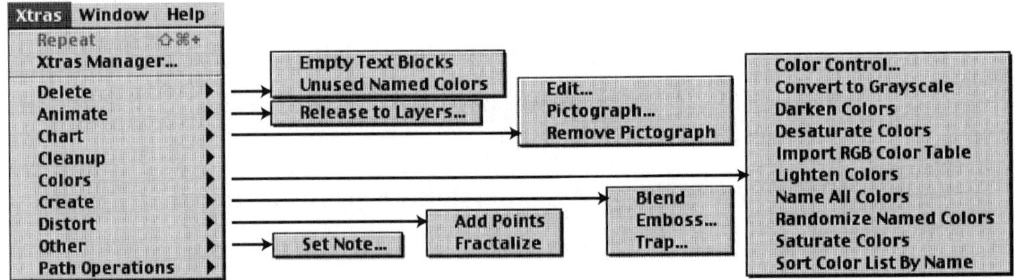

Additional Xtra Plug-ins are found in Window>Toolbars>Xtra tools, and in the Xtra Operations toolbar.

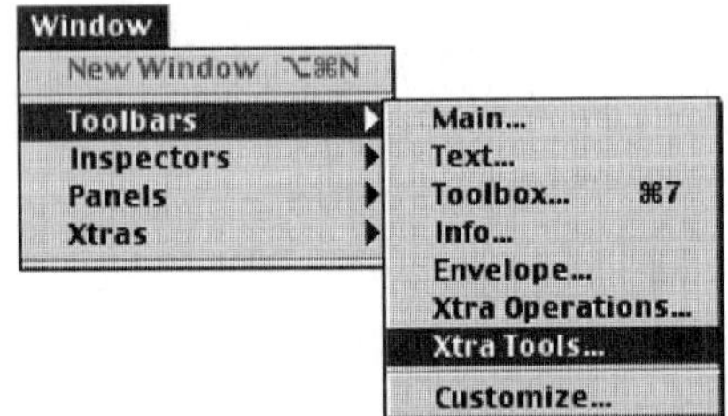

Xtras Manager

There are a total of 81 functions managed by the Xtras Manager (Xtras>Xtras Manager), falling under 13 categories — categories within the submenus, plus the Xtra Operations and Xtra Tools toolboxes. Since you can add Xtras in addition to these standard ones, the list could become quite long. To speed up your computer, turn off Xtras that you do not use.

Xtras that are checked in the Xtras Manager are turned on. Entire submenus may be turned on or off, or, through the Xtras Manager Options pop-up menu, you may turn them all on or all off. Managing Xtras in an on-the-fly operation. The Xtras are turned on or off immediately, with no need to relaunch FreeHand.

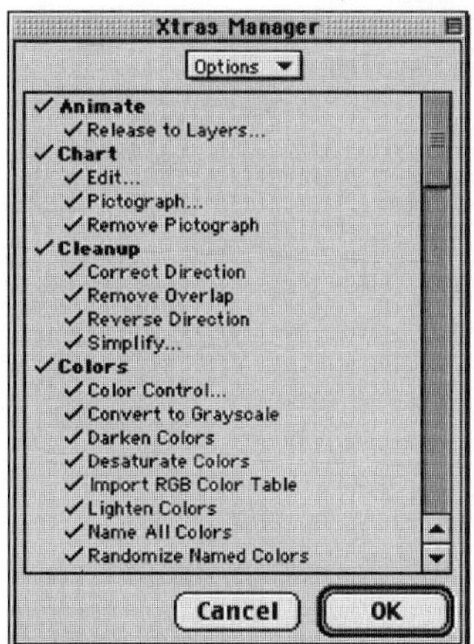

Categories of Xtras and their uses are as follows:

Animate	Creating Animations
Chart	Creating charts and pictograms
Cleanup	Improving path manipulation
Colors	Altering colors in a document
Create	Forming new objects
Delete	Removing unused elements from a document
Export	Filters for exporting files
Import	Filters for importing files
Other	Miscellaneous. Set Note ships with FreeHand and is used to create a non-printing label for an object.
Path Operations	Managing paths

Xtra Tools

Xtra Tools are a variety of operations that perform path modifications that would be either difficult or time-consuming to do by hand. Think of Xtra Tools as an extended and enhanced Toolbox. Usually, you just select an Xtra Tool and drag its crosshair cursor over an object, but some have dialog boxes that allow you to modify certain options to suit your particular needs.

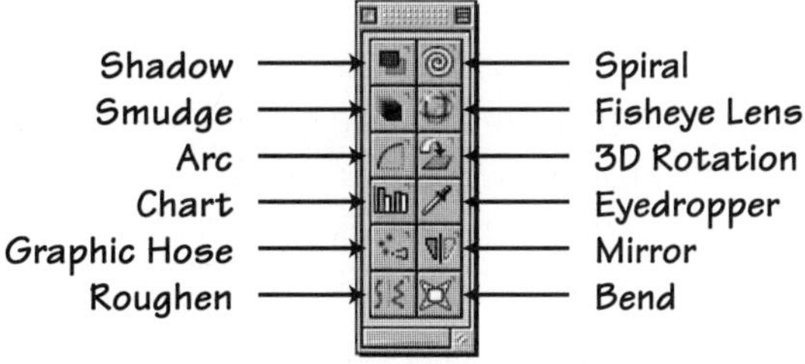

Xtra Tool icons that have angle brackets in the upper-right corners will show behavior-controlling dialog boxes.

We won't cover every Xtra tool, but we'll take a look at some of the more fun and useful ones that can make complex operations much easier.

Shadow 

The Shadow tool creates a shadowed copy of the original. The Shadow dialog box has several options and you can create some interesting effects by experimenting with them.

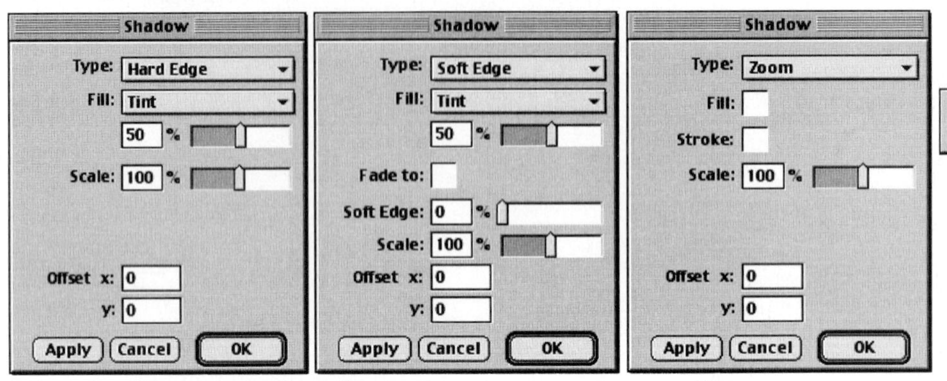

When the effects are applied, the resulting image can be very different.

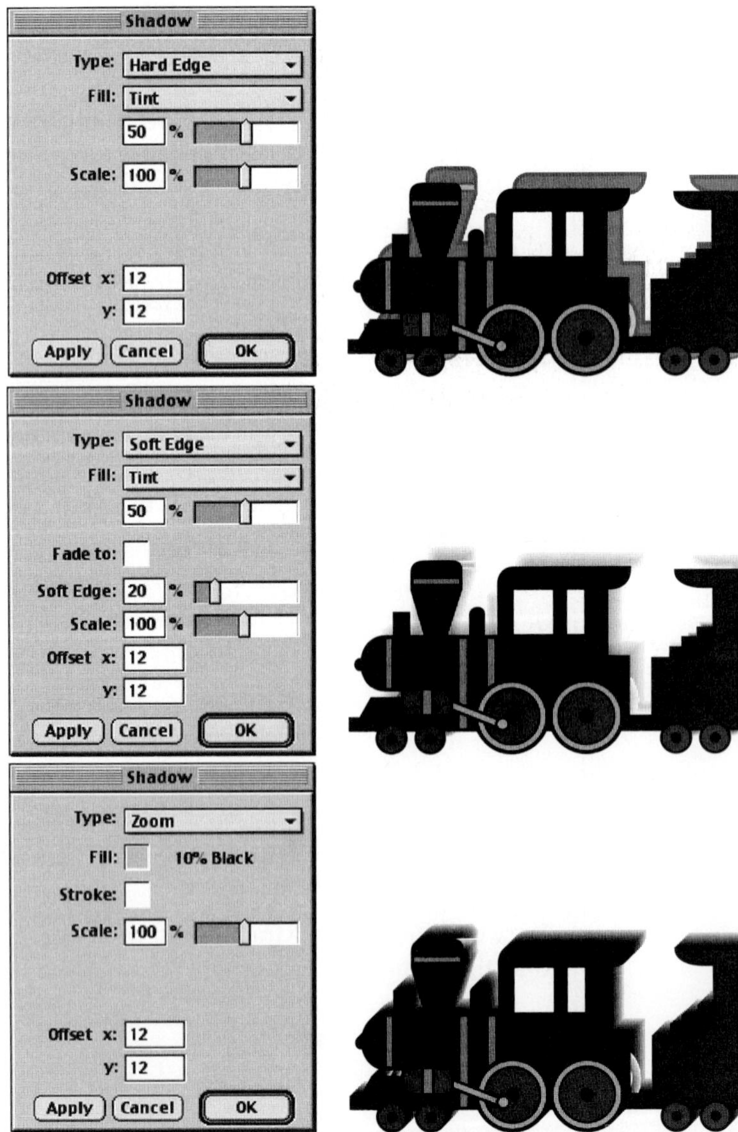

Spiral 

The Spiral tool draws a spiral much faster and more accurately than trying to draw one with the Pen tool. When the Spiral tool is double-clicked, its dialog box is displayed. The Spiral tool in the Xtras toolbar is identical to the one in the Toolbox.

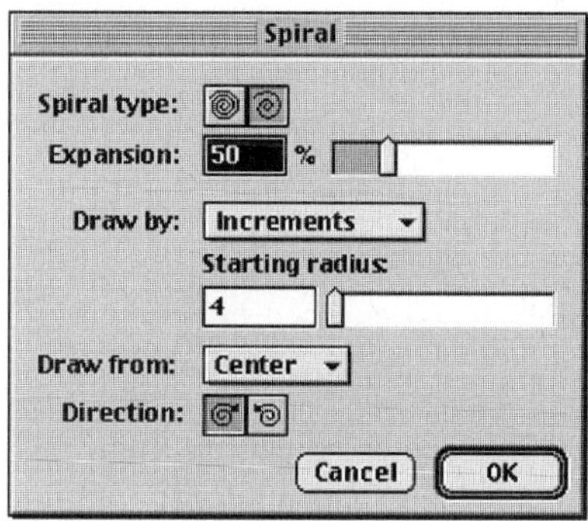

These settings will draw a spiral like the following:

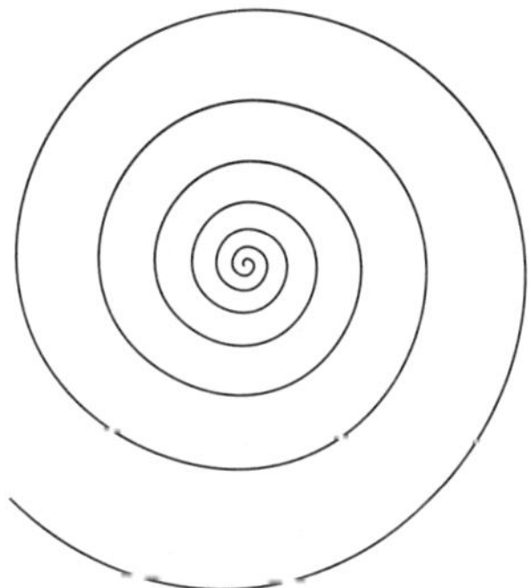

If you hold the Shift key while drawing, the origin of the spiral can be constrained to 45° angles. Interesting effects may be achieved when Modify>Expand Stroke is applied and interesting fills are used.

Smudge 

The Smudge tool creates graduated tones of the selected object. You can specify different fill and stroke colors in the Smudge dialog box. Double-click the Smudge tool icon to show the dialog box.

Colors to be smudged are dragged to the fill and stroke color wells in the dialog box.

Drag tool to set direction of smudge *After Smudging*

Fisheye Lens 

The Fisheye Lens magnifies portions of objects to look like they were viewed through a fisheye camera lens. You can set the curvature to be concave (inward) or convex (outward) in the Fisheye Lens dialog box.

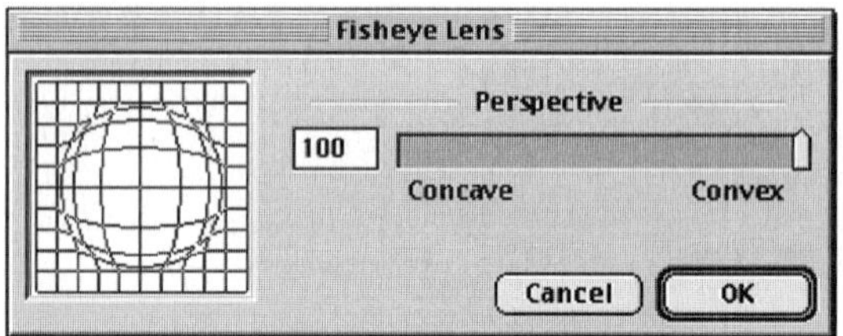

Original *After Convex Fisheye Lens* *After Concave Fisheye Lens*

Arc

The Arc tool draws several types of arcs. The way you drag the tool on the page determines the arc's orientation. Double-click on the Arc tool and experiment with the Arc settings to see the effects you can achieve.

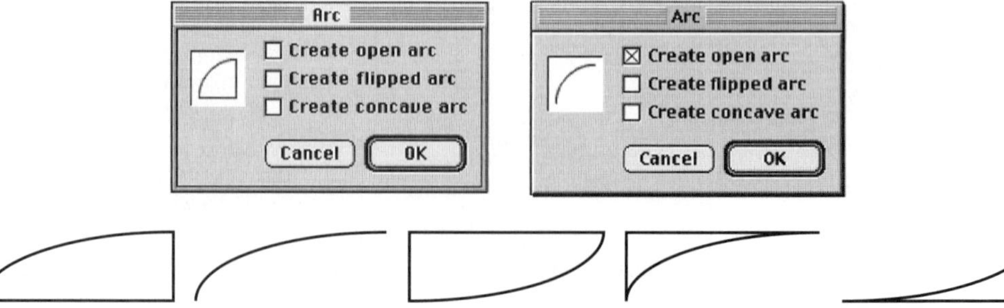

These arcs are standard (closed), open, standard flipped, concave, and concave flipped. These arcs were drawn from the lower-left corner to the upper-right corner.

3D Rotation 

The 3D tool skews objects, creating a three-dimensional effect. You can adjust the tool's behavior by double-clicking on it in the Xtra Tools toolbar.

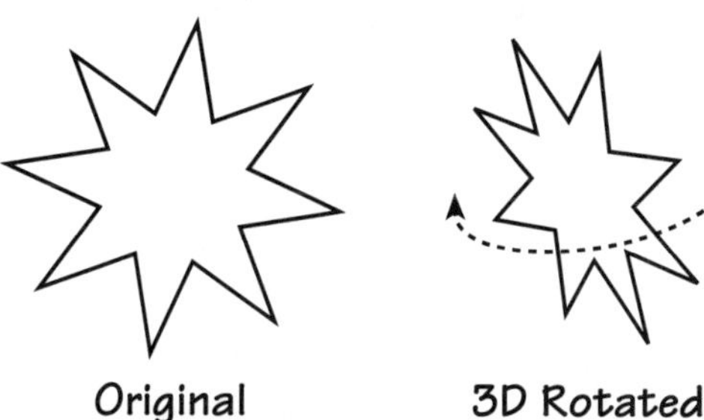

Double-click on the 3D Rotation icon to display its dialog box. It has two modes: Easy and Expert.

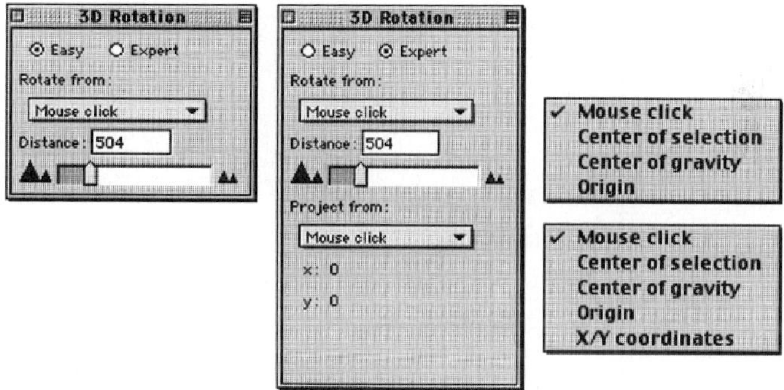

- Rotate from — Choose the point of origin of the rotation from this pop-up menu: Mouse click rotates the object with respect to where you click the mouse. Center of selection rotates from the center of the object. Center of gravity rotates by the apparent visual center of the object; and Origin rotates from the lower-left corner of the object.
- Distance — Drag the slider to the left to increase distortion or to the right to decrease distortion.

The expert menu includes the ability to define the projection (vanishing) point.

- Project from — Choose the vanishing point from this pop-up menu: Mouse click positions the vanishing point where you click your mouse; Center of selection positions the vanishing point in the center behind the object; Center of gravity positions the vanishing point behind the visual center of the object; Origin positions the vanishing point begin at the lower-left corner of the object; and X/Y coordinates allows you to type in the x and y positions of the vanishing point.

Press Option-Command-X (Macintosh) or Alt-Control-X (Windows) to show the Xtra Tools panel.

Chart 

The Chart Xtra creates a chart according to numeric data that you supply. To create a chart, click the Chart tool and drag a rectangle on the page. The Chart data input dialog box appears and the numeric chart data can be entered on the input line above the data cells. Type your information into the input line and press the Tab key to enter data across columns. Press Return/Enter to enter the data in a single column. Data entered across columns is considered to be multiple data sets. Data in a single column is considered a single data set, and will produce a chart with all bars, lines, or segments the same color. Click a cell and input a different value to change the data.

When you click OK, the chart will appear.

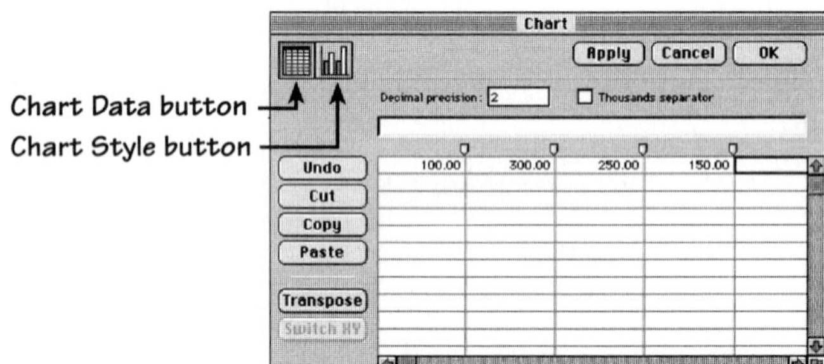

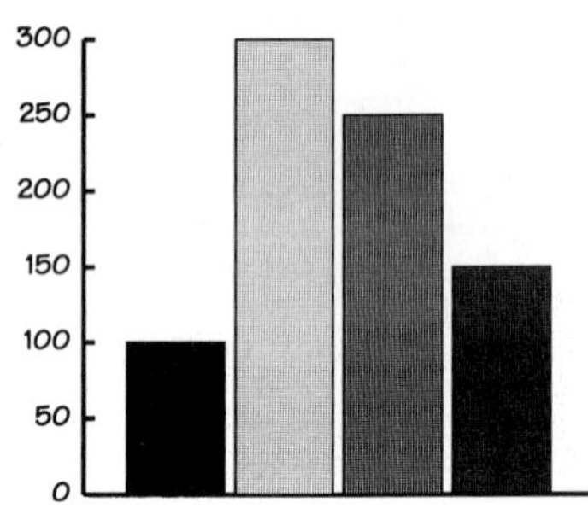

Editing Charts

Select the chart with the cursor and double-click the Chart tool to edit the chart's data or appearance. Click the Chart Style icon to change the chart's style.

The name of each chart appears when its icon is clicked.

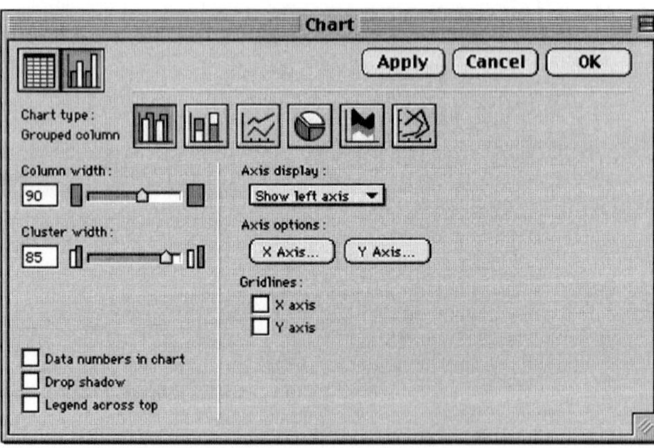

The changes will be applied to the chart when you click OK.

Pictograph

Pictograph replaces chart columns with artwork copied to the clipboard. To apply a pictograph, hold the Option/Alt key while selecting a column in the chart, then select Xtras>Chart>Pictograph to replace the columns of the chart with the objects in the clipboard.

The Pictograph works only with a single data set.

Eyedropper 

This tool is identical to the Eyedropper tool in the Toolbox. It is used to select a color from any object and apply it to another object.

Graphic Hose 

The Graphic Hose "shoots" an object with each click, or "sprays" one or more objects if the mouse button is held down. FreeHand comes with a few pre-made hose objects but you can easily add your own. To create a new hose, select New from the top pop-up menu of the Graphic Hose menu, then copy the object to the Clipboard and click Paste In. You can add up to ten FreeHand objects to a hose to create a series of hose "splats."

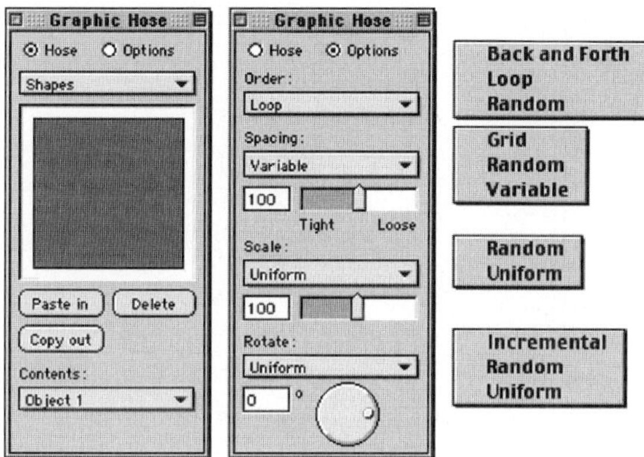

The manner in which the hose applies the objects is determined by the selections made in the Options menu. This is one of FreeHand's features that's a lot of fun to experiment with.

Mirror 

Used as an enhanced reflecting tool, Mirror reflects a duplicate across a 90° axis when clicked on or near a selected object. This eliminates the need to duplicate an object and reflect it. You can also set the mirroring across the x, y, or both axes in the Mirror dialog box and you can also rotate the objects while mirroring them. The Mirror dialog box has a few settings as follows:

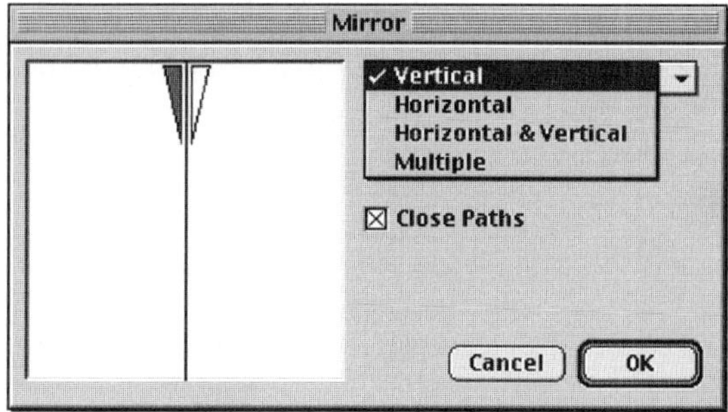

Choosing Multiple lets you also rotate the objects.

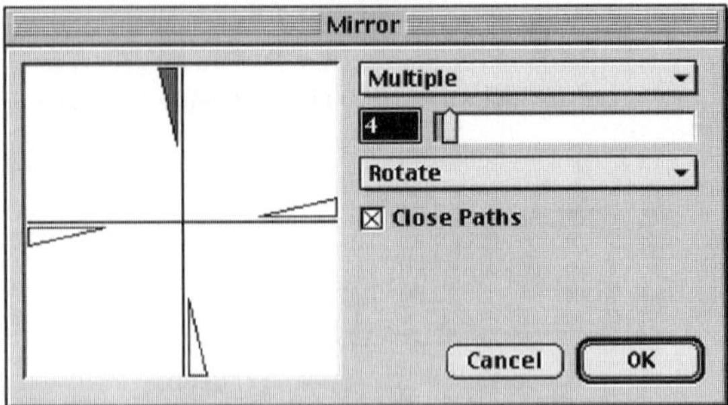

The following is the result of Multiple Mirror with Rotate:

Roughen 

Roughen takes the segments and anchor points of a path and breaks them into random anchors, making the edges of the object erratic or rough. You can set the amount of roughness in the Roughen dialog box. Moving the slider to the right creates finer gradations; moving it to the left creates coarser gradations.

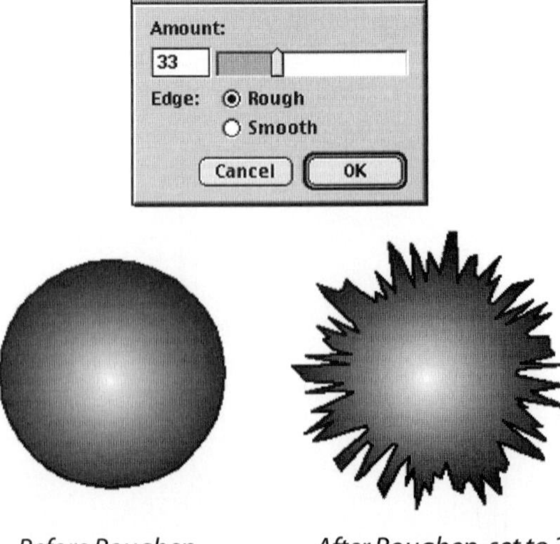

Before Roughen *After Roughen, set to 33*

Bend 

The Bend Xtra tool bends segments of a path depending upon how you drag the cursor. You can control the amount of bend with the slider in the Bend dialog box.

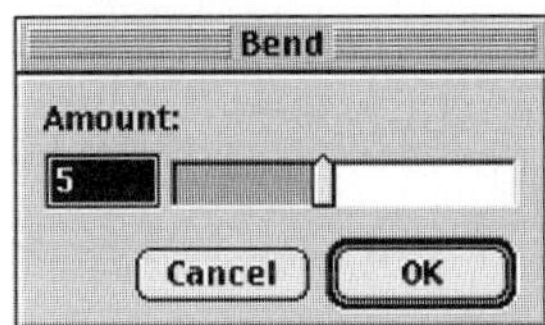

After clicking the Bend tool, you can drag anywhere around or on the selected object. If you pull the cursor down, the curves will round outward; if you pull the cursor up, they go inward.

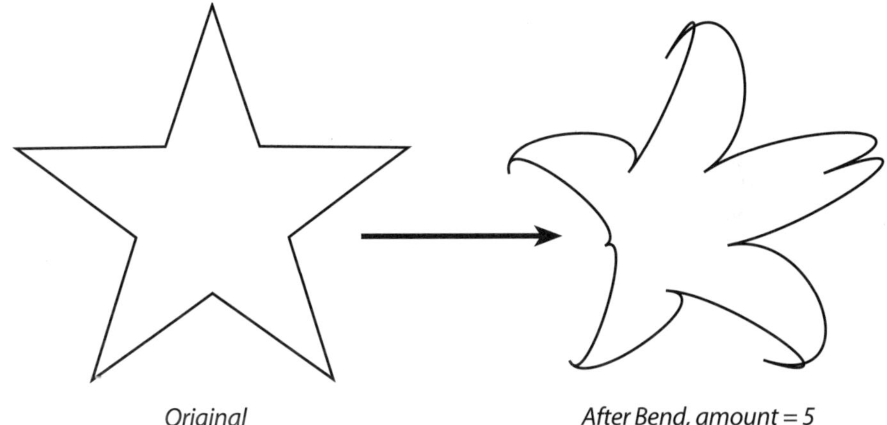

Original *After Bend, amount = 5*

Hose a Page

1. Create a new document.
2. Choose Windows>Toolbars>Xtras tools to show the Xtra Tools toolbar.
3. Double-click on the Graphic Hose tool to open the control box.

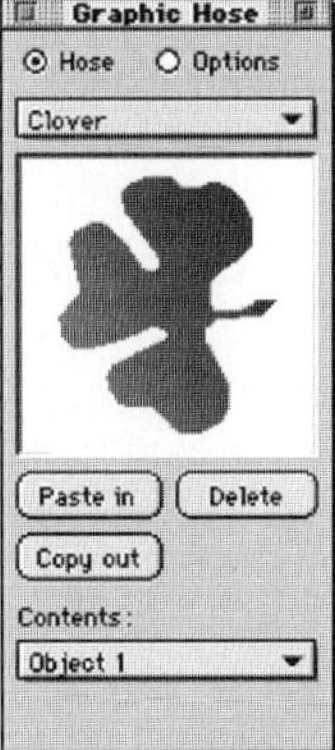

4. Choose Flowers from the pop-up menu and spray a few on the page.

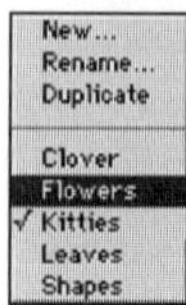

Choose Clover from the pop-up menu and place a few clover leaves on the page.

5. Open **Kitties.FH9** from your **SF-FreeHand** folder. Choose Edit>Select All and group the objects. Scale the cat down to about 20%. Copy the cat. Close the document without saving.

6. In the Graphic Hose control box, select New from the pop-up menu, and name the new hose pattern "Kitties". Click Paste In to paste the cat into the hose pattern.

7. Spray a number of cats on the page.

8. Experiment with the Graphic Hose settings. Click the Options button to reveal more hose controls. Try hosing other objects and changing the settings in the Options menu.

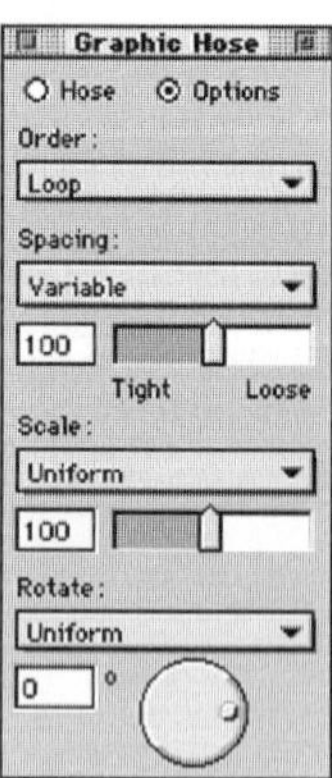

9. Close the document without saving.

Experiment with Xtras

1. Create a new document.
2. Draw an object of any shape and select it.
3. Select Window>Toolbars>Xtra tools and click the Roughen tool. Drag the crosshair cursor on or near your selected object. Watch what happens when you drag the object. Experiment with how the tool affects the object you have drawn. Press Command/Control-Z to Undo.
4. With the object selected, open the Xtra Tools toolbar and click on the Fisheye Lens tool. Drag the cursor on top of the object; the tool bends an object to look as if it were seen through a fisheye camera lens.

   Double-click on the Fisheye Lens tool to access its controls.

   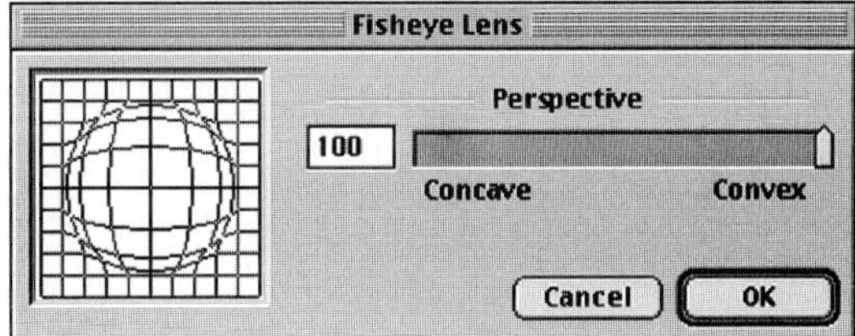

   Experiment with different settings and dragging this tool on various parts of an object to see the interesting effects that you can create. Delete the object when finished.
5. The default for the Arc tool is to create a closed arc. Double-click on the tool to ensure that the default setting (nothing checked) is currently in force. Click on the Arc tool in the Xtra Tools panels and drag the cursor on the page to draw an arc. Release the mouse when the arc is drawn.

6. Double-click on the Arc tool in the Xtra Tools toolbar. Click the Create open arc option to deselect it.

7. Drag the cursor on the page to draw another arc. The arc is now a closed path.

8. Select this path and click on the 3D Rotation tool in the Xtra Tools toolbar. Drag the cursor near the object and see it skew. You could use it to create a 3-dimensional look.

9. With the object selected, click on the Mirror tool in the Xtra Tools toolbar. Drag the cursor on the image and observe how it will reflect without the Reflect tool. Duplicate it, then select it and delete these objects.

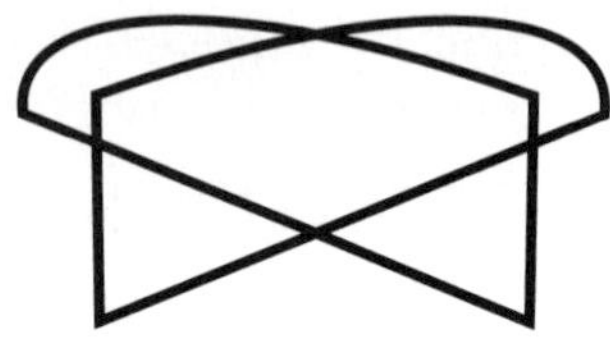

10. Click on the Spiral tool in the Xtra Tools toolbar. Drag its cursor on the page to draw a spiral.

11. Select the Smudge tool in the Xtra Tools toolbar. Drag the smudge cursor across the selected spiral. When you let go, you will see the smudge.

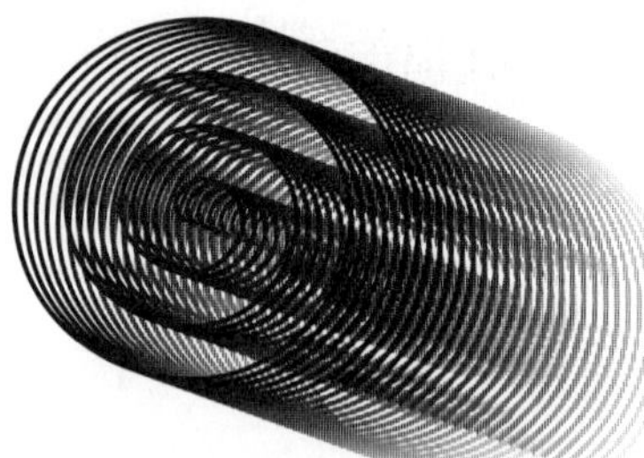

12. Delete the objects and leave the document open for the next exercise.

Work with Charts

1. Click on the Chart tool in the Xtra Tools toolbar.
2. With the Chart cursor, draw a square about 3″ across.
3. Click on the Chart Type icon and note the options available. Leave the Chart Type at the default, a simple bar chart, and return to the worksheet.
4. In the Chart worksheet, type the following information, creating a single data set:

   100 300 250 150

5. Press OK. FreeHand creates a simple bar chart based on the data entered.

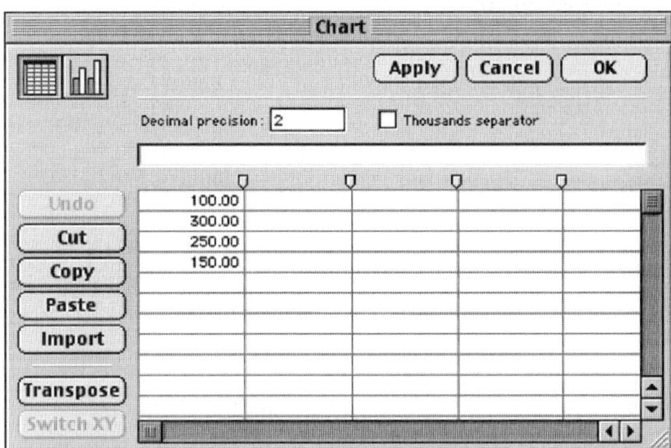

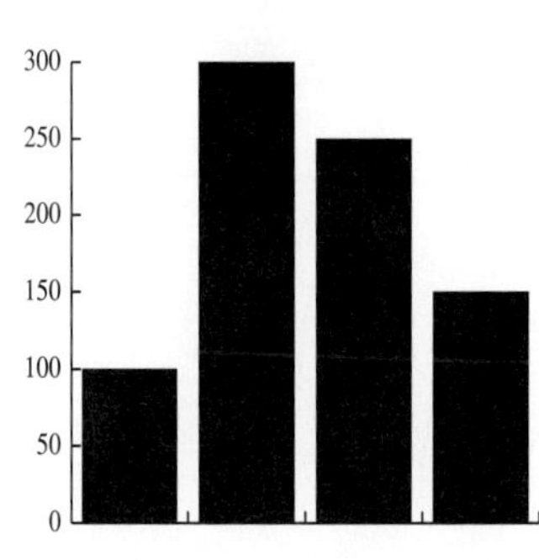

6. Open the file **Books.FH9**, select the grouped pile of books, and copy it to the clipboard. Close the **Books** file.
7. Hold down the Option/Alt key and select a column of the chart.
8. From the Xtras menu, select Chart>Pictograph>Paste In. Click the Repeating box to check it.

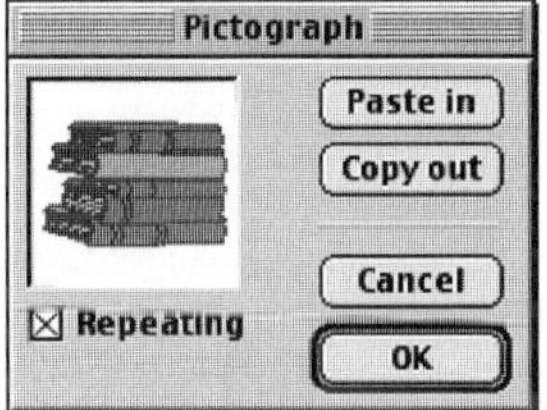

9. Click OK. The pictograph will be applied to all columns of the chart.

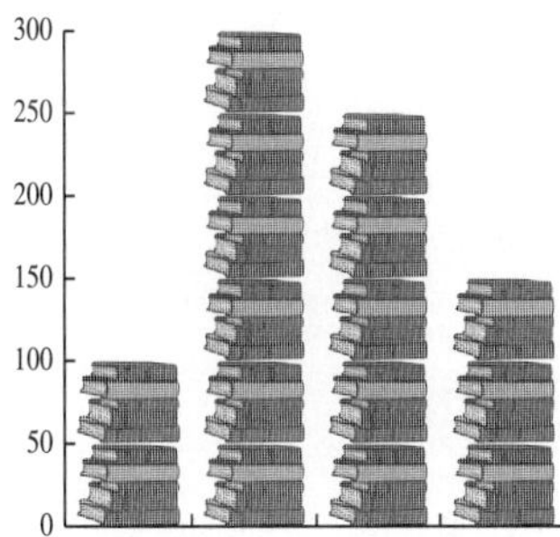

10. Close the document without saving.

Summary

You have explored the tools included in the Xtra Tools toolbar and have worked with most of them. These should give you an idea about how you can make working with FreeHand more productive, and should allow you to add diversity to your artwork — even statistical data such as charts and graphs.

Complete Project E: No Clowning Around

Notes:

Chapter 14

Importing and Exporting

Chapter Objective:

To learn how to import documents, and how to export documents for use in other applications. In Chapter 14, you will:

- Know why and when you need to export FreeHand documents.
- Learn how to import and export a document; understand how to exchange information between other applications.
- Understand the two main types of imported graphic files — vector and raster images — and the differences between them.
- Learn how a vector image is drawn in certain applications as path-oriented outlines; understand the screen appearance of a vector image.
- Learn how to edit vector EPS images with tools from within FreeHand.
- Understand how a vector image and FreeHand path image will differ in its on screen appearance.
- Learn how to modify raster images in FreeHand; study how the Object Inspector can provide information about a specific object.
- Understand how to link and embed imported graphics; how FreeHand copies the source graphic and stores it in the FreeHand document and the advantage that brings to you.
- Learn to alter raster images in FreeHand.
- Learn how to use FreeHand to create and export animations.

Projects to be Completed:

- Dinner Time (A)
- Mask Art (B)
- Tropical Treasure Logo (C)
- Grocery Ad (D)
- Ball and Mirror (E)
- No Clowning Around (F)

Importing and Exporting

Today's designers don't work in a vacuum. You may be expected to work with other designers and layout artists who may be using completely different applications (such as Adobe Illustrator, CorelDraw, QuarkXPress, or Adobe PageMaker) and computer platforms (Windows or Macintosh). There are established standards for exchanging information (text, images, drawings, or completed publications) between applications and platforms, and FreeHand is designed with these standards and realities in mind.

Getting Information into FreeHand

You can import a variety of graphic file formats into a FreeHand document, such as artwork from other drawing applications like Adobe Illustrator or CorelDraw, or photographic images from Photoshop or a desktop scanner. Different graphic formats have their advantages and their drawbacks. Knowing how an image is built, and how it can be modified, is the secret to confidently managing images.

There are two main formats for imported graphic files: vector and raster (bitmap). Vector and raster images are created in different ways. Artwork drawn in FreeHand, Illustrator, or CorelDraw is created in a vector format, made with points and paths. Raster images are bitmap, originating from a variety of sources, such as scanning, or from image-editing applications such as Adobe Photoshop or Corel Painter.

Vector Images

Vector images are made in programs such as FreeHand and Adobe Illustrator that draw path-oriented outlines based on mathematical algorithms. You can enlarge or reduce these images infinitely without suffering a loss of quality. Remember the old kids' game of Cat's Cradle? If not, it is played with a long piece of string laced between the fingers to form different patterns. Replacing the string with a big rubber band lets you pull your hands apart to make the pattern bigger; although the rubber band will become thinner, the curves and lines made with it remain smooth.

Vector images are similar to the rubber band: you can enlarge them as much as you like (and they won't snap). However, just as the rubber band gets thinner when stretched, vector images will reflect enlargement. Strokes become thinner relative to their placement, type may stretch unexpectedly, or patterns may distort. Similarly, when reduced, strokes may become too fat for the size of the art; type may plug up and vanish; or images may turn into formless blobs. If you plan to drastically enlarge or reduce artwork, you need to account for these variables in your design.

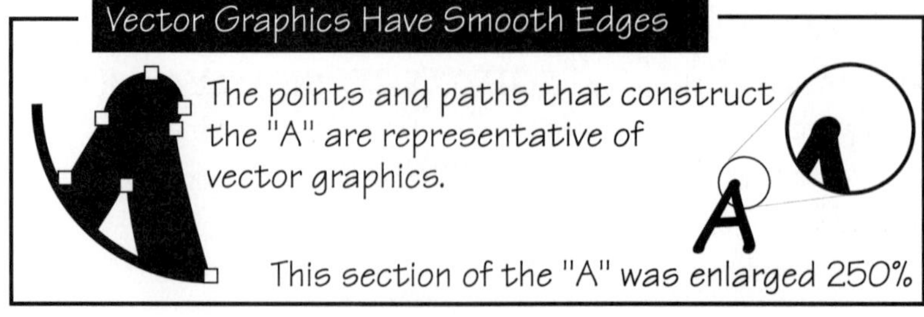

The Screen Appearance of Vector Images

When Vector images are imported, what you see on the screen is a low-resolution raster preview of the image. When printed, though, the image will reproduce as smoothly as your printer can possibly make it.

In this example, the left image is a screen shot of an imported vector EPS; the right image is a path residing in the document. Notice how the imported image has some jaggedness on its edges. The path on the right is much smoother because FreeHand displays resident objects as smooth vectors, not low-resolution raster previews.

The two objects appear as follows in Keyline mode. The imported EPS is on the left; the path is on the right.

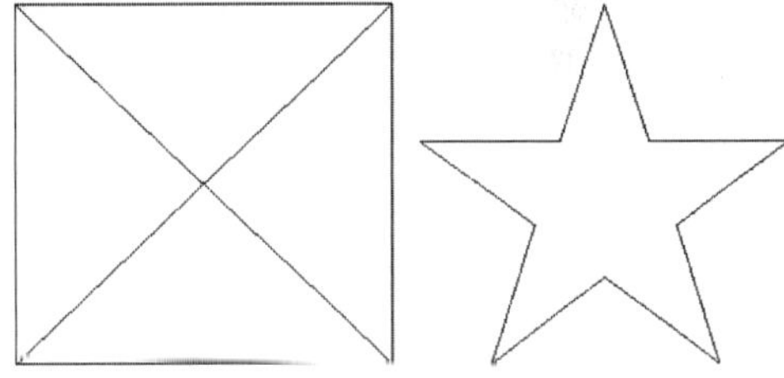

The bounding box with an "X" in it is also a way to identify an imported vector EPS in some programs.

Sometimes, FreeHand can't even import its own EPS files. Always keep the original artwork in the native FreeHand format and use EPS as an export format only, or save your work in the Editable EPS format.

You are better off copying an EPS file into FreeHand than importing it, especially if you will later save the FreeHand document as EPS for import into a page layout program.

Editing Vector EPS Images

Most vector EPS images, when imported, can be edited with tools from the Toolbox. This is controlled in the File>Preferences>Import option. The feature, Convert editable EPS when imported, must be clicked if you want the image to have editable paths. Otherwise, the graphic will be one single image on which you can only perform certain transformations.

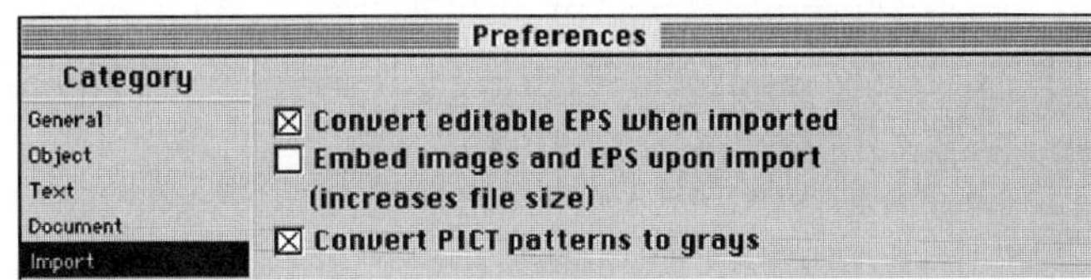

Other programs, such as PageMaker or QuarkXPress, have the ability to export their files as EPS, but this does not mean that they can be imported into FreeHand with editable paths. You must use discretion and your knowledge of the elements in the EPS file when you import them into FreeHand for editing.

In this example the left image was imported with Convert editable EPS when imported checked in Preferences; the right image was imported with this option off. The left image has paths that you modify, but the right image is a single, uneditable object and only limited FreeHand transformations can be performed on it.

Exporting Vector EPS Images Imported into FreeHand

You might have an imported vector EPS image as a part of your design. Then the client calls and wants a TIFF (a raster image format) file of the design to give to a newspaper for advertising. The job is simple enough in FreeHand — you simply export the design in TIFF format.

If you export a document as a raster (TIFF) file, make sure all the objects are vector paths. Placed EPS files that were not or could not be converted to editable artwork will render to a raster format with a coarse, low resolution.

But how is this TIFF image going to look? Look at this example. The left image was a path object in the document; the right image is a vector EPS image imported into the same document. Both images were exported as a TIFF, then printed here. The imported vector EPS has jagged edges and a faint pattern in it. This is because FreeHand is only exporting the low-resolution raster preview of the EPS, and not the defining vector information.

FreeHand Paths　　Placed Vector EPS

It is not recommended to export imported vector EPS images as raster formats. Vector EPS images should always be exported as EPS format, unless they will be used only in low resolution, such as a GIF image on the Web.

Raster (bitmap) Images

Raster graphics are represented as a fine grid of individual dots (pixels). Imagine a chessboard where each red and black square is a pixel. Imagine further that this chessboard is printed on a big balloon. As the balloon is inflated, the squares get bigger. Eventually the squares become distorted and no longer resemble what they looked like when you started.

Raster images behave the same way when enlarged. The pixels (squares) just get bigger and bigger, eventually to the point that the image looks very grainy and rough. Overly-enlarged raster art becomes *pixelated.* Raster images are very useful in the graphic arts to represent photographs or artwork created in a raster-based program like Photoshop. Raster images can be reduced without an apparent loss of quality, but cannot be enlarged much more than 5–10% without becoming pixelated. Consequently, raster images should be scanned or created as close to the finished size as possible.

While images may be exported as JPEG, this format, which uses a ***lossy*** *compression method, should be used at lower compression levels. Selecting a high compression level will result in a smaller file (which is good), and lower quality (which is not good).*

Raster Formats

The most common raster format used in the graphic arts industry is TIFF (Tagged Image File Format). Other raster formats used are JPEG, GIF, BMP, and PICT, but these are specialized for various purposes and, except for JPEG, aren't suitable for print reproduction. GIF and JPEG formats are widely used for graphics in web pages. If you are creating images for use on a web page for the Internet, you would probably select either JPEG or GIF format. Printed projects require the TIFF or JPEG format.

The Raster EPS Format

This file format encloses a raster image within an EPS "wrapper." Don't assume that the raster EPS format is going to smooth out jagged pixels when the image is enlarged; being raster in format, it will still become pixelized. If you need to create a raster EPS file to give to a printer, FreeHand is capable of exporting this graphic format.

Raster Images in FreeHand

Most raster images are only recognizable when viewing them in Preview mode. But you obviously can't always work in Preview mode, so you should be very careful if you have several raster images in a document along with squares and rectangles. You might get them mixed up.

Here's a quiz question: "Of the three objects shown in Keyline mode, without cheating by looking at the Object Inspector, which one was drawn by the Rectangle tool, the Pen tool, and which one is an imported raster image?"

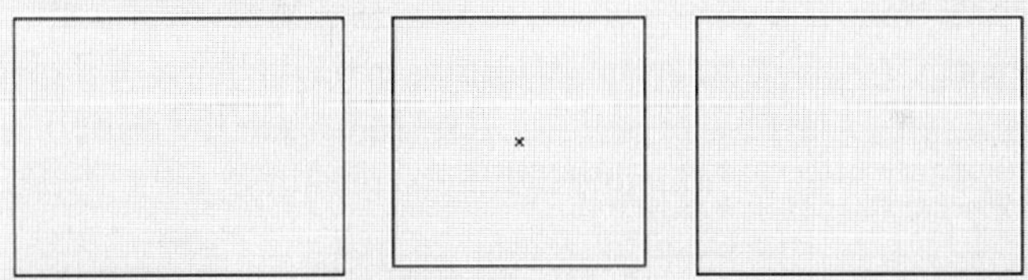

Answer: The only image that can be identified in Keyline mode is the middle object, because it has a center point. This means that it was created using the Rectangle tool. Otherwise, the other two images are indistinguishable in Keyline mode. If you were in a hurry and stretched and distorted the wrong image, Undo, Revert, re-importing, or redrawing the image would be the only alternatives.

The raster EPS file format, when viewed in Keyline mode is identified, just like a vector EPS, by the "X" in its bounding box.

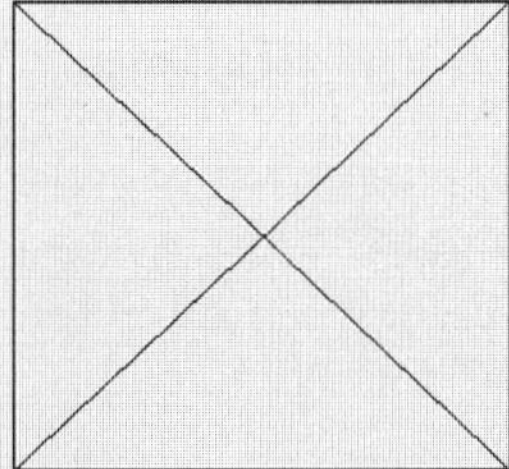

Modifying Raster Images in FreeHand

The Object Inspector can tell you a lot about a selected object, such as whether it is a path, a FreeHand group, a Grayscale TIFF, RGB TIFF, CMYK TIFF, or an imported EPS.

The Object Inspector shows selected objects by their type and format.

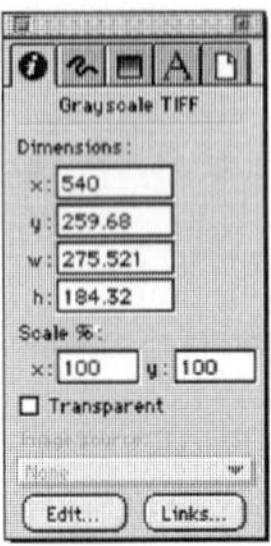

Make backup copies of embedded raster images in your document before applying effects. You might apply several modifications, then change your mind.

If the image is a Grayscale TIFF, Object Inspector lets you make certain modifications. This feature is found at the bottom of the Object Inspector, using the Edit button.

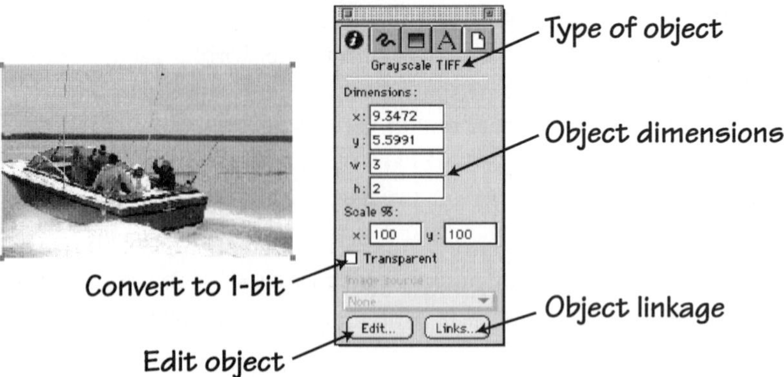

When you select the Edit option of the Object Inspector, a dialog box displays that allows you to lighten, darken, adjust contrast, and change effects of the image. The four buttons across the top give these changes:

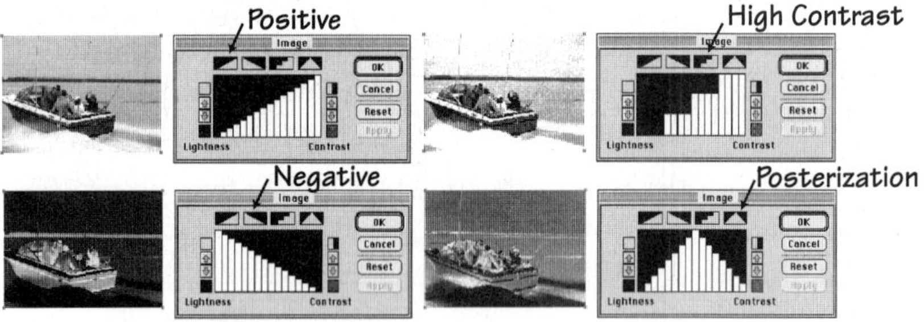

Under these buttons is the light-to-dark palette that shows you what the balance of the image is set for. The button to the right of this palette gives you control over adding or subtracting lightness, darkness, or contrast.

Clicking OK will apply the modifications you have made to the selected object. Remember, you can always undo these changes.

Linking and Embedding Imported Graphics

When importing graphics, FreeHand automatically creates a link to the image, controlled by the Edit>Links option. If you embed a graphic, FreeHand copies the source graphic and stores it in the FreeHand document and does not require the original image for print or display. Everything needed to reproduce the graphic is stored within the document.

If you choose to keep the imported graphic linked and not embedded, you will conserve disk space. Embedding graphics increases the file size of the document. When you import a graphic without embedding, FreeHand generates a low-resolution screen preview (a placeholder) to retain the position of the graphic and must locate the original to print or preview at high-resolution. When a graphic is linked, FreeHand updates the location and data from that link each time the document is opened.

An image link is simply the location of the image on your computer's hard disk, so FreeHand can find it to print a high resolution image.

Embedding is often used to transport completed documents. If your graphic files are embedded, you don't have to worry about collecting and managing them when you send your job to the service provider. Remember to create your settings for linking and embedding from Preferences>Import.

Use Command/Control-R to access the Import dialog box.

We heard of a situation where an entire series of bitmap images had to be recreated from scratch because they were embedded in file which became corrupted. There were no originals; they were all saved in the corrupted document. If they had been linked, the problem would not have occurred.

Always think about the organization of your environment; not just the document itself, the layers and measurements, but also the outside links that are established when working with imported graphics.

Drawbacks

There are advantages and disadvantages to linking and embedding. FreeHand won't change the name or location of the original imported file. A broken link makes all screen previews of imported images disappear, and the image will not print.

If you embed objects, your document file will grow in size, sometimes spectacularly. Large files require more memory and will make FreeHand run more slowly.

Managing Links

When you link or embed a graphic, FreeHand records the file name, size, disk location, and file type. This information is used whenever you open, export, or print the document; FreeHand checks to see that all links are still present. When opening a document with a linked image, FreeHand searches for the original graphic from where it was initially imported.

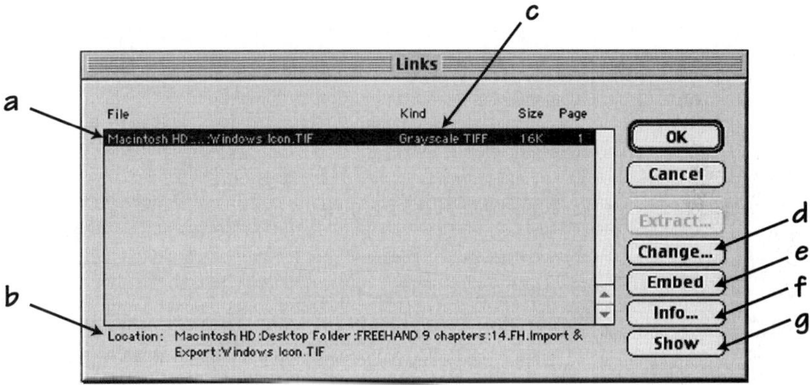

a — Name of the imported file.

b — Location of the file, on the computer.

c — The file format or kind.

d — Change lets you update or change the link to the imported file.

e — Embed will save a copy of the imported file into the document.

f — Info gives original file location, kind, last date modified, and file size.

g — Show will display the link at the location in the file.

The stored information on each graphic can be viewed from the Links dialog box. At any time you can select Edit>Links to display the Links dialog box to allow you to manage your links, repair broken links, search for missing links, update links, extract embedded objects, embed graphics, and view information about the graphic.

Be careful not to break a link by moving or deleting the source files. If FreeHand cannot locate the original graphic, you will be asked for the location of the file when you open the FreeHand document. Once you have again supplied FreeHand with this information, you will not be asked again.

If you see "????" listed under Size in the Links dialog box, the file's link has been broken. Click Change to select the file and locate it. This can happen if you move the source file to a different folder.

The Links dialog box can be accessed either by selecting Edit>Links, or selecting a linked or embedded object and clicking on the Links button in the Object Inspector.

Have the Computer Manage Your Links

If you are using FreeHand on the Macintosh you can have FreeHand reestablish links for you. Sometimes it is acceptable to have one graphics folder; this usually occurs when users create individual folders for categories of files (eg.: a folder for Documents, Applications, Graphics, etc.).

When a single folder contains all the files used for importing, change your Preferences>Document to "Search for missing links". This preference searches the specified folder and its subfolders to locate the missing links.

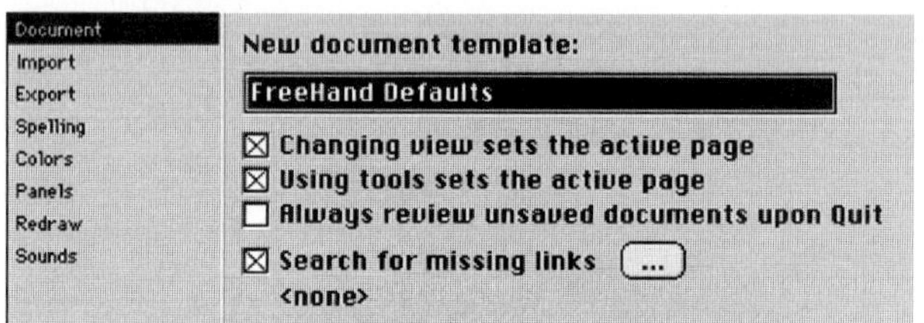

Exporting

It's easier to keep track of imported art if you save all imported files and the master document in the same folder. This will allow you to easily see all the file names, sizes, and types.

The need to transfer data between multiple applications and platforms as well as through the hands of many people involved in some aspect of the job requires a common file format. FreeHand can export data in more ways than you'll probably ever use. When you export a FreeHand document, you convert the illustration into a file format that is compatible with other applications on Windows or Macintosh computers. This is usually a vector EPS file, though it could also be a TIFF raster file for print, or GIF or JPEG for the Web.

Another important file format supported by FreeHand is Adobe's Portable Document Format (PDF). This format can be imported into many page layout programs, can be used on the web, and is used as a stand-alone format for document exchange.

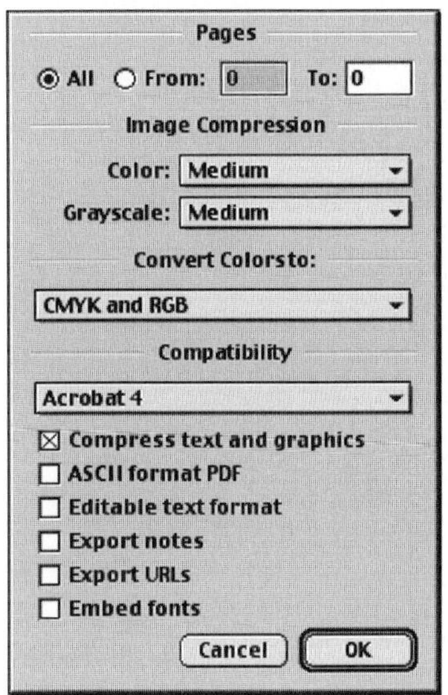

Supported File Formats for Exporting

Selecting the Format pop-up menu of the Export window will display a list of supported export file formats.

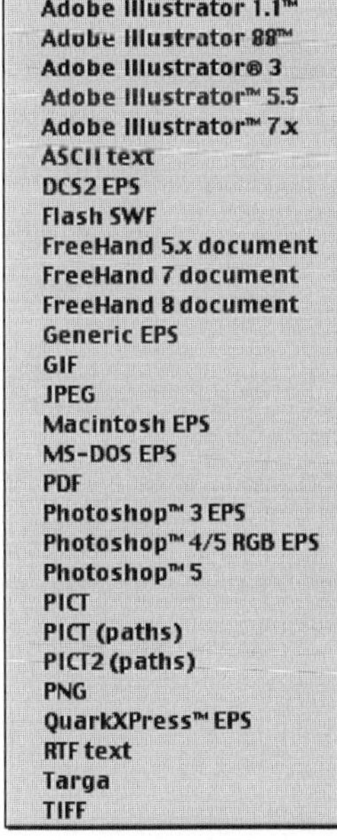

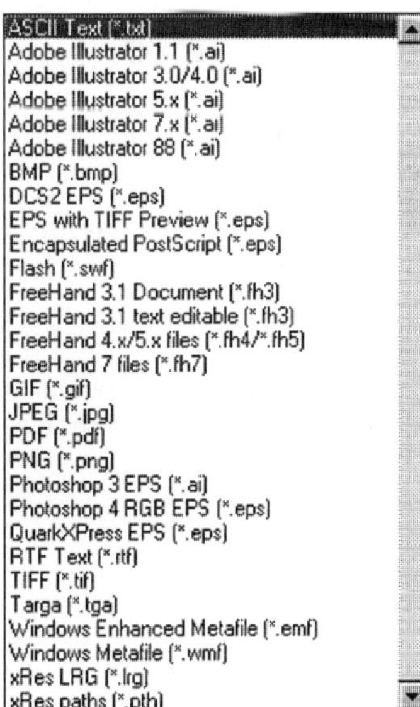

Macintosh *Windows*

If you are trying to export objects that are on the pasteboard, you might wonder why you aren't having any luck. Objects to be exported must be on a document page.

Import and Export Files

1. From the File menu, open the file **Exporting Files.FH9** from your **SF-FreeHand** folder.

2. The image is made up of paths, in FreeHand's vector format. To convert this to image formats suitable for external use, such as placing the image in other applications or use on a web page for the Internet, it must be exported.

3. Select File>Export. You will see the following window. Select the file format and name the file to be exported.

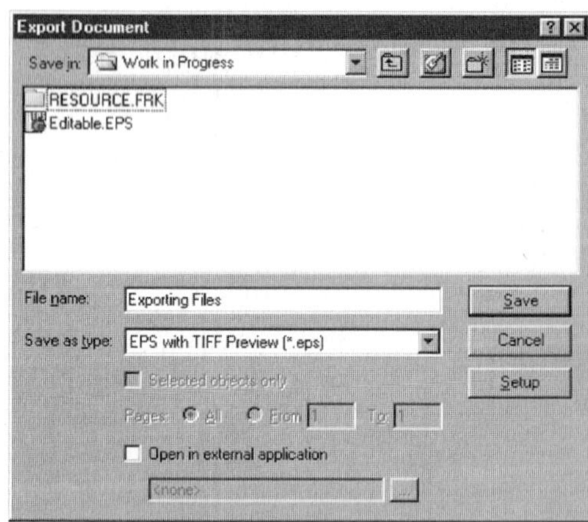

Macintosh (Left) and Windows (Right) File Export windows

If you don't know whether the computer that will import the file is a Macintosh, or is Windows-based always select the EPS with TIFF preview export option.

Both Macintosh and Windows computers can see the TIFF preview; only Macintosh computers can see the PICT image used in the Macintosh EPS format.

4. Leave the Format/Type set for Macintosh EPS (if you are using a Macintosh) or EPS with TIFF preview (for Windows users). The suffix .EPS is always added to the name of the file (even though, under Windows, it isn't always visible). If you want different names, you can always rename the file above the Format submenu (but remember to preserve the .EPS suffix). Leave the name as it is, locate your folder for saving work, and click Export/Save.

5. The original FreeHand document is unaffected. The exported file is a separate, external file saved to the folder you just specified.

6. Select File>Preferences>Import and turn off Convert editable EPS when imported, if it's on. Click OK.

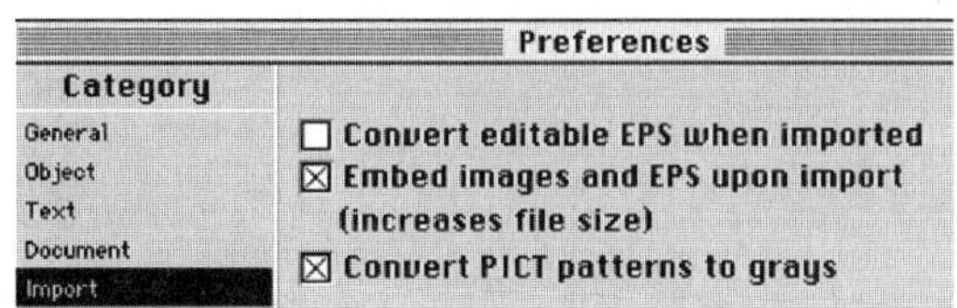

7. Select File>Import and choose the file you just saved. The image's preview appears (Macintosh only). Click Open to import this file.

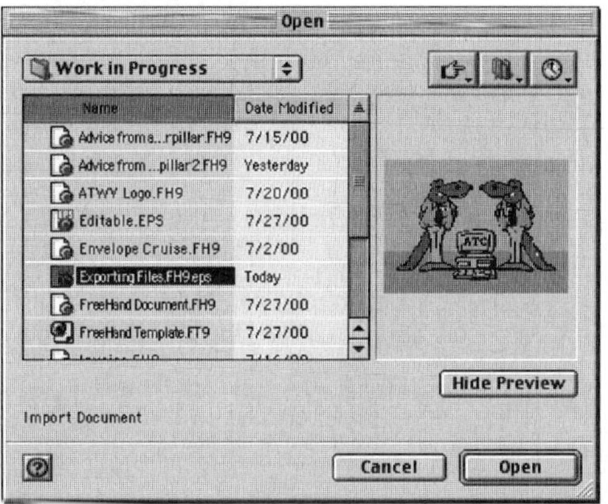

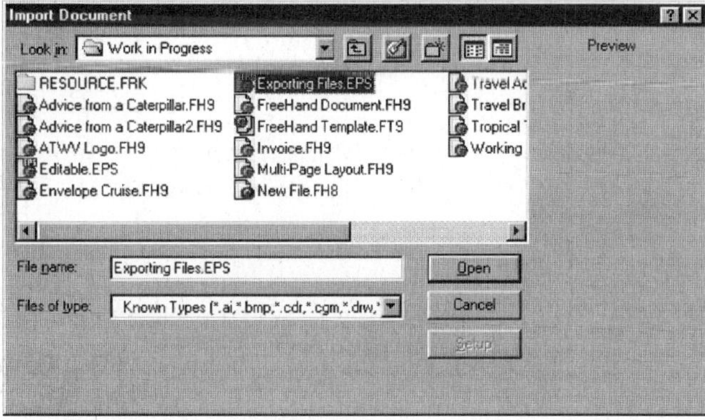

Macintosh (above) and Windows file Import windows

8. Back in the document, click the cursor to place this graphic on the page. Click on the image and try to ungroup it or select a path. What happened? It was imported as a single EPS image that can't be edited any further, except for scaling and similar transformations.

   Select File>Preferences>Import again and turn Convert editable EPS when imported back on. Leave this option on when you want imported images that you can edit, which is usually preferable. Click OK.

9. Select the imported image and delete it. Choose File>Import and import the same EPS file. Click the cursor on the page to place the image. It is now an editable FreeHand object that you can modify any way you like.

10. Delete the imported file. From File>Export, click on the Format/Save as Type submenu to choose GIF. The suffix .GIF is appended to the file name.

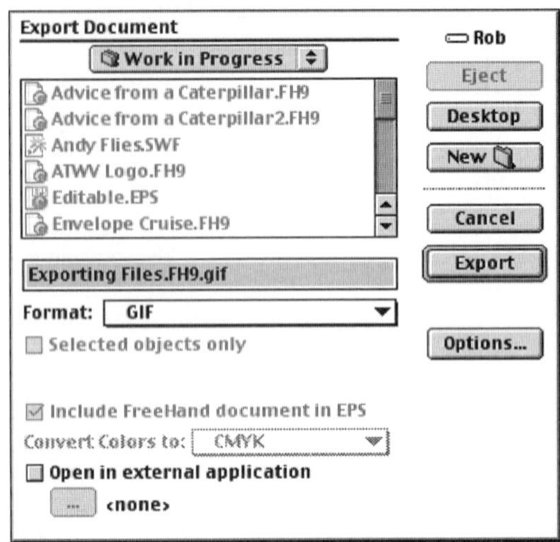

The Options (Macintosh) or Setup (Windows) feature is also accessible for raster formats. Click Options or Setup to display this dialog box. Set the Resolution for 72, then click OK. Return to the Export window, click Export/Save, and save the file in your **Work in Progress** folder.

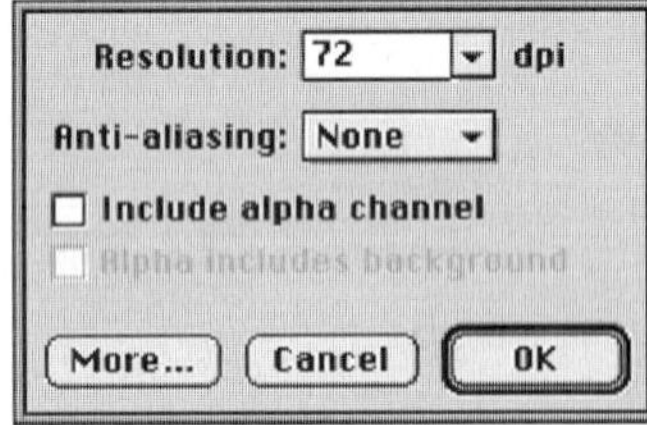

11. In the document, select File>Import and import the new GIF file. Click the cursor on the page to place the image.

12. Click on the placed image, then select View>Magnification 400%. This will enlarge the GIF image enough for you to see the pixelization (left image shown). Scroll the page upward to see the original vector image and how smooth its preview looks (right image shown).

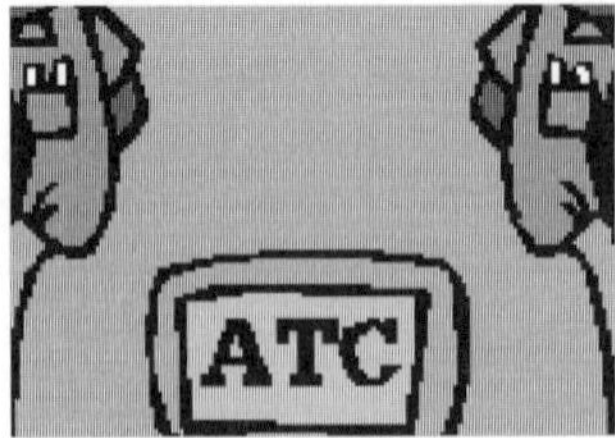

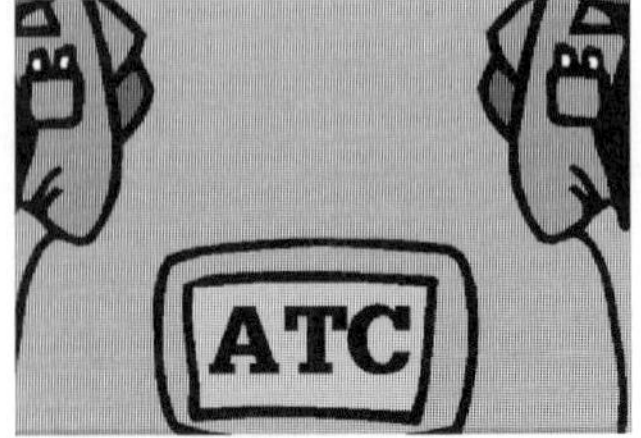

13. Use the Magnification pop-up menu to go to 50% view.

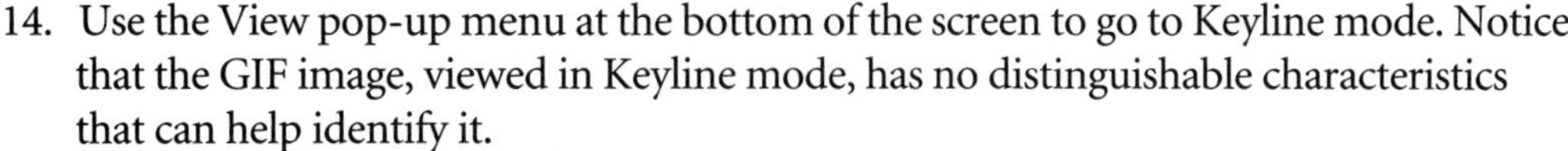

14. Use the View pop-up menu at the bottom of the screen to go to Keyline mode. Notice that the GIF image, viewed in Keyline mode, has no distinguishable characteristics that can help identify it.

Adjustments made to linked images in FreeHand do not affect the actual image, but merely apply the affects to it in the FreeHand document.

15. Delete the GIF image. Use the Rectangle tool to draw a simple square, keeping it selected. Select File>Export and, in the Export dialog box, click on the Selected objects only option. Set the Format/Type for TIFF. Click the Options (Macintosh) or Setup (Windows) button and set the Resolution for 300. Click OK and save the file to your **Work in Progress** folder.

16. In the document, select File>Import and import the TIFF image you just exported. Click the cursor on the page. Some thin-lined images do not show well on the screen at a small size; if parts of this square are not apparent, select View>Fit Selection to fill the screen with the image. Enlarged, you will see that it is intact. The Selected objects only option will export only those objects that are selected; this is a good method for singling out specific images for exporting.

17. You have now seen a sample of the power and versatility of the import and export features of FreeHand. Experiment with file formats and resolution of raster images such as JPEG, GIF, and TIFF.

18. Close the document without saving.

Alter Grayscale Raster Images

1. Open the document **Pelican.FH9** from your **SF-FreeHand** folder.

2. Click on the photo of the pelican to select it, and from the Object Inspector, click the Edit button to access the image controls.

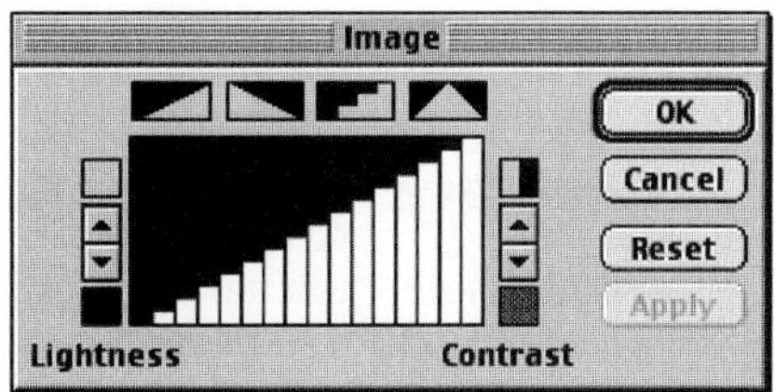

3. Scroll the Lightness and Contrast up and down. How does this affect the image?

4. Click on the second ramp at the top of the Image dialog box, then click Apply. The photograph becomes a negative.

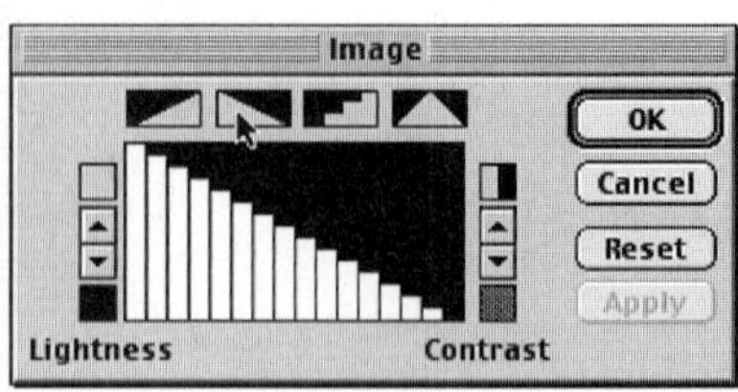

5. Click on the third ramp, the one that resembles stairsteps. Click Apply. The photograph becomes posterized.

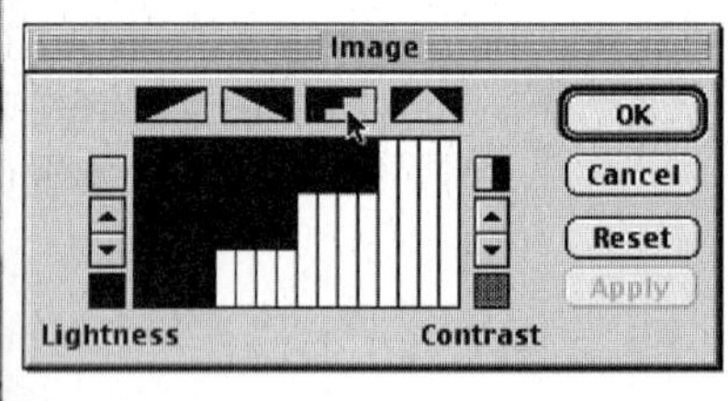

6. Click on the fourth ramp, which resembles a triangle to create a different posterization, brightening the mid-tones.

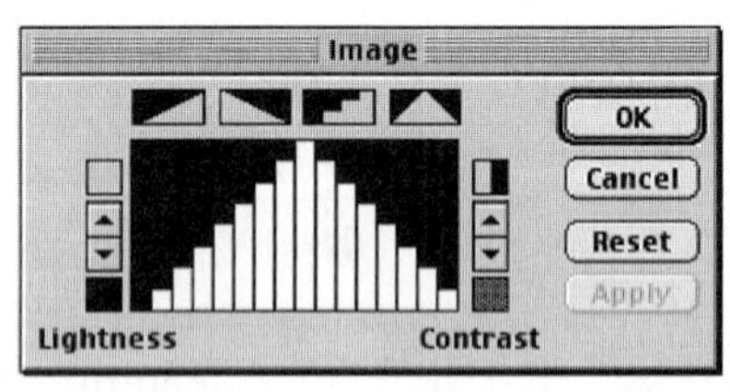

7. Click Cancel. Now drag the Brown color swatch from the Color List on top of the photograph and release. The photograph is colorized. Continue to experiment with other effects if you wish. Close the file without saving.

Summary

In this chapter, you have explored a number of formats used for importing and exporting files. You have learned which files are appropriate for print, and which should be used when preparing documents for the Web. You have imported and exported files, and have modified raster images within FreeHand.

CHAPTER 15

Printing and Separating

CHAPTER OBJECTIVE:

To understand how to print and separate from FreeHand. You will understand the basics of getting color on paper; page description languages; and screening. In Chapter 15, you will:

- Learn about page description languages, screening, screen rulings, screen angles, resolution, and trapping.
- Learn to use Find & Replace to change object attributes.
- Learn about dot gain, colored text, and checking gradients and blends.
- Learn about object-level halftones and printing separations.
- Learn how to print spot color separations.
- Familiarize yourself the Setup dialog options.
- Understand Print Setting, PPD's, UserPrep File, preview area, and pages and views.
- Understand separations; overprinting black, halftone screen/resolution, override objects, transfer function, and spread size.
- Understand imaging; labels and marks, imaging options, output options, and paper setup.

PROJECTS TO BE COMPLETED:

- Dinner Time (A)
- Mask Art (B)
- Tropical Treasure Logo (C)
- Grocery Ad (D)
- Ball and Mirror (E)
- No Clowning Around (F)

Printing and Separating

FreeHand's Print dialog box contains powerful prepress tools for creating press-ready color separations. In most cases, you'll use the Print dialog box to just print proofs to an inkjet or laser printer, and you really don't need to change anything in the Print dialog box to produce usable prints.

However, if you plan to use FreeHand as a production tool for the graphic arts, you need to learn more than just how to click the Print button. Even if you do not make your own color separations, this information will be valuable to you in the future when working with clients, prepress shops, and printers.

Adobe PostScript, like most programming languages, has different levels that have changed as the language has evolved. The current level is Level 3, which is just beginning to be used in printers and imagesetters. Most common is Level 2, which is widely supported in applications and equipment. Level 1 is the lowest common denominator and many types of prepress equipment and software are still limited to Level 1. In most cases, the PostScript level of your printer really isn't very important, although complex artwork may fail to print properly on a Level 1 printer.

Getting Color on Paper: The Basics

Color is put on paper in one of two ways: with spot color, which are pre-mixed inks of a specific color, or with four process colors, which means that the entire range of color in the printed piece is produced using percentages of Cyan, Magenta, Yellow and/or Black inks.

In this chapter, we will learn the process by which documents are prepared for printing and the underlying technologies used that make it possible.

Page Description Languages

Many laser printers and all professional graphic arts equipment generate pages by interpreting a *PostScript* file. PostScript is a programming language invented by Adobe Systems; they designed it specifically for the needs of the graphic arts industry. PostScript printers include a computer (called the *raster image processor)* and memory, which is one reason they're often more expensive than a standard printer. An imagesetter usually uses an external computer as its raster image processor (or RIP).

When you send a file from FreeHand to the printer, several things occur before the page is printed. Your computer uses a program called a *printer driver* that receives the information that FreeHand (and all other programs) sends to it, and converts this information to PostScript. The driver then sends the PostScript data to the printer. The printer's internal computer interprets the stream of PostScript language information from your computer and generates a precise pattern of dots on the printer's imaging surface. When the imaging process is finished, the printer prints the page.

PostScript is valuable to the graphic arts because it is *device-independent* and *resolution-independent.* This means that the same file, printed on any kind of PostScript printer, will still look more or less the same. PostScript drives *imagesetters*, which you may have heard of. An imagesetter is a very specialized, expensive piece of equipment designed for one purpose: to image PostScript onto photographic film or paper, which is then chemically processed and used to create plates for a printing press. Imagesetters can produce resolutions up to 5,000 dots per inch (dpi), resulting in the sharpest possible image. This is why nearly all jobs created on a computer are sent to an imagesetter for final output prior to being printed. Newer devices called *platesetters* bypass the film step entirely and image the pages directly to a printing plate. There are also *digital presses* that use a high-quality toner printing process.

Other page description languages in common use are PCL from Hewlett-Packard, and QuickDraw, from Apple Computer. Both do a good job of printing TIFF images and PostScript type (assuming you have a font rasterizer such as Adobe Type Manager), but they cannot print the curves and objects created in a PostScript-based illustration program such as FreeHand or Illustrator.

Screening in this context should not be confused with screen printing (sometimes called silk-screening). They are two completely different things, although artwork that will be screen printed must have a screen ruling applied to it, like any other printing process.

Other page description languages are used in inexpensive inkjet and laser printers. These printers are not used in professional applications although they may be adequate for rough proofing. FreeHand uses PostScript internally to represent anything you draw; if you print a document to most inkjet printers, the artwork will look jagged because the printer can only print the low-resolution preview that you see on the monitor. A PostScript printer is a requirement for professional graphic artists.

Screening

Screening is a basic graphic arts technique and tool that has been around for over a century. The invention of screening followed that of photography upon the realization that reproducing photographs with ink and paper on a printing press was impossible. Screening allows the continuous tones of a photograph to be broken down into dots, which you can plainly see in newspaper photos. Before computer-based screening was developed, a fine screen was placed over a sheet of unexposed film and a high-contrast photograph was taken of the original, resulting in film showing only a fine series of dots. Screen dots vary in size to represent changes in tone: darker areas of a photo will produce bigger dots than lighter areas of a photo. In the printing trade, a screened image is commonly called a *halftone*.

A black-and-white photograph prior to screening.

The same photograph with a very coarse screen. Notice how the dots represent areas of different tonality, or density.

Screening is necessary to reproduce photographs with a printing press. The continuous tones of photographs are only possible because of special papers and chemical processes that are far too cumbersome and expensive for mass reproduction.

Screens are also required to create tints of colors. A tint of 50% requires a screen that permits 50% of the light that strikes it to be reflected from the paper. A screen of 10% permits 90% of the light to be reflected. In most one- and two-color print jobs, photographs and tints are the only elements that require screening. Untinted type, fills, and artwork print at 100% of the ink.

Process color jobs, on the other hand, require that *every* element that is not 100% solid color (such as black type, or process colors such as Red, which is formed from overprinting 100% Yellow and 100% Magenta) be screened. Process color depends upon screening. A process color made of 25% Cyan, 55% Magenta, 5% Yellow, and 5% Black will be reproduced on press, after separation, as screened tints of those four inks. Similarly, color photographs are screened after separation and their tonal ranges converted into varying screened tints of the four process colors.

In a PostScript imagesetter, screens are determined by the application settings. The application performs the separation, sends the four (or however many) separations to the imagesetter as PostScript files, and the imagesetter generates screens of those files where necessary and plots the finished separations to film with a laser.

It's tempting to use a high screen ruling to get the most clear image, but the project's budget will dictate the paper quality and therefore the screen ruling. Lower-quality papers such as newsprint are very absorbent and will soak up and spread screen dots, so a low screen ruling must be used to compensate for this effect, called dot gain.

It is important to discuss these issues with your client and printer to determine the optimum screen ruling and paper stock for your project.

Screen Rulings

The number of lines of dpi on a screen determines the *screen ruling.* Screen rulings vary according to the press, the type of paper, and the intended use of the printed piece. They are measured in *lines per inch* (lpi) and you can specify the screen ruling when you setup the file for separation. Screen rulings apply to both spot and process color printing. Fine screen rulings, typically above 150 lpi, are used for high-quality pieces such as corporate reports, fine-art reproductions, and sales literature for expensive products. Medium rulings from 120–150 lpi are usually used for weekly glossy magazines, menus, inexpensive brochures, and similar items. Low rulings, from 65–110, are generally used for newspapers, junk mail, color tabloid papers, and other jobs printed on cheap paper where permanence isn't an issue.

Screen Angles

When color separations are printed, each individual screen is printed at a different angle. This is what creates the rosette pattern that you can see if you look at a magnification of a printed page. Black-and-white halftones are printed at a 45° angle. At 45°, the screening is not very noticeable, but if a black-and-white photo were printed in black ink at a 90° angle, you would definitely notice the screening. As a result, Black (or the darkest spot color) is always on a 45° angle, the next darkest color (for Magenta, or a second spot color) will be at a 75° angle, the third darkest will be at a 15° angle (Cyan in process, or a third spot color), and Yellow (or a light spot color), being very light, gets printed at 0°.

You should never change screen angles except when you are separating spot color art that has overlapping tints or gradients. The default screen angle values for process colors have been arrived at through years of refinement, so don't change them. Spot color screens default to a 45° angle, so this must be changed before the job is separated if there is more than one spot color, or if there are tints of black and one spot color that overlaps.

Resolution

In most cases, the resolution of the job will be determined by the prepress shop or printer. Most imagesetters range from 1200 dpi to over 5000 dpi; the time needed to generate film increases greatly with higher resolutions, resulting in higher costs. Imagesetters actually generate *raster lines* and use a laser and a high-speed shutter in combination to turn the laser on and off as it sweeps across the unexposed film.

In general, resolution is determined by the screen ruling chosen for the job. A higher screen ruling requires higher resolution. If the screen ruling is too high for a given resolution, visible banding or other unwanted artifacts can become apparent.

While you should never change the angles of process colors, you must usually change the angles of spot colors prior to printing separations.

The following table lists recommended resolution settings for a range of screen rulings:

Screen Ruling (lpi)	Imagesetter Resolution (dpi)
65 to 128	1200, 1270
90 to 150	2400, 2540
133 to 200	3360, 3600
175 and up	4000, 5000

Different prepress equipment may use variations of these resolutions. Again, your prepress shop and/or printer (many printers now incorporate prepress work such as film production and color separations) will usually determine the correct resolution for the screen ruling.

Trapping

We discussed trapping in the Color chapter. To reiterate, trapping of anything beyond Black and a spot color is best left to prepress professionals, but you can make things easier for them and for anyone who uses your artwork by making certain that all Black ink overprints. You can specify object-level overprinting with the Fill and Stroke Inspectors, or you can specify that all blacks overprint in the Print dialog box. Usually, you will not be printing your own separations, so it is important that your document is set up to trap properly to avoid unnecessary rework charges.

You can avoid trapping issues completely by designing artwork that does not use abutting colors. This isn't always possible, but it is the one sure method of eliminating trapping problems.

Failing that, design with restraint. Exuberant use of gradients, for example, can present trapping nightmares because they are very difficult to trap. Designing artwork that cannot be trapped (and sometimes cannot even be printed) is not all that hard, so use special effects cautiously.

Ask your printer or prepress shop to determine the optimal resolution for your screen ruling and to estimate production costs for your job.

Professional trapping is accomplished two ways: with specialized software running on a desktop computer, such as TrapWise from Imation, or with software running in the imagesetter's RIP, such as Linotype-Hell's Delta RIP or Scitex's Dolev system, which traps all incoming jobs automatically.

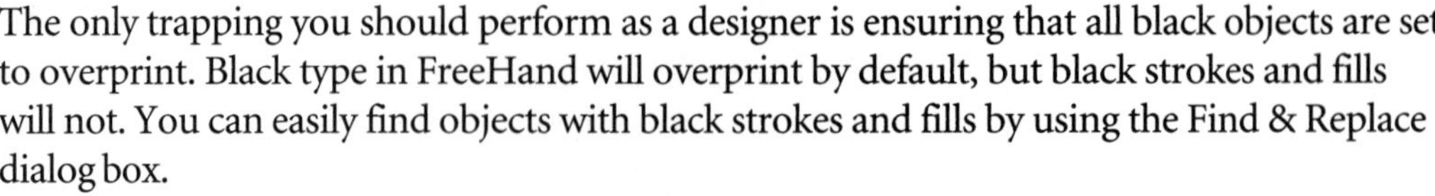

The only trapping you should perform as a designer is ensuring that all black objects are set to overprint. Black type in FreeHand will overprint by default, but black strokes and fills will not. You can easily find objects with black strokes and fills by using the Find & Replace dialog box.

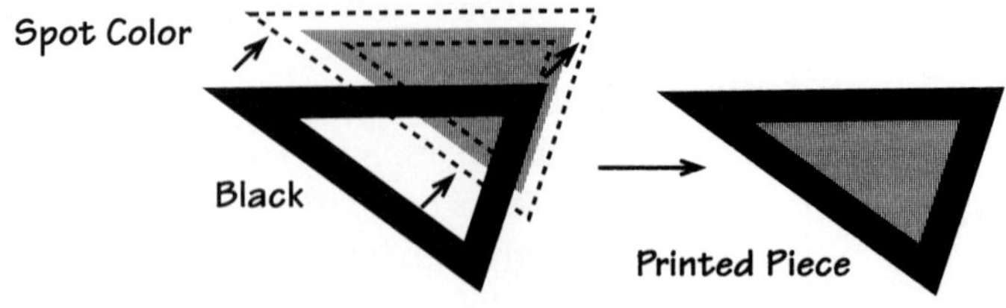

Overprinting a black stroke

Using Find & Replace to Change Object Attributes

1. Open the file **BlkStar.FH9** from the **SF-FreeHand** folder.
2. Choose Edit>Find & Replace>Graphics, and click on the Select tab.

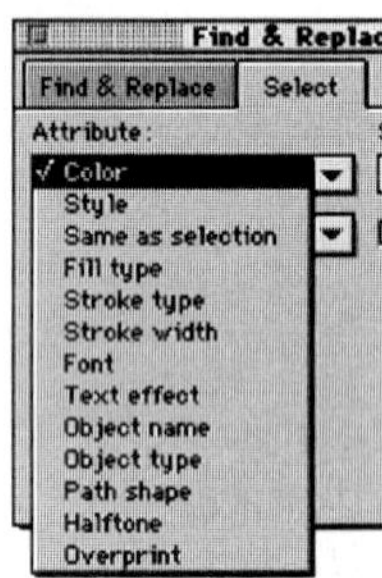

3. Select Color under the Attribute menu, then select Black from the Color menu.

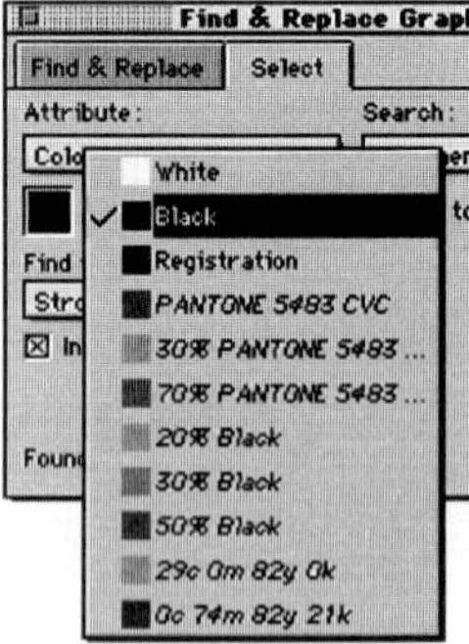

4. Select Strokes from the Find menu.

You can't change overprinting status in strokes and fills at the same time, so do one first, then the other.

5. Do not check the Include tints checkbox. Tints of black must be trapped traditionally.

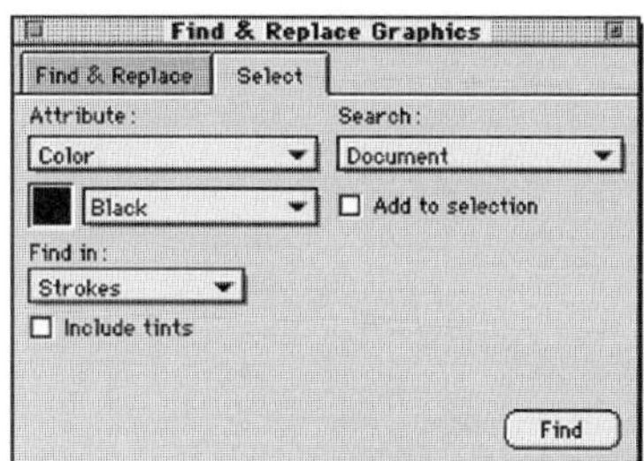

6. Click Find and FreeHand searches the entire document for any objects with a black stroke, and selects them for you.

7. Set all of the selected strokes to overprint by clicking the Overprint checkbox in the Stroke Inspector.

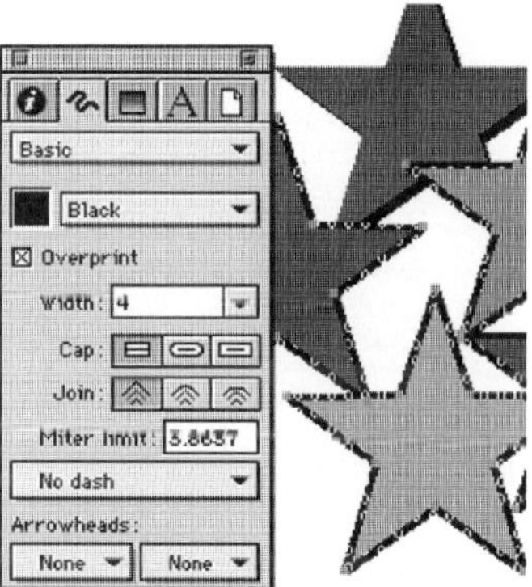

Find & Replace works similarly for finding, selecting, and overprinting black fills.

8. Close the file without saving.

The only time black should not overprint is if a black object has significant coverage over a multicolored object such as an imported TIFF image, because the image may be slightly visible through the black ink. In this case, if your job is to be printed with process colors, you can create a *rich black*, which is 100% black with smaller percentages of the other three process colors. Overprinted over an image, this eliminates show-through of the image under the black.

Here we have a black rectangle and black type overprinting a CMYK TIFF image (remember, the little "o"s indicate an object is overprinting; this is an option you can set in File>Preferences>Redraw>Display overprinting objects). To prevent a "ghost" of the image from showing through the rectangle, create a rich black.

The traditional formula for a rich black is 100% Black, and 60% Cyan. You can also add smaller percentages of Magenta and Yellow to obtain a very solid, saturated "super" Black, but check with your printer. Some paper stocks cannot tolerate heavy ink coverage and they may buckle or soak through, or simply come apart on the press. This is a particularly messy problem and requires a complete washup of the printing press.

Adding a rich black doesn't cost much more when printing process color, and is faster and cheaper than knocking out the image behind the black, which may require professional trapping.

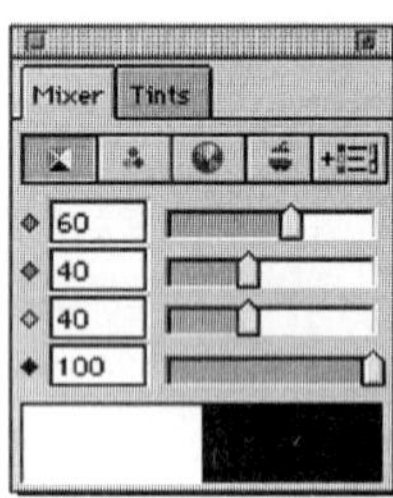

Formula for "super" black

Do not color overprinting text with rich black. Text covers a small percentage of a background, and any show-through will be negligible. Using rich black in text will make any misregistration of the press very obvious.

Dot Gain

When a halftone dot is printed on paper, it may swell slightly depending upon how absorbent the paper is. Newsprint will exhibit far more dot gain than an expensive glossy stock. Your printer or prepress shop should handle compensating for dot gain, the degree of which will be known to them based on the paper stock and printing equipment used.

Colored Text

Avoid using light tints or process colors in type unless the type is set in a large size, usually over 14 pt, or is set in a heavy, bold display typeface. For one thing, light tints can make type very hard to read. For similar reasons, type colored with process colors can also be difficult to read, especially at smaller sizes. Slight misregistration on the press can be very apparent in process-colored type, where it might not be noticeable in objects and TIFF images.

Solid, screened, and process type samples

Never use more than the percentages we specify for a rich black. Ask your printer to see what is recommended for their equipment and your paper stock. Total ink coverage should never exceed 300% (the total value of all four process color tints added together), and depending on the paper stock chosen may need to be adjusted for even less coverage.

Checking Gradients and Blends

Gradients and blends often cause the most trouble when jobs are sent to an imagesetter, even for those with only one color such as a black-to-white blend. Before separating jobs or sending them to a prepress shop, you should verify that your gradients and blends are compatible with the screen ruling and imagesetter resolution that you will be using.

Banded gradient or blend

Smooth, unbanded gradient or blend

General guidelines for reducing banding when creating your artwork:

- Use colors or tint values with a fairly wide range, for example, 10% to 90%, in a gradient. Narrow ranges of color, such as a tint from 30% to 50%, force the use of larger bands of tint, because fewer tints are available.
- Make your gradients a reasonable size. A short distance between two colors in a gradient results in a smoother transition because the available number of tints is larger.
- Specify a higher print resolution and/or a lower line screen value. A higher resolution produces more tints, as does a lower line screen value. If your art shows banding at 150 lpi and 1800 dpi resolution, increase the resolution (the best option), or reduce the line screen value to 120 lpi or 133 lpi (not a good option, because this will make your screens somewhat coarser).

You can use some mathematical formulae to calculate the available number of tints based upon the final output resolution and line screen ruling. Don't worry; they're simple.

To determine the *number of tints* your final output device can image (N), divide the printer resolution (P) by the screen ruling (R) and square the result.

$$N = (P/R)^2$$

If your printer's imagesetter will be run at 1800 dpi and 150 lpi (a good compromise between speed and quality), the number of tints available will be 144.

$$144 = (1800/150)^2$$

To determine *the actual number of tints* you can use with your gradient's selected colors or tints, multiply N by the difference between the tint values expressed as a decimal (Z). For example, your gradient starts with a 30% spot color tint and ends with a 60% tint of the same color. The difference is 30%, or 0.30 in decimal.

$$T = (NZ)$$

Using our value for N, this will make 43 available tints in your gradient. It doesn't sound like much, but if the gradient is small, it will not band.

$$43 = (144 \times 0.30)$$

Thin typefaces such as Futura Condensed are especially prone to illegibility if printed with process colors or tints of spot colors. Always use a solid spot or process color (containing at least 100% of Cyan or Magenta), or use Black, for best results with small or thin type.

Now see if the tint bands between the start and the end of the gradient are big enough to be visible. Divide the distance between the start and end of the gradient (D) by the actual number of tints available (T). A tint band size (S) of .05-in. or less is required to eliminate visible banding. For a gradient size of three inches, we can calculate *the tint band size* and see if it's small enough.

$$S=(D/T)$$

Using our previous values, S=0.069", which is too high and makes a tint band that's too fat.

$$0.69=(3/43)$$

Use gradients and blends sparingly and carefully. Banded gradients and blends are one of the most common causes of unusable color separations, which cost you time and especially money for bad film and a prepress operator's time for repairing the gradient.

Reducing the size of the gradient, or using a wider tint range, will help create smaller tint bands. Instead of using 60% for the end of the gradient, use 80%. This gives you 72 tints available, and will result in a desirable tint band size of 0.041". You should create your gradients with the tint distance and range of tint well in mind, since these options are under your control and imagesetter resolution and line screen ruling may not be.

For blends, use the same formulae. Once you arrive at a suitable tint band size, you can use the value for T to specify the number of steps in your blend.

If you are using a gradient of two colors, determine the tint differences using both colors. For example, a gradient might go from 30% Pantone 186 to 85% Pantone 116. Subtract 85 from 30, and convert the result, 55, to a decimal, 0.55. Process color blends usually don't create significant banding problems, but you should be aware of tonal differences here. A process color blend that starts with 0c 75m 55y 0k and ends with 30c 25m 10y 0k may exhibit banding because of the tint difference between the darkest inks, in this case, Cyan and Magenta. Base your tint difference value on the difference between these two inks.

Object-level Halftones

FreeHand's Halftones panel lets you set the line screen ruling and screen angle of most objects. You could specify that an object print at 65 lpi at an angle of 10°, even if the rest of the job will print at 133 lpi and 45°.

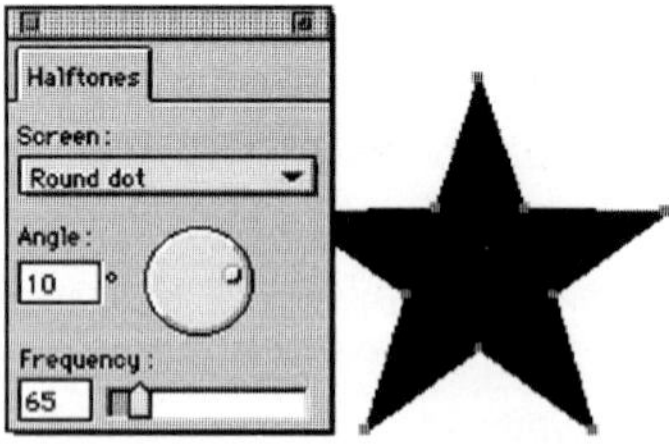

However, this is not a good idea because most imagesetters will override object-level halftone information, and also because if the object is colored with process color, all four separations will overprint each other at the specified angle, which won't look good. If you are uncertain if a document contains object-level halftones, you can override their set line screen and angle at print time in the Print Setup dialog box.

Printing Separations

This is where it all comes together. Every aspect of FreeHand's printing capability is controlled through the Print dialog box. You can follow the examples if you are connected to a PostScript laser printer. Separations cannot usually be printed on non-PostScript printers with any degree of accuracy.

FreeHand's Print Dialog Box

(Macintosh only) Macintosh computers use Apple's LaserWriter printer driver. There are many versions of the driver (currently, version 8.5.1), and different versions may present slightly different Print dialog boxes. The examples we use here are from LaserWriter 8.5.1, but the basic operations are the same for most versions still in use.

Windows users will probably have PostScript drivers already installed.

The initial Print dialog box is different on Macintosh and Windows computers, but the steps shown in Setup will be applicable to both.

Print Spot Color Separations

1. Open the file **SpotStar.FH9**. from the **SF-Freehand** folder It contains two spot colors plus Black. This requires that we change the screen angle of the non-black inks.

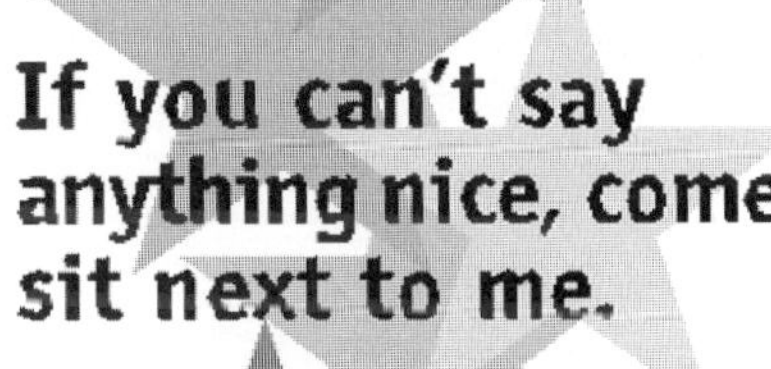

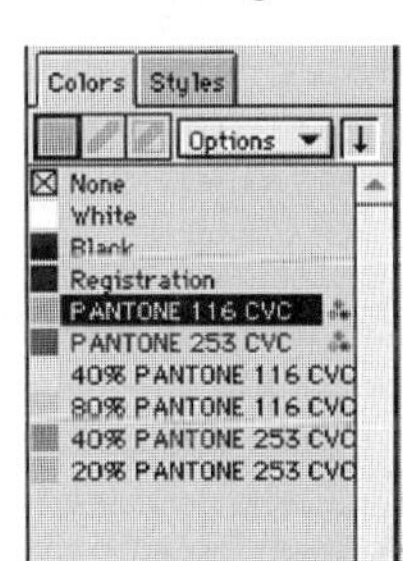

Note the colors used and the placement of colored objects. What does this file need? It needs to be trapped. Who should do it? Your printer. We can use the overprint method to trap the black ink, but because we have two abutting spot colors, trapping must be carefully done to prevent obvious overprinting from creating the impression of an edge or third color.

2. Press Command/Control-P to show the Print dialog box.

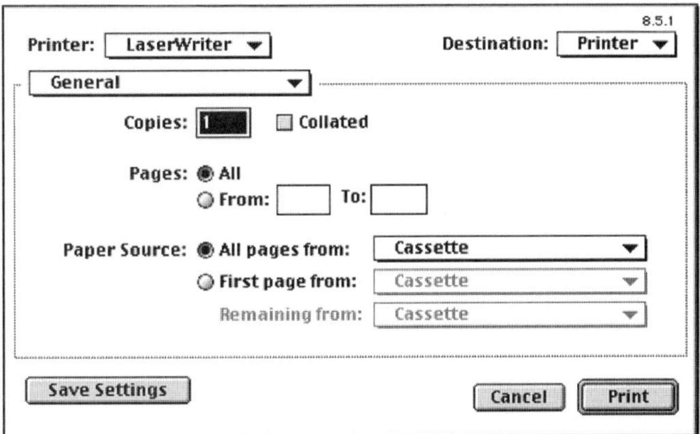

Both Windows and Macintosh computers rely upon a PostScript printer driver for creating separations. These drivers are many and varied and you should be using the most recent version available for your computer. Older versions may only support PostScript Level 1, or may have incompatibilities with certain types of printers, computer networks, or application programs such as FreeHand or QuarkXPress.

(Macintosh only) If your Print dialog box looks like the above, click and hold on the General drop-down menu, and choose FreeHand 9.

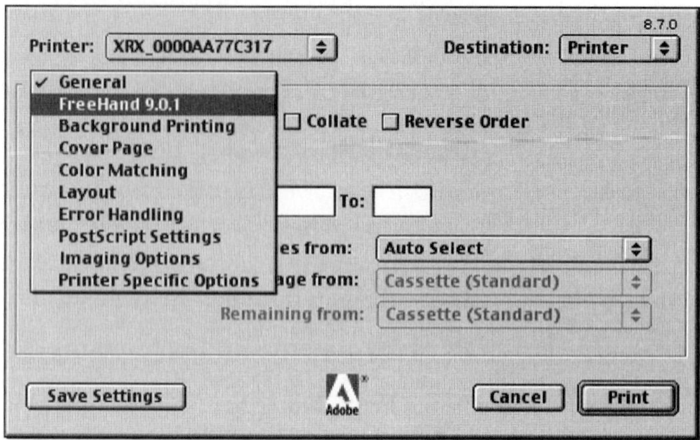

(Macintosh only) The Print dialog box in all LaserWriter versions should look similar to the following dialog box:

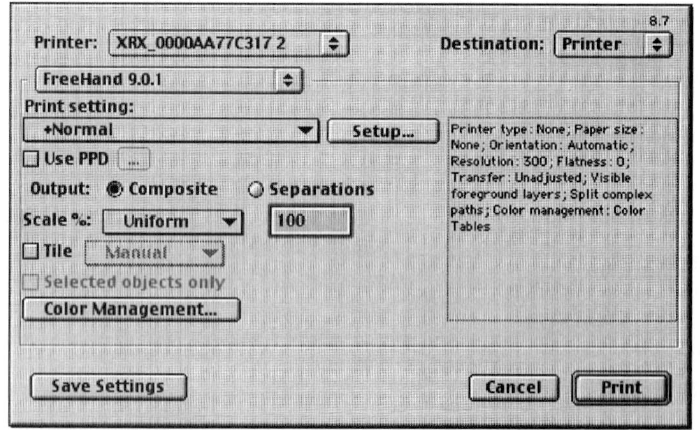

The Windows Print dialog box looks like the following dialog box:

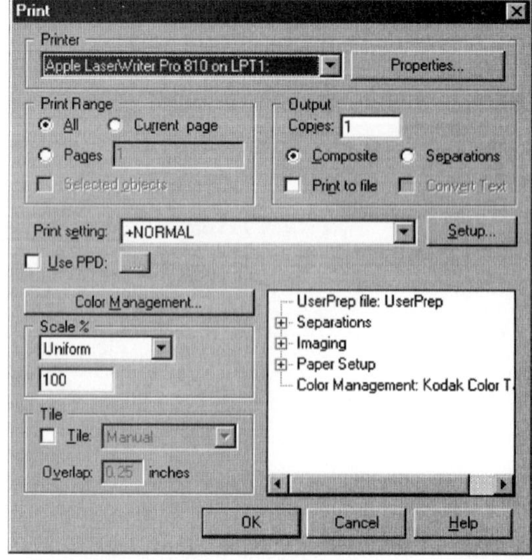

Most of the settings you make here will be overridden in the Setup dialog box. If you just want to send a normal printout to the printer, you could click Print and be done, but we're going to go through the steps of a separation, so there are more things that need to be done.

There are a few options in the initial Print dialog box that you can change. You can set scaling up or down or print separations without using the Setup dialog box (not recommended).

Macintosh users can select a printer through the Apple Menu>Chooser. Your Print dialog box may appear different from these examples due to the wide variety of printers and drivers. Windows users can select a printer through the Print dialog box.

3. Click the Setup button to display the Setup dialog box.

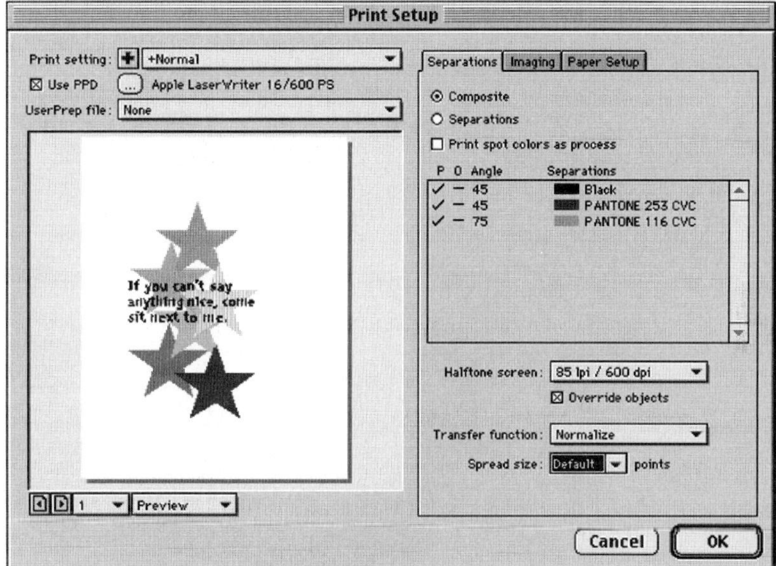

4. The Separations panel appears by default.

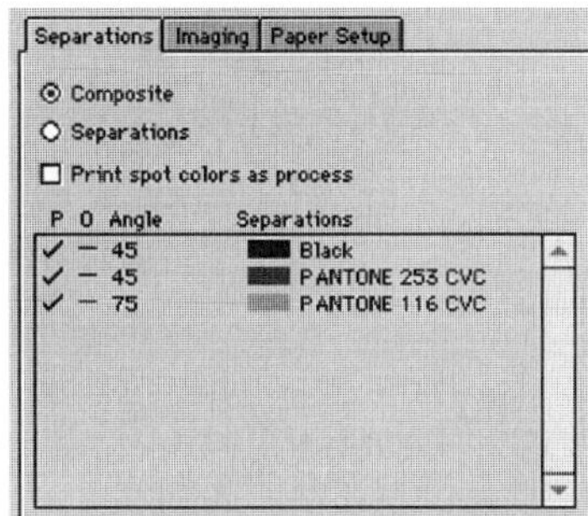

Color management is a fairly advanced topic and depends on a number of software extensions to your computer's operating system. The Color Management button will show the options available on your computer, if any, for invoking the color management software. Color management is beyond the scope of this course, and we recommend that you leave this option set to the default, which is "None."

Composite is selected by default. Change this to Separations. Leave Print spot colors as process unchecked. Click on the angle value for Pantone 253 CVC, which shows the Screen Angle dialog box.

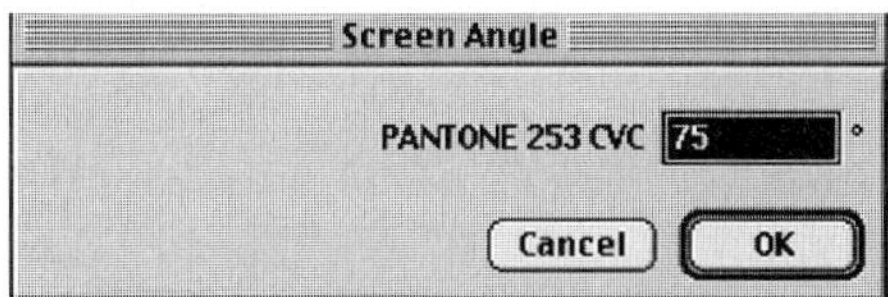

5. Type the angle of 75° in this dialog box and click OK.

6. Do the same for Pantone 116 CVC, changing it to 105°.

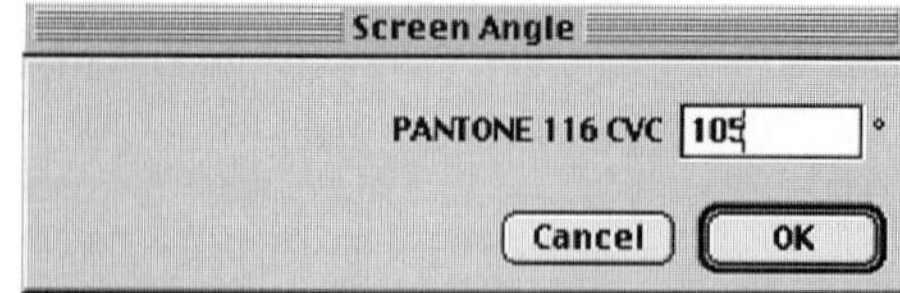

You only need to define different angles for spot color inks in your job if they abut and require trapping, as in this case, or if there are any overprinting inks. This applies to Black as well as to two or more spot colors.

7. Click the Imaging tab.

8. Click the checkboxes next to Separation names, Crop marks, and Registration marks.

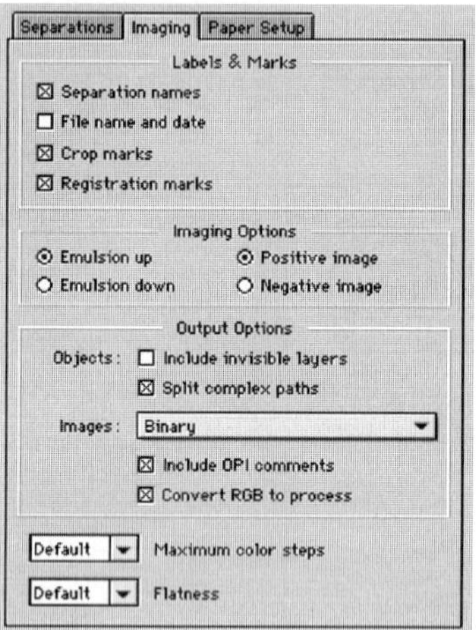

9. Click the Paper Setup tab.

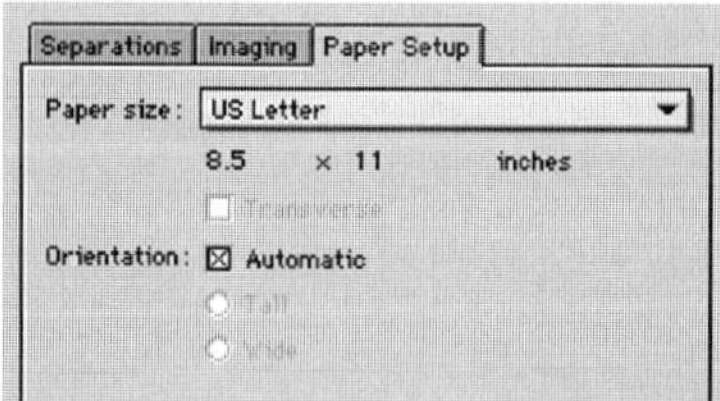

If the Paper size setting matches that of the paper in your printer, leave it alone. If not, click on the Paper Size pop-up menu to select the paper size of your printer.

10. Click OK to close the Setup dialog box, then click OK in the Print dialog box to send your file to the printer. Eventually, you will see three pages, each with crop and registration marks, the correct separation, and the names of the spot inks used.

11. Leave the file open.

The Setup Dialog Options

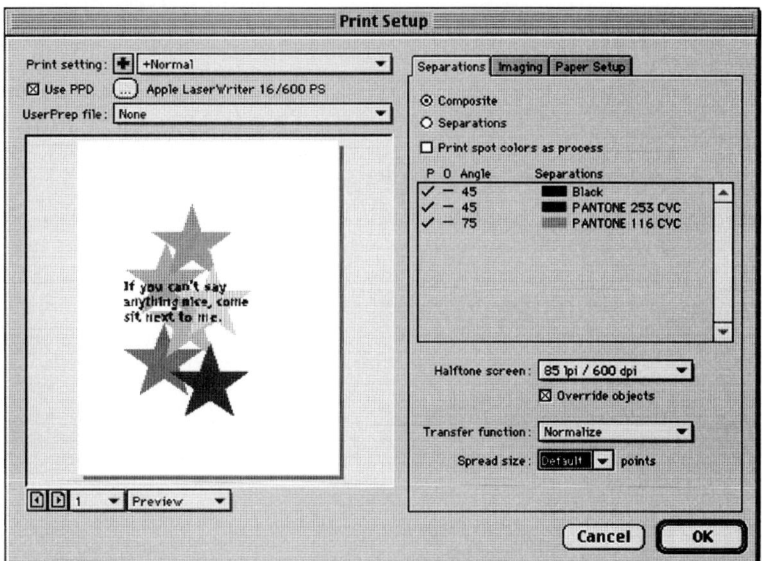

As you can see, there are a lot of options here. We'll begin at the upper-left corner of the dialog box and work our way across.

Print Setting

For nearly all output purposes, including separations sent to an imagesetter, leave this set at Normal. You can click the large + symbol to the left of the pop-up menu to save a particular set of print settings.

Using PPD

A PPD is a *PostScript Printer Description* file that contains information specific to your particular printer. PPDs are stored in a small file on your computer. Macintosh computers store these files in System Folder>Extensions>Printer Descriptions, and Windows computers store them in a few different places: in the Windows NT (or Windows 95/98) Directory/System32/spool/drivers/w32x86/ or in the FreeHand 9 Directory/English/PPDS/. Click the "Use PPD" checkbox, and FreeHand prompts you to select the PPD file that matches your printer.

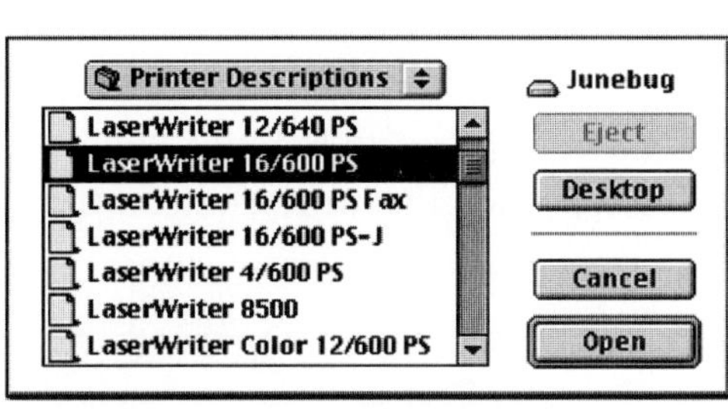

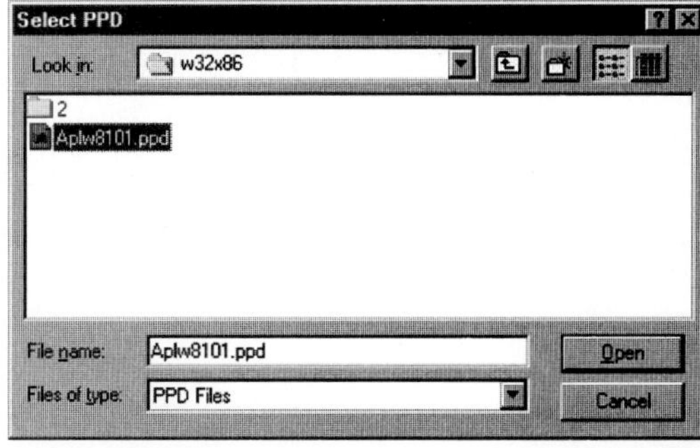

In the Macintosh example, we'll use the PPD for an Apple LaserWriter 16/600. For Windows, we'll use the PPD for an Apple LaserWriter Pro 810.

The PPD file contains information about your printer's maximum paper size, resolution, and the line screen rulings it is designed to print. Select the PPD for your printer and click Open to load the specific settings for your printer.

UserPrep File

FreeHand allows the inclusion of custom PostScript language files to be sent to the printer along with the print job. However, they are rarely required except for some specialized prepress equipment, so leave this set at None.

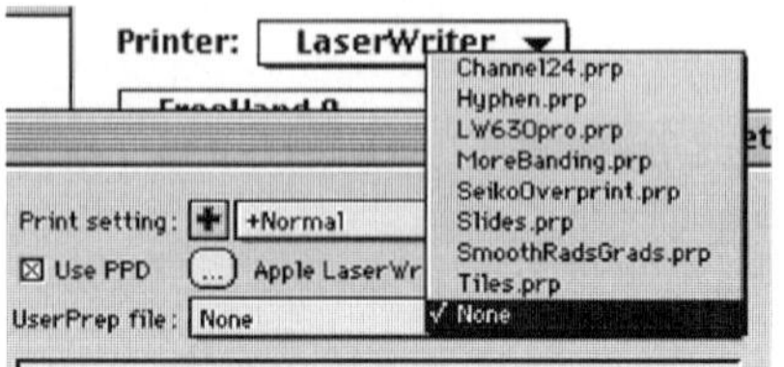

Preview area

FreeHand shows you a rough preview of what the printer will generate. This will change if you select different print options or a different paper size.

PPD files are usually installed automatically if you use the printer manufacturer's installation program. If you can't find a PPD file for your printer on the computer, you can usually download the most current PPDs from most printer manufacturer's web site, or from Adobe Systems' web site (http://www.adobe.com/).

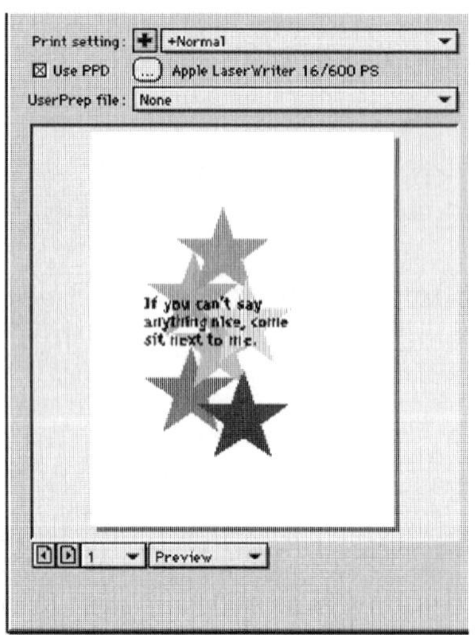

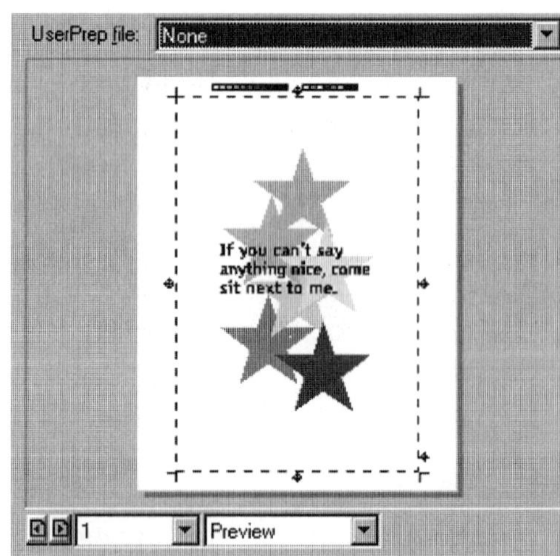

Pages and Views

You can use the Left/Right arrows keys or the Page pop-up menu to preview multiple pages, if any are present.

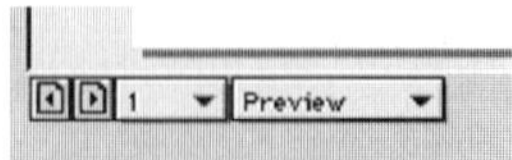

You can also choose the type of preview from the Preview pop-up menu. This lets you select a Keyline or X-Box preview that can be faster if your artwork is complex.

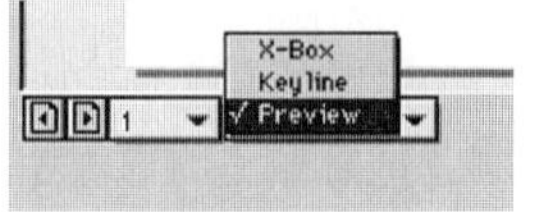

Overprinting Black

You can make a color overprint by clicking the dash under the "O" in the separations list. You should only have black overprint, never the others. This only applies to solid Black used in strokes and fills and does not change black used in TIFF images. Clicking the dash shows the Overprint Ink dialog box.

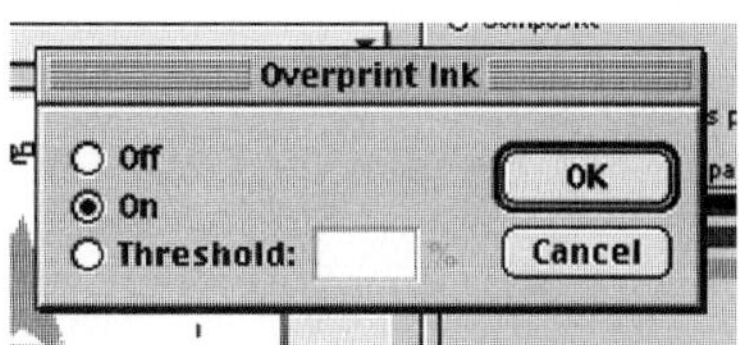

Set overprinting for On. If your document has overprinting tints of black, you can enter a value in the Threshold box at which the black tint will overprint; for example, if you want all black tints over 50% to overprint, enter 50 in the Threshold box.

Halftone Screen/Resolution

Clicking this pop-up menu will present the resolution(s) and line screen rulings that your printer can reproduce. If the pop-up menu appears grayed-out, you need to select a PPD to give FreeHand an idea of your printer's screen and resolution.

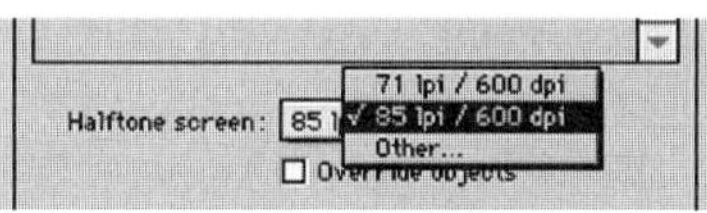

Override Objects

Checking this box makes FreeHand override all object-level halftones that may be present in a document. This should always be on.

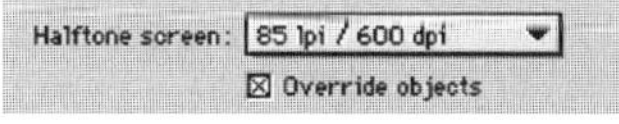

The X-Box preview lets you see the bounding box of the document page.

Transfer Function

For the vast majority of print jobs, leave this set at "Normalize." The Transfer function modifies dot values in halftones, and changing this could lead to unwanted results.

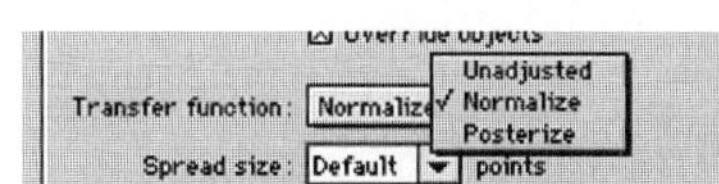

You may want to change this to Unadjusted when exporting a file containing color TIFF images to another application; or if printing color separations that will be used in a common document with the same image elsewhere. Color separations of CMYK TIFF images may appear different from FreeHand than from QuarkXPress, for example, so you should choose Unadjusted in these cases.

Spread Size

A value entered here will spread all basic strokes and fills. It is *not* an acceptable means of trapping files, and it should be left at the default setting.

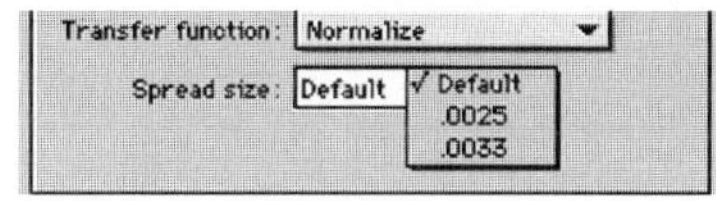

Imaging

Click the Imaging tab to show the Imaging dialog box.

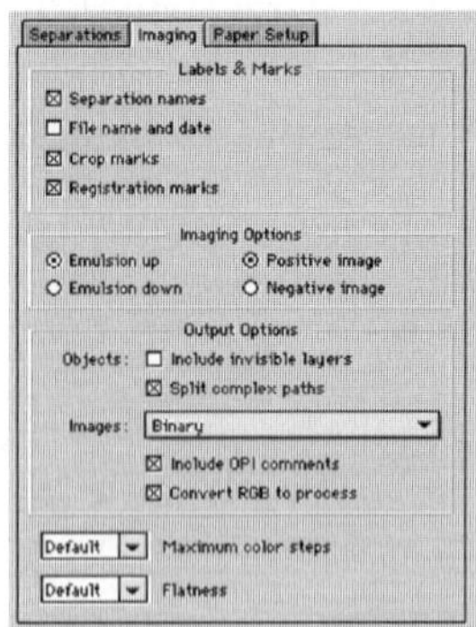

Labels and Marks

Here's where you tell FreeHand how you'd like your separations. In nearly all cases, you will want separation names, crop marks, and registration marks. The file name and the date are optional.

Your page preview may not reflect these choices. If your document is set up as a letter-size page (8.5″ × 11″), and your printer only prints letter-size pages, you won't get any marks or labels on the page. You will need to cancel printing and resize your document with the Page Inspector to accommodate these marks.

The following preview shows artwork properly sized to separate to a letter-size page.

Improper screen angles can result in muddy output, or just as bad, a moiré (pronounced "mor-ey"). Moirés produce a checker-board-like pattern in screened areas and are always unacceptable. Moirés can result from angle changes of even a few degrees. This is why you should never alter the screen angle settings for process color separations, and why you should be careful to set them correctly in spot color separations.

Imaging Options

Emulsion up/down only applies to film imagesetters. It refers to the relation of the film's emulsion to the image. Most shops will image films emulsion down, but leave it set at up (if you were to set it to down, and printed to a laser printer, you'd end up with a reversed or "flopped" image).

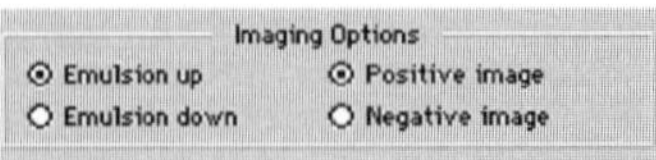

Positive/negative also applies to film imagesetters. A positive prints black on white, as usual; a negative prints white (or clear, really, in the case of film) on black. Leave this set at positive for laser printing.

Output Options

The default settings here should work for nearly all printers. You can include artwork on invisible layers if you wish. The Split complex paths option prevents long or complex paths from causing a PostScript error.

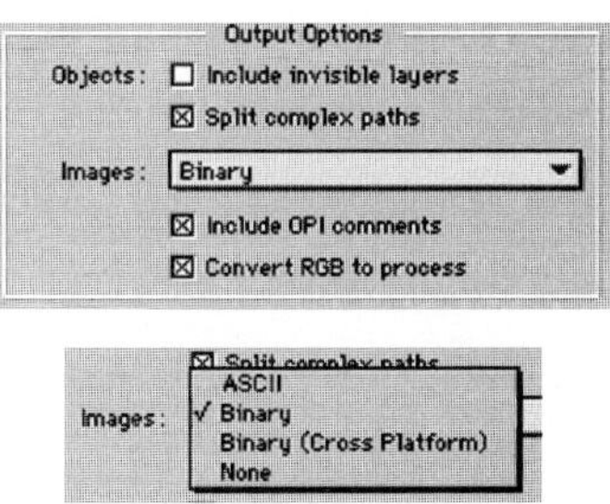

The Images pop-up menu should be left at Binary for Macintosh computers, or set to Binary/Cross platform if you are printing over a mixed Macintosh/Windows network. Windows users should select the default setting, usually Binary. A setting of None includes OPI data instead of image data. Uncheck the Include OPI comments option. The Convert RGB to process option will cause FreeHand to convert any RGB TIFF images in your file to CMYK values. Ideally, you should not have any RGB TIFF images in your document.

The Other option in the Halftone screen menu allows you to type in a specific resolution and line screen ruling, but it's not recommended because the choices shown in the pop-up menu reflect those that your printer is most capable of producing.

Paper Setup

Paper Setup allows you to choose from the paper sizes available in your printer (determined by information provided in the PPD file), and lets you change the orientation from tall to wide.

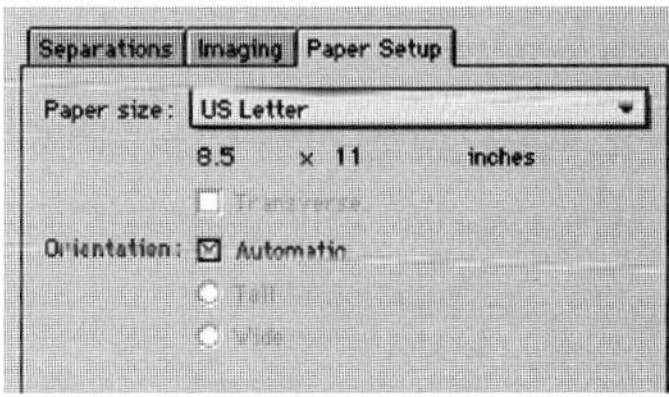

"Posterize" is a method of reducing gray levels in a halftone to create a special effect.

You choose the paper size from the pop-up menu. Select the paper size you want to use from the menu (if not letter, be certain to switch paper trays or provide a manual paper feed). These paper sizes may vary according to your particular printer and reflect those available for the LaserWriter 16/600.

You can have your document printed tall or wide. Usually, the default Automatic orientation setting will be correct, but if you want to change it, uncheck the Automatic box and select Tall or Wide. If you choose Wide, the preview reflects the new orientation, and you may end up cropping the top and bottom of your document.

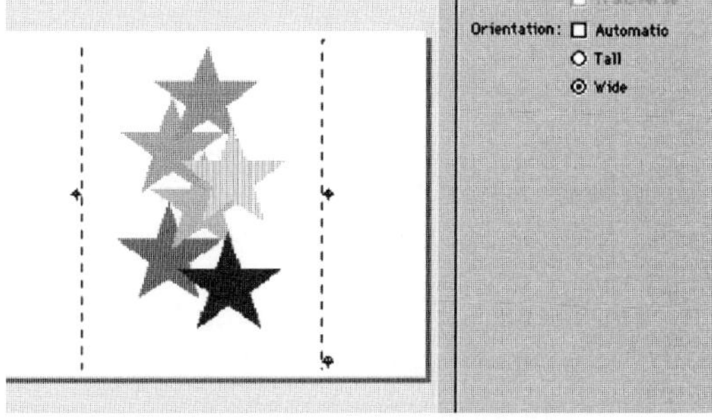

Wide should be used if your document is set up in the Wide orientation.

Most North American prepress shops will image negative, emulsion-down film. Positive, emulsion-down films are used almost exclusively outside of North America due to differences in printing tradition (the old "we've always done it that way" syndrome, which applies to the US and Canada as well).

OPI, or Open Prepress Initiative, is a means of substituting low-resolution TIFF images placed in your document with high-resolution equivalents. This lets you work faster and can dramatically shorten the time it takes your computer to send a large separation to a RIP, but it also requires specialized software and training to use.

Print Process Separations

This works the same way as printing spot color separations except for two things:

- Don't change the screen angles. FreeHand's default screen angles are correct, and you should not change them.
- You should set the Black plate to overprint if your artwork has black strokes or fills.

1. Continue with the open file "SpotStar.FH9". Press Command/Control-P to show the Print dialog box. Click Setup, then click the Separations tab. Click the Print spot colors as process option to convert the document to process colors. The four separations appear, along with the screen angles.

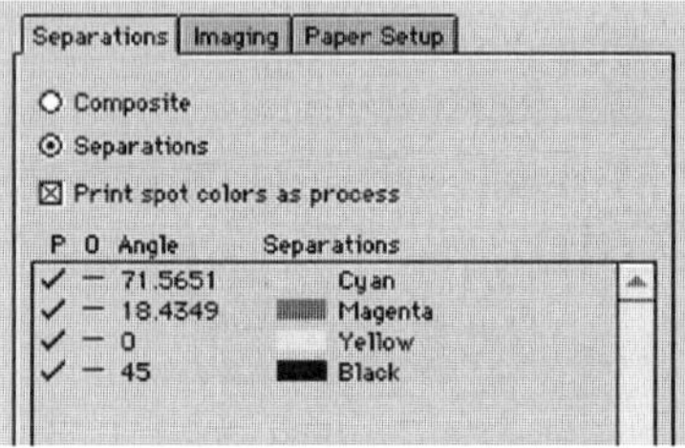

Note that the screen angles aren't the usual 45, 75, 105 and 90° values we discussed earlier. In this case, FreeHand has derived the screen angles from the printer's PPD file. These angles were arrived at through extensive testing and should not be altered. In real-world color separation, the correct angle for a process color can vary to some degree. This is normal, and your printer or prepress shop is used to it.

2. Set the entire black separation to overprint. Click the dash under the "O" column of the separation colors to show the Overprint dialog box.

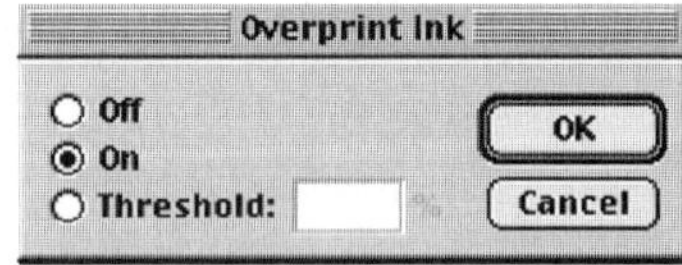

Click On, and then OK.

3. Other than these exceptions, printing process color separations is the same as printing with spot colors. Click OK to close the Setup dialog box, and then click Print to send the separations to your printer.
4. Compare the results with the spot color separations to see just how differently these color models operate.
5. Close the file without saving it.

Tiling

Tiling is a way of printing a document that is much larger than the size of the paper in your printer. If used, this option will break a large image down into tiles, or small pages that contain a portion of the entire document. You can then carefully tape them together to form the complete image. FreeHand can do this automatically for you, or you can specify tile breaks manually by repositioning the zero point of the page rulers.

Print Tiles of Large-format Documents

1. Open the file **Tiles.FH9.** This document is set up as a 22″ × 34″ page.
2. Choose File>Print, then if necessary select any options to show FreeHand's Print dialog box. Select your correct PPD.
3. Check the Tile box, and choose Automatic from the pop-up menu.

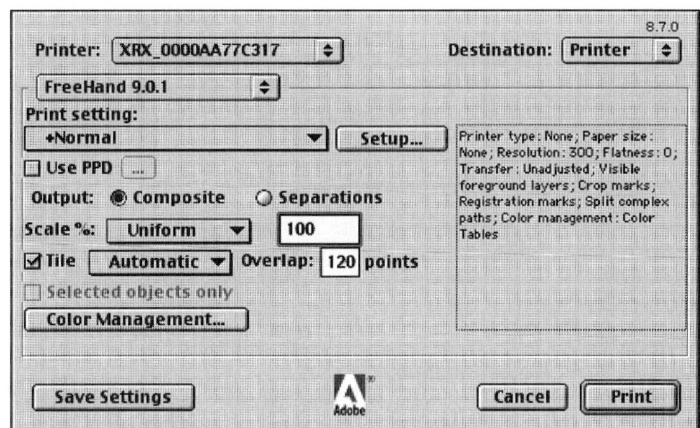

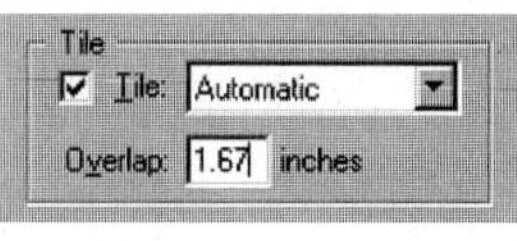

4. In the Overlap box, type in 120 (Macintosh) or 1.67 (Windows). The default 18 pt. overlap is far too small to be of any use because you must tape the tiled pages together with overlap and then cut through them in order for them to fit together properly.
5. Click the Setup button. In the preview, FreeHand displays the first tile of the entire page, sized to fit the currently-selected paper, which is probably US Letter.

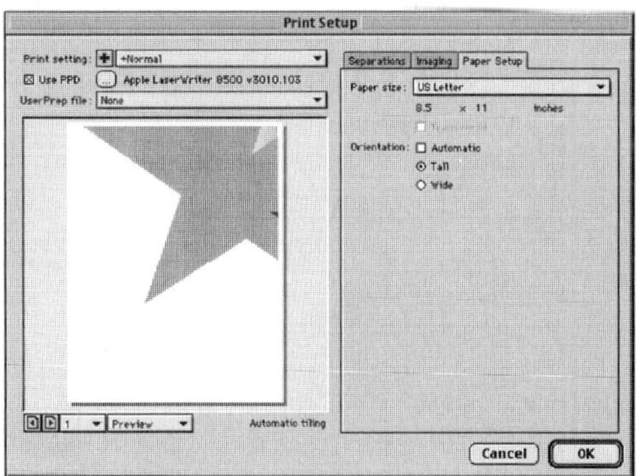

6. Click the Paper Setup tab and switch the paper size to something else, preferably smaller (our example printer has sizes called "Postcard" and "Statement," but yours may not). See how the tiling changes? It would take many more sheets of smaller paper to create the entire document.

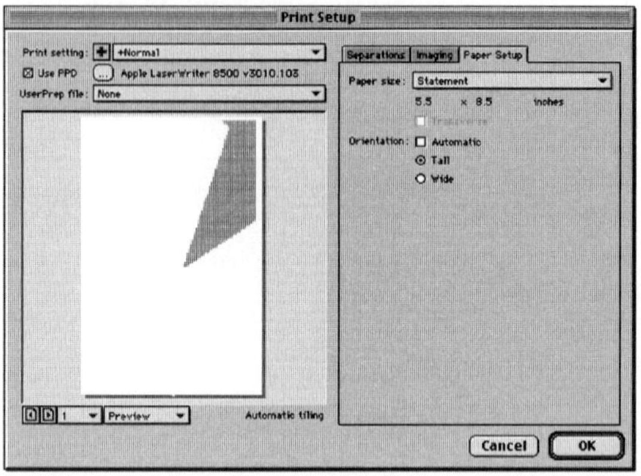

7. Switch the Paper size back to US Letter, then click on the Separations tab. Make certain that Composite is checked, and not Separations. Click on the Imaging tab, and check the Crop marks and Registration marks checkboxes. Uncheck Separation names, since we aren't separating this file. Click OK.

8. In the main Print dialog box, click Print to start printing.

On the Macintosh, overlap is always set in points, no matter what unit of measure you have selected. Windows uses the current unit of measurement.

9. Once the pages have printed, gather them up and arrange them *face down* on a light table, if available; tiling will be very difficult to do without one. Turn on the light and locate the special tiling registration marks that FreeHand creates on the edges of the pages. Overlap and line up these marks on two adjoining tiles, then tape the two sheets with a small piece of tape to make certain that they don't move out of register. Repeat this step for all the tiles.

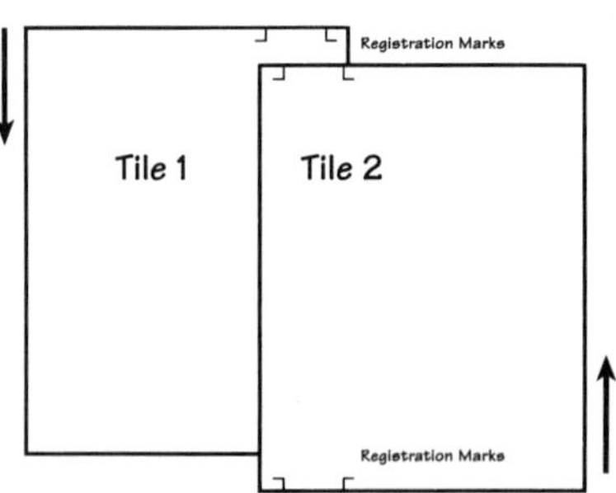

10. Using a sharp graphics knife and a steel ruler, cut the pages apart between the tiles. Because there is plenty of overlap, you don't have to be perfectly dead-center when cutting, but keep the cut neat and straight.

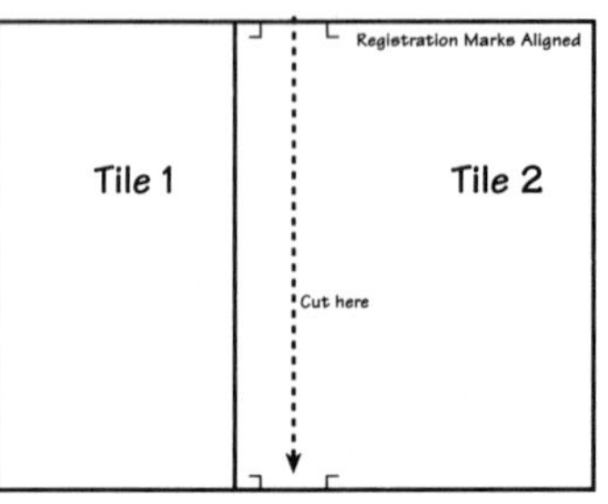

11. Remove the waste paper, butt the two edges of the two tiles together, and with a long piece of transparent tape, tape the sheets from edge to edge. Repeat this procedure with all of the other sheets until the entire page is finished. You can now use the crop marks to trim off the edges of the entire sheet.

12. Keep the file open.

    Manual tiling can be used to print just one tile of a large image, or to print multiple pages in a document on a single page.

Tile a Document Manually

1. In the open file "Tiles.FH9" drag the zero point to the middle of the page.

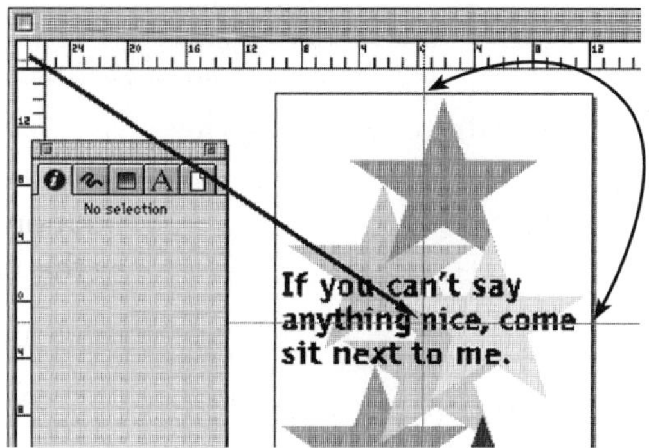

2. Choose File>Print, then if necessary select any options to show FreeHand's Print dialog box. Select your correct PPD.

3. Click the Setup button. In the preview, FreeHand displays the tile defined by the zero point.

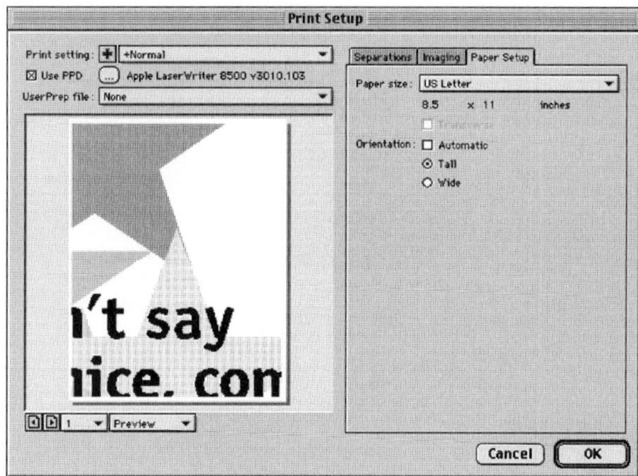

4. You can move the tile around in the preview to change the tiled area if you like. Click OK, then print the single tile. Close the file without saving it.

5. Open **Spot Star.FH9** from the **SF-FreeHand** folder.

6. Reduce the document window view until you can see all of the page. Drag the zero point to the lower-left corner of the page.

7. In the Print dialog box, choose Manual Tile. Check the preview to make certain that all of the page will fit on your chosen paper size. If not, you can select Fit on paper in the Print dialog box. Print the combined tile.

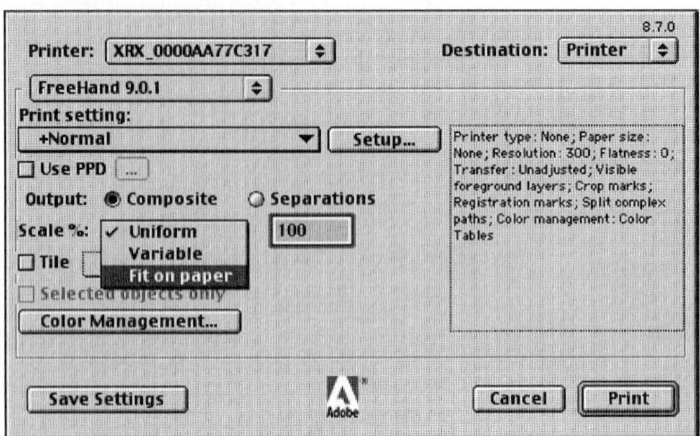

8. Close the file without saving.

Summary

In this chapter, you learned some principles of printing files to high resolution, including an exploration of page description languages and a discussion of screening and screen angles. You learned about trapping and got an understanding of the problems involved with printing gradients. You experienced using Find & Replace to change object attributes and learned how to print spot color separations and process separations. You also learned how to tile oversized documents to your proofing printer.

CHAPTER 16

Graphics for the Web

CHAPTER OBJECTIVE:

To understand how to prepare graphics for use on the Internet, using web-safe colors and to create animations. In Chapter 16, you will:

- Learn how publishing to the Web is different from creating graphics for print.
- Understand the difference between active and static pages.
- Understand the value of the Web-safe palette.
- Learn how to assign a URL to a graphic and to type.
- Learn about creating animations using pages and using layers.

PROJECTS TO BE COMPLETED:

- Dinner Time (A)
- Mask Art (B)
- Tropical Treasure Logo (C)
- Grocery Ad (D)
- Ball and Mirror (E)
- No Clowning Around (F)

Graphics for the Web

For the most part, we have discussed graphics designed for print. Indeed, that is what FreeHand was originally designed to create. However, as the World Wide Web has flourished, Macromedia has turned its attention to preparing files for that medium. Macromedia Flash is a program that accepts vector art for its animations; it is an ideal partner for FreeHand.

Because they are vector graphics, Flash files are smaller than raster images. As a result, they load faster. Since they are vector images, they can also be enlarged with no deterioration of quality. These are both highly-desirable qualities.

Web Publishing vs. Print

There are considerations for Web publishing that differ from publishing to print. When publishing to print, we have the entire spectrum of CMYK colors available to us. When publishing to the Web, however, we have a much more limited number of colors available — just 216. That is because only these colors are compatible with both Macintosh and Windows color space. The 216 colors are available from FreeHand's Web Safe Color Library, accessed through the Color List.

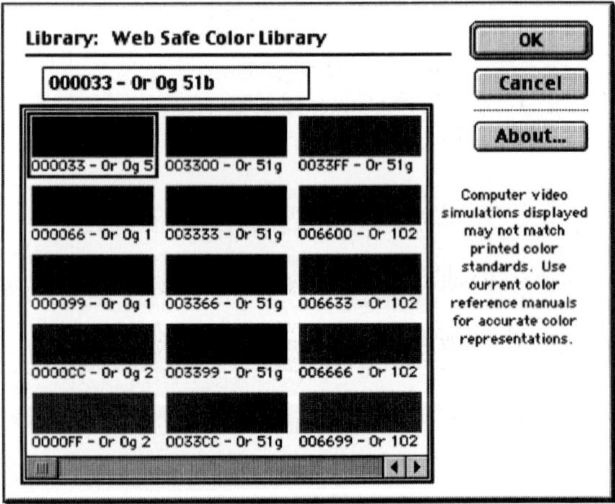

You'll note that the colors display somewhat differently than the colors used in CMYK printing. First of all, they are (and should remain) RGB, because they will be displayed on monitors, rather than printed on paper. Second, they are displayed with the parameters of their RGB equivalent in shorthand — a hexidecimal equivalent — in addition to the longer version giving RGB values.

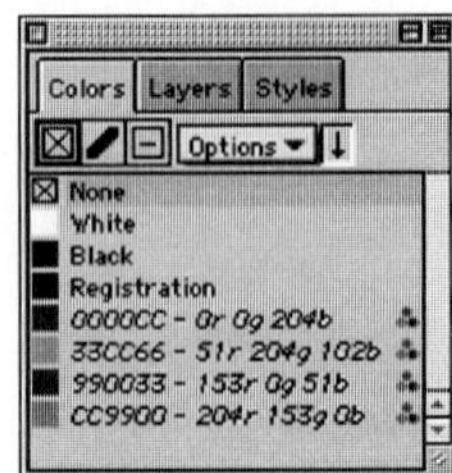

When the colors are defined in HTML code, they use different designations than you might expect. All designations are based on RGB values, ranging from 0 to 255, and are described as RRGGBB.

The 216 web-safe color palette is described as follows:

Web Color Designator		**# of Colors of 255**
00	=	0
33	=	51
66	=	102
99	=	153
CC	=	204
FF	=	255

If you were looking at the code for a web page, the background color might be set to a cream white, and designated: <BODY BGCOLOR="#FFFFCC">. Red type on a yellow background (the background, in this case, running under the type, not the entire page) could be designated <FONT COLOR="#FF0000" BACK="FFFF00">.

Static vs. Active Pages

When you design for print, you're very confident of the result: it will be what you designed and what you signed off on when you approved the proofs. There is nothing further to be done with a printed piece except to read it, or otherwise look at it.

On the other hand, documents designed for distribution on the Web are dynamic. They can contain hyperlinks, that take you from one spot in the document to another, or that deliver you to a web site completely separate from the one where you started.

FreeHand allows you to assign URLs (Universal Resource Locator) to objects and text, so when you click on them you are taken to the source they reference. URLs are attached through Windows>Xtras>URL Editor. To include a URL, select New from the Options menu and type the address in the entry field.

To apply a URL to an object or to text in the document, select the object or highlight the text, then click on the appropriate URL in the Editor. On the Macintosh you can also drag from the editor to the object or text. Text that has been linked to a URL appears in the Substring URLs section of the URL Editor.

Add Web-safe Color and Assign URL

1. Open the document **Alice on the Web.FH9** from your **SF-FreeHand** folder.

2. First, we want to add some color to this illustration. If it is not already open, open the Color List. From the Color List Options pop-up menu, select Web Safe Color Library. We want to select light blue, gold, and red colors to add to the graphic. We chose 3399FF, CC9900, and FF0000. We also added FFCCCC (pink) for the rabbit's eyes. Choose appropriate colors and click OK.

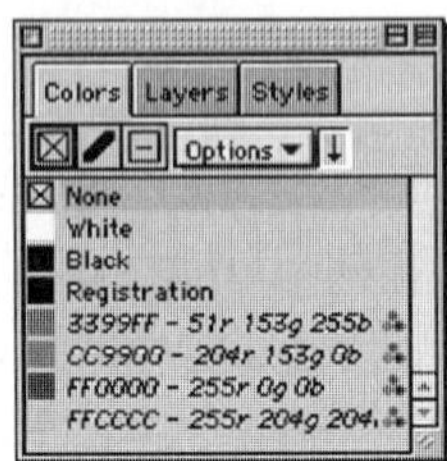

If you hold the Shift key down as you scroll through the library you can select all your colors at one time.

3. Apply the color to the graphic appropriately. We made the hearts in his tunic red, the ribbon around his neck blue, and the medal and the bugle gold.

4. Using the Pointer tool, draw a marquee to select the rabbit. Press Command/Control-G to group it. Deselect.

5. From Window>Xtras, open the URL Editor. Select New from the Options pop-up menu. Type in the address for the Alice in Wonderland website:

   http://www.ba.infn.it/~cirillo/lumenvitae/wonderland/wonder.html

   Click OK.

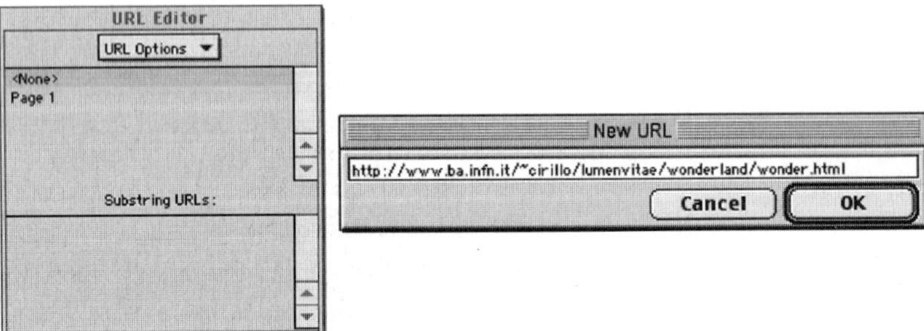

6. With the Text tool, highlight the text. Click on the URL to apply it. An abbreviated version of the text appears in the Substring URLs section of the URL Editor.

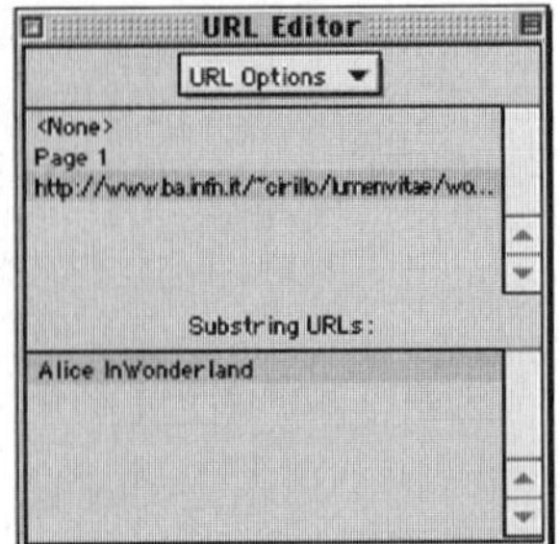

The following features are supported by Flash:

Basic strokes & fills

Lens fills

Gradient fills

CMYK & RGB TIFFs and embedded images

Blended paths

Composite paths

Clipping paths

Text blocks

Arrowheads

7. Deselect the text. If you're on the Macintosh, click on the name of the URL in the URL Editor and drag the white square over the rabbit and release. If you're working under Windows, click on the rabbit, then click on the name of the URL in the URL Editor. Deselect.

8. Alternately click on the title and the rabbit with the Pointer tool. Note that the URL becomes highlighted. Now click on the title with the text tool. The Substring URL appears.

9. Save the document to your **Work in Progress** folder and close it.

Creating Flash Graphics

Because FreeHand/Flash files are vector instead of raster, they are smaller and load faster than other file types. In addition, they can be enlarged, so more detail can be seen. Although Flash graphics can accept gradients and embedded raster elements, it's best to leave these out, when possible, to assure a faster-loading graphic.

To export a file as a Flash graphic, choose File>Export. Then, (Macintosh) from the pop-up menu, or (Windows) from the Save as Type pop-up menu, choose the Macromedia Flash (SWF) format.

If you checked the Open in External Application box, a dialog box will open telling you to Choose a File (Macintosh) or Please Select a Valid Application (Windows). You would open the Flash 4 Player from your FreeHand application folder.

Once the application is selected, you can click the Options button. Here you decide upon Path Compression, Image Compression (the choices are the same), how text will be handled, which pages to export, how animations will be executed, and Flash version compatibility. There is also an option to protect the file from being imported (protecting your intellectual property) and for high-quality printing.

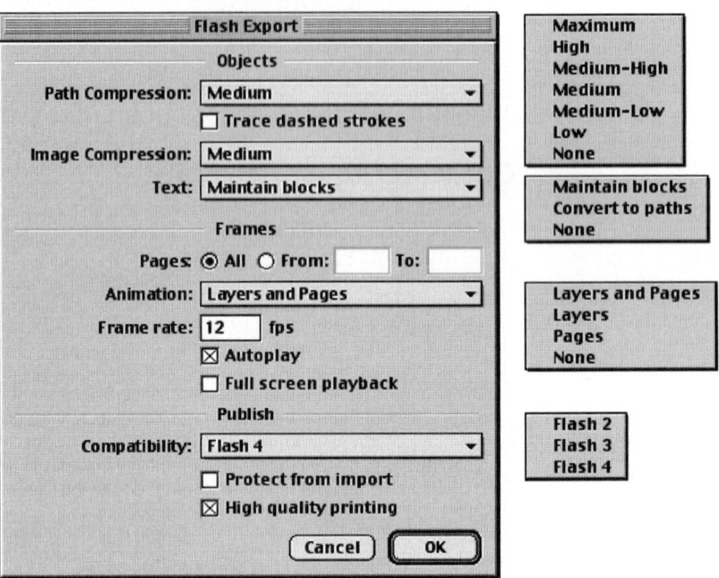

The first section in this menu deals with the objects in the document. The Path Compression pop-up controls the precision used to convert FreeHand paths to Flash paths. Maximum compression gives the smallest file, but the least precise conversion. None gives the most precise conversion. The Image Compression pop-up determines the quality and size of bitmap images. Maximum compression gives the smallest file, and None gives the best image. The Text pop-up menu gives you the option of maintaining the text blocks as text, converting to paths, or deleting the text from the file altogether.

The second section deals with how the animation is going to function. You may select all pages in the document or specific pages. Animation is determined by how you set up your document. If you animated by layers or pages, you should select those options. If you used both, you should select Layers and Pages. None performs no animation. The default Frame Rate of 12 frames per second creates a reasonably smooth animation for use on the Web.

Since the Flash 4 Player is freely distributed, it is the best choice for compatibility. The Protect from import checkbox may be used to disallow importing your image into another Flash movie.

Create a Flash Animation Using Pages

1. Open the document **Andy Flies.FH9** from your **SF-FreeHand** folder. This is a multi-page document that we're going to use to create a Flash animation.

2. From the View menu, select Fit All, so you get an idea of what we're working with.

3. Select File>Export (to your **Work in Progress** folder) and choose Macromedia Flash (SWF) as the format. Click Open in external application, and navigate to your FreeHand folder to select Flash 4 Player as the application.

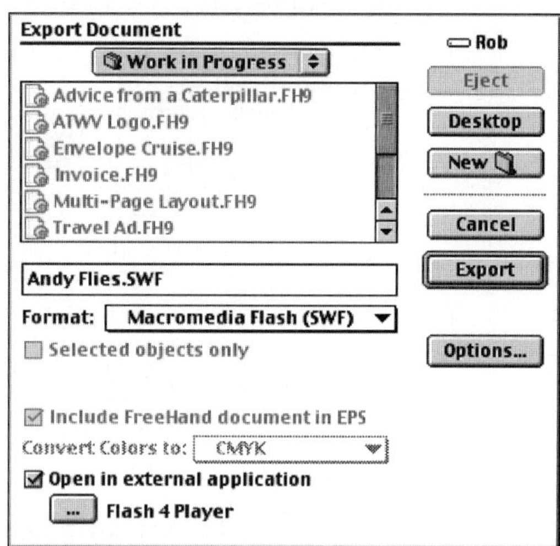

4. Click the Options/Setup button. Leave the compressions at Medium. Text has been converted to paths, so it can be left alone. Export All pages. Set the Animation to Pages, and the Frame rate at 8 frames per second. Leave the rest of the defaults. Click OK.

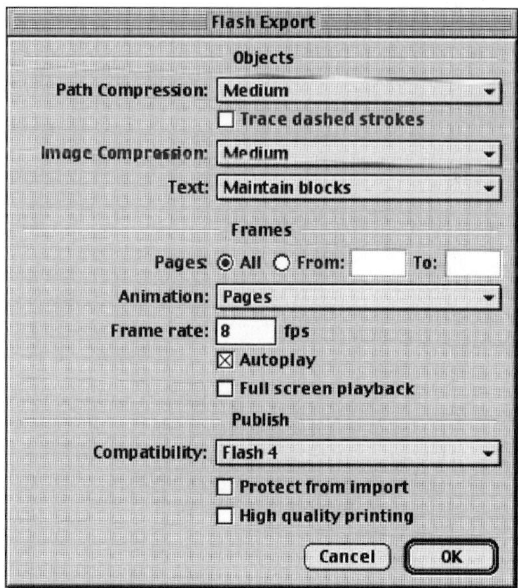

5. Click Export/Save. The Flash 4 Player defaults to playing a loop. You can alter this in the Control menu by unchecking it. Then click Rewind and Play to see the effect of a single playthrough of this animation. To play the animation frame by frame, click Step Forward (Command/Control->).

6. Close the FreeHand file without saving.

You probably noticed in viewing the file that it's a little jerky at 8 frames per second. The alternative was to increase the viewing rate to 12 frames per second, and to create another 7–9 pages. If you look at the FreeHand file, you'll see that the image was altered substantially in most of the frames. When creating animations such as this, be sure to keep a backup copy of the artwork.

Creating Animations Using Layers

Using FreeHand's blends, layers, and the Xtras>Animate>Release to Layers function allows you to easily create intermediate steps for an animation. The number of steps you create divided by the frames per second you stipulate in the export options will determine how long your animation will play. Remember, if you use the standard 12 frames per second, every second will involve 12 layers. There is a tradeoff between time and file size.

When Release to Layers is chosen, you have several options. It is important that you understand them in order to achieve the result you desire in your animation.

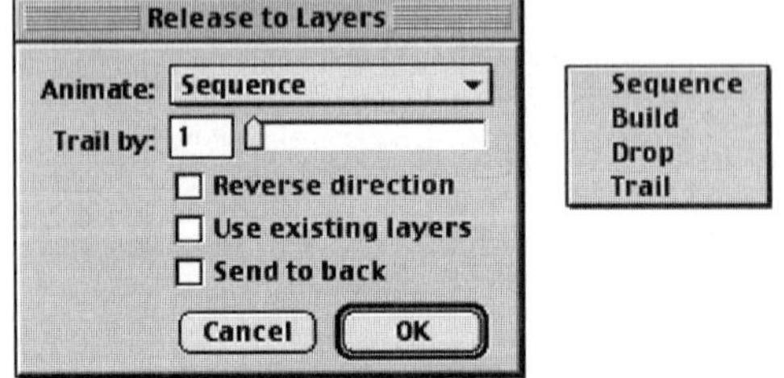

There are four Animate choices: Sequence, Build, Drop, and Trail.

- Sequence — All objects are released to separate layers in the sequence they were created.
- Build — Objects are released to layers to create a stacking or cumulative effect. Layer 2 will have the elements of layer 1 and layer 2; layer 3 will have the elements of all three layers.
- Drop — All objects are copied to all layers, except that one object is sequentially dropped from each layer. Layer 1 contains all but the first object. Layer 2 contains all but the second object, and so on.
- Trail — All objects are cloned and released to the number of layers specified in the Trail by field. If a group of three items is selected, and Trail by is set to 2, a total of five layers are created. Layer 1 contains object 1. Layer 2 contains objects 1 and 2. Layer 3 contains objects 1, 2, and 3. Layer 4 contains objects 2 and 3. Layer 5 contains object 3.

Trail by — This option determines the number of layers to which an object will be released. This option is available only when Animate is set to Trail.

Reverse Direction — releases the objects in reverse stacking order, and animates in reverse order.

Use existing layers — causes the Xtra to use the layers you have created. If additional layers are needed to perform the animation, it will create them.

Send to back — releases objects to the back of the stacking order. It is only available if Use existing layers has be checked.

In all likelihood, you will use the Sequence option for most of your animations. This allows FreeHand to do most of the work and frees you to create effective artwork.

When releasing an illustration to layers for the purposes of animation, the elements must be blends or groups.

Blend an Animation Using Layers

1. Open the document **Falling Leaves.FH9** from your **SF-FreeHand** folder. Activate the Xtra Operations toolbar from Window>Toolbars.
2. Using the Pen tool, draw a curving path from just above the top leaf to just below the bottom one.

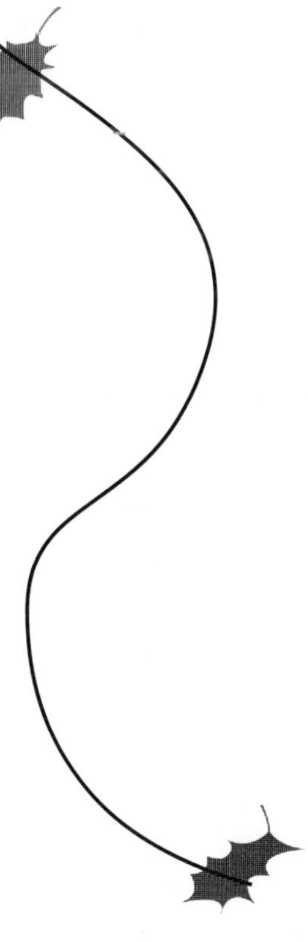

3. With the Pointer tool, select both the top and bottom leaf. Click on Blend in the Xtra Operations toolbar, or select it from Modify>Combine. From the Object Inspector, assign the Number of steps as 24.

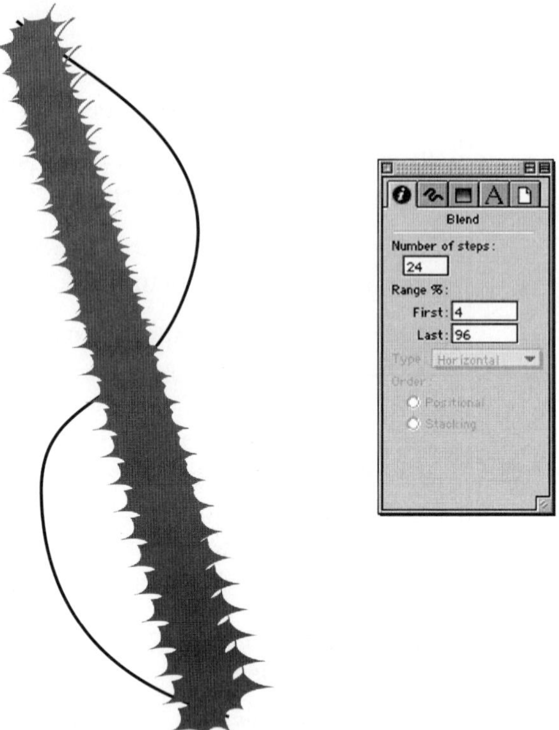

4. With the blend still selected, click on the path with the Pointer tool. Select Modify> Combine>Join blend to path.

5. With the blend selected, choose Xtras>Animate>Release to Layers. Each step of the blend will be on its own layer. Set Animate for Sequence.

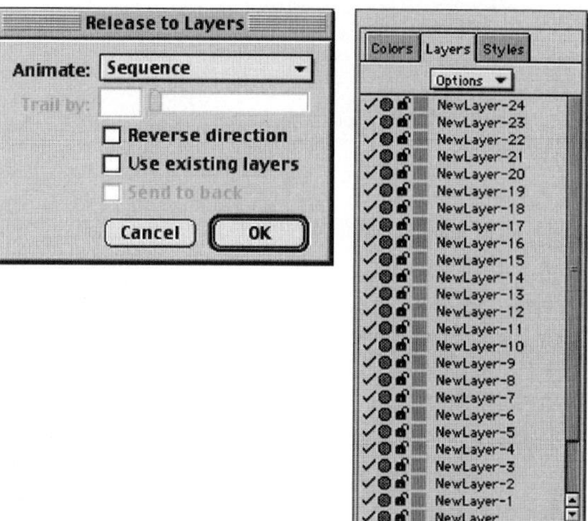

6. Now we're ready to export the file as a Flash movie. Select File>Export. Click the Options/Setup button. Leave the compression at the default. Export all pages; set Animation to Layers, and set the Frame rate at 12 frames per second. Click OK, then click Export/Save to export the file as a Macromedia Flash (SWF) file.

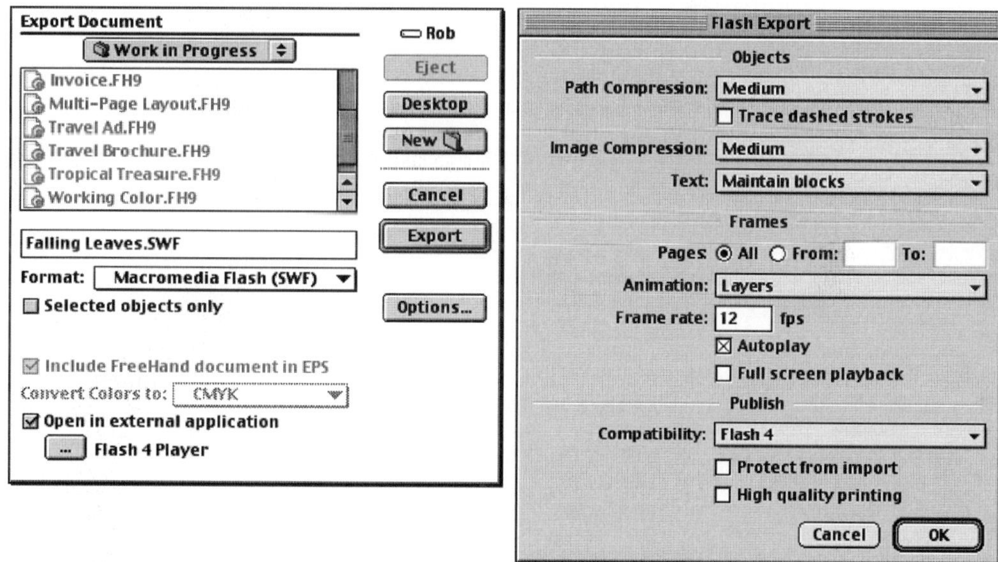

7. If Open in external application was checked, Flash 4 Player will launch and play the animation as a loop. Alter this default through the Control menu in Flash 4 Player. Save the FreeHand document to your **Work in Progress** folder.

Summary

In this chapter you learned some differences between publishing on the Web and publishing in print. You learned about and used the palette of 216 Web-safe colors and worked with a document to assign links from a URL to both text and graphics. You learned about Flash animations and created animation sequences using pages and using blends and layers. There is much more to learn about preparing documents for the Web, but what you have learned here will allow you to put your FreeHand skills to work creating Web graphics.

Notes:

PROJECT ASSIGNMENT #2

Assignment

A farm in Northern California is introducing a new line of seasoned vinegars in four flavors: garlic, thyme, cilantro, and basil. They want a contemporary logo to go along with this new line of products.

The client is a family-owned company with more than fifty years' experience in organic farming and the manufacture of bottled and canned foods are sold to a largely regional market. They're looking to introduce a modern look that's still able to convey a feeling of tradition, longevity, and commitment to the highest quality. They have a few professionally produced images of the flavoring agents that you can use if you want to.

Applying Your Skills

To develop the labels, you will need to use the following functions, methods, and features of Macromedia FreeHand:

- Using type and outlined-type elements combined with appropriate shapes and path functions to create a new logo for the client.
- Importing the copy supplied by the client for use on each of the four labels.
- Copying and pasting the nutritional information supplied on to the four labels and positioning it properly on the new designs.
- Using gradients and custom process colors to build subtle color and interest into each of the labels in the series.
- Using rotation and other transformations to position type and graphic elements vertically and horizontally to meet the requirements of the design.
- Selecting images from the files we've supplied and placing them into the labels, complete with whatever framing or outlining method you decide to choose for the labels.
- Printing test separations and a composite proof, along with the appropriate images and typefaces prior to packaging the job for delivery to a service provider.

Specifications

Each label will wrap around three sides of a bottle, and must be ten inches wide and five inches high. Each label must incorporate the supplied text, the nutrition label, and an image. Name each vinegar appropriately and use the same graphic treatment for all of the titles.

The labels are to be produced as a four-color process job, with no additional spot colors. Subtle colors and pastel shades are preferred, but don't limit your creativity — the client might like something surprising.

Included Files

We have supplied a full compliment of images and support files for this project. You must use these text and graphics.

There are various CMYK images supplied in TIFF format. You only need to use four of them, so you have some flexibility in your selections. There is also a text file containing the copy for the Celtic Farms label, called Copy for CF Labels.TXT. Lastly, use the Nutrition Label.FH9 file containing the information required by the FDA for food products. Make sure it's on all four labels.

Publisher's Comments

Labels are a true contemporary artistic venue — you can see the work of some of the nation's finest artists on food, record labels, and other forms of packaging. Many of the top awards in the graphics industry are awarded for unique and compelling packaging. Labels like the ones you're required to execute in this project are but one form.

This project is typical of many real-world assignments in that the client has supplied certain images that they feel are right for the look and feel they're trying to accomplish. Although you might have picked something different, it's up to you to incorporate what they're supplying with your own imagination to come up with something that will not only please the client but will help the product fly off the shelves.

This is ultimately the true purpose of the assignment — to make people notice your client's products in a sea of similar packages. A unique and compelling design that really stands out is the answer to this challenge.

REVIEW #2

CHAPTERS 9 THROUGH 16:

In Chapters 9–16 we explored the advanced features that FreeHand offers. We worked with type, examining its characteristics, and learned how it can be made to interact with paths and objects. We have also worked with the transformation tools, with which objects are scaled, rotated, skewed and reflected. We also learned a number of methods to alter a path to create special effects and to work with special tools, called Xtras. In addition, we explored a variety of import and export methods, to work with imported graphics, and how to print FreeHand documents. We explored the creation of vector graphics for the Web. By now, you should:

- Have a knowledge of typography, and know how to assign both text and paragraph attributes. Use the Text tool and the Text Inspector to efficiently incorporate text into your documents. Be able to import text, to link text blocks, and to meld text with graphics. You can to work with text on a path and to convert text into outlines.

- Use the Document Inspector to manage the elements of your document, including the bleed and the target resolution. You should be able to create FreeHand documents that have a variety of text and graphic elements.

- Understand the transformation modes, and have used the tools in the Transform palette to effect precise transformations. You also know how to interactively transform objects using the transformation tools. You have transformed object multiple times, duplicating the transformation last performed.

- Used the path altering tools to perform intricate tasks. You understand what a composite path is, and are able to use it to enhance your art. You have learned how to create blends, and know the importance of selecting points of the objects to be blended to achieve specific effects.

- Worked with a number of the plug-in tools that ship with FreeHand. You can perform 3D rotations, achieve smudge effects, and get a fisheye view of the object you are working with. You can create charts that are straightforward, or you can enhance them with graphics.

- Export FreeHand files in a variety of formats, and know the difference between vector and raster graphics. You know how to embed or to link images, and understand how to use the Object Inspector to gather information about the object you are examining. You learned how to alter imported raster images.

- Understand dot gain and trapping, and how to prepare your file for printing process or spot colors.

- Understand how to prepare graphics for use on the Internet, using web-safe colors, and how preparing files for the Web differs from preparing files for print. You learned how to create animations using layers and using pages.

Project A: Dinner Time

In this project you will use the skills you have learned to this point to draw the elements of this pet dinner scene, using a bitmap background element as your template.

Draw with Basic Shapes

1. Open the file **Dinner Time.FT9** from the **SF-FreeHand** folder.

   You will use the image on the locked background layer as a template for the drawing you will perform. All the work that you will do to this file will be performed on the Foreground layer.

2. Move the image to the top and center of the page.
3. Open the Layers panel (Window>Panels>Layers). With the image selected, click on the Background layer.
4. Click on the Padlock icon next to Background to lock the layer to avoid accidentally moving the template while you are drawing.

5. Double-click on the Foreground layer in the Layers panel and rename it "Dinner Time". Press Return/Enter to apply the name. Click on this layer to make it active. Any objects you make will be assigned to this layer only.

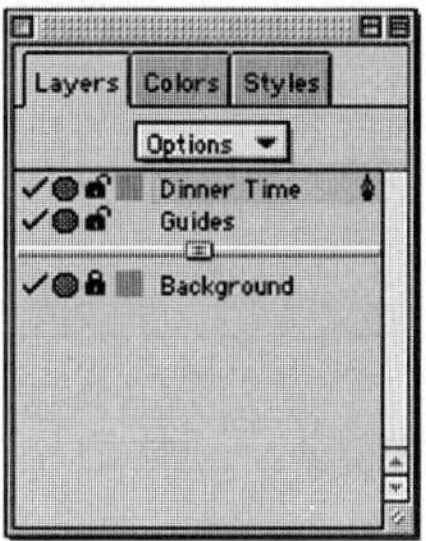

6. Double click on the Spiral tool in the Toolbox. Practice adjusting the settings and drawing sprirals until you create three spirals that are the same as in the imported image. When you are finished, move them into position with the Pointer tool.

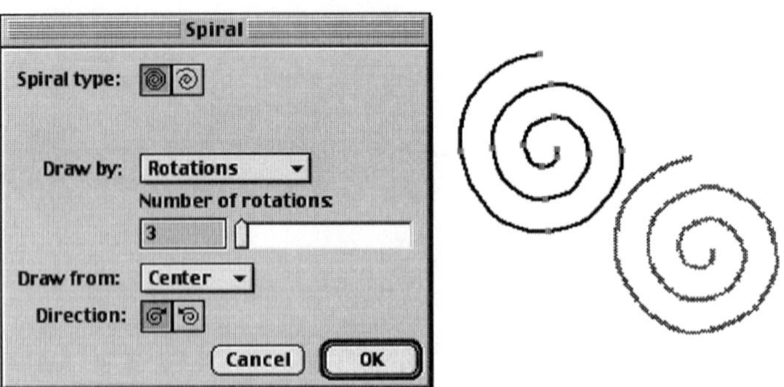

7. Zoom in on the face of the cat on the template with the Magnification tool by dragging it around that portion of the image with the tool selected.

Remember — holding Option/Alt draws from the center; holding the Shift key constrains the shape to a circle or square.

8. Select the Ellipse tool in the Toolbox and draw an ellipse for the cat's face. Continue using the Ellipse tool to draw parts of the cat's face that are circular in shape. Use the Pointer tool to adjust and refine the ellipses to fit the template as needed.

9. When you are finished creating the ellipse shapes for the cat, zoom into the dog area of the template and draw the ellipse shapes for the dog including the dog's eyes and nose.

10. When you are finished creating the ellipse shapes for the dog, use the Ellipse tool to create the eye of the mouse at the bottom of the template.

11. Zoom back into the cat and double-click on the Polygon tool in the Toolbox. Adjust the settings for a triangle and create the nose of the cat.

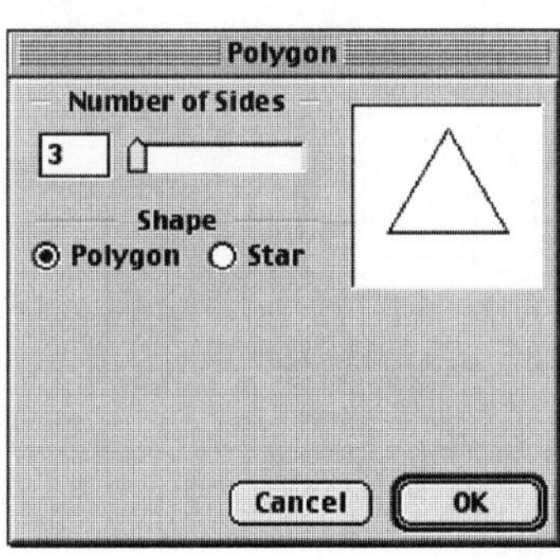

12. When you are finished creating the nose of the cat, use your Magnification tool to zoom around the bowl area of the template.

13. Double-click on the Polygon tool and adjust the settings for a five point star.

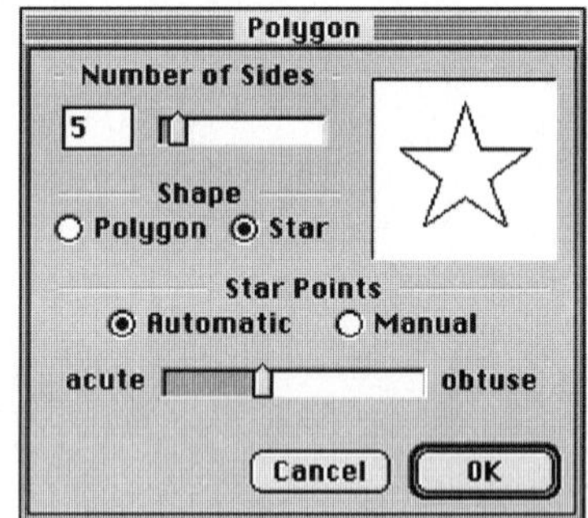

14. Draw the star shapes on the bowl using the Polygon tool with the new settings.

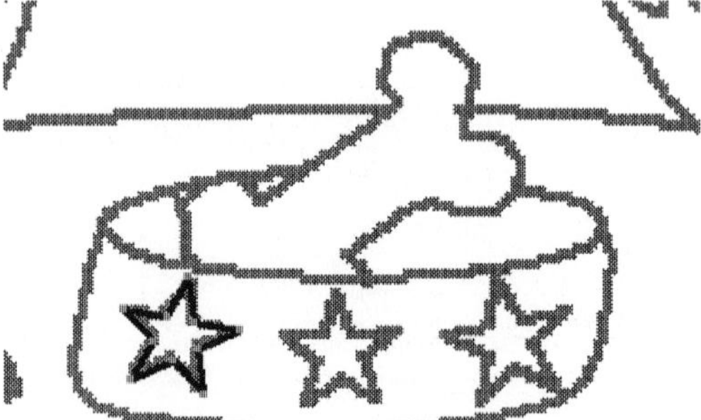

15. Use the Pointer tool to adjust and refine the polygons to fit the template as needed.

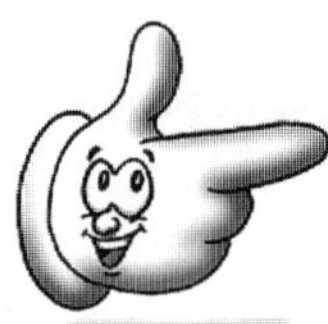

Use the Freehand Tool

1. Double click on the Freehand tool in the Toolbox. Make sure that the line settings are set to Freehand with the Precision slider set to 10.

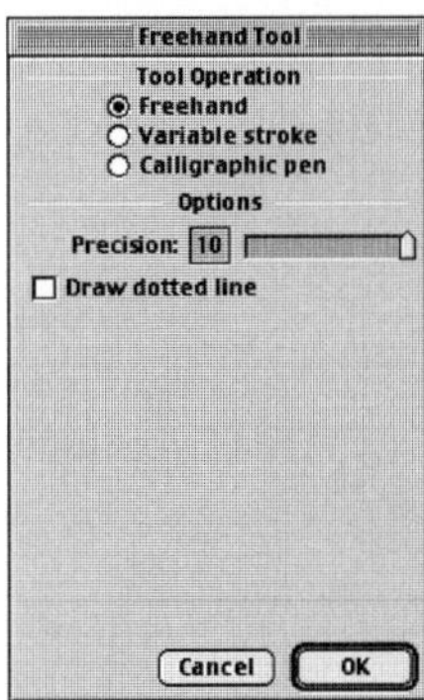

2. Zoom back around the face of the cat and draw the remainder of the cat's face using the Freehand tool. To do this, simply think of the Freehand tool as a pencil.

3. Zoom back out and use the Freehand tool to draw the remainder of the cat. When finished with the cat, draw the remainder of the bowl, dog, table top, and mouse, leaving only the table legs incomplete.

Create Basic Lines

1. Zoom into one of the table legs of the template and select the Pen tool from the Freehand toolbox.

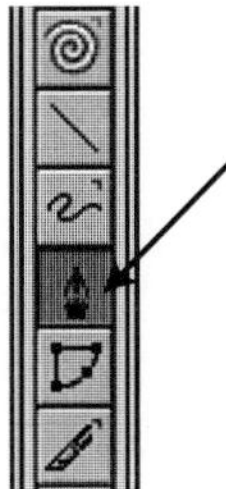

2. Using the Pen tool, create one of the table legs by clicking at each corner of the table leg to create the line .

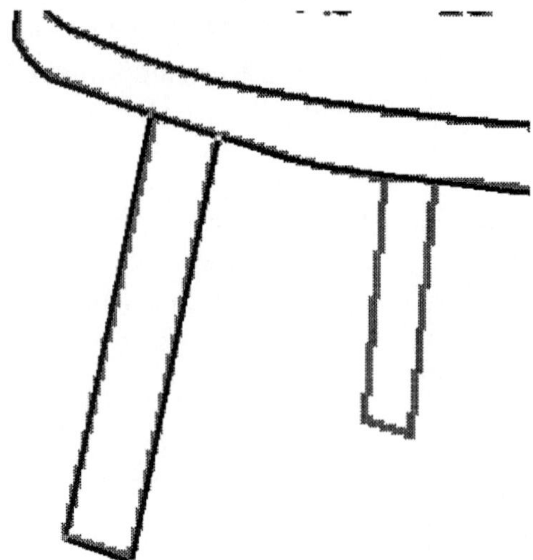

3. Create one more of the table legs with the Pen tool and then select the Bezigon tool in the Freehand toolbox.

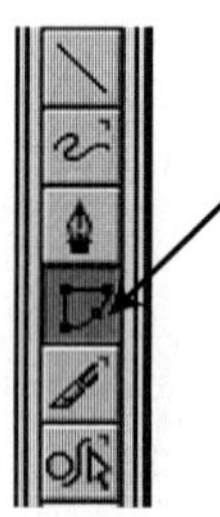

4. Draw the remaining two table legs using the Bezigon tool. You will see that they work basically the same when creating straight lines.

5. The design is complete. Select all the objects and group them by choosing Select>All, then Modify>Group.

6. Click the checkmark in front of the layer labeled "Background" in the Layers palette to view your work.

7. Use Save As to save the file in your **Work in Progress** folder. Save the file in the FreeHand Document format, and name it "Dinner Time.FH9".

8. Close the document.

Project B: Mask Art

Art such as that you will produce for this project could be used for greeting cards, CD covers, T-shirts, or any number of applications for which "practicality" isn't required — or for that matter, even desired.

Create Shapes with the Bezigon Tool

1. Open the **Mountains.FT9** file from the **SF-Freehand** folder. You will use the placed image as a guide to trace the background and the mountains.
2. Double-click on the Foreground layer in the Layers panel and rename it "Mountains". Press Return/Enter to apply the name. Click on this layer to make it active. Any objects you make will be assigned to this layer until another layer is chosen.

3. With the Rectangle tool, draw the border that surrounds the mountains in the template.
4. Once you have drawn the background, select the Bezigon tool and click where the left mountain touches the rectangle border (A). Continue to click along the template to draw the mountains (B). When the last click has been made to touch the rectangle border, move the mouse down slightly and, holding the Shift key, click on the border. Move the mouse directly across to the left side of the border, under the first click, and click again on the border, holding the Shift key. Make one final click on the first anchor point you clicked. The mountain is a closed path (C). Its left and right segments match the rectangle border. If the left and right segments do not match exactly, use the Pointer tool to fine-tune them to the rectangle border path.

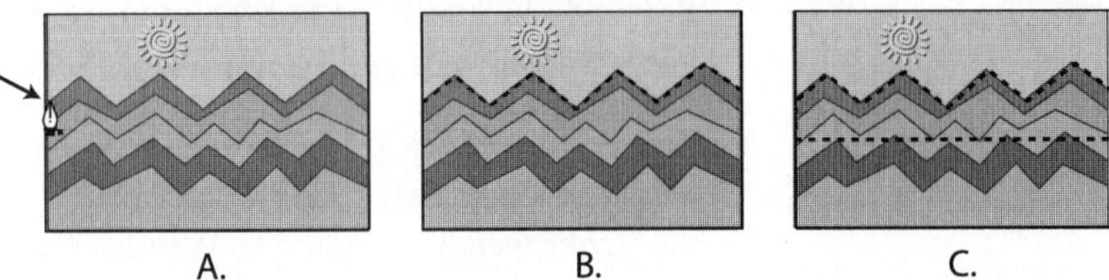

A. B. C.

5. Select this mountain path with the Pointer tool and select Edit>Clone to create a second copy of the shape. With the copy of the original selected, drag downward, holding the Shift key to constrain the move. Do not try to match the second level of mountains, but position the dragged path in its nearest vicinity. When in place, press Command/Control-D three times to repeat this duplication

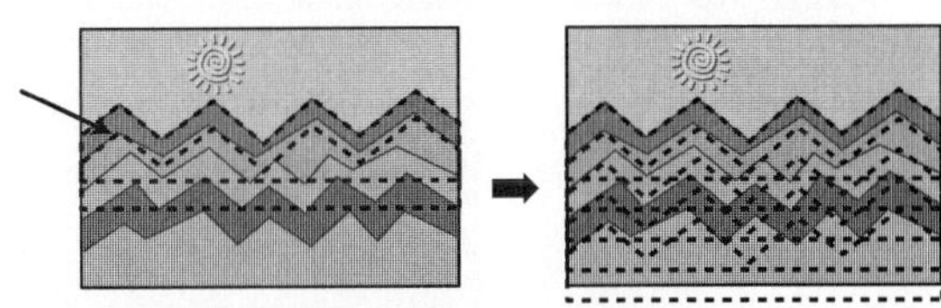

6. You will need to fine-tune the second mountain. Select the Pointer tool and click on the second mountain path to see its anchor points. Click on the individual anchor points with the Pointer tool and drag them to match the mountain.

7. Click on the third mountain path with the Pointer tool and move its anchor points to match the template. You will find that the path hasn't enough anchor points. Select the Bezigon tool and click it on the mountain segment when you need an additional anchor point.

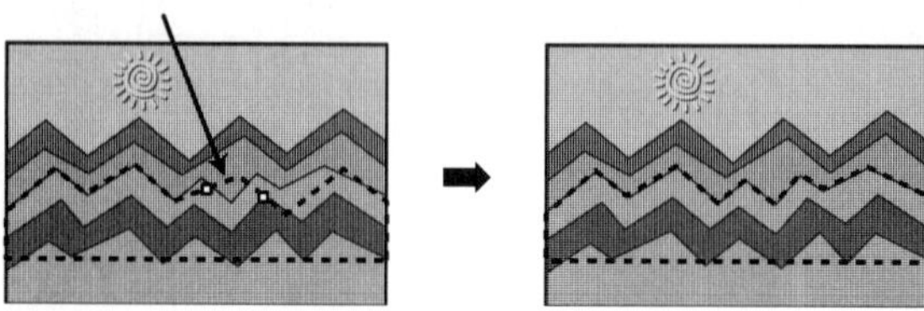

8. With the Pointer tool, fine-tune the fourth mountain path to match the template. Use the Bezigon tool to add anchor points when needed.
9. With the Pointer tool, fine-tune the fifth mountain path to match the template. Use the Bezigon tool to add anchor points when needed.
10. The fifth mountain will have to have its lower segment adjusted to match the rectangle border you drew first. Select the lower segment with the Pointer tool and to select both anchor points at the bottom corners of the segment. Click on the Up or Down Arrow key on your keyboard to move the bottom of the segment into place to match the template.

Build Mountains

1. You will now paint the border and mountains. From the Window menu, select Panels>Color List and Panels>Color Mixer.
2. Press Command/Control-A to select all the paths drawn. The border and mountains will retain their Black stroke color, but their weight needs to be changed to 3.5 pt. Set the stroke weight by going to Window>Inspector>Stroke and entering the new stroke weight. Remember to press Return/Enter on your keyboard to apply the change.

3. The fills of the paths will vary. Using the following list of paint attributes, select the object named and fill it with the listed colors using the Color Mixer. Make sure that your Color Mixer is set to CMYK and that you drag the colors into the Color List after they are mixed.

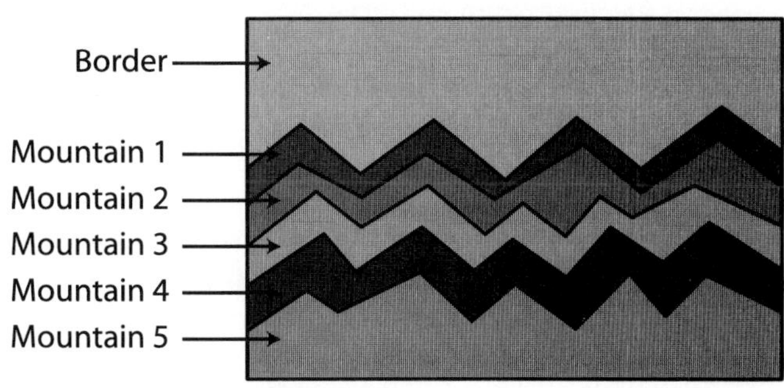

Border:	C 80, M 5, Y 0, K 0
Mountain 1:	C 45, M 90, Y 0, K 0
Mountain 2:	C 0, M 50, Y 100, K 0
Mountain 3:	C 75, M 5, Y 100, K 0
Mountain 4:	C 15, M 100, Y 100, K 0
Mountain 5:	C 75, M 5, Y 100, K 0

Applying the colors is easiest when they're applied front to back.

4. Select the border and mountains, then group them. Once they are grouped choose View>Hide Selection to hide them.

Here Comes The Sun

1. Double-click on the Spiral tool in the Toolbox and adjust your settings to draw a spiral that is very close to the size and orientation to that of the sun in the template (A). Enter 4 in the Number of Rotations field, and select the counterclockwise button. Use the Spiral tool to draw the spiral. With the Pointer tool, click on the path of the spiral to see its anchor points. Move these so the path matches the template sun more closely (B). The sun rays are single segments drawn by the Line tool. Select the sun and ray paths together, then select Window>Inspector>Stroke and increase the stroke Weight to 6.5 pt. and change the ends to Rounded caps (C).

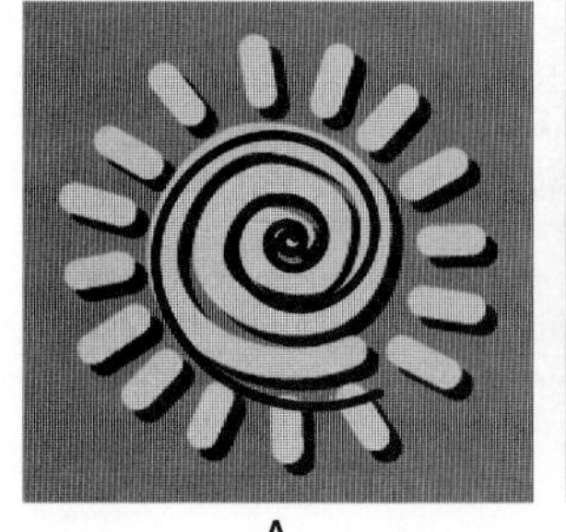
A.

B.

C.

2. With the sun and ray paths still selected, choose Modify>Group to group the sun and ray paths together. Copy these paths, and select Edit>Paste Behind. A duplicate will be pasted directly behind the original. Press the Right Arrow key two times, and the Down Arrow key two times.

3. Click on the original sun and ray group with the Pointer tool. Paint this group with a fill of None, and a stroke of 6.5 pt. C 0, M 10, Y 100, K 0 (CMYK Color Mixer palette).

4. Select both sun/ray groups and hide them.

Change Templates with Edit Link

1. The mountains are drawn now, so the complete template with the natives must replace the image you opened earlier.

2. Select Edit>Links to see the Links palette. Click on the **Mountains.TIF** option in the palette. At the right of the palette, click the Change button.

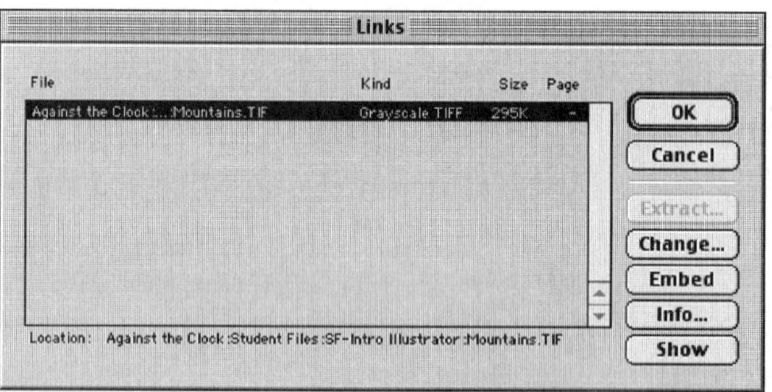

3. In the dialog box that appears, navigate to the **SF-Freehand** folder and select the **See No Evil.TIF** image. Click Open and then choose OK to replace the old image with the new. On the page, the image will be close to the same position as the former template image. Choose View>Show All to bring the mountain group back to view and move the group into place to match the template. Once they are grouped choose View> Hide Selection to hide them.

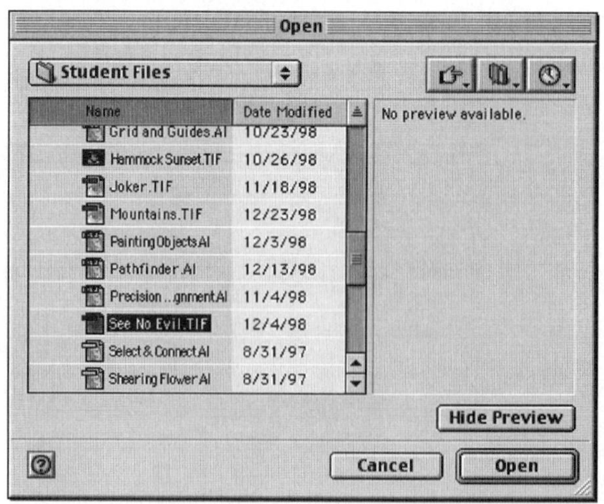

The Native Head

1. The three natives are actually one native figure that has been duplicated twice. You will create one figure less the arms, which will be added later. We will work on the center native, since we can see his eyes and other features.

2. Use the Pen tool to draw the curving lines of the hair. The area of the hair that goes behind the mask can be a straight line to complete the path. Adjust these points with the Pointer tool for a smoother, more rounded corner as needed.

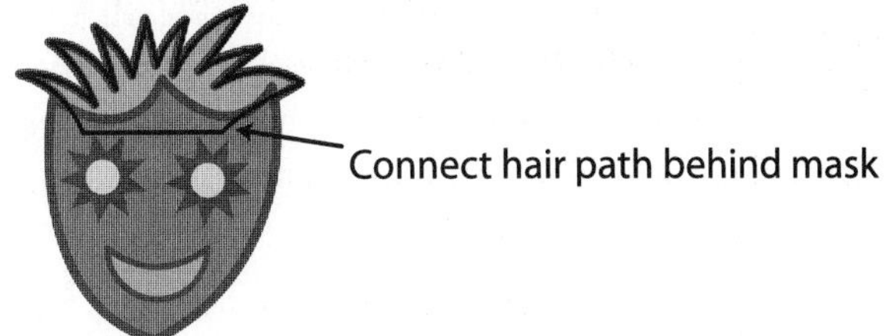

3. Select the Pen tool and trace the outline of the mask.

4. For the eyes, double click on the Polygon tool in the Toolbox and select a 9 pt. star. Click its cursor on the left eye and drag to draw the star. Paint the star with a fill of Black, and a stroke of None. Select the Ellipse tool, click the cursor on this star and drag to create the circle. Paint this circle from the Color List CMYK palette with a fill of C: 0, M: 10, Y: 100, and K: 0, and a stroke of None. Move the circle into the center of the star and group the circle and star together.

5. With the grouped eye selected choose Edit>Duplicate to duplicate the left eye. Drag the eye to the right to match the second eye in the template.

6. The mouth is drawn with an ellipses. Select the Ellipse tool. In the template, between the two corners of the mouth, click the cursor while holding the Option/Alt key, and draw from the center. Match the bottom half of the mouth. With the Pointer tool, click on the ellipse and choose Modify>Ungroup. Select the top anchor point of the ellipse and delete it. Drag the anchor point to the top of the mouth and collapse the handles of the end points of the mouth as needed.

7. From the Color Mixer CMYK palette, paint the outlines as follows:

   Mask — fill with C: 0, M: 50, Y: 100, K: 0; and a stroke of 3.5 pt. Black.

   Mouth —fill with C: 45, M: 90, Y: 0, K: 0; and a stroke of 2.5 pt. Black.

   Hair — fill with C: 0, M: 10, Y: 100, K: 0; stroke of 3.5 pt. Black.

   Select these paths and hide them be selecting View>Hide Selection.

8. The collar under the mask is drawn with the Pen tool. Be sure to trace along the jaw of the mask to fit the mask outline as close as possible. When the collar is finished, paint it with a fill of C: 75, M: 5, Y: 100, and K: 0; and a stroke of 3.5 pt. Black. Choose View>Show All to bring back the mask objects. Select the background, mountains, and sun, and hide them again. Select the hair, eyes, mouth, mask, and collar, group them, then hide the group.

The Native Body

1. The body of the native is made up of the torso, the grass skirt, and two legs. Start with the torso by tracing the template with the Pen tool. Extend the bottom of the torso so that it will be covered by the grass skirt, which will be in front of it. The navel is a simple Freehand tool segment.

2. The legs are closed paths and should be drawn with the Pen tool. Make sure they extend up behind the skirt, so the skirt will cover them

3. Continue with the Pen tool to trace the grass skirt in the template. The curving anchor points should be adjusted with the Pointer tool after the grass skirt is drawn.

4. From the Color Mixer CMYK palette, paint the components as follows:

   Torso and Legs — Fill with C: 0, M: 10, Y: 100, and K: 0; a stroke of 3.5 Black.

   Navel — fill with None and a stroke of 2.5 pt. Black.

   Grass Skirt — fill with C: 75, M: 5, Y: 100, and K: 0; a stroke of 3.5 pt. Black.

5. Select these objects and group them. Choose Show All to see the mask group. Select the mountain group and sun, and hide them again. Click on the torso group just drawn and choose Modify>Arrange>Send To Back to put it behind the mask and collar group.

6. Click on the two groups that make up this native and select Edit>Duplicate to duplicate them. Drag the duplicate group to the left to match the native on the left in the template. Repeat these steps to match the far right native. Select the groups of all three natives and hide them.

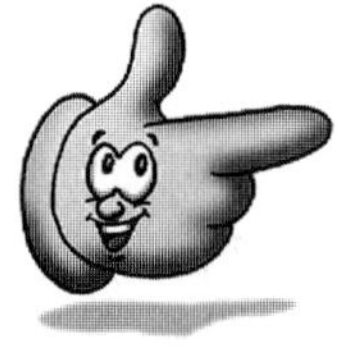

Draw the Native Arms

1. The arms of the natives should be drawn with the Pen tool. Select the tool and begin with the far left native's arms, then the middle native, followed by the far right one. The difference in drawing the arms is that they are not closed paths. This is to avoid unsightly black outlines where there should be a continuous fill. Draw the arm outlines so that their endpoints touch the torso, if seen, or go behind the collar to be hidden. Use the Pointer tool to adjust the anchor points as needed to fine-tune the fit.

2. When the arms are all drawn, select the Object Inspector and make the arms a closed path. Select the arms and the paint them with a fill of C: 0, M: 10, Y: 100, and K: 0; and a 3.5 pt. Black stroke.
3. Select View>Show All to show the native groups. Select the mountain and sun groups and hide them again. The Modify>Arrange>Send To Back option will need to be used to position the arms behind certain objects, while keeping them in front of others.

With the Pointer tool, click on the arms of the far left native. Press Command/Control-X to cut the arms. With the Pointer tool, Option/Alt-click on the collar of the native, and choose Edit>Paste Behind to paste it in back of the collar. The same procedure is done with the far right native. The arms are cut, the collar selected with the Pointer tool, then Edit>Paste Behind should be chosen. The middle native is slightly different. The arms are cut, the group is selected with the Pointer tool, then Edit>Paste Behind chosen. The design, so far, should look similar to the following:

When the Option/Alt keys are added to a click with the Pointer tool, individual elements of a group are selected.

Add a Little War Paint

1. The finishing touch of the natives is to paint their hair and garments with different colors. The middle native has been painted correctly. With the Eyedropper tool, click on this middle native's mask. Use the Eyedropper tool to drag the orange color over to the left native's hair, and then the left native's skirt. Now use the Eyedropper tool and click it on the middle native's collar. Drag the color over to the mask of the right native.

2. With the Pointer tool, Option/Alt-click on the mask of the left native. From the Color List, fill the mask with C: 45, M: 90, Y: 0, and K: 0. Use the same color on the hair, collar, and skirt of the right native.

3. With the Pointer tool, Option/Alt-click on the collar of the left native. From the Color List, change the fill to C: 15, M: 100, Y: 100, and K: 0.

4. With the Pointer tool, Shift- Option/Alt-click on the mouths of the left and right natives. From the Color List, change the fills to C: 0, M: 50, Y: 100, and K: 0.

5. Use View>Show All to reveal the hidden background, mountains, and sun. Use Modify>Arrange>Send To Back as needed to make sure these objects are sent behind the natives.

6. The artwork, now painted, should look like the following image:

7. Select Save As to save the file in your **Work in Progress** folder. Save in FreeHand Document format, and name your file "Mask Art.FH9". Close the document.

Project C: Tropical Treasure Logo

A company's logo is, perhaps, its most prized graphic possession. An incredible amount of time (and treasure) go into the creation and protection of logos. The Tropical Treasure logo simply conveys the look and feel of this Florida gift shop.

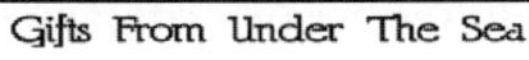

Creating Rules with the Pen Tool

1. Open the **Tropical Treasure.TIF** file from your **SF-FreeHand** folder.

2. Move the image to the center of the page and keep it selected.
3. Click on the embedded TIFF image. Select Window>Panels>Layers and click on the Background layer.
4. Click the Padlock icon on the Background layer to lock. When you click in the document, you're ready to work on the Foreground layer. Press Tab to deselect all, then click on the Foreground layer to continue.
5. Turn on Page Rulers and Guides from the View menu. From the left-side ruler, drag out vertical guides to mark the left and right sides of the logo template.

Command/Control-[hyphen] will clone an object without using the menu.

6. Begin with the rules at the top of the logo. With the Pen tool, click on the left end of the thick rule against the vertical guide. Holding the Shift key, go to the far right side of the rule and click.

7. Press the Tab key to deselect everything.
8. Select this segment with the Pointer tool and clone it. Press the Down Arrow key several times to move the duplicate segment downward, matching the position of the thin rule beneath the thick rule on the template.

9. Select the upper segment. In the Stroke Inspector panel, set the Width to 6 pt. Select the lower segment and set its Width to 2 pt.

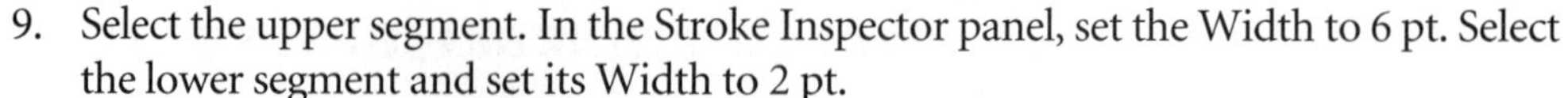

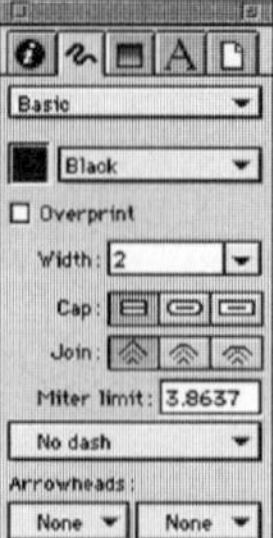

The keyboard shortcut for Clone is Command-"=" (Macintosh) or Control-Shift-C (Windows).

10. Select both segments and clone them. Move the clones down to match the bottom two rules of the template.

11. With the clones still selected, double-click on the Reflect tool. In the Transform panel, enter 180° for the Reflect axis, then click the Apply/Reflect button.

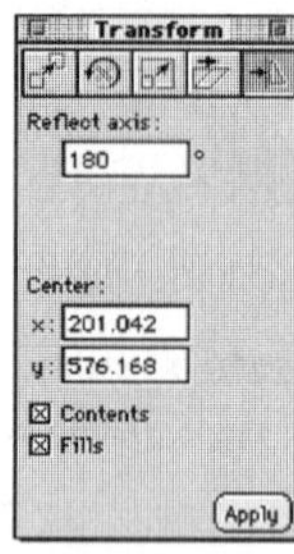

12. The cloned rules will Reflect. Use the Arrow keys to fine-tune the rules to better fit the template.

13. Select all of the rules by choosing Edit>Select All. Open the Color List. In the Options pop-up menu, select Pantone Uncoated. Enter the number 3155 and click OK. The color will be added to the Color List. Paint the rules with a fill of None, and a stroke of Pantone 3155 CVU.

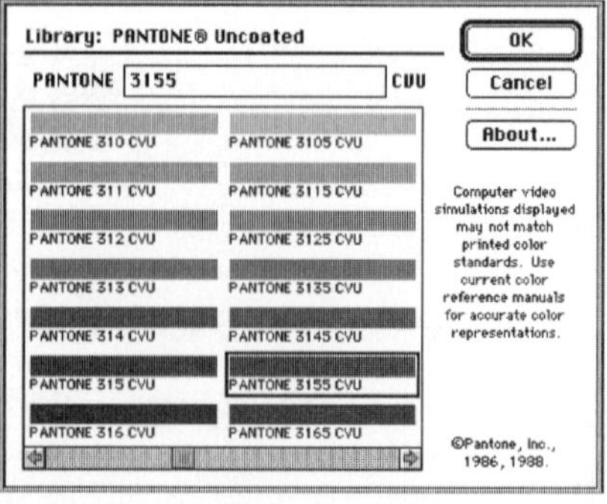

The keyboard shortcut for Select All is Command/Control-A.

You have now created and colored the rules of the logo. We will now draw and color the treasure chest.

In the Object Inspector, check to be sure that the width of the rectangles that make the top and bottom of the box are the same and that they have the same "X" position.

Pantone colors are generally referred to simply as PMS (Pantone Matching System) followed by their number.

Draw Shapes with the Rectangle Tool

1. In the Layers palette, create a new layer above the Foreground Layer.
2. Select the Rectangle tool and trace the template to create the treasure chest. There should be four rectangles — the trunk bottom, the trunk top, the plate, and the keyhole. The top of the trunk bottom should be equal with the top of the top rule. When it is in position, click the checkmark of the Foreground layer, turning it off, so you can see what you're doing.

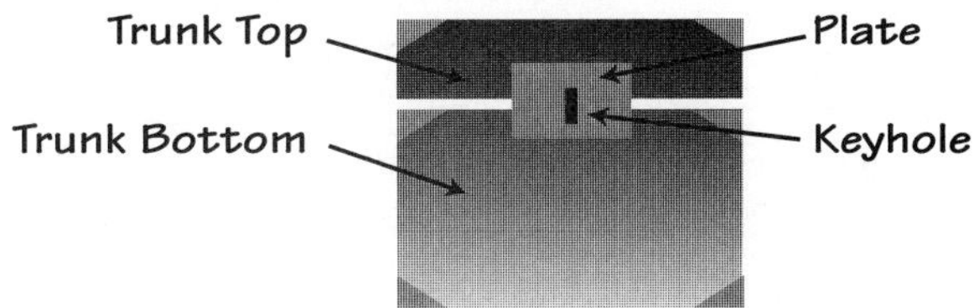

3. Select the Color List. In the Options pop-up menu, select the Crayon Library. Choose Pantone Uncoated 135, 169, 293, 410 Blue, Brown, Gold, and Salmon by holding the Shift/Control key. Click OK.
4. Select the two large rectangles (trunk top and bottom) and navigate to the Fill Inspector. Select Gradient from the pop-up menu.
5. Create a linear gradient of PMS 470 (top drop box) and PMS 169 (bottom drop box.) Fill the selected trunk top and bottom with this gradient. Set the stroke to None.

6. Fill the plate with PMS 135 and a stroke of None. Fill the keyhole with Black and a stroke of None.

Create the Brass Corners

1. Creating the brass corners of the trunk top and bottom is accomplished by drawing a square to fit the corner on which you are working. Objects drawn with the Rectangle tool must be ungrouped to make their anchor points accessible.

2. Draw a square to fit the upper-left corner of the trunk top. Select Modify>Ungroup to see the anchor points of this new square.

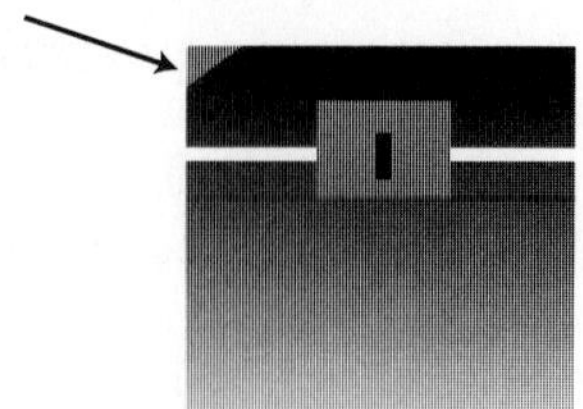

3. Select the bottom-right anchor point (A) and delete the selected anchor point (B) to create a triangle that fits the corner.

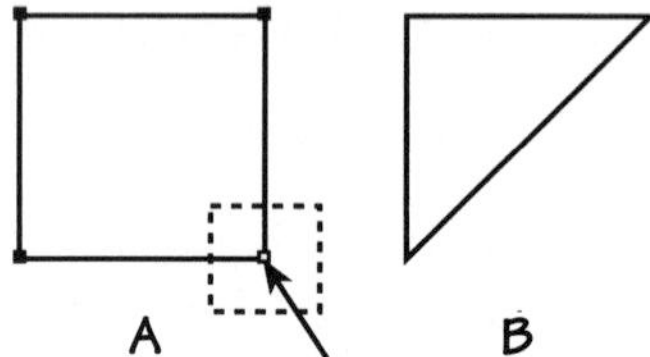

4. Select the triangle with the Pointer tool and drag a duplicate down to the trunk box corner while holding the Option/Alt key.

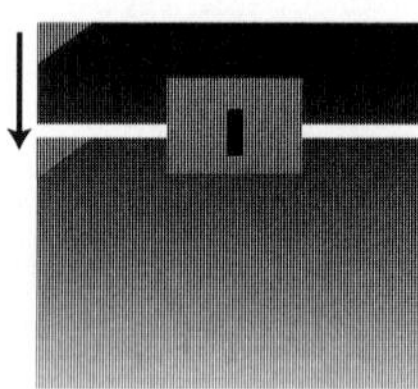

5. With duplicate selected, clone the triangle. Double-click the Reflect tool in the Toolbox and enter 180° for the Reflect axis. Click the Apply/Reflect button. Drag the reflected duplicate down to fit the bottom-left corner of the trunk.

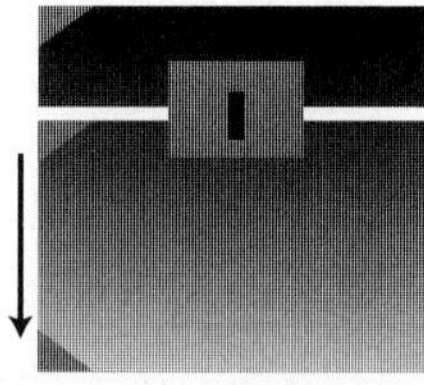

6. Select all three triangles. Drag a vertical guide to the center of the trunk's keyhole. With the Pointer tool, select the three corners. Choose Window>Toolbars>Xtra Tools. Select the Mirror tool and click on the vertical guide. This will automatically duplicate and reflect the corners to the right side. Deselect the left three triangles.

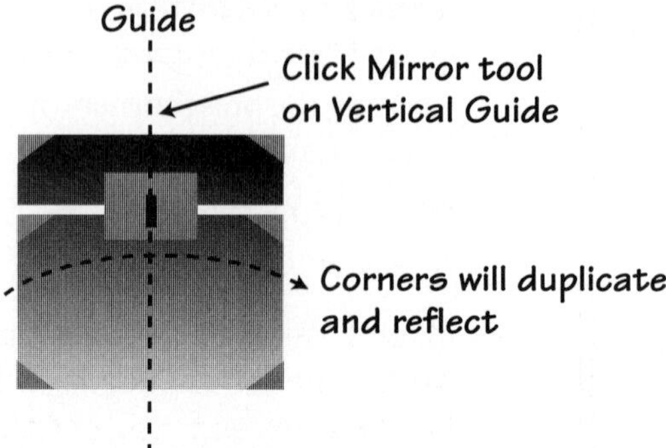

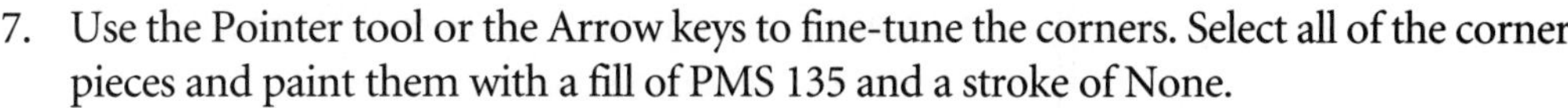

7. Use the Pointer tool or the Arrow keys to fine-tune the corners. Select all of the corner pieces and paint them with a fill of PMS 135 and a stroke of None.
8. Turn the Foreground layer back on.

Draw Shapes with the Ellipse Tool

1. Using the Ellipse tool, trace the coins at the bottom of the chest. With the Pointer tool, select all of the coins. From the Color List, click on the Fill icon. Select PMS 135 to paint the coins. Drag None to the Stroke icon.
2. Select Modify>Group to group the selected coins, and then clone them.
3. With the duplicate group selected, apply a fill of Black and a stroke of None.
4. Send this duplicate group to the back (Modify>Arrange>Send To Back) and press the Down and Right Arrow keys a few times for a shadow effect.

5. The chest and coins have been created. Select all of these objects and group them. Now it is time to work on the type.

Turn Type into Outlines

1. With the Text tool, click the cursor once on the page and type "TROPICAL TREASURE" in all capital letters.
2. Highlight the text with the Text tool and set the Font to ATC Tequila, 72 pt.
3. Click this text block with the Pointer tool to view the box handles. Drag the right-middle handle to the right side guide and drag the left-middle handle to the left side guide. This will space the letters evenly across the width of the text block.
4. Click the text cursor between the two words and use the Spacebar and/or the Kerning feature to adjust the words to fit the template. To kern the text, hold the Option (Macintosh) or Control-Alt (Windows) keys as you press either the left or right Arrow keys.
5. Once the letters are kerned, click on the text block with the Pointer tool. In the Text menu, choose the Convert To Paths option. The type will automatically be grouped. Paint the text with a fill of PMS 293, and a stroke of None.

6. With this group selected, choose Edit>Clone, then Modify>Arrange>Send To Back. This will be the first clone.
7. Press the Right Arrow key five times and the Down Arrow key five times to make a shadow effect. Paint this duplicate with a fill of Black and a stroke of None.

TROPICAL TREASURE

8. With this duplicate still selected, choose Edit>Clone. Clones move to the front when created.

Press Command-Shift (Macintosh)-P or Control-Shift -P (Windows) to convert selected text to paths.

9. To move this new clone, select Modify>Arrange>Move Backward. It will now be behind the original and in front of the first clone. Paint this new clone with a fill of White, and a stroke of None.
10. Press the Up Arrow key two times, then the Left Arrow key two times.
11. Your letters should look similar to the following image:

TROPICAL TREASURE

12. With the Text tool, click the cursor under the bottom rule lines in the logo.
13. Type "Gifts From Under The Sea".
14. Highlight the text, then go to the Text Inspector and set the font to ATC Daquiri, the size to 36 pt., and the horizontal scale to 120%. Be certain to use the Kerning feature to fit the letters to the template. Select the text block with the Pointer tool and choose Text>Convert To Paths.
15. Color the text with a fill of Pantone 3155 CVU, and a stroke of 1 pt. PMS 3155.

Gifts From Under The Sea

16. Move "Gifts From Under The Sea" in position on the template.
17. After moving the elements you have drawn onto the template, and after fine-tuning their positions, the logo should appear as follows:

18. In the Color List, select all of the colors in the document. From the Options menu, choose Make Process.
19. The logo is now complete. Select all of the objects and group them, then deselect.
20. Unlock the background, then click on it and press Delete/Backspace to remove it.
21. Save your file in the **Work in Progress** folder. Name the file "Tropical Treasure Logo.FH9" and choose the FreeHand Document format option. Close the document.

Project D: Grocery Ad

Grids, guides, and structured designs are helpful if you decide to use FreeHand as a page layout tool. The first step in building this relatively complex project is to create a set of grids and guides that split the page into regions.

To do this, we're going to rely on the Rows and Columns command combined with the use of layers. These techniques can be applied to a wide range of different layout and design requirements.

Build a Design Grid

1. Create a new letter-size document. Set the units of measurement to Inches. In the Document Inspector, set a Bleed of 0.25″ and a Printer Resolution of 1200 dpi.

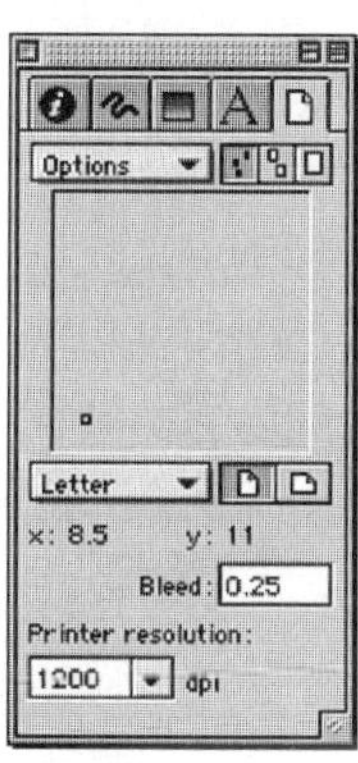

2. Select View>Page Rulers>Show, if the rulers do not appear on your page. Draw a rectangle and assign it following parameters in the Object Inspector: x: 0.5, y: 0.5, w: 7.5, h: 10.

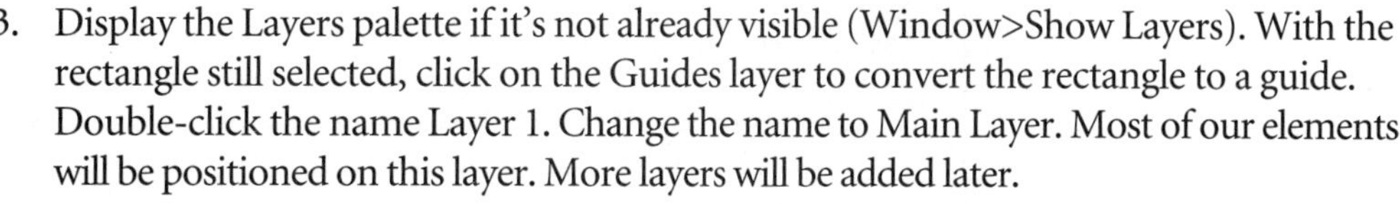

3. Display the Layers palette if it's not already visible (Window>Show Layers). With the rectangle still selected, click on the Guides layer to convert the rectangle to a guide. Double-click the name Layer 1. Change the name to Main Layer. Most of our elements will be positioned on this layer. More layers will be added later.

4. Change the units of measurement to Picas for the purpose of assigning guides. Select View>Guides>Edit.

5. Add vertical guides at 17p0, 18p6, 32p6, and 34p0. Click OK. You've added the guides for a basic 3-column grid.

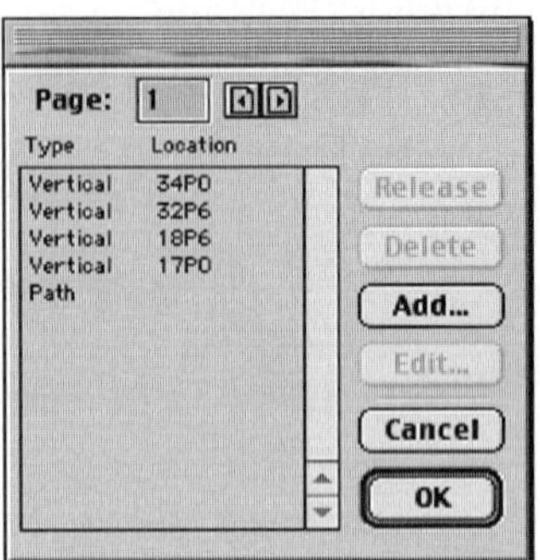

6. Now we'll add guides for the 4-column format. Select View>Guides>Edit to return to the Edit Guides dialog box and add vertical guides at 13p6, 14p6, 25p0, 26p0, 36p6, and 37p6.

   By now, the page is getting pretty well filled with guides. We still need one more set for positioning elements on the page.

7. This time create a set of guides that split the page vertically into thirds. Reactivate the Edit Guides dialog box and enter horizontal guides at 22p4, 23p4, 42p8, and 43p8.

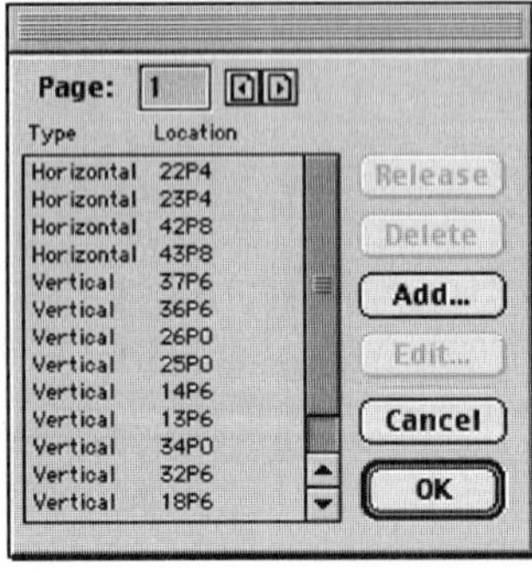

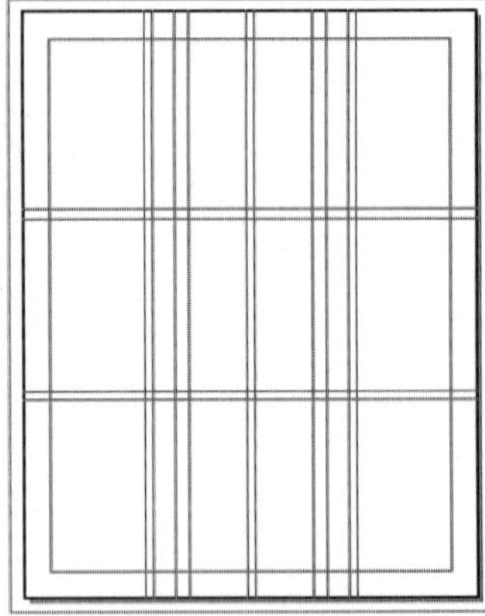

8. Save the file in your **Work in Progress** folder as "Grocery Ad.FH9" and continue to the next part of the exercise.

Building the Design

Although we're going to be building an advertisement for a grocery store, the grid that we created in the first portion of this project can be used repeatedly for a wide variety of design tasks. If you look at a lot of printed materials, you'll constantly see this basic grid in use.

The grid splits the page in fourths (which also establishes a column in the exact center of the page), and vertically and horizontally into thirds. You could also add a guide in the center of the page and split it into quarters or eighths, or almost any imaginable combination. It's a useful technique for using FreeHand for layout applications.

Add Components

1. Lock the Guides layer.
2. Switch to Keyline mode and draw a rectangle the exact size of the page. Drag horizontal and vertical ruler guides to mark the center of the page using the center point of this rectangle. With the rectangle selected, click on the guides layer to convert it to a guide.

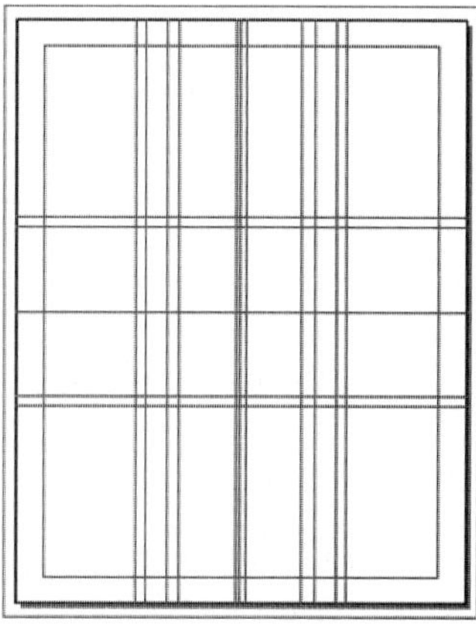

3. Using the Text tool, draw a rectangle in the lower left column (of the 4-column grid). Press Command-Option-Shift-M (Macintosh) or Control-Alt-Shift-M (Windows) to align the type to the center (middle) of the text block. Type three words on separate lines: "ITEM" <Return>, "$999" <Return>, and "Copy".
4. With the Type tool, highlight the word "ITEM" and set the font to ATC Papaya, the size to 36 pt., and set the leading at 32 pt. Highlight the word "Copy" and set the font to ATC Colada, the size to 12 pt., the leading at 13 pt., and the space above to 17 pt.
5. In the Adjust Columns Text Inspector, set the First line leading for 32 (fixed).
6. The "$999" will have two sizes applied. First, highlight the entire line and change the font to ATC Papaya, the size to 96 pt., and the leading at 78 pt.
7. Highlight the last two characters (99) and set the font to ATC Papaya, the size to 48 pt., and the baseline shift to 2p11. This will result in a nice looking price block.

There are plenty of reasons why one would choose to do a full page layout with nothing but FreeHand and a few high-quality scans. This project incorporates many of FreeHands's advanced features, and the results are identical to what you would achieve using traditional page layout applications such as QuarkXPress or Adobe PageMaker.

8. Click on this text block with the Pointer tool. From the Stroke Inspector, assign it a Black stroke with a weight of 2 pt. Choose the second dashed line for its border type.

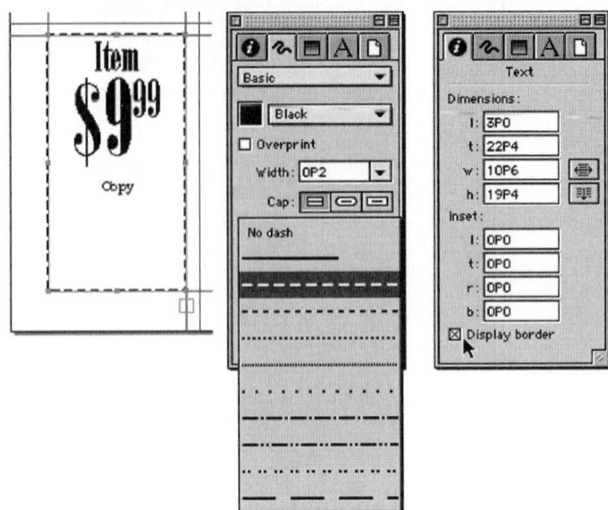

9. Select the text block and zoom out so that you can see the page. Drag the group to the right, holding the Shift key to constrain the move. When the dragged image matches the second column, hold the Option/Alt key and release the mouse button to duplicate. Press Command/Control-D two times to repeat the coupon across the bottom of the page.

10. Using the three-column grid, in the three columns directly above the coupons, choose File>Import to import the following three images from your **SF-FreeHand** folder: **Game Hens.TIF**, **Peppers and Corn.TIF**, and **Steak on Plate.TIF**. Use the Pointer tool (if needed) to squeeze them slightly to match the column guides. The adjustment is so slight that it won't visibly distort the images. When you're finished, turn off all the guides to view what you've accomplished.

11. Select View>Show Guides to view the guides again. Save the file.

Create the Header Graphics

1. Now we're going to create the page header. Select the Ellipse tool. While holding the Option/Alt key, click the crosshair where the first horizontal guide intersects the page's centerline. In the Object Inspector, enter x: 3p, y: 34p8, w: 45p0, and h: 18p0.
2. Select the Text tool in the Toolbox. Type the words "Angie and Angie's Gourmet Grocery". Highlight the text and set the font to ATC Tropical, and the size to 32 pt.

3. With the Pointer tool, click on both the text and the ellipse. Select Text>Attach To Path.
4. With the Selection tool, click on the left edge of the oval, where it intersects the top horizontal grid, and move it to the 51 pica mark on your vertical ruler. From the Text menu, select Text>Convert To Paths.
5. Copy the letters and apply a 3 pt. Black stroke to the selected outlines.

6. Select Edit>Paste in Front to paste the outlines in front. Apply a fill of None and a 2 pt. White stroke to the objects.

Use Command/Control-G to group objects.

Use Command/Control-L to lock objects.

7. Apply Paste in Front one more time to paste the original type in front of the other two.

8. With the Selection tool, select all three of these type outline groups and group them. Now select Modify>Lock to lock them.
9. With the Type tool, draw a thin rectangle using the horizontal guides above the photos as its boundaries. It should start at the left margin and cross the first two columns of the 4-column grid. If you check it in the Object Inspector, it will have a left margin of 3p0, a top margin of 43p8, a width of 22p0 and a height of 1p0.
10. In the Type Inspector, set the font to ATC Jamaica, and the size to 10 pt. Type the words "GOURMET MEALS READY TO GO", all in upper case.

11. Change the Fill of the type to White. Select the text block with the pointer tool and, from the Fill Inspector, assign a fill of None. In the Adjust Columns Text Inspector, assign a First Line Leading of 10 pt. (Fixed).

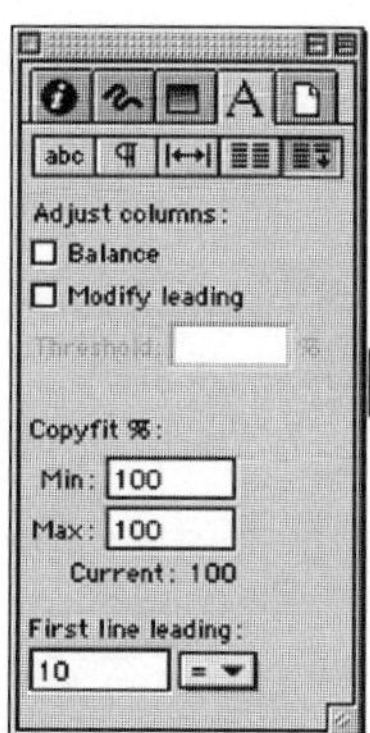

12. Select the text block. Drag it to the right, holding the Shift key to constrain the move. When in place on the two right column guides, hold the Option/Alt key and release the mouse button to duplicate the objects. Click the checkmark to turn off the Guides layer to see the page as it will appear when printed. The page should look like the image that follows. This is a good time to save.

Save your work as you go. Although we mention it only once or twice, we saved this document twenty times during development.

13. Display the guides again. Drag a set of horizontal ruler guides to 42p0 and 34p6 on the vertical ruler.

14. Choose File>Place and navigate to the **SF-FreeHand** folder to place the text file **Ready To Go.TXT**. Drag the Text tool to the space defined by the guides you just drew. The text will flow into the text block.

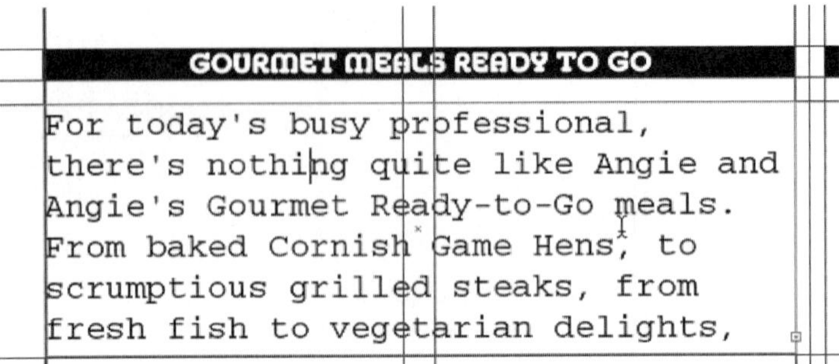

15. Set the font to ATC Mai Tai Normal, the size to 10 pt., the leading at 12 pt., and set the text to align left. It should fit perfectly into the space. If not, use range kerning (tracking) to tighten the letter spacing to fit.

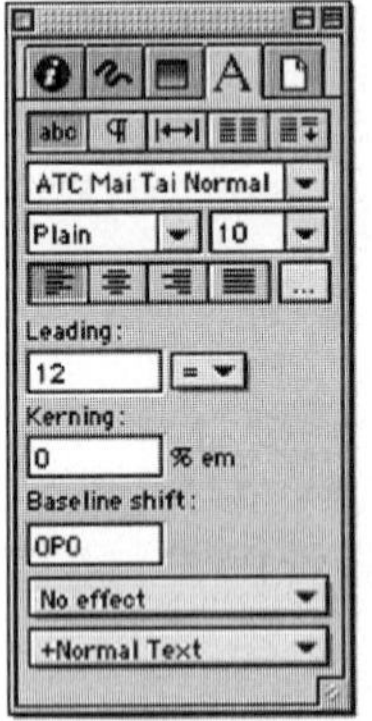

16. With the Type tool, highlight the GOURMET MEALS READY TO GO text in the duplicate that you dragged. Retype the words "CUSTOM CATERING SERVICES". Deselect the text block. Now select the Type tool and draw a text block below this text block, and place the file **Custom Catering.TXT** from the **SF-FreeHand** folder. Apply the same font and size settings as in step 18. Use the Spelling feature (from the Type menu) to check the text in both text blocks for errors.

17. From the File menu, navigate to the **SF-FreeHand** folder and place the file **Lobster Town.TIF.** Move it to the center of the page and drag it until it's just underneath the Angie's heading. Choose Modify>Arrange>Send To Back.

18. To complete the coupons on the bottom, use the Type tool to change the item text and prices to match the image below.

19. To add the final touch to the ad, use the Rectangle tool to draw a rectangle for the background. Start the rectangle off the page to the left of the reversed headers, using the 1/4″ bleed area, and drag it down to the bottom right, off the page to bottom of the bleed area. Make certain that it bleeds off three sides (left, right, and bottom). Send the rectangle to the back. Adjust the rectangle to fit the bleed guides, if needed. From the Color Mixer, create the rectangle's fill with the following settings: C: 10, M: 0, Y: 0, K: 10, and a stroke of None.

20. You're finished. Hide the guides to view the ad as it should appear when printed.

There really is no black border on the finished piece; we're showing it in this image so that you can see how the color rectangle will bleed (and be trimmed off) the final printed ad.

21. Save the file and close the document.

Project E: Ball and Mirror

Create the Ball & Mirror Design

1. Create a new document.
2. Navigate to the **SF-FreeHand** folder and import the **Ball & Mirror.TIF** image.
3. Center the image in the top half of the page.

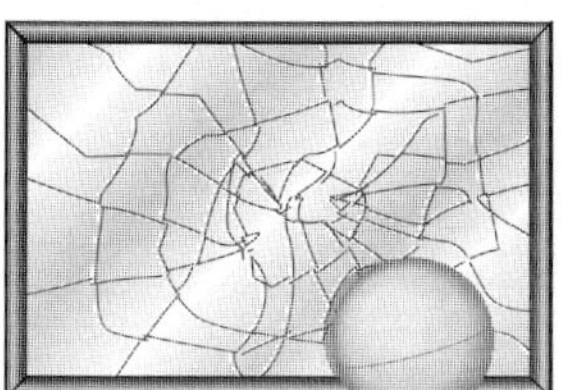

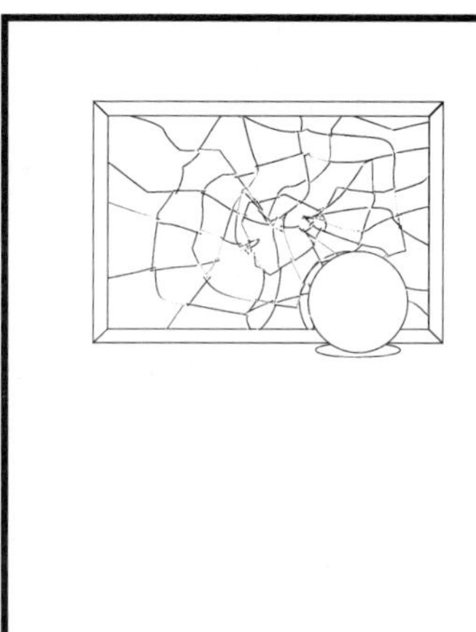

4. To create a template, access the Layers panel from Window>Panels. Select the imported graphic and click on the Background layer in the Layers panel.

   Click on the Padlock icon on the Background layer to lock the template.

5. FreeHand will return you to the Foreground layer.

Create the Frame

1. Double-click on the Foreground layer and rename it "Frame". Press the Return/Enter key to apply.

Objects drawn with the Rectangle tool must be ungrouped to make the anchor points accessible. The rectangles in this project must be ungrouped in order for the Divide operation to have anchor points to work with.

When positioning the 45° lines to the corners, it will help if you use View>Snap To Point toggled on. The lines will now snap to the anchor points of the rectangles.

2. Make certain that the units of measurement are set to Inches and that your page rulers are turned on. Double-click on the Rectangle tool and make sure its corner radius is set at 0. With the Rectangle tool, draw a 5.5″ × 3.75″ rectangle. Inside this rectangle, draw another rectangle that is 5.1″ × 3.35″. Select both rectangles and choose Window>Panels>Align to center the two rectangle on one another. Select Align center in both the vertical and horizontal pop-up menus, and then click Align/Apply.

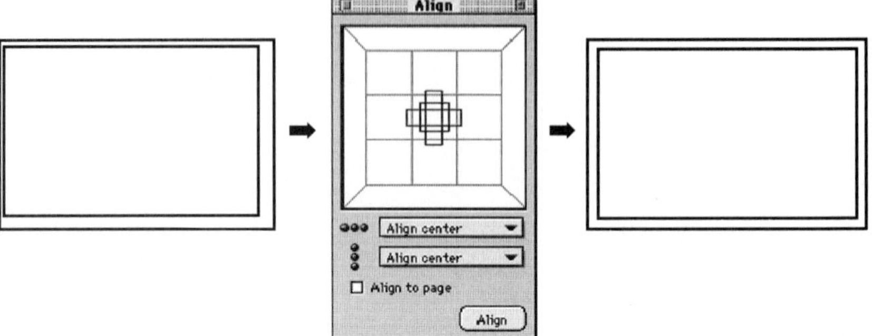

3. Ungroup the two rectangles by selecting them and choosing Modify>Ungroup. Select the Bezigon tool. Draw two lines bisecting the rectangles from the corners. Line them up at the corners so your cut through the corner will be at 45°. (Hold down the Shift key to constrain to that angle.)

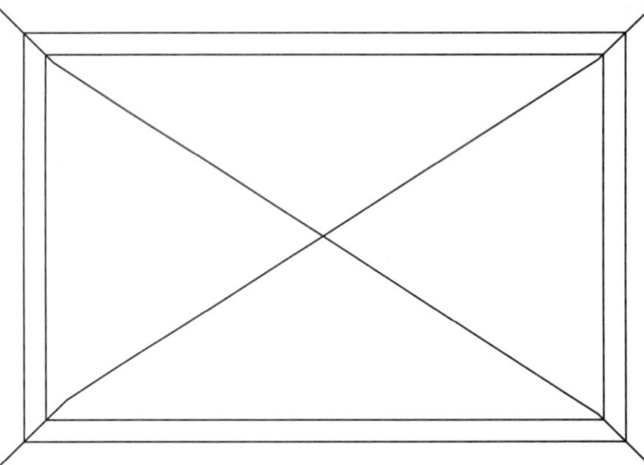

4. Once the lines are drawn, zoom in on each corner with the Magnification tool in Keyline mode to see the paths close-up. The line must touch the corner anchor points of both rectangles.

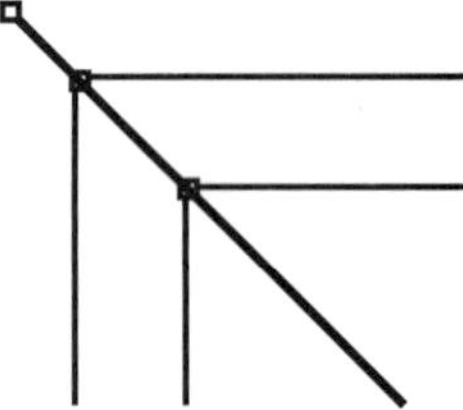

5. Select File>Preferences>Object. Make certain that Path operations consume original paths is not selected.

☐ Path operations consume original paths
☒ Option-drag copies paths

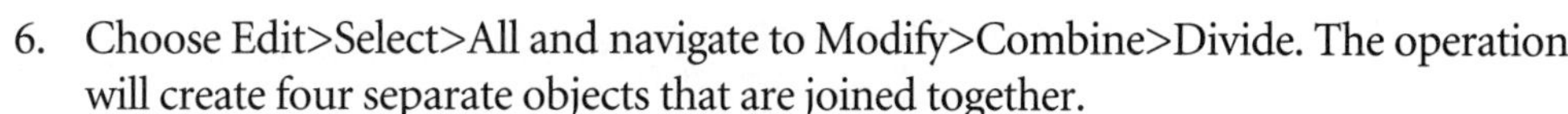

6. Choose Edit>Select>All and navigate to Modify>Combine>Divide. The operation will create four separate objects that are joined together.

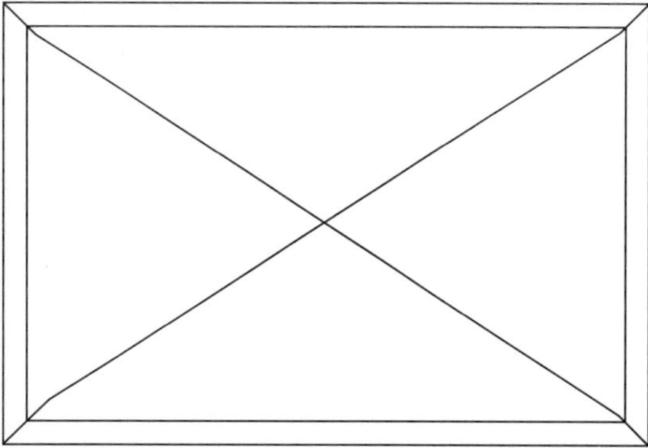

   With the new object still selected, navigate to View>Hide Selection. This will leave the original rectangles on screen. Click on the larger one and delete it; click on the remaining rectangle and cut it.

7. Select View>Show All to bring the new object back into view. With the entire object selected, choose Modify>Split. Delete the four triangles in the center and any extraneous lines from the frame.

Pantone colors are usually referred to as PMS (Pantone Matching System) and their number.

8. You will paint the frame with a multi-color gradient that you will now build. Select the Fill Inspector and, in the pop-up menu, select Gradient. Select all four frame pieces.

9. Select the Color List (Window>Panels). With its Options>Import function, select hold down the Shift/Control key and, from the Pantone Coated library, select PMS 217, 221, 278, 280, and 429. Click OK.

10. In the Fill Inspector>Gradient panel, click on the top gradient drop box and drag it down halfway along the color ramp; this will create a new drop box for a third color. Use the method of dragging a color to a drop box, color the three drop boxes in the Gradient panel as:

    Top drop box = 280.

    Middle drop box = 278.

    Bottom drop box = 280.

    Stroke all frame pieces with 1 pt. Black.

11. Select only the left and right frame pieces. In the gradient panel, set the Angle for 0 (zero). This will make the gradient colors flow from side to side. Press Return/Enter to apply.

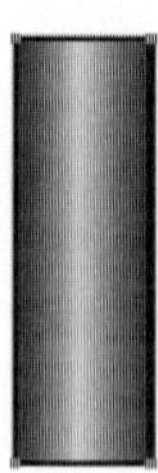

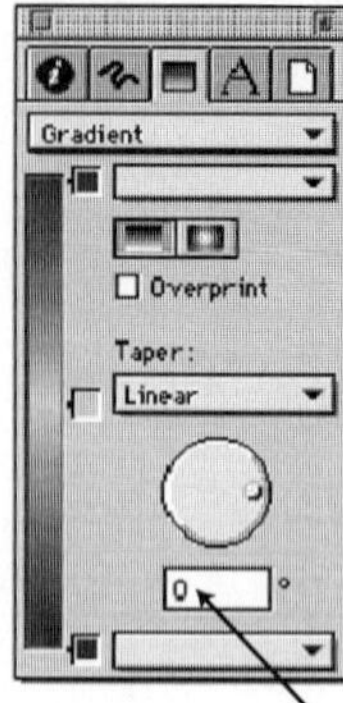

12. The frame is complete and painted. Select all four frame pieces and Modify>Group. Select the frame and Edit>Paste In Front to paste the rectangle that you copied earlier to the exact location on the page from where it was cut. Keep the pasted rectangle selected.

Create the Mirror

1. Create a new layer, naming it "Mirror". By creating the new layer, you have assigned the selected rectangle to this layer. Move the layer below the Frame layer.

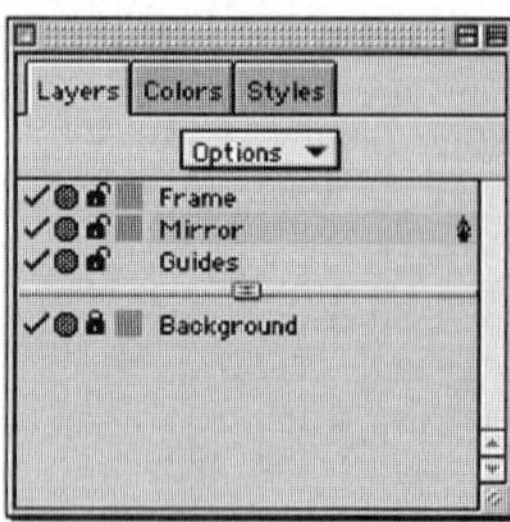

2. You will now create the mirror surface, which is a gradient.

3. Select Fill Inspector>Gradient and create a gradient that alternates between the colors PMS 278 and White, accessed in the Color List. To build the gradient, drag the top drop box down to make a new color drop box. Repeat this until you have five new drop boxes between the top and bottom drop boxes.

4. Select the top drop box and click the PMS 278 color name in the Color List. The next drop box is White. Alternate from 278 to White with the color drop boxes until you finish with a blue bottom drop box. Change the angle of the gradient to 315°.

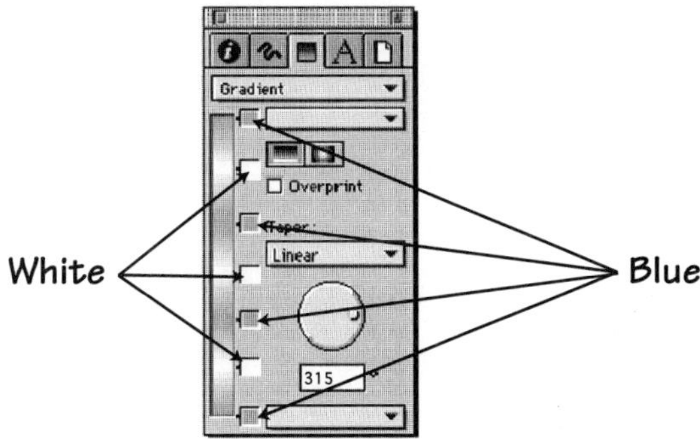

5. Press the Tab key to deselect all. The rectangle filled with this gradient will resemble a mirror.

Crack the Mirror

1. Click the Hide checkmark on the Mirror layer for a better view of the template to draw the mirror cracks. Create a new layer and name it "Cracks". Drag the Cracks layer down until it is under the Frame layer. Click on the Cracks layer to make it active.

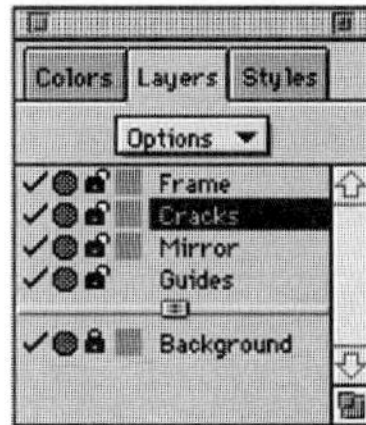

2. Select the Freehand tool and draw the cracks of the mirror to match the cracks in the template. Hold the Shift key and select all the cracks, then Modify>Group them. Color this group with: Fill = None, Stroke = 1 pt. PMS 280.

3. Use Edit>Clone on the cracks group and offset the clone by pressing the Left Arrow key three times. Color the cloned cracks with: Fill = None, Stroke = 1 pt. White. Deselect all by pressing the Tab key.

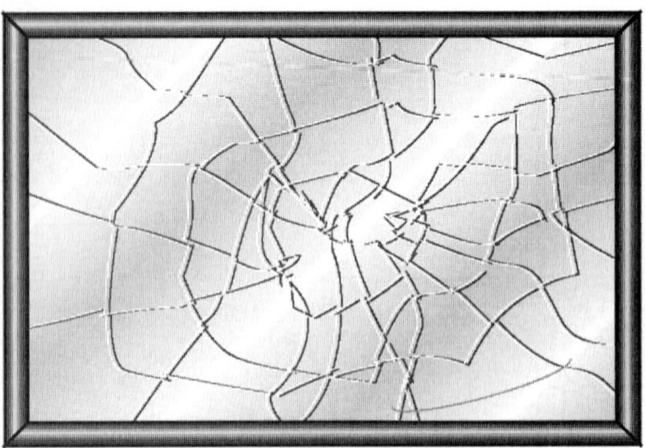

4. Make the Mirror layer active again by clicking the checkmark back on. This will display the background fill behind the cracks.

Create the Ball

1. Create a new layer and name it “Ball”. Keep it selected as the active layer.

2. With the Ellipse tool, draw a circle 1.6 inches in diameter. Set a stroke of None and fill the circle with a radial gradient built from:

Top drop box:	PMS 221
Bottom drop box:	PMS 217

Adjust the radial so the highlight is in the upper-left area to give the ball a round appearance.

3. Select the Ellipse tool and draw an ellipse 1.6 inches wide x 0.25 inches tall. Navigate to Modify>Ungroup to view the ellipse’s anchor points.

4. With the Knife tool, cut both side anchor points by clicking on both points with the knife tool selected. Delete the top half. Paint the remainder: Fill = None, Stroke = 2 pt. PMS 429. Move this path on top of the rubber ball and rotate the path 15°. Fine-tune the position to create the look of a ridge on the ball's surface.

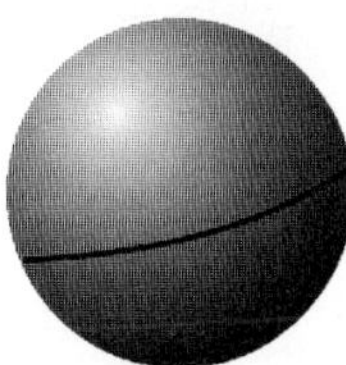

5. To create the reflection in the mirror, click on the ball and press Command-C (Macintosh) or Control-Shift-C (Windows) to clone the object.

6. In the Layers panel, click on the Cracks layer to assign the cloned ball to this layer. Select Modify>Arrange>Send To Back to send the shadow behind the cracks. Press the Left Arrow key six times to see it better. Paint the shadow: Fill = PMS 429, Stroke = None.

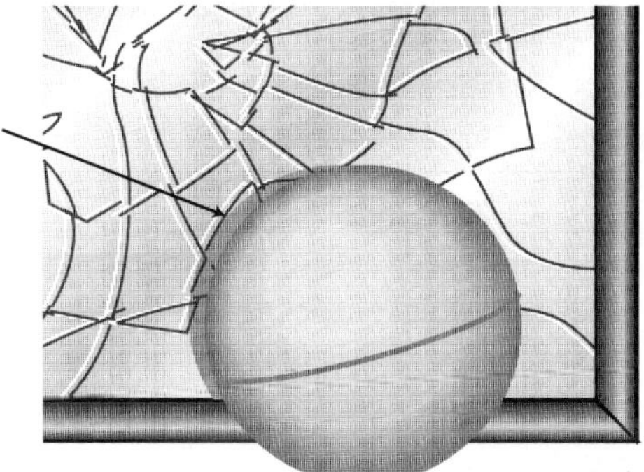

7. Deselect the shadow. Click on the Ball layer to create the shadow underneath the ball. With the Ellipse tool, draw another ellipse 1.6 inches x 0.25 inches. Paint it: Fill = White, Stroke = None. Clone the ellipse and Scale the clone 50%. Paint it: Fill = PMS429, Stroke = None.

8. Select both ellipses, and navigate to Modify>Combine>Blend.

   Select Modify>Arrange>Send To Back so that it will be behind the ball.

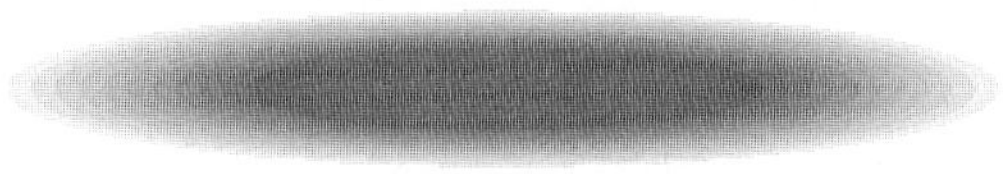

9. Position the shadow under the rubber ball. Fine-tune all objects for more accurate positioning in the design.

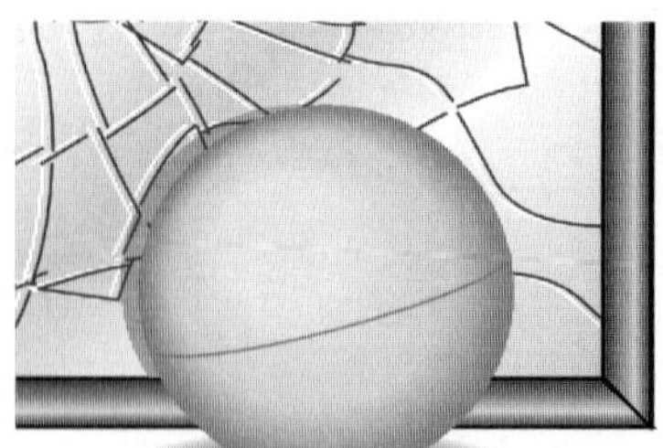

10. The design is now finished. It should appear as follows:

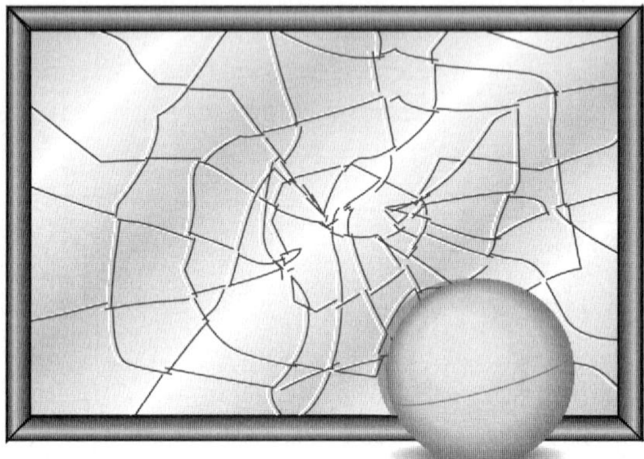

11. Lock all foreground layers. Unlock the Background layer. Press Command/Control-A to select all, and delete the underlying image.

12. Select Save As to save the document in your **Work in Progress** folder. Save in the FreeHand Document format, naming it "Ball & Mirror.FH9".

13. Close the document.

Project F: No Clowning Around

This is another image that could be created for a number of applications — from party invitations, to posters, to T-shirt designs. Although it is a relatively simple design, it will call for the use of many of the skills you have learned to date.

Create the Clown's Head and Collar

1. Open the document **Clown.FT9** from the **SF-Freehand** folder. Turn the Page Rulers on and set the units of measurement to Points.

Pantone colors are generally referred to as PMS (Pantone Matching System) and their number. That is how we refer to them here.

2. Double-click on the Foreground layer in the Layers panel and rename it "Clown". Press Return/Enter to apply the name.
3. In the Color List, select Options and select the PMS Uncoated library.
4. Hold down the Shift/Control key, and select PMS Process Yellow, PMS Process Cyan, PMS Orange 021, PMS Red 032, PMS 271, and PMS 326. Click OK to add them to your Color List.
5. Zoom in around the clown's head with the Magnification tool. Select the Ellipse tool in the Freehand Toolbox and begin by tracing around the head of the clown. Continue to use the Ellipse tool to draw the ears.

TIP: Hold down Option/Alt and Shift as you draw to draw circles from the center.

6. Select File>Preferences>Object and confirm that the Path operations consume original paths option is checked.
7. Select all three ellipses and choose Modify>Combine>Union. This will combine the three ellipses together into one shape. Paint the new shape with a fill of White, and a stroke of 1 pt. Black.

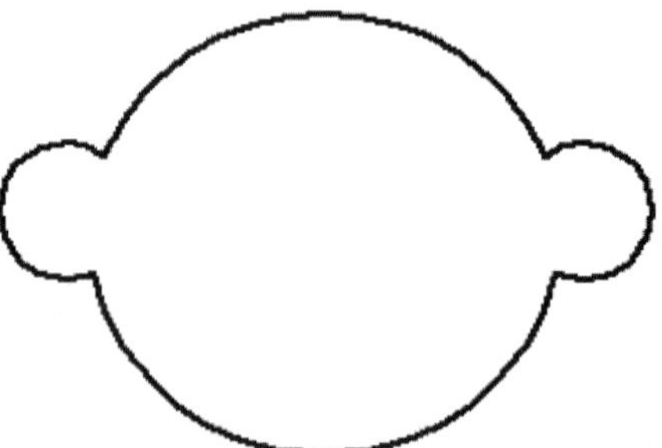

8. With the new shape selected, choose View>Hide Selection. This will eliminate any possible interference as you create the rest of the clown's face.
9. Continue to use the Ellipse tool to draw the eyes of the clown. Paint the eyes with a fill of White, and a stroke of 1 pt. Black. Paint the eyeballs with a fill of PMS Process Cyan, and a stroke of None. Paint the highlights with a fill of White and a stroke of None.

10. Use the Ellipse tool to draw the nose of the clown. Fill the nose with a radial gradient using PMS Red 032 and White, and apply a 1-pt. Black stroke.

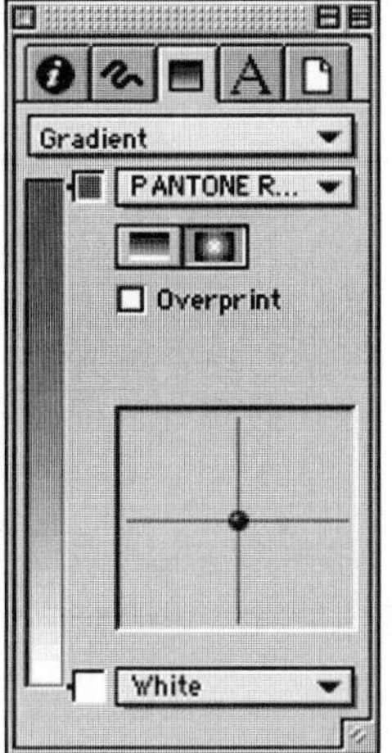

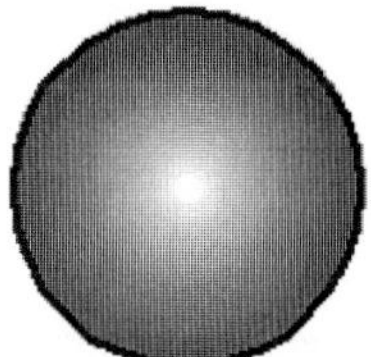

11. Select the Freehand tool from the Freehand Toolbox and draw the rest of the clown's face. Paint the area around the mouth with a fill of PMS Process Yellow, and a stroke of 1 pt. Black. Paint the mouth with a fill of None, and a stroke of 1 pt. Black. Paint the eyebrows with a fill of Black, and a stroke of 1 pt. Black.

    Choose Modify>Arrange>Move Backward to send objects behind other objects. You may need to do this depending on the order in which you draw the objects.

12. Use View>Show All to display the clown's face. Use Modify>Arrange>Send To Back to send objects behind other objects as needed. Select all of the objects you have drawn so far, then group them. Use View>Hide Selection to Hide the group.

13. Drag a guideline to the center of the clown in between the clown's eyes. Next, use the Freehand tool to draw one half of the clown's hair. Paint the hair with a fill of Blue Green, and a stroke of 1 pt. Select the clown hair with the Pointer tool and use the Mirror tool (Window>Toolbars>Xtra Tools) to reflect the hair by clicking on the guideline to create the other half of the clown's hair.

14. The Pen tool is used to draw the curving lines of the hat. Adjust these points with the Pointer tool for a smoother, more rounded corner as needed. Remember to use Modify>Arrange>Move Backward to send objects behind other objects. You may need to do this with the hat top to send it behind the bill. Paint both the top and bottom of the hat with a fill of PMS Process Cyan, and a stroke of 1 pt. Black.

15. Use the Pen tool to draw the curving strip of the hat. Adjust these points with the Pointer tool for a smoother, more rounded corner as needed. Fill the strip with a linear gradient using PMS Process Yellow and White, and a stroke of 1 pt Black.

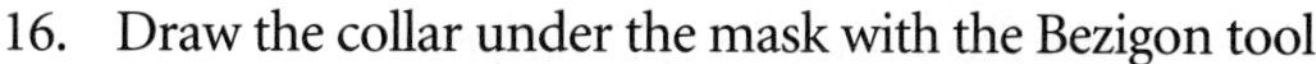

16. Draw the collar under the mask with the Bezigon tool.

17. When you have finished drawing the collar send it behind the other objects. Paint the collar with a fill of PMS 320, and a stroke of 1 pt. Black.

18. Use View>Show All to bring all the objects back. Uncheck the Background layer so you can see your work more clearly. Make any necessary changes now. Select all the objects and group them. Use View>Hide Selection to hide the group.

The Clown Body

The body of the clown is made up of the polka dot outfit, the puffy collar buttons, the sleeve and pant cuffs, the shadow on the ground, and the hands and shoes. Start with the puffy collar buttons.

1. Use the Pen tool to create the clown's outfit. Leave the suit unpainted for now. We need to be able to see to place the buttons and the polka dots.

2. Use the Freehand tool to trace around the puffy buttons. Color them with a fill of White, and a stroke of 1 pt. Black.

3. Use the Ellipse tool to create one of the polka dots. Paint the polka dot with a fill of PMS Process Yellow, and a stroke of None. With the polka dot selected with the Pointer tool, hold the Option/Alt key and duplicate to create several more polka dots, positioning them as you go.

4. Paint the suit with a fill of PMS Red 032 and a stroke of 1 pt. Black

5. Select all the polka dots with the Pointer tool by holding the Shift key down as you select each one. Choose Edit>Cut. Select the clown's outfit and choose Edit>Paste Inside. This will place the polka dots inside of the clown's outfit. With the clown's outfit still selected choose Modify>Arrange>Send To Back to send the outfit to the back.

6. Use the Pen tool to create the sleeve and pant cuffs. Paint the sleeve cuffs with a fill of PMS Orange 021, and a stroke of 1 pt. Black. Paint the pant cuffs with a fill of White, and a stroke of 1 pt. Black.

7. Use the Pen tool to create the hands and shoes. Start with the left hand by tracing around the outside shape of the hand.

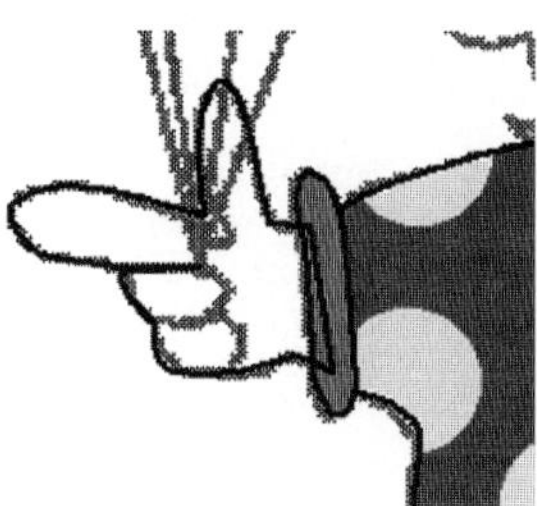

8. Use the Freehand tool to draw in the fingers of the left hand using a 1 pt. Black stroke.

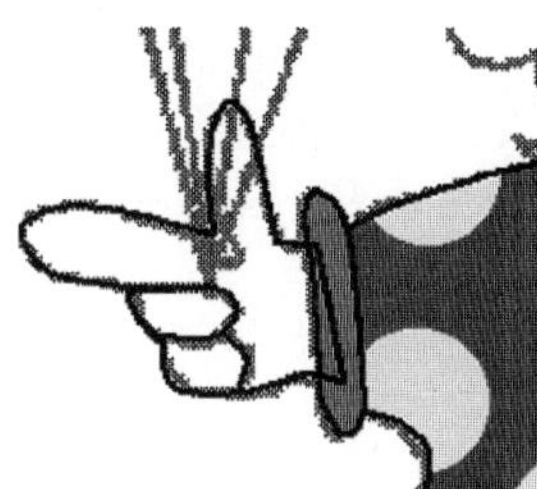

9. Select the outline of the hand with the Pointer tool. Paint the left hand with a fill of White and a stroke of 1 pt. Black. With the left hand selected, choose Modify> Arrange>Send To Back. Repeat the steps used to create the left hand to create the right.

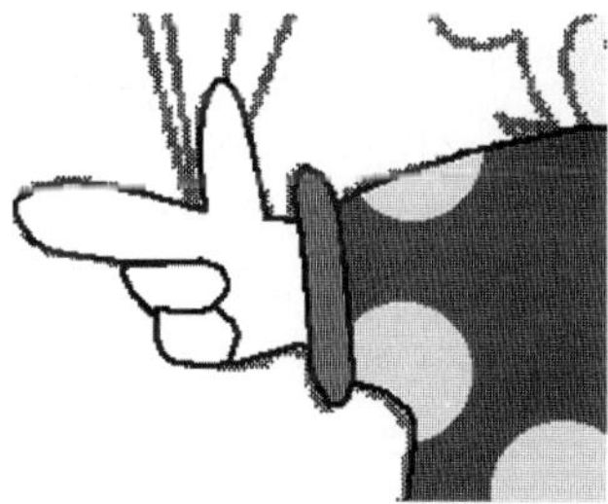

10. Use the Pen tool to create the shoes. Use the same steps as you used with the hands, drawing the shape of the shoes first with the Pen tool, then creating the line inside the shoes with the Freehand tool. Paint the shoes with a fill of PMS Orange 021, and a stroke of 1 pt. Black.

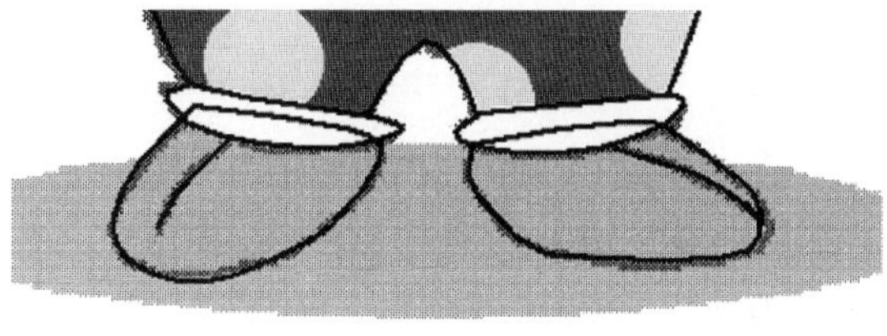

11. When you are finished drawing the shoes, select them and choose Modify>Arrange> Send To Back.

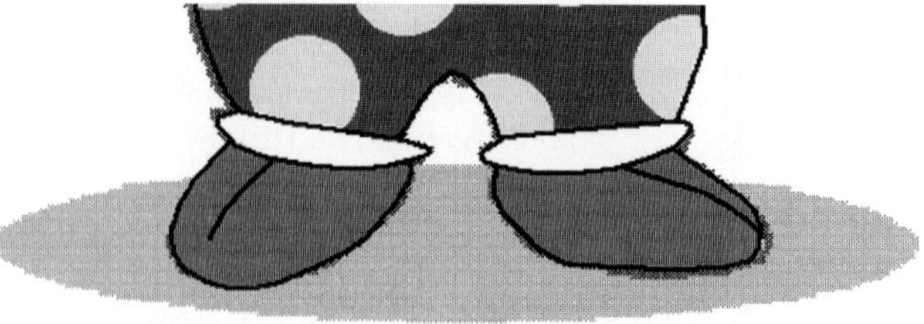

12. Use the Ellipse tool to create the shadow on the ground. Paint the shadow with a fill of Cornflower, and a stroke of None. When you are finished drawing the shadow, select it and send it to the back.

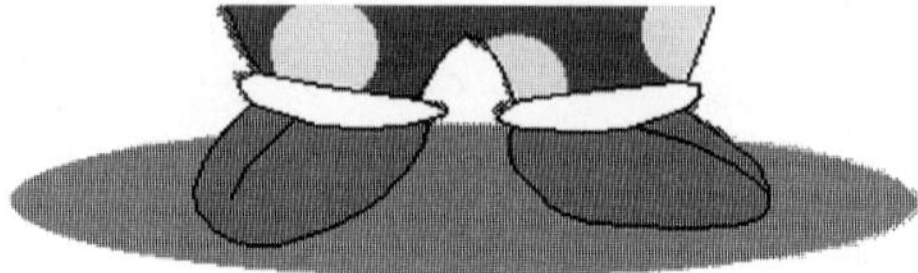

13. You have now drawn the clown body. Choose Show All to display all of the objects. Select the grouped clown head objects and bring them to the front. Select the top collar puffy button and bring it to the front of the collar. The completed clown body should appear as shown.

14. Select all the objects you have created and group them. Hide the group.

Creating The Balloons

1. The balloons are created by using the Ellipse tool and then choosing Send To Back. Select Keyline mode to get a clear view of the objects. Use the Ellipse tool to draw the balloons one at a time.

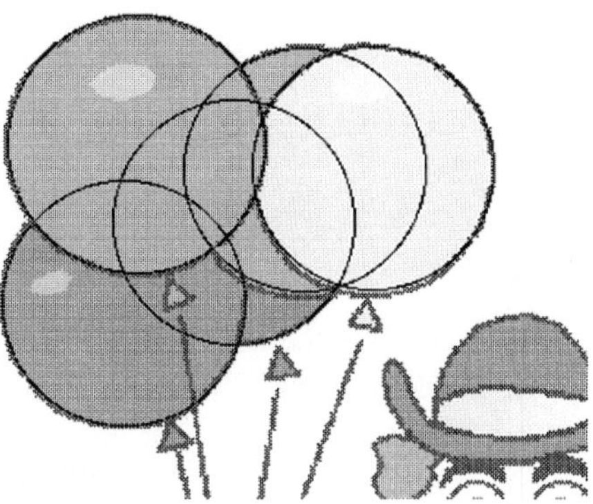

2. Three of the balloons have highlights. Use the Ellipse tool to draw the highlights one at a time. Use the Pen tool to create the triangle shapes at the bottom of the balloons.

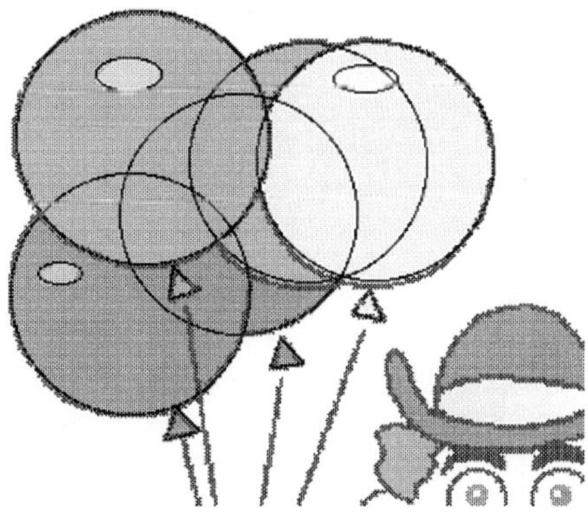

3. Return to Preview mode. The balloons are all different colors. Using the following list of paint attributes, select the balloons named and fill them with the colors from the Color List. Make sure that you also color the balloon string holders at the bottom of each balloon. The balloons all have a 1pt. Black stroke.

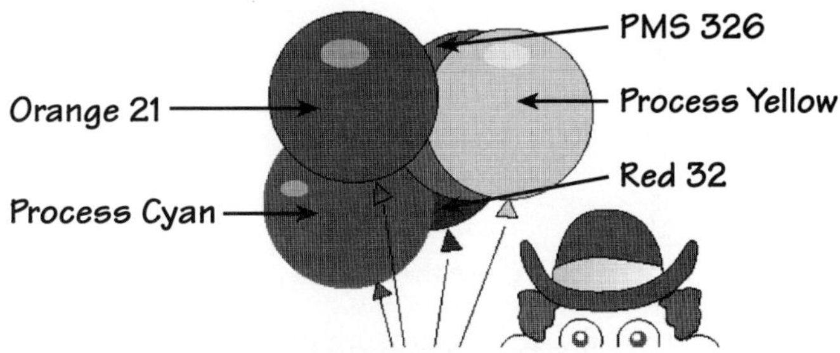

4. For the three balloons that have highlights, use the Color Mixer to give the highlights a 50% tint of the its color. The highlights should have no stroke.

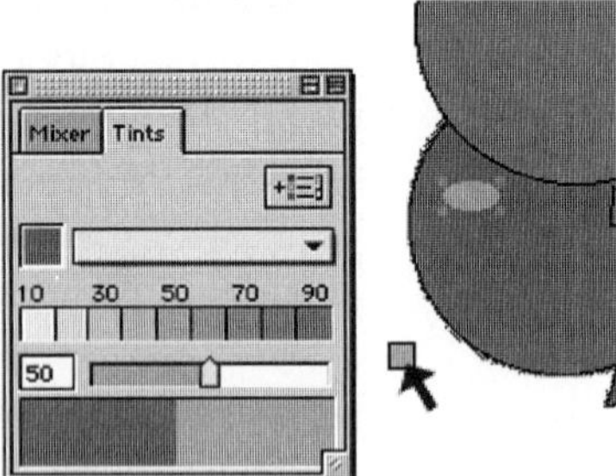

5. Use the Line tool to draw in the strings from the clown's hand to the balloon's string holders. Give the strings a 1-pt. Black stroke.

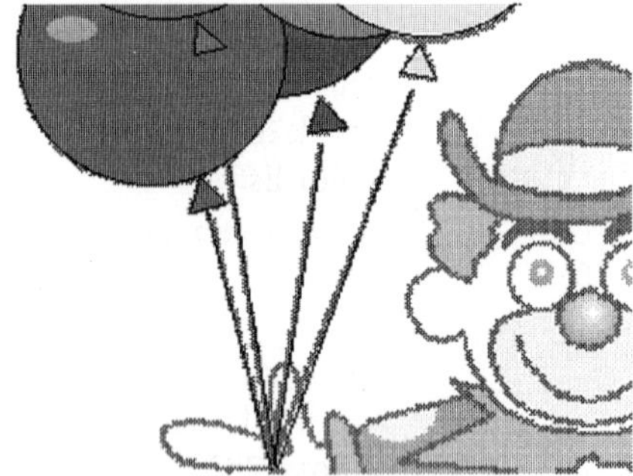

6. Display all of the objects. You have now created the artwork. The finished artwork should appear as shown.

7. To use the art in a printed document, convert it to CMYK.
8. Save your work into your **Work in Progress** folder. Choose FreeHand Document format, and name the file "No Clowning Around". Close the document

Index